THE STUDIA PHILONICA ANNUAL

THE STUDIA PHILONICA ANNUAL
STUDIES IN HELLENISTIC JUDAISM

Contributions should be sent to the Editor, Prof. G. E. Sterling, Yale Divinity School, 409 Prospect Street, New Haven, CT 06511, USA; email: gregory.sterling@ yale.edu. Please send books for review to the Book Review Editor, Prof. Michael Cover, Department of Theology, Marquette University, P.O. Box 1881, Milwaukee, WI 53201-1881, U.S.A.; email michael.cover@marquette.edu.

Contributors are requested to observe the "Instructions to Contributors" located at the end of the volume. These can also be consulted on the Annual's website: http://divinity.yale.edu/philo-alexandria. Articles which do not conform to these instructions cannot be accepted for inclusion.

The Studia Philonica Monograph series accepts monographs in the area of Hellenistic Judaism, with special emphasis on Philo and his *Umwelt*. Proposals for books in this series should be sent to the Editor, Prof. Thomas H. Tobin, S.J., Theology Department, Loyola University Chicago, 1032 West Sheridan Road, Chicago, IL 60660-1537, U.S.A.; email: ttobin@luc.edu.

THE STUDIA PHILONICA ANNUAL
Studies in Hellenistic Judaism

Volume XXXI

2019

EDITORS
David T. Runia
Gregory E. Sterling

ASSOCIATE EDITOR
Sarah J. K. Pearce

BOOK REVIEW EDITOR
Michael Cover

SBL Press
Atlanta

THE STUDIA PHILONICA ANNUAL
Studies in Hellenistic Judaism

The financial support of

C. J. de Vogel Foundation, Utrecht
Yale University
Freed-Hardeman University

is gratefully acknowledged.

ISBN: 9781628372649 (hardcover: alk. paper)
ISBN: 9780884144205 (electronic book)
ISSN : 1052-4533

Printed on acid-free paper.

∞

CONTENTS

ARTICLES

ABRAHAM TERIAN, Philo about the Contemplative Life: Conybeare
Revisited 1
MIKOLAJ DOMARADZKI, The Value and Variety of Allegory: A Glance at
Philo's *De Gigantibus* 13
GÁBOR BUZÁSI, Pilpul and Eros: Philo's Platonic Interpretation of the Law
Concerning the Garment Taken in Pledge (*De Somniis* 1.92–114) 29
EKATERINA MATUSOVA, Genesis 1–2 in *De Opificio Mundi* and Its
Exegetical Content 57
BEATRICE WYSS, Philo of Alexandria: Interpreter or Teacher? 95
DAVID T. RUNIA, Is Philo Committed to the Doctrine of Reincarnation?. 107
THOMAS R. BLANTON IV, The Expressive Prepuce: Philo's Defense of
Judaic Circumcision in Greek and Roman Contexts 127
ALEXANDER E. STEWART, The Rhetorical Use of Divine Threat in Philo of
Alexandria... 163
EVERETT FERGUSON, Philo and the Fathers on Music 185
ZE'EV STRAUSS, Solomon Judah Rapoport's Maskilic Revival of Philo
of Alexandria: Rabbi Yedidya Ha-Alexandri as a Pioneer of Jewish
Philosophy 201

BIBLIOGRAPHY SECTION

D. T. RUNIA, M. ALESSO, E. BIRNBAUM, A. C. GELJON, H. M. KEIZER,
J. LEONHARDT-BALZER, M. R. NIEHOFF, S. J. K. PEARCE, S. WEISSER, S. YLI-
KARJANMAA, Philo of Alexandria: An Annotated Bibliography 2016 . 227
SUPPLEMENT: A Provisional Bibliography 2017–2019 278

BOOK REVIEW SECTION

GEORGE BOYS-STONES, *Platonist Philosophy 80 BC to AD 250: An Introduction
and Collection of Sources in Translation*
REVIEWED BY DAVID T. RUNIA 297
JOSÉ PABLO MARTÍN, Pura Nieto Hernández, and Sofía Torallas Tovar,
eds., *Filón de Alejandría: Obras Completas*
Reviewed by PAOLA DRUILLE.. 300
JANG RYU, *Knowledge of God in Philo of Alexandria*
Reviewed by SCOTT D. MACKIE.. 303
CHRISTIANE BÖHM, *Die Rezeption der Psalmen in den Qumranschriften, bei
Philo von Alexandrien und im Corpus Paulinum*

Reviewed by MICHAEL B. COVER.. 307

SEAN A. ADAMS AND SETH M. EHORN, EDS., *Composite Citations in Antiquity.*
Volume One: Jewish, Graeco-Roman, and Early Christian Uses
Reviewed by JUSTIN M. ROGERS.. 310

PIETER B. HARTOG, *Pesher and Hypomnema: A Comparison of Two*
Commentary Traditions from the Hellenistic-Roman Period
Reviewed by MICHAEL GRAVES 313

MARTIN GOODMAN, *A History of Judaism*
Reviewed by DAVID T. RUNIA.. 317

ANDREI A. ORLOV, *Yahoel and Metatron: Aural Apocalypticism and the*
Origins of Early Jewish Mysticism
Reviewed by KEVIN SULLIVAN 319

GUDRUN HOLTZ, *Die Nichtigkeit des Menschen und die Übermacht Gottes:*
Studien zur Gottes- und Selbsterkenntnis bei Paulus, Philo und in der Stoa
Reviewed by DANIEL LANZINGER... 322

JENNIFER OTTO, *Philo of Alexandria and the Construction of Jewishness*
in Early Christian Writings
Reviewed by ILARIA L. E. RAMELLI 325

NEWS AND NOTES.. 330

NOTES ON CONTRIBUTORS 336

INSTRUCTIONS TO CONTRIBUTORS 340

NOTE. The editors wish to thank the typesetter Gonni Runia once again for her tireless work on this volume. They wish to express their thanks to Dr. Lisa Marie Belz, O.S.U, Ph.D., Zachariah P. Eberhart, Chris Atkins and Oana Captiva for meticulously proof-reading the final manuscript. As in previous years we are deeply grateful to our publisher, SBL Press, and to its staff, with a special mention of Nicole Tilford.

The Studia Philonica Annual 31 (2019): 1–11

PHILO ABOUT THE CONTEMPLATIVE LIFE: CONYBEARE REVISITED

ABRAHAM TERIAN

Frederick C. Conybeare's *Philo about the Contemplative Life* is one of the most exhaustive studies on any work of Philo of Alexandria.[1] However, nearly every subject it deals with has long been settled in scholarship, and that quite differently. Half of the four-hundred-page book deals with the Greek text and textual issues, including the Eusebian excerpts and the old Latin and Armenian versions. This half of the book was superseded within two decades by the Cohn-Wendland critical edition of Philo's works (PCW, vol. 6 esp.) and the somewhat critical adoption of the latter text by the translators for the Loeb Classical Library edition of Philo (PLCL, vol. 9 esp.). Together, these two editions pushed Conybeare's painstaking work into virtual oblivion. A fourth of the book is a rebuttal of old arguments against the authenticity of the work and its Philonic authorship, introductory questions that are no longer asked by Philonists. The most useful part of the book is the remaining fourth, with sixty pages of commentary showing where Philo's thought is paralleled elsewhere in his writings, and some forty pages of glossaries and indices. Were it not for the mounting interest in the subject of this Philonic treatise in the comparative study of the descriptions of the Essenes, brought to wider circles of scholarly discussion since the discovery of the Dead Sea Scrolls and the more recent interest in the history of asceticism, Conybeare's work would have merited only a footnote in the history of scholarship on *De vita contemplativa*. This, and a recent reprint driven more by the market for reprints than by current scholarly interest in the mostly outdated work, justified anew its space on the shelves of libraries.

---

[1] Frederick C. Conybeare, *Philo about the Contemplative Life, or the Fourth Book of the Treatise Concerning Virtues* (Oxford: Clarendon, 1895; repr., New York: Garland, 1987). For the early reviews, see the references in Howard L. Goodhart and Erwin R. Goodenough, "A General Bibliography of Philo Judaeus," in Erwin R. Goodenough, *The Politics of Philo Judaeus: Practice and Theory* (New Haven: Yale University Press, 1938), 194. Hereafter G-G.

Conybeare's work warrants a second look because of his remarks on the value of the Armenian text of *De vita contemplative* to help emend perceived corruptions in the Greek text,[2] and more so because he failed—every now and then—to discern such corruptions where the Armenian reading could have been helpful. His remarks on the Armenian text are not to be taken lightly, for besides his renown in New Testament and Philo scholarship, the Oxford philologist was also a respected Armenologist. His pioneering studies in the latter field are too numerous to cite. It would be sufficient to say that they encompass nearly every aspect of ancient Armenian studies, including history, literature, theology, liturgy, and codicology.[3]

Two major observations in the Armenian text of Philo's *De vita contemplativa* persuaded Conybeare to declare its superiority over all extant Greek manuscripts of this work.[4] He noticed that unlike the Greek manuscripts, the Armenian text and the Eusebian excerpt (*Hist. eccl.* 2.17–18) share a common lacuna at 483.46 of Mangey's edition (§78; omitting ἐν ᾧ ἤρξατο ἡ λογικὴ ψυχὴ διαφερόντως τὰ οἰκεῖα θεωρεῖν).[5] A related observation was that all the Greek manuscripts of Philo have a common lacuna at 483.18 of Mangey's edition (§75; omitting ὁ πρόεδρος αὐτῶν, πολλῆς ἁπάντων ἡσυχίας γενομένης—supplied from the Armenian version). Conybeare's observations led him to conclude that at least in this treatise of Philo the Greek archetype of the Armenian translation is more akin to that used by Eusebius than to that of the existing Greek manuscripts.[6] These sightings drove him to give the Armenian text greater attention and to assign it a special place in textual considerations, a criterion he seems to have failed to maintain—as

---

[2] "As a version it is marvelously faithful, reproducing the Greek original word for word, and as a rule without any change in the order. Hence its great value as a means of determining the Greek text. The family of text represented by the Armenian version has been already dwelt upon in my introductory chapter. But it should be added that my inferences as stated in that chapter only applied to the D.V.C., and not to the rest of the treatises preserved in this version" (G-G 155).

[3] See his collected reviews and articles on Armenian subjects, compiled with introduction by Nerses Vrej Nersessian under the title *The Armenian Church: Heritage and Identity* (New York: St. Vartan Press, 2001); for his Philonic studies in periodical literature, see pp. 3–121, and 417–26 on the affinities between the Armenian text of Philo and that of Irenaeus; see also Robert W. Thomson, *A Bibliography of Classical Armenian Literature to 1500 A.D.*, Corpus Christianorum (Turnhout: Brepols, 1995), 305.

[4] Conybeare, *Philo about the Contemplative Life*, 7–10, 154–55.

[5] For this early edition of Philo's works, see Thomas Mangey, *Philonis Judaei opera quae reperiri potuerunt omnia*, 2 vols. (London: William Bowyer, 1742); its pagination is retained in the PCW edition.

[6] Conybeare, *Philo about the Contemplative Life*, 155.

he acknowledges at one point in the preface, obviously written after the pages in question were set or printed already:

> I have begun with an essay on the sources of the text. I regret that in writing §§18 and 19 of the same, I failed to see as clearly as afterwards (see p. 250) the true significance of the Eusebian text at 483.42.[7] Both the Armenian text and that of Eusebius had here the same lacuna and are therefore derived from a common archetype, distinct from the other archetype Σ from which all the Greek books with their common lacuna at 483.18 have flowed.[8]

To the distinctive omissions / additions observed by him we may add several others that he missed, especially the omission in all the Greek manuscripts at 483.33 of Mangey's edition (PCW 66.15–16 [§77]): τὰ ὦτα καὶ τοὺς ὀφθαλμοὺς ἀνατετακότες, an adopted reading in PCW and others thereafter, from the Armenian version.

Conybeare also missed taking full note of the shorter titles of the Philonic treatise. The Armenian version has the simplest form: Φίλωνος περὶ βίου θεωρητικοῦ, whereas in the Eusebian excerpts the title appears twice with the addition ἢ ἱκετῶν. The Greek manuscripts, without exception, present a variety of subtitles and further complicate the problem of Philo's historical works in "five books."[9] Of the two shorter titles, the one in Armenian seems to be primary and that in Eusebius secondary, if we may pursue the following remarks on the Eusebian title by Colson: "It is difficult to see why Philo substituted ἱκετῶν for θεραπευτῶν. It does not occur in the treatise itself and though as Conybeare shows there are many passages where ἱκεταί and θεραπευταί are coupled, they are not exactly the same and ἱκεταί does not suit the sense of healing which he gives as an alternative meaning for Therapeutae."[10] It would be enough to point out that the Armenian text and Eusebius omit the subtitle(s) so prominent in the Greek manuscripts, where they seem to be tertiary.

---

[7] He probably meant line 46, see Conybeare, *Philo about the Contemplative Life*, 119–20.

[8] Conybeare, *Philo about the Contemplative Life*, vii. The codices of Philo are fully discussed by Cohn in the PCW edition (1:i–xlix), including those used for establishing the text of *De vita contemplativa* (cf. 6:xi–xii, on the Armenian version).

[9] Φίλωνος ἱκέται ἢ περὶ ἀρετῶν δ' (C); Φίλωνος περὶ βίου θεωρητικοῦ ἢ ἱκετῶν τὸ δ' (MG); τοῦ αὐτοῦ περὶ βίου θεωρητικοῦ ἢ ἱκετῶν ἀρετῶν τὸ δ' (F); Φίλωνος ἰουδαίου περὶ βίου θεωρητικοῦ ἢ ἱκετῶν ἀρετῆς τὸ τέταρτον (A); περὶ βίου θεωρητικοῦ ἢ ἱκετῶν ἀρετῶν (HPv). On the problem of the five books *On Virtue*, see E. Mary Smallwood, *Philonis Alexandrini Legatio ad Gaium* (Leiden: Brill, 1970), 36–43, concluding: "The problem of the structure of Philo's historical works and his 'five books' is one for which a certain solution is probably unattainable." The Latin seems to have lost the original title completely, for it has: *Philonis Judaei liber de statu Essaeorum, id est Monachorum, qui temporibus Agrippae regis monasteria sibi fecerunt.*

[10] PLCL 9:518.

There are several other shared readings between the Armenian version and Eusebius; for example, at 52.3 (§22), where both have εὐκαίρως (adopted reading in PCW) against εὐκαίρου of the Greek codices. Certain other Armenian-Eusebian readings also have the backing of the Old Latin against the Greek manuscripts; for example, at 55.4 (§34) all three have σώματος (adopted reading in PCW) against σωματικάς in the Greek manuscripts.[11] But not always are the affinities between Eusebius and the Armenian version discerned by either Conybeare or the editors of PCW. For example, the Armenian reading զոր ... յարմարմամբ (*zor ... yarmarmamb*) corresponds to ἃ ῥυθμοῖς at 54.2 (§29), in agreement with the Philo codices against the distorted readings of the Eusebian manuscripts (ἀριθμοῖς or ῥυθμοῖς).[12] Moreover, Eusebius alone is said to have at 67.6 (§78) ἐμφαινόμενα (adopted reading in PCW) against the Greek manuscripts, which have ἐμφερόμενα.[13] No mention is made of the Armenian reading տեսանելով (*tesanelov*, meaning "seeing," i.e., of what has been revealed), which seems to corroborate the preferred and adopted Eusebian reading. To be sure, the Armenian text does not always agree with the Eusebian excerpts.[14]

Conybeare went so far with his enthusiasm about the Armenian version that he somewhat exaggerated its true significance "as a means of determining the Greek text," adding: "Throughout, the same Greek expressions are interpreted by the same Armenian equivalents."[15] The words "determining" and "throughout" are somewhat exaggerative terms for the place of the Armenian version in providing valuable control over the Greek text in textual assessments. While as a rule the Armenian translation of Philo maintains the syntax of the Greek, the interlinear character of the translation is inconsistent. Also, notwithstanding the translator(s)' more or less systematic choice of words to render the Greek, the Armenian translation does not always convey the meaning of the Greek, and that not only because of differences in the inherent meaning(s) of equivalent terms in the respective languages, but also because the translation is full of inflectional inconsistencies especially when rendering verbs and participles. Surely, if

[11] Cf. the Armenian reading արբեալ (*arbeal*, Gk. πίοντες) at 56.15 (§40, adopted reading in PCW), supported by the Latin against all the Greek manuscripts, which have πίνοντες.

[12] Yet in the same section (§29) the editors of PCW take note of the Philonic-Armenian-Eusebian reading of ἐν τοῖς ἀλληγορουμένοις, against the reading of two Philonic manuscripts accepted by Mangey (ἀλληγορουμένης).

[13] Conybeare failed to recognize the relationship of the Armenian reading to that in Eusebius (*Philo about the Contemplative Life,*-19).

[14] See, e.g., PCW 52.14 (§24), 54.1–2 (§29), 64.5 (§68).

[15] Conybeare, *Philo about the Contemplative Life,* 155.

one were to translate the Armenian *De vita contemplativa* literally and apart from the Greek, the resultant translation would be considerably different from a literal translation of the Greek, as Sgarbi has demonstrated convincingly.[16] What this amounts to is that at times the controlling value of the Armenian text over the Greek is not as significant as at other times; that sometimes the nuances of morphology, including inflections and derivatives, have to be winked at in favor of the Greek reading. Consequently, omissions and additions gain added significance in this sort of textual criticism. Yet even here, caution is to be exercised since the Armenian translation often has several words strung together (syndetic and asyndetic) for a single Greek word.[17] Now that the style of the translator(s) is almost thoroughly studied and the question of textual relations is better understood, there has to be some downgrading of the syntactical and morphological value of the Armenian version vis-à-vis the Greek.

Nor does the translation date given by Conybeare (fifth century, based on two wrongly dated works that seem to utilize the Armenian Philo[18]) hold true: "Lastly, the language and diction of the version testifies to the same date. It is unmistakably that of the golden age of Armenian literature, of what is called the age of the Translators, which lasted, roughly speaking, from 350–500 A.D."[19] He is not only off by at least a century in dating the translation of Philo, which belongs to the second half of the sixth century, but also in gross error in equating the language and diction of this translation with the language and diction of the "golden age" of Armenian literature (fifth century, following the invention of the Armenian alphabet in 404/6). There is a vast syntactical difference in the writings and translations of these successive periods, with gross grammatical anomalies— imitative of Greek—that characterize works from the latter period.[20]

---

[16] Romano Sgarbi, *Problemi linguistici e di critica del testo nel* De vita contemplativa *di Filone alla luce della versione armena*. Memorie, Instituto Lombardo – Classe Lettere, vol. 40 fasc. 1 (Milan: Istituto Lombardo, 1992).

[17] Abraham Terian, "Syntactical Peculiarities in the Translations of the Hellenizing School," in *First International Conference on Armenian Linguistics (11–14, July 1979): Proceedings*, ed. John A. C. Greppin (Delmar, N.Y.: Caravan, 1980), 197–207; cf. Terian, *Alexander, vel de rationem quam habere etiam bruta animalia*, PAPM 36 (Paris: Cerf, 1988), 25–26.

[18] An observation first made by Jean-Baptiste Aucher (below, n. 22) and perpetuated in Armenian apologetic scholarship committed to preserving the traditional date(s) of these authors (Eghishē and Movsēs Khorenats'i). See the studies cited at the outset by Gohar Muradyan, including her own (below, n. 20).

[19] Conybeare, *Philo about the Contemplative Life*, 155.

[20] Bernard Coulie, "Style et traduction: Réflexions sur les versions arméniennes des textes grecs," *REArm* 25 (1994–1995): 43–62. For more on the latter period, see C. Mercier, "L'école hellénistique dans la littérature arménienne," *REArm* 13 (1978–1979): 59–75; Abraham Terian, "The Hellenizing School: Its Time, Place, and Scope of Activities

For his diplomatic edition Conybeare used four manuscripts, including the royal manuscript of King Het'um II of Armenian Cilicia (1289–1293, 1295–1297) as his *codex optimus* (Venice, Mekhitarist Library, manuscript no. 1040, dated 1296).[21] This is the same manuscript used earlier in the nineteenth century by Jean-Baptiste Aucher for the edition of Philo's works extant in Armenian only.[22] Conybeare, however, had previously persuaded an experienced editor at the Mekhitarist establishment in Venice, the philologist Garegin Zarphanalian, to publish the rest of the Armenian version of Philo containing those works the Greek of which is extant, including *De vita contemplativa*[23] The "anonymous" editor, whose identity is well known in Armenian scholarship, used the same *codex optimus*, against which he collated the other Philo manuscript in the Mekhitarist collection (Conybeare's D). The same editor thanks in an appendix the Oxford professor by name for sponsoring the publication of the volume. Consequently, the Armenian text published by Conybeare, except for its elaborate apparatus that contributes nothing to a better understanding of the text, is the

---

Reconsidered," in *East of Byzantium: Syria and Armenia in the Formative Period*, ed. Nina G. Garsoïan, Thomas F. Mathews, and Robert W. Thomson, Dumbarton Oaks Symposium 1980 (Washington, DC: Dumbarton Oaks, 1982), 175–86; Romano Sgarbi, *Analisi linguistico-filologica dell'interpretazione armena della trattazione greca filoniana intorno all'altare*, Memorie, Istituto Lombardo – Classe Lettere, vol. 39 fasc. 3 (Milan: Istituto Lombardo, 1989). For an overview of the "Hellenizing" tendencies, with a survey of scholarship including contributions in Armenian, see Gohar Muradyan, "The Armenian Version of Philo Alexandrinus: Translation Technique, Biblical Citations," in *Studies on the Ancient Armenian Version of Philo's Works*, ed. Sara Mancini Lombardi and Paola Pontani, SPhA 6 (Leiden: Brill, 2011), 51–85; Muradyan, *Grecisms in Ancient Armenian*, Hebrew University Armenian Studies 13 (Leuven: Peeters, 2011).

[21] The other three are: Erevan, Matenadaran no. 2100 (formerly Ejmiatsin no. 2049.5), dated 1325, Conybeare's B; no. 2057 (formerly Ejmiatsin no. 2046.2), dated 1328, his C; and Venice, Mekhitarist Library no. 1334, early fourteenth century, his D. For a description of these manuscripts, see my introduction to *Alexander*, 30–35, in PAPM (cited above, n. 17).

[22] Jean-Baptiste Aucher, *Philonis Judaei sermones tres hactenus inediti, I. et II. De Providentia et III. De Animalibus* (Venetiis: Typis coenobi p. Armenorum in insula s. Lazari, 1822); Aucher, *Philonis Judaei paralipomena armena: Libri videlicet quatuor in Genesin [sic], libri duo in Exodum, sermo unus de Sampsone, alter de Jona, tertius de tribus angelis Abraamo apparentibus* (Venetiis: Typis coenobi p. Armenorum in insula s. Lazari, 1826).

[23] Փիլոնի Հեբրայեցւոյ ճառք թարգմանեալք ի նախնեաց մերոց որոց Հելլէն բնագիրք հասին առ մեզ (*P'iloni Hebrayec'woy čaṙk' t'argmanealk' i nakhneac' meroc' oroc' Hellen bnagirk' hasin aṙ mez* [Works of Philo Judaeus, translated by our ancients, the Greek originals of which have come down to us]), ed. Garegin Zarphanalian (Venice: Mekhitarist Press, 1892), 286. The contents of this edition are as follows: pp. 5–32 = *De vita contemplativa*; pp. 33–104 = *De Abrahamo*; pp. 105–177 = *Legum allegoriae* 1–2; pp. 178–200 = *Spec.* 1.79–161; pp. 201–219 = *Spec.* 1.285–345; pp. 220–222 = *Spec.* 3.1–7; pp. 222–223 = fragment from *De numeris*; pp. 223–267 = *Decal.*; pp. 268–284 = *Spec.* 3.8–64.

same as that published three years earlier by the Venetian Mekhitarists.[24] Unfortunately, the Armenian text of the Philonic works in this edition has not been studied alongside the Greek text as Conybeare probably had wished to undertake following his observations in the Armenian version of *De vita contemplativa*. A major reason for this *status quaestionis* is that Zarphanalian's edition lacks both the pagination of Mangey's edition and the section divisions enumerated in subsequent editions of the Greek text, thus hampering any quick comparison between the Greek and Armenian texts.[25]

There are 176 variant readings from the Armenian version indicated in the critical apparatus of the PCW edition of *De vita contemplativa*. Whereas 65 of these have parallel readings in one or another of the Greek manuscripts and 33 of them have been adopted in the text,[26] including two where the Armenian is in harmony with Eusebius (52.3 [§22]) and also with the Latin (55.4 [§34]), 111 variants stand alone against the Greek witnesses. Of these 111, only 19 have been adopted[27]—including 3 of the 21 additions (62.8 [§61], 66.4 [§75], 66.15–16 [§77]), but none of the 30 omissions. The remaining 44 readings peculiar to the Armenian have corresponding Greek words but differ either in their inflection or in the syntactical sequence. Nearly one fourth of these are simple transpositions, possibly later scribal adaptations of the artificial syntax; e.g., 47.8 (§3), 47.13 (§3, twice), 48.2 (§6), 51.2 (§18), leaving some openness as to how they should be construed in Greek.[28]

---

[24] Strangely, unacknowledged by Conybeare.

[25] It was in the course of my marking the section divisions in the margin of this edition that I happened to discover an inserted folio at pp. 222–23 belonging possibly to the lost Περὶ ἀριθμῶν (*De numeris*); see my article "A Philonic Fragment on the Decad," in *Nourished with Peace: Studies in Hellenistic Judaism in Memory of Samuel Sandmel*, ed. Frederick E. Greenspahn, Earle Hilgert, and Burton L. Mack, Scholars Press Homage Series 9 (Chico, CA: Scholars Press, 1984), 173–82.

[26] See 48.14 (§9), 48.16 (§9), 48.19 (§10), 49.14 (§14), 52.3 (§22), 52.5 (§23), 52.7 (§23), 52.14 (§24), 53.7 (§27), 53.14 (§29), 54.23 (§33), 55.4 (§34), 55.11 (§36), 55.15 (§37), 59.8 (§50), 59.12 (§51), 59.20 (§52), 61.16 (§59), 62.6 (§61), 62.13 (§62), 62.17 (§63), 63.10 (§65), 64.5 (§68), 64.6 (§68), 66.5 (§75), 67.11 (§79), 69.3 (§83), 69.8 (§84), 69.8 (§85), 69.8 (§85), 69.16 (§86), 70.4 (§87), 70.1 (§90). Rejected: 46.1 (§1), 48.21 (§10), 50.9 (§16), 52.2 (§22), 52.11 (§24), 52.11 (§24), 52.12 (§24), 55.1 (§34), 55.2 (§34), 56.4 (§38), 56.5 (§38), 56.8 (§38), 56.12 (§39), 57.1 (§40), 57.19 (§44), 58.3 (§44), 58.4 (§45), 58.7 (§45), 58.7 (§45), 60.1 (§53), 60.11 (§54), 60.11–12 (§54), 61.1 (§56), 61.4 (§57), 61.5 (§57), 62.12 (§62), 65.5 (§71), 65.20 (§73), 66.3 (§75), 68.13 (§81), 69.5 (§84), 70.1 (§90).

[27] See 47.20 (§6), 49.9 (§13), 50.8 (§16), 56.15 (§40), 57.12–13 (§42), 58.18 (§49), 59.17 (§51–52), 60.4 (§53), 62.14 (§62), 63.23 (§67), 65.11 (§72), 66.4 (§75), 66.15–16 (§77), 68.14–15 (§82), 68.16 (§82), 69.7 (§84), 70.10 (§88), 70.18 (§89).

[28] See 46 (Title), 47.8 (§3), 47.13 (§3), 47.13 (§3), 48.2 (§6), 48.8 (§8), 49.2 (§11), 51.2 (§18), 51.10 (§20), 51.10–11 (§20), 52.6 (§23), 52.12 (§24), 53.11 (§28), 54.20 (§33), 57.4 (§40), 57.11 (§42), 58.3 (§44), 58.18 (§48), 59.15 (§51), 60.6 (§53), 60.14 (§55), 60.18 (§56), 61.13 (§58),

The following lists show all such omissions and additions, beginning with the page and line number in the PCW edition, followed by the section number in parenthesis.

Omissions in the Armenian text as noted in PCW

46.6	(§1)	τοῖς
49.4	(§12)	ἢ παρακλήσεως
49.7	(§13)	καὶ μακαρίας
49.8	(§13)	ἤδη
49.8–9	(§13)	υἱοῖς ἢ θυγατράσιν εἴτε καὶ ἄλλοις
50.11	(§16)	τὸν ἰατρόν
51.9	(§19)	ἀχθείς
54.3	(§30)	χωρίς
54.6	(§30)	ἑξῆς
59.8	(§50)	ἔτι
60.6	(§53)	ἐπαινέσαντες
60.15	(§55)	οὕτως
62.7	(§61)	μόνον
63.5	(§64)	τις
63.7–8	(§64)	καὶ ἑαυτούς
63.12	(§65)	ἦν
63.12	(§65)	ἔλαχεν
64.1	(§67)	ἀλλ᾽ ἔτι κομιδῇ νέους παῖδας
64.2–3	(§67)	ἐνηβήσαντας καί
64.8–9	(§68)	ἀφ᾽ ἑαυτῆς
64.13	(§69)	καὶ ἀστείοις
65.11	(§72)	οἳ
65.13	(§72)	αὐτῶν
66.7	(§75)	ἢ καὶ ὑπ᾽ ἄλλου
67.5	(§78)	ἤρξατο ἡ λογικὴ ψυχὴ διαφερόντως τὰ οἰκεῖα θεωρεῖν
68.17–69.1	(§83)	ἄγεται δὲ ἡ παννυχίς
69.2	(§83)	τὸ πρῶτον
70.3	(§86)	δέ
70.4	(§87)	ἦν
70.16	(§89)	ἀνίσχοντα

Several of these Armenian omissions could well be explicable by later additions in Greek, where they appear to be either superfluous or parenthetical, for example, at 49.4, 8–9, 50.11, 64.1. As for the last example, Cohn brackets the questionable words on the basis of the Armenian text.[29] Moreover, one

---

61.18 (§59), 62.4 (§60), 62.8 (§61), 62.11 (§62), 63.1 (§63), 63.7 (§64), 63.13 (§65), 63.14 (§66), 63.16 (§66), 64.6 (§68), 64.7 (§68), 64.14 (§69), 64.18 (§69), 65.18 (§73), 67.1–2 (§78), 68.1 (§80), 69.5 (§84), 69.15 (§86), 70.7 (§88), 70.17 (§89), 70.21 (§90).

[29] That these parenthesized words are to be expunged is argued by Cohn in a later study ("Kritische Bemerkungen zu Philo," *Hermes* 51 [1916]: 161–68, esp. 179; noted by Colson, PLCL 9:523).

could easily point out several other omissions in the Armenian text that are unaccounted for in PCW. These six from Conybeare's list have been overlooked:[30] 51.8 (§19) ἅπαξ, 53.6 (§27) αὐτῶν, 57.6 (§41) ἠμύνετο, 59.4 (§49) ἕτερα, 60.6 (§53) οὐκ, 62.19 (§63) ταῦτα. These and other omissions in the Armenian text deserve further attention.

Additions in the Armenian text as noted in PCW[31]

47.7	(§2)	ὄντως	(էապէս)
47.12	(§3)	εἶναι	(լինելոյ)
48.19	(§10)	αὐτοῖς	(առ նոսա)
52.6	(§23)	αἱ	(որք)
53.15–16	(§29)	αὐτῶν	(նոցա)
59.7	(§50)	γάρ	(քանզի)
59.16	(§51)	καί	(եւ)
60.15	(§55)	αὐτῶν	(նոցա)
61.13	(§58)	δέ	(եւ)
62.8	(§61)	τὰ δὲ σώματα	(եւ մարմիներն)
		(vel τὸ δὲ σῶμα)	
63.16	(§66)	αὐτοῖς	(նոցա)
63.22	(§66)	αὐτῶν	(հրեանց)
65.5	(§71)	ἦν	(էր)
65.11	(§72)	καί	(եւ)
65.11	(§72)	τήν	(-ն)
65.13	(§72)	καί	(եւս)
66.4	(§75)	ὁ πρόεδρος αὐτῶν,	([եւ] զահերեցն ի նոսանէ՝
		πολλῆς ἁπάντων	հասարակ իրրու
		ἡσυχίας	լռութիւն
		γενομένης	եղեւ)
66.15–16	(§77)	τὰ ὦτα καὶ	(զականջսն եւ
		τοὺς ὀφθαλμοὺς	զաչսն
		ἀνατετακότες	ի նմա կառուցանէն)
68.5	(§80)	καί	(եւ)
68.6	(§80)	καὶ καθ᾽ ἡλικίαν	(եւ ըստ հասակի
			վայելչականան զարդու)
70.11	(§88)	ἦσαν (vel ἦν)	(էին)

---

[30] Conybeare, *Philo about the Contemplative Life*, 7–9. The list contains two erroneous "omissions": at 57.15 (§43 [478.6 Mangey]): μέσος; and at 70.6–7 (§87 [485.29 Mangey]): τοῦ προφήτου.

[31] Not all are marked with the abbreviation for additions "add.," but all are found in the apparatus under "Arm." It is indeed difficult to consider the occasional periphrastics of auxiliary verbs as additions to the Greek text, since very often they are necessitated by the translation; e.g., Arm. adds εἶναι after τὸ ποτόν (47.12), and ἐστι after ἀκίνετος (47.15) and after ἄξιον (47.21); etc. (the last two are not in the apparatus; were all such verbs to be considered, the list of additions would have been considerably longer).

We see readily how, except for the three words at 62.8 and the two longer additions at 66.4, 15–16, which fill lacunae in the Greek text and which have been duly adopted (Conybeare being oblivious of the latter), the majority of the Armenian additions indicated in this edition emanate from simple translational necessities—even in this artificially imposed style of translating.

Like most every major subject Conybeare addresses in his *Philo about the Contemplative Life,* his overestimation and unsystematic utilization of the Armenian version in the textual criticism of the Greek original gives reason to designate this part of his work also as a thing of the past; or, at best, a pioneering work that calls for considerable revision. Contrary to his statements on its significance, the Armenian text has to be used with great caution as a control over the Greek text. The interlinear character of the translation is deceptive, for the rendering is replete with inexact equivalents—however consistent—and abounds in frequent inconsistencies in inflections of words. These features of the translation seldom lend it to emend corruptions in the Greek text, especially in instances where the Armenian reading stands alone. It is not at all surprising that the majority of Conybeare's emendations, especially when based on the Armenian text alone, were systematically rejected in the PCW edition and relegated to the apparatus. Equally questionable, however, is the use made of the Armenian version in the latter edition of the Greek text: not only for not taking Conybeare more seriously where his emendations are justifiable (as Colson at times observes in his annotations in PLCL) but also for treating the Armenian version inflexibly. Whereas Conybeare errs in going overboard in both estimation and utilization, the German editors err in their minimalist approach to the Armenian version even though they cite it 176 times in the apparatus. With their primary focus on the Greek text, they seem to have sought the likely contributions of the Armenian version in instances where its reading is attested also by one or another of the Greek witnesses. They have not exhausted the full significance of the Armenian variants— much less accounted for them all; nor have they been consistent with their criteria for adopting Armenian readings.[32]

---

[32] Illustrative of this are the three uses of ἐρημία in this treatise: at 51.10 (§20), 52.12 (§24), and 62.11 (§62). All three are translated accurately in Armenian (both lexically, albeit amplified, and contextually): the first as յապահով վայր զհանդարտութեան (*yapahov vayr zhandartut'ean,* §20), the second as զյապահով հանդարտութիւնն (*zyapahov handartut'iwnn,* §24), and the third as անմարդութիւն եւ ամայութիւն (*anmardut'iwn ew amayut'iwn,* §62). Yet the respective editors have supposed that in the first two instances the Armenian is the equivalent of ἠρεμία, and consequently the supposed Armenian reading stands alone in

It follows that Conybeare's work on the Armenian version of *De vita contemplative* stands in need of some revision vis-à-vis its relation to the Greek text, as also the critical apparatus in the PCW edition—even certain readings of its main text.

St. Nersess Armenian Seminary, NY
National Academy of Sciences, Armenia

---

these two cases in the critical apparatus. It is very unlikely that the same word was misspelled twice in the Greek exemplar of the Armenian, or that the translator(s) did not quite know the meaning of the word these two instances but knew it the third time around. Elsewhere in the works of Philo where both the Greek and the Armenian texts could be compared, ἐρημία is translated in somewhat similar, multiple Armenian words.

The Studia Philonica Annual 31 (2019): 13–28

THE VALUE AND VARIETY OF ALLEGORY: A GLANCE AT PHILO'S *DE GIGANTIBUS*[*]

MIKOLAJ DOMARADZKI

Philo's fascinating account of allegory has received a great deal of well-deserved scholarly attention in diverse aspects. Thus, for example, his exegetical nomenclature and his original criteria for identifying figurative expressions have been carefully examined.[1] His pivotal role in the history of allegorical interpretation and his profound influence on the development of later allegoresis have likewise been convincingly demonstrated.[2] More recently, Philo's relation to Jewish Bible exegesis and to Homeric scholar-

---

[*] This work was supported by the National Science Centre, Poland [grant number 2017/25/B/HS1/00559]. I would like to thank *SPhiloA*'s editor Gregory E. Sterling and the anonymous reviewer for their helpful suggestions and inspiring criticisms.

[1] See, e.g., the classic work by Carl Siegfried, *Philo von Alexandria als Ausleger des Alten Testaments an sich selbst und nach seinem geschichtlichen Einfluss betrachtet. Nebst Untersuchungen über die Graecitaet Philo's* (Jena: Hermann Dufft, 1875), esp. 31–137 (on Philo's "Sprache") and 160–97 (on Philo's "hermeneutischen Grundsätze," i.e., his "Regeln vom Ausschlüsse des Wortsinns" and his "Regeln der Allegorie") or the seminal study by Jean Pépin "Remarques sur la théorie de l'exégèse allégorique chez Philon," in *Philon d'Alexandrie. Lyon. 11–15 septembre 1966*, ed. Roger Arnaldez, Claude Mondésert, Jean Pouilloux, and Antoine Guillaumont (Paris: Éditions du CNRS, 1967), 131–67. For a more recent and extremely useful discussion, see Adam Kamesar, "Biblical Interpretation in Philo," in *The Cambridge Companion to Philo*, ed. Adam Kamesar, (Cambridge: Cambridge University Press, 2009), 65–91, esp. 77–85 (on the "Rationale for Allegorical Interpretation").

[2] While the literature on the topic is abundant (see, e.g., Jean Pépin, *Mythe et allégorie: Les origines grecques et les contestations judéo-chrétiennes* [Paris: Études augustiniennes, 1976] or Christoph Blönnigen, *Der griechische Ursprung der jüdisch-hellenistischen Allegorese und ihre Rezeption in der alexandrinischen Patristik* [Frankfurt a. M.: Lang, 1992]), important work on Philo's reception has been done by Annewies van den Hoek and David T. Runia. See esp. Annewies van den Hoek, *Clement of Alexandria and His Use of Philo in the* Stromateis: *An Early Christian Reshaping of a Jewish Model* (Leiden: Brill, 1988); David T. Runia, *Philo in Early Christian Literature: A Survey*, CRINT 3.3 (Assen: Van Gorcum; Minneapolis: Fortress, 1993); Runia, *Philo and the Church Fathers: A Collection of Papers* (Leiden: Brill, 1995); Annewies van den Hoek, "Philo and the Grigen: A Descriptive Catalogue of Their Relationship," *SPhiloA* 12 (2000): 44–121; David T. Runia, "Philo in Byzantium," *VC* 70 (2016): 259–81.

ship in Alexandria has also been extensively investigated.[3] While Philonic research has greatly advanced in all these areas, the modest purpose of the present article is to look at the types and functions of allegory in a text that nicely illustrates the idiosyncrasy and complexity of Philo's approach.

On the Giants and its twin treatise *On the Unchangeableness of God* belong to the most frequently discussed works of Philo.[4] While David Winston and John Dillon have produced a detailed commentary that covers the formal, stylistic and philosophical aspects of the pair of tracts,[5] it is their structure that has been particularly thoroughly examined.[6] As things stand, it may not be an exaggeration to say that this is still as—David T. Runia has once diagnosed—one of Philo's best known works.[7] This does not mean, however, that there is complete consensus on every issue. Consider this following observation:

> Nul n'est tenu d'aimer l'allégorie comme moyen de compréhension. Nul ne doit non plus la dénigrer ou la réduire, sans l'avoir longtemps mesurée. Elle a chez Philon la puissance régulatrice de l'aimant : il ordonne en lignes de force répondant à une structure unique et constante tous les atomes du métal. Il ne semble pas qu'on puisse trouver dans le *De gigantibus* une seule phrase qui ne participe étroitement à la Cité unifiée, pleine, des deux traités réunis.[8]

---

[3] See esp. Maren R. Niehoff, "Homeric Scholarship and Bible Exegesis in Ancient Alexandria: Evidence from Philo's 'Quarrelsome' Colleagues," *CQ* 57 (2007): 166–82; Niehoff, *Jewish Exegesis and Homeric Scholarship in Alexandria* (Cambridge: Cambridge University Press, 2011); Niehoff, "Philo and Plutarch on Homer," in *Homer and the Bible in the Eyes of Ancient Interpreters*, Jerusalem Studies in Religion and Culture 16, Maren R. Niehoff (Leiden: Brill, 2012), 127–53.

[4] The testimony of Eusebius (*Hist. eccl.* 2.18.4) makes it clear that the two were originally one.

[5] David Winston and John Dillon, *Two Treatises of Philo of Alexandria: A Commentary on* De Gigantibus *and* Quod Deus Sit Immutabilis, BJS 25 (Chico, CA: Scholars Press, 1983).

[6] Among the most important contributions are the following: Valentin Nikiprowetzky, "L'exégèse de Philon d'Alexandrie dans le *De Gigantibus* et le *Quod Deus sit Immutabilis*," in *Two Treatises*, 5–75 (this study develops ideas presented already in: Nikiprowetzky, *Le commentaire de l'écriture chez Philon d'Alexandrie: Son caractère et sa portée; Observations philologiques* [Leiden: Brill, 1977], esp. 170–80); David T. Runia, "The Structure of Philo's Allegorical Treatises: A Review of Two Recent Studies and Some Additional Comments," *VC* 38 (1984): 209–56; Runia, "Further Observations on the Structure of Philo's Allegorical Treatises," *VC* 41 (1987): 105–38 (both papers reprinted in: Runia, *Exegesis and Philosophy: Studies on Philo of Alexandria* [Aldershot: Variorum, 1990]) and Peder Borgen, *Philo of Alexandria: An Exegete for his Time* (Leiden: Brill, 1997), esp. 102–23.

[7] Cf. Runia, "Further Observations," 106.

[8] Jacques Cazeaux, *La trame et la chaîne, II: Le cycle de Noé dans Philon d'Alexandrie*, ALGHJ 20 (Leiden: Brill, 1989), 56–57. This work is a continuation of Cazeaux, *La trame et la chaîne ou les Structures littéraires et l'Exégèse dans cinq des Traités de Philon d'Alexandrie*, ALGHJ 15 (Leiden: Brill, 1983). Cf. also the next note.

While much has been written about the problems of reading Philo's works through the lens of structuralist literary criticism,[9] the present paper will focus on Philonic allegory understood as "moyen de compréhension" rather than "puissance régulatrice." Of course, this is not to deny that there is a systematic structure in Philo's works: modelled on Middle Platonist interpretations of the *Odyssey*, Philo's exegeses build on the assumption that the Pentateuch is an allegory of the soul's ascent to the divine.[10] Thus, the belief that Scripture contains guidance for the soul provides also *De gigantibus* with a fairly consistent structure. However, this article will be concerned primarily with an "instructive" or—*sit venia verbo*—"explanatory" value that Philo ascribes to allegory in his treatise: whether he interprets a biblical verse, etymologizes a scriptural name or appropriates a philosophical concept, Philo often employs allegory for elucidatory purposes. Accordingly, this article will touch upon three issues in *Gig.*: (1) the interaction between allegorical expressions and allegorical interpretations, (2) the coalescence of allegoresis and etymology, and (3) the difference between literal and allegorical appropriation in Philo. It will be argued that *De gigantibus* shows allegory to take many forms in Philo, as it helps him to make his exegeses more accessible and compelling.

1. *The Interrelationship between Allegorical Expressions and Allegorical Interpretations*

A remarkable feature of Philo's exegeses is a constant movement between allegory and allegoresis. Following the established tradition, we may characterize the former as a mode of *composing* a text (i.e., an *expression*) and the latter—as a mode of *reading* (i.e., an *interpretation*). The distinction has been aptly put by Jean Pépin, according to whom the former "consiste à cacher un message sous le revêtement d'une figure," whereas the latter—"à décrypter la figure pour retrouver le message."[11] It is a distinctive feature of

---

[9] See, e.g., Runia, "The Structure," 211–26 or John Dillon's review in *VC* 46 (1992): 83–87.

[10] See, e.g., Borgen, *Philo of Alexandria*, 11; Kamesar, "Biblical Interpretation," 86 or, more recently, Gregory E. Sterling, "When the Beginning Is the End: The Place of Genesis in the Commentaries of Philo," in *The Book of Genesis: Composition, Reception, and Interpretation*, ed. Craig A. Evans, Joel N. Lohr, and David L. Petersen, V T Sup 152 (Leiden: Brill, 2012), 440.

[11] Pépin, *Mythe et allégorie*, 488. See further Mikolaj Domaradzki, "The Sophists and Allegoresis," *AncPhil* 35 (2015): 247–58; Domaradzki, "The Beginnings of Greek Allegoresis," *CW* 110 (2017): 299–321 and Domaradzki, "Democritus and Allegoresis," *CQ* 69 (forthcoming).

his exegeses that Philo frequently makes the two interact so that his allegorical interpretations are interspersed with and supported by various allegorical expressions.[12] Thus, two important traditions converge in Philo: that of allegorical interpretation and that of allegorical composition.[13]

Allegory is, of course, primarily the achievement of Moses: Philo sees himself as merely elucidating this allegorical composition. But if allegory was of great didactic value for the prophet, would it not (at least sometimes) be a useful tool of explanation for his interpreter? That Philo makes frequent and abundant use of various metaphors and personifications in his exegeses is common knowledge. Whether his strongly figurative language is categorized as "allegorical" depends, obviously, on how one understands the term "allegory."[14] In what follows, it will be assumed that it is legitimate to speak of allegorical *composition* in Philo when his continuous interweaving of personifications and other metaphors produces a sustained figurative meaning.[15] Indeed, *On the Giants* shows that in his

---

[12] To this best of my knowledge, this interplay between allegorical interpretations and allegorical expressions in Philo has not received any special attention in Philonic research. Needless to say, however, various scholars have stressed that Philo employs diverse techniques of instruction. Thus, for example, in his exquisite discussion of Philo's style and diction (*Two Treatises*, 129–78), John Leopold frequently emphasizes the illustrative purpose and unique richness of poetic imagery in Philo (metaphors, personifications, similes, extended comparisons, etc.). See, esp. his "Philo's Vocabulary and Word Choice," 137–40; "Characteristics of Philo's style in the *De Gigantibus* and *Quod Deus*," 141–54 and "Rhetoric and Allegory," 155–70. Also, Adam Kamesar has convincingly shown Philo's assumption about the educational or pedagogic value of the Pentateuch (the pan-Scriptural didacticism). See esp. his "The Literary Genres of the Pentateuch as Seen from the Greek Perspective: The Testimony of Philo of Alexandria," *SPhiloA* 9 (1997): 143–89 and "Philo, the Presence of 'Paideutic' Myth in the Pentateuch, and the 'Principles' or *Kephalaia* of Mosaic Discourse," *SPhiloA* 10 (1998): 34–65.

[13] On the two traditions, see esp. Jon Whitman, *Allegory. The Dynamics of an Ancient and Medieval Technique* (Cambridge, MA: Harvard University Press, 1987), 3–10. While the scholar argues that the two allegorical traditions converge in Bernard Silvestris's *Cosmographia* (218–60), the present paper suggests that the process—at least in embryonic form—can also be found in Philo. Importantly, Whitman uses the term "allegory" in relation to both the technique of interpretation and the technique of composition. However, I side with those scholars who prefer to reserve the term "allegory" for the strategy of *expressing* an idea and the term "allegoresis" for the strategy of *revealing* it (see, e.g., my "The Beginnings," 300–302).

[14] For example, Leopold, "Characteristics of Philo's style," points briefly to the use of allegorical language "in both Moses and Philo" (143–44), but does not pursue the matter further.

[15] See Whitman, *Allegory*, to whose excellent discussion this paper is greatly indebted here.

exegeses Philo often employs this strategy in the service of allegorical *interpretation*. Let us look at some examples.[16]

The second exegetical unit in *Gig.* 6–18 deals with Gen 6:2, which reports that the "angels (ἄγγελοι) of God"[17] took to themselves wives from the "daughters (θυγατέρας) of men." While the problem resides naturally in how disembodied spirits can marry mortals, the answer is provided by a sophisticated allegoresis, in the course of which the angels are equated (§§6, 16) with "demons" (δαίμονες) and "souls" (ψυχαί), whereas the daughters are identified (§§17–18) with "pleasures" (ἡδοναί). The upshot is that the biblical lemma is revealed to actually depict a seduction of wicked individuals (fallen souls) by various sensual pleasures: those who descend into the body "as though into a river" (ὥσπερ εἰς ποταμόν)[18] and abandon philosophy, make various unwise choices, which is why they are defeated by corporeality and drown in spiritless hedonism. While the explanation builds on what is customarily referred to as "Philo's demonology" (§§6–16),[19] the argument is also buttressed (§17) by a quotation from Ps 77:49

---

[16] In what follows, all quotations from *Gig.* (at times modified) are taken from David Winston, *Philo of Alexandria: The Contemplative Life, The Giants, and Selections* (New York: Paulist, 1981).

[17] On the substitution of οἱ ἄγγελοι τοῦ θεοῦ for οἱ υἱοὶ τοῦ θεοῦ, see, e.g., Peter Katz, *Philo's Bible: The Aberrant Text of Bible Quotations in Some Philonic Writings and Its Place in the Textual History of the Greek Bible* (Cambridge: Cambridge University Press, 1950), 20–21 or David Gooding and Valentin Nikiprowetzky, "Philo's Bible in the *De Gigantibus* and the *Quod Deus sit Immutabilis*," in *Two Treatises*, 106–7.

[18] *Gig.* 13. This is an appropriation from *Tim.* 43a6. For a survey of other uses of this imagery, see David T. Runia, *Philo of Alexandria and the Timaeus of Plato* (Leiden: Brill, 1986), 260–61.

[19] See, e.g., Valentin Nikiprowetzky, "Sur une lecture démonologique de Philon d'Alexandrie, *De Gigantibus* 6–18," in *Hommage à Georges Vajda. Études d'histoire et de pensée juives*, ed. Gérard Nahon and Charles Touati (Louvain: Peeters, 1980), 43–71; John Dillon, "Philo's Doctrine of Angels," in *Two Treatises*, 197–205 and, more recently, Francesca Calabi, *God's Acting, Man's Acting: Tradition and Philosophy in Philo of Alexandria* (Leiden: Brill, 2008), 111–25. Philo's demonology has been classified as "essentially Middle Platonic" (John Dillon, *The Middle Platonists: A Study of Platonism 80 B.C. to A.D. 220* [London: Duckworth, 1977; rev. ed., Ithaca, NY: Cornell University Press, 1996], 174). For further discussions of the question whether Philo can be categorized as a Middle Platonist, see, e.g., Runia, *Philo of Alexandria and the Timaeus of Plato*, 505–19; Gregory E. Sterling, "Platonizing Moses: Philo and Middle Platonism," *SPhiloA* 5 (1993): 96–111; David T. Runia, "Was Philo a Middle Platonist? A Difficult Question Revisited," *SPhiloA* 5 (1993): 112–40 and Thomas H. Tobin, "Was Philo a Middle Platonist? Some Suggestions," *SPhiloA* 5 (1993): 147–50. Finally, it is worth noting that the above passage in *Gig.* (along with such parallel texts as *Plant.* 14 and *Somn.* 1.138–141) sheds some light on Philo's view of reincarnation. For an extensive discussion, see Sami Yli-Karjanmaa, *Reincarnation in Philo of Alexandria*, SPhiloM 7 (Atlanta: SBL Press, 2015) and Yli-Karjanmaa, "The Significance of Reading Philonic Parallels: Examples from the *De plantatione*," *SPhiloA* 29 (2017): 159–84.

[78:49] about the sending of "evil angels" (ἀγγέλων πονηρῶν).[20] Hence, the bad angels/demons are deciphered as allegories of incarnated souls that choose the life of pleasures ("wed the daughters of humans").

Notably, this allegoresis is intertwined with various figurative expressions that help to elucidate the point. For example, the wicked ones are diagnosed (§17) not to know the "daughters of right reason" (ὀρθοῦ λόγου θυγατέρας), that is, "sciences and virtues" (ἐπιστήμας καὶ ἀρετάς), which is why they "woo the pleasures" (ἡδονὰς μετερχόμενοι), that is, "mortal descendants of mortal men" (τῶν ἀνθρώπων θνητὰς θνητῶν ἀπογόνους). Thus, Philo allegorically interprets the Genesis story, while at the same time creating suggestive allegorical agents. He thereby uses the strategy of personification for the purpose of explaining his interpretation, and in the course of doing so he produces an extended non-literal sense. The resulting allegory conveys that the souls who become enamored of the daughters of right reason (i.e., "marry sciences and virtues") strive to liberate themselves from incarnation by virtue of philosophy (i.e., the art of dying to the life in the body). The figurative expression used to designate the sciences and virtues reinforces the explanation put forward: the evil angels (i.e., seduced souls) are the enemies of right reason, because their love for pleasure is antithetical to science and virtue. Thus, in this exegesis the "daughters of humans" from the biblical lemma are *interpreted* as "sensual pleasures," whilst the aforementioned "sciences and virtues" are allegorically *portrayed* as the "daughters of right reason." The exegesis illustrates, then, how Philo lets the technique of *interpretation* ("allegoresis") interact with the technique of *composition* ("allegory") so that the personification of the daughters of right reason explicates the allegoresis of the daughters of humans from the biblical lemma. This shows that Philo's allegorical exegeses can have a compositional dimension: in *Gig.* 17 the Alexandrian not only unveils the hidden meaning of the Genesis story, but also makes use of personification combined with other metaphors to elucidate and strengthen his point. This is not an isolated case.

The first exegetical unit in *Gig.* 1–5 deals with Gen 6:1, which has it that "men (ἄνθρωποι) began to become numerous (πολλοί) on earth and daughters (θυγατέρες) were born to them." Philo raises (§1) the question about the "numerous population" (πολυανθρωπία) that followed Noah and his sons (though later discussion shows that the problem resides not only in the multiplication of the human race, but also in the appearance of *female*

---

[20] On which, see Naomi G. Cohen, *Philo's Scriptures: Citations from the Prophets and Writings: Evidence for a Haftarah Cycle in Second Temple Judaism* (Leiden: Brill, 2007), 141, 147, 155.

progeny) and proposes the following solution: the existence of that which is "rare" (σπάνιον) highlights the presence of that which is "very numerous" (πάμπολυ). While the ensuing allegoresis reveals that the biblical lemma in fact concerns a spiritual procreation, the explanation builds precisely on the idea that the scarcity of justice brings out the widespread prevalence of injustice.

The allegorical interpretation that Philo puts forward (§§4–5) has it that the just Noah fathers "sons" (i.e., virtues), whereas the numerous unjust ones can only be parents of "daughters" (i.e., vices and passions). The explanation that Noah's descendants are few and virtuous presupposes obviously the superiority of the male (i.e., "just") over the female (i.e., "unjust"), which is pervasive in Philo's writings.[21] However, it is note-worthy that the allegorical interpretation (few sons = virtues, numerous daughters = vices and passions) is, again, reinforced and explicated by a host of non-literal expressions that yield a sustained figurative meaning. The following deserve to be mentioned: the begetting of "male offspring in the soul" (ἄρρενα γενεὰν ἐν ψυχῇ), the thoughts that are "unmanly, emascu-late and effeminate" (ἄνανδροι καὶ κατεαγότες καὶ θηλυδρίαι), the tree "of vir-tue" (ἀρετῆς) and the trees of "vice and passions" (κακίας καὶ παθῶν), whose "shoots" (βλάσται) are "feminine" (γυναικώδεις), the "male" (ἄρρενα) reason that the just Noah pursues and the injustice of the many that is "bearing females" (θηλυτόκος). Again, there is an interplay between allegoresis and allegory, which results in that the latter elucidates the former and makes the explanation more appealing and vivid. One more time, then, Philo's approach has at once an interpretative and a compositional aspect: his allegorical interpretation of the Genesis story is supported by an extended figurative description.

Interestingly, the two above exegeses are slightly inconsistent. On the one hand, the daughters in *Gig.* 4–5 signify vices and passions (the impli-cation being that "female is bad" and "reason is male") and, on the other, *Gig.* 17 mentions the "daughters of right reason" (which entails that—at least sometimes—"female can be good and rational"). While such incon-gruities abound in Philo, they can easily be accounted for in terms of the primacy of the biblical text and the modesty of the Philonic text.[22] As the task of an exegete is first and foremost to explain Scripture inspired by

---

[21] As has been stressed by Carl Siegfried, *Philo von Alexandria als Ausleger,* 189: "Das Männliche ist das Tüchtigere, Bessere, daher sind männliche Geburten Tugenden." For a more recent discussion, see Richard A. Baer, *Philo's Use of the Categories Male and Female* (Leiden: Brill, 1970), esp. 40–44.

[22] See Runia, "The Structure," 237–38.

God, philosophical coherence is hardly the first priority.[23] Thus, we can say that Philo allows his allegories to be somewhat at odds with one another when he focuses on the different aspects of an issue and/or highlights its distinct characteristics.[24] The first exegesis (§§1–5) deals with daughters in general (contrasted with Noah's son), whereas the second one (§§6–18) deals with specific daughters (those that the "angels" choose). That is why in the former case the female as such is valued negatively (the unjust ones have no male offspring, their thoughts are unmanly, emasculate and effeminate, they plant solely trees of vice and passions, etc.), whereas in the latter case the female can be virtuous (as is testified by the aforementioned personification: the daughters of right reason = sciences and virtues).

2. *The Coalescence of Allegoresis and Etymology*

Philo's proclivity for using etymology as a technique of allegorical interpretation has been generally recognized.[25] Notwithstanding this, some scholars have opposed etymology and allegorical interpretation. David Dawson, for example, has stressed that the two should be clearly distinguished, since etymology "lacks a narrative dimension."[26] Anthony A. Long has even more forcefully argued that etymology explains "atomic units of language," whilst allegory requires "a whole story, a narrative."[27]

---

[23] As has been aptly emphasized by Giovanni Reale and Roberto Radice, "La genesi e la natura della filosofia mosaica. Struttura, metodo e fondamenti del pensiero filosofico e teologico di Filone di Alessandria. Monografia introduttiva ai diciannove trattati del «Commentario allegorico alla Bibbia»," in *Filone di Alessandria: Tutti i trattati del Commentario allegorico alla Bibbia*, ed. Roberto Radice, in collaboration with Giovanni Reale, Clara Kraus Reggiani and Claudio Mazzarelli (Milano: Bompiani, 2005), XXXI: "la coerenza filosofica è subordinata all'intenzione e alla finalità esegetica."

[24] This seems to be corroborated by the fact that Philo's hermeneutics allows a shift of focus and emphasis. While Gen 6:2 is not discussed in *QG*, Gen 6:1 is. *QG* 1.89 also wrestles with the question about the multiplication of the human race, but here the question is placed in the context of the imminent flood (not the preceding birth of Noah and his sons), and the answer points not to the rarity of justice, but to the fact God's favors precede His judgments.

[25] See esp. David T. Runia, "Etymology as an Allegorical Technique in Philo of Alexandria," *SPhiloA* 16 (2004): 101–21 or, more recently, Tessa Rajak, "Philo's Knowledge of Hebrew: The Meaning of the Etymologies," in *The Jewish-Greek Tradition in Antiquity and the Byzantine Empire*, ed. James K. Aitken and James Carleton Paget (Cambridge: Cambridge University Press, 2014), 173–87.

[26] David Dawson, *Allegorical Readers and Cultural Revision in Ancient Alexandria* (Berkeley, CA: University of California Press, 1992), 6–7.

[27] Anthony A. Long, "Stoic Readings of Homer," in *Homer's Ancient Readers: The Hermeneutics of Greek Epic's Earliest Exegetes*, ed. Robert Lamberton and John J. Keaney

Although it goes without saying that one should not indiscriminately equate allegoresis with etymology, Philo's hermeneutics shows that it would be misguided to radically oppose the two. What deserves to be particularly highlighted here is that positing a sharp opposition between etymology and allegoresis frequently leads to an unwarranted denigration of the importance of the former interpretative strategy. Tellingly, Anthony A. Long asserts that etymology "plays but a small role in Philo's exegesis."[28] This assessment is difficult to reconcile with what we find in *De gigantibus*.

Let us briefly look at the fourth exegetical unit in *Gig.* 58–67.[29] The exegesis deals with Gen 6:4, which relates that "the giants (γίγαντες) were on the earth in those days." While the exegesis begins with a flat dismissal of the idea that the Lawgiver "hints enigmatically" (αἰνίττεσθαι) at the myths of the poets (§58), it provides the solution that Moses shows humans to divide into three distinct classes: the earth-born, the heaven-born and the God-born (§60). In the course of ensuing discussion, etymology plays an instrumental role in Philo's exegesis and often transmogrifies into a type of allegoresis.

(Princeton, NJ: Princeton University Press, 1992), 54. In his later paper, the scholar specifically opposed Stoic etymology to Philo's allegorical interpretation: Long, "Allegory in Philo and Etymology in Stoicism: A Plea for Drawing Distinctions," *SPhiloA* 9 (1997): 198–210. Cf. also the next note.

[28] Long, "Allegory in Philo," 206–7. For an excellent discussion of the role of etymology in Philo's allegoresis, see Runia, "Etymology as an Allegorical Technique," 101–21. For scholars who stress the coalescence of etymology with allegoresis (particularly in Stoicism) and explicitly reject Long's positon, see, e.g., Ilaria Ramelli and Giulio Lucchetta, *Allegoria.* vol. 1: *L'età classica* (Milano: Vita e Pensiero, 2004), esp. 79–81, 98–99, 458–59, 464–69; Richard Goulet, "La méthode allégorique chez les stoïciens," in *Les stoïciens*, ed. Gilbert Romeyer Dherbey and Jean-Baptiste Gourinat (Paris: Vrin, 2005), 112–17; Jean-Baptiste Gourinat, *"Explicatio fabularum*: La place de l'allégorie dans l'interprétation stoïcienne de la mythologie," in *Allégorie des poètes, allégorie des philosophes: Études sur la poétique et l'herméneutique de l'allégorie de l'Antiquité à la Réforme*, ed. Gilbert Dahan and Richard Goulet (Paris: Vrin: 2005), 11–12, 25–26; Ilaria Ramelli, "The Philosophical Stance of Allegory in Stoicism and Its Reception in Platonism, Pagan and Christian: Origen in Dialogue with the Stoics and Plato," *IJCT* 18 (2011): 339–40 and Mikolaj Domaradzki, "Theological Etymologizing in the Early Stoa," *Kernos* 25 (2012): 139–41.

[29] The present paper follows scholars who regard *Gig.* 19–57 as a single unit rather than two separate sections. See, e.g., Winston and Dillon "Commentary," 244–66; Runia, "Further Observations," 121, 133–34; Borgen, *Philo of Alexandria*, 107–11. David Runia has persuasively argued that the exegetical problem of *Gen* 6.3b is here integrated into that of *Gen.* 6.3a ("Further Observations," 121). For scholars who consider §§19–55 and 55–57 to be two separate sections, see, e.g., Nikiprowetzky, "L'exégèse de Philon d'Alexandrie," 13–21; Cazeaux, *La trame et la chaîne, II*, 17–21 or Radice, *Filone di Alessandria: Tutti i trattati del Commentario allegorico alla Bibbia*, 637–38.

First, the "giants" (γίγαντες) from the biblical lemma are not only derived from the "earth-born" (γηγενεῖς), but also allegorized as those who "hunt after the pleasures of the body" (θηρευτικοὶ τῶν σώματος ἡδονῶν) and preoccupy themselves solely with their enjoyment. This means that these "men of earth" (i.e., slaves of the sensual and carnal) are very much like those who previously were said (§§17–18) to have "married the daughters of humans" (i.e., embraced the life of pleasures).[30] Not only does this etymology have a clear narrative dimension, but it also combines with other etymological interpretations and gradually metamorphoses into a complex allegoresis that additionally utilizes several allegories.

Philo gives Nimrod as an example (§65) of those "sons of earth" (γῆς παῖδες) who abandon God for pleasures of the flesh, upon which he etymologizes this name (§66) as signifying "desertion" (αὐτομόλησις).[31] This interpretation reveals, then, that Nimrod symbolizes rebellion against God: the giant strays from the path of God (the "royal road"), breaks the covenant with Him (ceases to be "God's ally") and wages war against Him (becomes "God's enemy"). It is for this reason that giants are called "deserters." While Nimrod represents the soul/mind overwhelmed by the flesh, this etymological allegoresis makes it now possible for Philo to explain ((§66) why Moses ascribes Babylon to Nimrod: the name "Babylon" stands for "alteration" (μετάθεσις), i.e., something "akin to desertion" (συγγενὲς αὐτομολία), since every desertion commences with a "change and alteration of judgment" (γνώμης μεταβολὴ καὶ μετάθεσις). Hence, the beginning of Nimrod's reign is termed "Babylon," because it means a change of heart that results in a repudiation of God. Thus, the giants' rejection of the spiritual corresponds to the fall of the aforementioned "angels" that likewise choose the carnal.

Evidently, the three etymological interpretations are woven into the fabric of a complex allegoresis: (1) the giants are "men of earth" who seek bodily pleasures rather than God, (2) the first man to begin this betrayal has appropriately been called a "defector," and (3) the kingdom he reigns over has fittingly been named "conversion." Far from playing a minor role, etymology validates the entire allegorical exegesis. While similar coalescence of etymology with allegoresis can be observed in Philo's explana-

[30] It may not be superfluous to note that in *QG* 1.92 the giants are sons of angels and mortal women.

[31] To support his interpretation Philo adduces (§66) Gen 10:8, which has it that Nimrod "began to be a giant (γίγας) on the earth." While in *QG* 1.82 Nimrod is also a paradigm of opposition to God, the passage further suggests that the name means "Ethiopian," on which see Lester L. Grabbe, *Etymology in Early Jewish Interpretation: The Hebrew Names in Philo*, BJS 115 (Atlanta: Scholars Press, 1988), 130.

tions of Abram (§62), Abraham (§63) and many others, it is a characteristic feature of ancient ἐτυμολογία in general that (more often than not) this etymologizing transforms into some sort of allegorizing.[32] Philo's hermeneutics is no exception here.

What is exceptional about Philo's etymological allegoresis (or allegorical etymology) is that it is frequently interspersed with and supported by various non-literal expressions that often produce an extended figurative meaning. Thus, for example the giants are said (§65) to have "derailed the mind from the tracks of reason" (τὸν νοῦν ἐκβιβάσαντες τοῦ λογίζεσθαι)[33] and "adulterated the best coinage" (τὸ ἄριστον ἐκιβδήλευσαν νόμισμα). Again, these expressions help to clarify and bolster the explanation put forward: they indicate figuratively that the men of earth subjugate the higher (i.e., mind) to the lower (i.e., body) and exchange the superior (i.e., reason) for the inferior (i.e., flesh). Hence, this composition strengthens the interpretation which unravels that the giants from the biblical lemma are opponents of God who value the carnal over the spiritual and, thereby, desert Him.

The foregoing analyses suggest that in his exegeses Philo frequently integrates the act of allegorical interpretation with an act of allegorical composition: whether he explains a biblical verse (section 1) or etymologizes a scriptural name (section 2), he often has recourse to various non-literal expressions that frequently produce a sustained figurative meaning. It is important to note here, though, that while Philo takes the whole Pentateuch to be an allegory of the soul's progress towards virtue, he is prepared neither to allegorize everything (e.g., the figure of God) nor to completely deny the literal meaning of Scripture (e.g., observance of the Law). Indeed, in a well-known passage, Philo compares (*Migr.* 89–93) the literal meaning of the text to the body and the allegorical one to the soul, thus, putting it in no uncertain terms that the literal sense is not to be

---

[32] This has been well established in research on the history of allegoresis. For example, Andrew Ford has aptly observed that when the ancients interpreted poetry "there was little difference between allegorizing a divine figure in the tradition of Theagenes or etymologizing an apparently opaque word in the tradition of the sophists and grammarians" (*The Origins of Criticism: Literary Culture and Poetic Theory in Classical Greece* [Princeton, NJ: Princeton University Press, 2002], 88). In a similar vein, Monique Dixsaut stresses that etymology frequently becomes "même exégèse" (*Platon et la question de la pensée* [Paris: Vrin, 2000], 162), whereas David Sedley emphasizes that ancient etymology is "more closely analogous to modern literary criticism than to modern etymology" (*Plato's Cratylus* [Cambridge: Cambridge University Press, 2003], 37).

[33] This is buttressed by quotation of Gen 2:24 ("the two became one flesh"), which is taken to illustrate how one becomes a giant. *Leg.* 2.49 further informs us that the mind (symbolized by Adam) becomes ensnared by the irrational part of the soul (symbolized by Eve), which leads to abandoning God, virtue and wisdom.

discarded: one must not neglect the "body," as it is the "abode" of the "soul" (cf. also *Contempl.* 78). Hence, it is necessary to examine how the literal meaning is preserved in *De gigantibus*.

3. The Literal and Allegorical Appropriation

The distinction between a literal and an allegorical exegesis in Philo is of paramount importance for understanding his hermeneutics.[34] While the difference may at first sight seem rather obvious, it should be borne in mind that our understanding of the literal/allegorical opposition does not have to tally with that of Philo. Indeed, this point has been brilliantly made by Jaap Mansfeld in his study on Philo's exegetical strategies:

> Some of the interpretations called literal by Philo may strike us as being allegorical, for instance the one concerned with the Platonic cosmology, which he finds in the first chapters of Genesis. For Philo, however, the allegorical or, as he often calls it, the deeper interpretation pertains to the inner, not the outer, world. It follows that philosophical theories that are useful at the literal level need not be so at the allegorical, and conversely.[35]

Let us take another example from the second exegetical unit. In the course of his exposition, Philo makes (§8) two important identifications: first, the "stars" (ἀστέρας) are equated with "souls divine and pure throughout" (ψυχαὶ ὅλαι δι' ὅλων ἀκήρατοί τε καὶ θεῖαι) and, then, each of the stars is also characterized as "most immaculate mind" (νοῦς ἀκραιφνέστατος).[36] While both these identifications may look quite allegorical to us, they would not be perceived as such by Philo, since they build heavily on Plato's cosmology (see esp. *Tim.* 40a–d),[37] which was taken literally not figuratively. The first equation reflects the view that in the beginning all souls are pure and unsullied, whereas the second—that every star is a rational mind.[38] On the

---

[34] On this issue, see esp. the collection of essays in David M. Hay, ed., *Both Literal and Allegorical: Studies in Philo of Alexandria's* Questions and Answers on Genesis and Exodus, BJS 232 (Atlanta: Scholars Press, 1991).

[35] Jaap Mansfeld, "Philosophy in the Service of Scripture: Philo's Exegetical Strategies," in *The Question of "Eclecticism": Studies in Later Greek Philosophy*, ed. John M. Dillon and Anthony A. Long (Berkeley, CA: University of California Press, 1988), 71.

[36] This sentence does not appear in Winston's (otherwise excellent) translation.

[37] On Philo's appropriation thereof, see esp. Runia, *Philo of Alexandria and the* Timaeus *of Plato*, 227–31.

[38] This characterization of the stars as pure souls/minds has given rise to the controversy as to whether the stars are here regarded as incorporeal and invisible (see esp. Harry A. Wolfson, *Philo: Foundations of Religious Philosophy in Judaism, Christianity, and Islam*, 2 vols., rev. ed. [Cambridge, MA: Harvard University Press, 1968], 1:364; but cf.

other hand, the above discussed identification of the angels from Gen 6:2 with demons and souls is clearly allegorical: as is characteristic of allegoresis, this equation extracts a hidden (esoteric) meaning from the biblical lemma. Thus, if we compare the two identifications, we can see that for Philo the former represents a relatively uncontroversial ("Middle Platonist") view (stars = souls = minds), whereas the latter represents a highly unpalatable one (disembodied angels have mortal spouses), which requires an (allegorical) explanation.

The two equations illustrate an important exegetical strategy frequently employed by Philo: appropriation. Basically, the strategy consists in adopting and adapting a concept to suit the exegete's needs.[39] This often involves a modification of meaning and/or conflation with another doctrine, which leads to the result that the appropriated concept is reinterpreted and integrated into the new context.[40] While the aforementioned identifications instantiate cases of allegorical and literal appropriation, Philo's hermeneutics in general has a strong appropriative dimension. Obviously, this has ramifications for our assessment of Philo as a historian of philosophy: although Philo should not be dismissed as completely unreliable in this area, his reliability must be approached with a great deal of caution. What

---

already Siegfried, *Philo von Alexandria als Ausleger*, 306: "die Sterne gewissermassen zu Leibern haben"). David Winston has persuasively argued that *Gig.* 8 presents the stars as "completely rational," rather than disembodied (*Logos and Mystical Theology in Philo of Alexandria* [Cincinnati: Hebrew Union College Press, 1985], 33). This argument is particularly compelling in light of the ensuing description of the fallen souls/demons as the enemies of right reason (see above in the main text).

[39] The strategy is a hallmark of the Hellenistic age and it has been extensively covered in existing literature. In connection with Philo's sources and/or techniques of appropriation, the works of Carlos Lévy and Gregory E. Sterling deserve special mention here. See, e.g., Carlos Lévy, "Le concept de *doxa* des Stoïciens à Philon d'Alexandrie: Essai d'étude diachronique," in *Passions and Perceptions: Studies in Hellenistic Philosophy of Mind. Proceedings of the Fifth Symposium Hellenisticum*, ed. Jacques Brunschwig and Martha C. Nussbaum (Cambridge: Cambridge University Press, 1993), 250–84; Levy, "Éthique de l'immanence, éthique de la transcendence: Le problème de l'*oikeiôsis* chez Philon," in *Philon d'Alexandrie et le langage de la philosophie*, ed. Levy, (Turnhout: Brepols, 1998), 153–64; idem, "La conversion du scepticisme chez Philon d'Alexandrie," in *Philo of Alexandria and Post-Aristotelian Philosophy*, ed. Francesca Alesse (Leiden: Brill, 2008), 103–20; Gregory E. Sterling, "'The Jewish Philosophy': Reading Moses via Hellenistic Philosophy according to Philo," in *Reading Philo: A Handbook to Philo of Alexandria*, ed. Torrey Seland (Grand Rapids: Eerdmans, 2014), 129–54; Sterling, "Philo's Hellenistic and Hellenistic-Jewish Sources," *SPhiloA* 26 (2014): 93–97; Sterling, "From the Thick Marshes of the Nile to the Throne of God: Moses in Ezekiel the Tragedian and Philo of Alexandria," *SPhiloA* 26 (2014): 115–33. Cf. also the next note.

[40] Though sometimes this new use is foreign or even contrary to original one. Thus, e.g., Carlos Lévy examines how Philo can use the concept οἰκείωσις "d'une manière étrangère, ou même contraire à la doctrine stoïcienne" ("Éthique de l'immanence," 153).

sometimes makes Philo a problematic source for reconstructing the views of earlier thinkers is that—as noted above—he saw his task as being to explain Scripture inspired by God rather than to give an objective account of a philosophical doctrine. This means that Philo accommodates various views for the purpose of elucidating the Bible rather than presenting a historically faithful and unbiased account of them. Let us consider another example.

In his fourth exegesis, Philo ingeniously appropriates Plato's notorious denunciation of poetry. Having emphasized Moses's aversion to myth-making (§58), Philo stresses that the Lawgiver is equally critical of visual arts (§59). Thus, he explains that Moses has banished painting and sculpture from his *politeia*—as Plato exiled (*Resp.* 398a) poetry from his—because they belie the nature of truth and beguile the souls (§59). That Philo echoes here Plato is evident.[41] As is well known, Plato levels two charges (*Resp.* 603a–b) against poetic mimesis: imitative art is "far from" (πόρρω) all "truth" (ἀληθείας) and all "intellect" (φρονήσεως). These accusations reflect Plato's epistemological and ethical concerns, respectively: (1) by describing the sensible world, the poets produce merely copies of the copies and (2) their deceptive phantoms appeal to our emotions rather than to reason (*Resp.* 598b–605c). While Philo's use of Platonic criticism must be placed in the context of the Second Commandment,[42] it instantiates a literal appronpriation of a pagan view in the service of Jewish monotheism: this reference to πολιτεία is not figurative. There is, however, a reference to the term in the fourth exegesis that is allegorical.

When discussing the God-born (exemplified by priests and prophets), Philo explains (§61) that these men of God leave the *politeia* of this world, rise above the Cynic-Stoic ideal of becoming a *cosmopolites* (see, e.g., Diogenes Laertius 6.63; 7.88), transcend the sensible sphere and "migrate to the noetic cosmos" (εἰς τὸν νοητὸν κόσμον μετανέστησαν), where they "dwell

---

[41] The Platonic origins of this criticism have already been emphasized by Émile Bréhier: "dans cette exclusion des mythes de la cité mosaïque, Philon suit incontestablement Platon" (*Les idées philosophiques et religieuses de Philon d'Alexandrie* [Paris: Picard, 1908], 65).

[42] The context of the Second Commandment has been stressed, for example, by Monique Alexandre: "Le rejet de la fabulation est ici lié au second commandement du Décalogue proscrivant les représentations" ("Monarchie divine et dieux des nations chez Philon d'Alexandrie," in *Philon d'Alexandrie: un penseur à l'intersection des cultures gréco-romaine, orientale, juive et chrétienne*, ed. Sabrina Inowlocki and Baudouin Decharneux [Turnhout: Brepols, 2011], 121). For a general discussion of Philo's account of the Second Commandment, see Sarah Pearce, "Philo of Alexandria on the Second Commandment," in *The Image and Its Prohibition in Jewish Antiquity*, JJSSup Series 2, ed. Sarah Pearce (Oxford, Journal of Jewish Studies, 2013), 49–76.

enrolled as citizens of the *politeia* of incorruptible and incorporeal ideas" (ᾤκησαν ἐγγραφέντες ἀφθάρτων <καὶ> ἀσωμάτων ἰδεῶν πολιτείᾳ). Thus, we see again how Philo combines various figurative expressions to allegorically convey that the men of God overcome Cynic-Stoic materialism and nominalism: as the God-born engage in contemplation of the intelligible world, they disengage from the realm of sense-perceptible reality. The fourth exegesis shows, then, that when appropriating a philosophical concept, Philo would often incorporate it in a non-literal description.

4. *Conclusion*

The foregoing discussion has been confined to only a few passages from the first part of Philo's beautiful double-treatise. Still, if the above remarks are correct, then Philo (at least sometimes) employs allegory in a function that can be characterized as "instructive" or—even better—"explanatory": when interpreting a biblical verse, etymologizing a scriptural name or appropriating a philosophical concept, Philo has frequently recourse to allegory for explicative purposes. Thus, instead of being simple rhetorical embellishments or stylistic ornaments that merely spice up his style, Philo's allegories enable him to clarify his exegeses and/or make his arguments more cogent. It is for this reason that one so often encounters series of figurative expressions in Philo's complex exegeses.

Allegory in Philo is neither accidental nor incidental, but stems from the very nature of his exegetical project. The few passages of *Gig.* that have been analyzed here show the variety of Philo's allegory (which can be embedded in a complex allegoresis, etymology or appropriation). However, this diversity of allegory manifests itself not only in its form but also in its function: Philo's use of allegory for elucidatory purposes is obviously not the whole picture. Clearly, the apologetic dimension must always be borne in mind. To exonerate Scripture from the charges of irrationality, implausibility or inconsistency, Philo brings to light the latent meaning of various biblical lemmata so that a profound wisdom is excavated from underneath these *prima facie* embarrassing and/or outrageous passages. The hidden sense that Philo unveils is, then, explicated by a host of non-literal expressions that often yield an extended allegorical meaning. But ultimately Philo wants his reader not only to understand the law of Moses but also to live by it. Thus, Philonic allegory is supposed to help one pass from flesh (the literal) to spirit (the figurative). This "salvific"—so to say—function of allegory is as important as is the apologetic and/or the explanatory one. Hence, Philo's allegory emerges as a dynamic interplay of

Mikolaj Domaradzki

various types and functions. Needless to say, however, more empirical analyses of Philo's exegetical practice will have to be conducted to corroborate this observation.

Adam Mickiewicz University in Poznan

The Studia Philonica Annual 31 (2019): 29–55

PILPUL AND EROS:
PHILO'S PLATONIC INTERPRETATION OF THE
LAW CONCERNING THE GARMENT TAKEN IN
PLEDGE (*DE SOMNIIS* 1.92–114)*

GÁBOR BUZÁSI

The Mosaic legislation concerning the garment taken in pledge (Exod 22:25–26[1]) is a minor ordinance in the book of Exodus. The passion with which Philo defends its proper interpretation is therefore surprising. As we shall see, his vehemence is prompted precisely by the triviality of the regulation—at least when taken in the literal sense. For Philo is convinced that in reality Moses did not attribute to the Creator of the universe a petty concern about a rag to be returned to its original owner before sunset. In his argument Philo, quite uniquely in his oeuvre, refutes the literal sense of a biblical law in the form of a veritable *pilpul*: an array of dialectic arguments based on a meticulous analysis of the text. For Philo, however, the *sensus litteralis* is neither the only, nor the most relevant sense of the biblical text. The real meaning, he argues in the second part of his exegesis, concerns the ascent of the soul to God by using *logos* as one's most inherent property. In this allegorical interpretation Philo makes subtle allusions to Plato's *erotic* dialogues without referring to the philosopher explicitly. The reconstruction of these hitherto unrecognized allusions sheds new light on the meaning and scope of the Philonic passage. Moreover, a reflection on the place of the passage in Philo's treatise *De Somniis* also enables us to

* The final version of this article was written in Salzburg where I enjoyed the kind hospitality of Prof. Kristin De Troyer at the Department of Biblical Studies and Church History. My research was generously supported by OMAA / AÖU (Stiftung Aktion Öster-reich – Ungarn). I am grateful for the comments on earlier versions by Gábor Betegh, Alex Leonas, Steve Mason, Stefan Schorch, and above all to Gregory Sterling and the anony-mous reader of *SPhiloA* for their invaluable suggestions.

[1] These are the verse numbers of the Hebrew Bible and the Septuagint. In the Vulgate and in most modern translations, our verses are numbered as 26–27 (because they count Exod 21:37 as 22:1). In the following, I will use the verse numbers of the Septuagint and the Masoretic Text, indicating the Vulgate numbers in brackets (or square brackets).

propose an explanation of his passionate attack on the literal reading of the halakhic regulation. The immediate context in Philo is a discussion of the Sun as the symbol of God, embedded in the exegesis of another biblical passage: the sunset preceding Jacob's dream of the heavenly ladder (Gen 28:11). After a close reading of Philo's relatively intricate argument I will propose a hypothesis about the identity of his opponents; it will also be argued that Philo's passion in this little studied section of *De Somniis* is related to the dilemma whether it is legitimate to consider the Sun as the most genuine visible image of God.[2]

1. *The Biblical Passage*

Philo quotes the Exodus passage (22:25–26 [26–27]) as follows:

ἐὰν ἐνεχύρασμα ἐνεχυράσῃς τὸ ἱμάτιον τοῦ πλησίον, πρὸ δυσμῶν ἡλίου ἀποδώσεις αὐτῷ· / ἔστι γὰρ τοῦτο περιβόλαιον αὐτοῦ μόνον, τοῦτο τὸ ἱμάτιον ἀσχημοσύνης αὐτοῦ· ἐν τίνι κοιμηθήσεται; ἐὰν οὖν καταβοήσῃ πρός μέ, εἰσακούσομαι αὐτοῦ· ἐλεήμων γάρ εἰμι. (§ 92)[3]

If thou take thy neighbour's garment to pledge thou shalt restore it to him before the setting of the sun; for this is his only covering, it is the garment of his shame. Wherein shall he sleep? If then he cry unto Me, I will hear him, for I am compassionate.[4]

---

[2] *Somn.* 1.92–114 has been relatively neglected in modern research, notable exceptions being Clara Kraus Reggiani and Giovanni Reale, *Filone di Alessandria: L'uomo e Dio; Il connubio con gli studi preliminari; La fuga e il ritrovamento; Il mutamento dei nom;. I sogni sono mandate da Dio* (Milano: Università Cattolica di Sacro Cuore, 1986); Benedetto Bravo, "Sulân: Représailles et justice privée contre des étrangers dans les cités grecques," *Annali della Scuola Normale Superiore, Classe di lettere e filosofia,* 3/10.3 (1980): 788–90; and Georg Korting, *Das Vaterunser und die Unheilabwehr: Ein Beitrag zur ἐπιούσιον-Debatte (Mt 6,11/Lk 11,3)* (Münster: Aschendorff, 2004), 637–94 (Bravo and Korting discuss our passage in the context of an analysis of ῥύσιον, one of the terms for 'pledge'). For further reflections on *Somn.* 1.92–114 (other than the annotations in PLCL, PAPM, and PCH) cf. Erwin R. Goodenough, *By Light, Light: The Mystic Gospel of Hellenistic Judaism* (New Haven: Yale University Press, 1935), 169 ("a long allegory that adds little to the argument"); Harry A. Wolfson, *Philo,* 2 vols. (Cambridge, MA: Harvard University Press, 1947), 1:129 (a brief summary of the argument); and Franz-Norbert Klein, *Die Lichtterminologie bei Philon von Alexandrien und in den hermetischen Schriften: Untersuchungen zur religiösen Sprache der hellenistischen Mystik* (Leiden: Brill, 1962), 28 ("[eine] dunkle Stelle[, die] in dem von uns behandelten Rahmen ohne Wichtigkeit [ist]."

[3] Philo is quoted according to PLCL, the Greek text being based on PCW. Numbers preceded by §, unless otherwise indicated, refer to the paragraphs of *Somn.* 1. Philo does not discuss this biblical passage elsewhere.

[4] The translations, unless noted otherwise, are those of PLCL, who later on also translate ἐνεχυράζω as "hold in pawn" (§ 105) and ἀσχημοσύνη as "unseemliness" (§ 109).

Apart from minor orthographical variations, Philo reproduces the text of the Septuagint, which for him famously replaces the Hebrew original.[5] The Greek, while preserving most features of the Hebrew, exhibits some divergences with a potential impact on its interpretation:

אם חבל תחבל שלמת רעך עד בא השמש תשיבנו לו. כי הוא כסותה לבדה הוא שמלתו לערו במה
ישכב והיה כי יצעק אלי ושמעתי כי חנון אני

If thou *at all* take thy neighbour's garment to pledge thou shalt restore it to him before the *going* of the sun; for this is his only covering, it is the garment *for his skin*. Wherein shall he sleep? If then he cry unto Me, I will hear him, for I am compassionate.[6]

First, the etymological figure of the Hebrew (אם חבל תחבל) is reproduced in the Septuagint (ἐὰν ἐνεχύρασμα ἐνεχυράσῃς), but the emphasis on the hypothetical overtone of the condition ("if you *do* take—i.e., take *at all*[7]—a pledge") is lost, at least in Philo. *Second*, the reference to the sunset (עד בא השמש / πρὸ δυσμῶν ἡλίου) may also be ambiguous: while the Greek explicitly indicates "setting," that is, "going down," in Hebrew בא may also mean "coming," that is, rising.[8] *Third*, the garment "of his shame" (ἀσχημοσύνης αὐτοῦ) is לערו in Hebrew, which literally means "for his skin."[9] As we shall

---

[5] The differences, according to the edition of Rahlfs: ἐὰν δὲ ἐνεχύρασμα; ἔστιν γὰρ; αὐτοῦ, μόνον τοῦτο; πρὸς με. Alain Le Boulluec and Pierre Sandevoir, *La Bible d'Alexandrie: L'Exode* (Paris: Cerf, 1989), 230, place the comma with Philo and P. de Lagarde after μόνον pace Rahlfs ("his only covering" instead of "the only garment of his shame"). On the LXX as the inspired text of the Bible for Philo cf. Folker Siegert, "Early Jewish interpretation in a Hellenistic style," in *Hebrew Bible / Old Testament: The History of Its Interpretation*, vol. 1, ed. Magne Saebø (Göttingen: Vandenhoeck & Ruprecht, 1996), 172–76; and Adam Kamesar, "Biblical interpretation in Philo," in *The Cambridge Companion to Philo*, ed. Adam Kamesar (Cambridge: Cambridge University Press, 2009), 65–72; occasionally, however, Philo seems to take the Hebrew also into account, cf. § 106 (ἐν χρῷ) with my comments below.

[6] PLCL, modifications in italics.

[7] Cf. the renderings of Lauterbach in *Mekhilta de-Rabbi Ishmael*, ed. and tr. Jacob Z. Lauterbach (Philadelphia: The Jewish Publication Society, 2004²), 2:460 or Nehama Leibowitz in her *Studies in Shemot (Exodus)*, part 2 (Jerusalem: The World Zionist Organization, 1976), 415; this is also the translation of the King James Version and many other English Bibles.

[8] As a phrase, בא השמש normally refers to sunset, but the verb alone more often indicates arrival than departure.

[9] This is how, e.g., Nehama Leibowitz in her *Studies in Shemot (Exodus)* 415 and Nahum M. Sarna, *Exodus/שמות* (Philadelphia: The Jewish Publication Society, 1991), translate the phrase, while the Vulgate has "his flesh" (*carnis eius*). Cf. Christoph Dohmen, *Exodus 19–40* (Freiburg: Herder, 2004), 142, "für seinen Körper"; and Korting, *Das Vaterunser und die Unheilabwehr*, 641 "bloßen Leib." The difference between "shame" and "skin" is also noted by Le Boulluec and Sandevoir, *La Bible d'Alexandrie: L'Exode*, 230, who refer to it as one of the reasons for Philo's rejection of the literal interpretation (for shame is manifest by daylight rather than at night).

see, some rabbinic interpretations diverge from those of Philo precisely on account of these differences.

As for the biblical context, our passage is part of the Covenant Code (Exod 20:22–23:33), the first large collection of legal material in the Pentateuch, framed by the two theophanies at Mt. Sinai (Exod 19 and 24) as the culmination of the liberation from Egypt.[10] The connection of these specific regulations with the historical event of the Exodus is indicated by the fact that the first ordinance in the Covenant Code (following the prohibition of idolatry and a cultic decree) pertains to the liberation of slaves (Exod 21:2–11). Most of the laws in this halakhic collection focus on the regulation of everyday life within the Israelite society: injuries, property rights, sexual offences, religious and social questions. It may be that the overarching narrative context of liberation and revelation provides these laws with a symbolic dimension but taken at face value most of them are certainly pragmatic.

The immediate context of our passage is a legislation concerning the disadvantaged of society (Exod 22:20–24 [21–25]): strangers, widows, orphans, and the poor. It is therefore quite natural to interpret the law of the pledge in a social and humanitarian sense, especially since in a parallel passage (Deut 24:10–13) the debtor is explicitly said to be "a needy man."[11] The obvious similarity of both regulations does not imply for Philo (and other ancient exegetes) that they should be read as mutually explaining each other.[12] Nonetheless, if we consider these texts from a historical point of view, we can find further biblical passages providing evidence of a practice described in these laws. Amos mentions people who "lay themselves down beside every altar on garments taken in pledge" (2:8) (בגדים חבלים); Proverbs dissuades one from giving security to foreigners by encouraging

---

[10] The Decalogue (Exod 20:1–17) is distinguished from these special ordinances.

[11] "When you make a loan (משאת / ὀφείλημα) of any sort to your countryman, you must not enter his house to seize his pledge (לעבט עבטו / ἐνεχυράσαι τὸ ἐνέχυρον). You must remain outside, while the man to whom you made the loan brings the pledge (העבט / τὸ ἐνέχυρον) out to you. And if he is a needy man (איש עני / ὁ ἄνθρωπος πένηται), you shall not go to sleep in his pledge (לא תשכב בעבטו / οὐ κοιμηθήσῃ ἐν τῷ ἐνεχύρῳ αὐτοῦ). You must return the pledge (העבט / τὸ ἐνέχυρον) to him at sundown (כבא השמש / περὶ δυσμὰς ἡλίου), that he may sleep in his cloth (בשלמתו / ἐν τῷ ἱματίῳ αὐτοῦ) and bless you; and it will be to your merit (צדקה, ἐλεημοσύνη) before the Lord your God." (Jeffrey H. Tigay, *Deuteronomy*/דברים, Philadelphia: The Jewish Publication Society, 1996), 225–26. For Philo's interpretation of this passage see *Virt.* 88–89, discussed in n. 21.

[12] From a historical point of view, Deut 24:10–13 seems to be an interpretative elaboration of our passage, cf. Leibowitz, *Studies in Shemot (Exodus)*, 415; Eckart Otto, *Das Deuteronomium. Politische Theologie und Rechtsreform in Juda und in Assyrien* (Berlin: de Gruyter, 1999), 294–98.

others to take such a person's garment as a punishment[13]; and among the (false) accusations of Job's friends we find the following: "For you have exacted pledges (תחבל) of your brothers for nothing and stripped the naked of their clothing" (22:6) (בגדי ערומים תפשיט).[14] Moreover, an ostracon dated to the seventh century BCE has preserved the petition of a reaper addressed to the governor for having been stripped of his garment by his commander.[15] None of these parallels depict exactly the legal situation addressed in our passage but there are overlapping elements which confirm that taking away (parts of) one's garment as a pledge or punishment was indeed customary in biblical times. Yet, if one subjects the passage in itself to serious scrutiny as Philo does, one will find various incongruities in its literal level of meaning, although solutions proposed may be different.[16]

2. *Philo's Interpretation*

Philo discusses our biblical passage in a context rather different from the one suggested by the biblical canon and modern research. In the context of *De Somniis*, Exod 22:25–26 (26–27) is part of an intricate web of primary, secondary and tertiary biblical passages (lemmata) explaining each other. The case of the garment taken in pledge (§§ 92–114) is embedded in a series of biblical interpretations of the Sun in the Bible (§§ 72–119), the most ambitious among them being the claim that the Sun refers to God himself; the discussion of the garment to be returned before sunset is introduced as an exegetical support of this interpretation of the Sun.[17] The occasion for the insertion of this 'solar treatise' is a sunset in the Jacob narrative (Gen

---

[13] Prov 20:16 and 27:13. The LXX version differs from the Masoretic Text significantly.

[14] Philo does not reflect on these passages.

[15] The text was first edited and translated by Joseph Naveh, "A Hebrew Letter from the Seventh Century B. C.," *IEJ* 10 (1960): 129–39; cf. also Herbert Donner and Wolfgang Röllig, *Kanaanäische und aramäische Inschriften* (Wiesbaden: Harrassowitz, 1962), nr. 200; on the interpretation of the letter cf. Jonathan Ben-Dov, "The Poor's Curse: Exodus XXII 25–26 and Curse Literature in the Ancient World," *VT* 56 (2006). 436.

[16] Among modern scholars Samson Raphael Hirsch, *Der Pentateuch: Exodus*, 6th ed. (Frankfurt: Kaufmann, 1920), 176; Brevard S. Childs, *Exodus: A Commentary* (London: SCM, 1974), 479; and Christoph Dohmen, *Exodus 19–40* (Freiburg: Herder, 2004), 175–78, agree that the counter intuitive details of the legislation point to an emphasis on social sensitivity and compassion rather than on legal regulation. These explanations are compatible with Philo's exegesis of a parallel passage, Deut 24:10–13 in *Virt.* 82–89.

[17] The discussion of this meaning (§§ 72–76 and 92–117) occupies the greatest part (ca. 2/3) of the 'treatise' (§§ 72–119) on the Sun; the alternative meanings of the Sun include (1) the human intellect (§§ 77–78 and 118–119); (2) sense perception (§§ 79–84, and 118–119); and (3) the *logos* of God (§§ 85–86).

28:11, § 72), significant because of the dream of the heavenly ladder the patriarch saw at Beth El ("the house of God") after he had fallen asleep.[18] Jacob's dream of the ladder, and especially the situation in which he saw it, is discussed in great detail (§§ 2–188), with our passage playing a pivotal role in Philo's exegesis.[19] Thus in Philo the legislation concerning the garment is examined in a multiple context involving Jacob's dream, his journey and his character, as well as the significance of the sunset preparing his dream, other biblical sunsets and sunrises, and the symbolism of the Sun in general. If we want to appraise Philo's interpretation we need to keep in mind that his hermeneutical approach diverges significantly from the historical critical approach of modern scholarship. Philo is not interested in questions such as the evolution of Pentateuchal legislation or its Near Eastern parallels, therefore the context he deems relevant is constituted neither by the Prophets and the Hagiographa nor by Canaanite, Mesopotamian or Egyptian legal texts. What the Philonic context certainly does is to establish a surprising connection between the garment taken in pledge and the Sun, preparing the way for the allegorical interpretation of the biblical passage (§§ 102–114), a method which Philo believes is capable of revealing its deeper and more fundamental registers. Prior to this, however, Philo rejects the literal sense forcefully. It is worth analyzing Philo's argument before turning to his allegorical exegesis and to the problem of his rejection of the literal sense (the *peshat*) of the biblical text.

2.1. *Rejecting the Literal Sense (§§ 93–101)*

Philo declares quite clearly at the very beginning of his exegesis that he considers the literal sense (ἡ ῥητὴ πραγματεία) of the passage untenable.[20] He criticises, at this point still almost politely, those who "suppose that the lawgiver feels all this concern (σπουδή) about a cloak (ἀμπεχόνη)" (§ 93). A

---

[18] "[...] and he met with (ἀπήντησεν / ויפגע, lit. "lighted upon" or "came across") a place; for the sun set (ἔδυ γὰρ ὁ ἥλιος / כי בא השמש); and he took one from the stones of the place, and put it under his head, and he slept in that place." (Gen 28:11 = § 4) For another (more indirect) interpretation of Jacob's dream and the sunset cf. *Praem.* 36–40. On a typology of dream visions as the structuring principle, and on the original structure, of the treatise see Sofía Torallas Tovar, "Philo of Alexandria's Dream Classification," *Archiv für Religionsgeschichte* 15 (2014): 67–82.

[19] Interestingly enough, of the 187 chapters devoted to the dream of the ladder (§§ 2–188), 140 discuss the narrative context, while the dream itself is explained in merely 47 chapters (§§ 133–179). For a summary of the context in *De somniis* cf. Korting, *Das Vaterunser und die Unheilabwehr*, 639–42.

[20] For ῥητὴ πραγματεία cf. § 102 and § 120. Other terms referring to the literal/plain sense include προκείμενον ("obvious," cf. *Leg.* 3.4) and πρόχειρον ("at hand," cf. *Det.* 155).

quarrel about a cloak taken in pledge, he argues, is an embarrassingly "trifling (εὐτελής) matter" for "the Creator and Ruler of the universe" to be compassionate about, and attributing such "human pettiness" (ἀνθρωπίνη μικρολογία) to God is "a mark of men who have utterly failed to see" the greatness of God's excellence (ἀρετή) (§ 94).[21] With this the main point of the refutation is stated: God's real nature and majesty is incommensurable with the triviality of the problem—at least according to the literal meaning. The remaining arguments (§§ 95–101) against the plain sense are largely refutations of objections, potential or real, in defence of the literal reading.[22]

Two remarks are necessary here. On the one hand, it must be pointed out that the utter rejection of the literal sense of a biblical law is rather unusual in Philo who is said to be "the earliest example that we have of a writer who tries to maintain the validity of both the allegorical and the non-allegorical levels of interpretation."[23] On the other hand, Philo's failure to sympathise with those who insist that God's care about the most basic human needs is indeed a remarkable sign of compassion might be embarrassing not only for our sensitivities but also according to the standards of Philo's own time.[24] Both questions will be addressed below. First, however, it is worth recapitulating Philo's arguments against the literal sense, this fine example of Philonic *pilpul*.[25]

1. It is only natural in such transactions that lenders (δανεισταί) keep the securities (τὰ ῥύσια) until they have gotten back what they had lent as the

---

[21] μικρολογία (σμικρολογία in some manuscripts), "pettiness" or "hair-splitting" is a hapax in Philo, but certain forms of it are frequent in Plato, e.g., *Symp.* 210d3 (in a passage important for Philo's argument, cf. 2.2.2 [e] below, p. 42); the term is also related to μικροπολίτης ("citizen of a little/narrow world"), cf. § 39. Philo does not consider God's concern with the needy as "pettiness" since in *Virt.* 82–89 he interprets the parallel passage (Deut 24:10–13) as an expression of social sensitivity. What he finds too insignificant for the Deity to deal with is the rag itself and the absurd legal situation surrounding it.

[22] I will argue below that these objections are real rather than fictitious, cf. n.45 and 2.2.3.

[23] Thomas H. Tobin, *The Creation of Man: Philo and the History of Interpretation* (Washington DC: Catholic University of America Press, 1983), 155. Cf. my discussion below, 3.1.

[24] Cf. Matt 25:35–36, 42–43. Early Christian exegetes combine the literal and the allegorical interpretation of our passage, cf. Ambrose, *De Tobia* 14, § 47, p. 545 Schenkl (CSEL 32, 2).

[25] Philo's argument targets each term of the commandment (the transaction, the legislator, the debtor, the creditor, and the garment) one by one, and reflects also on the literary genre. In his recapitulation, Wolfson, *Philo*, 1:129 only mentions the triviality of the literal meaning and the wording of the law. Cf. also Korting, *Das Vaterunser und die Unheilabwehr*, 642–44. I do not use *pilpul* in its pejorative sense ('casuistic hair-splitting') but rather in its original meaning: 'sharp analysis' (the term is etymologically related to 'pepper').

latter is their own (τὰ ἴδια) (§ 95).[26] Philo does not take it for granted that the debtor is socially disadvantaged; and indeed, neither does the text contain any *explicit* reference to the financial situation of the debtor, nor does Philo apparently consider the parallel passage Deut 24:10–13 as relevant here. Yet, he raises a whole series of objections to his own statement based on the hypothesis that the debtor is poor, which is precisely the case in the parallel passage.

2. Thus the first objection (§ 95) is that the law in fact refers to debtors who are poor (πένητες) and therefore deserve pity (ἐλεεῖν αὐτούς). This, however, is unlikely, Philo counters, for if this were the case then it would have been much more reasonable for Moses either to prescribe donations to those in need instead of making them debtors, or to prevent them (κωλῦσαι) from lending on security to the poor.[27] Once he permitted lending, the lawgiver cannot be indignant with lenders taking pledge, as this is what distinguishes lending from donating. It follows that if he is indignant it is not because of the situation suggested by the plain sense but due to the real, allegorical meaning.

3. The second objection (§§ 96–97) pushes the previous one to the extreme and focuses on the debtor. Suppose he is so poor that his rag (ῥάκιον) is his only property, that is, we are dealing with an exceptional situation.[28] Why then would he prefer to be indebted rather than accept the donations people in such extreme situations are normally ready to give?[29] What does he aim to get in turn for his rag, Philo asks not without sarcasm, perhaps a better garment? Moreover, and here he stresses one point which is emphatic in the Greek text but only implicit in the Hebrew: does it

---

[26] As we have seen, some modern exegetes base their interpretation precisely on the assumption that the circumstances described by the law are not natural. In *Mekhilta de-Rabbi Ishmael*, 2:460 (*Kaspa*), on the other hand, R. Ishmael interprets this verse in a vein similar to Philo's: "Scripture comes to teach you that you should do your duty, but you may (also) take what is yours." (בא הכתוב ללמדך שתהא עושה מצוה ותהא נוטל את שלך).

[27] Εἶτ' οὐκ ἄμεινον ἦν γράψαι νόμον, δι' οὗ τούτους ἐρανιοῦσι μᾶλλον ἢ χρεώστας ἀποφανοῦσιν ἢ ἐπ' ἐνεχύροις τοῦ δανείζειν κωλῦσαι; The last word is Mangey's plausible conjecture for the κωλύσουσιν of the manuscripts, which requires a modification (in italics) in the translation of Colson in PLCL 5: "In that case would it not be better to make a law for contributing to the needs of such people instead of making them debtors, or *to prohibit* (instead of "for prohibiting," Colson's translation of the conjecture κωλύσονται) lending upon security?" The translation of the Hebrew etymological figure by Lauterbach or Leibowitz (see n. 7) implicitly agrees with Philo's objection: "If thou *at all* take to pledge"—i.e., you should preferably not do so.

[28] ῥάκιον, "ragged, tattered garment," first attested in Aristophanes (*Ach.* 412, 415), is a hapax in Philo.

[29] This remark implies that either Alexandrian economy or civil (Jewish) solidarity was strong in Philo's Alexandria.

present no problem for the debtor to expose his shame (αἰδώς) in daylight?[30] Consequently, such a debtor is very unlikely to exist even under exceptional circumstances.

4. Focusing now (§ 98) on the creditor, Philo points out that his behaviour is not only absurd but also disgraceful, assuming that the debtor is exceedingly poor (πενιχρός). Why cannot the creditor afford a penny (τετράδραχμον), or even less, as a free gift to someone so miserable? What kind of person would take one's only garment as a security? This is again something other than lending: it is robbery, and those who commit such crime are called "coat-snatchers" (λωποδύτης) instead of creditors.[31] It is implied that such transactions should be prohibited rather than regulated, for someone's most vital property must not be taken away even temporarily. This is the bottom line in Philo's interpretation of the transaction: it is completely illegitimate robbery. This conclusion will be the starting point of his allegorical exegesis.

5. Turning from the participants of the transaction to the garment itself, Philo raises the further point (§ 99) that it is no less problematic to keep one's garment for the day than for the night. Uncovering one's nakedness when it is visible is indecent—Philo highlights the term used in the Septuagint (ἀσχημοσύνη, ἀσχημονεῖν) for Hebrew "skin" (עֹר). Decency, it seems, is not so much an external moral requirement as the opposite of defenselessness which, at least, is eliminated by the darkness of the night.[32]

---

[30] See above, n.9. On the problem of nudity see below, § 99 (our 2.1.5).

[31] For λωποδύτης in a less specific sense (translated as "foot-pads" in PLCL) cf. *Ios.* 84; *Spec.* 4.87, 121. Our passage uses the word in the original sense as λῶπος / λώπη means "covering," "robe," or "mantle."

[32] Apparently, from Philo's Egyptian perspective nights do not seriously endanger one's health by their cold (contrast *Exodus Rabbah* 31:6, p. 385–86 Lehrman or *Midrash Tanhumah* in Nehama Leibowitz in her *Studies in Shemot (Exodus)*, 419). Philo discusses nakedness extensively in *Ebr.* 4–6 and *Leg.* 2.53–71. There are parallel rabbinic reflections on the problem of decency in case the garment is taken to pledge during the day. Following the principle that there is no needless repetition in the Torah, Rabbis applied the parallel passages Exod 22:25–26 (26–27) and Deut 24:10–13 to two different situations—to daytime ("up to the setting of the sun") and to nighttime ("when the sun goes down"): "Thou Shalt Restore It unto Him Up to the Time of the Setting of the Sun (עד בא השמש). This refers to a garment worn during the day (כסות יום) which you must restore to him for the whole day (כל היום). I thus know only about the garment worn during the day that you must restore it to him for the whole day. How do I know about the garment worn during the night that you must restore it to him for the whole night? Scripture says: Thou shalt surely restore to him the pledge when the sun goeth down (כבא השמש) (Deut 24:13). On the basis of this the Sages said: During the night one may take as a pledge a garment worn by day, and during the day one may take as a pledge a garment worn by night." (*Mekhilta de-Rabbi Ishmael* 2:460 [*Kaspa*]). Leibowitz in her *Studies in Shemot (Exodus)*, 416–24, gives an overview of subsequent rabbinic interpretations.

6. The next difficulty reiterates (cf. 2.1.1 above) that the pledge is legally in the possession of the creditor rather than the debtor. Philo concentrates (§ 100) on the term "to return" (ἀποδιδόναι, Hebrew להשיב), which, in view of the above consideration, is out of place (διδόναι / לתת, "to give" would be fitting) and therefore it must refer to something more inherently belonging to the original owner.

7. Neither does it escape Philo's scrupulous eyes (§ 100) that, curiously enough, the decree does not oblige the debtor to return (κομίσαι) the garment to the creditor the following morning, which obviously renders the whole transaction pointless.[33]

8. Philo's last objection against the relevance of the plain sense of our passage is that of the literary critic (§ 101). The peculiar form of the law (τὸ τῆς ἑρμηνείας ἰδιότροπον), he observes, reminds one of an aphorism (ἀφορισμός)[34] rather than a specific command (παραίνεσις),[35] that is, it belongs to the genre of sayings rather than *halakha*—in other words, this is not a law to be observed at all![36]

Having refuted—as he certainly believed he did—every attempt to force this ethical maxim into the narrow mould of a practical commandment, Philo once again, and not without sarcasm, refers to his literalist opponents as "the sophists of literalism" (τοὺς τῆς ῥητῆς πραγματείας σοφιστάς) who "keep their eyebrows very high" (λίαν τὰς ὀφρῦς ἀνεσπακότας) (§ 102).[37] They are unlikely to read the biblical text more scrupulously than

---

[33] In b. B Metz 115a it is presupposed that the pledge is to be taken again by the creditor, and a reason is also given: in order that the sabbatical year should not cancel the debt (שלו תהא שביעית משמטתו).

[34] Ἀφορισμός literally means "definition," cf. *Leg.* 1.65, i.e., "an explanatory statement" (PLCL)—in this case concerning the necessities of life and compassion.

[35] Παραίνεσις, lit. "exhortation," refers to a specific command as in *Leg.* 1.97, 101 (on the prohibition to eat from the tree).

[36] Philo even rephrases the biblical passage in the form of an exhortation. Since there he uses imperative instead of future forms, Colson *ad. loc.* and Wolfson, *Philo*, 1:179, citing *Fug.* 171 and *Ebr.* 138, argue that the difference between the literary genres is based on the verbal modes. However, there are other passages with verbs in the future which Philo treats as laws in the literal sense (cf. Deut 24:13). Therefore, it must be the general style of the statement, together with the future tense, which brings Philo to this conclusion.

[37] What Colson translates as "self-satisfied" literally means "those raising their eyebrows too high." In other contexts, Philo uses the same phrase to describe teachers boasting of their power and rejecting poor students (*Congr.* 127) or people priding in their prosperity and mocking widowhood and orphanhood (*Mos.* 2.240). There is a debate about the identity of the sophists in Philo. Bruce W. Winter, *Philo and Paul among the Sophists: Alexandrian and Corinthian Responses to a Julio-Claudian Movement*, 2nd ed. (Grand Rapids, MI: Eerdmans, 2002) argued that they were representatives of the Second Sophistic. Most Philonists believe, however, that they refer to those who prefer rhetoric over substance. (I am grateful for Gregory Sterling for this reference.)

Philo but they meticulously ward off any attempt to discover its deeper meaning. Philo's approach is very much akin to that of textual critics but instead of emending the text or rejecting it as inauthentic he saves it by offering a figurative interpretation following, as he says, "the rules of allegory" (τοῖς ἀλληγορίας νόμοις).[38]

2.2. The Allegorical (Figurative) Meaning (§§ 102–114)

Philo's method in establishing the allegorical meaning of the passage is similar to the one he has been using in his refutation of the literal sense: he once again focuses on the individual terms, although only partly the same ones as above.[39] These details are more intricately interwoven, resulting in a passionate rhetorical piece.

1. The central tenet and starting point of Philo's exegesis is his identification of the garment with *logos*, which in our passage means both "speech" and "reason."[40] The hermeneutical procedure by which Philo arrives at his conclusion is an inquiry into what one may call the essential meaning of terms, a method which he finds more fitting than contextual or historical interpretation. What is a garment, *essentially?*—Philo asks. A garment, his answer goes, does three things: it protects, covers, and embellishes the body.[41] It protects the body "from frost and heat," "conceals nature's secret parts (τὰ τῆς φύσεως ἀπόρρητα)," and it is "a fitting adornment (κόσμος)" for the body (§ 102). Ascending further from this intermediate

---

[38] The following exegesis is a fine example of Philo's method. For the expression cf. *Abr.* 68 and Siegert, "Early Jewish interpretation in a Hellenistic style," 184.

[39] Garment (§§ 102–104), taking in pledge (§§ 105–107), one's only covering (§§ 107–108), unseemliness (§ 109), sleep (§§ 110–112), and returning the garment before sunset (§§ 112–114).

[40] Reasoning is an inner speech (λόγος ἐνδιάθετος), as opposed to the one pronounced (λόγος προφορικός); cf. *Migr.* 78 (identified with Moses and Aaron, respectively). Due to the complexity of the term I do not translate it. As we shall see, *logos* is related to the rational and 'erotic' faculty of the soul as a gift of God by which it may ascend to him. On *logos* in Philo cf. David Winston, *Logos and Mystical Theology in Philo of Alexandria* (Cincinnati: Hebrew Union College Press, 1985) and Manuel Alexandre Júnior, "Twofold Human Logos in Philo of Alexandria: the Power of Expressing Thought Through Language," in *Pouvoir et puissances chez Philon d'Alexandrie*, ed. Francesca Calabi, et. al. (Turnhout: Brepols, 2015), 37–59.

[41] Some ancient and modern exegetes also believe that the garment is merely an example of essential things ("lebensnotwendige Dinge"; so Christoph Dohmen, *Exodus 19–40* [Freiburg: Herder, 2004], 177), cf. Deut 24:6: "No one shall take a handmill or an upper millstone in pledge, for he would be taking a life (נפש) in pledge." The Midrash Rabbah on Exodus (31:7, p. 385 Lehrman) mentions the pin of the plough as another example (based on the *figura etymologica*, cf. p. 31 above).

level of abstraction Philo implicitly asks what it is that has the same three functions for the benefit of the person in a different and (according to Philo) even more vital sense. The result of this exegetical equation is *logos*, which equally protects—against aggressors (κατὰ τῶν νεωτεριζόντων, § 103);[42] hides up "matters of shame and reproach," especially sins (ἁμαρτίαι); and it is an adornment (κόσμος) of life as a whole as it compels us to become more excellent (§ 104). For Philo, this allegorical meaning of "garment" fits more smoothly in the fabric of the biblical passage: *logos* does belong to the original owner, it is not to be returned the next morning, and it is a human being's "most peculiar prerogative" (τὸ ἴδιον ἀνθρώπου κτῆμα, § 113).

2. The most interesting part of Philo's exegesis is his interpretation of "taking in pledge" as referring to *logos* (§§ 105–107). This is the point where he associates the Mosaic regulation with Platonic doctrines and it is here that his exegesis turns dramatic and passionate.[43] *Logos* is an eminently personal property, related to one's faculty of reasoning, arguing, and ascent to God. Philo's argumentation reveals that for him taking this most inherent faculty "in pledge" is illegitimate, to say the least, and akin to what he has called above "coat-snatching" (§ 98). Philo's interpretation of this looting is an impressive sequence or 'fugue' of metaphors subtly transiting one from the other while preserving the original theme.[44] He opens with surprisingly harsh words describing those who commit such crime: they are called "mischievous pests" (λῶβαι καὶ κῆρες ἀνθρώπων)[45] and the chain of

[42] The primary meaning of νεωτερίζω in Philo seems to be youthful, immature behaviour (cf. *Ebr.* 146; *Sobr.* 15) rather than innovation. This restlessness is manifested as rebellion, revolution or tyranny in society (cf. *Agr.* 40; *Sobr.* 10; *Mos.* 2.13; *Spec.* 3.63) or as physical harm in nature (cf. *Opif.* 80; *Somn.* 1.124; *Mos.* 1.216; 2.65). In a specific sense, it has the connotation of sacrilege (cf. *Praem.* 77; *Flacc.* 48; *Legat.* 208).

[43] These Platonic allusions are not listed in David Lincicum, "A Preliminary Index to Philo's Non-Biblical Citations and Allusions," *SPhiloA* 25 (2013): 139–67 and Lincicum, "Philo's Library," *SPhiloA* 26 (2014): 99–114. On Philo's use of the *Phaedrus* see Anita Méasson, *Du char ailé de Zeus à l'Arche d'Alliance: Images et mythes platoniciens chez Philon d'Alexandrie* (Paris: Études Augustiniennes, 1986) and Michael Cover, "The Sun and the Chariot: The *Republic* and the *Phaedrus* as Sources for Rival Platonic Paradigms of Psychic Vision in Philo's Biblical Commentaries," *SPhiloA* 26 (2014): 151–67.

[44] The metaphors are indicated by letters (a) to (h).

[45] Lit.: "disgraces and blemishes among humankind"; λώβη in Philo's vocabulary primarily means bodily or (more rarely) mental damages, cf. *Cher.* 96; *Agr.* 130; *Plant.* 164; *Her.* 284; *Somn.* 1.226; 2.64; *Spec.* 1.80, 167, 254, 260; *Contempl.* 55; λῶβαι ἀνθρώπων is not attested elsewhere. κῆρες ἀνθρώπων has a Platonic pedigree (*Leg.* 9.937d6–8) and it is relatively frequent in Philo (cf. *Sacr.* 111; *Sobr.* 38; *Spec.* 4.200). In some manuscripts the gender of the relative pronoun and the participle is feminine (αἴ MA, ἀφαιρούμεναι A), suggesting impersonal evil forces rather than real persons, cf. PLCL 5:352–353. But in §§ 106–107 these are definitely real people and I do not see a change of subject at § 114, *pace* PLCL 5:356, note *a*. Cf. David M. Hay, "References to Other Exegetes," in *Both Literal and*

metaphors is designed to describe the various aspects of their single crime—holding *logos* in pawn.

(a) Instead of fostering the growth (συναυξῆσαι) of *logos* they cut it utterly down (ὅλον ὑποτέμνονται) (§ 105); *logos*, therefore, is presented as a dynamic entity which, in contrast with a coat, is capable of growing or diminishing according to external influences. (b) The dynamic character of *logos* is likened in a second step to wheat and other crops (σῖτον καὶ τὸν ἄλλον καρπόν) ravaged by the enemy (§ 105)—a reference to the scorched earth policy. They cut down *logos*, which, according to this image, is also capable of serving as food,[46] in order that neither its owner nor the enemy may take advantage of it.[47] (c) Now that we are in a military context (indicated already in § 103), Philo makes it explicit that there is indeed a total, war ("without truce and declaration/herald" [ἄσπονδος καὶ ἀκήρυκτος[48]]) waged by "certain people" (ἐνίοις) against "rational nature" (τὴν λογικὴν φύσιν) (§ 106). With this image Philo not only dramatizes and intensifies the wickedness of his unidentified targets but also specifies that the real owner of *logos* is "rational nature," i.e. the upper and most noble part of the human soul.[49] In light of the previous metaphor, the soul now appears as a field into which seeds of logos have been sown in order that they may grow and bring fruit.

(d) Philo, however, translates this image into yet another metaphor which serves his exegetical objective much better. Initially, the shift is clandestine as the metaphor is ambiguous: these people, he says, "cut down to the ground its (i.e. rational nature's) first shoots" (τὰς βλάστας αὐτῆς ἀποκείρουσιν ἐν χρῷ), which, in a more literal translation, means they "clip/shear/shave close to the skin its (first) shoots" (§ 106).[50] The image

---

Allegorical: Studies in Philo of Alexandria's Questions and Answers (Atlanta: Scholars Press, 1991), 87, against John Dillon's suggestion that Philo's opponents are imaginary "straw men." For a similar invective against creditors in a literal context cf. *Virt.* 86.

[46] Philo consistently identifies the manna with *logos*, cf. *Leg.* 2.86; 3.175; *Sacr.* 86; *Det.* 118; and *Her.* 79, emphasizing its transcendent origin.

[47] Deut 20:19–20 prohibits this tactic, which Philo discusses extensively in *Virt.* 148–159; cf. also *Spcc.* 4.226–229.

[48] The phrase is characteristic of Philo: cf. *Sacr.* 18 (against the passions); *Fug.* 114 (the High Priest against profane women); *Somn.* 2.166 (among the effects of alcohol); and *Praem.* 87 (wild animals against men).

[49] λογικὴ φύσις in Philo refers to the reasoning power of the soul (*Opif.* 149–150), identified with νοῦς or intellect (*Her.* 232; *QG* 2.62). It is the image of God in the human being (*Det.* 83) and the 'mother' of the two main types of *logos*, i.e., inner and external (*Migr.* 68). The translation in PCH "das natürliche Wachsen der Sprache" is certainly too narrow.

[50] ἐν χρῷ (hapax in Philo but frequent otherwise) often refers to a haircut explicitly, while the translations in PCH, PLCL and PAPM suggest the cutting of a plant. The other

emerging in place of a landscape of war is that of a living being the shoots and growths of which are hair or feathers (again referring to *logos*), without which it will somehow be rendered "barren and unproductive" (ἄγονον καὶ στεῖραν) of "noble doings" (καλῶν ἐπιτηδευμάτων).[51]

(e) "Noble doings" is in virtual quotation marks in Philo's own text as well (introduced by ὡς ἔπος εἰπεῖν, "as it were"), as the phrase is borrowed from Diotima's speech about Eros in Plato's *Symposium* (211c5).[52] More particularly, the expression refers to a stage in the soul's ascent to ultimate Beauty, the contemplation of which makes life really "worthwhile to live" (βιωτόν) and which inspires people "to give birth" to (τίκτειν) truly excellent deeds (211d–212a).[53] (f) Realising that Philo has surreptitiously guided us from the war scene to the imagery of the Platonic ascent of the soul towards the first cause (clearly identified with the biblical God, § 92), we have more confidence to identify the creature to which he compares the rational human soul. It is a winged animal since it is said to "take a deep breath and rise on high" (μεγάλα πνεύσασα καὶ ἐπὶ μήκιστον ἀρθεῖσα[54]) "smitten with a passionate love" (πληχθεῖσαν ἔρωτι[55]) for, and soaring towards, "objects of philosophical contemplation" (τῶν φιλοσοφίας θεωρημάτων), that is, beautiful intellectual realities (§ 106). In Plato's myth of the charioteer (Socrates's palinode in *Phaedr.* 246a–256e), it is precisely the soul which, represented by the charioteer and the pair of winged horses drawing the chariot (253c7–d1), strives to ascend to the divine realm to contemplate the beauty of "the place above the heaven" (τὸν ὑπερουράνιον τόπον) which "was never worthily

metaphor "sqeeze the life out of its earliest growths" (τὰς πρώτας ἐπιφύσεις ἐκθλίβουσιν) may be applied both to a plant and an animal.

[51] "Barrenness" in the physical sense is hardly the direct consequence of losing hair or feathers, see below, nn. 53, 63.

[52] Καλὰ ἐπιτηδεύματα is frequent in Isocrates, and Plato himself also uses it on a number of occasions (e.g., *Resp.* 4.444e3; 8.560b7; *Leg.* 1.638a6; and often in *Hipp. maj.*) but Philo's subsequent argument (§ 107) clearly shows that Diotima's speech is his relevant source here (cf. also σμικρολόγος, 210d2). For Diotima's speech see *Symp.* 201e–212c; for Philo's references to Plato cf. Lincicum, "A Preliminary Index to Philo's Non-Biblical Citations and Allusions," 139–167 and Lincicum, "Philo's Library," 99–114 (those in our passage have not been identified as such). Korting, *Das Vaterunser und die Unheilabwehr*, does not discuss §§ 105–107.

[53] This last point explains Philo's reference to barrenness above. For the description of the "stages" (ἐπαναβασμοί, cf. 211c3) of the soul's ascent (corporeal beauties—psychic/spiritual/intellectual beauties—the Beautiful itself) see 210a–d; the "Beautiful itself" is described at 210e–212a.

[54] Colson translates the phrases more figuratively: "grandly inspired and highly exalted," which expresses Philo's argument fittingly but misses the allusion to the imagery of Plato. For μεγάλα πνεύσασα cf. *Mut.* 215 (in a pejorative sense); ἐπὶ μήκιστον ἀρθεῖσα cf. *Aet.* 135 (on a volcanic eruption).

[55] For πληχθεῖσαν ἔρωτι cf. *Opif.* 77. Eros is a key term in Philo, attested dozens of times.

sung by any poet, nor will it ever be" (247c3–4). It is the vision of this intelligible beauty which nourishes the feathers (πτέρωμα, 246e2) of the soul's metaphorical wings and, once fallen into incarnation and the ensuing oblivion, it is the perceptible resemblances (ὁμοίωμα, 250a6) of transcendent beauty itself which remind the souls—but only some of them—of their celestial origin (249d–250a), elevating them to their true home.[56] In such moments the souls are "smitten" (ἐκπλήττονται, 250a6) by desire, and the feathers of their souls' wings start to grow (251b1–252a1). Key terms in Philo's account resemble, or even coincide with, those of Plato's myth,[57] the imagery of which is based on the metaphor of wings.[58] It is against this Platonic background that Philo's interpretation of the biblical legislation becomes clear, and it is undoubtedly these Platonic passages with a view to which he composed his exegetical argument.[59]

(g) Since the original context is the illegitimate seizure of *logos* (without which the soul is prevented from ascending to God), Philo integrates these Platonic metaphors into the earlier imagery of conflict.[60] Instead of feathers (of the soul) shorn to the skin, Philo now likens the powerful impulse of the erotically inspired soul towards learning (παιδεία, § 107)[61] to a sweeping torrent (χειμάρρους)—a symbol of the power of *logos*. Since this irresistible rush (ἀκατάσχετος ῥύμη) is impossible to halt, the only tactic the enemy can resort to is changing its course (τὴν φορὰν ἔτρεψαν) and channeling it to low and illiberal activities (εἰς βαναύσους καὶ ἀνελευθέρους τέχνας μετοχετευσάμενοι).[62] In this way they finally manage to neutralise the impetus of the

---

[56] The divine charioteers freely contemplate supracelestial reality (246e–247e); cf. *Praem.* 38 where Philo depicts God as a charioteer surrounded by dazzling light (cf. Cover, "The Sun and the Chariot," 163–64). Philo, unlike Socrates, does not mention the contemplation of intermediary grades of beauty.

[57] ἐκπλήττονται, 250a6, cf. also 255b4; τὴν βλάστην τοῦ πτεροῦ (251d3); ἀναπνοὴν λαβοῦσα (251e4), ἐξαναπνεύσας (254c6).

[58] The gods call Eros Pteros (πτέρως) on account of his power to grow feathers (πτεροφύτωρ, 252b9); cf. also 255c4–d3.

[59] In Philo, just as in *Phaedrus* and *Symposium*, the aim is the vision of God (§ 114), on which cf. Scott D. Mackie, "Seeing God in Philo of Alexandria: Means, Methods and Mysticism," *JSJ* 43 (2012): 147–79. On the vision of God and the flight of the mind see Gregory E. Sterling, "Dancing with the Stars: The Ascent of the Mind in Philo of Alexandria," in *Apocalyptic Literature and Mysticism*, ed. Pieter G. R. de Villiers, Adela Collins, and John Collins, Exstasis: Religious Experience from Antiquity to the Middle Ages (Berlin: de Gruyter, 2019), 155–66.

[60] Cf. above, (b)–(c).

[61] PCW notes that some manuscripts (piously) add τὴν ἱερὰν ('holy') after παιδείαν, just as they add ἀληθοῦς ('true') after φιλοσοφίας.

[62] In Philo, βάναυσοι τέχναι often has a neutral or mildly pejorative sense of "practical/mechanical arts/sciences" (cf. *Leg.* 1.57; 2.107; *Mos.* 2.219; *Spec.* 1.335; 2.65) but it may also assume the more negative overtone of "meanness" or "vulgarity" (cf. *Sacr.* 32; *Fug.* 83). In

soul, leaving it behind exhausted and unproductive despite its natural capability of great achievements (μεγαλοφυές).[63] (h) The last metaphor Philo employs to depict the situation is that of a fertile land of orphans allowed by bad guardians to become dry and barren. (§ 107).

Only at this point does Philo return to the original image of the garment taken in pledge—by now clearly just one among an array of symbols— which, in light of this sequence of metaphors, unequivocally comes to refer to the stripping (περισυλάω) of *logos*, that is, one's only real "garment." (§ 107).

3. Who are the malicious perpetrators? Philo does not tell us but he characterises them as people motivated by "jealousy and envy" (βασκανίας καὶ φθόνου[64]), panicking that the genuine impulse of these exalted souls "should sweep over their hair-splittings and plausible inventions against the truth" (γλισχρολογίας, πιθανὰς κατὰ τῆς ἀληθείας εὑρέσεις).[65] I will argue below that this is a reference to the literalists who prevent noble souls from discovering the magnificent and inspiring truths of the Bible by insisting on the literal sense.[66]

4. Philo's allegorical-psychological interpretation of the remaining terms is less revealing in its exegetical procedure, therefore we may concentrate on its results: the *only* covering (περιβόλαιον μόνον, § 108) refers to *logos* as the uniquely inherent property (ἴδιον § 108, ἴδιον κτῆμα § 113) of a human being; indecency (ἀσχημοσύνη, § 109) refers to shameful deeds (§ 104); and sleeping or rest (κοιμηθήσεται, § 110) to the security provided by *logos* as a guard. Philo emphasizes that *logos* is "bound up with us, or rather

Prob. 34 Philo describes a "peace-time war" in which men are forced under duress to undertake "menial tasks."

[63] This is the point where barrenness (cf. n. 53) becomes meaningful.

[64] By contrast, in the *Phaedrus* envy is far from the gods (247a7; cf. *Timaeus* 23d4). For βασκανία and φθόνος cf. *Cher.* 33; *Mut.* 95, 112; *Abr.* 21; *Ios.* 144; *Mos.* 1.246; *Virt.* 170, *Flacc.* 29; *QG* 4.191b.

[65] γλισχρολογία, lit. "sticky/stingy *logos*," i.e., stickiness of mind or intellectual pettiness, is Philo's neologism (in some MSS we have αἰσχρολογία), attested also in *Congr.* 52 ("sceptics who do not concern themselves with the best things in nature ... but spend themselves on petty quibbles [μικρὰ σοφίσματα] and trifling disputes [γλισχρολογούμενοι]"); *Somn.* 2.301 ("some perhaps may say scoffingly that such points [the 'lip' of the river in Exod 7:15] should not be brought into our inquiries, as savouring of petty trifling [γλισχρολογία] rather than any profitable process [ὠφέλεια]"); cf. later in Origen, *Exhort. ad mart.* 2.19; and Diogenes Laertius, *Vitae* 2.30; γλίσχρος is frequent in Plato. πιθαναὶ εὑρέσεις goes back to Plato (cf. *Apol.* 17a3–4); for Philo cf. *Post.* 52 (Cain's arguments); *Conf.* 39; and *Migr.* 171 (sophists).

[66] I do not agree with PLCL that in § 114 the personified agents turn into "evil forces within us." Nevertheless, the "we" in § 114 implies that anyone can act like these anonymous people.

cemented and united with us by an invisible and indissoluble natural glue" (ἐνδεδεμένος, μᾶλλον δὲ ἡρμοσμένος καὶ ἡνωμένος κόλλῃ τινὶ φύσεως ἀλύτῳ καὶ ἀοράτῳ, § 111).[67] By emphasizing this Philo anticipates his main conclusion (§ 114) that *logos* is by nature inseparable from the nobler part of the soul ("rational nature"), and therefore "taking it in pledge," while a vicious attempt, cannot result in complete separation.

5. The last point in Philo's allegorical exegesis pertains to the obligation to restore *logos* to its real owner before sunset; this is also where he resumes his interpretation of the Sun as a symbol of God (§§ 112–114) interrupted by this long excursus starting at § 92.[68] The point of connection between the Sun and God is their respective illuminative power—God's incorporeal (ἀσώματος) rays being directed to the human mind / soul (νοῦν τὸν ἀνθρώπινον; ἐν ψυχῇ) as a merciful act (δι' ἔλεον).[69] However, from what Philo has said so far it is not obvious in what sense the presence of God is necessary for the restoration of *logos*. In the biblical passage it is the debtor who is in need of his cloak for the night, while here the focus shifts to the creditor, whom Philo addresses in the second person:

> While, then, God still pours upon you the rays of sacred light [τὸ ἱερὸν φέγγος],[70] hasten while it is day [ἐν ἡμέρᾳ] to restore to its owner [τῷ κυρίῳ][71] the pledge [τὸ ῥύσιον] you have seized. For when he has set [δύντος γάρ],[72] you, like "all Egypt"[73] will experience for ever a tangible [ψηλαφητὸν[74]] darkness, and smitten [πληχθεὶς[75]] with sightlessness and ignorance[76] will be deprived of the possessions of all of which you deemed yourself master, and be perforce[(ἀνάγκῃ]

---

[67] The *logos*, whether fostered or incapacitated, inherently belongs to the human soul.

[68] Cf. τοῦτον δὴ τὸν δόλιχον ἀπεμηκύναμεν ("this long course we have run," § 115), cf. *Det.* 15.

[69] ἔλεος is a reference to the biblical text (ἐλεήμων γάρ εἰμι, 'for I am compassionate,' Exod 22:26 [27]). Plato, *Leg.* 2.653c9–d5 is also a possible reminiscence, cf. θεοὶ δὲ οἰκτίραντες τὸ τῶν ἀνθρώπων ἐπίπονον πεφυκὸς γένος ... with Philo's δι' ἔλεον τοῦ γένους ἡμῶν. In *Post.* 30 Philo depicts God as going down with the sons of Israel to Egypt "in pity for rational nature (διὰ φύσεως οἶκτον λογικῆς), that it may be caused to rise out of the nether world of passion into the upper region of virtue."

[70] "His sacred light." (PLCL)

[71] "Dem Herrn" in PCH, implying the Lord, is misleading.

[72] The subject is ambiguous and both PLCL and PAPM refer it to "that light"; however, it is more likely that the implied subject is God (τοῦ θεοῦ) as symbolized by the Sun.

[73] Exod 10:21; in *Mos.* 1.123–125 Philo discusses the plague of darkness in the literal sense.

[74] The term is first attested in the Septuagint (Exod 10:21) but other forms occur in Plato (*Phaed.* 99b4), Homer (*Od.* 9.416, on the blinded Cyclops), and elsewhere.

[75] The same expression as above, § 107, referring to *eros*.

[76] Note that blindness is present on two levels: physical and spiritual/intellectual.

enslaved by Israel, the Seeing One [τοῦ βλέποντος],[77] whom, though by nature immune from bondage, you tried to plunder [ἐρρυσίαζες]." [78]

In this last passage Philo translates the legal case into yet another metaphor, evoking a new biblical context, the slavery in Egypt and the liberation of the Exodus.[79] Restoring the *logos* to its owner corresponds here to Pharaoh's permission to restore freedom to Israel, enabling God's people to leave the house of slavery for the mountain of revelation. Pharaoh in this context is the equivalent of the evil creditor, Israel that of the human soul ("rational nature"), freedom corresponds to *logos*, while God is the source of intellectual light in the metaphor of the sunset, and the source of revelation on the mountain[80] in the historical setting of the Exodus.[81] It remains to draw our conclusions from these metaphors projected upon, and mutually explaining, each other.

In this multiple prism, those perverting the impetus of others towards God by depriving them of the faculty which provides them with wings hold their victims in an intellectual/spiritual slavery. They believe, wrongly, that in this way they manage to degrade them to their own lowly outlook. They do not, or no longer, possess the erotic desire to mount on high but they are afraid of the irresistible impetus of others. This is the point when the "creditor" refuses to restore the most peculiar property to its natural owner. However, this is not the end of the biblical "aphorism." For the "owner of the garment," in his pain and justified resentment, "cries

---

[77] Philo consistently interprets the name Israel as "the one who sees"; cf. Ellen Birnbaum, *The Place of Judaism in Philo's Thought: Israel, Jews, and Proselytes*, BJS 290, SPhiloM 2 (Atlanta: Scholars Press, 1996), 61–127 (Chapters 2 and 3), and C. T. Robert Hayward, *Interpretation of the Name Israel in Ancient Judaism and Some Early Christian Writings: From Victorious Athlete to Heavenly Champion* (Oxford: Oxford University Press, 2005), 156–93.

[78] Lit. "you tried to make him your debtor by taking a pledge from him." Translating this term as referring to Israel as a pledge has caused difficulties in the interpretation of the passage (PLCL: "you seized as your chattel"; PCH: "den du auspfändetest"; PAPM: "que tu retenais en gage"; Reggiani and Reale, *Filone di Alessandria: L'uomo e Dio. Il connubio con gli studi preliminari*, 467–68, explains the returning of the pledge as the recognition [il riconoscimento] that *logos* is granted by God to humanity; Korting, *Das Vaterunser und die Unheilabwehr*, 692: "den du mit Beschlag belegtest"). It is much more plausible to identify Pharaoh with the "coat-snatchers," and Israel's freedom as the "garment."

[79] This final context is closely related to the original setting of the law concerning the pledge in the Book of Exodus (cf. section 1 above).

[80] On Philo's avoidance of the name Sinai see Gregory E. Sterling, "Thunderous Silence: The Omission of the Sinai Pericope in Philo of Alexandria," *JSJ* 49 (2018): 1–26.

[81] Alternatively, *logos* could correspond to Israel (cf. PLCL, PAPM, or Bravo, "Sulân," 789); however, it would be very much out of place to make God an equivalent of the person whose garment ("Israel") had been forcefully taken away.

onto" the Lord and He "will hear him." In the language of the concluding metaphor, God listens to the voice and the longing of the looted and humiliated soul by sending his light to him. The miracle of light in Egypt symbolizes that God restores the *logos* to the human mind by which it can see. Philo also explains the nature of this substitute light when he comes back to Jacob's dream: "When that glorious undiluted light (ἄκρατον φέγγος) sank out of their sky, they obtained that which has been diluted (τὸ κεκρα-μένον)" (§ 117), comparable to the light of the Moon's dimmer (ἀμυδρότερον) illumination (§ 116).

Thus, although deprived of the primary source of light, the soul, which cannot be entirely bereft of illumination, receives a consolation in the weaker light of the *logoi* sent by God. Those, however, who committed the crime of attempting to withhold the access of others to light, are smitten by complete darkness as a punishment. The darkness surrounding them is clearly spiritual in nature ("sightlessness and ignorance," § 114), and it is the consequence of their γλισχρολογία (§ 107) or narrow-mindedness, jealousy and envy (§ 107) which, despite their forceful acquisition of other people's *logoi*, leaves them without intellectual clarity and illumination. These people, we may infer, are themselves deprived of an active and operating *logos*, their feathers are not growing and their wings are not spread out. Therefore, no matter how many other *logoi* they incarcerate, they will not come closer to light and to God.

It follows that just as the plague of darkness, so also the sunset affects primarily those who debase themselves by attempting to deprive others of their freedom to use their proper intellectual and spiritual capacities. For their innocent victims—Israel, the seeing one, that is, the soul—who had been prevented from ascending to God by external oppressors, God's light will shine nevertheless: in Egypt in the form of the miracle, at the mountain through God's epiphany, and, in the imagery of the Platonic myths, when the soul grows its feathers again and flies up to the luminous divine realm above the heaven or, to use another Platonic metaphor, ascends from the cave.[82] Thus the soul's potential capability of vision is perfected by God's light, a sign of God's compassion for the souls of the poor.[83] The sunset before Jacob's dream refers to the situation when someone is deprived by malicious oppressors of God's illuminative power but, crying in his need to

[82] Plato, *Resp.* 7.514a–520a.

[83] Cf. Plato's theory of vision in *Tim.* 45b–46c. In the myth of the *Phaedrus* Socrates also claims that every human soul by nature has an experience of (divine) reality or else it would not have incarnated as a human being but something else (249e4–250a1: πᾶσα μὲν ἀνθρώπου ψυχὴ φύσει τεθέαται τὰ ὄντα, ἢ οὐκ ἂν ἦλθεν εἰς τόδε τὸ ζῷον).

God, receives as a consolation the secondary lights of angels walking up and down on the heavenly ladder.[84]

3. Conclusions

3.1. Philo's Rejection of the Literal Sense of a Mosaic Law

In view of our analysis, the first problem to be addressed is Philo's forceful rejection of the literal sense in the case of Exod 22:25–26 (26–27). In most cases, the Alexandrian exegete, while giving preference to the allegorical, considers the plain sense as a legitimate or even a fundamental level of Scriptural interpretation.[85] These two levels of meaning, Philo explains in a famous passage, are like body and soul, coexisting in an organic unity.[86] Those who suppress the literal sense, he warns his "extreme allegorist" opponents,

> as though they were living alone by themselves in the wilderness, or as though they had become disembodied souls [ἀσώματοι ψυχαί], and knew neither city nor village nor household nor any company of human beings at all, overlooking all that the mass of men regard [τὰ δοκοῦντα τοῖς πολλοῖς], [they] explore reality in its naked absoluteness [γυμνὴν αὐτὴν ἐφ᾽ ἑαυτῆς].[87]

[84] In Exod. Rab. 31 10 (p. 389–90 Lehrman) we find an allegorical interpretation of our passage. Based on a word play, the midrash uses the garment as a symbol of the Temple (משכן) given in pledge (משכון) to the heathen nations for Israel's sins (without making God indebted to them) "until the Sun appears" (עד בא השמש), "that is, till the coming of the Messiah (שיבוא המשיח עד)" since the sun of righteousness (שמש צדקה / ἥλιος δικαιοσύνης / sol iustitiae) in Maleachi 3:20 (in some versions 4:2) was famously interpreted as referring to the Messiah (בא השמש here means the arrival of the sun). Ambrose (cf. n. 24 above) also identifies the Sun in Exod 22:26 (27) with the sol iustitiae which goes down for those not doing justice to their neighbours. Ambrose's negative example, instead of Pharaoh, is Judas.

[85] On Philo's exegetical methods cf. Wolfson, Philo, 1:115–38; Tobin, The Creation of Man, 154–61; Burton L. Mack, "Philo of Alexandria and Exegetical Traditions in Alexandria," in ANRW 21.1: 249–67; David Instone Brewer, Techniques and Assumptions in Jewish Exegesis Before 70 CE (Tübingen: Mohr Siebeck, 1992), 198–212; Siegert, "Early Jewish interpretation in a Hellenistic style," 182–87; Kamesar, "Biblical interpretation in Philo," 65–91.

[86] Migr. 89–93; cf. David M. Hay, "Putting Extremism in Context: The Case of Philo, De Migratione 89–93," SPhiloA 9 (1997): 126–42.

[87] Migr. 90. It reveals Philo's ambivalence that in Abr. 236 (in a non-legal context) he uses the same metaphor of nakedness in a positive sense.

Philo makes it explicit that by observing the laws of Sabbath, festivals, circumcision, and Temple worship, even if we are aware of their true symbolic or inner meaning,

> we shall gain a clearer [ἀριδηλότερον] conception of those things of which these are the symbols [σύμβολα]; and besides that we shall not incur the censure of the many and the charges they are sure to bring against us [τὰς ἀπὸ τῶν πολλῶν μέμψεις καὶ κατηγορίας].[88]

In his exegetical praxis Philo normally follows his own hermeneutical principle by keeping and explaining the literal sense (ἡ ῥητὴ ἀπόδοσις) of biblical passages—not only in *Questions and Answers* and *Exposition*, but also in his *Allegorical Commentary*.[89] At the same time, we find quite a number of instances when he criticises or rejects the literal sense.[90] To be sure, most of these passages do not involve legal material and thus the principle expounded above is not violated.[91] In some cases, however, Philo's criticism of the literal sense extends to Mosaic legislation as well, although elsewhere he does not go beyond taking a distance from a literal interpretation.[92] In view of the relevant passages we may conclude that our passage is really unique. Philo does not only reject the literal sense of a Mosaic law more categorically than anywhere else, but even ridicules the plain sense of a biblical passage, attacking its defenders with a vehemence he normally reserves for those undermining it.[93] Who were Philo's oppo-

---

[88] *Migr.* 93. For the charges referred to see below, 3.2.

[89] Cf. *Leg.* 2.14; *Ebr.* 130; *Agr.* 157; *Sobr.* 65. For the *Exposition* cf. e.g. *Abr.* 20, 68, 88, 119, 131, 200, 217, 236; *Jos.* 125; *Spec.* 1.23, 200 (with a general hermeneutical principle), 287, 2.29, 146–147, 3.178 (reference to Philo's allegorist teachers), *Praem.* 65.

[90] Cf. Siegert, "Early Jewish Interpretation in a Hellenistic style," 184.

[91] E.g., in the story of the paradise (Gen 2–3) the trees of life and understanding cannot be physical trees (*Opif.* 154; cf. *Plant.* 32), God cannot literally take one of Adam's "sides" (*Leg.* 2.19, this is μυθῶδες); Adam cannot literally hide from God (*Leg.* 3.4; cf. *Det.* 155)—these are mythical elements. Cf. Philo's reflections on further narrative details in *Det.* 11–16 (with Ekaterina Matusova, "Allegorical Interpretation of the Pentateuch in Alexandria: Inscribing Aristobulus and Philo in a Wider Literary Context," *SPhiloA* 22 [2010]: 37–38), *Det.* 95, 167; *Post.* 1, 50, *Conf.* 190; *Congr.* 44, 126.

[92] Cf. *Deus* 133 (cf. below, n. 101); *Agr.* 131 (on Lev 11:4: "if we fix our eyes on the literal way of regarding the matter [πρὸς τὴν ῥητὴν ἐπίσκεψιν], I do not know what principle there is in the reason given for the camel's uncleanness"); *Plant.* 113 (on Lev 19:23–25: "the literal interpretation being quite out of keeping with the facts [τοῦ ῥητοῦ μὴ σφόδρα συνᾴδοντος]); *Fuga* 106 (on Num 35:25: "If taken literally, this point presents, I feel, great difficulty [πολλὴν ἐν τῷ ῥητῷ μοι παρέχουσα δυσκολίαν]).

[93] The uniqueness of Philo's attitude to the literal sense and its proponents in our passage has been rightly noticed by Valentin Nikiprowetzky, *Le commentaire de l'Écriture chez Philon d'Alexandrie*, (Leiden: Brill, 1977), 228: "Mais c'est là, semble-t-il, un cas à peu près unique chez notre auteur." Perhaps Philo's ridicule of the literal sense was motivated

nents and what prompted him to this passionate attack, even contradicting his general principles?[94] His reasons seem to be twofold: first, as we have seen, the paradoxical details of the literal sense and the presence of a parallel passage (Deut 24:10–13) gave Philo an opportunity to reserve Exod 22:25–26 (26–27) for the specific purpose of condemning those who question the validity of the allegorical sense;[95] second, Philo's symbolic interpretation of the Sun as an image of God intensified the conflict between him and the literalists.[96] We shall see the impact of the solar context at the end of the article (III C); let us now briefly focus on Philo's enemies.

3.2. Who Are Philo's Enemies?

For the profile of Philo's literalist opponents as well as his attitude against them it is essential to recognize that, by all likelihood, they are identical with those whom he, in the course of his exegesis, charges with taking others' *logos* in pledge.

Philo characterises his literalist opponents by an all too human pettiness of mind (ἀνθρωπίνη μικρολογία), since their insistence on the material interpretation of the garment is incommensurate with the greatness of God (§§ 93–94). The objections attributed to these literalists also imply a narrow-minded and niggardly attitude: the literalists are unable to conceive of generous people voluntarily supporting the poor (§§ 96, 98); neither is their Moses magnanimous enough to prescribe donations instead of forcing the needy into humiliating legal transactions (§ 95). The literalists are worse than the "slowest-witted reader" (βραδύτατος) as even the latter understands that this law cannot possibly be meant literally (§ 101). The narrow-mindedness and slow-wittedness of the literalists is accompanied by a boastful and insensitive attitude ("raising their eyebrows too high" [λίαν τὰς ὀφρῦς ἀνεσπακότας]) based on their pseudo-science or sophistry (cf. σοφισταί) (§ 102). No wonder that such people also insist on an interpretation which tactlessly exposes the debtors' nakedness to the public (§ 98). These literalists obviously hold that the allegorical interpretation suggested by Philo

---

by a fear that the literalists would criticize the passage along similar lines; in this case his critical attitude was preemptive.

[94] *Migr.* 89–93, see above.

[95] Philo gives a non–allegorical ethical interpretation of Deut 24:10–13 in *Virt.* 88–89.

[96] On other possible reasons of inconsistency in Philo cf. Scott D. Mackie, "Seeing God in Philo of Alexandria: the Logos, the Powers, or the Existent One?," *SPhiloA* 21 (2009): 45–47.

himself is to be rejected; the rejection by these boastful people cannot have been less than scornful.

Strikingly similar to the profile of the literalists is that of the enemies of "rational nature" who prevent others from ascending to the realm of God (§§ 105–107 *passim*). This sort of harmful people (ἄνθρωποι) cut the growth and block the rapture of the soul inspired by a passionate love (ἔρως) of divine reality. They fear that the inspired soul in its irresistible impulse will sweep away their stinginess of mind (γλισχρολογία) and plausible inventions with which they attempt to overthrow truth (πιθανὰς κατὰ τῆς ἀληθείας εὑρέσεις), that is, that truth which the soul discovers in its erotic and enthusiastic state of mind. It is this stinginess of mind to which these people, by their malevolence (κακοτεχνίαι, "perversions of art") want to drag down and debase these exalted souls in order to enslave them.

In view of these similarities we may conclude that Philo's literalist adversaries are to be identified with the enemies of *logos*. The latter is probably a broader category including anyone preventing others (or themselves) from a spiritual elevation to God; but literalists who deny that there is a spiritual dimension in our passage or elsewhere in Scripture certainly belong to this group of people. It follows that the "truth," the object of the soul's erotic desire, implies the true meaning of Scripture, whereas "illiberal arts and sciences" include the narrow-minded literalism of Philo's opponents. Consequently, the vehemence of Philo's attack on those taking *logos* in pledge is in reality a passionate defense of the allegorical sense against literalists. It is possible that even the "aggressors" (νεωτερίζοντες) against whom *logos* is a weapon of defence (§ 103) are those literalists who intimidate others when they do their first steps towards the deeper understanding of the subtle message of God, compatible with Plato's doctrines. On this interpretation, Philo's exposition of Exod 22:25–26 (26–27) is both programmatic and paradigmatic: the exegete singles out this law to interpret it as a plea for the right to access the deeper and "erotic" sense of Scripture.[97]

---

[97] Philo reflects on a similar situation in *Conf.* 39: "Now there are many who though they have not the capacity to demolish by sheer force the plausible inventions of the sophists (τὰς πιθανὰς τῶν σοφιστῶν εὑρέσεις), because their occupation has lain continuously in active life (διὰ τὴν ἐν τοῖς ἔργοις συνεχῆ μελέτην) and thus they are not trained in any high degree to deal with words (τῷ μὴ σφόδρα περὶ λόγους ... γεγυμνάσθαι), find refuge (κατέφυγον) in the support (συμμαχίαν) of the solely Wise Being and beseech Him to become their helper." Elsewhere he compares blindness to literalism, e.g., *Somn.* 1.164: "these and like lessons would cause even those who were blind in their understanding to grow keen-sighted, receiving from the most sacred oracles (i.e., Scripture) the gift of eyesight, enabling them to judge the real nature of things, and not merely rely on the literal sense (τοῖς ῥητοῖς)."

The identification of Philo's literalist opponents with those taking *logos* in pledge has added significant details to the profile of these people. Whether they can be identified with an actual group of exegetes is another question. As David Hay points out concerning *Questions and Answers*, Philo's "failure to name any other exegete suggests that for him the questions and answers are to be evaluated with little regard for the identity of those who created them."[98] We cannot even be absolutely certain that these exegetes are Jewish, although it is unlikely that a non-Jewish reader would have engaged in such a detailed analysis of a Mosaic law.[99] Since we do not hear about arguments based on the Hebrew original we may reasonably suppose that Philo's opponents are Greek-speaking Jews, most probably fellow Alexandrians. Profiles of groups or groupings of Alexandrian Jewish literalist exegetes have been identified by scholars.[100] Unfortunately, we do not know their social status, let alone their individual representatives.[101] It is clear, however, that we have at least two extreme tendencies, perhaps represented by actual groups, whose principles and methods were at odds with those of Philo: the extreme allegorists in *Migr.* 89–93 as well as the extreme literalists, his opponents in the present context. Philo's own position is in between, but closer to the former.

M. J. Shroyer proposed a fourfold classification of the literalists mentioned by Philo:[102] the simpletons (uncritical readers), the conservatives (opponents of critical investigation), the mythologists (looking about extra-Scriptural parallels) and the aggressive literalists who insist on the plain sense in order to ridicule and undermine the authority of Scripture.[103]

[98] Hay, "References to Other Exegetes," 97.
[99] Cf. Maren R. Niehoff, "Homeric Scholarship and Bible Exegesis in Ancient Alexandria: Evidence from Philo's 'Quarrelsome' Colleagues," *CQ* 57 (2007): 168.
[100] Cf. M. J. Shroyer, "Alexandrian Jewish literalists," *JBL* 55 (1936): 261–84; Hay, "References to Other Exegetes"; Brewer, *Techniques and Assumptions in Jewish Exegesis Before 70 CE*, 205–7; Siegert, "Early Jewish Interpretation in a Hellenistic Style," 189–97; Niehoff, "Homeric Scholarship and Bible Exegesis in Ancient Alexandria," 166–82; Peder Borgen, "Philo: An Interpreter of the Laws of Moses," in *Reading Philo: A Handbook to Philo of Alexandria*, ed. Torrey Seland (Grand Rapids, MI: Eerdmans, 2014), 86–87.
[101] Cf. Hay, "Putting Extremism in Context," 141. On a number of other occasions Philo refers to the literalists with sarcasm, cf. *Deus* 133 on Lev 14:34–36; sometimes he uses harsh words against literalists, cf. *QG* 4.168. On such passages cf. Nikiprowetzky, *Le commentaire de l'Écriture chez Philon d'Alexandrie*, 228; Brewer, *Techniques and Assumptions in Jewish Exegesis Before 70 CE*, 205–7; Matusova, "Allegorical Interpretation of the Pentateuch in Alexandria," 39.
[102] Shroyer, "Alexandrian Jewish literalists," 273–79.
[103] For the latter cf. *Conf.* 2, 142; *Ebr.* 65; *Her.* 81; *Mut.* 60–61 (with Niehoff, "Homeric Scholarship and Bible Exegesis in Ancient Alexandria," 172–76). The same strategy was applied on the Bible by pagan critics in Late Antiquity (esp. Celsus, Porphyry, and

Philo's opponents may be characterized as ultra-conservatives, and his passion may be explained by a fear of criticism, oppression or even persecution.[104] His warning to his "extreme allegorist" colleagues that those suspicious of allegorical interpretation are likely to bring charges against them seems to be applied here, under attack by extreme literalists, to himself and his disciples.[105]

3.3. *What Is the Significance of the Sun in Philo's Anti-Literalist Polemic?*

I have proposed an explanation of Philo's unprecedented rejection of the literal sense specifically in his exegesis of Exod 22:25–26 (26–27). Finally, we also need to consider the impact of the 'solar' context in *De Somniis*, more particularly of the allegorical identification of the Sun with God himself, on Philo's polemic. I will argue that Philo's vehemence is motivated by his frustration with his literalist opponents who prevented him from carrying his Platonic solar symbolism to some of its logical conclusions.

As we have seen, our passage is part of a small treatise on the significance of the Sun in the Bible. According to one of the four meanings mentioned, and clearly the most important one, the Sun is the symbol of God himself.[106] In §§ 73–76 Philo offers various exegetical arguments to support this interpretation of the Sun.[107] Most importantly, he declares that although in reality nothing is like God, there exist two entities resembling Him: the human soul and the Sun (§ 73). Since the former is invisible, with his statement Philo subscribes to the Platonic doctrine according to which the Sun is the par excellence visible image of the invisible Deity himself.[108]

Emperor Julian), cf. Wolfram Kinzig, "Pagans and the Bible," in *The New Cambridge History of the Bible*, vol. 1, ed. James Carleton Paget and Joachim L. W. Schaper (Cambridge: Cambridge University Press, 2013), 752–74. Philo's critical remarks against the literalists in *QG* cf. Hay, "References to Other Exegetes," 85.

[104] *Migr.* 93, cf. Hay, "Putting Extremism in Context," 129, 131. In his own classification, Shroyer, "Alexandrian Jewish literalists," 275, should have associated Philo's opponents in our passage with "ultra-conservativism"; however, he mistakenly attributes Philo's own argument, based on the incommensurability of God with the garment, to the literalists (p. 279).

[105] Cf. *Migr.* 93 quoted on p. 49 above.

[106] The fact that Philo almost never assigns the Deity an allegorical meaning underlines the rarity of this symbolism. I am grateful to my reader for pointing this out.

[107] On this passage cf. Francesca Calabi, *God's Acting, Man's Acting: Tradition and Philosophy in Philo of Alexandria* (Leiden: Brill, 2008), 62–65; Catherine Hezser, "'For the Lord God Is a Sun and a Shield' (Ps. 84.12): Sun Symbolism in Hellenistic Jewish Literature and in Amoraic Midrashim," in *Jewish Art in Its Late Antique Context*, ed. Uzi Leibner and Catherine Hezser (Tübingen: Mohr Siebeck, 2016), 219.

[108] Cf. *Resp.* 6.508c.

As obvious it is in Plato's famous analogy of the Sun and the Good, and the Platonic tradition based on it, this contention cannot be easily demonstrated from the biblical text.[109] Philo takes Ps 26 (27):1 ("The Lord is my illumination [φωτισμός]") as his starting point (§ 75), but his other proof texts are more indirect. In an interpretation of Gen 1:4 ("God separated between light and between darkness"), he establishes an analogy between God and the Sun, as the latter obviously has the function of distinguishing day from night. At this point Philo gives a remarkable paraphrase of Plato's analogy:

> And above all, as the Sun when it rises makes visible objects which had been hidden [τὰ κεκρυμμένα τῶν σωμάτων ἐπιδεικνύται], so God when He gave birth [γεννήσας] to all things, not only brought them into sight [εἰς τοὐμφανὲς ἤγαγεν], but also made [ἐποίησεν] things which before were not, not just handling material as an artificer [δημιουργός], but being Himself its creator [κτίστης]. (§ 76)

The Socrates of Plato's *Republic* elaborates systematically the analogy between the Good and the Sun. As the Sun not only illuminates physical objects but also causes them to become, so the Good both enlightens invisible-intelligible reality (with truth) and also constitutes it as such.[110] Philo, on the other hand, invests the Sun only with the function of illuminating visible reality, while it is God whom he emphatically declares to be the demiurge and creator of things visible. In doing so Philo not only confuses the functions of Plato's Good (the first Cause, Philo's God, § 92) with those of the Sun, but only partly succeeds to prove that the Sun is the most obvious visible image of the invisible God.[111] Philo's reasons for not bringing the Platonic analogy to its logical conclusion most probably included his dismay with his conservative adversaries, which he vented by an unusually passionate attack on literalists diplomatically cast in the role of the "coat-snatchers" implied in the Mosaic law.

Why would literalists most likely have raised their eyebrows, had Philo developed the analogy of the Sun and God more fully? It is well known that Deuteronomy (4:19, 17:5) forbids any form of heliolatry as part of its general prohibition of idolatry. How dangerous a preoccupation with the Sun could be, especially when the resemblance of the Sun with the invisible

---

[109] Plato's analogy: *Resp.* 6.506e–509d; on the exegetical tradition cf. Matthias Baltes, "Is the Idea of the Good in Plato's *Republic* Beyond Being?" in *Studies in Plato and the Platonic Tradition: Essays Presented to John Whittaker*, ed. Mark A. Joyal (Aldershot: Ashgate, 1997), 3–23.

[110] *Resp.* 6.509b2–10.

[111] Calabi, *God's Acting, Man's Acting*, 63, while reflecting on the divergence of *Opif.* 29–31 (another important Philonic interpretation of the Sun) from Plato's analogy, does not note this anomaly in the context of *Somn.* 1.76.

God was pointed out, is documented in biblical narratives about actual Sun worship in the Temple of Jerusalem. King Josiah is reported to have removed the horses and burned the chariots of the Sun that the kings of Judah had dedicated to it, either as an image of God or as a deity in its own right (2 Kgs 23:11); and Ezekiel describes similar practice most vividly (8:16).[112] Thus, even though God is often described in the Bible with metaphors of fire and light, those concerned with observing the Law could not tolerate a Platonic theology of the Sun even with precautions provided by conscientious allegorists. In view of the traces of their polemic preserved in *De Somniis*, both Philo and his literalist opponents were concerned about the sanctity of Scripture as well as the most basic human needs. What brought them into conflict was their different opinion about what constituted these core values of the biblical tradition.

Eötvös Loránd University,
Budapest

---

[112] On heliolatry in ancient Israel cf. J. Glen Taylor, *Yahweh and the Sun: Biblical and Archaeological Evidence for Sun Worship in Ancient Israel* (Sheffield: Sheffield Academic Press, 1993); Hezser, "'For the Lord God Is a Sun and a Shield' (Ps. 84.12)," 216–17.

The Studia Philonica Annual 31 (2019): 57–94

GENESIS 1–2 IN *DE OPIFICIO MUNDI* AND ITS EXEGETICAL CONTEXT

EKATERINA MATUSOVA

1. *The Position of* De opificio mundi *in the Philonic Corpus*

Biblical treatises in Philo's corpus are traditionally subdivided into the "Allegorical Commentary" and the "Exposition of the Law." The Allegorical Commentary is understood as constituting a running commentary on Genesis, starting from Gen 2:1 (*Legum allegoriae*), and going up to 18:4, with the inclusion of later texts from Genesis in the latter treatises. It interprets the Bible verse by verse (with several omissions), using extensive excurses into (and links outwards to) other books of the LXX. The Exposition of the Law consists of thematic treatises that are devoted to the interpretation of the laws themselves; Philo understands these as embodied in the lives of the patriarchs (before the law was given—*De Abrahamo, De Iosepho*), and comments upon the specific law given to Moses (*De Decalogo, De specialibus legibus, De virtutibus*); *De praemiis* then logically closes the series by directly imitating the end of Deuteronomy (where rewards and punishments for those loyal and not loyal to the law are described). It would be absolutely incorrect to say that allegory is not used or neglected in this latter series, but it is true that its use is diminished here in comparison to "Allegorical Commentary," if only because Philo is elaborating on particular themes in these treatises rather than writing line by line commentary.

According to the point of view represented by Greg Sterling, "Modern editors have misled readers by placing *De opificio mundi* with the Allegorical Commentary rather than the Exposition of the Law."[1] According to him, *De opificio mundi* takes the second position in the Exposition of the Law after *De vita Mosis*, then follow the treatises on the lives of the

---

[1] Gregory E. Sterling, "'Prolific in Expression and Broad in Thought': Internal References to Philo's Allegorical Commentary and Exposition of the Law," *Euphrosyne* 40 (2012): 63.

patriarchs (*De Abrahamo*, etc.) and those on specific laws.[2] A more common position has often been to classify *De opificio mundi* as the first treatise in the Exposition of the Law.[3] This is despite the fact that the treatise does not discuss laws, in contrast to the other treatises in this series.

It has been suggested by some scholars that the initial treatise in the Allegorical Commentary has been lost.[4] This is despite the fact that no external evidence exists that such a treatise was ever written by Philo, in contrast to other lost treatises where we do have such evidence. This lack of evidence is stressed even by those who advocate the view that the lost beginning of *Legum allegoriae* once existed.[5]

The main arguments against *De opificio mundi* being the initial treatise of the Allegorical Commentary are as follows:

---

[2] Gregory E. Sterling, "General Introduction to the Philo of Alexandria Commentary Series," in Philo of Alexandria, *On Cultivation*, Introduction, Translation and Commentary by Albert C. Geljon and David T. Runia, PACS 4 (Leiden: Brill, 2013), xi–xvi, xiv. Recently, Sterling has nuanced his opinion, suggesting that *De vita Mosis* is "an introductory biography to the Exposition," meant to introduce the listeners to the Exposition, which in reality begins with *De opificio* (Gregory E. Sterling, "Philo of Alexandria's *Life of Moses*: An Introduction to the Exposition of the Law," *SPhiloA* 30 [2018]: 31–45).

[3] Valentin Nikiprowetzky, *Le commentaire de l'Écriture chez Philon d'Alexandrie. Son caractère et sa portée. Observations philologiques* (Leiden: Brill, 1977), 197: "L'on considère d'habitude que ce traité qui, selon l'ordre traditionnel, est placé en tête de tous le commentaires philoniens, appartient en realté non au commentaire allégorique, mais à l'exposition de la loi." This view is advocated in the French edition by R. Arnaldez (PAMP 1, *De opificio mundi*, 115), in the German translation by Cohn-Heinemann (L. Cohn, I. Heinemann et W. Theiler, *Philo von Alexandria: die Werke in deutscher Übersetzung*, 7 vols. [Breslau: Marcus Verlag, 1909–1938; Berlin: de Gruyter, 1964], 1:25–89); in the more recent scholarship by Abraham Terian, "Back to Creation: the Beginning of Philo's third Grand Commentary," *SPhiloA* 9 (1997): 19–36 and David T. Runia, *Philo of Alexandria: On the Creation of the Cosmos according to Moses; Introduction, Translation and Commentary*, PACS 1 (Leiden: Brill, 2001), 2–4, who puts it on the second position, between *Mos.* and *Abr.*

[4] Emile Bréhier, *Les idées philosophiques et religieuses de Philon d'Alexandrie*, Études de philosophie medieval 8, 3rd ed. (Paris: Vrin, 1950), III; Thomas H. Tobin, "The Beginning of Philo's Legum Allegoriae," *SPhiloA* 12 (2000): 29–43; Sterling, "'Prolific in Expression and Broad in Thought,'" 64. Emile Schürer, *A History of the Jewish People in the Time of Jewish Christ*, transl. S. Taylor and rev. P. Christie, section 2.3, 3rd ed. (Edinburgh: T&T Clark, 1998), 331; and Valentine Nikiprowetzky (see the main text below) reject this possibility.

[5] See Tobin, "The Beginning of Philo's Legum Allegoriae," 30: "It must be clear, however, that the reasons for favoring the view that such a treatise once existed are of a different sort than those for the other two lost treatises. There is no manuscript evidence for such a treatise as there is for *Leg.* IV. Nor are there any parallel interpretations for Gen 1:1–31 in the *QG*, as there are for the other two lost treatises. In addition the lists of treatises found in the manuscript tradition of Philo offer no clues that such a treatise ever existed. Nor is there evidence from ancient testimonia about Philo that any such treatise ever existed."

1. The first part of the treatise (devoted to Gen 1) does not appear to be an allegorical commentary in the strict sense (the second part, starting from *Opif.* 154, and from Gen 2 in terms of the Bible, seems to constitute allegory in a much more apparent way in the manner of the remainder of the Allegorical Commentary). Nor is *De opificio mundi* structured by lemmata where the biblical text is cited and commented upon verse by verse as in the Allegorical Commentary.

2. The biblical verses commented upon at the beginning of *Legum allegoriae* overlap with the biblical verses commented upon last in *De opificio mundi*. The treatises thus do not cohere fittingly.

3. In its somewhat abrupt beginning, *Legum allegoriae* starts with the comment on Gen 2:1 ("The heavens and the earth were completed with everything that was in them" [NETS]) and connects it to Gen 1:1.[6] Philo suggests that "the heaven and the earth" first introduced in Gen 1:1 are symbols of mind and sense-perception. This is an interpretation that we first see in *Legum allegoriae* and that is absent in *De opificio mundi*. This makes some scholars think that an extensive alternative interpretation of Gen 1 in these terms might have existed.

4. Also the point has been made that *De Abrahamo,* which is one of the treatises in the "Exposition of the Law," seems to be directly associated with *De opificio mundi* which is referred to as its "preceding treatise" (*Abr.* 2).

However, even at first glance, many of these points can be countered by arguments that offer different interpretations or explanations.

---

[6] *Leg.* 1.1 Καὶ συνετελέσθησαν ὁ οὐρανὸς καὶ ἡ γῆ καὶ πᾶς ὁ κόσμος αὐτῶν" (Gen 2:1). νοῦ καὶ αἰσθήσεως γένεσιν εἰπὼν πάλαι, νῦν δὴ ἀμφοτέρων τελείωσιν διασυνίστησιν. "'And the heaven and the earth and all their world were completed.' He had already told of the creation of mind and sense-perception; he now claims the perfection of both" (transl. Colson with my emendation based on Sterling,"'Prolific in Expression and Broad in Thought,'" 64). This phrase has Moses as its agent and, hence refers to what is said *in the biblical text*, rather than in its interpretation, although its interpretation by Philo is already *proleptically* present in the first sentence and clearly explained in the next sentence using γὰρ: συμβολικῶς μὲν γὰρ τὸν νοῦν οὐρανόν, ἐπειδὴ αἱ νοηταὶ φύσεις ἐν οὐρανῷ, τὴν δὲ αἴσθησιν καλεῖ γῆν. "For using symbolical language he calls the mind heaven, since heaven is the abode of natures discerned only by mind, but sense-perception he calls earth..." (PLCL 1:147). Thus, I think, that the correct way of understanding the εἰπὼν πάλαι is as a reference to Gen 1:1, where the origin of the heaven and the earth is introduced ("In the beginning God created the heavens and the earth." [NETS]); an additional consideration of this being so is that, in my opinion, εἰπὼν can hardly mean here "having discussed" (cf. Sterling, "'Prolific in Expression and Broad in Thought,'" 64).

1. As mentioned above, allegory is explicitly used starting from *Opif.* 154 and until *Opif.* 169 (the end of the treatise). It is introduced in a manifesto-like way in *Opif.* 157:

> Now these are no *mythical fictions* [οὐ μύθου πλάσματα], such as poets and sophists delight in, *but patterns which invite allegorical and indirect understanding* [δείγματα τύπων ἐπ' ἀλληγορίαν παρακαλοῦντα κατὰ τὰς δι' ὑπονοιῶν ἀποδόσεις].[7]

Given Philo's declared orientation toward the ethical allegory of the LXX (that is, one that refers to the conditions of human soul),[8] the introduction of allegory in a manifesto-like form here is readily explainable. Here ethical interpretation becomes possible for the first time in the discourse, the previous part having been devoted to the description of cosmology rather than to a discussion of the human soul. However, even at first glance, the first part is not entirely "non-allegorical" either, as has been noted by several scholars.[9] A serious reinterpretation of the literal meaning of Gen 1 follows as a result. (I will dwell on the allegorical import of the cosmo-logical part in more detail below.)

2. The overlapping of the verses between *De opificio mundi* and *Legum allegoriae* is plausibly explained by Nikiprowetzky, who suggested that the inclusion of verses referring to the creation and the expulsion of man was necessary if we consider the definition of *kosmopoiia* given in *Praem.* 1: "The story of the creation [κοσμοποιία] is told throughout with an excellence worthy of the divine subject, beginning with the genesis of the cosmos [ἀπὸ γενέσεως οὐρανοῦ] and ending with the framing of man [εἰς ἀνθρώπου κατασκευήν]."[10] This definition of *kosmopoiia* corresponds exactly to how Plato defines the content of the *Timaeus*.[11] Hence, it was necessary that *De*

---

[7] PLCL 1:125 (with my emendation).

[8] See Ekaterina Matusova, "Allegorical Interpretation of the Pentateuch in Alexan-dria: Inscribing Aristobulus and Philo in a Wider Literary Context," *SPhiloA* 22 (2010): 44–48.

[9] Cf. Nikiprowetzky, *Le commentaire de l'Écriture chez Philon d'Alexandrie*, 198: "Ajou-tons, que le character litteral dont, par contraste avec le *Legum Allegoriae*, serait marquée le *De Opificio Mundi* nous parait loin d'être demontré." Runia, *On the Creation of Cosmos according to Moses*, 17: "In the case of *Opif.* it is crucial that the reader keep this deeper symbolical exegesis in mind at all times, since without it many features of the treatise remain obscure or even confused."

[10] Transl. Colson with my emendation (PLCL 8:313).

[11] Plato, *Tim.* 27a: "Seeing that Timaeus is our best astronomer and has made it his special task to learn about the nature of the Universe, it seems good to us that he should speak first, *beginning with the origin of the Cosmos and ending with the generation of mankind*"; *Tim.* 90e: "And now the task prescribed for us at the beginning *to give a description of the Universe up to the production of mankind*, would appear to be wellnigh completed." (transl.

opificio mundi embrace Gen in conformity with the Platonic model. Thus, *De opificio mundi*, conforming to the definition in *De praemiis*, covers the history of Adam and Eve down to their expulsion from the Garden of Eden (until 3:24). On the other hand, *Post.* 64–65, *Fug.* 78, and *QG* 1.1 show that Philo admitted a subdivision of these three chapters. The passage running from Gen 1:1 to Gen 2:1 (or 4) constitutes in his eyes the account of *kosmopoiia* in the strict sense. The two following chapters were for him a recapitulation of the account of the Creation of anthropological and psychological nature. Thus, if *De opificio mundi* discusses the account of Creation in its totality, *Legum allegoriae* applies the account of Creation to "the small universe" of man."[12]

3. In stressing the difference between *De opificio mundi* and *Legum allegoriae* in their interpretations of the heaven and the earth (cosmologically in *De opificio mundi*, psychologically in *Legum allegoriae*) scholars have not paid attention to a striking similarity between these two treatises in their interpretation of the creation account. Not only is the interpretation of Gen 2:1 (*Leg.* 1.1) essentially akin to the interpretation of this biblical verse in *Opif.* 129–30 (as stressed by Thomas Tobin),[13] but also *Legum allegoriae* systematically resumes all the main points of the inter-pretation of the creation account specific to *De opificio mundi*. Thus, *Legum allegoriae* essentially keeps to the idea of the double creation introduced in *Opif.* 16–19 (cf. *Leg.* 1.1, 19, 21–22); *Legum allegoriae* resumes the idea of the Divine mind (λόγος) which replaces the biblical creation by command or saying in *Opif.* 8, 20–25 (cf. *Leg.* 1.19, 21); *Legum allegoriae* is anxious to remove the notion of the creation in time, in six days, as well as the related notion of God resting from his work (*Leg.* 1.2–20 cf. *Opif.* 13, 28, 67). All these elements in *De opificio mundi* are essential for understanding the strategy of interpretation followed in this treatise (as the reader will see in my argument below in par. 2 and 3.1) and they are introduced under the strong influence of the *Timaeus* which is another specific feature of *De opificio mundi*. Also, *Legum allegoriae* resumes Pythagorizing arithmology of the numbers 6 and 7 (*Leg.* 1.3–5, 8–15 cf. *Opif.* 13–15, 90–128), in a much more concise form than *De opificio mundi*, but sometimes preserving even the similarity of expressions (cf., for instance, *Leg.* 1.15 and *Opif.* 100). All these points are systematically introduced and extensively explained in *De opificio mundi* from a theoretical point of view. A brief reference to them

---

R. G. Bury, *Plato*, vol. 5, LCL, 5th ed. [London: William Heinemann LTD; Cambridge, MA: Harvard University Press, 1966], 47, 249).

[12] Nikiprowetzky, *Le commentaire de l'Écriture chez Philon d'Alexandrie*, 198.

[13] Tobin, "The Beginning of Philo's Legum Allegoriae," 29, 32, 33, 34, 43.

and building upon them in the beginning of *Legum allegoriae* conveys a strong impression that the cosmological interpretation in the manner of *De opificio mundi* is re-used here.

However, what is specific to the *Legum allegoriae* interpretation of the creation account is emphasized by Philo himself. In *Leg.* 1.16, which offers an interpretation of Gen 2:2, he gives a cosmological interpretation of the verse and then signals a turn to ethical interpretation: "however, in terms of ethics this should be understood in the following way" (ἡ δὲ πρὸς τὸ ἦθος ἀπόδοσίς ἐστι τοιαύτη).[14] By this he indicates his intention to deviate from cosmology to ethics, even if the primary meaning of Genesis 2:1 invites a cosmological reading.[15] This is Philo's program for the entire *Legum allegoriae* which interprets Genesis in psychological terms as an allegory of the soul (applied to Gen 2 from verse 8 already in *Opif.* 154–169).[16] Hence, Philo's specific concern in *Legum allegoriae* is to introduce a general foundation for the ideas of intelligible and sense-perceptible, which are the key-notions of Platonic psychology. Thus, he assigns the notion of mind to the heaven and that of sense-perception to the earth (both notions introduced in the first sentence of the Bible). But this is all that he essentially needs to continue his interpretation of Genesis in psychological terms. No one familiar with Philo's writing technique would doubt his ability to give diverse interpretations to the same textual element, when it is required by his context. But is it necessary to imply on this basis that a whole psychological interpretation of the hexameron was executed as a separate treatise?

4. Finally, the reference to *De opificio mundi* in *Abr.* 2 which, according to Terian, "leaves no reason to resort to exegesis" because of "the absolute clarity of the Greek text, with this excellent translation by Colson,"[17] is precisely the opposite, in my opinion: the phrase admits various interpretations and requires exegesis.

---

[14] Translation is mine.

[15] This turn is paralleled in Philo's programmatic deviation from astronomical to ethical interpretation as well (See Matusova, " Allegorical Interpretation of the Pentateuch in Alexandria," 42–50).

[16] Tobin, "The Beginning of Philo's Legum Allegoriae," 33–34: "But in one essential respect Philo's interpretation in Leg. 1.1. is significantly different. Philo's Platonic interpretations (of *Opif.* 129–30 as well as *Opif.* 15–88) are both cosmological.... But the interpretation in *Leg* 1.1. is not really about the creation of the world. Rather, it is about the division between the creation of the ideas of mind and of sense-perception.... More specifically, Philo's interpretation in *Leg.* 1.1. is of a piece with his allegory of the soul which is the dominant pattern of interpretation in the whole *Legum Allegoriae*."

[17] Terian, "Back to Creation," 31.

ὃν μὲν οὖν τρόπον ἡ κοσμοποιία διατέτακται, διὰ τῆς προτέρας συντάξεως, ὡς οἷόν τε | ἦν, ἠκριβώσαμεν. (*Abr.* 2)

The story of the order in which the world was made has been set forth in detail by us as well as was possible in the preceding treatise. (Transl. by Colson[18])

The expression διὰ τῆς προτέρας συντάξεως translated by Colson as "the preceding treatise" could also be translated as "an earlier treatise" (cf. LSJ, s.v. "πρότερος II"). As an expression, it can correspond to the expression Ἐν μὲν τῇ πρὸ ταύτης συντάξει (*Her.* 1.1; *Spec.* 2.1), which would mean the immediately preceding text, but it can also be used as a variant of the expression used in *De Virtutibus* in reference to *De Vita Mosis*: πρότερον ἐν δυσὶ | συντάξεσιν (*Virt.* 52). These treatises have never been taken by scholars to follow each other in direct sequential order; the phrase in *Virt.* refers to *Mos.* as an already-existing treatise which is simply written earlier than the one at hand. Most tellingly, *De Abrahamo* uses the expression διὰ τῆς προτέρας συντάξεως twice—once in the beginning, in reference to the *kosmopoiia* subject, that is, apparently to the treatise *De opificio mundi*, and second, in *Abr.* 13, in this sentence:

ἐν ἀριθμοῖς δὲ ἡ τετρὰς τετίμηται παρά τε τοῖς ἄλλοις φιλοσόφοις, ὅσοι τὰς ἀσωμάτους οὐσίας καὶ νοητὰς ἠσπάσαντο, καὶ μάλιστα παρὰ Μωυσεῖ τῷ πανσόφῳ, ὃς σεμνύνων τὸν τέταρτον ἀριθμόν φησιν, ὅτι „ἅγιός ἐστι καὶ αἰνετός" (Lev. 19:24)· δι' ἃς δ' αἰτίας ἐλέχθη, διὰ τῆς προτέρας συντάξεως εἴρηται. ἅγιος δὲ καὶ ἐπαινετός ὁ εὔελπις..

Now the number four has been held in high honour by the other philosophers who devoted themselves to the study of immaterial and conceptual realities, and especially by the all-wise Moses who when glorifying that number *speaks* (φησιν) of it as "holy and for praise" [ἅγιός ἐστι καὶ αἰνετός] (Lev. 19:24), *and why he so called it* [δι' ἃς δ' αἰτίας ἐλέχθη] has been shown *in a former treatise* [διὰ τῆς προτέρας συντάξεως]. "Holy," too, and "praiseworthy" [ἅγιος δὲ καὶ ἐπαινετός]... [19]

In the phrase "and why he so called it," the verb "to call" (ἐλέχθη) refers to the preceding verb "speaks" (φησι), and hence specifically to the quotation from Lev 19:24. This is also confirmed by the repetition of the expression "holy and praiseworthy" in the beginning of the next sentence. However, Lev 19:24 is not quoted, discussed or even alluded to in *De opificio mundi*, whereas there are, for instance, a good fifteen paragraphs devoted to the interpretation of this verse in *Plant.* 117–132 (in connection with the number four). It is less important whether *Plant.* is referred to here specifically, or whether it may be some other, lost, treatise. The important fact is that two *different* treatises are referred to using the same phrase: this

18 PLCL, 6:5.
19 PLCL, 6:11.

confirms that the expression διὰ τῆς προτέρας συντάξεως does not necessarily imply immediate antecedence. It is the case that either one of the treatises, or both, were written not *immediately* before *De Abrahamo*, but simply earlier. [20]

It is true that in the beginning of *De opificio mundi* Philo refers to the Pentateuch as the laws and links the cosmological part with the legislative part by making recourse to the notion of the law of nature, which will play an important part in the treatises on the lives of the patriarchs in the "Exposition of the Law." This might be taken to suggest that Philo planned *De opificio mundi* as the introduction to *De Abrahamo* and *De Iosepho*. However, we should not forget that in Hellenistic Egypt Moses is considered a νομοθέτης and the Bible νόμοι or νομοθεσία since time immemorial (cf. *Let. Aris.* 15.2; 30.2; 31.3; Aristobulos apud Eusebius, *Praep. ev.* 13.12.1). It was hardly possible to introduce the subject of the creation by removing it from its general and natural framework. That necessitates a reference to the legislative character of the text, as well as a basic explanation of how the two correspond. Alternatively, if accepting the theory of secondary prefaces, suggested by Greg Sterling,[21] one might suggest that *Opif.* 1–3 is a typical example of this secondary introduction, added to an already existing treatise by way of connecting it (also) to the "embodied laws" series. One might also observe that the reference to the treatise on *kosmopoiia* in the beginning of the treatise *De Abrahamo*—the first in the line of treatises devoted to the laws embodied in the exemplary lives and in the particular commands—can be explained by the logic of the introduction of this subject matter in accordance with Philo's general vision of the structure of the Scripture, in which both "genealogy" and "legislation" follow the introductory part, the *kosmopoiia* (*Mos.* 2.45–48; *Praem.* 1–4; *Abr.* 1–5). In other words, Philo necessarily refers to the treatise about creation in order to *organize* his work (a tendency clearly visible in his non-biblical writings

[20] Gregory Sterling suggested that *Abr.* 2 is a so called "secondary preface." By "secondary preface" he means the practice of ancient writers to include a preface at a later stage, after completion of their work, to show to the reader how the treatises in their corpus are related to each other (Sterling, "'Prolific in Expression and Broad in Thought,'" 60, 67). Even if I am not entirely convinced that *Abr.* 2 was added to the text later (because *Abr.*1 seems to me to be an organic part of the treatise that follows), I certainly think that this preface is meant to structure Philo's work (see below in the text). This, however, does not alter the fact, demonstrated above, that the phrase διὰ τῆς προτέρας συντάξεως does not necessarily imply immediate chronological antecedence. Philo does want to connect *De Abrahamo* and *De opificio*. However, *De opificio* might have already existed for a while, before *De Abrahamo* was written.

[21] See the previous footnote.

as well), that is, to introduce his actual subject properly, assigning to it a proper place in the whole outline of the Bible.

On this understanding, nothing prevents the treatise *De opificio mundi* from being written by Philo as the initial work in the whole corpus—the Allegorical Commentary and the Exposition of the Law included—as, for instance, has been suggested by Nikiprowetzky.[22] However, as mentioned above, this understanding has not won out in modern scholarship. If Nikiprowetzky rejected the hypothesis of a lost "allegorical" treatise on Gen 1, scholars such as Thomas Tobin, Abraham Terian, David Runia and Gregory Sterling do support this idea. The latter three scholars are resolute in classifying *De opificio mundi* exclusively under the Exposition of the Law.[23]

---

[22] "Nous pensons qu'ayant d'abord projeté de faire du *De Opificio Mundi* le premier des traités qu'il voulait consacrer à la partie législative du Pentateuque, il aurait décidé ensuite de transformer le *De Opificio* en préface générale à l'ensemble du commentaire, fonction à laquelle, comme le notait Colson, ainsi qu'on l'a vu, il était parfaitement propre" ("We think that Philo, having planned to write *De Opificio Mundi* as the first treatise in the legislative series, subsequently changed his mind and decided to transform it into a general introduction to the whole commentary, a function to which, as Colson noted, and as we have seen, it was absolutely apt" [Nikiprowetzky, *Le commentaire de l'Écriture chez Philon d'Alexandrie*, 99; transl. is mine]).

[23] Terian, "Back to Creation," 21: "However, *De opificio* is a thematic exposition, like the rest of the treatises in the Exposition, whereas those of the Allegorical Commentary are more exegetical and overly allegorical commentaries—especially *Legum allegoriae;*" and 34: "The *Opificio* is so unlike *Leg.* that it couldn't have been a part of the same commentary." Runia, *On the Creation of Cosmos according to Moses*, 4: "In this commentary *Opif.* will be rigorously treated as belonging to the Exposition of the Law." In addition to the arguments discussed in the main text, there are two other arguments used by these two scholars, which are nonetheless evaluated differently even among them, with the result that their discrepancies make the argument far from being conclusive. Terian has analyzed the evidence of manuscripts, stressing cases where *Opif.* is or might have been connected to the Exposition of the Law. He suggests that in the majority of mss. *Opif.* is connected to this last series. He himself admits, however, that "Certainly, the manuscript tradition does not of itself constitute conclusive evidence regarding the place of *De opificio* in the Philonic corpus, especially when the partiality of some works and the total loss of others are reckoned and the existing medieval manuscripts are traced to a single archetype" (Terian, "Back to Creation," 29). This argument works for him only in combination with "the internal evidence." But this is precisely what we are questioning in this article. On the contrary, Runia omits Terian's restriction, and refers to the evidence from mss. as a strong argument (Runia, *On the Creation of Cosmos according to Moses*, 3). And the other way round, Terian says that *Opif.* was written after *QG* and *QE* and the Allegorical commentary ("Back to Creation," 35), whereas Runia does not think that it is possible to determine their mutual chronology. The argument, however, on which he himself dates the treatise to 30–40 CE implies that any series is necessarily written *en bloc*, which, in my opinion, is another chronological oversimplification (Runia, *On the Creation of Cosmos according to Moses*, 4).

In this article I am not going to question the formal difference in structure between *De opificio mundi* and *Legum allegoriae* (quotations by lemmata in *Legum allegoriae* vs. the narrative of *De opificio mundi*), nor argue against a connection between *De opificio mundi* and *De Abrahamo*, given that this was emphasized by Philo himself—even if its character is rather formal, and the first treatise may have been written significantly earlier than *De Abrahamo*. Rather, I am going to highlight that Philo's main approach to the interpretation of the Genesis account in *De opificio mundi* is congruent with the history of *allegorical interpretation* of the type of text to which Gen 1 belongs. It works as the representative of the genre of allegorical commentary on the creation account in Philo's corpus, and therefore there is no need to postulate a different (lost) allegorical commentary on Gen 1. I will also try to explain why we do not find allegorical terminology in this treatise until *Opif.* 154. As part of this explanation I will also draw attention to a specific use of Genesis in the Pseudo-Pythagorean treatises and suggest how this fact could have influenced Philo's approach too.

As mentioned above, in detaching the treatise from the Allegorical Commentary, two major points are stressed: first, the *non-allegorical* character of *De opificio mundi.*, and second, its *thematic* character. I will start by discussing the allegorical import of the treatise. To that end, we have to recall my outline of the origins and purpose of allegory, and its first implementation in the work of Aristobulos, in particular with reference to Gen 1.

2. *Gen 1 in Aristobulos*

In my article of 2010 in *SPhiloA* 22, I discussed the principles of allegorical commentary applied to the Old Testament in Aristobulos and Philo. I asserted that this commentary originated as part of the Hellenistic approach to the barbarian sacred texts that were considered to be connected with mysteries.[24]

Methodologically, a particular literary pattern stands at the origin of the tradition: the allegorical commentary in the Derveni papyrus. In this commentary, written in the fourth century BCE at the latest, a cosmogonic Orphic poem is interpreted allegorically. The commentator tries to reconcile the Orphic poem with contemporary Greek philosophy. In Greek culture, epic mythology, including a particular genre of cosmogony, faced

---

[24] See also Ekaterina Matusova, *The Meaning of the 'Letter of Aristeas' in Light of Biblical Interpretation and Grammatical Tradition*, FRLANT 260 (Göttingen: Vandenhoeck & Ruprecht, 2015), 91–96.

long-standing criticism from as early as Heraclitus and Xenophanes in the seventh century BCE. According to this trend in philosophy, these poetic accounts are not true; they are often obscene, and have nothing to do with the notion of God that was slowly developing within Greek philosophical tradition. They are *mythology*—with all the negative connotations of the word implying each of the failings I have just listed—in contrast to *philosophy*, or *philosophical theology*, which offers an account of the true notion of the Divine.[25] In the fourth century BCE, one of the most important representatives of such criticism of poetic mythology was Plato (the second book of *The Republic*). Both Homer and the Orphic tradition met with his disapproval. A younger contemporary of Plato, Isocrates, refers to the Orphic poems as obscene texts that are paradigmatically non-philosophical.[26] On the other hand, "Orphic rites" were becoming more and more widespread and popular in fifth and fourth-century Athens. Thus, it is not surprising that, along with earlier sporadic and partial attempts to interpret Homer indirectly,[27] we find in the fourth century BCE (terminus ante quem) an allegorical commentary on an Orphic cosmogonic poem that is trying to reconcile its content with contemporary philosophy.

The author of the Derveni Papyrus was compelled to declare that the plain meaning was actually *intentional allegory* used by Orpheus in order *to hide the sacred meaning from the non-initiated* (P. Derv. 7.5–11; 13.5). He shows how the true philosophical sense becomes apparent through indirect interpretation. He refers to the text of the poem as *hieros logos,* and claims to understand every element in the text allegorically (right down to the level of individual words) (P. Derv. 7.7–8 KPT (also P. Derv. 7.2 Betegh, Janko).[28]

This is the strategy applied to the Bible by Aristobulos (and subsequently by Philo), who argues *against mythological* understanding of the text (Fr. 2 Holladay = Eusebius, *Praep. ev.* 8.10.2). He alludes to the Old Testament *and an Orphic poem,* which he refers to in his commentary as being of a similar nature and classifies them under the generic title of *hieros logos* (Fr. 4a Holladay = Eusebius, *Praep. ev.* 13.12.4). He claims that Moses composed it as such *intentionally* (Fr. 2.3 Holladay = Eusebius, *Praep. ev.* 8.10.1–4). He

---

[25] See W. K. C. Guthrie, *A History of Greek Philosophy* (Cambridge: Cambridge University Press, 1962), 370–80; Sarah Broadie, "Rational Theology," in: *The Cambridge Companion to Early Greek Philosophy,* ed. by A.A. Long (Cambridge: Cambridge University Press, 1999), 205–24.

[26] Isocrates, *Bus.* 39.

[27] See David Konstan and Illaria L. E. Ramelli, "Allegory I (Graeco-Roman Antiquity)," in *EBR* 1:780–85.

[28] See in detail Matusova, "Allegorical Interpretation of the Pentateuch in Alexandria," 22–24.

sets out the principles of a comprehensive indirect commentary word by word, or line by line (καθ' ἕκαστον) formulated in the Derveni Papyrus (Fr. 2 Holladay = Eusebius, *Praep. ev.* 8.10.6). Also particular interpretations used by Aristobulos are suspiciously similar to those found in the Orphic commentary (see note 8 for details).

However, the most important observation in our case is that the text that the author of the Derveni Papyrus comments upon is a Theogony—an account of the generations of primordial deities. It already contains a good deal of *cosmogony* in itself, and is reinterpreted by the author of the Derveni Papyrus as a *philosophical cosmogony*, or, rather, as *an account of the physical system of the world*.

Thus, a cosmogonic religious text stands at the beginning of this line of the development in allegorical interpretation. Accordingly, Gen 1, a cosmogony in the religious text of the Jews, implicitly demands allegorization. Unsurprisingly, Aristobulos is very consistent in rejecting a direct understanding of the principal elements of the narrative of the cosmological part, Gen 1. Such things as "And God said ... and it was so," which accompany every act of creation, resemble pure mythology, and must be radically reinterpreted.

> The voice of God should be taken not as a spoken word, but as the constitution of things [Δεῖ γὰρ λαμβάνειν τὴν θείαν φωνὴν οὐ ῥητὸν λόγον, ἀλλ' ἔργων κατασκευάς,], just as Moses, in our Law, has spoken of the entire coming to be of the cosmos as the words of God [τὴν γένεσιν τοῦ κόσμου θεοῦ λόγους εἴρηκεν ὁ Μωσῆς], because he continually says of each instance: "And God said, and it came to be" [συνεχῶς γάρ φησιν ἐφ' ἑκάστου· 'καὶ εἶπεν ὁ θεός, καὶ ἐγένετο]. It seems to me that Pythagoras, Socrates and Plato, having diligently sought everywhere, followed him when they say that they hear the voice of God [ἀκούειν φωνῆς θεοῦ], because they precisely knew that the constitution of all things came to be by God, and is constantly sustained by Him [τὴν κατασκευὴν τῶν ὅλων συνθεωροῦντες ἀκριβῶς ὑπὸ θεοῦ γεγονυῖαν καὶ συνεχομένην ἀδιαλείπτως]. (Fr. 4, 4a Holladay = Eusebius, *Praep. ev.* 13.12.3–4; transl. is mine)

Aristobulos comments on the phrase "And God said, and it came to be" (καὶ εἶπεν ὁ θεός, καὶ ἐγένετο), which he refuses to take in its literal meaning as an oral command or saying. He says that "The voice of God should be taken not as a spoken word [οὐ ῥητὸν λόγον]," which means that the idea of God's *logos* in the biblical account of the creation either pre-existed for Aristobulos, or was deduced by him from the verb λέγω/εἶπον. Aristobulos chooses the notion of the harmonious voice, φωνή, to interpret λόγος, immediately connecting it with the notion used by the Pythagoreans to explain the harmonious order in the world (cf. "It seems to me that Pythagoras, Socrates and Plato ... followed him when they say that they hear the voice of God [ἀκούειν φωνῆς θεοῦ]"]. This notion is known as a specific Pythagorean concept as we learn from Aristotle's *De Caelo* 290b21–25: "they (sc. the Pythagoreans) affirm that *the sound* [τὴν φωνὴν] of the stars as they revolve is concordant [ἐναρμόνιον]."[29] Its influence can be also seen in the description of the harmonious world soul in the *Timaeus* (Plato, *Tim.* 37a-c). This concept of the musical harmony of the world (which is interwoven with the idea of φωνή) comes up again in the pseudo-Aristotelian treatise *De Mundo* as one of its important theological notions.[30] The fragments of Aristobulos show several important parallels with this pseudo-Aristotelian treatise.[31] Remarkably, in *De Mundo* 400a4 the notion of the world harmony is applied to the notion of the λόγος *of God* which, of course, only formally coincides with the biblical logos of God, meaning here instead the "principle" or "relation" which God has to the cosmos: "τοῦτον οὖν ἔχει τὸν λόγον ὁ θεὸς ἐν κόσμῳ, συνέχων τὴν τῶν ὅλων ἁρμονίαν τε καὶ σωτηρίαν..." ("The position of God in the universe is analogous to this, for he preserves the harmony and permanence of all things"). Given other distinctive coincidences with the treatise, I suggest that it was an attentive reading of this sentence that may have prompted Aristobulos to apply the teaching of the harmonious voice to the notion of the biblical *logos*. Aristobulos reinterpreted the term in *De Mundo* by exploiting its polysemy and by making it overlap with the *logos* of the biblical narrative.

Anyway, it is by reinterpreting the λόγος of God through the notion of voice that always sounds in the world, and represents its eternal harmony, that Aristobulos not only eliminates the notion of a "command" orally given by God from the narrative, but at the same time also removes the notion of a temporal creation of the world (as the musical harmony of the world is a notion to which temporal categories do not apply). Both elements in the biblical text appear to be too similar to a mythological cosmogony. God for Aristobulos is the cause of the world, but not in a temporal sense, which is in full accord with the Peripatetic doctrine (and using late terminology can be described as *creatio aeterna*).

---

[29] Transl. by W.K.C. Guthrie, *Aristotle*, Vol. 6. *On Heavens*, LCL, 6th ed. (Cambridge, Mass.: Harvard University Press, 1968), 193.

[30] *Mund.* 396b 25; 399a 12–17 (in particular); 399b 31; 400a4.

[31] See Roberto Radice, *La filosofia di Aristobulo e i suoi nessi con il "De mundo" attribuito ad Aristotele*, 2nd ed. (Milano: Vita e pensiero, 1995); Ekaterina Matusova, "'Seeing' God in Alexandrian Exegesis of the Bible: From Aristobulos to Philo," in *Gottesschau–Gotteserkentnis*, ed. Evangelia Dafni, WUNT 387 (Tübingen: Mohr Siebeck, 2017) 64–66. It is also useful to keep in mind that the notions of συνέχεια and κατασκευή, both used by Aristobulos in his interpretation (cf. συνεχομένην and ἔργων κατασκευάς, τὴν κατασκευὴν τῶν ὅλων), also belong to the vocabulary of this treatise (*Mund.*, 398b24, 399a6,30)

This reinterpretation automatically brings him to reinterpret other temporal elements in the narrative, in particular, that God "rested from all His work" (Gen 2:3), and the account of the temporal creation of the cosmos over 6 days:

What the Law *highlights* [τὸ δὲ διασαφούμενον διὰ τῆς νομοθεσίας], saying that God rested [ἀποπεπαυκέναι] on this day, does not mean, as some understand it, that God has never done anything since then, but by saying "having stopped" it is meant that He set out their order (sc. the order of things) for all the time [ἀλλ' ἐπὶ τῷ καταπεπαυκέναι τὴν τάξιν αὐτῶν οὕτως εἰς πάντα τὸν χρόνον τεταχέναι], since Moses *signals* [σημαίνει] that He made the heaven and the earth and everything therein over six days, in order to reveal the times and order of what precedes what. Having thus set out their order, He keeps them together and changes them accordingly (τὴν τάξιν προείπῃ τί τίνος προτερεῖ. τάξας γάρ, οὕτως αὐτὰ συνέχει καὶ μεταποιεῖ.). (Fr. 5 Holladay = Eusebius, *Praep. ev.* 13.12.11–12; transl. is mine)

"(God) rested" (ἀποπεπαυκέναι) refers to the fixation of the order of things (τάξις), and the sequence of the six days refers to their rank (both are aspects of the Greek notion of τάξις). This interpretation is suggested to Aristobulos by an alternative definition of the cosmos as τάξις in the Peripatetic tradition, in particular, also in *De Mundo*.[32]

As the author of the Derveni Papyrus, who was drawing on Diogenes of Apollonia and Anaxagoras in reinterpreting the Orphic cosmogony sometimes using expressions literally found in their fragments,[33] Aristobulos draws on a particular philosophic tradition (the late Peripatetic tradition tinted with Pythagoreanism) and on a particular philosophic text (*De Mundo*), which he then uses for the reinterpretation of Gen 1. A large part of his exegesis is a philosophical 'reading-in' of this text into Genesis. Drawing on this text, he transforms the notion of *logos* into that of an immanent harmonious order in the world, and links it with a philosophically cognate notion of *taxis*. This way he transforms a religious ("mythological") cosmogony into a philosophical description of the cosmos and its Cause.

However, he understands it as an allegorical interpretation offered within the framework of his program as set out at the beginning of his treatise (Fr. 2 Holladay = Eusebius, *Praep. ev.* 8.10.1–6). Thus, he explicitly

[32] In particular, *Mund.* 391b9–12: Λέγεται δὲ καὶ ἑτέρως κόσμος ἡ τῶν ὅλων τάξις τε καὶ διακόσμησις, ὑπὸ θεοῦ τε καὶ διὰ θεὸν φυλαττομένη (Cf. *De Mundo* 391–397; *Cael.* 296a34: ἡ δέ γε τοῦ κόσμου τάξις ἀΐδιος). This definition also chimes with some biblical and para-biblical passages (Job 16:3; 28:3; 28a:2; 38:12; Hab 3:11; 1 En. 2.1–2).

[33] On Diogenes of Apollonia in the Derveni Papyrus see Gabor Betegh, *The Derveni Papyrus: Cosmology, Theology and Interpretation* (Cambridge: Cambridge University Press, 2004), 308ff, 318; Ekaterina Matusova, "Between Exegesis and Philosophy: Philosophical Generalisations in cols. XVI, XVII and XIX of the Derveni Papyrus in Light of Interpretative Strategy," *AGPh* 98 (2016): 137, n.54.

used the words διασαφούμενον, "highlighted," and σημαίνει, "signals," of the six days creation account. In the language of allegory starting from the Derveni Papyrus both words have the force of technical terms. A more modern διασαφέω replaces the more archaic δηλόω, which refers to the revelation of a hidden meaning (P. Derv. 8.1.3: 11.11; 17.9; 18.1; 21.1; 22.13; 24.2; 26.2). σημαίνω is a technical term referring to a sign or allusion to a hidden meaning, given in the plain, direct meaning of the text, which has to be reinterpreted (P. Derv. 16.7; 17.11; 23.7; 25.13; 26.3; cf. Aristobulos's use in Eusebius, *Praep. ev.* 8.10. 6).

3. Aristobulos's Legacy in Philo and New Elements in Philo's Approach

3.1. Aristobulos's Legacy in Philo

We shall now see in what measure Philo in *De opificio mundi* subscribes to this tradition of allegorical interpretation of Gen 1 inherited from Aristobulos, and where he deviates from it.

According to this tradition, Philo starts with the far from surprising claim that the laws of Moses are devoid of any *mythology*, but represent a pious *theology* (i.e., *philosophy*):

> If you consider the other lawgivers, you will find that some drew up the regulations that they regarded as just in an unadorned and naked fashion, while others enclothed their thoughts with a mass of verbiage and so deceived the masses by concealing the truth with mythical fictions [μυθικοῖς πλάσμασι]. Moses surpassed both groups, regarding the former as lacking reflection, indolent and unphilosophical, the latter as mendacious and full of trickery. Instead he made a splendid and awe-inspiring start to his laws. He did not immediately state what should be done and what not, nor did he, since it was necessary to form in advance the minds of those who were to make use of the laws, *invent myths* [μήτ ... μύθους πλασάμενος] or expressed approval of those composed by others. (*Opif.* 1–2)

> Hence he was not off the mark in also giving a description of it (the cosmos) becoming, thereby *speaking about God in a truly reverent manner* [μάλα σεμνῶς θεολογήσας]. (*Opif.* 12)[34]

Philo repeats the claim that the Genesis account is not mythology in *Opif.* 157, when he comes to his interpretation of Gen 2, more specifically of the passage concerning the creation of man and woman and banishment from Paradise. Here, however, as one would expect, he declares that allegory is a means of avoiding a mythological understanding of the text (see above).

---

[34] Transl. by Runia, *On the Creation of Cosmos according to Moses*, 49.

True, that the words which would traditionally indicate an allegorical approach in Philo do not appear in the first part of the text (so the words συμβολικῶς and αἰνίττομαι appear first in *Opif.* 154); however, within this part he keeps to the two main elements introduced by Aristobulos: the reinterpretation of the *logos* of God, away from the literal meaning of an utterance; and the reinterpretation of the creation in time, as occurring over six days.

Like Aristobulos, Philo indirectly interprets the recurrent expressions "and God said … and it was so." According to Philo, this was an act of divine thought taking place in His mind. Unlike Aristobulos, however, Philo reinterprets the *logos* of God not in phonological, but in intellectual terms, as God's reason (*Opif.* 8, 20–25).

Just like Aristobulos, Philo does not accept the narrative that describes the creation of the cosmos over six days. Moreover, he is drawing closely on the interpretation proposed by Aristobulos, that is, the notion that the number of days refers to the *taxis* in the world (*Opif.* 13, 28, 67). Unlike Aristobulos, he accepts that the world came to be in a single instant: creation happened in actual fact, but at once, rather than over six days.

Philo carefully preserves the principal elements taken over from the allegorical tradition, that is he maintains a reinterpretation of the literal meaning of the elements in the text that were rejected by Aristobulos. It is not difficult to see that Philo's deviations from Aristobulos's pattern are caused not by a different approach to the biblical narrative, but by a different philosophical framework chosen to reinterpret it—one that is not the Aristotelian model of the world, but the *Timaeus* of Plato (in conjunction with contemporary Middle Platonic theories of its interpretation).[35]

---

[35] Cf. Illaria Ramelli's assessment of Philo's approach: "Thus, he (Philo) reads Scripture as an allegorical exposition of fundamentally Platonic doctrines, both in his writings devoted to the exposition of the Mosaic Law, in which the allegorical reading is sprinkled among general literal explanation, and, above all, in his great allegorical commentary on Genesis, in which Philo provides a running allegorical exegesis of the biblical account." (Ilaria L. E. Ramelli, "Allegory II (Judaism)," *EBR* 1:786. This is contrary to Dawson's unwarranted statements, that "Rather than synthesizing scriptural and nonscriptural meanings, Hellenistic Jewish writers thus subordinate formerly nonscriptural meanings to scripture" (David Dawson, *Allegorical Readers and Cultural Revision in Ancient Alexandria* [Berkeley: University of California Press, 1992], 82; cf. pp. 102, 108, 113. Hellenistic writers practicing allegory do subordinate scriptural meanings to Greek philosophy, sometimes in a very violent way, as the tradition of allegory coming from the Derveni commentary prescribes (e.g., reworking the idea of God "saying" at creation, or of the notion of creation in time, over six days); but they also seek to find a genuine synthesis between them, as much as their larger Jewish context and reading techniques encourage them. On that see par. 3.2 below and, especially, Matusova, "'Seeing' God in Alexandrian Exegesis of the Bible," 74–85.

It is one of the main postulates in the *Timaeus* that the world came to be by the Demiurge at one particular point (*Tim.* 28b 5–7), and that previously it existed in the realm of ideas (*Tim.* 28c4–29a5). In conjunction with the Middle Platonic theories that ideas are thoughts of God, the place where they existed before is understood by Philo as God's mind.

Not only does Philo keep to the need to reinterpret the two mentioned elements in the narrative, but the orientation on the pattern given in the *Timaeus* brings him to introduce the third major change in the literal meaning of the text: the creation in chapter 1 (and partly 2) is presented by him as the creation of ideas, rather than as a creation of the visible world.

The general approach of Philo's reading is as follows:

According to the *Timaeus*, our visible world must have been created according to the pattern of an ideal, intelligible world, as Plato says: πρὸς τὸ λόγῳ καὶ φρονήσει περιληπτὸν (*Tim.* 29a: "after the pattern of that which is apprehensible by reason and thought"). Compare an even more provocative reformulation of this passage in Timaeus Locrus (206.11 Thesleff): Πρὶν ὦν ὡρανὸν λόγῳ γενέσθαι ἤστην ἰδέα τε καὶ ὕλα καὶ ὁ θεὸς δαμιουργὸς τῷ βελτίονος ("Before the world came to be in the word/reason [through the word/reason], there was idea and matter and God, the demiurge of the better"). It can be easily deduced from the context of the *Timaeus* that λόγῳ καὶ φρονήσει refers to the mind of God (as no one other *logos* and reason existed at the time of the creation of the cosmos). Based on this suggestion, and on the Middle Platonic understanding of God as Mind, Philo reinterprets the *logos* of God through the Platonic phrase in intellectual terms as God's reason. The identification made by Philo is supported by two Middle Platonic doctrines recorded in Alcinous (and in many places in Philo), which state that ideas are thoughts of God,[36] and that God's *logos* is an instrument and criterion of divine judgement (κρίσις).[37] Thus, Philo interprets all things created in Gen 1 as God's ideas, existing in his mind, and the process by which the ideal world is created as the intellectual process in God's Mind

---

[36] Alcinous, *Did.* 9.2: "For the forms are eternal and perfect thoughts of God" (εἶναι γὰρ τὰς ἰδέας νοήσεις θεοῦ αἰωνίους τε καὶ αὐτοτελεῖς). (Here and below the translations are by John Dillon, in: *Alcinous: The Handbook of Platonism; Transl. with an Introduction and Commentary* [Oxford: Clarendon, 1993], 16).

[37] Alcinous, *Did.* 4.2: "To take a clearer view of the matter, the judging agent might be said to be the philosopher, by whom things are judged, but equally well it could be taken to be the reason, by means of which the truth is judged, and which was what we declared to be the instrument of judgement[(κριτὴς δὲ καὶ ὁ λόγος, δι' οὗ τὸ ἀληθὲς κρίνεται, ὃ καὶ ὄργανον ἔφαμεν εἶναι]. Reason in turn takes two forms [Διττὸς δ' ἐστὶν ὁ λόγος]: the one is completely ungraspable and unerring, while the other is only free from error when it is engaged in the cognition of reality. Of these the former is possible for God [τούτων δὲ ὁ μὲν πρότερος θεῷ δυνατός,], but impossible for men, while the second is possible also for men" (p. 5–6).

(λογισμός- *Opif.* 25). In particular, Philo alludes to the theory of *criterion* (as he uses the verb διακρίνω to describe God's intellectual actions in the process of creation in *Opif.* 76, 154, and refers explicitly to the notion of criterion in *Opif.* 62), and to the dialectical method of *diaeresis*, in which mind continuously divides reality into two halves (δίχα, δύο).

Roberto Radice, having identified the method of *diaeresis* in the background of Philo's theory of *logos* in *Quis rerum divimarum Heres sit*, remarks that Philo surprisingly doesn't allude to this method in *De opificio mundi*, although the text of Genesis should have suggested this idea to Philo.[38] Indeed, it is reiterated in the text of Genesis that God created the world by separating (διαχωρίζω) something from something which could be taken as a synonym of διαιρέω. In my opinion, Radice fails to see the method of *diaeresis* being alluded to in *De opificio mundi* because he only has in mind the original Platonic definition and use of it. A different picture presents itself if we take into account the definition that is recorded in *The Handbook of Platonism* written by Alcinous (*Didaskalikos*). In it *Diaresis*, which comes first in Alcinous's classification of dialectical procedures, is an intellectual process whereby mind *divides genera* into *species*:

"Division may consist in dividing a genus into species, or a whole into parts [Διαίρεσις μὲν τοίνυν ἐστὶν ἡ μὲν γένους εἰς εἴδη τομή, ἡ δὲ ὅλου εἰς μέρη]. An instance would be when we divide [τέμνομεν] the soul into a rational part and a passionate part, and the passionate in turn into a spirit and the appetitive." (Alcinous, *Did.* 5.2)

And:

"It is primarily, however, the division of the genus into species [τοῦ γένους πρῶτον εἰς εἴδη τομῇ χρῆσθαι δεῖ] that one must make use of for the purpose of discerning what each thing is in itself by virtue of its essence." (Alcinous, *Did.* 5.3)

The words having the power of terms here are: τέμνω, τομή, γένος, εἶδος. It is evident that Philo is aware of this doctrine from his reference to the results of the creational separation as τμήματα:

Opif. 15: "Now to each of the days he assigned some of the *portions* [τμημάτων] of the whole"

Opif. 56:"All the time having been divided *into two portions* [εἰς δύο τμήματα], day and night"

---

38 Roberto Radice, *Platonismo e Creazionismo in Filone di Alessandria*, introduction by Giovanni Reale, Vita e pensiero (Milano: Universita Cattolica del Sacro Cuore, 1989), 67–71, 218.

Opif. 57: "one and alone it has by itself separately had day *apportioned* to it, half of the whole time [ἥμισυ τμῆμα ... κεκλήρωται]" [39]

and, particularly, from how he represents the creation of the idea of man in *Opif* 76:

> And when Moses had called the genus "man," quite admirably, did he distinguish its species [τὸ γένος ἄνθρωπον εἰπὼν διέκρινε τὰ εἴδη], adding that it had been created "male and female," and this though its individual members had not yet taken shape."[40]

Thus, when interpreting the creation of humans, Philo uses the verb διακρίνω which is connected to the theory of logos as criterion and interprets male and female as species (εἴδη) of one genus (γένος) of human being (ἄνθρωπος). Apparently, the recurrent use of the verb διαχωρίζω together with the constant mention of the γένη that appear as a result of the division have been taken by Philo as virtual parallels to the doctrine of *diairesis*.

Thus, Philo builds his interpretation on the creational account of the *Timaeus* and on the Middle-Platonic theories that help him to develop the theory of the divine logos-criterion that thinks reality by dividing it.[41]

Philo's text is much more extensive than the tiny fragments of Aristobulos, and when studying it, we can see that the *Timaeus* is being read into the interpretation to a much stronger degree. As Runia finely put it: "in Philo's view, the structure and subject matter of the *Timaeus* illuminate Moses' intentions in the composition of the Pentateuch."[42] *De opificio mundi* not only abounds in other themes, references and allusions to the *Timaeus*,[43]

---

[39] PLCL, 1:43

[40] PLCL, 1:61

[41] Radice's underestimation of the importance of the late Platonic handbooks (such as Alcinous's *Didaskalikos*) as evidence for an earlier stage of the Platonic tradition not only makes him overlook the traces of the method of Diaeresis in *De Opificio*, but also makes him suggest that Philo invented the theory that ideas are thoughts of God and that it later influenced Platonism (Roberto Radice, "Observations on the Theory of the Ideas as the Thoughts of God in Philo of Alexandria," *SPhiloA* 3 [1991]: 126–34). Although the reading of Philo by later Platonists cannot be excluded on a-priori grounds (cf. David T. Runia, "Witness or Participant," in *Philo and the Church Fathers: A Collection of Papers* [Leiden: Brill, 1995], 182–205; Runia, *Philo in Early Christian Literature: A Survey*, CRINT 3 [Assen: Van Gorcum, 1993], 9–11), nevertheless, following systematically Radice's methodology, we will be constrained to acknowledge Philo's influence on almost all Platonic doctrines that developed in Platonism after Plato, even if their presence in Philo is fragmentary and can be reconstructed only with the help of these Platonic handbooks.

[42] David T. Runia, *Philo of Alexandria and the Timaeus of Plato*, PhilAntS 44 (Leiden: Brill, 1986), 87.

[43] Runia, *Philo of Alexandria and the Timaeus of Plato*, and Runia, *On the Creation of Cosmos according to Moses*, passim.

including literal coincidence in expressions, but its holy status is also apparent in details such as the neutral references to the multiple gods dwelling in the sky (*Opif.* 27), or interpreting Gen 1:26 (καὶ εἶπεν ὁ θεός Ποιήσωμεν ἄνθρωπον, "And God said, Let us make man" [KJV]) through *Tim.* 41a–d as subordinate gods helping God in creating man (*Opif.* 72–75).[44] A simple comparison with Philo's other treatises which contain an interpretation of ποιήσωμεν, "let us make," in Gen 1:26 and refer to multiple gods dwelling in the sky makes it clear that Philo usually prefers the interpretation of the plural in terms of a notion more closely linked to the Jewish context, i.e., *dynameis* of God, while any other mention of visible gods, stars, planets and other gods of the Greek pantheon is always accompanied by a comment explaining their untrue nature (*Conf.* 169–176; *Fug.* 68–70; *Mos.* 1.13–17; *Virt.* 211–214; *Decal.* 54–59).

There is one parallel text where Philo refers to the "younger gods" in an entirely neutral tone and quotes the famous passage in the *Timaeus*, "Θεοὶ θεῶν, ὧν ἐγὼ δημιουργὸς πατήρ τε ἔργων, δι' ἐμοῦ γενόμενα ἄλυτα ἐμοῦ γε μὴ ἐθέλοντος ..." ("Gods of gods, those works whereof I am framer and father, you came into being by me, but you are indissoluble as I am unwilling") (Plato, *Tim.* 41a), namely, *De Aeternitate Mundi* (*Aet.* 13; cf. 112), which is a treatise offering a school philosophical exercise on a given subject, and one that is not intended for a Jewish religious community at all (if only because the Jews are referred to only once and in the third person). Similar neutrality of references to Greek sources can also be found in *Quod omnis probus liber sit*, which is also a purely philosophical treatise. In my view, it is remarkable to find a passage that is neutral with respect to standard polytheism (as it is present in the *Timaeus*) in a biblical treatise devoted to the commentary on the first chapters of the Bible.

However, building onto a philosophical text for the reinterpretation of the narrative is also methodologically congruent with Aristobulos's strategy and the allegorical approach to a text that is considered to be a religious (that is mythological) cosmogony. In view of our outline of the history of allegory, this use of the *Timaeus* can best be explained as a paradigmatic use

---

[44] A particular attachment to the *Timaeus* in this passage was also stressed by Dillon (John Dillon, *The Middle Platonists: A Study of Platonis;. 80 b.C. to A.D. 220*, 2nd ed. (Ithaca, NY: Cornell University Press, 1996), 171–72) and Radice (Radice, *Platonismo e creazionismo*, 161). Runia says, with the intention to undermine Dillon's point, that in Philo the identity of helpers "remains rather obscure" (Runia, *On the Creation of Cosmos according to Moses*, 238). However, compared to other relevant places in Philo, the very lack of explanatory comments thereupon is rather eloquent. For educated readers, the parallel with the *Timaeus* was lucid. As a tactics of reference, it chimes with the notoriously neutral reference to the "gods dwelling in sky" in *Opif.* 27.

of the text as the legitimizing force in transforming a religious creation account into a philosophic cosmogony (cf. Philo's explicit warning against taking the creation account as ἀφιλόσοφον ["non-philosophical"] [*Opif.* 2, 8, 12, 26]).

Building onto the *Timaeus* must be acknowledged as a smart choice. Plato is known to Philo as the most trenchant critic of religious mythology (which criticism at a stage earlier than Plato provoked the response of the author of the Derveni papyrus in the form of the theory of allegory), and the philosopher *par excellence*. However, Plato himself offered his own account of the creation of the cosmos by a Demiurge, that is, by God in person. In terms of theological tensions with mythology, his decision was paradoxical and challenging. Although there were always philosophical cosmogonies in Greek philosophy starting from the seventh century onwards, one of their specific features in comparison to mythological accounts was the absence of the figure of the God-Creator. From that point of view, Plato's account in the *Timaeus* was a challenge. It was very wise of Philo to use that crucial change in the philosophical discourse for the philosophical legitimization of the creation account in the Bible. In order to show that the biblical account of the creation is true philosophy, Philo needed to show that it is essentially identical with the account of the *Timaeus*. That explains the close associations Philo draws with that dialogue, extending to the toleration of multiple gods, which, as I have mentioned, never goes uncommented upon by Philo elsewhere.

Thus, Philo resumes the traditional strategy in three main points. First, an opening claim for the text's non-mythological, philosophical character; second, the transformation of its content into a philosophical cosmogony by changing its plain meaning (Philo keeps the two elements in the narrative changed by Aristobulos, and adds the third important change—the creation of an ideal world, rather than the real one in Gen 1);[45] and third, the carrying out of this transformation by drawing on a particular, recognizable, philosophic text. Thus, in *De opificio mundi* Philo offers his own specific reading of the creation account in terms of the tradition inherited from Aristobulos.

The best evidence that Philo is perfectly aware of the strategy of interpretation he is following and the purpose of this genre is the way he arranges all three major elements compositionally. As said, Philo begins

---

[45] Cf. also Runia's note in *On the Creation of Cosmos according to Moses*, 16: "Since Philo wants to relate the Mosaic text to current thinking, all features relating to the archaic Hebraic or Near-Eastern cosmology and zoology of the account are passed over in silence, except in day one, where they are radically reinterpreted."

with the starting point of philosophical allegory by saying that the creation account is not mythology, but philosophy and theology (*Opif.* 1, 8, 12). He introduces the three major reinterpretation topics immediately after that in a declarative and consecutive way. Thus, the reinterpretation of the creation over six days follows in *Opif.* 13–15; the reinterpretation of the creation in the sense of the creation of the ideal, rather than the real world follows in *Opif.* 16–19; the reinterpretation of God's word in the sense of His reason follows in *Opif.* 20–25. All these subjects will appear in the text of the treatises further down, as Philo's text proceeds, but he feels it is necessary to put them all together at the beginning of the treatise, thus marking out its main *agenda*. Having done this, he then starts commenting on the first verse of the Bible (*Opif.* 26).

What is also remarkable, however, is that, whereas the author of the Derveni Papyrus and Aristobulos claimed that they were revealing hidden meanings, because Orpheus and Moses intentionally concealed them, Philo only claims the non-mythological character of the text of Genesis, but avoids using specific allegorical terminology until *Opif.* 154 (where ethical allegory starts). A point can be made that he presents his discourse as similar to the Platonic discourse in the *Timaeus*, which probably would not be incorrect. However, I think that Philo had some particular grounds to do so, rather than a mere wish to imitate Plato.

3.2 *Philo's Reading through Ben Sira*

In fact, it would seem to be a natural strategy for advocates of Jewish Scripture to build upon Plato in attempts to give a philosophical basis for the account of creation in the Bible, but we see that Aristobulos did not do so. This is not the first occasion in my studies of Hellenistic Judaism that I have to note a drastic change of the philosophic paradigm in the time period between Aristobulos and Philo which led to the change of philosophical scenery in favour of Platonism. This phenomenon has a twofold nature. On the one side, it is connected to the rise and development of philosophical schools in Alexandria; on the other hand, as I suggested elsewhere, it might be also connected to the changes in the appearance of the corpus of authoritative Jewish texts available to the Alexandrian authors. In my article devoted to this subject, I spoke about a possible influence of the ideas found in the Qumran texts,[46] but it certainly refers to the translated texts which kept completing the LXX corpus as well. One of

---

[46] See Matusova, "'Seeing' God in Alexandrian Exegesis of the Bible," 86.

them was the translation of Ben Sira, done at some point after 132 BCE, that is, later than the presumed period of Aristobulos' activity.[47] In this translation we find an excellent legitimation for Philo's theory of God's logos as described above. Ben Sira's grandson, speaking about the creation of the world, says that things ἐν γνώσει κυρίου διεχωρίσθησαν, "By the Lord's knowledge they were marked off (or "separated" – E. M.)" (NETS) (33:8 and uses the verb διαχωρίζώ again in connection to knowledge in 33:11); he uses the word κρίσις ("judgement, separation") in the same context (33:13), stressing that all things in the world are divided in pairs as opposites: δύο δύο, ἓν κατέναντι τοῦ ἑνός, "two by two, one opposite the other one" (NETS) (33:15), πάντα δισσά, ἓν κατέναντι τοῦ ἑνός, "Everything is in pairs, one opposite one" (NETS) (42:24). And, finally, he explicitly correlates God's logos with his λογισμός, "reasoning" (Λογισμῷ αὐτοῦ ἐκόπασεν ἄβυσσον, "By his reasoning he abated the abyss and planted islands in it" (NETS) (43:23), adding a phrase that allows for several interpretations, but perfectly squares with the Philonic one that implies that created things are ideas existing in God's mind: καὶ ἐν λόγῳ αὐτοῦ σύγκειται τὰ πάντα, "and by (or: in) his word all things consist" (KJV 43:26). Needless to say that, when stressing the importance of the wording of Ben Sira's grandson, I do not want to say that he was influenced by Platonism. What we have here is a mere coincidence: the grandson's translational choice may have happened to be highly stimulating when read by anyone trained in Platonic philosophy. Thus, in the context of wisdom discourse, Logos of God that was at creation is interpreted by Ben Sira's grandson in intellectual terms—as γνῶσις, ἐπιστήμη ("knowledge"), λογισμός ("reasoning"). At the same time, by using the verb διαχωρίζω ("to separate") and the notion of κρίσις ("judgement, separation") together with them, as well as declaring that everything is divided into opposites, he might have suggested a clear link to the theory of logical division (*diakrisis*) in halves and opposites. We can suggest that these elements in Ben Sira's translation prompted Philo for an easy adaptation of the Platonic account of creation *in mind* combined with a specific Middle-Platonic theory of logical division.

---

[47] Apparently, Ben Sira's translation was an important text in the Egyptian Diaspora. For instance, it is important for understanding the *Wisdom of Solomon* (see Ekaterina Matusova, "The Making of the Theme of Immortality in the *Wisdom of Solomon*," in *Bookish Circles: Social Contexts of Literacy in the Greco-Roman Mediterranean*, ed. J. D. H. Norton, L. A. Askin, and G. V. Allen [Cambridge: Cambridge University Press forthcoming]). While its influence on Philo still awaits a proper study, for some basic parallels one can consult *Philon d'Alexandrie*, Biblia Patristica. Supplément, ed. J. Allenbach et al. (Paris: Éditions du centre national de la recherche scientifique, 1982), 91.

However, if Philo's Platonizing intepretation of the creation account is based on such a solid foundation as Ben Sira's text (which he must have assumed was faithfully rendered in the translation), this would mean that he could not actually see his Platonizing interpretation as allegorical in the strict sense. Allegory ascribed to Orpheus in the Derveni Papyrus and to Moses by Aristobulos in his treatise implies *intentional hiding of the sacred meaning from the non-initiated by speaking about something different than actually meant* which gives rise to the terminology of signs, hints, *hieros logos* etc. present in any allegorical commentary in this tradition (which we also see starting from *Opif.* 154). But from Philo's point of view, Gen 1 as rendered by Ben Sira, was indeed speaking in unmistakably Platonic terms. For him this was a variant of the creation account, coming from the depths of the ancestral tradition.

This awareness must have been increased by his own reading of Gen 1, in which, as Runia also noted, several elements also support a Platonic interpretation of the passage. For instance, it is said in Gen 1:1–2 that "In the beginning God created the heaven and the earth, and the earth was invisible and shapeless" (ἡ δὲ γῆ ἦν ἀόρατος καὶ ἀκατασκεύαστος). The phrase, in its Greek translation, has a strange meaning: the earth was created, but it was invisible and "unfurnished" (or "unprepared"). What does this mean? It is correctly noted by Runia in his commentary on the treatise that the word ἀόρατος is a Platonic term used as an epithet of ideas, εἴδη (Plato, *Resp.* 529b5; *Soph.* 246b7; *Tim.* 52a3; Alc. *Did.* 7.4).[48] The same applies to Philo's understanding of Gen 2:4–5 in *Opif.* 129.[49]

As I noted earlier, most probably, with a strong support on the part of Ben Sira, the verb διαχωρίζω was perceived by Philo as an indication of the Platonic doctrine of the division of genera into species (τοῦ γένους εἰς εἴδη τομή). This doctrine is used by Philo most explicitly in his interpretation of the creation of the genus of an ideal man, with its species of man and woman (*Opif.* 67). But in this example too, Philo's interpretation was more sensitive to what the Greek text actually says than it appears. The expression zākār ûnǝqēbâ used in the Hebrew text of Gen 1:27 are rendered in the LXX using words ἄρσεν καὶ θῆλυ (in the phrase καὶ ἐποίησεν ὁ θεὸς τὸν ἄνθρωπον, κατ' εἰκόνα θεοῦ ἐποίησεν αὐτόν, ἄρσεν καὶ θῆλυ ἐποίησεν αὐτούς). However, in Greek these words are not simply equivalents of "male and female" as in English. As neuter adjectives, they are notions too abstract to be properly used of male and female, so that Philo had sufficient reason to envisage the neuter word *eidos* behind them.

---

[48] Runia, *On the Creation of Cosmos according to Moses*, 165.
[49] For details, see Runia, *On the Creation of Cosmos according to Moses*, 309–12.

The title Γένεσις itself, which distinctively recalls one of the key terms in Platonism, must have been taken as a striking coincidence from that point of view (and Philo makes full use of the possibility to set the word within the context of Platonic philosophy as his first argument in *Opif.* 12).

The Greek text of the first chapters, when seen through the eyes of a person educated in Platonic philosophy, may have given hints toward the Platonic interpretation more so than to the mind of someone who is untrained in ancient philosophy. I think that Philo's own reading of Gen 1 through the lenses of his philosophical education complemented his understanding deriving from Ben Sira's translation, so that he was rather positive that Platonic philosophy was present in the narrative of Gen 1 in actual fact, although the plain meaning of the text may seem to be different. This persuasion about the virtual sameness of the accounts did not allow him to speak about Moses concealing the deep meaning here and consequently made him to suppress allegorical terminology until the expulsion from Paradise (where this similarity ends). All that does not undermine the fact that Philo was very well aware of the rules of the mainstream genre in which he was due to inscribe an explanation of the Jewish creation account. The best sign of it is his strong demythologizing pathos throughout the treatise, which is a signature of allegorical approach. Hence his marking out of elements rejected in their literal meaning by Aristobulos and the emphasizing of his bold reading of creation as creation of ideas first, his strong clinging to the *Timaeus* and his ready switch to allegorical terminology at the interpretation of Gen 2.

4. *Philo's Non-Allegorical Attitude in Context: Gen 1–2 in Pythagorean Sources*

The other reason for the change of the focus among Jewish Alexandrian authors toward Platonism was the development of Platonism in Alexandria itself.

This development can be connected to the activity of the school of Eudorus (fl. ca. 50–25 BCE), who is also known for his vivid interest in Pythagoreanism (which notion includes pseudo-Pythagorean writings).[50] In what follows I will turn to two treatises from the corpus *Pseudopythagorica ethica* which, as W. Burkert and B. Centrone have suggested, contain references to Gen 1 and 2.

[50] Dillon, *The Middle Platonists,* 115–39. Dillon, "Pythagoreanism in the Academic Tradition," in *A History of Pythagoreanism,* ed. C. A. Huffman (Cambridge: Cambridge University Press, 2014), 261–263.

Ekaterina Matusova

4.1 *Pseudopythagorica Ethica—The Time and Place of Origin*

The treatises in question were written in the Doric dialect under the names of ancient Pythagoreans. Ultimately, the philosophy of the treatises represents a mixture of Aristotelian and Platonic doctrines. In dating the corpus, there have been two extreme tendencies, one of which tends to date the corpus to the early Hellenistic period, with South Italy, Alexandria and Asia Minor as possible places of origin, and the other which dates it to the first century CE (or even later), with Rome as the birthplace.[51] However, several scholars who studied the pseudo-Pythagorean treatises noted a remarkable similarity between them and Philo (Bréhier, Delatte, Centrone, Mansfeld, Dillon).[52] Although Bruno Centrone, the most recent editor of the corpus, admits that some of the coincidences may result from a use of common sources and a common milieu, he is resolute in stressing the fact that some texts were written earlier than Philo and were known to him. This includes not only the non-Doric pseudo-Pythagorean authors to whom Philo *refers by name* (as for instance, to Philolaus in *Opif.* 100 and to Ocellus Lucanus in *Aet.* 12), but also Doric material that is not explicitly referred to (for instance, the unique similarity of thought between *Ebr.* 201 and Ps.-Archites's *De Viro Bono* 11, 12–7, or *Decal.* 30 and Ps.-Archites's *On Opposites* 23, 17 ff).[53] This particular connection with Philo serves for Centrone as important grounds for taking his own position on their date

[51] For the first tendency see: Holger Thessleff, *An Introduction to the Pythagorean Writings of the Hellenistic Period*, AAA, Ser. A/30.1 (Åbo: Åbo Akademi, 1965); Thessleff, "On the Problem on Doric Pseudopythagorica: An Alternative Theory of Date and Purpose," in *Pseudepigrapha I. Pseudipythagorica – Lettres de Platon – Littérature pseudépigraphique juive*, ed. Karl von Fritz, EAC 18 (Vandoeuvres-Genève: Fondation Hardt pour l'Étude de l'Antiquité Classique, 1971), 57–88; For the second one: Walter Burkert, "Zur geisgeschichtlicher Einordnung einiger pseudepigrapha," in Fritz, *Pseudepigrapha* I, 25–55. L. Delatte (Louis Delatte, *Les Traités de la Royalité d' Ecphante, Diotgène et Sthénidas* [Liège: Fac. de Philos. et Lettres, 1942], 284–88) argued for an even later date in the second century CE, but his opinion has not become influential.

[52] Emile Bréhier, *Les idées philosophiques et religieuses de Philon d'Alexandrie*, 18–23; Delatte, *Les Traités de la Royalité d' Ecphante, Diotgène et Sthénidas*, 179–80 Bruno Centrone, *Pseudopythagorica ethica. I trattati morali di Archita, Metopo, Teage, Eurifamo. Introduzione, edizione, traduzione e commento a cura di B. Centrone* (Napoli: Bibliopolis 1990), 30–34, also n. 64, 69, 43, 233–34 and passim in the commentary; Delatte, "The pseudo–Pythagorean Writings," in *A History of Pythagoreanism*, ed. Carl A. Huffman (Cambridge: Cambridge University Press, 2014), 325; Jaap Mansfeld, *Heresiography in Context. Hippolytus'Elenchos as a Source for Greek Philosophy*, Philosophia antiqua 56 (Leiden: Brill, 1992), 67. Dillon, "Pythagoreanism in the Academic Tradition," 265–66.

[53] Centrone, *Pseudopythagorica ethica*, 43–44; Centrone, "The pseudo–Pythagorean Writings," 325; Mansfeld, *Heresiography in Context*, 67.

and place of origin, or circulation. Centrone takes the first century BC as the most probable *terminus a quo*[54] and retains Alexandria as their possible place of origin:

> In relazione al problema della cronologia è di una qualche importanza il confronto con Filone d'Alessandria, che è, come si avuto modo di vedere, l'autore con il quale globalmente gli *pseudopythagorica* etici mostrano maggiori somiglianze.[55]

> Se in molti casi le analogie tra Filone a gli *pseudopythagorica* risalgono probabilmente ad una fonte commune, assai verosimile è comunque che essi si collochino in uno medesimo *milieu* culturale. Ritengo dunque che il I secolo a.C. rappresenti la data piu probabile di composizione degli ethica e che l'ipotesi di Alessandria quale possibile luogo di origine mantegna ancora la sua validita.[56]

4.2. *Gen 1–2 in Ekphantos and Euryphampos*

I turn now to the discussion of the places in the treatises of Ekphantos *On Kingship* (*Peri Basileias/De Regno*) and Euriphamos *On Life* (*Peri Biou, De Vita*) which, according to the suggestion of Burkert and Centrone, contain allusions to the Old Testament, in particular, to Gen 1 and 2.[57] I will examine these texts from the point of view as to whether Genesis is alluded to in them indeed and if so, how precisely it is treated and used.

Ekphantos *On Kingship*:

> 1. Ἐπὶ δὲ γᾶς ἄνθρωποι ἀπῳκισμένον χρῆμα καὶ πολὺ τᾶς καθαρωτέρας φύσιος ἐλαττούμενον καὶ πολλᾷ τᾷ γᾷ βαρυνόμενον, ὡς ἀπὸ τᾶς ματρὸς αὐτὸ μόγις ἐπᾶρθαι <ἄν>, αἰ μὴ θεόμοιρός τις ἐμπνοίησις ἐλέῳ ζῴῳ συνᾶψεν αὐτὸ τῷ κρέσσονι μέρει δεικνῦσα τὰν ἱερὰν τῶ γεννάτορος πότοψιν, ὡς ἀδύνατον ἐκείναν θεάσασθαι. (Stob. 4.6.22 p. 244 He.; Thesleff, 79)

> Upon the earth humans are in exile and much inferior to purer nature and they are weighed *down by much earth* [πολλᾷ τᾷ γᾷ βαρυνόμενον], so that man would hardly have risen from his mother by himself, *had not a divine inbreathing* [αἰ μὴ θεόμοιρός τις ἐμπνοίησις] united him with the eternal living being, having shown

---

[54] This is also the position of Heinrich Dörrle, Art. Pythagoras 1C, RE XXIV 2 (1963), 271 and Dillon, *Middle Platonists*, 119: "We do not know who wrote them, or when, or why. On the basis of the appearance of some of them in Philo (of surviving writers), and from the fact of the revival of Pythagoreanism in Cicero's time, we may conjecture that there was a corpus of these works in existence some time before the middle of the first century B.C." Cf. Paul Moraux, *Der Aristotelismus bei den Griechen von Andronikos bis Alexander von Aphrodisias*, vol.. 2, Peripatoi 6 (Berlin: de Gruyter, 1984), 605–7.

[55] Centrone, *Pseudopythagorica ethica*, 43.

[56] Centrone, *Pseudopythagorica ethica*, 44.

[57] Burkert, "Zur geisgeschichtlicher Einordnung," 49–53; Centrone, *Pseudopythagorica ethica*, 16, 31–34.

to his better part the holy appearance of the parent, so that it was impossible to look at Him.[58]

2. ἐν δὲ τᾷ γᾷ καὶ παρ' ἁμῖν ἀριστοφυέστατον μὲν ἄνθρωπος, θειότερον δὲ ὁ βασιλεὺς ἐν τᾷ κοινᾷ φύσει πλεονεκτῶν τῷ κρέσσονι. τὸ μὲν σκᾶνος τοῖς λοιποῖς ὅμοιος, οἷα γεγονὼς ἐκ τᾶς αὐτᾶς ὕλας, ὑπὸ τεχνίτα δ' εἰργασμένος λῴστω, ὃς ἐτεχνίτευσεν αὐτὸν ἀρχετύπῳ χρώμενος ἑαυτῷ. (Stob. 4.6.22 p. 244 He.; Thesleff, 80)

On the earth and here the human beings have the best nature, but the king is more divine, as, having the same nature as all humans, he abounds in the better part (i.e., mind—E.M.). Bodily, he is similar to all others, because he has come into being from the same matter, but he is created by the best master, who mastered him *using himself as an archetype* (pattern; ἀρχετύπῳ χρώμενος ἑαυτῷ).

The first part of the fragment refers to (1) earth as an essential element of humans and as their origin, and (2) to the divine inbreathing that allows the human being to rise from the earth and (3) to be united with the "living being." All three points correspond to Gen 2:7:

And God formed man, dust from the earth, and breathed into his face a breath of life, and the man became a living being. (NETS)

Although all these thoughts have parallels in Plato to some extent, they have particular, non-Platonic aspects here. Thus, for instance, while in Plato earth is said to be the element of the bones and one of the elements of the flesh (*Tim.* 64 c1; 73 e–74 d), it is by no means the only element of the human body. In contradistinction to the anthropology of the *Timaeus*, in Ekphantos' text earth is thought to be the only element (or the only mentioned element) of the human body (which corresponds to Gen 2:7). It appears that the body is thought to be created first and then the soul is blown into it, whereas it is the other way round in Plato. Although the notions that the substance of the world soul was partly used for the creation of the soul of the human being (*Tim.* 41 d–e) and that mind enters the human being from outside were known in the Greek tradition (*Tim.* 90 b1; Arist. *De gen.an.* 736b28; Timaeus Locrus 45; Atticus 7.13 Des Places), *inbreathing* specifically (ἐμπνοίησις) is not a notion used in Greek philosophy. It does, however, clearly correspond to ἐνεφύσησεν... πνοὴν ζωῆς in Gen 2:7 (besides, it should be noted that Ekphantos does not specify soul or mind here; instead he speaks about something indeterminate, like πνοή in the biblical text); and finally, although the idea that this inbreathing causes life and unites the human being "with the eternal living being" alludes to the idea from the *Timaeus* that humans and *kosmos* are united by partly having a common soul (*Tim.* 90a5), it emphatically also corresponds to the

---

[58] Here and below translation of the pseudo-Pythagorean sources is mine.

sequence of the biblical ideas, where the thought of becoming a "living being" is introduced after the creation from earth and inbreathing. It seems therefore that ideas not alien to, or even derived from, Platonic anthropology in the *Timaeus* appear here in a form influenced by the Old Testament.

The opposite is true of the next thought in the second part of the fragment, namely, that God created the king "using himself as an archetype (pattern)." Contrary to what we have just observed, the terminology is not biblical here. Instead it is notably Platonic. Ἀρχέτυπος and τύπος are terms traditionally used in reference to the ideal and material worlds in Platonic philosophy, but the thought is not Platonic orthodoxy. Although humans have acquired part of their soul or—in the peripatetic interpretation—mind from outside, which makes them cognate with the divine macrocosm, and becoming similar to God is the goal of human life, with humans in their ideal state supposed to be divine rather than human, we do not find these partially metaphorical thoughts expressed as God being the archetype of man and as having created man as a copy of himself. In Platonism humans are encouraged somehow to approach divine status, while being bestowed with some of the prerequisites for doing so, but there is not such straight-forward dependence on God as being created as his copy. Thus, this thought is remarkably biblical. It corresponds to Gen 1:26–27:

> And God said, Let us make man in our image, after our likeness: (Gen 1:26 KJV)

> So God created man in his *own* image, in the image of God created he him; male and female created he them. (Gen 1:27 KJV)

> καὶ εἶπεν ὁ θεός ποιήσωμεν ἄνθρωπον κατ᾽ εἰκόνα ἡμετέραν καὶ καθ᾽ ὁμοίωσιν (Gen 1:26)

> καὶ ἐποίησεν ὁ θεὸς τὸν ἄνθρωπον κατ᾽ εἰκόνα θεοῦ ἐποίησεν αὐτόν ἄρσεν καὶ θῆλυ ἐποίησεν αὐτούς (Gen 1:27)

We can even suggest what may have prompted the Pythagorean author to adopt this verse (thought) from the Bible, although it differs in content from orthodox Platonic anthropology. It is plausible that he was inspired by the word ὁμοίωσιν which is used in the LXX translation. This word has the force of a term in Platonism. According to Platonic philosophy, the goal of humans in life is to become as similar to God as possible (ὁμοίωσις θεῷ κατὰ τὸ δυνατόν, *Theaet.* 176a). Ekphantos may have read the biblical context through the prism of this philosophical vocabulary, which may have encouraged him to blend Platonic doctrine with the Gen 1:26–27 notion by further reformulating the latter in Platonic terms.

Thus, my analysis of the text leads me to agree with Burkert, who asserted that Ekphantos no longer belonged to the pure Greek line in the development of Greek literature, but was imprinted by contact with Judaism.[59]

Bruno Centrone pointed out the similarity to the Bible in another text from the same corpus, namely *On Life* (*Peri Biou, De Vita*) by Euryphamos (Stob. 4.39.27 p. 914 He. [Thesleff, 85–87; Centrone, 103–104]). In listing gifts that humans have acquired from God, Euryphamos says that these gifts include:

τὸ μὲν γὰρ λόγῳ τυπωτικὸς ἦμεν καὶ καλῶν καὶ αἰσχρῶν νοητικός, καὶ τὸ ὀρθὸς ἀπὸ γᾶς ἀνακεκλίσθαι καὶ ἐς τὸν οὐρανὸν ἀποβλέπεν καὶ θεῶν τῶν ἀνωτάτω νοητικὸς ἦμεν ἔχει γὰρ οὕτως ὁ σύμπας λόγος· τὸ θῆον ἄνθρωπον πολυφρονέστατον ζῷον ἐς τὸν κόσμον ἐσώκισεν, ἀντίμιμον μὲν τᾶς ἰδίας φύσιος, ὀφθαλμὸν δὲ τᾶς τῶν ἐόντων διακοσμάσιος· διὸ καὶ ὀνύματα μὲν ἔθηκε τοῖς πράγμασι, χαρακτῆρι αὐτῶν ἐπόμενος (Thesleff, 86; Centrone, 104)

to be able to give the imprint of logos [τὸ μὲν γὰρ λόγῳ τυπωτικὸς ἦμεν] *and to understand good and evil and to rise up right from the earth and to look at the sky and think about gods...because that is what the entire logos speaks about: God has settled man, the most intelligent living being, in the world as an imitation of His own nature* [ἀντίμιμον μὲν τᾶς ἰδίας φύσιος] *and as an eye of the order of beings. For this reason he gave names to things, according to their character.*

The reference to the possibility "to give the imprint of logos" connects to the thought that man is created in "imitation of His own nature," and alludes to the thought in Ekphantos that God created man "using himself as an archetype," ἀρχετύπῳ χρώμενος ἑαυτῷ. God imprinted τύπος in man, and man himself is able to carry out this same thing ("to give the imprint of logos," τὸ μὲν γὰρ λόγῳ τυπωτικὸς ἦμεν), for instance, in giving birth to other human beings[60]—although a more broad understanding of the phrase in the sense of "rationally organizing the world around him" cannot be excluded either. In explaining this statement, however, Euryphamos refers to a source which he simply calls λόγος ("because that is what *the entire logos* speaks about"). In it the first thought is that God "has settled man ... in the world as an imitation of His own nature," which must be an allusion to Gen 1:26–27, as discussed above. The further sequence of thoughts in this source is not less remarkable. Man is an imitation of the nature of God; he is the supervisor of all living beings ("an eye of the order of beings"). That confirms the suggestion of a reference to Gen 1:26 lying behind it as a

---

[59] Burkert, "Zur geisgeschichtlicher Einordnung," 53.

[60] Aristotle comes to mind here with his definition of *eidos* of a human being as "human being gives birth to a human being" (*M.* 1033b26–1034a8) and Ps.-Archites defines *eidos* as τύπωσις (*On Intelligence*, 38.10–12). Cf. also Philo's interpretation of the male seed as logos (*Deus* 16).

source, as it corresponds exactly to the sequence of thoughts in this verse, where the idea of ruling is introduced after the idea of creation according to the pattern ("Let us make humankind according to our image and according to likeness, and let them rule the fish of the sea and the birds of the sky and the cattle and all the earth and all the creeping things that creep upon the earth" [NETS]). Then he gave them names which corresponds to Gen 2:20: "And Adam gave names to all the cattle, and to all the birds of the sky and to all the animals of the field" [NETS]). The idea of man giving names to things is not alien to Greek philosophy (it appears in the Orphic tradition starting from the Derveni papyrus and then in Plato's "Cratylus," probably under the influence of this tradition, and sporadically elsewhere), but it does not appear in Plato or elsewhere in connection with the creation of humans. We see this clearly in connection only in the Bible and in this source referred to by Euryphamos as *logos*. This definition is, of course, quite universal and could potentially refer to any authoritative text (which, for instance, already incorporated some biblical ideas on an earlier stage), but it is rather remarkable that the Bible is also called directly and simply *logos* in another source which betrays a similar mixture of "Pythagorean" (i.e., Platonic-Aristotelian) and biblical elements—in the so called *Testamentum Orphei* (Eusebius *Praep. ev.* 13.12.5):

ὡς λόγος ἀρχαίων, ὡς ὑδογενὴς διέταξεν,
ἐκ θεόθεν γνώμῃσι λαβὼν κατὰ δίπλακα θεσμόν.

"So (says) the word [λόγος] of the ancients, so the one born in the water set it forth,/ After receiving it in his mind from God on the two-tablet law."[61] (refers to Moses – E.M.)

Euriphamos' expression (ἔχει γὰρ οὕτως ὁ σύμπας λόγος) also directly corresponds to how Philo refers to the Bible in *Opif.* 153:

φυτευθῆναι *λόγος ἔχει* παράδεισον ὑπὸ θεοῦ τοῖς παρ' ἡμῖν οὐδὲν προσεοικότα (refers to Gen 2:8).

"A parc or pleasaunce, we are told, was planted by God, quite unlike the pleasaunces with which we are familiar."[62]

---

[61] Translation of C. R. Hollady with my emendations. See Carl R. Holladay, *Aristobulos*, vol. 3 of *Fragments from Hellenistic Jewish Authors*, SBLTT 39 (Atlanta: Scholars Press, 1995), 170–71; Cf. Christoph Riedweg, *Jüdisch-hellenistische Imitation eines orphischen Hieros Logos. Beobachtungen zu OF245 und 247 (sog. Testament des Orpheus)*, Classica Monacensia 7 (Tübingen: Günter Narr Verlag, 1993), 34, 40–41.

[62] PLCL, 1:121

The expression λόγος ἔχει is ambiguous and may carry an idiomatic meaning of "people say," but hardly so in this context where Philo is actually commenting on the Bible.

4.3. *Ekphantos and Eryphamos and Their Legacy in Philo*

It is a known fact that the Pythagorean element in *De opificio mundi* is quite strong. Traditionally it is recognized in the section devoted to numbers in the creation account. As David Runia notes "more than a quarter of the entire work is taken up with this material," and he does not doubt that "The interpretation of biblical numbers patently draws on a Pythagorean background."[63] Philo's open reference to Philolaos also derives from this work (*Opif.* 100). However, I think that the Pythagorean background is present here to a much stronger degree, and that the treatises of Ekphantos and Euryphamos play an important part in it. Let me demonstrate the connection between them and Philo using the example of just one subject, Philo's anthropology.

We noted Platonic terminology in how Ekphantos put the idea of the creation according to God's pattern: "mastered him using himself as an archetype." ὃς ἐτεχνίτευσεν αὐτὸν ἀρχετύπῳ χρώμενος ἑαυτῷ. To express the same idea Euryphamos uses a peculiar expression "an imitation of his own nature," ἀντίμιμον μὲν τᾶς ἰδίας φύσιος.

Philo uses both expressions:

> After all the rest, as I have said, Moses tells us that man was created after the image of God and after His likeness (Gen 1:26) (...) for after the pattern of a single Mind, even the Mind of the Universe *as an archetype* (ὡς ἂν ἀρχέτυπον), the mind of the individuals was molded (*Opif.* 69).[64]

> ...mankind, that highest form of life, which has received dominion over everything whatsoever upon earth, born to be the likeness of God's power and image of His nature, the visible of the Invisible, the created of the Eternal [ἀντίμιμον γεγονὸς θεοῦ δυνάμεως, εἰκὼν τῆς ἀοράτου φύσεως ἐμφανής, ἀιδίου γενητή]. (*Mos.* 2.65)[65]

Ekphantos uses the word *inbreathing* (ἐμπνόησις) to paraphrase the expression in the LXX ἐνεφύσησεν ... πνοὴν ζωῆς in Gen 2:7. So does Philo

---

[63] Runia, *On the Creation of Cosmos according to Moses*, 25–26.

[64] PLCL, 1:55.

[65] PLCL, 6:481. In this phrase, Philo clearly elaborates on the expression ἀντίμιμον τᾶς ἰδίας φύσιος by expanding it into a bigger phrase. It is tempting to suggest that a variant ἀιδίας instead of ἰδίας was present in the text of Euryphamus available to him, which would include ἀιδίου in the number of Philo's allusions too (ἀίδιος can be of three endings as well, see LSJ s.v., so ἀιδίας could easily stand in the manuscripts instead of ἰδίας).

using the word ἐμπνευσθέντα (τὸν ἄνθρωπον ἐμπνευσθέντα εἰς τὸ πρόσωπον, *Opif.* 139).

In both Pythagorean authors, the idea of creation according to the pattern of God is interpreted in the sense that mind in humans is formed after the pattern of God's mind. So, for instance, in Ekphantos "inbreathing," ἐμπνοίησις, transforms "the better part," τὸ κρέσσον μέρος, of a man, i.e. mind; and in Euryphamos imitation of the nature of God implies that an "imprint," τύπος, received by man, is that of logos.

Similarly, Philo insists that likeness to God implies *only* the likeness of the human mind, created according to the pattern of God's mind:

> After all the rest, as I have said, Moses tells us that man was created after the image of God and after His likeness. Right well does he say this, for nothing earth-born is more like God than man. Let no one represent the likeness as one to a bodily form; for neither is God in human form, nor is the human body God-like. *No, it is in respect of the Mind,* the sovereign element of the soul, that the word image is used [ἡ δὲ εἰκὼν λέλεκται κατὰ τὸν τῆς ψυχῆς ἡγεμόνα νοῦν]; for after the pattern of a single Mind, even the Mind of the Universe as an archetype, the mind of the individuals was molded. (*Opif.* 69) [66]

We know from a parallel interpretation of the biblical verse in the *Wisdom of Solomon* (2:22–24) (probably reflected by Philo in *Opif.* 154–155) that the philosophical interpretation of likeness chosen by Philo was by far not the only one (or not the only one which was obvious) in Hellenistic Judaism, even if it is tinted with Platonism. Thus, the author of *Wisdom* explains it in terms of immortality that human beings were meant to share with God.

In the Pythagorean authors, an immediate consequence of the intellectual likeness to God is the possibility of *contemplation,* that is, thinking of invisible things and ultimately about God. Euryphamos: "to understand good and evil ... to look at the sky and think about gods," whereas Ekphantos stresses that this possibility of contemplation reaches its limits when it comes close to the contemplation of God Himself: "had not a divine inbreathing united him with the eternal living being, *having shown to his better part (i.e. to the mind) the holy appearance of the parent, so that it was impossible to look at Him.*"

In full accord with this, Philo develops the idea of likeness to God into that of the possibility of contemplation, that is, theoretical thinking, up to the thinking about God Himself:

> (Mind) is invisible while itself seeing all things, and while comprehending the substances of others, it is as to its own substance unperceived; and while it opens by arts and sciences roads branching in many directions, all of them

[66] PLCL, 1: 55.

great highways, it comes through land and sea, investigating what either
element contains.... Wafted by this to the topmost arch of the things perceptible
to mind, it seems to be on its way to *the Great King Himself*; but, amid its
longing to see Him, pure and untempered rays of concentrated light stream
forth like a torrent, so that by its gleams the eye of the understanding is *dazzled*
[ὡς ταῖς μαρμαρυγαῖς τὸ τῆς διανοίας ὄμμα σκοτοδινιᾶν].[67] (*Opif.* 69–71)

Exactly as in Ekphantos, the contemplation has its limits, and fails when
coming close to the Great King, that is, God Himself. The image, partly
inspired by Plato (*Resp.* 518 a–b) seems, however, even at the lexical level,
to be strongly influenced by the next passage in Ekphantos's text, where
dazzling and *dizziness* (μαρμαρυγαί τε γὰρ πολλαὶ καὶ σκοτοδινιάσεις) are said to
seize those approaching too close to divine kingship:

> And this can be applied to kingship: it is divine and difficult to look at for all
> but the genuine ones due to its excessive shine. Much *dazzling* and *dizziness*
> [μαρμαρυγαί τε γὰρ πολλαὶ καὶ σκοτοδινιάσεις] reveal the false ones as if they have
> ascended to an abnormal height. (Ekphantos Stob. 4.7.64, p. 273 He; Thesleff,
> 80)

God is not only alluded to, but explicitly called "the upper king" or "the
heavenly king" in Ekphantos (τῶ ἀνωτέρω βασιλέως, τῶ κατ' ὠρανὸν βασιλέως),
so that Philo's passage, when referring to God as *Megas Basileus* (*Opif.* 71; cf.
Opif. 88, 144), together with a lexically similar description of impossibility
to see him, seems to reflect the main themes of this Pythagorean treatise
very closely.

The ideology of the treatise of Ekphantos implies that the king is the
highest form of humans:

> On the earth and here the human beings have the best nature, but the king is
> more divine, as, having the same nature as all humans, he abounds in the better
> part (i.e., mind – EM). Bodily, he is similar to all others, because he has come
> into being from the same matter, but he is created by the best master, who
> mastered him using himself as an archetype (pattern). Thus, the king is the one
> and only creation that is like an imprint of the higher king, being always close
> to his Creator, but being visible to his subjects in the light of his kingship. (Stob.
> 4.7.64, p. 273 He; Thesleff, 80)

All the biblically-related ideas of creation according to God's pattern and of
the government on earth as a representative of God are developed in
relation to the king, βασιλεύς, as the highest form of man. It is remarkable in
this connection that Philo applies the epithet βασιλεύς to man several times
(*Opif.* 84, 86, 148), although it is only said in the Bible that man ἄρχει
"governs" (Gen 1:26, 28) living beings, with that verb not necessarily

---

[67] PLCL, 1:55-56.

implying royal rule in the Greek language. It can be suggested that Philo develops the idea of royalty in reference to man under the influence of Ekphantos' treatise. That influence of royal ideology and the reasoning of Euryphamos are evident in how Philo comments on man giving names to things in *Opif.* 148:

> Quite excellently does Moses ascribe the bestowal of names also to the first man: for this is the business of wisdom and *royalty*, and the first man was wise with a self-taught wisdom, as he came into being by divine hands, he was moreover the *king* [βασιλεύς] and it befits a ruler to give names to everyone of his subordinates.[68]

The expression "he came into being by divine hands" corresponds to Ekphantos' phrase "but he is created by the best master, who mastered him using himself as an archetype (pattern)" which refers to the king in the Pythagorean treatise. Therefore the idea of royalty immediately appears in Philo's text ("he was moreover the *king*"). But this "Ekphantized" interpretation is presented in the chain of arguments that closely follows a parallel passage in Euryphamos:

> God has settled man, the most intelligent living being, in the world as an imitation of His own nature and as an eye of the order of beings. For this reason he gave names to things, according to their character (Thesleff, 86; Centrone, 104)

When discussing this passage of Euryphamos I noted that the idea of giving names should be explained by the biblical context here, rather than by the general Greek one, because it is only the Bible that connects the idea of giving names with the creation of humans. However, in the Bible the verse speaking about the creation of man and that speaking about giving names are separated by twenty other verses. Euryphamos, unlike the Bible, links them together immediately. And this is the connection in Philo's passage: man is created by God, he is the ruler on earth, and *therefore* he gives names to the ruled ones. Only the idea of ruling (expressed by Euryphamos using the more general language "an eye of the order of beings") is stressed by Philo in terms of royalty.

It should be also added that Philo and Ekphantos speak of man being of the best nature among living beings (τὸ πάντων ἄριστον (sc. τὴν φύσιν) (*Opif.* 67, 68); ἀριστοφυέστατον μὲν ἄνθρωπος (Ekphantos Thesleff 80,1), and both use the noteworthy word ἐπίκαρον/ἐπίκηρον, "mortal," in reference to him ἄνθρωπον δὲ βραχὺ ζῷον οὕτως καὶ ἐπίκηρον (*Opif.* 72); ἐπίκαρον ὂν τὸ ζῷον (Ekphantos Thesleff 83,3–4).

---

[68] PLCL, 1:117.

Thus, if some of the elements just listed, taken separately and individually, can be explained by the Platonic–Aristotelian background (to which the Pythagorean treatises also ultimately go back), the cumulative effect of the parallels clearly shows that the treatises in question are an important background to Philo.

Finally, probably an even stronger argument for this position is that Philo's treatise *De opificio mundi*, which is meant to give a systematic interpretation of Gen 1–2, gives as the first quotation from the Bible Gen 1:26–27 (*Opif.* 25), rather than the first verses of Gen 1 (which only appears in *Opif.* 26). The impression is that the treatise formally opens with the verse which, by being adopted and alluded to by both Pythagorean authors, obviously became a biblically-inspired element of Pythagorean literature.

5. *Conclusion: Philo's Writing Strategy*

The Pythagorean treatises just discussed do not apply allegory to the text of the LXX. Rather, they amalgamate the text of the Bible with that of the *Timaeus* (as well as with other important texts, although the *Timaeus* visibly predominates). It would take another article to explain the reasons for this attitude. Summarizing it briefly, based on my previous work, it can be said that Peripatetic doxography starting from the fourth century BCE always included teachers from the east among philosophical predecessors of Pythagoras. The Jews joined this line starting from Hermippus (the second century BCE). [69] Hence, the late Pythagoreans considered these sources as being closely related to their own tradition, whereas the goal of Pseudepigrapha was to show that the teaching of Plato and Aristotle is already contained in ancient Pythagorean texts. This way sources from the east may have come together with Plato and Aristotle in the late Pseudepigraha written under the names of ancient Pythagoreans. The idea was to show that these sources and Plato and Aristotle basically translate the same message (being all the teaching of the Pythagoreans). This way, Plato and Aristotle were amalgamated with the pieces of eastern wisdom locally available to these later writers.

---

[69] For the Jews in ancient Pythagorean doxography, see Ekaterina Matusova, "The Jews as "Chaldeans" in Egypt," in *Gegenspieler. Zur Auseinandersetzung mit dem Gegner in frühjüdischer uund urchristlicher Literatur*, ed. M. Tilly and U. Mell, WUNT (Tübingen: Mohr Siebeck, 2019), 43–59; (in print)); and for those who read Russian: Е. Матусова, "Филон Александрийский и греческая доксография," Вестник Древней Истории 2001 (1): 40–52.

Given the closeness of Philo to the corpus in general, and to Ekphantos and Euryphamos in particular, it would be logical to suggest that he was well aware of the Pythagorean approach to the Bible. This approach may have created a broader context for his reading together of Genesis 1 and Platonism, according to the principles described above. Not only does he borrow from this tradition a particular interpretation of likeness to God as likeness in the logical part of the soul, but he also shares with these authors their main intention: to show that Plato and the Jewish cosmogony basically transmit the same message.

He also partially shares their technique. As we have seen, in the Pythagorean texts, sometimes a biblical wording expresses a thought that is genuinely Platonic, but sometimes Platonic wording is superimposed onto a distinctively biblical thought. One of the methods is to read a Platonic doctrine into a biblical phrase, based on the similarity of terms, as happens in the case of the term ὁμοίωσις in Gen 1:26. The word is not used as a philosophical term in the Bible; but rather is interpreted through the Platonic doctrine ὁμοίωσις θεῷ κατὰ τὸ δυνατόν (*Theaet.* 176a), as I suggested. In precisely the same way as the Pseudo-Pythagorean treatises in question, Philo reads Genesis and Plato together, restating the biblical doctrine in philosophic, Platonic terms, drawing from the lexical and etymological hints given in the text of the LXX (see above, par. 3.2).

However, unlike the Pseudo-Pythagorean texts, we will not find in *De opificio mundi* examples where Philo restates a Platonic doctrine in the LXX terms as the Pythagoreans sometimes do. On the contrary, he is consistent in his strategy of always reformulating a biblical thought in Platonic terms. (This chimes with his meticulous subjection of the biblical account to the *Timaeus* in terms of doctrine, whenever possible.)

The reason is clear: whatever genuine closeness Philo may have thought existed between Platonism and the Bible (and, as I said above in part 3, I think that this essential similarity was one of his most earnest convictions), he was perfectly aware of the rules of the genre in which he was going to inscribe his interpretation. He works within the general framework of the allegorical tradition, the main intention of which consists in philosophizing a religious (or mythological) text. Cosmogony stands at the core of the genre, and requires a philosophizing transformation in the first place. Philo thus uses the intentions and technique found in Ps.-Pythagorean writings consciously, but cautiously, subjecting it to the scope and goal of his allegorical undertaking. Thus, one can say that the strategy shared with the Pythagoreans is not opposed to allegorical approach, but complements it in achieving its main goal. It is *harnessed* to the main goal of allegory, as it is used in the form which is meant to demonstrate the philosophical character of the Bible (rather than the "oriental" character of Plato).

In his treatment of Gen 1–2 Philo masterfully developed two possible approaches to philosophizing creation account that had foundations in the earlier traditions: one which is allegorical, and which comes from the Derveni Papyrus via Aristobulos, and the other which implies reading Gen 1–2 through Platonic lenses drawing on their virtual doctrinal compatibility and finds its broader context in the Pythagorean attempts to adapt the Bible, in particular Gen 1–2 to the *Timaeus*. Partially in terms of content and generally in terms of strategy, the Philonic reading is strictly conforming to what we find elsewhere on interpretations of Gen 1, but it is also summarizing the previous experience in one mixed treatment. This leads scholars to express the equally mixed opinion that although the treatise is "thematic," it is not devoid of allegory either.

Thus, Philo's treatment of Gen 1 is not only well explainable from its exegetical context, but also the study of this context does not allow me to imagine what other *systematic* "allegorical" reading this chapter could potentially have. On the historical understanding of the treatise from within the approaches available to Philo, nothing prevents *De opificio mundi* from being the representative of an allegorical approach to the creation account and a treatise that paves the way to the strategy pursued in the so called "Allegorical Commentary." While not being written in the same manner from a formal point of view as the Allegorical commentary, this treatise fulfills all the requirements of the genre of allegory. It also goes a step further in showing that the sort of allegorical interpretation in the spirit of Platonic philosophy which is offered in the Allegorical Commentary is not a forced strategy imposed on the Bible, but instead follows from the essential identity of the Bible and Platonism revealed in *De opificio mundi*. In that sense too, the interpretation of Gen 1 proposed in the treatise *De opificio mundi* is a logical beginning for the entire allegorical interpretation of Genesis, and does not need to be artificially detached from it or to be dated to a later period.

Institut für Antikes Judentum und
Hellenistische Religionsgeschichte
Tübingen, Germany

The Studia Philonica Annual 31 (2019): 95–105

PHILO OF ALEXANDRIA: INTERPRETER OR TEACHER?

BEATRICE WYSS

Gregory Sterling argues in a series of articles (convincingly in my opinion) that Philo of Alexandria ran his own private "School of Moses."[1] Although we have no proofs of the *Sitz im Leben* of Philo's voluminous and multifaceted oeuvre, cumulative evidence points toward a private school. Sterling corroborates his 1999-thesis that "Philo had a private school in his home or personally owned structure for advanced students which was similar to schools of higher education run by individuals throughout the Greco-Roman world"[2] with the existence of an exegetical tradition (without a tradition of thought there is no school), Philo's own statements, for example *Anim.* 6[3] and the genre of commentary that was used in philosophical schools. The setting of the literary genre "commentary" lies in an educational milieu, as he argued in comparing Philo's commentaries with the remains of the commentaries of Aristarchus of Samothrace (third–second century BCE), the *pesharim* at Qumran (Second Temple period), and commentaries on Plato, especially the anonymous Commentary on *Theaetetus*.[4] Comparing Philo's work with the work of Epictetus second century CE), Plotinus (third century CE) and Proclus (fifth century CE), he

---

[1] Gregory E. Sterling, "'The School of Sacred Laws': The Social Setting of Philo's Treatises," *VC* 53 (1999): 148–64; Sterling, "Philo's School: The Social Setting of Ancient Commentaries," in *Sophisten in Hellenismus und Kaiserzeit: Orte, Methoden und Personen der Bildungsvermittlung,* ed. Beatrice Wyss, Rainer Hirsch-Luipold, and Solmeng-Jonas Hirschi (Tübingen: Mohr Siebeck, 2017), 121–42; Sterling, "The School of Moses in Alexandria: An Attempt to Reconstruct the School of Philo," in *Second Temple Jewish "Paideia" in Context,* ed. Jason M. Zurawski and Gabriele Boccaccini (Berlin: de Gruyter, 2017), 144 n. 11.

[2] Sterling, "The School of Sacred Laws," 150.

[3] Lysimachus, Philo's grand-nephew, is speaking: "So here I sit quietly, modestly, and with restored humility as is proper for a student; and here you are seated in front of me on a platform looking dignified, respectable, and erudite, ready to begin to teach your teachings" (cited by Sterling, "The School of Sacred Laws," 157–58). The translation is by Abraham Terian, *Philonis Alexandrini De animalibus: The Armenian Text with an Introduction, Translation, and Commentary* (Chico: Scholars Press, 1981), 69.

[4] Sterling, "Philo's School," 128–38.

concludes that the philosophy according to Moses was the content of Philo's teaching, whereas the three commentary series aimed at three different groups of students/hearers and the philosophical treatises furnished basic knowledge in philosophy for beginners.[5] Together with but independently of Sterling, Sean A. Adams argues that Philo's *Questions and Answers in Genesis and Exodus* stem from the Greek philosophical curriculum and were used as a classroom text.[6]

So far so nice. But what do we do with Philo's own claim (*Anim.* 7, immediately following the polite remark of his grand-nephew Lysimachus cited in note 3):

> I shall begin to interpret but I will not teach, since I am an interpreter and not a teacher. Those who teach impart their own knowledge to others, but those who interpret present through accurate recall the things heard from others. And they do not do this just to a few Alexandrians and Romans—the eminent or the excellent, the privileged, the elite of the upper class, and those distinguished in music and other learning—gathered at a given place.[7]

Does Philo's statement not contradict every claim of his being a teacher? I thought first we have Julius Pollux (second century CE), who gave the following definition (4.41): Σοφιστής, διδάσκαλος, παιδευτής, ἐξηγητής, ὑφηγητής, ἡγεμών. Sophist, teacher, tutor, commentator, exegete, master (my translation).

From Julius Pollux we learn that sophist, teacher and exegete are all synonyms and I could stop here. But the case is not that easy: Although *De animalibus* is preserved completely in Armenian, the second sentence is extant in its Greek original and reads as follows: Διδάσκουσι μὲν οἱ τὰς ἰδίας τέχνας μυοῦντες ἑτέρους, ἑρμηνεύουσι δὲ οἱ ἀλλοτρίαν ἀκοὴν εὐστοχίᾳ μνήμης ἀπαγγέλλοντες.[8]

The dichotomy thus is not between teacher and exegete, but between teacher and interpreter (ἑρμηνεύς, as I would guess the noun was, cf. ἑρμηνεύουσι).

The first part of my argument is devoted to show that Philo's statement (*Anim.* 7) does not contradict his being a teacher of philosophy like Socra-

---

[5] Sterling, "School of Moses," 162–63.

[6] Sean A. Adams, "Philo's Questions and the Adaptation of Greek Philosophical Curriculum," in *Second Temple Jewish "Paideia,"* 167–84, containing a useful history of scholarship on the present topic (167–70).

[7] Terian, *De animalibus*, 69.

[8] "They teach, they who initiate others their own art, but they interpret, they who report by sagacity of memory what they heard from others" (my translation). Greek text: Terian, *De animalibus*, 263, a transcription from Vaticanus gr. 1553, introduced as Φίλωνος ἐκ τοῦ περὶ τῶν ἀλόγων ζώων ("from Philo's *On Irrational Animals*").

tes. The second part of my argument tackles Philo's polemic against sophists and adds from this point of view further evidence of Philo's self-image as the only true philosopher like Socrates.

Now let us see the conceptual frame from which the term "interpreter" comes, and who "the others" are, whose interpreter Philo pretends to be. I will give a very short sketch of the platonic background Terian worked out.[9]

(1) The motifs (not the wording) used in the introductory and transitory dialogues preceding and following Alexander's arguments in Philo's *De animalibus* (1–9.72–76) resemble those used in the introductory and transitory dialogues preceding and following Lysias's arguments in Plato's *Phaedrus* (227a–230e.234d–237a).[10] Our passage resembles *Phaedrus*, (235cd) insofar as Socrates is pretending that he knows nothing, but instead is full of what he has heard from the elders Sappho, Anacreon and others.

(2) The idea that the interpreter's knowledge is not his own is reminiscent of Plato's *Ion* (530a–542b),[11] especially 533c–536d.

(3) Philo has a prominent predecessor in refusing to call himself "teacher" (διδάσκαλος), namely, Socrates.[12]

(4) The insistence that the interpreter refuses to present his findings only to some chosen few of the privileged classes recalls the attitude of Socrates, who sought to render his services to all his fellow-citizens.[13]

(5) Terian also notes that the "question of interpretation in Philo is invariably tied to that of inspiration—as seen in his understanding of the prophets as inspired interpreters of divine pronouncements and in his claim to inspiration with regards to his own interpretation."[14]

Now, let us consider the subtexts Terian found: The *Apology, Ion,* and *Phaedrus*. In what follows, I will not give a thorough interpretation of Plato or Philo, instead, I will point to some concepts that are found in the works

---

[9] Terian, *De animalibus*, 116–18.

[10] Terian, *De animalibus*, 267.

[11] Terian, *De animalibus*, 116–17. The next passage is from Terian, too.

[12] Plato, *Apol.* 33a ἐγὼ δὲ διδάσκαλος μὲν οὐδενὸς πώποτ' ἐγενόμην—"In fact, I have never been teacher of anyone." Translation by R. E. Allen, *The Dialogues of Plato, Volume 1, Euthyphro, Apology, Crito, Meno, Gorgias, Menexenus: Translation with Analysis* (New Haven: Yale University Press, 1984).

[13] Plato, *Apol.* 33b, "To rich and poor alike I offer myself as a questioner; and if anyone wishes to answer, he may then hear what I have to say" (translated by Allen); cf. Xenophon, *Mem.* 1.10; Terian, *De animalibus*, 118.

[14] Terian, *De animalibus*, 117 with older literature. See also his "Inspiration and Originality: Philo's Distinctive Exclamations," *SPhiloA* 7 (1995): 56–62.

of both authors, albeit in different manner. The aim is to show that the topics of inspiration and interpretation are interconnected both in Plato's aforementioned works and in Philo's oeuvre and that Philo fashions himself as a second Socrates.

(1) I will begin with the *Phaedrus*, but not with 235cd, because Terian has already written what is necessary, but let us consider 244a–245a. Here, Plato through Socrates expounds a theory about "good" mania, that means, a god-sent frenzy that inspires prophets, the priestess of the Delphian oracle, and also poets. It is this theory of frenzy that Philo in a modified manner took over in *Her.* 258–266.[15] The *Phaedrus* provided Philo with a theory of frenzy and divine inspiration (244a–245a) and with a Socrates, who pretends that he knows nothing of his own (235cd).

(2) Now let us turn to the *Ion*, a short dialogue, a work of the young Plato.[16] Plato presents Socrates as questioning the once-famous rhapsode Ion of Ephesus about his art, hence the title, *Ion*. One passage is, as I think, fundamental for Philo's understanding of the art of an interpreter as being inspired by God (*Ion* 533c–536d) and also for his understanding of himself as an interpreter: Socrates states that "the rhapsode must interpret the poet's thought to his audience" (530c τὸν γὰρ ῥαψῳδὸν ἑρμηνέα δεῖ τοῦ ποιητοῦ τῆς διανοίας γίνεσθαι τοῖς ἀκούουσι). In other words: The interpreter (ἑρμηνεύς) knows nothing of his own, but only "interprets" the thought (διάνοια) of the poet. Socrates repeats this point later: "and that poets are nothing other than messengers of the gods" (534e οἱ δὲ ποιηταὶ οὐδὲν ἀλλ' ἢ ἑρμηνῆς εἰσιν τῶν θεῶν). Philo, in using the verb ἑρμηνεύειν, inscribes himself in this tradition of the inspired—in his case, not poet, but interpreter of divine words (that means, words uttered by the divinely inspired Moses).

Later, Socrates says: "For your speaking well about Homer is not an art ... but a divine power which moves you" (533δ ἔστι γὰρ τοῦτο τέχνη μὲν οὐκ ὂν παρὰ σοὶ περὶ Ὁμήρου εὖ λέγειν ... θεία δὲ δύναμις ἥ σε κινεῖ).[17] Socrates opposes

---

[15] This has long been seen by Hans Leisegang, *Der Heilige Geist: Die vorchristlichen Anschauungen und Lehren vom Pneuma und der mystisch-intuitiven Erkenntnis* (Leipzig: Teubner, 1919), 1.166 with Aleknienés thorough analysis, "L''extase mystique' dans la tradition platonicienne: Philon d'Alexandrie et Plotin," *SPhiloA* 22 (2010): 67–75. She demonstrates that in Philo's thinking the poetic ecstasy, as introduced in the *Ion*, has the highest place, and replaces the philosophical ecstasy, that ranked first in Plato's *Phaedrus*.

[16] Ernst Heitsch, *Platon. Ion oder Über die Ilias: Übersetzung und Kommentar* (Göttingen: Vandenhoeck & Ruprecht, 2017), 29–34. R. E. Allen, *Plato. Ion, Hippias Minor, Laches, Protagoras, Translated with Commentary* (New Haven: Yale University Press, 1996), 1–22, esp. 5, gives a short and thoughtful commentary on our topic. The translations are from Allen.

[17] Similar statements 534c, 536cd, 542ab, here θεία μοῖρα. There is a long discussion about Philo's own experience of ecstasy, mysticism, being an inspired interpreter. Because

τέχνη and θεία δύναμις, art and divine power. In Socrates's view two sets of knowledge exist: one consisting of an orally transmitted or written set of concepts that one can learn (the τέχνη, art), and one kind of knowledge that is the result of divine power and is not under human control. Both belong to the realm of transmitting knowledge, but differ in the method of transmitting and in the content of the transmitted knowledge.

In the next passage, we find the idea of the mind that is taken out of man while he is in ecstasy (cf. Philo, *Her.* 258–266). Socrates is speaking: "This is why the god takes the mind out of them and uses them as his servants, as he uses oracles and divine prophets: so that we their hearers may know it is not they, in whom mind is not present, who tell things of such great value, but the god himself who speaks, making utterance to us through them."[18]

I think, here we find a productive misunderstanding concerning the singular ὁ θεός, for in a polytheistic system, the audience knew well, which of the gods was "the god" who inspired the poet, it was the appropriate Muse. The monotheistic Philo also knew well, which was "the god," namely the only one. Note that in this passage, God is the subject of the phrase, so the grammatical structure reproduces the content of the argument, that God is active and not human. To be sure, so far Socrates examined the connection between the god and the poet, the Muse and Homer. Now, neither Ion the rhapsode nor Philo are poets, but they are interpreters of poets or Moses. Socrates compares this relationship to the magnet that attracts many iron rings. God, the Muse, is like the magnet who inspires the poet, the poet inspires the interpreter, the interpreter inspires the audience.[19] Applied to Philo, this means: God inspires Moses, the prophet and perfect lawgiver (note, that also Plato in *Meno* 99c sees

---

I will not enter this topic, I name only a few articles: David M. Hay, "Two Types of Mosaic Inspiration," *JSP* 2 (1989): 49–67 (with John R. Levison, "Two Types of Ecstatic Prophecy according to Philo," *SPhiloA* 6 [1994]: 83–89); Hay, "Philo's View of Himself as an Exegete: Inspired, but not Authoritative" *SPhiloA* 3 (1991): 40–70. Sze–Kar Wan, "Charismatic Exegesis: Philo and Paul Compared," *SPhiloA* 6 (1994): 54–82. David Winston, "Philo's Mysticism," *SPhiloA* 8 (1996): 74–82. Tatjana Aleknienė, "L' extase mystique."

[18] 534cd διὰ ταῦτα δὲ ὁ θεὸς ἐξαιρούμενος τούτων τὸν νοῦν τούτοις χρῆται ὑπηρέταις καὶ τοῖς χρησμῳδοῖς καὶ τοῖς μάντεσι τοῖς θείοις, ἵνα ἡμεῖς οἱ ἀκούοντες εἰδῶμεν ὅτι οὐχ οὗτοί εἰσιν οἱ ταῦτα λέγοντες οὕτω πολλοῦ ἄξια, οἷς νοῦς μὴ πάρεστιν, ἀλλ ὁ θεὸς αὐτός ἐστιν ὁ λέγων, διὰ τούτων δὲ φθέγγεται πρὸς ἡμᾶς.

[19] Plato *Ion* 536a "Do you also know then that the spectator is the last of those rings I spoke of as receiving power by the Heraclean stone? You, the rhapsode and actor, are the middle ring; the first ring is the poet himself. But it's the god who draws the soul of men through all of them in whatever direction he may wish, making the power of one depend upon the other" (trans. Allen).

politicians in a state of frenzy, like prophets and poets), Moses inspires the interpreter Philo. In this chain there is no direct inspiration of the interpreter by God. This is important to notice: Philo never pretends to be a prophet, he distinguishes between his abilities and those of the supreme Moses,[20] and he does not directly claim divine authorship for his interpretations of scripture, though he links his concept of God's two powers up to his own experience of divine rapture.[21]

(3) and (4) The third text is the *Apology* of Socrates, where Socrates pretends that he has never been a teacher, that he did not teach only a few but that he was accessible for everyone who wished it (*Apol.* 33ab). In the *Apology*, one finds also a mention of the divine inspiration of prophets and poets (*Apol.* 22bc). So, the topics of "not being a teacher" and "divine inspiration" are once more found in one work.

(5) Having taken into account the platonic subtexts, I think, it is evident why the questions of teaching, interpreting and divine inspiration are interconnected: Philo was in the same conceptual frame he found in Plato's work. With this in mind, it becomes evident that Philo's statement in *Anim.* 7 ("but those who interpret present through accurate recall the things heard from others") is only on a very superficial level a modest one; in fact, on the contrary, Philo implicitly claims the highest possible source for his knowledge, albeit in an indirect way, namely God who inspires Moses.

Socrates who in the words of Plato (*Apol.* 33a) refuses to be called a teacher, was of course a kind of teacher. Plato and Xenophon were his most famous pupils. Other pupils of Socrates are called the "Socratics" like Aeschines, Antisthenes, Aristippus of Cyrene, Euclides, and Phaidon. They are not well known today, because they suffered serious damage of written records; only scanty fragments and paraphrases are extant.[22] Socrates set his teaching against the teachings of his contemporaries, the sophists, whom he accused of taking money for teaching and teaching only the rich and wealthy.[23] When Philo fashions himself in the manner of Socrates, he

---

[20] Terian, "Interpretation," 56–62.

[21] *Cher.* 27–28; *Somn.* 2.250–254; and Wan, "Charismatic Exegesis," 62–71. Cf. *Migr.* 34–35; *Spec.* 3.1–6; and Wan, "Charismatic Exegesis," 56–71.

[22] Gabriele Giannantoni, *Socratis et Socraticorum reliquiae*, 4 vols. (Naples: Bibliopolis, 1990).

[23] David Blank, "Socratics vs Sophists on Payment for Teaching," *Classical Antiquity* 4 (1985): 1–49.

follows not only a trend in contemporary pagan philosophy,[24] but for the attentive reader, he presents himself as the true philosopher.

Now, in the second part of my argument, I will put in another conceptual frame found in Philo's oeuvre to accentuate Philo's image of himself as a second Socrates and only true philosopher. As Socrates, he is engaged in a constant battle against so called sophists, especially in his Allegorical Commentary.[25] For all who are not aware of this topic,[26] I will add more

[24] Klaus Döring, *Exemplum Socratis: Studien zur Sokratesnachwirkung in der kynisch-stoischen Populärphilosophie der frühen Kaiserzeit und des frühen Christentums* (Wiesbaden: Steiner, 1979), an old but still useful work.

[25] *Aet.* 132 (philosophers); *Agr.* 136 (γραμματικοί, Lev 11:4), 143–144 (Lev 11:7), 159 (Deut 20:5–7), *Leg.* 3.232 (bis, king of the Amorites, Num 21:28); *Cher.* 8 (Ismael, Gen 21:14); *Conf.* 39 (Egyptians, Exod 14:30); *Congr.* 67 (Gen 16:2), 129 (Ismael, Gen 21:20); *Contempl.* 4 (stoic philosophers), 31 (rhetors); *Det.* 38–39 (Pharaoh's experts of rituals, Exod 4:10), 71–72 (Balaam, Num 23:8); *Ebr.* 71 (Exod 32:27–28); *Fug.* 209, 211 (Ismael, Gen 16:12), *Her.* 246 (philosophers, Gen 15:11); *Ios.* 103.106 (Pharaoh's experts, *Gen* 41:24); *Migr.* 72 (Gen 12:3), 76 (Pharaoh's experts, Exod 4:10), 171 (Exod 33:15); *Mut.* 10 (philosophers, Exod 33:23), 208 (Exod 6:27), 257 (teachers, Gen 29:31), *Post.* 35 (Protagoras, Gen 4:17), 86 (Deut 30:11–14), 131 (Ismael, Gen 21:20), 150 (Exod 22:27), 220 (sophists of Egypt, augurs, ventriloquists, soothsayers, Gen 37:3), *Somn.* 2.281 (Egyptians, Exod 14:30); *Mos.* 1.92 (Pharaoh's experts, Exod 7:12); 2.212 (Exod 20:11); QG 3.33 (Ismael, Academy and Scepticism, Gen 21:20). It is not always possible to identify the σοφισταί. —Most of the occurrences of the term "sophist" are found in the Allegorical Commentary. See Gregory Sterling, "Review of *Paul's Anthropology in Context: The Image of God, Assimilation to God, and Tripartite Man in Ancient Judaism, Ancient Philosophy and Early Christianity*, by George H. Van Kooten, *SPhiloA* 22 (2010): 296–97; and see my own explanation of this fact: "Philon und die Sophisten—Philons Sophistendiskurs vor dem Hintergrund des alexandrinischen Bildungsumfelds," in *Jüdisch-hellenistische Literatur in ihrem interkulturellen Kontext*, ed. Martina Hirschberger (Frankfurt a.M.: Lang, 2012), 98 n. 23).

[26] Philo's sophists are not of great interest in research: Valentin Nikiprowetzky, *Le commentaire de l'écriture chez Philon d'Alexandrie* (Leiden: Brill, 1977), 183–92 (very lucid about the connection of scepticism and the sophists); Bruce Winter, *Philo and Paul among the Sophists*, 2nd ed. (Cambridge: Cambridge University Press, 2002), followed by George H. van Kooten, "Balaam as the Sophist par Excellence in Philo of Alexandria. Philo's Projection of an Urgent Contemporary Debate onto Moses' Pentateuchal Narratives," in *The Prestige of the Pagan Prophet Balaam in Judaism, Early Christianity and Islam*, ed. George H. van Kooten and Jacques van Ruiten (Leiden: Brill, 2008), 131–61. Winter and Van Kooten take Philo's sophists as members of the Roman elite, also known as Second Sophistic and downplay the polemic Philo uses in denigrating the sophists. I criticized this view in my 2011-article "Philon und die Sophisten," as did Erkki Koskenniemi indepen dently of me in his article "Philo and the Sophists," in *Greeks, Jews, and Christians. Historical, Religious and Philological Studies in Honor of Jesús Peláez del Rosal*, ed. Lautaro Roig Lanzillota and Israel Muñoz Gallarte, EFN 10 (Córdoba: Ediciones el Almendro, 2013), 253–79.

information. If we take into account the exegetical background,[27] we see that from the beginning in Gen 1 (*Opif.* 45) through Deuteronomy (*Post.* 86, Deut 30:11–14), crucial as well as minor figures of the Pentateuchal narrative represent the sophist. Cain (*Agr.* 159–165), Ismael (e.g., *Fug.* 209), the experts at Pharaoh's court and adversaries of Joseph (*Ios.* 103, 106) and Moses,[28] Balaam (e.g., *Det.* 71) and the King of the Amorites (*Leg.* 3.232) symbolize the sophist. The soul who became pregnant without wisdom either miscarries or the offspring is the quarrelsome sophist who shoots with the bow (*Cong.* 129, Gen 21:20). The sophist transgresses the boundary of truth (*Leg.* 3.232, Num 21:28), he is mimicking and debasing the authentic coin (*Mut.* 208, Exod 7:11), sophists are like pigs (*Agr.* 144). In the command "slay each his brother and each his neighbour and each him that is nearest to him" (*Ebr.* 68, Exod 32:29) the "nearest" is the sophist according to Philo's speech. So he concludes (*Ebr.* 71): "Why, then, should we not at once take vengeance on him too, sophist and miscreant that he is, by sentencing him to the death that befits him—that is to silence, for silence is the death of speech?"

If we open the conceptual frame and add the noun σοφιστεία, the adjective σοφιστικός and the verb σοφιστεύειν, the importance of the sophistic thread becomes more evident: The serpent in Paradise is tricky like a sophist (*Agr.* 96), Babel is the city of godlessness, impiety, self-love, arrogance, false opinion, unfairness, licentiousness, audacity, immoderate indulgence in pleasures, in one word: a city of sophists, "until such time as God takes counsel (Gen 11:6) and brings upon their sophistic devices a great and complete confusion" (*Post.* 53). Jacob's secondary wife Zilpa represents "the art of devising clever arguments whose easy persuasiveness is a means of deception" (*Cong.* 29 ἡ λογικὴ σοφισμάτων εὕρεσις εὐστόχῳ πιθανότητι καταγοητεύουσα, Gen 30:3). The actual meaning of Aaron's rod that swallowed up the rods of Pharaoh's experts (Exod 7:12) is that the sophistic arguments are devoured and done away with by nature (*Migr.* 85); Balaam only has mantic or magic σοφιστεία and not a real knowledge of God.[29] Sophists haunt creation from the beginning (*Opif.* 45, Gen 1:14–19) till Philo's own days (*Post.* 101 ὁ νῦν ἀνθρώπων σοφιστικὸς ὅμιλος).

There are some points of contact in Plato's critic and polemic against sophists and Philo's, as we will see. Plato knows of one "Egyptian sophist,"

---

[27] This point is correctly emphasized George H. Van Kooten, *Paul's Anthropology in Context* (Tübingen: Mohr-Siebeck, 2008), 230–37.

[28] *Det.* 38; *Migr.* 76; *Mos.* 1.92; *Somn.* 1.220; Sarah J.K. Pearce, *The Land of the Body: Studies in Philo's Representation of Egypt* (Tübingen: Mohr-Siebeck, 2007).

[29] Σοφιστεία μαγική / μαντική *Mut.* 203 (Num 31:8); *Mos.* 1.277 (Num 23:1).

Proteus (*Euthd.* 288b τὸν Πρωτέα μιμεῖσθον τὸν Αἰγύπτιον σοφιστὴν imitate Proteus, the Egyptian sophist); Egypt is the homeland of Philo's sophists.³⁰ But the polemical pattern Philo uses in denigrating the sophists is not only based on Plato's works, it is far more widespread in Greek literature.³¹

(1) The sophists are many, crowds of sophists haunt the cities and their quarrels are uncountable.³²

(2) Sophists are bad teachers or teachers of bad things.³³

(3) Sophists are greedy; they sell their teachings like chandlers and they teach only the young and rich.³⁴

(4) Sophists are skilled in speaking and fond of words and speeches, they tire up the ears of their hearers.³⁵

(5) Sophists are well-versed in arguing and use fallacies and tricks.³⁶

(6) Sophists are polemical and aggressive, constantly and fervently attacking everybody.³⁷

³⁰ See n. 28. There is a link to scripture as well, Exod 7:11 συνεκάλεσεν δὲ Φαραω τοὺς σοφιστὰς Αἰγύπτου καὶ τοὺς φαρμακούς, καὶ ἐποίησαν καὶ οἱ ἐπαοιδοὶ τῶν Αἰγυπτίων ταῖς φαρμακείαις αὐτῶν ὡσαύτως.

³¹ I am preparing a monograph on this topic; a shortcut is available: "Der gekreuzigte Sophist," *EC* 4 (2014): 503–28; Wyss, "Lukians sophistische Philosophen in den Fugitivi," in *Munera Friburgensia: Festschrift zu Ehren von Margarethe Billerbeck*, ed. Arlette Neumann-Hartmann and Thomas S. Schmidt (Bern: Peter Lang, 2016), 62–63.

³² *Agr.* 136, ὁ πανταχοῦ τῶν σοφιστῶν ὅμιλος ("the swarm of sophists to be found everywhere"); *Post.* 101, ὁ νῦν ἀνθρώπων σοφιστικὸς ὅμιλος ("the sophistic group of present day people"); cf. *Mut.* 10, ἡ ἀδηλότης μυρίας ἔριδας σοφισταῖς ἐγέννησεν ("that mystery which has bred numberless contentions among the sophists");—Cf. also Cratinos fr. 2 K./A. = Clement of Alexandria, *Strom.* 1.3.242, σοφιστῶν σμῆνος ("a swarm of sophists"); Iophon fr. 1 TGrF = Clement of Alexandria, *Strom.* 1.3.24.3, πολλῶν σοφιστῶν ὄχλος ("a mob of many sophists"). Plutarch, *Frater. Amor.* 478b, τὸ πλῆθος τῶν σοφιστῶν ("plenty of sophists"); Dio Chrysostom, *Or.* 8.9, πολλῶν μὲν σοφιστῶν κακοδαιμόνων ("many wretched sophists"). These and the following non-Philonic references are taken from "Der gekreuzigte Sophist," 512–19. The translations of Philo are by F.H. Colson and G.H. Whitaker, PLCL.

³³ *Mut.* 257; *Post.* 150. Cf. Isocr. *Or.* 13.9.

³⁴ Teaching for money: Plato, e.g., *Apol.* 20a, 33a, *Crat.* 391b; cf. *Lach.* 186c; *Prot.* 311e; *Soph.* 224de; *Resp.* 6,493a; and Philo, *Post.* 150; cf. *Ios.* 125; *Mos.* 2.212; Plato, *Prot.* 313c; and Paul, 2 Cor 2:17; Plato, *Soph.* 231d, νέων καὶ πλουσίων ἔμμισθος θηρευτής ("a hired hunter of the young and rich"); Maximus of Tyre 27.8, Pollux 4.42–43.

³⁵ *Contempl.* 31; *Agr.* 143; *Leg.* 1.74; *Migr.* 72. Cf. Clement of Alexandria, *Strom.* 1.3.22.5, ποταμὸς ἀτεχνῶς ῥημάτων, νοῦ δὲ σταλαγμός ("unsystematically a flood of words but a drop of mind"); Isocrates, *Or.* 15.197; Dionysius of Halicarnassus, *Dem.* 44. Philo, *Agr.* 136; *Det.* 72; Clement of Alexandria, *Strom.* 1.3.22.4–5.

³⁶ *Agr.* 143; *Leg.* 3.232; *Mos.* 2.212; Λόγοι σοφιστικοί, *Opif.* 157; *Leg.* 1.74; 3.41 (Gen 15:5); *Her.* 304; *Migr.* 85. Plato, *Euthyd.* 297c; Plutarch, *Pericl.* 36.5; Antiphanes fr. 120 K/A; Aulus Gellius 5.10.3; 6.3.34–35.

³⁷ *Agr.* 159; *Det.* 39.71; *Congr.* 129; *Fug.* 211; *Her.* 246; *Mut.* 10; *Post.* 131; *Somn.* 2.281. *Agr.* 162 (τῷ φιλέριδι καὶ σοφιστικῷ στίφει ["with the strife-loving band of sophists"]); *Det.* 41–42 (σοφιστικῶν παλαισμάτων ["the tricks of the sophistic wrestling"]; παρελθὼν δ' ὡς Ἄβελ

(7) Sophists act contrary to what they preach (*Congr.* 67; *Post.* 86). Plato works with a contradistinction between δόξα, whose expert is the sophist, and being, whose expert is the philosopher (*Soph.* 254a); Philo's opposites are σοφιστεία and σοφία.[38]

(8) Sophists are like sorcerers; the sophist Protagoras charms his hearers like Orpheus.[39]

Some years ago, I argued in a paper, that the sophists in Philo's oeuvre are not the representatives of Roman or Greek elite culture, that are known mainly in the second century, often from Asia minor, and well represented in Flavius Philostratus's *Vitae sophistarum* (*Lives of the sophists*).[40] Instead, I argued that the sophists Philo despised are teachers of a quite wide range of knowledge, for example, grammar (*Agr.* 143), but also Stoic philosophy (*Contempl.* 4; *Migr.* 171), and (as I overlooked in my paper) in one case Jewish literalists (*Somn.* 1.102). In general, the sophist belongs to the realm of propaedeutic education (*Mut.* 263, τὸν κύκλον καὶ τὸν χορὸν ἅπαντα τῶν σοφιστικῶν προπαιδευμάτων ["the whole round and train of the early branches of the professional schools"]; cf. *Mut.* 257). I still think I was correct in suspecting social grounds for the polemic: Philo criticized teachers who ran their own private schools as a business (*Mos.* 2.212) and as a means to earn money (a need Philo maybe did not have, being the brother of the very well-to-do Alexander the Alabarch), who came from the lower classes of society (e.g., manumitted slaves),[41] who tried to attract pupils with their rhetorical and argumentative skills. Of course, I have to admit, that I came to this conclusion in reading Philo across the grain, so to speak, in not

---

εἰς σοφιστικὸν ἀγῶνα ["when like Abel he steps out for a contest of wits"]); *Migr.* 82 (πρὸς ἀγῶνα σοφιστικόν). Cf. Plato, *Euthd.* 297c; *Prot.* 342b; *Tht.* 154e and: δεινὸς σοφιστής, τῶν ἀγυμνάστων σφαγεύς "a terrible sophist, slayer of the untrained" (323* K./S. TGrF 2.79 = Numenius fr. 25 [Des Places = Eusebius, *PE* 14.6.1]); Hermeias, *Irrisio* 2.7.

38 Σοφιστεία vs σοφία *Opif.* 45; *Cher.* 9; *Migr.* 85; *Praem.* 8; *Prob.* 4; *Prov.* Frg. 1.28; cf. *Leg.* 3.206; *Spec.* 3.54.

39 Σοφιστεία and γοήτεια *Cong.* 29; *Praem.* 8; *Somn.* 2.40. Plato, *Soph.* 234e; *Prot.* 315a; Aesch. *Or.* 3.137; Dem. *Or.* 19.250; Dio Chrysostom, *Or.* 32.39; Maximus of Tyre 18.4. There is much more behind this than I can say here, see Walter Burkert, "ΓΟΗΣ: Zum griechischen 'Schamanismus,'" *Rheinisches Museum* 105 (1962): 36–55; he remarks that in a certain sense the sophist of the second century CE is the successor of the archaic *goes*; Jacqueline de Romilly, *Magic and Rhetoric in Ancient Greece* (Cambridge, Mass.: Harvard University Press, 1974) and my "Der gekreuzigte Sophist," 517–28.

40 *Philon und die Sophisten* against Winter *Philo and Paul among the Sophists* and Van Kooten, "Balaam as the Sophist par Excellence."

41 Johannes Christes, *Sklaven und Freigelassene als Grammatiker und Philologen im antiken Rom* (Wiesbaden: Steiner, 1979); on the social background of sophists in the first century CE see also my "ΣΟΦΙΣΤΗΣ in der Kaiserzeit," in *Sophisten in Hellenismus und Kaiserzeit*, 186–210.

believing what he literally says. But this is sometime the task of the historian.

It is time to weave the strings together: Philo, who fashions himself as a second Socrates, and this means, the true philosopher who knows nothing, teaches no one, but is accessible for everyone who wishes it, is, as Socrates, a kind of teacher, although both pretend the contrary. Socrates pretends that he knows nothing of his own, and Philo pretends that he does not impart his knowledge to his hearers, as teachers do. Socrates presents a theory of divine inspiration, to which Philo adheres and which he uses in his works; Philo claims *expressis verbis* divine inspiration for his interpretation of God's two powers. As Socrates struggled against sophists, so Philo struggles against sophists, that means, teachers who run their own school for earning money and who teach grammar, rhetoric, philosophy, but not in the same way as Philo teaches philosophy. The fashioning as Socrates and the constant struggle against the sophists put Philo on the side of the true philosopher. His teaching is hence true philosophy, the philosophy according to Moses, as Sterling correctly put it.

University of Bern
Switzerland

The Studia Philonica Annual 31 (2019): 107–125

IS PHILO COMMITTED TO THE DOCTRINE
OF REINCARNATION?*

DAVID T. RUNIA

1. *A Highly Significant Study*

When I was asked a few years ago to examine the dissertation of a Finnish scholar, I very soon realized that this was a highly significant study, arguably the most innovative piece of research to be carried out on Philo's thought in recent years.[1] Sami Yli-Karjanmaa's study is the first ever to specifically address the question of whether the theme of reincarnation is present in Philo's writings and whether the Alexandrian accepts the doctrine. It is characteristic of his careful method that he defines the term "accepts" (or its alternatives "adopts," "approves," "endorses"), taking it to mean "receive with favour" or "receive as valid" (p. 4). The conclusion of his investigation is that Philo indeed accepts the doctrine. A survey of previous scholarship shows that this was the view of the majority of nineteenth century scholars but lost favour in the twentieth century (pp. 13–29). For the most part, however, scholars have just made brief comments on the question, not regarding it as of very great importance. Yli-Karjanmaa takes a different approach, studying it in meticulous and fascinating detail.

A laudable feature of the study's method is that it wishes to take all the available evidence into account regardless of which answer to the main question of the work it tends to support (p. 7). The evidence is divided into two categories, indirect and direct, and the two resultant treatments form

---

* This article is the revised text of a paper presented to the Philo of Alexandria Seminar at the Annual Meeting of the Society of Biblical Literature held in San Antonio in November 2016. My thanks go to Dr Sami Yli-Karjanmaa for his thought-provoking comments on the text.

[1] Sami Yli-Karjanmaa, *Reincarnation in Philo of Alexandria*, SPhiloM 7 (Atlanta: SBL Press, 2015). See also his article "'Call Him Earth:' On Philo's Allegorization of Adam in the *Legum allegoriae*," in *The Adam and Eve Story in the Hebrew Bible and in Ancient Jewish Writings Including the New Testament*, ed. Antti Laato and Lotta Valve, Studies in the Reception History of the Bible 7 (Turku: Åbo Akademi University, 2016), 253–93.

the main parts of the study. The third and final part, entitled Synthesis, applies the results of the earlier parts and attempts to show that they present a feasible reconstruction of Philo's thought.

In the first main part Yli-Karjanmaa sets out the indirect evidence for the doctrine of reincarnation and this necessitates a wide-ranging examination of themes in Philo's psychology and eschatology. Naturally there is a strong focus on the texts of the Allegorical Commentary, which is wholly focused on the life-journey of the soul, but numerous texts in the *Quaestiones* are also adduced, as well as some important passages in the Exposition of the Law. The starting-point has to be the dualistic make-up of the human being, consisting of soul and body (p. 30). Following a fundamental tenet of Platonic philosophy, Philo is committed to the view that the soul exists before it enters the body and, being immortal, will outlive its association with the body (p. 32). But the human being is more complex than just consisting of soul and body. The soul itself has a complex structure involving parts or faculties that interact with the body. There are on the one hand the senses and the lower parts of the soul, which experience passions and pleasures. There is also the higher part of the soul, its rational part or mind, which must guide the human being so that he or she can lead a life of piety and virtue (pp. 36–37).

In order to conceptualize the process which the soul undergoes, Yli-Karjanmaa introduces two key terms for his argument. The former refers to the process of salvation whereby the soul shakes off the influence of the body and becomes purely rational, i.e. a mind (νοῦς). This process he calls "monadization," defined as "the salvific phenomenon whereby the soul's (sic) becoming pure mind through dismissal of its other constituent parts" (p. 41). The term is based on the description of Moses's death in *Mos.* 2.288. When the mind is in such a state it is able, as in the case of Jacob–Israel, to "see God," that is to know him and to reside with him. This is the ultimate stage of the soul's life and represents the climactic stage of Philo's eschatology.

The second key term focuses more directly on the soul's experience of the body once it is incarnated. Yli-Karjanmaa speaks of the "corporealization of the mind," which is "the phenomenon whereby the mind (or soul) orientates towards, and desires to experience, the world of matter in general and a physical body in particular" (p. 70). Philo uses it to explain the transgression and fall of the first human being Adam, but it also characterizes the life of any human being, bringing about that, when death takes place, it may happen that the soul does not rise to heaven and God, but has to submit to the process of reincarnation. A key text here is *Leg.* 1.105 (exeg. Gen 2:17), where Philo says that death is of two kinds: for the human being it is the separation of body and soul (cf. Plato, *Phd.* 64c, 67d), but for the soul it is the destruction of virtue and the taking up of wickedness. The death of the soul is a punishment (*Leg.* 1.107), and by implication it involves the process of reincarnation (pp. 57–70), perhaps not just once but as many times as needed until the soul is purified and reaches its goal in residing with God.

Examination of a large number of passages, mainly in *Leg.* and *QG* (esp. 1.51 on Gen 3:19), leads Yli-Karjanmaa to arrive at a compact schema of Philo's conception of the journey of the soul involving six stages (p. 73):

(1) incorporeal existence with God;
(2) incarnation;
(3) corporealization and transgression;
(4) reincarnation until the prerequisites of salvation are met;
(5) liberation from the life in the body; and
(6) eternal incorporeal existence with God.

He emphasizes that such a schema runs the risk of simplification and over-systematization.[2] Nevertheless it has the virtue of clarity, showing in the clearest possible way how reincarnation can be fitted in to a journey of the soul that extends far beyond the confines of the single life of the human being.

In the final section of the presentation of the indirect evidence Yli-Karjanmaa approaches his subject from a different angle. He sets out in impressive and fascinating detail Philo's use of Platonic reincarnational terminology and imagery in Philo's writings. Primarily drawn from three dialogues, the *Phaedo*, the *Timaeus*, and the *Phaedrus*, it is focused on themes such as being bound to a mortal body, being plunged in a river, paying back the borrowed elements of which the body consists at fixed periods, the body as a grave or a prison, changing to animal form, practising death, and being weighed down by earthiness (pp. 111–27). Such extensive use of literary means is typical of Philo's use of Plato. For Philo, Moses provides the basic (and faultless) framework, but Plato (and also the Stoics) allows him to flesh out that framework. Philo takes over major ways of thinking from the Athenian philosopher, but it is done in bits and pieces through the exegetical process (p. 112).

In the second main part of the study Yli-Karjanmaa examines the direct evidence on reincarnation in Philo's writings. This is confined to four texts. The first is the *locus classicus* for the presence of the doctrine in the Philonic

---

[2] The schema is repeated in "'Call Him Earth'," 261.

corpus, *Somn*. 1.137–139 (cited on p. 131). In explaining the meaning of the ladder (κλῖμαξ) in Jacob's dream at Gen 28:12, it describes the descent and ascent of the discarnate souls, making use of a good deal of Platonist terminology and explicitly stating that some souls "hurry back again" (παλινδρομοῦσιν αὖθις) to the life in the body. The second text is found at *Cher.* 114 (cited on pp. 153–54), part of a long allegorical reflection on God's sovereignty and the fact that we human beings are God's possession (and not our own, as impiously thought by Cain, whose name means "possession," *Cher*. 52). What, Philo asks, really belongs to us? He asks a number of questions about our make-up. In the case of soul, do we possess it as our own? What about after death takes place? But then we shall exist no longer, but "hasten to a regeneration" (εἰς παλιγγενεσίαν ὁρμήσομεν).[3] The third text is found at *QE* 2.40 and is preserved in full in the Armenian translation and partly in a Greek fragment (cited at pp. 169–70). Yli-Karjanmaa argues that when the text speaks of the souls "being dragged down to Tartarus," it is an explicit reference to a new reincarnation. The final text is even more difficult. It is one of the texts from Byzantine florilegia collected by J. Rendel Harris and is located in a section entitled "Fragments from the lost fourth book of the Allegories of the Sacred Laws" as fr. 7.3 (cited on p. 187). The text is only six lines long in Harris's collection. In an impressive display of philological expertise Yli-Karjanmaa demonstrates that it is very likely to be authentic and argues that the comparison of sleeping and awakening with the salvific rebirth after death points to the process of reincarnation. He concludes (p. 212) that in all four texts Philo speaks of the idea of reincarnation with approval.

The final part of Yli-Karjanmaa's study is entitled Synthesis. He emphasizes that in his view it can be assumed that "when Philo uses similar vocabulary in simlar contexts in different texts, he is speaking of the same things, and that therefore we are entitled to read these texts together. This means assuming that the texts form a whole, and that what is said in one text is, in the absence of evidence to the contrary, implied in the others" (p. 215). The task for the scholar is to "explain Philo by Philo," i.e. do what Philo fails to do and build up a description of his views (cf. p. 244). This method allows a synthesis of reincarnational passages to be put together which also gives us an understanding of Philo's individual eschatology. The fate of the soul is intimately tied to what it determines to be the object of its love, whether that be God or earthly things which are primarily associated with the body and its desires (p. 220). There are four reasons

---

[3] The passage is difficult to summarize accurately and needs to be consulted in the original.

why the soul fails to leave the bodily realm and keeps on returning to it: ignorance, unwillingness, inability and a lack of God's grace. The first three are obstacles for the soul as it makes progress towards perfection. Philo's soteriology is synergistic: "the soul needs to make progress on its own but recognize its dependence on God's grace in order to be saved" (p. 243). Ultimately it is God who determines whether the soul has to return to the earth and to the body.

A final question that remains to be answered is why Philo is so reticent about speaking in explicit terms about reincarnation. After all, he never makes any clear pronouncements on the subject and even when the theme is mentioned explicitly in the four passages it is only done so in passing. Nevertheless, Yli-Karjanmaa argues, he did wish to communicate his view that souls transmigrate and his vagueness is not impenetrable. A good explanation for this approach is Winston's view that Philo was reluctant "to give undue prominence to a Platonic conception that was essentially alien to Jewish tradition" (p. 246),[4] with the proviso that we do not know a lot about what Jewish tradition is in the case of Alexandrian Judaism. Given that the theory of reincarnation is closely linked to the allegorical tradition, which met with opposition in the Alexandrian community, it is probable that "reincarnation was for Philo an esoteric tradition" (p. 247), only to be disclosed to those who had the required level of understanding of the hidden meaning of scripture.

2. Three Significant Advances in Our Understanding of Philo

There can be no doubt, therefore, that this monograph has made a highly significant contribution to Philonic studies. It has placed the subject of the place of the doctrine of reincarnation in Philo's mental universe firmly on the map. No study of his views on psychology and anthropology will want to set it aside. Among the many advances that it makes in our understanding of Philo, there are three aspects which I would like to emphasise in particular.

Firstly Yli-Karjanmaa introduces a clear distinction between two kinds of allegory, protological and universal.[5] The former, protological allegory,

[4] Yli-Karjanmaa cites here David Winston, *Logos and Mystical Theology in Philo of Alexandria* (Cincinatti: Hebrew Union College Press, 1985), 42.
[5] Yli-Karjanmaa, *Reincarnation* 4–5, 35; cf. also "'Call Him Earth,'" 255. At *Reincarnation*, 5 n.10 he states that it is related to the distinction made between history and actualization in David T. Runia, *Philo on the Creation of the Cosmos According to Moses*, PACS 1 (Leiden: Brill, 2001), 333–34.

is related primarily to the creation account in Gen 1–3, so refers to events *in illo tempore*, to use Mircea Eliade's famous phrase. These happened at the beginning of time and in the early history of humankind, but still have a direct significance for human life through the recognition that the cosmos and the human beings in it owe their existence to God's creative activity and that human life is most often not conducted on earth in a way that corresponds to what God wishes it to be. The latter, universal allegory, denotes explanations of the biblical text in terms of how life is *in hoc tempore*, as human beings live and conduct their lives, whether on earth or potentially beyond it. This distinction is particularly relevant to the jump from the limited allegory at the end of *Opif.* and the commencement of full-blown allegory in *Leg.* Of course, as is now generally recognised, most of our editions and translations err in suggesting a continuity between these two works.[6] This involves crossing over from the Exposition of the Law to the Allegorical Commentary, which have long been recognised as being different, if sometimes overlapping, commentary series. It does not help that we appear to be missing an allegorical commentary on the first chapter of Genesis.[7] *Leg.* 1 certainly does seem to start *in medias res*, without any kind of introductory section. I vividly recall how disconcerting I found the first book of *Leg.* when I first started to read Philo. Yli-Karjanmaa's analyses do much to clarify the train of thought of the early books of the Allegorical commentary, where Philo regularly elaborates on foundational matters pertaining to the human make-up, but not from a protological viewpoint, even though he is commenting on the creation account.

Secondly Yli-Karjanmaa's research has improved our understanding of Philo's appropriation of the dialogues of Plato. The main relevant dialogues for his subject are the *Phaedo*, the *Phaedrus*, and the *Timaeus*. He rightly points out deficiencies in my treatment of the passages describing reincarnation in the *Timaeus*. For example, my treatment focused too much on the subject of the transmigration of human souls into animals.[8] For the

[6] See Abraham Terian, "Back to Creation: The Beginning of Philo's Third Grand Commentary," in *Wisdom and Logos: Studies in Jewish Thought in Honor of David Winston*, ed. David T. Runia and Gregory E. Sterling, BJS 312, SPhiloA 9 (Atlanta: Scholars Press), 19–36; James R. Royse, "The Works of Philo," *The Cambridge Companion to Philo*, ed. Adam Kamesar (Cambridge: Cambridge University Press), 46–47.

[7] As argued by Thomas Tobin, S.J., "The Beginning of Philo's *Legum Allegoriae*," *SPhiloA* 12 (2009): 29–43; Gregory E. Sterling, "'Prolific in Expression and Broad in Thought': Internal References to Philo's Allegorical Commentary and Exposition of the Law," *Euphrosyne* 40 (2012): 63–64.

[8] David T. Runia, *Philo of Alexandria and the Timaeus of Plato*, Philosophia Antiqua 44, 2nd ed. (Leiden: Brill, 1986), 260–66, 346–51; see Yli-Karjanmaa, *Reincarnation*, 20–25 and passim.

Phaedrus he usefully augments the research of Anita Méasson.[9] But for the *Phaedo* he is the first scholar to show in detail how extensive the use is that Philo makes of this seminal dialogue, far surpassing the unsatisfactory treatment in the dissertation of Billings published nearly a century ago.[10] For Philo the dialogue is fundamental in supplying language, imagery and thematics that describe the relation between the body and the soul, the journey of the soul, the nature of the philosophical life and the meaning of death for the soul.[11] Yli-Karjanmaa is right when he says that the relative importance of Plato's dialogues for Philo depends on the subject matter at hand. It might be fair to say, using the distinction between protological and universal accounts introduced above, that the *Timaeus* is the key dialogue for his explanation of the creation account and what happened *in illo tempore*, but that the *Phaedo* leads the way when Philo explores the life and journey of the soul once it has been created and resides in the material realm. When reading Philo's allegories in the Allegorical Commentary and in the *Quaestiones*, the presence of the *Phaedo* in the background must be constantly borne in mind.

The third advance that Yli-Karjanmaa's study makes to our knowledge flows on directly from the second. His research clearly demonstrates that Philo makes very considerable use of the language and conceptuality of the reincarnation of the soul in his allegory of the soul. This has never been previously shown in anything like the kind of detail that we find in his study. It appears in his use of technical terms such as παλιγγενησία and παλινδρομέω,[12] in the frequent language of descent, in the descriptions of the soul being bound to, imprisoned in or tainted by the body, in the imagery of immersion and drowning, in the conception of the death of the soul while in the body, and so on. This language and conceptuality describes a fundamental experience of the soul, i.e. what happens to it when it is corrupted by the association with the body, its sense-organs and its passions. To use Yli-Karjanmaa's terminology, it expresses the process of corporealization of the soul. It is also relevant to the life of the soul when it

---

[9] Anita Méasson, *Du char ailé de Zeus à l'Arche d'Alliance: Images et mythes platoniciens chez Philon d'Alexandrie* (Paris: Études Augustiniennes, 1986).

[10] Thomas H. Billings, *The Platonism of Philo Judaeus* (Chicago: University of Chicago Press, 1919).

[11] See now also David T. Runia, "La receptíon del *Fedón* de Platón en Filón de Alejandría (translated by M. Alesso)," *Circe de clásicos y modernos* 20 (2016): 91–112 (English version not yet published).

[12] For παλιγγενησία see *Cher.* 114, *Post.* 124, *Legat.* 325, discussed at Yli-Karjanmaa, *Reincarnation*, 163–166; παλινδρομέω *Post.* 156, *Somn.* 1.139, *QE* 2.40 etc., discussed at Yli-Karjanmaa, *Reincarnation*, 140, 252–54.

leaves the body behind or departs from the body, when it undergoes a process of purification, and when it ascends to the heavens or ultimately to God. These notions too are integral to Philo's allegory of the soul. They might be summarised under the term "decorporealization" of the soul, even if Yli-Karjanmaa does not express it in this way. In analysing Philo's use of the language and conceptuality of reincarnation he goes far beyond anything that has been achieved in Philonic research on this topic previously. It will prove indispensable for anyone working on Philo's allegorical system in the future.

3. *Is Reincarnation a Fundamental Part of Philo's Views on the Soul?*

The question before us now is whether we can follow Yli-Karjanmaa when he takes the decisive further step and claims that the doctrine of reincarnation, "was a fundamental part of Philo's views on the soul."[13] The doctrine can be formulated as follows. Originally the soul was created by God, placed in a body and endowed with mind to form the human being. There then took place an initial transgression *in illo tempore* caused by the corporeal environment that the human being found himself in.[14] As a consequence humanity enters a process which follows the six stages of the schema outlined above[15] involving incorporeal existence with God, incarnation, transgression, reincarnation, liberation and return to existence with God. Utilizing the distinction between protology and universal experience,[16] one can say that, when Philo speaks of God as creator in relation to humanity, he will sometimes be thinking of the original creation of Adam and Eve as the beginning of humanity, but his allegories most of the time are working with a history of the soul involving pre-existence, life in the body, post-existence and reincarnation in an unspecified number of iterations, before ending for some souls at least in an eschatological future with God. This cosmic history of the soul is seldom alluded to, but can be discerned in the background by the reader who knows his or her Plato and has been initiated into this esoteric knowledge in Philo's school. It will be agreed that the renewed focus on this neglected area of Philo's psychology

---

[13] Yli-Karjanmaa, "'Call Him Earth'," 259, summarizing the main argument of his dissertation.

[14] Yli-Karjanmaa rightly argues ("'Call Him Earth'," 260) that love of the body cannot be the original cause of the soul's incarnation. It must have been God's creative act.

[15] See above section 2.

[16] A legitimate extension of the earlier distinction between protological and universal allegory. See above section 2.

and anthropology, if Yli-Karjanmaa's thesis is accepted, has important consequences. It considerably strengthens the influence of Platonic philosophy on his thought, but aligns him with a minority of thinkers in the Jewish tradition. It separates him from Patristic authors that followed him, but perhaps not entirely in the case of the early Alexandrians Clement and Origen.[17]

I would wish to put forward an alternative interpretation, which recognizes the three important advances in our understanding of Philo that were outlined above, but takes them in a less radical direction. It is possible to argue, I submit, that Philo is *not committed* to the Pythagorean-Platonic doctrine of metempsychosis. By "committed" here I mean that for Philo it would be an essential component of how scripture should be interpreted on the fate of the soul after (and also before) death. I would argue instead that he uses its language and conceptuality to illustrate the journey and fate of the soul while it is joined with the body in the συναμφότερον that is the human being. The allegory of the soul focuses on the universal experience of the life of the soul in the body and its struggle to shake off the influences of the body which prevent it from living the good life and ascending to the divine. The decisive notion on which the allegory turns is that of orientation. The soul can orientate itself towards heaven and God or it can do so towards earth and the corporeal. Philo illustrates the former with descriptions of the ascent of the soul to the heavens, using imagery from the *Phaedrus*. The earth and the body are left behind and can even be gazed upon from above, but this experience need not take place only after physical death. It can take place while in the body but only after removing all traces of its negative influence. This is the kind of language that Philo uses of his own experience in the rare autobiographical passage *Spec.* 3.1–6.[18] In contrast the soul can also be dragged down to the earthly and corporeal realm by giving into the desires and passions associated with the body. This is the death of the soul while joined with the body,[19] dying to the life of virtue and suffering the penalty associated with the life of wickedness (equivalent to death in allegorical terms). This process can be

[17] See Yli-Karjanmaa, *Reincarnation* 249, the final lines of the book.

[18] On such experiences see now Gregory E. Sterling, "Dancing with the Stars: The Ascent of the Mind," in *Apocalypticism and Mysticism in Ancient Judaism and Early Christianity*, ed. John J. Collins, Pieter G. R. De Villiers, and Adela Yarbro Collins, Ekstasis. Religious Experience from Antiquity to the Middle Ages 7 (Berlin: de Gruyter, 2018), 155–66. Sterling does not, however, dwell on the conditions that allow such experiences to occur.

[19] *Leg.* 1.105–108, where at §106 Yli-Karjanmaa rightly interprets σύνοδος as "union" (*Reincarnation*, 57).

interpreted as occurring during human life in the physical sense of living on earth, but the language of entombment of the soul in the body as if in a grave, which in the Pythagorean-Platonic tradition refer to the trajectory of reincarnation, is used to illustrate it. It is a particularly vivid way of expressing the descent of the soul into a life of bodily passion and wickedness, in which the progression to a better life is thwarted. We might compare how in modern parlance, for example, we speak of people being caught in a downward spiral of drug addiction or crime. The language of ascent and descent uses a vertical metaphor, whereas the language of migration stays on a horizontal plane of journeying away from or turning back.[20] These are rich metaphors and the complex way that Philo weaves them into the tapestry of his allegorical exegesis is, to our knowledge at least, unmatched in antiquity.

It is an incontrovertible fact that in Philo's extant writings, he never makes an explicit pronouncement on the truth and validity of the doctrine of metempsychosis. It would not have been difficult for him to do so. As far as we know he never wrote anything like a systematic work of theology. At most one can point to a list of key doctrines at *Opif.* 170–172, but it is in fact quite limited, being confined to theology and cosmology and making no reference to mind or soul. Particularly valuable are corrective statements that he makes through an appeal to Mosaic scripture, as he does in the case of the Stoic doctrines of ἐκπύρωσις at *Her.* 228 or πνεῦμα as moving air at *Det.* 83. Of course we have to bear in mind that we may be missing such comments in works that are no longer extant, for example the lost books of the *Legum allegoriae.*[21]

Given the centrality of scriptural exegesis in Philo's understanding of his task as thinker and teacher, it can be pointed out that not only does he not tell us whether the doctrine of reincarnation is scriptural or not, but also that there were undoubted opportunities to base the doctrine on scriptural texts. A case in point is the text at Gen 3:19 when God is reported as saying to Adam "by the sweat of your brow you will eat your bread until returning to the earth from which you were taken, for you are earth and to earth you will turn back."[22] Of course a literal protological interpretation of the verse would not have been difficult. The words ἐξ ἧς ἐλήμφης can be taken to refer to the creation of the human body in Gen 2:7

---

[20] Of course they can be combined when there is emigration to heaven and God and migration back to or down to the corporeal or to Egypt.

[21] There appear to be two books (or long sections of a book) missing, covering the texts Gen 3:1b–8a and 3:20–23.

[22] NETS translation (modified). The LXX text is: ἐν ἱδρῶτι τοῦ προσώπου σου φάγῃ τὸν ἄρτον σου ἕως τοῦ ἀποστρέψαι σε εἰς τὴν γῆν, ἐξ ἧς ἐλήμφης· ὅτι γῆ εἶ καὶ εἰς γῆν ἀπελεύσῃ.

and the return to earth as the dissolving of the corpse into the elements, as appears to be indicated in *Leg.* 3.253 and *QG* 2.61. But in both the former passage and in *QG* 1.51, Philo also appears to give a universal interpretation about the corrupted man who undergoes 'spiritual death" (*QG* 1.51, Marcus's translation) or the foolish mind which turns away from the right principle (*Leg.* 3.252), so that beginning and end are one. Yli-Karjanmaa argues that both texts point to the six-stage model of the soul's fall and rise, and he thinks that the change to the future indicative in his paraphrase at *Leg.* 3.253 to μεχρὶ ἀποστρέψεις εἰς τὴν γῆν points to a translation "for as long as you return to earth" rather than "until" as in all existing translations, thereby hinting at the doctrine of reincarnation.[23] My point here is that the text could easily furnish Mosaic authority for the doctrine, but Philo does not take the opportunity to make this at all clear. Similarly the ladder in Jacob's dream could be used for the same purpose and maybe Philo does make this clear, depending on how we read the passage at *Somn.* 1.133–156, to which I will return shortly. Yli-Karjanmaa's explanation is that Philo is being deliberately reticent and writes for the discerning initiated reader. In my view a simpler reading is possible, whereby the text is taken in universal terms to refer to the foolish mind who devotes itself wholly to the earth, i.e. the body and its bodily concerns.

When I was rereading Yli-Karjanmaa's monograph for the purposes of this paper, there was a passage that struck me forcibly. It commences a section on "Afterlife and Salvation":[24]

> Explicit speculation on the hereafter is not one of Philo's main concerns. Termini's statement that Philo "spiritualizes the very notions of life and death, and minimizes the importance of physical death" is valid. In my view the background for this minimization lies in the view that the details of afterlife do not in themselves determine the way in which the life on earth should be lived. In his thought the orientation must in any case be away from the corporeal and towards the divine; this brings happiness, its opposite misery. This is sufficient for Philo to be able to justify his ethical standards.
>
> This is not, however, the entire picture, for the above does not mean that Philo had no concept of the after-life; nor does it follow that he had no view of what the misery resulting from body-oriented life leads to *post mortem*, nor that he was uninterested in these issues. But for some reason, when he expresses his thought of what follows the death of a "wicked" person, he usually does so quite sparingly and inexactly.

[23] Yli-Karjanmaa, *Reincarnation*, 76–78.
[24] Yli-Karjanmaa, *Reincarnation*, 81–82. The reference is to Cristina Termini, "Philo's Thought within the Context of Middle Judaism," in Kamesar, *Cambridge Companion*, 108.

I would argue that in his universal allegory, Philo indeed does not show any great interest in eschatological issues. The main focus is on the orientation of the soul while in the body, whether towards the corporeal and spiritual death or towards the incorporeal and spiritual life. Punishment (and perhaps even damnation) can occur in this life through what human beings do to themselves. Salvation similarly can start to occur during one's life through an orientation towards the divine. The language and conceptuality of metempsychosis taken over from the Pythagorean-Platonic tradition are powerful literary instruments in depicting these processes, but for Philo the doctrine itself is not essential. It is to be agreed that it would be going too far if we were to conclude that he had no views on the eschatological process. The question is how can we determine what they are if he is so vague about them.

4. *A Closer Look at Two Key Passages*

It will not be possible in the present context to examine all the magnificently explored detail of Yli-Karjanmaa's examination of allegorical passages. Particularly in his exposition of texts in the *Quaestiones* he breaks much new ground. Every scholar who makes a serious study of Philo's writings and thought must read his book. At this point I want to zoom in on two passages in the Allegorical Commentary which are important for his thesis and on which I have made pronouncements in the past.

The first is at *Agr.* 89, taken together with §169 and §174, located in a treatise on which Albert Geljon and I have written a commentary.[25] It is not one of the four passages in which Yli-Karjanmaa sees a direct reference to reincarnation. But when summarizing his treatment of those passages he claims that when read together with some other passages "we have all the reason to consider especially the *Agr.* passage as an allusion to reincarnation."[26]

The passage is part of the exegesis of a secondary lemma Deut 17:15b–16a in which Israel is told that it will not be able to establish a foreign ruler over itself "for the reason that he will not multiply for himself cavalry, nor will he return the people back to Egypt." We note that the verb translated

---

[25] Albert Geljon and David T. Runia, *Philo On Cultivation: Introduction, Translation and Commentary*, PACS 4 (Brill: Leiden, 2013). It is the first commentary on an allegorical treatise published in the Philo of Alexandria Commentary Series.

[26] Yli-Karjanmaa, *Reincarnation*, 213.

"return" here is ἀποστρέφω, the same verb used in the text on Adam in Gen 3:19 discussed above.[27] The text reads as follows:[28]

(§88) ... (the passage) is concerned ... with the irrational, uncontrolled and disobedient motion in the soul, which it will be advantageous to restrain, lest "it return all its people back to Egypt," the region of the body, and by force make it a lover of pleasure and passion rather than a lover of excellence and of God. For, as Moses himself has said, the one who has acquired a multitude of horses must necessarily make his way to Egypt. (§89) For whenever the soul, like a boat, is buffeted and slung, now to the one side of the intellect and now to the other side of sense-perception, by the violence of the passions and the evil deeds that blow over it and it is overwhelmed by the looming wave, then as is likely the intellect becomes waterlogged and drowns. The depths [βυθός] into which it sinks and drowns is the body that is likened to Egypt.

The text in Deuteronomy does not speak of being drowned in the depths, and as Yakir Paz already pointed out in a review of our commentary,[29] there is probably an allusion to Exod 15:5 which we missed, where the Egyptian horse and rider "sank to the depths like a stone," incidentally the only time in the Pentateuch that the word βυθός occurs.[30] Philo had given an exposition of this incident just before the present passage in §§79–83. A further mention of the ἔσχατος βυθός is found at §169 with reference to those had reached perfection but had believed that their improvement was due their own efforts and so disappeared into the "deepest abyss," while in §174 the metaphor of the boat is continued but there is no mention of sinking, only of not reaching the harbour.

In a note Yli-Karjanmaa draws attention to the fact that in our commentary on §89, we "do not comment on the issue of returning to the body."[31] Most certainly, if we were writing our commentary now, we would mention the possibility that in the final words of this passage Philo is hinting at the process of reincarnation, as proposed in his study. We might, however, still hesitate to take the passage as evidence that Philo himself was committed to the doctrine. In the context of the allegory the passage can be

---

[27] This link is, I think, not mentioned by Yli-Karjanmaa. The verb is common in the Pentateuch and Philo's treatment deserves further examination.

[28] My translation at Geljon and Runia, *Philo On Cultivation*, 60–61. Yli-Karjanmaa offers a partly different translation at *Reincarnation*, 182, but there are no essential divergences between the two, except perhaps that he translates βυθός with "bottom." The NETS translation reads "into the deep."

[29] Yakir Paz, Review of *Philo On Cultivation* by A. C. Geljon and D. T. Runia, *Bryn Mawr Classical Review* (2013): no. 10.61.

[30] It also occurs only once in Plato's works in a literary expression ("abyss of nonsense") at *Parm.* 130d7.

[31] Yli-Karjanmaa, *Reincarnation*, 183 n. 587.

taken to refer to a severe setback that the soul experiences when over-whelmed by the force of passion, interpreted as sinking back into the body's sphere of influence. One might compare the exegesis of the "return to Egypt" in Num 4:14 at *Leg.* 3.175 (where the return is to "passion") and especially at *Post.* 156, where the return is to "the shelter of a dissolute and licentious life" and this might have happened if the saviour had not thrown into the soul a "sweetening tree" (cf. Exod 15:25) which produced a love of hard work (φιλοπονία) rather than a hatred of it. Yli-Karjanmaa argues that the reference to βυθός in §89 (and also §169) becomes clearer as a reference to reincarnation in the body when read together with texts such as *QG* 4.234 and *QE* 2.40.[32] One may legitimately ask whether the reader of the treatise is meant to make this link. Is this the way that Philo's allegorical method works? If the *Quaestiones* are to be regarded as preliminary notes for composing exegetical treatises or a repository of exegetical themes,[33] does this mean that the readers of the allegorical commentary are assumed to have the contents of that work at the back of their minds? Or should one appeal to teaching that Philo might have carried out in a school setting?[34]

On the other hand, I believe that Yli-Karjanmaa's interpretation of the three passages in *Agr.* that they indicate progress on the part of the soul is illuminating and gives us insight into Philo's intentions when composing the allegorical structure.[35] §89 is located in the first part of the treatise, in which there is an antithesis between Noah the cultivator who is on the path to being a sage and workers of the earth focused on the body and its passions. The other two texts, §§167 and 174, are located in the treatise's second part, in which Noah is interpreted as a beginner who makes pro-gress on the path of perfection. It is to be agreed that the two later passages are meant to be linked up with the earlier one. Philo uses language and imagery that in other contexts could be taken to refer to the soul departing from and returning to the body, but can equally be taken as imagery

---

[32] Yli-Karjanmaa, *Reincarnation*, 69, 83, 181. Note that the main discussion of *Agr.* 89 is part of his interpretation of *QE* 2.40 and its reference to Tartarus as direct evidence of Philo's endorsement of the doctrine.

[33] Cf. Runia, *Philo of Alexandria*, 381; Gregory E. Sterling, 'Philo's *Quaestiones*: Prolegomena or Afterthought?,' in *Both Literal and Allegorical: Studies in Philo of Alexandria's Questions and Answers on Genesis and Exodus*, ed. David M. Hay, BJS 232 (Atlanta: Scholars Press, 1991), 122.

[34] See Gregory E. Sterling, "Philo's School: The Social Setting of Ancient Commen-taries," in *Sophisten in Hellenismus und Kaiserzeit: Orte, Methoden und Personen der Bildungs-vermittlung*, ed. Beatrice Wyss, Rainier Hirsch-Luipold, and Solmeng-Jonas Hirschi, STAC 101 (Tübingen: Mohr Siebeck, 2017), 123–42.

[35] On the treatise's structure see Geljon and Runia, *Philo On Cultivation*, 10–16.

illustrating the death of the soul to virtue or a setback on the path to the ultimate goal.

In our commentary on §89 Geljon and I drew attention to the possible background of the allegorization of the nautical adventures of Odysseus in Homer's *Odyssey* in terms of the quest of the soul for virtue and perfection. Unfortunately references to such allegorical themes are scattered, both in Philo and elsewhere, and they have to my knowledge never been systematically collected.[36] The only extant example of the allegorization of a substantial piece of the text of the Odyssey is Porphyry's essay *De antro nympharum*, based at least in part on earlier interpretation by Numenius. Reincarnation figures prominently in the exegesis. Porphyry outlines (§11) various kinds of souls, including those who drag a body with them and become embodied through an attraction to moisture. The nymphs in *Od.* 13.104 for whom the cave is a sacred place are then identified as "souls proceeding to becoming" (αἱ εἰς τὴν γένεσιν ἰοῦσαι ψυχαί, §12). Both Porphyry and Numenius are much later than Philo, but there are already references to allegorization of themes from Odysseus's travels in Cicero, as pointed out by Boyancé,[37] so the method in fact precedes Philo. It is thus possible though as yet unproven that the covert references to reincarnation that Yli-Karjanmaa discovers in the texts in *Agr.* make use of language and themes used in this Greek allegorical tradition.

I turn now to the second passage at *Somn.* 1.137–139. As Yli-Karjanmaa states, this text is the *locus classicus* for the view that Philo espoused the doctrine of reincarnation. It is part of a long section of text interpreting the ladder in Jacob's dream in Gen 28:12. In giving a typology of souls which ascend and descend in the air, Philo includes a category which, "longing for the familiar and accustomed ways of mortal life, hurry back again"[38] and by implication return to the body. Philo uses the verb παλινδρομέω here. As was noted earlier,[39] it appears to be a technical term for the process of moving back from the higher to the lower and from the incorporeal to the

[36] In addition to the references given at Geljon and Runia, *Philo On Cultivation*, 182, see also Pierre Boyancé, "Études Philoniennes," *REG* 76 (1963): 67–79; Robert Lamberton, "The Neoplatonists and the Spiritualization of Homer," in *Homer's Ancient Readers: The Hermeneutics of Greek Epic's Earliest Exegetes*, ed. Robert Lamberton and John J. Keaney (Princeton: Princeton University Press, 1992), 115–33.

[37] Boyancé, "Études," 73. Note also the interpretation of the transformation of Odysseus's men into swine at *Od.* 10.239–240 in terms of reincarnation at Plutarch fr. 200 Sandbach (probably erroneously attributed to Porphyry by Stobaeus).

[38] Yli-Karjanmaa's translation at *Reincarnation*, 131.

[39] See above at n. 12.

corporeal.[40] In my dissertation I noted this text and stated that Philo appeared not to have "fully integrated" the doctrine it alludes to in his thought. Yli-Karjanmaa is rightly critical of my treatment of the question, which was indeed superficial and apodictic to a fault.[41] Nevertheless I would persist in saying that there are puzzling aspects to this text, not in what it says, but in how it is used.

The passage in *Somn.* is one of four in which Philo sets out a cosmological interpretation of the angels which play such a prominent role in the Pentateuch.[42] In each case there is reference to incorporeal souls which range through the air (and heaven in *Conf.* 176). Only in *Somn.* is there an explicit reference to reincarnation. There seem to me to be two difficulties. Firstly it is difficult to give a reason why the return of the souls to bodies is mentioned in only one of the passages and not in the others. Secondly, no exegetical application is made of the detail of the return of the souls who are lovers of the body (φιλοσώματοι).[43] In each of these passages Philo is focused on explaining the references to angels in the biblical texts in terms of incorporeal souls and by comparing them with the role of δαίμονες in Greek philosophy. Yli-Karjanmaa persuasively suggests this might be a theme that was "part of a Hellenistic *Jewish* tradition."[44] After quoting the biblical text in Gen 28:12 Philo gives no less than four explanations of what the "ladder" symbolises (§§134–156). The first of these (§§134–145) is cosmological and identified with the air. Philo explains how the air is full of souls and how these ascend and descend. The verbs in §138 κατίασαν and ἀνέρχονται are patently inspired by the biblical text which speaks of the angels who ascend and descend (ἀνέβαινον καὶ κατέβαινον), though the order has been reversed). When Philo applies the explanation in §142 he cites these words again and explains how they apply to the angels as messengers of God. The ladder is then also taken to symbolise the soul (§§146–149), the life of the practiser (§§150–152) and the affairs of human beings (§§153–156). As Anne Boiché has recently shown,[45] this is an example of how Philo

---

[40] Yli-Karjanmaa, *Reincarnation*, 140, 251–54; noted earlier by Jaap Mansfeld, "Heraclitus, Empedocles, and Others in a Middle Platonist Cento in Philo of Alexandria," *VC* 39 (1985): 144.

[41] Yli-Karjanmaa, *Reincarnation*, 144, referring to Runia, *Philo of* Alexandri,a 348.

[42] See the useful table at Yli-Karjanmaa, *Reincarnation*, 145, which does not however contain all the common elements. As he notes in n. 460, a passage in *QG* 4.188 also refers to the interpretation of "angels" without all the cosmological details. On these texts see also Runia, *Philo of Alexandria*, 228–\29.

[43] A Platonic term, used uniquely in his corpus at *Phd.* 68c1.

[44] Yli-Karjanmaa, *Reincarnation*, 145 n. 461 (his emphasis).

[45] Anne Boiché, *L'écriture de l'exégèse dans le* De somniis *de Philon d'Alexandrie* (diss. Sorbonne, Paris 2018), 273.

sometimes piles up multiple explanations of the same text, the one not excluding the other but rather enriching the understanding of the text. In the first explanation there is certainly a reference to the reincarnation of certain souls (not explicitly identified), but exegetically nothing is done with this detail. It is not applied to human life, since the biblical text is speaking about angels. Human beings come into the picture in relation to the angels' role as messengers from and to God.

Yli-Karjanmaa argues that "with regard to *Somn.* 1.134–151 and its parallels, I think that simply copying but not really digesting what he had copied would not fit well the kind of thinker Philo was, one who paid so much attention to textual detail in the Bible."[46] Most certainly Philo is a careful reader of the biblical text. The references to the verbs in Gen 28:12 that we just noted is a small case in point. But his exegeses generally focus on specific and detailed aspects of the text or questions raised by it, once again as in the case just discussed. In addition, it is also a feature of Philo's exegesis that he sometimes cites extensive slabs of philosophical material in order to illustrate or give background for biblical exposition. Two very striking cases are found at *Opif.* 89–128 (the long exposition of arithmological material on the hebdomad) and *Ebr.* 167–202 (the sceptical tropes), but there are many others.[47] This means that some aspects of this illustratory material are more relevant to Philo's purpose than others. This is how I took the undoubted reference to the process of reincarnation in this particular passage.

6. Concluding Remarks

There is much that we cannot be certain about when we have to determine Philo's views on the Greek religious and philosophical doctrine of reincarnation and decide whether he regarded it as a fundamental part of Mosaic thought. We do not have all the texts that Philo wrote. He may have indicated more clearly his views on reincarnation, whether positively or negatively in a treatise now lost.[48] A single critical remark like the one about ἐκπύρωσις in *Her.* 228 or a positive application linked to a biblical text would have put the matter beyond doubt. As already noted,[49] we do not

---

[46] Yli-Karjanmaa, *Reincarnation*, 144.
[47] For example the copious explanation of the function of division in *Agr.* 131–145.
[48] The fragment that Yli-Karjanmaa analyses in depth at *Reincarnation* 186–212 is most likely from the lost Book 4 of *Leg.* Given the lack of context, a full interpretation of the fragment's seemingly positive reference to reincarnation is not possible.
[49] See above n. 44 and text thereto.

really know enough about Alexandrian Judaism to be able to determine
whether it had groups of thinkers who were an exception to the general
rule that the doctrine of reincarnation was "essentially alien to Jewish
tradition."[50] It would also be helpful to know a lot more about the role that
reincarnation played in Greek philosophical allegories, for example of the
wanderings of Odysseus.[51] Above all, it is difficult to determine which
doctrines are regarded as essential for an understanding of the deeper
meaning of scripture which the allegorical method of interpretation laid
bare. Philo never wrote a work comparable to the Περὶ ἀρχῶν of Origen,
which aims to present the "rule of faith" containing the key doctrines
handed down from the apostles, among which is the resurrection of the
body, but not the reincarnation of the soul.[52]

But we have to work with the texts that we have. These reveal, in my
view, that Philo was not committed to the doctrine of reincarnation, the
reason being that it was not essential for what he was trying to achieve in
his allegorical interpretations. At most its language might illustrate the
process whereby the incarnate soul becomes "corporealized"—to use Yli-
Karjanmaa's very useful term—when it comes under the baleful influence
of the body, its senses and its passions. Philo had many opportunities to be
more explicit about this doctrine if he was committed to it in his role as
exegete, but he did not make use of them. It is of course possible that he
was being deliberately secretive, as Yli-Karjanmaa argues,[53] but I am (as
yet) not convinced.

In the end the answer we give to the question posed by the title of this
paper turns on how we think we should read Philo. Do we need to connect
some of the dots that he leaves scattered throughout his writings, bearing
in mind that we do not have them all (though what we do have is quite
copious)?[54] This is certainly the way that he himself reads Mosaic scripture,
which he regards as forming a coherent whole, but one that is not immediately accessible in all the riches of its meaning. Yli-Karjanmaa argues that
Philo must have regarded the Bible as a "model for his lack of explicit-

---

[50] Winston's phrase cited by Yli-Karjanmaa as noted above in n. 4. The most striking
exception is the use of the doctrine in the Kabbalistic tradition, where it is invoked as a
punishment for sin.

[51] See above n. 36 and text thereto.

[52] An expansion of the δόγματα εὐσεβείας καὶ ὁσιότητος set out in Opif. 170–172 would
have been a good start. Origen accepts the ἐνσωμάτωσις of pre-existent intellects, but not the
μετενσωμάτωσις of human souls.

[53] Yli-Karjanmaa, Reincarnation, 247 concludes: "These considerations favor the
possibility that reincarnation was for Philo an esoteric teaching."

[54] As argued by Yli-Karjanmaa, Reincarnation, xi.

ness."[55] In a sense his method is a return to a more dogmatic reading of Philo, though done with a much greater sensitivity to genre and context. The alternative is that we adhere to the view that Philo regards himself as an interpreter and even a servant of scripture, unfolding its hidden meaning to the best of his ability and especially as it relates to the moral and spiritual life of his readers. For this purpose the doctrines of Greek philosophy give valuable assistance, but ultimately they are only acceptable if they derive their authority from scripture, taking into account how it can and should be interpreted. Philo's method entails that his thought will always remain to some degree obscured and enigmatic. The discussions on how we should read him will long continue. Sami Yli-Karjanmaa has made a very substantial contribution to these discussions and all Philonists should be very grateful to him.

The University of Melbourne
Australian Catholic University

---

[55] Yli-Karjanmaa, *Reincarnation*, 246.

The Studia Philonica Annual 31 (2019): 127–161

THE EXPRESSIVE PREPUCE:
PHILO'S DEFENSE OF JUDAIC CIRCUMCISION IN GREEK AND ROMAN CONTEXTS*

THOMAS R. BLANTON IV

As it has been thoroughly documented in a number of works, from Menahem Stern's monumental *Greek and Latin Authors on Jews and Judaism*, first published in 1974, to Andreas Blaschke's exhaustive treatment in *Beschneidung: Zeugnisse der Bibel und verwandter Texte* (1998) and Simon Claude Mimouni's *La circoncision dans le monde judéen aux époques grecque et romaine* (2007), the history of circumcision as portrayed in Greco-Roman literary sources commenting on Jews and in Jewish literature itself is well known.[1] What is not frequently brought into discussions of Jewish circumcision, however, is the wealth of evidence from Greek art and comedy and Roman visual humor, where we discover elaborate systems of signification attached to the phallus, and more specifically, to the prepuce and exposed

---

* Earlier versions of this paper were presented in a public lecture at the University of Fribourg on Oct. 11, 2018, and at the "Abraham as Ritual Model" workshop held at the Kleine Synagoge under the auspices of the Max-Weber-Kolleg für kultur- und sozialwissenschaftliche Studien, University of Erfurt, on Dec. 17, 2018. My gratitude goes to Sandra Jaeggi and Philippe Guillaume for organizing the public lecture, to Philippe for his kind hospitality after the lecture, and to Claudia Bergmann, with whom I organized the workshop in Erfurt. Much of the research for this paper was completed as a fellow in the Research Centre "Dynamics of Jewish Ritual Practices in Pluralistic Contexts from Antiquity to the Present" at the University of Erfurt from July through December, 2018. Thanks, too, to Jan Bremmer for offering helpful criticism of an earlier draft of this paper; and to Troy Martin for sharing with me material related to his paper "Christianity and Conflicting Cultural Conceptions Concerning Circumcision," presented at the 2015 Society of Biblical Literature Annual Meeting in Atlanta on Nov. 22, 2015. Lastly I thank Greg Sterling and an anonymous reader for offering helpful criticism and alerting me to several errors that stood in need of correction in the text.

[1] Menahem Stern, *Greek and Latin Authors on Jews and Judaism*, 3 vols., Fontes ad res Judaicas spectantes (Jerusalem: Israel Academy of Arts and Sciences, 1974); Andreas Blaschke, *Beschneidung: Zeugnisse der Bibel und verwandter Texte*, TANZ 28 (Tübingen: Francke, 1998); Simon Claude Mimouni, *La circoncision dans le monde judéen aux époques grecque et romaine: Histoire d'un conflit interne au judaïsme*, Collection de la Revue des Études juives (Leuven: Peeters, 2007).

glans of the phallus. The visual material both confirms perceptions evident in the literary material—for example, the association of circumcision with the "barbaric" customs of non-Greeks—and introduces relevant information not evident in the literary sources.

Perhaps due to an academic division of labor between art historians and specialists in textual analysis, when discussing circumcision, scholars of the Hebrew Bible, early Judaism, and early Christianity tend to overlook artistic material, focusing solely on the analysis of relevant Judaic, Christian, and Greco-Roman texts—an approach followed in the foundational studies of Stern, Blaschke, and Mimouni, for example. It is probably not coincidental that the most significant exception to this trend occurs in an article penned by neither an art historian nor a scholar of ancient Judaism, but a historian of medicine, Frederick Mansfield Hodges. In a seminal article, Hodges shows how "Greeks valued the longer prepuce and pathologized the penis characterized by a deficient prepuce—especially one that had been surgically ablated" through circumcision.[2] Although Hodges's insights have been developed in a series of articles by Robert G. Hall, the wealth of information provided by Greek and Roman art and statuary remains underexploited and largely neglected in studies of circumcision in the Hebrew Bible, early Judaism, and early Christianity.[3]

Despite the significance of Hodges's work to the study of early Judaism, however, he seems overly harsh in his treatment of Judaic sources. One may speculate that this harsh treatment is colored by his opposition to the practice of circumcision on medical, aesthetic, and human rights grounds, unfamiliarity with the Judaic sources, or both.[4] Hodges

---

[2] Frederick Mansfield Hodges, "The Ideal Prepuce in Ancient Greece and Rome: Male Genital Aesthetics and Their Relation to *Lipodermos*, Circumcision, Foreskin Restoration, and the *Kynodesmē*," *Bulletin of the History of Medicine* 75 (2001): 375.

[3] Robert G. Hall, "Epispasm and the Dating of Ancient Jewish Writings," *JSP* 2 (1988): 71–86; Hall, "Circumcision," *ABD* 1:1025–31; Hall, "Epispasm: Circumcision in Reverse," *Bible Review* 8.4 (1992): 52–57. Troy W. Martin ("Paul and Circumcision," in *Paul in the Greco-Roman World: A Handbook*, ed. J. Paul Sampley, 2nd ed., 2 vols. [London: T&T Clark, 2016], 1:113–31) also recognizes the importance of the artistic material for Judaic and early Christian studies, largely depending on Dover and Hodges.

[4] Hodges notes a broader trend in European medicine in which there is an "increasing move towards establishing … tissue-preserving surgeries that, like their classical antecedents, are focused on treating underlying pathology, maintaining foreskin function, and preserving natural cosmesis" (Frederick Mansfield Hodges, "Phimosis in Antiquity," *World Journal of Urology* 17.3 [1999]: 136). One may note that ritual circumcision treats no pathology, is not tissue-preserving, eradicates foreskin function, and does not preserve natural cosmesis, and thus runs directly counter to the medical trend that Hodges describes. Moreover, Hodges utilizes a framework of human rights: "Simply stated, every human has the right to keep every body part with which he or she was born" (George C.

comments, for example, that Philo of Alexandria's "dismissal of opposition to circumcision as 'childish mockery' betrays his failure to understand the philosophical and aesthetic underpinnings of the Greeks' high regard for the cultivation of physical health and beauty."[5] This brief study has two goals: First, it seeks to reiterate Hodges's fundamental but underappreciated insight that Greco-Roman artistic depictions are highly relevant to the understanding of Judaic circumcision during the Greco-Roman period; to this end, we examine some of the material that Hodges took into account and supplement it with additional, Roman material that he did not consider. Second, even while supporting and supplementing Hodges's argument in some respects, this study seeks to establish that contrary to Hodges's view, Philo was thoroughly cognizant of the "philosophical and aesthetic underpinnings" of both Greek and Roman attitudes toward circumcision, and in fact incorporated Greco-Roman philosophical, ethical, medical, and geographical reasoning into his defense of the ritual practice.

The Phallus and Its Symbolism in Greece and Rome

Like the eye, hair, and skin, the phallus was a part of the human body that acquired a wide array of symbolic associations in antiquity: it could connote beauty or ugliness, civilization or barbarism; it could be viewed as protective or threatening; it was frequently associated with production and fertility, and, of course, with sex. In what Larissa Bonfante has argued was a seventh-century-BCE cultural innovation associated with the "athletic nudity" exemplified both by ephebes exercising in the gymnasium and hoplites training for war, the Greeks often portrayed the male body

---

Denniston, Frederick M. Hodges, and Marilyn Fayre Milos, preface to *Genital Cutting: Protecting Children from Medical, Cultural, and Religious Infringements: Proceedings of the 11th International Symposium on Circumcision, Genital Integrity, and Human Rights, 29–31 July 2010, University of California–Berkeley* [London: Springer, 2013]). See also the prefaces to *Genital Autonomy: Protecting Personal Choice,* ed. George C. Denniston, Frederick M. Hodges, and Marilyn Fayre Milos (London: Springer, 2010), and *Circumcision and Human Rights,* ed. George C. Denniston, Frederick M. Hodges, and Marilyn Fayre Milos (London: Springer, 2009). Relevant to the question of Hodges's familiarity with Judaism, the medical historian seems to confuse Josephus with Philo when he refers to the former as an "Alexandrine" (Hodges, "Ideal Prepuce," 403). It is worth noting that my intention in this article is not to comment on whether or not circumcision ought to be practiced in contemporary societies, but better to understand the positions espoused by one ancient Judaic writer, Philo of Alexandria, in a situation of cultural complexity and contestation.

[5] Hodges, "Ideal Prepuce," 387.

unclothed.⁶ Classicist Kenneth Dover demonstrated that the Greek aesthetic ideal prized the youthful, athletic male body possessed of a small penis whose glans was amply covered by a long, tapering foreskin, or prepuce.⁷

As Hodges points out, the Greek beauty ideal that required the *glans penis* to be amply covered by a long, tapering foreskin is evident, for example, in the depiction of the binding of Patroclus's wound by Achilles on a vase attributed to the Sosias painter, who was active around 510 to 490 BCE.⁸ The younger, beardless Achilles wraps a bandage around the left arm of the older, bearded Patroclus, whose arm had evidently been pierced by the arrow pictured resting at an angle just below his right shin.⁹ Patroclus's *akroposthion*, the Greek term designating the portion of the prepuce that extends beyond the tip of the glans, is shown elegantly draped over his right ankle.

Figure 1. Achilles binds the wound of Patroklus (Source: "Akhilleus Patroklos Antikensammlung Berlin F2278 resized solid black bg.png," Wikimedia Commons. Image in the public domain under the Creative Commons CC0 1.0 Universal Public Domain license.)

⁶ Larissa Bonfante, "Nudity as a Costume in Classical Art," *American Journal of Archaeology* 93 (1989): 543–70.

⁷ Kenneth J. Dover, *Greek Homosexuality* (Cambridge: Harvard University Press, 1977).

⁸ Hodges, "Ideal Prepuce," 376.

⁹ Homer depicts Patroclus as being older than and a mentor to Achilles (*Il.* 11.785–789).

Like that of the wounded warrior Patroclus, the glans of the idealized male form of what is a Greek god, most likely Zeus, is entirely covered by the prepuce in the bronze statue found off Cape Artemision and dated around 460 BCE.[10] The god stands poised to hurl a lightning bolt, or perhaps a trident if, as some scholars have argued, the figure represents Poseidon.[11] The projectile, whether lightning bolt or trident, is now lost.

Figure 2. Artemision Bronze Zeus (or Poseideon). (Source: "Zeus [or Poseidon] of Cape Artemision," National Archaeological Museum of Athens. Image (X 15161) courtesy of National Archaeological Museum, Athens. © Hellenic Ministry of Culture and Sports / Archaeological Receipts Fund.)

Like the Greeks of the sixth and fifth century BCE, Romans half a millennium later understood the prepuce as a significant feature of the ideal male form. The Greek physician Galen, working in the second half of the second century, for example, lists the prepuce among the most splendid of nature's means of adorning the human body:

> Nature out of her abundance ornaments all the members, especially in man. In many parts there is manifest ornamentation, though at times this is obscured by the brilliance of their usefulness. The ears show obvious ornamentation, and so, I suppose, does the skin called the prepuce [πόσθη] at the end of the penis and the flesh of the buttocks.[12]

---

[10] Discussed in William R. Biers, *The Archaeology of Greece: An Introduction*, 2nd ed. (Ithaca: Cornell University Press, 1996), 215–16; and briefly described by Hodges ("Ideal Prepuce," 377 n. 6).

[11] See *Thespiades-Zodiacus et supplementum Abila-Thersites*, vol. 8.2 of *Lexicon Iconographicum Mythologiae Classicae (LIMC)*, ed. Fondation pour le lexicon iconographicum mythologiae classicae (Zurich: Artemis, 1997), 353: "Poseidon 28"; 452: B28.

[12] Galen, *De usu partium corporis humani* 11.13; cited in Hodges, "Ideal Prepuce," 376.

In contrast, the partially exposed glans of the penis, deficient or lacking with respect to the prepuce, could be depicted by Greeks and Romans to indicate the foreign, and therefore barbaric, "other." According to Herodotus, Colchians (from the eastern shore of the Black Sea, in present-day Georgia), Egyptians, Phoenicians, Syro-Palestinians, and Ethiopians practiced circumcision; although, he indicates, some Phoenicians abandoned the practice under Greek influence (*Histories* 2.104.2–4). An Attic red-figure amphora attributed to the Pan painter around 470 BCE depicts Herakles defeating the Egyptian King Busiris and his priests. The vase recalls a story otherwise attested by Isocrates (*Busiris* 31, 36–37) in which the Egyptian king, rather than welcoming strangers with hospitality, instead sacrificed them to the gods of Egypt. Herakles, outraged by such inhospitable treatment, killed Busiris and his entourage. As Hodges notes:

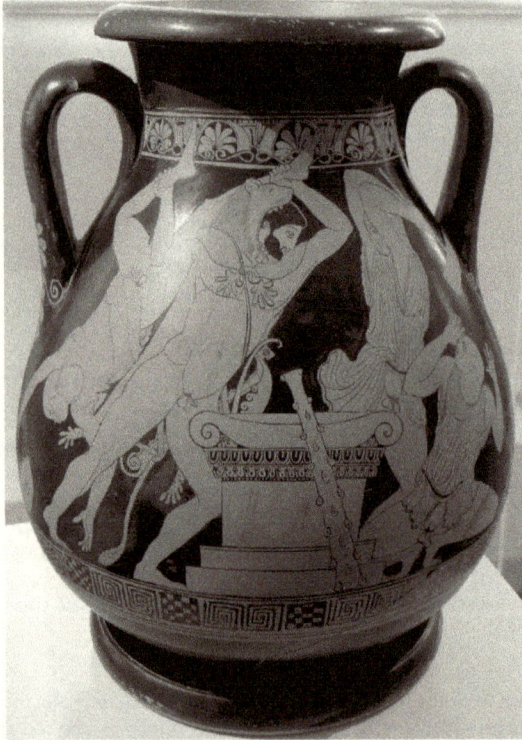

Figure 3. Herakles defeats the Egyptian king, Busiris, and his priests (Source: "Herakles fighting Busiris; Attic red-figure pelike [wine-holding vessel]," Wikimedia Commons, photo by Marsyas, Dec. 22, 2005. Image licensed under the Creative Commons Attribution-Share Alike 2.5 Generic license.)

The painter has taken great pains to depict the priests as having fat, ugly, wrinkled, circumcised penises with a bulbous externalized glans, which contrast sharply with the neat and attractive penis of Herakles, with its elegantly long and tapered prepuce. Likewise, the snubbed noses and monkey-like faces of the Egyptians could hardly be more dissimilar to the heroic Greek profile of Herakles.[13]

An array of cultural significations is displayed in the image: the superiority of Greek culture over Egyptian (symbolized by the triumphant Herakles); Greek hospitality juxtaposed to imagined Egyptian inhospitality; the prominent, aquiline nose of Herakles juxtaposed to the small, snubbed noses of the Egyptians; and, more importantly, Herakles's small, thin penis adorned with an ample *akroposthion* juxtaposed to the larger, thick phalluses of the Egyptians, with glandes indecently exposed. The prepuce bears an array of significations that, interacting with signals associated with other body parts as well as the legendary narrative depicted, signal to Greek onlookers the superiority of their own culture over that of the barbaric Egyptians.[14]

One encounters another of the groups listed by Herodotus as practicing circumcision in a much later image from the Roman Period in the House of Menander at Pompeii, on a mosaic tiled between 40 and 20 BCE.[15] On the floor at the entrance leading to the *caldarium*, a room for hot baths, was the mosaic image of, appropriately, a bath attendant—in this case an Ethiopian slave, depicted as an ethnic "other" with very dark skin, large phallus, and exposed glans. Both Andrew Clarke and Claudia Moser have plausibly interpreted the figure as an apotropaic symbol, meant to ward off the evil eye of envy, which was believed to exert ill effects, both magical and social, against the one on whom a malevolent gaze fell.[16] It was understood that the best remedy for the evil eye was to avert the gaze by drawing the attention of the onlooker toward a fixed comic image; comedy dissipates

---

[13] Hodges, "Ideal Prepuce," 385–86.

[14] For a different image apparently signaling the superiority of Greek culture over the barbarian "other," see the picture of an Attic red-figure vase that has been interpreted as a Greek man, erect phallus in hand, running toward a sexually submissive Persian male, apparently to sodomize him; the latter figure is accompanied by the caption "I am bend-over"; so Dover, *Greek Homosexuality*, 105. G. Ferrari Pinney ("For the Heroes Are at Hand," *Journal of Hellenic Studies* 104 [1984]: 181–83, with plate), on the other hand, interprets the scene as a parodic depiction of the epic figure Eurymedon and his Scythian squire.

[15] John R. Clarke, *Looking at Lovemaking: Construction of Roman Sexuality in Roman Art, 100 B.C.–A.D. 250* (Berkeley: University of California Press, 1998), 129.

[16] Clarke, *Looking at Lovemaking*; Claudia Moser, "Naked Power: The Phallus as an Apotropaic Symbol in the Images and Texts of Roman Italy," Undergraduate Humanities Forum 2005–2006: Word & Image, https://repository.upenn.edu/uhf_2006/11/, 47–48.

envy and malice by evoking laughter.[17] Clarke notes that the Ethiopian's "un-Roman body type caused laughter—all the more so when he had an enormous phallus."[18] We may add that the comedic value of the image is enhanced by the slave's indecorously exposed glans—a point to which we will return. In the mosaic, the *glans penis* is colored with purple tesserae, emphasizing its exposure.[19]

Figure 4. Ethiopian bath attendant with large phallus and exposed glans; House of the Mendander, Pompeii (Source: "Pompeii - House of Menander - Caldarium - Mosaic 1.jpg," Wikimedia Commons. Image in the public domain under the CC0 1.0 Universal Public Domain license.)

In addition to characterizing the non-Greek or non-Roman barbarian or slave, categories that overlap in the mosaic from Pompeii depicting the Ethiopian bath attendant, the large phallus with exposed glans was a stock

---

[17] See, for example, Clarke, *Looking at Lovemaking*, 131.

[18] Clarke, *Looking at Lovemaking*, 131; also cited in Moser, *Phallus as Apotropaic Symbol*, 48.

[19] According to Clarke, *Looking at Lovemaking*, 133.

image in Greek comedy.[20] This is evident in a list of comic motifs enumerated by Aristophanes, who ironically likens his own comedies to a modest
young woman:[21]

> Look how naturally decent she is: first of all, she hasn't come with any
> dangling leathern phallus [σκύτινον] stitched to her, red at the tip [ἐρυθὸν ἐξ
> ἄκρου] and thick, for the boys a cause for laughter [τοῖς παιδίοις ἵν᾽ ᾖ γέλως]; nor
> does she mock bald men, nor dance the *kordax*; nor does an old man, while
> speaking his lines, cover up bad jokes by beating the interlocutor with his stick.
> (*Clouds* 537–42; trans. Henderson, LCL, modified)[22]

Aristophanes makes reference to one of the props deployed in Old
Comedy, the large, thick, leathern phallus, exposed glans painted red, that
was stitched to leotards worn by comic actors.[23] The phallus prop is
designated by the term σκύτινον, a substantive formed from the adjective
meaning "leathern," which in this passage refers to a "leathern phallus," as
the *Greek-English Lexicon* of Liddell and Scott makes clear.[24] The sight of the
red, exposed glans "at the tip" (ἐξ ἄκρου) of the phallus is described as a
"cause for laughter" (γέλως). We can see this comic prop depicted in a red
figure bell krater attributed to the McDaniel painter from Puglia, Italy,
around 380 to 370 BCE. The painting depicts a scene from South Italian
comedy that parodies the mythic association of the centaur Chiron with
Apollo and the healing art.[25]

---

[20] Timothy J. McNiven, "The Unheroic Penis: Otherness Exposed," *SOURCE: Notes in
the History of Art* 15 (1995): 10–16, shows that in Greek art the large phallus is associated
with the elderly, slaves, manual laborers, those guilty of hubris, foreigners, and drunk-
ards.

[21] The irony of the passage becomes clear when one recognizes that Aristophanes
uses most of the stock motifs in his own comedies; see Laura M. Stone, *Costume in
Aristophanic Comedy*, Monographs in Classical Studies (Salem, NH: Ayer, 1984).

[22] Aristophanes, *Clouds; Wasps; Peace*, ed. and trans. Jeffrey Henderson, LCL
(Cambridge: Harvard University Press, 1998).

[23] On the use of the phallus prop in Greek comedy, see Laura M. Stone, *Costume in
Aristophanic Comedy*, Monographs in Classical Studies (Salem, NH: Ayer, 1984), 72–126;
Gwendolyn Compton-Engle, *Costume in the Comedies of Aristophanes* (Cambridge: Cam-
bridge University Press, 2015), 24–25.

[24] LSJ, s.v. σκύτινος.

[25] Xenophon, *Cynegeticus* 1.1–6; Philostratus, *Heroicus* 33.1–2; Pindar, *Pythian Odes*,
3.1–7. For the identification of the characters and scene depicted in the painting, see
"Pottery: Red-figured Bell-krater Showing a Scene from South Italian Comedy," Collection
Online, The British Museum, https://www.britishmuseum.org/research/collection_
online/collection_object_details.aspx?assetId=6123003&objectId=463873&partId=1,   ©
Trustees of the British Museum.

Figure 5. Scene from South Italian comedy; underhanging phallus props prominently on display (Source: "Pottery: red-figured bell-krater…," British Museum Collection Online. Image courtesy of the British Museum. © The Trustees of the British Museum. All rights reserved.)

Chiron is depicted as a paunchy, elderly man with white hair and beard ascending a staircase apparently leading to the temple of Apollo at Delphi, being pulled and pushed by two slaves who stand in front of and behind him. Aside from the lone figure who stands to the right watching the scene, who is probably Chiron's student Achilles, all the characters portrayed are depicted as grotesque and ugly, with grossly protruding noses, mouths, and lips, huge padded buttocks; and, in the case of the males, large, thick phalluses. The glans of Chiron is decorously concealed beneath the *akroposthion*, while the glandes of the two slaves, in contrast, are comically exposed. The comedic effect is heightened by the portrayal of wrinkles in the phalluses of the two characters coded as elderly, as indicated by their grey hair, Chiron and the slave who stands behind and below him. The slave who stands above Chiron, in contrast, is portrayed as middle-aged: balding but not yet grey, with a phallus not yet so wrinkled.

The stock comedic motif of the elderly male is likewise combined with that of the exposed glans in a Boeotian black-figure ware from the sixth or fifth century BCE that depicts a hunter—a figure that Dover mistook to be the god Zeus—as elderly, white-bearded, and balding, with a paunchy stomach and exaggerated buttocks recalling the padded costumes of comedic actors, and with a bulbous glans partially exposed. In a parodic hunting scene, the man stalks a boar that is apparently cornered, preparing to throw the crooked spear that he brandishes.[26] As Alexandre Mitchell observes, "Even the boar is made to look like a plump defenseless domesticated pig on the run."[27] Note the stark contrast between the comedic image of the hunter poised to throw his spear depicted in the Boeotian black-figure ware—elderly, paunchy, balding, glans exposed—and the dignified, athletic image of Zeus in the Artemesion bronze statue, poised to throw the lightning bolt—an adult in his prime, fit, muscular, and athletic, with a full head of hair and ample *akroposthion* (see fig. 8).

Figure 6. Caricatured hunter, bulbous glans partially exposed for comedic effect (Source: Alexandre G. Mitchell, *Greek Vase-Painting and the Origins of Visual Humour* [New York: Cambridge University Press, 2009], 257, fig. 129. Vectorised drawing by Alexandre G. Mitchell. Reprinted by permission of Alexandre Mitchell and Cambridge University Press.)

In addition to connoting foreignness, slavery, or comedic laughter, the exposed glans could also indicate a state of arousal resulting from the anticipation of a sexual encounter. In such cases, the penis is pictured erect. A drinking cup attributed to the Pedieus Painter (ca. 520–510 BCE), for

---

[26] On the visual humor involved in the Beotian black ware vases, see Alexandre G. Mitchell, *Greek Vase-Painting and the Origins of Visual Humour* (New York: Cambridge University Press, 2009); for discussion of parodic hunting scenes: 261–63; image: 257, fig. 129. For Dover's mistaken identification of the figure as Zeus, see Dover, *Greek Homosexuality*, 71, 128; image: BB16.

[27] Mitchell, *Greek Vase-Painting*, 263.

example, depicts a beardless youth being prepared by a female, perhaps a prostitute, for irrumation (fellatio) or, more likely given the postures of the two figures, to be mounted. The female grasps the right knee of the man, instructing him to assume a sexual posture with his legs bent beneath him, weight borne on the balls of his feet, while in her right hand she grasps his erect phallus, glans exposed.

Figure 7. Woman prepares youthful male for intercourse; the glans of the young man's phallus is exposed (Source: "Attic Red-Figure Kylix," side A, Phintias, c. 510 BCE, The J. Paul Getty Museum, Villa Collection. Digital image courtesy of the Getty's Open Content Program.)

Moreover, images of satyrs, part animal and part human beings who are associated with revelry, drunkenness, and an overabundance of sexual desire, are frequently depicted ithyphallic, or erect, with glans alternately covered by the prepuce or exposed. An Athenian black-figure drinking cup attributed to the Amasis Painter around 520 BCE, for example, depicts two satyrs masturbating amicably. The glans of the satyr on the left is covered by the *akroposthion*, while that of the satyr on the right is exposed; the collocation suggests the successive covering and uncovering of the glans during manual stimulation of the phallus (see fig. 8).

In addition to the pursuit of sexual pleasures, satyrs are associated with revelry, the drinking of wine, intoxication, and song; and frequently portrayed as associates of the god Dionysus. In these respects, they represent the converse of the Greek aesthetic ideal: the fully human, and therefore rational, self-controlled young male, small phallus flaccid and decorously hidden beneath its prepuce, and tipped by an elongated *akroposthion*. Timothy McNiven has shown that Greek art associated the small phallus with the characteristic of *sophrosyne*, or self-controlled moderation, the very characteristic that satyrs notably lack.[28] A red-figured vase attributed to Douris around 500 to 490 BCE depicts a satyr balancing a drinking cup on his large, erect phallus during a *symposion*. Note that the ideal of the *akroposthion* is observed, despite the satyr's erection; and it is in fact the rigid *akroposthion* that supports the drinking cup: a feat possible only in the artistic imagination. (see fig. 9)

Figure 8. Two satyrs masturbating amicably (Source: "Drinking cup [kylix] depicting two satyrs," Museum of Fine Arts, Boston. Photograph © 2019, Museum of Fine Arts, Boston. Reprinted by permission.)

The erect phallus connotes not only the pursuit of sexual pleasure but also procreation, fertility, productivity, and, by extension, even success in mercantile endeavors. The primary bearer of this symbolism was the god Priapus, the son of Aphrodite and Dionysus or, alternatively, of Dionysus and Chione, cursed by Hera with a condition of permanent erection (hence the modern medical term *priapism*).[29] The god's existence in a continual state of

---

[28] McNiven, "Unheroic Penis," 13, writes, "Gods, heroes, and men of the upper class are in control of themselves, and their *sophrosune* [sic] is indicated in Greek art by a dainty penis." Conversely, lack of self-control is associated with the large penis.

[29] For an overview, see *Aara-Aphlad*, vol. 1.1 of *Lexicon Iconographicum Mythologiae Classicae (LIMC)*, ed. Fondation pour le lexicon iconographicum mythologiae classicae

Figure 9. Satyr balances a drinking cup on his erect phallus (Source: "Komos Douris BM E768.jpg," Wikimedia Commons, https://en.wikipedia.org/wiki/Satyr#/media/File:Komos_Douris_ BM_E768.jpg. Image in the public domain under the CC0 1.0 Universal Public Domain license.)

sexual arousal facilitated his association with fertility; consequently, his image frequented Roman gardens. Moreover, as the erect phallus of Priapus bore a similarity to the Greek herm, and indeed was often portrayed in herm-like fashion, with a head and torso emerging from a square pole, as depicted in a fresco in the House of the Surgeon in Pompeii.[30] Like the herm, Priapus serves a protective function; for example, in the *Priapea*, a collection of verses from the late first century or early second century CE, he is understood to protect from sexual violation women and children, both male and female, in the garden over which he presides, and to protect the garden and household against thieves.[31]

A marble statue from the late second or early third century CE portrays Priapus dressed in matronly tunics and hooded. He lifts up the tunics to expose his erect phallus. The abundance of fruits supported by the phallus

---

(Zurich: Artemis, 1981), 1028–29; Theodor Heinze, "Priapus," *BNP*: http://referenceworks. brillonline.com/ browse/brill-s-new-pauly.

[30] For an image, see "Pompeii – Casa del Chirurgo – Paintress," Wikimedia Commons, https://commons.wikimedia.org/wiki/File:Pompeii_-_Casa_del_Chirurgo_- _Paintress_-_MAN.jpg. See also Moser, "Naked Power," 40, who discusses a herm-pillar from Tivoli with an inscription to Priapus.

[31] Recent editions of the *Priapea* include those of W. H. Parker, *Priapea: Poems for a Phallic God* (London: Croom Helm, 1988); Christiana Goldberg, *Carmina Priapea: Einleitung, Übersetzung, Interpretation und Kommentar* (Heidelberg: Winter, 1992); Louis Callebat and Jean Soubiran, *Priapées* (Paris: Les Belles Lettres, 2012); Carmen Condoñer and Juan Antonio González, *Priapea*, Exemplaria Classica Sup 3 (Huelva: Universidad de Huelva, 2015).

are indicative of the god's association with fertility. The garments and pose appear to be borrowed from Aphroditus *anasyromenos* statues depicting the gender nonbinary god, breasted and wearing female clothing, lifting the skirts (*anasyromenos*) to expose a phallus in an apotropaic gesture.[32] Except for the presence of the large phallus, one might suppose the image shown here to represent Aphroditus rather than Priapus.

Figure 10. Priapus with vegetation around genitals (Source: "Statue of Priapus," Museum of Fine Arts Boston.Photograph © 2019, Museum of Fine Arts, Boston. Reprinted by permission.)

Priapus's association with fertility could extended outside the garden even to signify success in mercantile endeavors, as indicated by a well-known fresco from the House of the Vettii in Pompeii. The basket of fruit at Priapus's feet, indicative of fertility and abundance, creates a visual parallel with the large bag of money, indicative of mercantile success, against which Pripaus weights his semi-turgid phallus. The grotesque proportions of the phallus indicate that the image may have served apotropaic functions, averting the evil eye of envy both by suggesting that the wealth of

---

[32] Theodor Heinze, "Hemaphroditus," *BNP*: http://referenceworks.brillonline.com/browse/brill-s-new-pauly; image and discussion in *LIMC* 1.1: 685: "Priapus 69"; 1034: A69.

the Vettii is attributable to the beneficial influence of the god and by evoking laughter. In spite of its comedic proportions, the phallus of Priapus retains its decorum, as the glans remains hidden beneath the *akroposthion*.

Figure 11. Priapus with phallus on scale; fresco, House of the Vettii, Pompeii
(Source: "Pompeya erótica6.jpg," Wikimedia Commons.
Image in the public domain under the CC0 1.0 Universal Public Domain license.)

Life Imitates Art: Medical Interventions

The Greek artistic ideal of the glans fully covered by an ample prepuce apparently exerted an effect on the lives of Greek and Roman males. Modern physicians have noted that the length of the prepuce may naturally change over time; its maximum length is reached during puberty. Moreover, due to natural variation, some males are born with more, and others with less ample foreskins. Therefore, it was deemed desirable to extend the length of the prepuce in cases where its amplitude was insufficient to fully cover the glans. As Hodges notes, "Greeks valued the longer prepuce and pathologized the penis characterized by a deficient prepuce—especially one that had been surgically ablated—under the disease concept of *lipodermos.*"[33] The medical term *lipodermos* derives from Greek verb *leipō*, "to be wanting, missing, or lacking," combined with the noun *derma*, "skin." He who suffers from the condition "lacks skin" to sufficiently cover the glans.

Various medical treatments were devised to remedy the condition. In his *De Materia Medica*, first century CE physician and herbalist Pedanius Dioscorides of Cilicia recommends the herb thapsia, to which he attributes both laxative and purgative qualities: "It is useful for the prepuce of those suffering from *lipodermos*, providing it not be as a result of circumcision. It induces swelling, which when bathed and anointed, restores the defect of the *posthē* [foreskin]."[34] Dioscorides's exemption of circumcision indicates that amputated prepuces were not amenable to herbal treatment as were congenitally foreshortened ones. Soranus of Ephesus, who practiced medicine in the late first and early second centuries CE, recommends a different remedy for infants judged to have been born with defective foreskins: the wet nurse should stretch the foreskin forward over the glans and tie it in place with thread, "for if gradually stretched and continuously drawn forward, it [the foreskin] easily stretches and assumes its normal length and covers the glans and becomes accustomed to keep the natural good shape."[35]

In his work *De Medicina* (*On Medicine*), Roman encyclopedist Aulus Cornelius Celsus (ca. 25 BCE–ca. 50 CE) describes two surgical remedies for *lipodermos* and one additional procedure to secure the prepuce over the glans. The latter procedure, known as infibulation, is the least invasive. It involves making perforations on either side of the prepuce and securing the prepuce over the glans penis with thread until the perforations are cicatrized, at which time a light pin (*fibula*) is inserted through the perforations, holding the prepuce in place so that the glans is completely covered. Celsus notes, however, that the procedure, which is performed "either for the sake of the voice, or for health's sake" is "more often superfluous than necessary."[36]

The more invasive surgical remedy for *lipodermos* involved stretching the prepuce so that it covered the glans, tying it in place, and subsequently making one incision around the base of the penis near the pubes so that the

---

[33] Hodges, "Ideal Prepuce," 375.

[34] Trans. of Hodges, "Ideal Prepuce," 395.

[35] *Gynecology* 2.34, quoted in Hall, "Epispasm," 2.

[36] Celsus, *De Medicina* 7.25; trans. W. G. Spencer, Loeb Classical Library (Cambridge: Harvard University Press, 1971).

detached skin slid forward toward the tip; the result was that "a sort of small ring is laid bare in front of the pubes, to which lint is applied in order that flesh [i.e., scar tissue] may grow and fill it up." This procedure, which was applied in cases in which the prepuce was congenitally foreshortened, resulted in an enhancement of the *akroposthion*.

Epispasm, the recommended treatment in cases in which the foreskin was not foreshortened congenitally but removed surgically, "after the custom of certain races," involved not one but two incisions. The first, extending around the penis at its base near the pubes, corresponds with the procedure already described. The second incision was made around the penis just below the glans. Celsus assures his readers that "this is not so very painful, for once the margin [adjacent to the glans] has been freed, it can be stripped up by hand as far back as the pubes, nor in so doing is there any bleeding."[37] The entire section of penile skin, thus severed at both ends, was slid forward to cover the glans. Affusions, plasters, and bandages were applied to prevent infection and to hold the skin in place until the wounds healed.

The sustained attention to and variety of treatments for *lipodermos* indicate the pervasiveness of the aesthetic ideal of the lengthy prepuce. If nature did not furnish a suitably ample covering for the glans, the herbalist's chest, the wet nurse's thread, and the physician's needle and scalpel offered measures to remedy the defect.

The Chronic Exposure of the Glans: Judaic Circumcision according to Philo

Although, as indicated earlier, Hodges viewed Jewish writers like Philo as being fundamentally out of touch the Greco-Roman preputial aesthetic, this seems highly unlikely. Hodges claims that Philo's "dismissal of opposition to circumcision as 'childish mockery' betrays his failure to understand the philosophical and aesthetic underpinnings of the Greeks' high regard for the cultivation of physical health and beauty."[38] However, the claim that Philo fails to understand the philosophical and aesthetic underpinnings of the preference for the intact phallus among Greeks and Romans is on the face of it a strange assertion to make, especially given that Philo wrote in Greek, was deeply imbued by Platonic philosophical ideals, and lived in Alexandria, a thoroughly Hellenized metropolis during first century BCE

---

[37] Celsus, *De Medicina* 7.25 (trans. Spencer).
[38] Hodges, "Ideal Prepuce," 387.

and first century CE. In what follows, we briefly describe Philo's Alexandrian context and show that he was, contrary to Hodges's claim, both well aware of and engaged with Greek and Roman perceptions of the phallus and foreskin.

Philo's Alexandria

The city of Alexandria in which Philo lived around the turn of the era was marked by diverse cultural influences. The native Egyptian population, who during the Roman period were required to pay a *laographia*, a tax on *laoi*, or "natives," were represented, as were Greeks, who had held sway for three centuries during the Hellenistic, Ptolemaic Dynasty. During the reign of Augustus Ceasar (27 BCE–14 CE), Alexandria became a Roman province tasked to provide grain to Rome.[39] A sizeable population of Judeans or Jews were present in the city; their number in the first century CE has been estimated to have been around 180,000, or even as high as half a million, ten to twenty percent of whom were Judean.[40] As Jan Bremmer noted, the Alexandrian population was organized according a sociopolitical hierarchy that privileged Romans, Greeks, Judeans, and Egyptians, in that order.[41] Philo himself was thoroughly conversant with Greek (Platonic) philosophy, rhetoric, and arithmetic; Daniel Schwartz opines that "it can hardly be doubted that Philo attended a gymnasium, especially in light of his rhetorical abilities and his fondness for athletic imagery."[42] Moreover, Philo's brother, Alexander the Alabarch, was a wealthy merchant who held a post collecting taxes on produce imported to Egypt from Arabia; and his nephew Tiberius Julius Alexander would eventually become governor of Egypt under Nero, would play a role in the sack of Jerusalem under Titus, and would take a position as praetorian prefect in Rome. And Philo himself was selected to lead a Jewish delegation to Gaius Caligula in Rome in 38/39 CE.[43] Maren Niehoff has recently argued that after visiting Rome, Philo began to distance himself somewhat from Platonic traditions in favor

[39] I rely for this brief history on Daniel R. Schwartz, "Philo, His Family, and His Times," in *The Cambridge Companion to Philo*, ed. Adam Kamesar (Cambridge: Cambridge University Press, 2009), 14–24.
[40] Positing 180,000: Schwartz, "Philo," 15 n. 20; positing 500,000, 10–20 percent Judean: Jan N. Bremmer, "The First Pogrom? Religious Violence in Alexandria AD 38?," in Jörg Frey et al., eds., *Alexandria: Hub of the Hellenistic World* (Tübingen: Mohr Siebeck, forthcoming).
[41] Bremmer, "First Pogrom?"
[42] Schwartz, "Philo," 18.
[43] Schwartz, "Philo," 10–14.

of enhanced engagement with Roman Stoicism.[44] Although Niehoff may have overstated the case for Philo's break with Platonic traditions in favor of interaction with Stoic ones, Philonists agree that the Alexandrine was familiar with both Greek and Roman philosophical traditions.[45] In view of his Greek education, his interaction with both Platonism and Stoicism, his ties to the gymnasium, his family connection to highly placed Roman officials, and his own participation in a delegation sent from Alexandria to Rome, it is demonstrable that Philo was thoroughly conversant with Greek and Roman attitudes; and it is likely that this familiarity extended beyond philosophy to encompass Greek and Roman perceptions regarding the significance of the prepuce and its absence. As we will see in the following discussion, far from being ignorant of the "philosophical and ethical underpinnings" of the Greek and Roman preference for the intact prepuce, Philo's writings evidence both a keen awareness of and an intensive interaction with Greco-Roman discourses regarding both phallus and foreskin.

Philo's Defense of Circumcision in Its Greco-Roman Context

Philo interacts knowledgeably with Greek and Roman philosophy, ethics, medicine, and geography in relation to the practice of circumcision. This interaction is particularly evident in Philo's *On the Special Laws* and *Questions and Answers on Genesis*. Of these two texts, Philo's treatment of circumcision in *On the Special Laws* constitutes a suitable starting point for discussion, since Hodges refers to that text when he writes that Philo's "dismissal of opposition to circumcision as 'childish mockery' betrays his failure to understand the philosophical and aesthetic underpinnings" of the Greek aversion to circumcision. Philo's characterization of Greek opposition to circumcision as "childish," however, ought not be taken to imply that he fails to grasp "underpinnings" of the Greek (and Roman) preputial aesthetic. It is not misunderstanding that prompts Philo to characterize opposition to circumcision in this way, but rather what he characterizes as an unwise and disrespectful dismissal of the practice that "impugn[s] the good sense of great nations." We examine the text of *Spec.* 1.1–3 in more detail below. Before examining the text, however, two relevant issues must

[44] Maren R. Niehoff, *Philo of Alexandria: An Intellectual Biography*, Anchor Yale Bible Reference Library (New Haven: Yale University Press, 2018).

[45] See, for example, the following reviews of Niehoff's work: Carlos Lévy, review of Niehoff, *Philo of Alexandria*, SPhiloA 30 (2018): 183–91; René Bloch, review of Niehoff, *Philo of Alexandria*, AJSR 43 (2019): 201–4; Stephan Hecht, review of Niehoff, *Philo of Alexandria*, RQ 113 (2019): 273–75.

be addressed: How are we to identify the party or parties that engage in "childish mockery" of the practice of circumcision in the text, and why does circumcision occupy first place in the discussion in *On the Special Laws*?

Maren Niehoff has argued that the mockery that Philo refers to in *Spec.* 1.3 originated not from Greeks or Romans, as Hodges's statement implies, but from other Jews. Niehoff writes:

> While Philo in *De Specialibus Legibus* does not give any clues regarding the background of these critics, he provides some information in *De Migrationi Abrahami*. It clearly emerges here that he has Jews in mind. He accuses them of overly indulging in the allegorical meaning of Mosaic law and thus becoming oblivious to its actual performance (*Migr.* 89)."[46]

Niehoff's view, however, is extremely unlikely. *Migr.* 89, which Niehoff cites as evidence, nowhere refers to mockery of circumcision. On the contrary, the Jewish interpreters referred to in that text agreed with Philo in holding circumcision in high regard; they understood that one could follow God's injunction to become circumcised without severing the physical foreskin, a position that Philo unequivocally rejected (*Migr.* 92). "Overly indulging in the allegorical meaning of Mosaic law," however, hardly constitutes mockery of the practice of circumcision. On the contrary, the exegetical procedure itself indicates the high regard in which the biblical text advocating circumcision was held. Secondly, it is unlikely that Philo would refer to the position of his Judaic interlocutors in *Migr.* 89 as "childish and unwise," as he characterizes the mockers addressed in *Spec.* 1.3. The Platonizing hermeneutical strategy of interpreting biblical texts as metaphors indicating rational self-control over the passions is one in which Philo himself engages extensively, and which he elsewhere associates with wisdom (see, e.g., *Decal.* 1). The metaphorical reception of Philo's Judaic interlocutors in *Migr.* 89 must therefore be distinguished from the "childish and unwise" mockery addressed in *Spec.* 1.3. Moreover, Philo's notice that the mockery originates with οἱ πολλοί in 1.1 and his identification of circumcision as a practice of "great nations" (μεγάλα ἔθνη) in 1.3 strongly suggest that he writes to defend a regional and ethnic practice against criticism by a majority of outsiders. Lastly, Niehoff points to no parallels as examples of *Jews* mocking circumcision. On the other hand, the mockery of circumcision is amply attested in non-Judaic sources, a point to which we will return below. It is therefore highly likely—if not almost certain—that it

---

[46] Maren R. Niehoff, "Circumcision as a Marker of Identity: Philo, Origen and the Rabbis on Gen 17: 1—14," *Jewish Studies Quarterly* 10 (2003): 101.

was non-Jews rather than Jews who engaged in the "mockery" of circumcision that Philo addressed in *Spec.* 1.3.

Another contested issue concerns the reasons why Philo addressed circumcision in the prolegomenon to his *On the Special Laws*, a document that treats the Decalogue or Ten Commandments as a framing device to discuss an assortment of biblical injunctions. An influential argument in regard to that question was advanced by Richard Hecht, who sought to demonstrate that two factors account for Philo's placement of the material at the beginning of the treatise: first, circumcision represents the removal of arrogance and conceit, or the presumption "that man is something more than a creature of God," and therefore represents the "'vestibule' or portal through which one must pass if one is to understand properly the nature of the *nomos* and its special laws"; and second, that by associating circumcision with other nations like Egypt, Philo combats charges of "Jewish particularism."[47] Hecht's position, however, is untenable for two reasons. First, it overlooks the clear statements and grammatical structure of *Spec.* 1.1: ἄρξομαι δ'ἀπὸ τοῦ γελωμένου παρὰ τοῖς πολλοῖς ("And I will begin with that which is laughed at among many people"). "Laughter" is listed as the issue of prime concern in connection with Philo's choice to "begin" his discussion with circumcision. Hecht ignores this. Philo continues: even that ancient, philosophically-minded people, the Egyptians, practiced circumcision. And then: παρὸ καὶ προσῆκον ἦν παιδικὴν χλευεῖν μεθεμενοῦς ... ἀναζητῆσαι τὰς αἰτίας, ὧν χάριν ἐκράτησε τὸ ἔθος ("And for that reason it would be proper to give up childish joking ... to seek the causes on account of which the custom prevailed..."). Philo uses παρό, a contracted form of παρὰ ὅ, to introduce "a proposition that is *logically* deduced from a preceding proposition ... that was *made as its basis*": thus the translation "for that reason" or "in consequence of that fact."[48] In consequence of the fact that Egyptians, like Judeans, practice circumcision, Philo reasons that it would be "proper" to "give up childish joking" in order to seek out the reasons for the practice;

[47] Richard D. Hecht, "The Exegetical Contexts of Philo's Interpretation of Circumcision," in *Nourished with Peace: Studies in Hellenistic Judaism in Memory of Samuel Sandmel*, ed. Frederick E. Greenspahn, Earle Hilgert, and Burton L. Mack, Scholars Press Homage Series (Chico, CA: Scholars Press, 1984), 75. Hecht's arguments are cited approvingly by Feldman, *Jew and Gentile*, 155, 157.

[48] G. K. Beale, Daniel J. Brendsel, and William A. Ross, *An Interpretive Lexicon of New Testament Greek: Analysis of Prepositions, Particles, Relative Pronouns, and Conjunctions* (Grand Rapids: Zondervan, 2014), 8, where the authors define the logical relationship of "inference" between clauses or sentences (emphasis is that of Beale et al.). The Greek lexicon of Liddell and Scott clearly indicates that παρό serves an inferential function, glossing it "wherefore" (LSJ, s.v. "παρό")—a usage that does not, however, occur in the New Testament material surveyed by Beale, Brendsel, and Ross.

reasons that Philo subsequently enumerates. The clear import of Philo's statements is that he begins (ἄρξομαι) his discussion of the "special laws" with circumcision precisely because it provokes the "laughter" of "the many."

While Hecht's exegesis of Philo is otherwise highly instructive, his main arguments to account for the placement of circumcision at the beginning of *On the Special Laws* must be rejected, as they fail to grapple sufficiently with the clear wording of *Spec.* 1.1. When stating reasons for opening the treatise with a discussion of circumcision, Philo does not mention the presumption "that man is something more than a creature of God." The question of whether Philo attempted to counter charges of Jewish particularism in the prologue needs to be approached judiciously: whereas circumcision was certainly perceived as a marker of ethnic particularity, it would be a strange way for Philo to argue if, as Hecht suggests, he attempted to "universalize" the law by associating circumcision with Egypt, as Egyptians, too, were identified as ethnically "other" (or, "particular") by Greeks and Romans, in part based on their practice of circumcision, as we have seen. Instead, Philo explicitly states a very specific ground for beginning *On the Special Laws* as he did: he wished to address the derision of circumcision, expressed in the form of mocking laughter, by Greeks and Romans.

In his important study tracing the history of Judaic circumcision from Genesis through the Talmuds, Simon Mimouni registers surprise at the fact that Philo begins *On the Special Laws* with a discussion of circumcision. This is "astonishing" (étonnant), writes Mimouni, because circumcision does not appear to be numbered among the "special laws" that form Philo's subject matter; the subject does not recur later in the treatise. Mimouni continues: the position of Philo's discussion of circumcision at the beginning of this treatise "is perhaps indicative of the problem this practice poses in the world in which he lives. Moreover, Philo himself points out that circumcision is the object of 'mockery of the crowd,' and that it has indeed been an easy joke in the Greek-Roman milieu."[49] Although Mimouni does not elaborate the observation that circumcision offered opportunity for "an easy joke" in the Greco-Roman milieu, the data provided by Greek and Roman art and statuary amply justify such a statement. As we have seen, Old Comedy regularly made use of the image of the phallus with

---

[49] Mimouni, *Circoncision*, 100: "Cette position première dans le traité est peut-être l'indication du problème que pose cette pratique dans le monde où il vit. D'ailleurs, Philon, lui-même, relève que la circoncision est objet de 'railleries de la foule,' et qu'elle a été effectivement un thème de plaisanterie facile dans le milieu gréco-romain." The translation is mine. Martin, "Paul and Circumcision," 123–24, also views Greco-Roman ridicule as the reason why Philo begins his treatise with a discussion of circumcision.

indecently exposed glans as a comic motif; Aristophanes refers to it as a "cause for laughter" (γέλως). This is evident in the fourth century BCE vase painting depicting the healing of Chiron, although there the comedic effect was produced by the indecent exposure of the glans due to an insufficient prepuce rather than an amputated one. Moreover, visual humor involved in Roman apotropaic images depicting the circumcised phallus, including the image of the Ethiopian bath attendant in the House of the Vettii, is of particular significance: the apotropaic power believed to inhere in the image of the enlarged and/or circumcised phallus derived in part from its ability to mollify envy, and thus to ward off the evil eye, by producing laughter.[50] Further confirmation is provided by Josephus, who complains that the "Hellenizing" Egyptian Apion "denounces us [i.e., Judeans] for sacrificing domestic animals and for not eating pork, and he jeers at [χλευάζει] the practice of circumcision" (*Ag. Apion* 2.13).[51] In the second century CE, Marcion would cite circumcision as a hindrance to missionary activity because "everybody turns away from pain and flees from the derisive mockery which results from shameful ugliness."[52] The circumcised phallus connoted, from the Greek and Roman perspectives, barbarism and comedic laughter; laughter that from the Judaic perspective was experienced as "jeering" and "mockery." Thus Mimouni is probably correct in his surmise that it was due to "the problem this practice [i.e., circumcision] poses in the world in which he lives" that prompted Philo to place it in the prominent first position in *On the Special Laws*: circumcision posed a notable problem that Philo wished to address directly as a central issue of Judaic law.

Having established both that it was the widespread mockery of circumcision that prompted Philo to insert it into the prominent first position in *On the Special Laws* and that the mockery originated with Greco-Roman rather than Judaic groups, we turn to examine the text in more detail, as it provides the rationale for Philo's attempts to justify the ritual practice. The relevant text occurs in the prologue to *On the Special Laws*, which reads as follows:

---

[50] Moser, "Naked Power," 46, writes: "Laughter, according to a widespread belief in the ancient world, was considered an effective method to avert the Evil Eye, for 'laughter is itself apotropaic' and 'sexual imagery could be a source of mirth, releasing tension and anxiety'" (citing Marilyn B. Skinner, *Sexuality in Greek and Roman Culture* [Malden: Blackwell Publishing, 2005], 260).

[51] Josephus, *Against Apion*, trans. Henry St. James Thackeray, LCL (Cambridge: Harvard University Press; London: Heinemann, 1962).

[52] Cited in Niehoff, "Circumcision as a Marker of Identity," 114.

And I will begin with that which is laughed at among many people [ἀπὸ τοῦ γελωμένου παρὰ τοῖς πολλοῖς]. Now the practice which it laughed to scorn [γελᾶται], namely the circumcision of the genital organs, is very zealously observed by many other nations, particularly by the Egyptians, a race regarded as pre-eminent by its populousness, its antiquity, and its attachment to philosophy. And for that reason, it would be proper to give up childish joking [παιδικὴν χλεύην] and to enquire in a wiser and more respectful spirit [φρονιμώτερον καὶ σεμνότερον] into the causes on account of which the custom prevailed, instead of dismissing the matter prematurely and impugning the good sense of great nations [καταγινώσκειν μεγάλων ἐθνῶν εὐχέρειαν]. (*Spec.* 1.1–3)[53]

The lines constitute a preamble to Philo's discussion of Judaic laws. Given the association of the exposed *glans penis* with laughter in Greek comedy and, in Roman art, with attempts to use visual humor to ward off the evil eye, it is perhaps not as astonishing as Mimouni thought that Philo chose to open his discourse with a defense of circumcision. In response to what he characterizes as the "childish joking" and "derisive laughter" with which the image of the circumcised phallus was pervasively greeted, Philo attempted to provide a sense of legitimacy to the circumcision ritual in a "wiser and more serious spirit." As Louis Feldman notes, "a kind of 'Egyptomania' had swept through some of the most fashionable circles of Roman society in the last half of the first century B.C.E.; hence, Philo's retort that circumcision was also practiced by the Egyptians was a most effective reply to those who ridiculed it."[54] Moreover, Philo's mention of "wisdom" in the passage is apropos, since *philosophia*, philosophy or the "love of wisdom," is the primary witness that he enlisted in his defense of circumcision. Far from ignoring the "philosophical and aesthetic underpinnings" of the Greek and Roman preputial aesthetic as Hodges suggested, Philo both deployed and reinterpreted philosophical traditions in his defense of the ancestral Judaic practice of circumcision.

Philo's philosophical defense of circumcision was to interpret it as a metaphor for the "excision of the pleasures of the body" (*Migr.* 89–93). He agreed with the Judaic interlocutors described above that biblical laws held metaphorical or allegorical meanings; he disagreed by retaining the observance of the laws in their literal sense. Following Platonic traditions, he reasoned that the bodily passions tied the immortal soul too closely to earthly pursuits and hindered the philosophical contemplation of transcen-

---

[53] Philo, *The Special Laws*, trans. F. H. Colson, LCL (Cambridge: Harvard University Press, 1984), 101 (modified).

[54] Louis H. Feldman, *Jew and Gentile in the Ancient Word: Attitudes and Interactions from Alexander to Justinian* (Princeton: Princeton University Press, 1993), 155. Feldman appears to rely directly on Hecht, "Philo's Interpretation of Circumcision," 77, here.

dent truths (compare, e.g., Plato, *Phaedr.* 249–251; *Symp.* 210–212 A). One needed to be metaphorically circumcised, that is, to remove one's passions, in order properly to pursue philosophy as Philo understands it.

In his *QG* 3.46, for example, Philo likens circumcision to the removal of "superfluous growths" so that the mind (*nous*) might be "pure and naked of every evil and passion" and so become "free and unbound." Free of the passions that impede it, the mind could ascend to the heavenly realm to attain a vision of transcendent truth (see, e.g., *Her.* 69–70; *Migr.* 9). Philo depicted circumcision as having a twofold significance: literally, it involves the excision of penile foreskin, and metaphorically, it involves the excision of passions from the soul. As Mimouni notes, "The two circumcisions advanced in the Philonian interpretation of Genesis 17 suggest an allegorical reading directly related to the philosophical theme of the ascension of the soul."[55] Philo advocates the Platonic view that the physical body and its passions "weigh down" the soul, hindering it from accomplishing its upward journey toward the ideal, heavenly realm that is evident only on the basis of philosophical contemplation. Philo's metaphor thus links the Judaic ritual practice of circumcision with Greek philosophical attempts to attain insights that transcend those of the mundane world.

Philo's notion of the twofold circumcision is expressed clearly in *Questions and Answers on Genesis*. The full text of this philosophico-exegetical is extant only in Armenian, although some Greek fragments remain. In cases in which Greek fragments are lacking, retroversion of the Armenian into Greek offers an indication of the original terms and phrases used. In *QG* 3.46, Philo expounds Gen 17:10b–11a:

> What is the meaning of the words, "There shall be circumcised every male of you, and you shall be circumcised in the flesh of your foreskin"? I see two circumcisions, one of the male, and the other of the flesh; that of the flesh is by way of the genitals, while that of the male, it seems to me, is by way of reason. For that which is, one might say, naturally male in us is the mind [ὁ νοῦς], whose superfluous growths it is necessary to cut off and throw away in order that it may become pure and naked or every evil and passion, and be a priest of God. Now this is what He indicated by the second circumcision, stating (in) the Law that "you shall circumcise your hardness of heart," which means your hard and rebellious and refractory thoughts, and by cutting off and removing

---

[55] Translation of the author. The original reads (Mimouni, *Circoncision*, 103): "Les deux circoncisions avancées dans l'interprétation philonienne de Gn 17 suggèrent une lecture allégorique mise directement en relation avec le thème philosophique de l'ascension de l'âme."

arrogance, you shall make the sovereign part [τὸ ἡγεμονικόν; i.e., the mind] free and unbound.[56]

Philo relies here on the notion that humans have a twofold nature, subsisting from a combination of perishable body (i.e., "flesh") and immortal mind (νοῦς/διάνοια): the human being "was created at once both mortal and immortal: mortal with respect to the body, and immortal with respect to the mind" (*Opif.* 46.135: γεγενῆσθαι θνητὸν ὁμοῦ καὶ ἀθάνατον, θνητὸν μὲν κατὰ τὸ σῶμα, κατὰ δὲ τὴν διάνοιαν ἀθάνατον). He genders the mind male and the body or "flesh," albeit implicitly, female.[57] The physical body is circumcised when tissue is removed from the prepuce, whereas the "male creature," mind, is metaphorically circumcised when "superfluous shoots," connected with what is wicked and vile, are "pruned away and to cast off." Philo mixes the metaphor of circumcision with that of arboriculture here; the two metaphors are linked by the aspect of excision. He is aided in his metaphorical interpretation of circumcision by the idea, persistent in earlier, biblical literature, of the "circumcision of the heart" (e.g., Deut 10:16; 30:6), which he interprets as referring to the removal of "rebellious thoughts and ambition," thus rendering the mind "free" to pursue a vision of heaven through contemplation of Judaic Scriptures in a philosophical mode.

Philo's views on of the excision of the passions take on additional significance when he interprets circumcision as a metaphor for the excision specifically of sexual desire. As we have seen, the pulling back of the foreskin to expose the glans was associated with sexual activity, and this connotation may be present even in the absence of an erection. For example, hypersexual satyrs were sometimes pictured with glans exposed even when the penis was flaccid.[58] The chronic exposure of the glans by circumcision could thus be associated with chronic lewdness. As Troy Martin aptly notes, "Circumcision … permanently exposes the glans and renders the male perpetually sexually aroused."[59] Nor was this point lost on the Romans. The historian Tacitus writes that "as a nation, they [Judeans] are very inclined to lust" (*proiectissima ad libidinem gens*), although, he concedes,

---

[56] Philo, *Questions and Answers on Genesis*, trans. Ralph Marcus, LCL (Cambridge: Harvard University Press, 2002), 240–41, slightly modified.
[57] On the gendering of the mind as male and body as female, Niehoff, "Circumcision as a Marker of Identity," 95–96.
[58] Dover, *Greek Homosexuality*, image B80; see also the amphora of satyrs treading out wine with Dionysus by the Amasis Painter; photo in Biers, *The Archaeology of Greece*, 184, no. 7.33.
[59] Martin, "Paul and Circumcision," 116.

"they abstain from intercourse with foreign women" (*Hist.* 5.2).[60] Martial's jests about the genitalia of Jewish males in his *Epigrams* likewise suggest that Jews were seen as sexually hyperpotent.[61] In *Epigram* 7.55, for example, the poet contrasts his own phallus, which he coyly characterizes as "well-behaved and small" (*proba et pusilla*) with that of a Judean, whose member is presumed to have just the opposite characteristics.[62]

In stark contrast, Philo asserts that the exposed glans of the circumcised Jewish phallus represents not a chronic state of lust, but chronic self-control and a rejection of lust. Commenting on Gen 17:24–25, which indicates that Abraham's son Ishmael was circumcised just at the onset of puberty at age thirteen, Philo writes:

> [God] instructs him who is about to undertake marriage by all means to circumcise his sense-pleasures [ἡδονάς] and amorous desires, rebuking those who are lascivious and lustful, in order that they may restrain their excessive embraces, which usually come about not for the sake of begetting children but for the sake of unrestrained pleasure. (*QG* 3.61)[63]

Arguing that circumcision represents the excision of sensual pleasure and sexual desire, and therefore functions as a "rebuke" to lustful persons. The

---

[60] Trans. of C. H. Moore, Loeb Classical Library (modified); cited in Stern, *Greek and Latin Authors* 2:26. On the Roman perception that the exposed glans signaled sexual insatiability, see Pierre Cordier, "Les Romains et la circoncision," *Revue des Études juives* 160 (2001): 337–55. The factor of ethnicity is also certainly involved; as Stern, *Greek and Latin Authors*, 2:40, notes, "the notion is mostly based on the common typology of the strong sexual passions credited to barbarians, especially to those of the East."

[61] On *Epig.* 7.82, see Marie Roux, "Martial, *Epigrams* VII.55," Judaism and Rome: Re-thinking Judaism's Encounter with the Roman Empire, http://judaism-and-rome.cnrs.fr/martial-epigrams%C2%A0vii82, who notes that "the pulling back of the foreskin of the Jews may have become a humorous and provocative motif because their sex organs were associated with some kind of priapism and unrestrained sexuality totally opposed to the self-control which characterized the Roman citizen with good morals." Commenting on *Epig.* 7.35, Dwora Gilula, "Did Martial Have a Jewish Slave?," *Classical Quarterly* 37.2 (1987): 532–33, writes, "Martial and his slave have a true super-*mentula*, such as is typical of lustful, sexually potent Jews" (533). See also Peter Schäfer, *Judeophobia: Attitudes toward the Jews in the Ancient World* (Cambridge: Harvard University Press, 1997), 99–102. For an important discussion of the significance of the terms ψωλός, *verpus*, and *recutitus* (all referring to the uncovering of the glans, either due to sexual arousal or to circumcision), see Martin, "Paul and Circumcision," 117–18.

[62] Martial, *Epig.* 7.55; see also Marie Roux, "Martial, *Epigrams* VII.55," Judaism and Rome: Re-thinking Judaism's Encounter with the Roman Empire, http://judaism-and-rome.cnrs.fr/martial-epigrams%C2%A0vii55.

[63] Philo, *Questions and Answers on Genesis*, trans. Ralph Marcus, LCL (Cambridge: Harvard University Press, 2002), 264. Only fragments remain of the Greek version of *Questions and Answers on Genesis*; the extant sixth century Armenian version that Marcus translates was based on a Greek exemplar.

sexual use of the Jewish phallus, Philo opines, is not to gratify sensual desires but to sire children; it is thus both restrained and goal oriented.

Philo opines that circumcision, rather than signaling a chronic state of libidinousness, signals an effective remedy for lewdness. Reflecting on Gen 17:10, which indicates that only males and not females were to undergo the rite of circumcision, Philo addresses the evident gender disparity as follows:

> But the divine legislator ordained circumcision for males alone for many reasons. The first of these is that the male has more pleasure in, and desire for, mating than does the female, and he is more ready for it. Therefore He rightly leaves out the female, and suppresses the undue impulses of the male by the sign of circumcision. (*QG* 3.47; trans. Marcus, LCL)

Again Philo inverts the stereotypical Greek and Roman association of circumcision with an overabundance of sexual desire; in his view, circumcision rather "suppresses the undue impulses" characteristic of sexual desire. In both *QG* 3.61 and 3.47, Philo understands the significance of the circumcised Jewish phallus in a manner that is the converse of the views expressed by Tacitus and Martial.

Closely related to the notion of the circumcised Judean as hypersexualized, exposed glans signaling a chronic state of sexual anticipation is the notion that Judeans and other circumcised are especially prolific, undoubtedly as the result of their chronic concupiscence. In his *Histories*, Tacitus writes:

> Still they [i.e., Judeans] provide for the increase of their numbers. It is a crime among them to kill any newly-born infant. They hold that the souls of all who perish in battle or by the hands of the executioner are immortal. Hence a passion for propagating their race and a contempt for death. (*Hist.* 5.5; trans. Godley, LCL)

Alongside their "inclination to lust," mentioned earlier, Tacitus lists an interdiction against infanticide and the belief in the immortality of the soul as factors contributing to Judean prolificness, as both are held to "provide for the increase in their [i.e., Judeans'] numbers."

Philo accepts the stereotype that Judeans, like their circumcised Egyptian counterparts, are more prolific than peoples whose males remain uncircumcised. Indeed, in *Virt.* 64, he goes so far as to state that Jews are the "most populous" (πολυανθρωπότατος) of all the nations on earth! In a tellingly contradictory statement, he makes the same claim about another circumcised group, the Egyptians (*Spec.* 1.2). Philo is clearly aware of the stereotype of the prolific, circumcised male, and he not only accepts it, but lists it as a point of Jewish pride.

Rather than attributing prolificacy to chronic concupiscence as signaled by the exposed glans, however, Philo develops an elaborate, rationalizing explanation that involves medical, philosophical, and geographic components. In his *Questions and Answers on Genesis*, for example, Philo writes that Abraham and the other Judaic patriarchs instituted the rite of circumcision

> for the sake of populousness [ἕνεκα τῆς πολυανθρωπίας], for we see that nature is a living thing and very well disposed toward man [φιλάνθρωπον]. Now as wise men they knew that as the seed often flows into the fold of the foreskin, it likely that it will be scattered unfruitfully; but if there is no obstacle to prevent [it], it will succeed in reaching its proper place. For this reason such nations as practice circumcision increase greatly in population. (*QG* 3.48)[64]

Philo supports his contention that circumcision is performed in order to increase the population by providing a medical rationale. Judeans are especially prolific, writes Philo, because the foreskin is not present to impede the free flow of semen into the vaginal canal, preventing it from being "scattered unfruitfully." We may note that Philo's explanation links fertility to the physical characteristics of the phallus. In his *On the Generation of Animals*, the philosopher Aristotle had similarly provided a "scientific" rationale as to why, in his view, the smaller phallus valued in classical Athens was particularly fecund: "This does in fact happen with men who have a large penis [τῶν μέγα τὸ αἰδοῖον ἐχόντων]: they are less fertile than those who have a moderately sized one [τῶν μετριαζόντων], because the semen gets cooled off by being transported too great a distance, and cold semen is not generative" (*Gen. an.* 1.7; trans. Peck, LCL, modified).[65] While Philo's explanation is quite different from Aristotle's, both philosophers suggest that the physical characteristics of the phallus directly effect fertility; for Philo, the circumcised phallus facilitates the unimpeded transmission of semen; for Aristotle, the smaller phallus prevents its cooling.

In addition to his medical rationale, Philo suggests a philosophical justification for circumcision by prefacing his discussion in *QG* 3.48 with the notice that "nature is a living thing and very well disposed toward man." This formulation hews closely to a Stoic formulation recorded by Diogenes Laertius, who writes, "They [the Stoics] say that God is a living thing [θεὸν δ' εἶναι ζῷον] that is immortal and rational and intelligent, perfect in happiness [τέλειον ἐν εὐδαιμονία], not admitting of any evil, [and]

---

[64] All translations of *Questions and Answers on Genesis* are those of Ralph Marcus, LCL.

[65] Aristotle, *Generation of Animals*, trans. A. L. Peck, LCL (Cambridge: Harvard University Press, 1963).

provident [προνοητικόν] toward the world and its inhabitants."[66] Laertius's language thus parallels that of Philo, although God, rather than nature, is referred to as the "living being" who is "provident" toward humans.[67] However, the Stoics regularly identified God (i.e., Zeus) or the gods in general with nature. Cicero writes that according to Chrysippus, "God is the world itself [*ipsumque mundum deum*] ... he is the common nature of all things [*naturam universam*], universal and all-embracing" (*Nat. d.* 1.39).[68] Similarly, Alexander of Aphrodisias writes: "[The Stoics say that] the world [τὸν κόσμον] is a unity which includes all existing things in itself and is governed by a living, rational, intelligent nature [ὑπὸ φύσεως διοικούμενον ζωτικῆς τε καὶ λογικῆς καὶ νοερᾶς]" (*Fat.* 191.1).[69] The cosmos is understood as a well-ordered being that may be identified with God or with nature, which are taken to be synonymous.[70] The notion that God, Zeus, or nature is well-disposed toward humans is nicely captured by Plutarch, who, albeit in the context of an anti-Stoic argument, reports that the Stoics "says that God is ... benevolent, caring, and beneficent [φιλάνθρωπον καὶ κηδεμονικὸν καὶ ὠφέλιμον]" (*Comm. not.* 1075E).[71]

Philo similarly interacts with the Stoic idea of nature in *On the Creation of the World*, where he writes: "The world is in harmony with the law and the law with the world, and ... the man who observes the law is thus a citizen of the world, directing his actions in relation to the [rational] purpose of nature [πρὸς τὸ βούλημα τῆς φύσεως], in accordance with which the entire world is also administered" (*Opif.* 3).[72] Maren Niehoff has shown how Philo reinterprets the laws of the Decalogue in conversation with Stoic precepts. The result, however, is not simply a recapitulation of Stoic ideas, but a more complex interaction between Stoicism and biblical traditions

---

[66] Trans. of A. A. Long and D. N. Sedley, *The Hellenistic Philosophers*, 2 vols. (Cambridge: Cambridge University Press, 1987), 323 (slightly modified). The Greek text appears in the same work (2:321).

[67] As Dirk Baltzly notes, in Stoic cosmology, "The entire cosmos is a living thing and God stands to the cosmos as an animal's life force stands to the animal's body, enlivening, moving and directing it by its presence throughout" (Dirk Baltzly, "Stoicism," *Stanford Encyclopedia of Philosophy*, https://plato.stanford.edu/entries/stoicism/).

[68] Trans. of Long and Sedley, *Hellenistic Philosophers*, 1:323; Greek text: 2:321–22.

[69] Trans. of Long and Sedley, *Hellenistic Philosophers*, 1:337; Greek text: 2:338.

[70] A variant on the idea occurs in Cleanthes's Hymn to Zeus, where Zeus is not identified with nature, but rules and orders it: "Zeus, originator [or, "chief"] of nature, steering all things with law"; see Long and Sedley, *Hellenistic Philosophers*, Greek text: 2:326–27.

[71] Trans. of Long and Sedley, *Hellenistic Philosophers*, 1:327; Greek text: 2:327–28.

[72] Cited according to the translation of Niehoff, *Philo of Alexandria*, 155.

such that "Philo's philosophical reinterpretation of Mosaic law offers an enlightened form of [Judaic] ethnicity."[73]

Philo's notice that "nature is a living thing" that is "well-disposed toward humans" thus has an identifiably Stoic ring and is in keeping with the generally Stoicizing approach that he takes in his later writings. This conclusion is justified in spite of partial Judaic parallels, including the description of Israel's god as a "living God" in passages such as Deut. 5:25; 2 Kgs 19:16; Jer 10:10; and Dan 6:27, and an emphasis on God's kind disposition toward humanity, for example, in Exod 34:6 and Matt 6:25–33. The Stoic influence in Philo's formulation is apparent in the mention of *physis* rather than God, per se, as an active power with concern for humanity. Moreover, the term *zōon*, "living thing," is to be contrasted to the more typically Judaic formulation "the living God" (ὁ θεὸς ζῶν), a phrase that frequently occurs in contrasts to "lifeless" idols (Isa 37:14–20; Bel 5). The Stoic usage, therefore, is quite distinct. Moreover, the juxtapostion of *physis*, *zōon*, and divine *philanthrōpia* in a single passage clearly indicate Philo interacts with Stoic formulations in QG 3.48. A caveat must be registered, however: although in some passages, Philo "virtually identifies nature with God,"[74] he generally recognizes "the most fundamental divide of all ... between God, transcendent eternal Being and sole first principle, and that which receives the benefit of his creative activity, belonging to the realm of genesis."[75] Thus Philo does not in principle adhere to the Stoic view that God and nature are to be equated.

Philo's use of the term "nature" also hints beyond Stoic cosmology to Stoic ethics, with which it is closely related. In the Stoic view, "happiness" (*eudaimonia*) and "living well" are to be achieved by "living in accordance with nature [κατὰ φύσιν ζῆν]" (Stobaeus, *Ecl.* 2.77);[76] that is, living "in accordance with the nature of oneself and that of the whole [ordered cosmos], engaging in no activity wont to be forbidden by the universal law, which is the right reason pervading everything and identical to Zeus" (Diogenes Laertius, *Vitae* 7.87–89).[77] Philo's placement of the reference to nature, which is "well-disposed toward humanity" just after the notice that circumcision was instituted "for the sake of populousness" (ἕνεκα τῆς

---

[73] Niehoff, *Philo of Alexandria*, 170.

[74] David T. Runia, *Philo of Alexandria: On the Creation of the Cosmos according to Moses*, Philo of Alexandria Commentary Series (Leiden: Brill, 2001), 219, citing *Spec.* 1.100; 3.184.

[75] Runia, *Philo of Alexandria*, 22.

[76] Greek text in Long and Sedley, *Hellenistic Philosophers*, 2:389.

[77] Trans. of Long and Sedley, *Hellenistic Philosophers*, 1:395. On "living well," see David Sedley, "The Goal," §17 of "Stoicism," *Routledge Encyclopedia of Philosophy*, https://www.rep.routledge.com/articles/thematic/stoicism/v-1/sections/the-goal.

πολυανθρωπίας) and just before his medical explanation of exactly how the rite serves to facilitate procreation strongly suggests that circumcision is practiced "in accordance with nature," and thus, in accordance with "the right reason pervading everything." Unlike the Stoics, however, Philo attributes this "right reason" to the God of Israel rather than to Zeus. Thus his suggestion that circumcision was practice "in accordance with nature" is in keeping with biblical passages indicating that the God of Israel enjoined the practice (Gen 17:10–11), passages that Philo cites.

In addition to his argument that circumcision promotes fertility and his Stoicizing suggestion that it is performed "in accordance with nature," Philo develops a medico-environmental rationale for the practice, combining medical and environmental justifications. In *QG* 3.48, Philo writes:

> Not only the Jews but also the Egyptians, Arabs and Ethiopians and nearly all those who inhabit the southern regions near the torrid zone are circumcised. And what is the particular reason if not that in these places, especially in summer, the foreskin of the genitals, which is the skin that surrounds and covers (them), becomes inflamed and infected. But when this is cut off, by being laid bare (the penis) is restored, and the affliction is resisted and expelled. For this reason the nations which are in the northern regions and all those to whom has been allotted a portion in those regions of the earth which are windy are not circumcised. For in those regions, as the heat of the sun is relaxed and diminished, so too is the disease which is produced by heat in the skin of the parts of the body. (*QG* 3.48)

Philo here relies on the knowledge that physicians would sometimes amputate not only the foreskin, but even—in cases of severe infection—the entire *glans penis*. In his treatise *De Medicina*, the first century CE encyclopedist Aulus Cornelius Celsus devotes substantial passages to the treatment of ulcers of the testicles and penis, a "lesion that the Greeks call *phimosis*" (*Med.* 7.25; see also 6.18; 25.2).[78] The condition could be treated by the application of lineaments, poultices, or, in more extreme cases, by cauterization or the incision or removal of the foreskin, or even of the glans itself if gangrene had set in (*Med.* 6.18).

Philo combines the knowledge that Roman medicine recognized the value of removing parts of the phallus in cases of extreme infection with the observation that the climate tends to be hotter in the "southern regions" (i.e., those situated closer to the equator), and, based on the view that infection is facilitated by warm weather, reasons that Egyptians, Arabians, and Ethiopians, like Judeans, circumcised their males preemptively as public health precaution. He thus recognized the fact that circumcision was, from

---

[78] On this condition, see Hodges, "Phimosis in Antiquity," 133–36.

Greek and Roman perspectives, a marker of ethnic "otherness," while at the same time seeking to displace that interpretation by supplying an alternative, medico-environmental rationale that justified circumcision as a salutary accommodation to a torrid environment. On this view, environment is the salient factor distinguishing the circumcised from the uncircumcised, and not, as in the more typical Greek and Roman views, the contrast between civilization and barbarism. Philo's medico-environmental rationale suggests that the practice of circumcision is nothing less than a medical treatment prophylactically applied to avoid penile infection in hot climates.

Conclusion

In summary, Philo's Platonizing attempt to reinterpret circumcision philosophically as a metaphor for the "excision of the passions," his Stoicizing suggestion that it is performed "in accordance with nature," his medical explanation linking it to enhanced fertility, and his medico-environmental explanation that it prevented penile infection in hot southern climates, all constitute attempts by a well-educated Jew to provide "wiser and more serious" interpretations of circumcision that could, at least in theory, serve to counter the "derisive laughter" and "scorn" associated with the ritual practice by his Greek and Roman contemporaries. Frederick Hodges is to be commended for pointing to a significant amount of Greek art and indicating its relevance to the understanding of Judaic circumcision in its Hellenistic context; this material significantly adds to perspectives otherwise known from the literary material that is more familiar to scholars of ancient Judaism. Moreover, the Greek material that Hodges pointed to can be supplemented with depictions of the circumcised ethnic "other" as apotropaic symbols to ward off the evil eye of envy by invoking laughter in Roman art. On the other hand, Hodges was quite wrong to characterize Philo as failing to understand the "philosophical and aesthetic underpinnings" of Greek disapproval of circumcision. Quite the contrary: Philo's apologias for circumcision indicate deep interaction with Platonic and Stoic philosophy, Stoic ethics, and Roman medicine and geography. Philo, however, did not simply adopt Greco-Roman discourses tout court; rather he modified and adapted them to serve the Judaic agenda of defending circumcision in view of the very negative evaluation placed upon it by non-Judaic interpreters. The examination of the evidence provided by Greek art and comedy, and Roman visual and poetic humor allows contemporary interpreters, two millennia later, more fully to appreciate the social and cultural pressures that could impel some Jews to abandon the practice of circumcision in favor of a purely metaphorical understanding, and that elicited Philo's attempts to provide respectable philosophical and medical justifications for the ancestral rite whose practice he defended.

University of Erfurt

The Studia Philonica Annual 31 (2019): 163–183

THE RHETORICAL USE OF DIVINE THREAT IN PHILO OF ALEXANDRIA

ALEXANDER E. STEWART

The past two decades have witnessed an increased interest in fear appeals. Argumentation theorists are seeking to understand the structure and provide guidelines for evaluating fear appeals.[1] Social scientists and marketers are exploring the effectiveness of fear appeals on social behavior.[2] Ethicists are weighing the benefits versus harm of using fear as motivation.[3] Classicists are describing the role of fear in Greco-Roman religion.[4] The cognitive

---

[1] Douglas N. Walton, *Scare Tactics: Arguments that Appeal to Fear and Threats*, Argumentation Library 3 (Dordrecht: Kluwer Academic, 2000); John Woods, "Appeal to Force," in *Fallacies: Classical and Contemporary Readings*, ed. Hans V. Hansen and Robert C. Pinto (University Park, PA: The Pennsylvania State University Press, 1995), 240–50; Alexander E. Hooke, "Tortuous Logic and Tortured Bodies: Why is *Ad Baculum* a Fallacy?," in *Proceedings of the Second International Conference on Argumentation*, ed. Frans H. van Eemeren (Amsterdam: International Centre for the Study of Argumentation, 1991), 391–96.

[2] Melanie B. Tannenbaum et al., "Appealing to Fear: A Meta-Analysis of Fear Appeal Effectiveness and Theories," *Psychological Bulletin* 141 (2015): 1178–1204; Kim Witte and M. Allen, "A Meta-Analysis of Fear Appeals: Implications for Effective Public Health Campaigns," *Health Education and Behavior* 27 (2000): 591–615; P. A. Mongeau, "Another Look at Fear-Arousing Persuasive Appeals," in *Persuasion: Advances Through Meta-Analysis*, ed. M. Allen and R. W. Preiss (Cresskill, NJ: Hampton Press, 1998), 53–68.

[3] Nurit Guttman and Charles T. Salmon, "Guilt, Fear, Stigma and Knowledge Gaps: Ethical Issues in Public Health Communication Interventions," *Bioethics* 18 (2004): 531–52; Ronald Bayer and Amy L. Fairchild, "Means, Ends and the Ethics of Fear-Based Public Health Campaigns," *Journal of Medical Ethics* 42 (2016): 391–96; Gerard Hastings, Martine Stead, and John Webb, "Fear Appeals in Social Marketing: Strategic and Ethical Reasons for Concern," *Psychology and Marketing* 21 (2004): 961–86; Stephen L. Brown and Demian Whiting, "The Ethics of Distress: Toward a Framework for Determining the Ethical Acceptability of Distressing Health Promotion Advertising," *International Journal of Psychology* 49 (2014): 89–97.

[4] Maria Patera, "Reflections on the Discourse of Fear in Greek Sources," in *Unveiling Emotions II: Emotions in Greece and Rome: Texts, Images, Material Culture*, ed. Angelos Chaniotis and Pierre Ducrey (Stuttgart: Franz Steiner Verlag, 2014), 109–34; Angelos Chaniotis, "Constructing the Fear of Gods: Epigraphic Evidence from Sanctuaries of Greece and Asia Minor," in *Unveiling Emotions: Sources and Methods for the Study of Emotions in the Greek World*, ed. Angelos Chaniotis (Stuttgart: Franz Steiner Verlag, 2013), 205–34.

turn in psychological understandings of emotion has renewed interest in how emotions, including fear, relate to moral development.[5] Finally, biblical scholars are reevaluating the meaning and role of fear in biblical texts (see below).

Although there are many capable practitioners of religious fear appeals in antiquity, particularly in apocalyptic authors, it is rarer to find an ancient author reflect on the logic and methodology of religious fear appeals. Philo provides philosophical reflection on the necessity of fear appeals grounded in God's judgment and the beneficial results of fear for individuals and the community. Philo's philosophical reflection on the benefits of fear likely reveal unarticulated attitudes toward divine threat in the broader Greco-Roman world.[6] In contrast to many other ancient Jewish and later Christian authors, Philo approached the problem of human weakness as a philosopher and sought to help his hearers move toward perfection and immortality through philosophy and the pursuit of virtues.[7]

This article will contribute to the growing multi-disciplinary research on religious fear appeals by focusing on Philo's attitude toward threats, fear appeals, and scare tactics in moral and religious instruction as evidenced from the Philonic corpus. Because Philo's convictions regarding fear appeals are generally expressed in passing as he develops other arguments and pursues other agendas, this topic has not received extensive focus in prior Philonic scholarship. Nevertheless, Philo's perspectives on the rhetorical use of divine threat can make a positive contribution to ongoing research on fear appeals in at least two ways. First, exploring ancient approaches to perennial questions often can provide new insights and perspectives. For example, the four main constructs in the Extended Parallel Process Model used for developing and evaluating fear appeal

---

[5] Martha C. Nussbaum, *Upheavals of Thought: The Intelligence of Emotions* (Cambridge: Cambridge University Press, 2001); Paul Lauritzen, "Emotions and Religious Ethics," *JRE* 16 (1988): 307–24.

[6] Older debates about whether Philo was primarily a Greek or a Jew have given way in the last few decades to studies which acknowledge both—he was a Jew in the Greek speaking Diaspora. See Ellen Birnbaum, "Two Millennia Later: General Resources and Particular Perspectives on Philo the Jew," *CBR* 4 (2006): 262; Earle Hilgert, "Central Issues in Contemporary Philo Studies," *BR* 23 (1978): 17–20. N. G. Cohen, *Philo Judaeus: His Universe of Discourse*, Beiträge zur Erforschung des Alten Testaments und des antiken Judentums 24 (Frankfurt am Main: Peter Lang, 1995), 10. Gert J. Steyn writes, "The extensive extant Corpus Philonicum provides an important window into the world of Second Temple Judaism(s) and its place during Greco-Roman times" ("Some Observations on Philo of Alexandria's Sensitivity to Strangers," in *Sensitivity to Outsiders: Exploring the Dynamic Relationship between Mission and Ethics in the New Testament and Early Christianity*, ed. Jakobus Kok et al., WUNT 2.364 [Tübingen: Mohr Siebeck, 2014], 59–60).

[7] Michael L. Satlow, "Philo on Human Perfection," *JTS* 59 (2008): 501, 518.

effectiveness in the social sciences (perceived threat severity, perceived threat susceptibility, perceived response efficacy, and perceived self-efficacy) are all discussed by Philo (cf. Aristotle, *Rhet.* 2.5.1–22).[8] What is new often turns out to be quite old and the old continues to have relevance. Second, Philo's discussions of the rhetorical use of divine threat is particularly helpful for understanding the role of religious fear appeals in early Christianity. Jesus and the earliest Christians all employed religious fear appeals but rarely engage in deeper reflection on the logic of the fear appeals.[9] This leaves us with clear examples of divine threat employed in moral exhortation but little theoretical justification or reflection on the warrants underlying the logic. Philo differs from Aristotle and the Stoics in his ability to shed light on the positive role of fear in New Testament moral exhortation because he shares a generally similar religious orientation based on the same foundational religious texts.

This article will begin by considering the foundational worldview conviction undergirding Philo's approach to religious fear appeals: God's right as creator to punish. We will then consider Philo's consideration of the benefits associated with proper fear of punishment, his own utilization of fear appeals, his awareness of the audience-specific nature of appropriate fear appeals, and his negative comments on fear. We will seek throughout to position Philo in dialogue with the multi-disciplinary research on fear appeals noted in this introduction.

---

[8] On the Extended Parallel Process Model see Erin K. Maloney, Maria K. Lapinski, and Kim Witte, "Fear Appeals and Persuasion: A Review and Update of the Extended Parallel Process Model," *Social and Personality Psychology Compass* 5 (2011): 206–19; Kim Witte, "Putting the Fear Back into Fear Appeals: The Extended Parallel Process Model," *Communication Monographs* 59 (1992): 329–49; Kim Witte, "Fear Control and Danger Control: A Test of the Extended Parallel Process Model (EPPM)," *Communication Monographs* 61 (1994): 113–34.

[9] On Jesus see F. Scott Spencer, "To Fear and Not to Fear the Creator God: A Theological and Therapeutic Interpretation of Luke 12:4–34," *Journal of Theological Interpretation* 8 (2014): 229–49. On Paul see Euichang Kim, *The Fear of God in 2 Corinthians 7:1: Its Meaning, Function, and Eschatological Context*, LNTS 605 (London: T&T Clark, 2019). On Peter see Katherine M. Hockey, *The Role of Emotion in 1 Peter*, SNTSMS 173 (Cambridge: Cambridge University Press, 2019), 179–225. On Hebrews see Amy Peeler, "'A Fearful Thing to Fall into the Hands of the Living God': A Study of Fear in the Epistle to the Hebrews," *RevExp* 115 (2018): 40–49. On Revelation see Michael Labahn, "'Gottesfurcht' in der Johannesoffenbarung: Emotionspsychologische Skizzen zur Funktion von 'Furcht' und Angst in der Textpragmatik der Johannesoffenbarung," in *New Perspectives on the Book of Revelation*, ed. Adela Yarbro Collins, BETL 291 (Leuven: Peeters, 2017), 433–60.

God's Right to Punish and Cause Fear

For Philo it was self-evident that God had the right to judge, punish, and motivate obedience through fear. God's rights over creation are linked to his role in creation.[10] As creator, God is both the benefactor and master of all that exists.

> Quite naturally, then, does God give the commandments and exhortations before us to the earthly man.... To enforce the exhortation, both Divine titles are employed, both "Lord" and "God," for it says "God the Lord commanded him." This is in order that, should he obey the exhortations, he may be deemed worthy by God of his benefactions; but that, *should he rebel, he may be driven from the presence of the Lord who has a Master's authority over him.* For this reason again, when he is being cast out of the garden, the sacred writer has introduced the same titles, for he says, "And the Lord God sent him forth out of the garden of delight, to till the ground, out of which he was taken." This is to show that, since "the Lord" as Master and "God" as benefactor had issued the commands, so *in both capacities does He inflict punishment on him who had disobeyed them. For he dismisses the disobedient by the exercise of the very powers which He had exercised in urging him to obedience.* (*Leg.* 1.95–96; italics added) [11]

Philo argues that the two names for God reflect God's dual role as benefactor and master. As the master of every human being God has authority over humanity and the right to punish disobedience. This understanding of God sets the framework for Philo's understanding of the positive role of fear in development toward perfection.

Philo develops God's dual role as Benefactor and Master elsewhere.

> Addressing himself to the mind of man he says, "God asks nothing from thee that is heavy or complicated or difficult, but only something quite simple and easy. And this is just to love Him as a benefactor [εὐεργέτην], or failing this to fear Him at least as a ruler and lord [εἰ δὲ μή, φοβεῖσθαι γοῦν ὡς ἄρχοντα καὶ κύριον], and to tread in every way that will lead thee to please Him, to serve Him not half-heartedly but with thy whole soul filled with the determination to love Him and to cling to His commandments and to honour justice. (*Spec.* 1.299–300; italics added)

As humanity's benefactor, God wants what is best for human beings and seeks to motivate piety through commands and prohibitions. The best

---

[10] On God and creation in Philo see Abraham P. Bos, "Philo on God as 'archê geneseôs,'" *JJS* 60 (2009): 32–47.

[11] Unless otherwise noted, all translations of Philo and Greek excerpts are from PLCL.

possible response is to love God as a benefactor but, if that is not possible, to at least fear him as a ruler and lord and obey through fear.[12]

Philo further brings together God's severe punishment with his benevolence in *On Providence*.

> God is not a tyrant who has made a practice of cruelty and violence and all the deeds committed by a despot who rules by ruthlessness, but a king invested with a kindly and law-abiding sovereignty who governs the whole heaven and earth with justice. Now for a king there is no fitter name than father, for what the father in family life is to the children the king is to the state and God is to the world, God who under the immutable laws of nature has joined in indissoluble union two things most excellent, governorship and guardianship. (*Prov.* 2.2–3)

God is justified in his punishment because he rules the world with lawful authority and exercises this authority as one in a caring relationship to humanity. This understanding of God provides the foundation for Philo to understand God's punishments and fear producing threats.

Parallels could also be noted here to the Roman concept of *pater familias* in which the father of the household had absolute authority over his household and ideally sought to increase the well-being of the household.

Moving down the hierarchy of authority Philo draws an explicit parallel between God as humanity's ruler and master and parents as the rightful rulers and masters of their children.[13] Both God and parents have the right and obligation to motivate their children with threats and punishment when necessary. His comments on the command for children to fear parents in Lev 19:3 are instructive.

> Admirable too, as it seems to me, is that other ordinance where he says, "Let each fear his father and mother." Here *he sets fear before affection* [φόβον πρὸ εὐνοίας τιθείς], not as better in every way, but as more serviceable and profitable for the occasion which he has before him. For in the first place, persons subject to instruction and admonition are in fact wanting in sense, *and want of sense is only cured by fear* [ἀφροσύνη δ᾽ οὐκ ἄλλῳ ἢ φόβῳ θεραπεύεται] ... *but [the law] did enjoin fear for the sake of those who are in the habit of neglecting their duty*. ... But these parents also must be exhorted to employ *more active and*

---

[12] Jutta Leonhardt comments, "Thus the love of God is the first and best way to please Him; however, if this stage has not been reached, the Jewish rituals of worship and the obedience to the Law are the next best way to serve Him as the ruler of all" (*Jewish Worship in Philo of Alexandria*, Texts and Studies in Ancient Judaism 84 [Tübingen: Mohr Siebeck, 2001], 13).

[13] This ordered view of authority in the cosmos is also extended to the future hope of humankind's rule over violent and dangerous animals: "they will no longer as heretofore be roused to ferocity by the sight, but will be awe-struck into respectful fear of him as their natural lord and master [ἄρχοντα καὶ φύσει δεσπότην εὐλαβῶς ἕξει], while others will grow gentle in emulation of the docility and affection for the master" (*Praem.* 89).

severe admonitions to cure the wastage of their children, and the children also that they may stand in awe of those who begot them, *fearing them both as rulers and masters* [δεδιότες καὶ ὡς ἄρχοντας καὶ ὡς φύσει δεσπότας]. For only so, and that hardly, will they *shrink from wrongdoing.* (*Spec.* 2.239–41; italics added) [14]

Philo's views about parents and children parallel his perception of the relationship between God and human beings. There is a role for affection in the relationship but fear is necessary because it alone is able to deal with folly: "and want of sense is only cured by fear" (*Spec.* 2.239).

Fear was the natural, fitting, and necessary response of human beings to their human rulers, of animals to human beings, of children to parents, and of human beings to God. For Philo, God was at the very top of an ordered structure of authority, and as the ultimate authority God had every right to punish and threaten those under him for their good.

The legitimate authority of the threatener is widely recognized today as essential for justifying the use of threat as motivation. Building on the work of Milburn and Watman, Douglas Walton argues that the legitimacy of a threat "has to do with how the occupant of a particular status position who has a role in a given network of social norms uses a threat in accord with the norms of the position and situation. Thus, legitimacy has to do with the social context in which the threat is made, and the relationship of the respondent and the proponent in some system of contractual and social norms."[15] In addition, for a threat to be credible and capable of producing behavioral change the respondent must believe the proponent is able and willing to carry out the threat.[16] Within Philo's worldview God is the ultimate legitimate authority who seeks what is best for humanity and is not adverse to using fear-producing threats to benefit his creatures.

---

[14] In *Spec.* 2.232 Philo draws more attention to the role of threats and punishment in the production of fear and obedience in children: "And therefore fathers have the right to upbraid their children and admonish them severely and if they do not submit to threats conveyed in words to beat and degrade them and put them in bonds. And further if in the face of this they continue to rebel, and carried away by their incorrigible depravity refuse the yoke, the law permits the parents to extend the punishment to death." Philo elsewhere compares the role of political leaders with that of a parent, guardian, or teacher. Everyone in authority must be strict with those under their authority in the hope that they could be improved. This would naturally involve rebuke and punishment. "He who does not gladly receive improving advice must to be consistent censure parents and guardians and teachers and all persons in charge, because they reprimand and sometimes even beat their own children or orphan-wards or pupils, though really it is against all morality to call such treatment evil-speaking or outrage instead of friendliness and benevolence" (*Ios.* 74).

[15] Walton, *Scare Tactics*, 179; Thomas W. Milburn and Kenneth H. Watman, *On the Nature of Threat: A Social Psychological Analysis* (New York: Praeger Publishers, 1981), 49.

[16] Walton, *Scare Tactics*, 120; Milburn and Watman, *On the Nature of Threat*, 17.

Legitimate authority, however, is not sufficient by itself to ethically justify the use of threat and fear appeals. A legitimate authority could still be critiqued for acting in a cruel, vindictive, or oppressive manner. The character and intentions of the threatener are important considerations in ethically evaluating the rhetorical use of threats. Drawing "partly from virtue theory in ethics and epistemology and partly from Kantian principles of respect for persons as ends-in-themselves," Robert Kimball seeks to identify minimal universal norms which could be used to evaluate a threat in any dialogical context.[17] "In general, what's wrong with *argumentum ad baculum* should be explained in terms of the intentions, purposes, and character of threateners, and the differences in intentions and purposes for which threats are made. The character of those who make the threats will provide the criteria for distinguishing benign and malicious threats."[18] Philo's stress on God as humanity's benefactor who employs fear-producing threats for the benefit of humanity seems to indicate that he was aware of the ethical problems associated with fear appeals employed by cruel tyrants. For Philo, however, God is not a vindictive and irrational tyrant who delights in cruelty and suffering; God instead wants what is best for his creatures.

The Benefits of Fearing Punishment

Philo argues that fear could also be very beneficial for the the community. The severe punishments the law required were justified because not only would they prevent the sinner from committing the action again, they would prevent others with fear from committing the same offense.

In §§22–50 of *On the Virtues* Philo focuses on the virtue of courage in wartime. In order to emphasize the important connection of courage with σωφροσύνη (rationality, moderation, sound judgment) and εὐσέβεια (piety, devoutness) Philo retells the story of the Israelite victory over the Midianites (Num 25; 31).[19] Philo does not focus on any of the characters from the biblical account popular in other retellings (Phinehas, Balaam, Balak) but uses the story to focus on the seduction of the Israelite soldiers by the

---

[17] Robert Kimball, "What's Wrong with *Argumentum ad Baculum*? Reasons, Threats, and Logical Norms," *Argumentation* 20 (2006): 89. Cf. Douglas Walton and Fabrizio Macagno, "The Fallaciousness of Threats: Character and *Ad Baculum*," *Argumentation* 21 (2007): 63–81.

[18] Kimball, "What's Wrong with *Argumentum ad Baculum*?," 89.

[19] Walter T. Wilson, *Philo of Alexandria: On Virtues: Introduction, Translation, and Commentary*, PACS 3 (Leiden: Brill, 2011), 122–23.

Midianite women, divine punishment of 24,000 youth who succumb to temptation, and victory by 1,000 pious warriors from each tribe. In Philo's retelling, things could have deteriorated further if God had not intervened.

> And they would have enticed others also of the less stable kind had not God the beneficent and merciful, taking pity for their sad condition, lost no time in punishing the mad folly of the offenders, 24,000 in number, and restrained those who were like to be overwhelmed as by a torrent, but were brought by Him to their senses through fear [φόβῳ νουθετήσας]. (*Virt.* 41)

Several important observations can be made. First, Philo interprets God's judgment of the 24,000 as a beneficial act of mercy and pity on the community as a whole. The just judgment of some is mercy on others. Second, judgment as mercy works by keeping the majority from the actions which would lead to God's judgment. Third, judgment is effective as mercy by motivating those in danger of succumbing through fear and terror. Philo presents all of this in a very positive and approving manner; motivation to godliness and self-control by fear of divine wrath is effective, praiseworthy, and, at least sometimes, necessary.

The communal benefits of fear inducing punishment is also evident in Philo's comments about the need to cut off the hand of a woman who grabbed the genitals of a man in a quarrel.

> The fact that she does so with the evident intention of helping her husband must not absolve her. To restrain her over-boldness she must pay a penalty which will incapacitate herself, if she wishes to repeat the offense, and *frighten the more reckless members of her sex into proper behaviour* [φόβῳ μετριάσουσιν]. And the penalty shall be this—that the hand shall be cut off which has touched what decency forbids it to touch. (*Spec.* 3.175; italics added)

Fear producing punishments were beneficial to the broader community by instilling healthy fear.[20] Philo also recognizes the value of severity in warfare "to intimidate and so admonish the neighboring peoples [καὶ ὑπὲρ τοῦ νουθετῆσαι φόβῳ τοὺς ὁμόρους], for men learn to behave wisely from the sufferings of others [ἐπειδὴ τοῖς ἑτέρων πάθεσιν ἄνθρωποι διδάσκονται σωφρονεῖν]" (*Spec* 4.223).

In addition to warning others, fear producing punishments had a restorative, and not just punitive, function. Reflecting on the Deuteronomistic curses he argues that "if however they accept these chastisements as a warning rather than as intending their perdition, if shamed into a whole-hearted conversion, they reproach themselves for going thus astray, and

---

[20] On these convictions in the broader Greco-Roman world see Patera, "Reflections on the Discourse of Fear," 123–26. Cf. Aristotle, *Eth. nic.* 10.10.1179b7–14; Aeschylus, *Eum.* 690, 698; Plato, *Gorg.* 525b.

make a full confession and acknowledgement of all their sin ... then they will find favour with God the Savior, the Merciful" (*Praem.* 163).,,

The apparent harshness of Philo's comments about chopping off a woman's hand in *Spec.* 3.175 and his positive evaluation of social shaming in *Praem.* 163 is cause for ethical concern; ethicists have argued that fear appeals can cause active harm by stigmatizing, humiliating, and marginalizing target populations:[21] "Once stereotypes and stigmas are established, they can result in individuals being feared, avoided, regarded as deviant, and even blamed for engaging in the immoral behaviors that must have elicited the 'punishment' of their affliction."[22] Stigmatization can cause the internalization of self-blame, destroy self-esteem, produce shame, guilt, and isolation, and lead to abuse, ridicule, and social exclusion by the broader society.[23] Philo is not afraid to use shame and fear as motivation and he seems to employ a utilitarian ethic; the punishment of some will prevent greater harm to many. Philo's general attitude is not idiosyncratic and ethicists generally hold the view that "considerations of benefit can override worries relating to harm."[24] Although almost universally viewed negatively, stigmatization through social norming could lead to positive benefits to the broader public if it pressures individuals to change destructive behavior.[25] Philo would agree with these pragmatic and utilitarian approaches to the potential negative side effects of the use of fear appeals.

Several of the ideas mentioned so far are combined in Philo's discussion in *On the Embassy to Gaius*:,God's correction of human beings is actually an expression of his beneficence, punishment often leads to the instruction and improvement of sinners, and if not, it at least functions to motivate others to proper behavior through fear.

> Assuming that the punitive are to be classed among the beneficial, not only on the ground that they are a part of laws and statutes, since no law can be complete unless it includes two provisions—honours for things good and punishment for things evil, but because the punishment of others often admonishes offenders and calls them to wisdom [ἡ κόλασις νουθετεῖ καὶ σωφρονίζει πολλάκις μὲν καὶ τοὺς ἁμαρτάνοντας], or, certainly at any rate, their neighbours. For

---

[21] Guttman and Salmon, "Guilt, Fear, Stigma and Knowledge Gaps," 547; Brown and Whiting, "The Ethics of Distress," 91.

[22] Guttman and Salmon, "Guilt, Fear, Stigma and Knowledge Gaps," 547.

[23] Guttman and Salmon, "Guilt, Fear, Stigma and Knowledge Gaps," 547; Brown and Whiting, "The Ethics of Distress," 91.

[24] Brown and Whiting, "The Ethics of Distress," 91.

[25] Cf. Hyunyi Cho and Charles T. Salmon, "Unintended Effects of Health Communication Campaigns," *Journal of Communication* 57 (2007): 305–6; Claudia Amonini, Simone Pettigrew, and Cassandra Clayforth, "The Potential of Shame as a Message Appeal in Antismoking Television Advertisements," *Tobacco Control* 24 (2015): 436.

penalties are good for the morals of the multitude, who fear to suffer the like [φόβῳ τοῦ μὴ παραπλήσια παθεῖν]. (*Legat.* 7)

For Philo, fear of punishment thus plays an important part in the moral formation of community members and fear appeals are an expression of God's kindness.

Philo's Rhetorical Use of Threat and Fear

We have seen that Philo views God as holding legitimate authority to punish but that God is motivated by benevolence and kindness in the use of fear to instruct humankind. Building upon this, Philo himself utilizes fear appeals to motivate his readers in moral and spiritual development. Unlike, for example, the Apocalypse of John, Philo does this as a philosopher and exegete and not as a prophet.[26] Nevertheless, the consequential logic of the rhetorical use of divine threat is quite similar.

Philo's discussion of the death of the soul clearly illustrates his use of fear appeals as motivation for virtue and moral progress (*Post.* 71–74; *Her.* 53; 201; *Leg.* 1.105–108; 2.77; 3.35, 52, 72; *Fug.* 54–64; *QG* 2.12; *Spec.* 1.345; *Agr.* 67–77; 94–101).[27] The death of the soul is a death to virtue which is described by Philo as a punishment (*Leg.* 1.107).[28] Zurawski synthesizes the material and argues that the "sins Philo most often claims are responsible for the death of the soul are blasphemy, devotion to pleasure, and lack of education."[29] A more general but over-arching explanation would be that the death of one's soul is caused by extreme wickedness.[30]

---

[26] On John's use of threats and fear appeals see Alexander E. Stewart, "*Argumentum ad Baculum* in the Apocalypse of John: Toward an Evaluation of John's Use of Threats," in *New Perspectives on the Book of Revelation*, ed. Adela Yarbro Collins, BETL 291 (Leuven, Peeters, 2017), 461–72.

[27] On the death of the soul in Philo see Sami Yli-Karjanmaa, *Reincarnation in Philo of Alexandria*, SPhiloMS 7 (Atlanta: SBL Press, 2015), 57–70; D. Zeller, "The Life and Death of the Soul in Philo of Alexandria: The Use and Origin of a Metaphor," *SPhiloA* 7 (1995): 19–55; John T. Conroy, "Philo's 'Death of the Soul': Is This Only a Metaphor?" *SPhiloA* 23 (2011): 23–40; Emma Wasserman, *The Death of the Soul in Romans 7: Sin, Death, and the Law in Light of Hellenistic Moral Psychology*, WUNT 2.256 (Tübingen: Mohr Siebeck, 2008), 60–76; Jason M. Zurawski, "Hell on Earth: Corporeal Existence as the Ultimate Punishment of the Wicked in Philo of Alexandria and the Wisdom of Solomon," in *Heaven, Hell, and the Afterlife: Eternity in Judaism, Christianity, and Islam: Volume 1: End Time and Afterlife in Judaism*, ed. J. Harold Ellens (Santa Barbara, CA: Praeger, 2013), 193–226.

[28] Cf. Zeller, "The Life and Death of the Soul in Philo," 21.

[29] Zurawski, "Hell on Earth," 196.

[30] Wasserman, *The Death of the Soul*, 65–66.

Moving beyond specific warnings related to the death of the soul, in *On the Cherubim* Philo employs a divine threat formulated in a conditional clause: if we do not do this, God will do this. Most explicit threats exhibit consistent formal features and "find expression as a single statement, many times on the order of 'If you (or he or she) doesn't ..., then ____.'"[31] Philo presents the conditional threat as a general precept by including himself among those in danger. "Seeing then that our souls are a region open to His invisible entrance, let us make that place as beautiful as we may, to be a lodging fit for God. *Else [εἰ δὲ μή] He will pass silently into some other home*, where He judges that the builder's hands have wrought something worthier" (*Cher.* 98; italics added). If Philo and his hearers did not adequately prepare their souls to be fitting abodes for God he would abandon them. For Philo, the real and possible negative outcome should motivate himself and others to pursue moral and spiritual development. Fear of loss should motivate positive action; this is the common logical structure of a fear appeal.

In the examples we have looked at so far Philo uses fear of divine action (punishment) as motivation for action but he also often used argumentation from the consequences of an action to try to motivate through fear without explicit mention of divine punishment.[32]

In *On the Sacrifices of Cain and Abel* we encounter perhaps the fullest articulation of an evil person ever composed by an author or speaker. Philo begins with a conditional clause: if his hearers worshipped pleasure, they would become terrible people (*Sacr.* 32). This conditional argumentation motivates with fear of the consequences. It is fascinating to note that in such a long list of terrible results of worshipping pleasure there is no mention of divine final judgment. It is assumed that God would judge such a person, but it is also evident that becoming such a person was in itself the punishment because it led to the death of the soul.

Philo uses such "if, then" consequentialism as motivation elsewhere.

[F]or *if one has not a clear view* of what is farther on, of what is worth seeing and hearing, of virtues, that is to say, and virtuous actions, but turns round to look at what is behind and at his back; *if he pursues* the deafness of glory, the blindness of wealth, the stupidity of bodily robustness, and the empty-mindedness of external beauty, and all that is akin to these, *he will be set up as a*

---

[31] Michael J. Wreen, "A Bolt of Fear," *Philosophy and Rhetoric* 22 (1989): 138. In contrast to a threat, a warning includes a statement of intentionality. Cf. Walton, *Scare Tactics*, 113–14; Bruce Fraser, "Warning and Threatening," *Centrum* 3 (1975): 173.

[32] Fear appeals are widely recognized as arguments from the consequences. Cf. Walton, *Scare Tactics*, 191.

soulless pillar, with its substance streaming down from it; for salt has no firmness. (*Somn.* 1.248; italics added)

If anyone fails to look in the direction of the virtues and looks backward instead he will be like a lifeless pillar of salt melting away. In this example Philo uses fear-inducing consequentialism focused on the consequences of one's trajectory in moral development.

Another example of this common conditional argumentation is evident in a brief section in *On the Special Laws*: "And if anyone renders the worship due to the Eternal, the Creator, to a created being and one later in time, he must stand recorded as infatuated and guilty of impiety in the highest degree" (*Spec.* 1.20). This rhetorical "if, then" construction shames any readers who may be contemplating idolatry with the threat of being charged with impiety and whatever consequences such a charge might bring.[33] ,

Philo elsewhere explicitly distinguishes between normal consequences inflicted by humans in authority and the punishment that proceeds from God in his attempt to scare his readers with the consequences of not informing against an oath breaker.

If anyone knows that another has perjured himself, and influenced by friendship or shame or fear rather than piety, fails to inform against him or bring him to justice, he must be liable to the same penalties as the perjurer. For to range oneself on the side of the wrongdoer is just the same as committing the wrong. *As to the penalties of perjury, some proceed from God, others from man. The highest and greatest are from God, Who is not gentle to such impiety,* but suffers the guilty to remain for ever in their well-nigh hopeless uncleanness, a just and fitting penalty, I hold. (*Spec.* 2.26–27; italics added)

The increased severity in God's punishment lies first and foremost in the fact that God allows them to remain forever in their unpurified state. He does not come to their aid to help them change. Philo also affirms the justice and propriety of God's judgment; God has the right and duty to judge.

In *On Dreams* Philo again uses an "if, then" fear producing argument to focus on God's role in bringing the punishment.

Yet, *if they pass* from this intoxication to sobriety, and become themselves again; if realizing the sottishness of their past they feel shame and self-reproach for the sins to which their ill-judging judgment has led them; if they take repentance for their counsellor, a counsellor impervious to flattery and bribery; if they propitiate the merciful power of Him that is by recantations in which holiness replaces profanity, they will obtain full pardon. But *if they continue* for ever to plunge and prance like stiff-necked horses disobedient to the rein, as though they were free and independent and rulers of others, necessity inexo-

---

[33] On Philo's views of idolatry see Karl-Gustav Sandelin, "The Danger of Idolatry according to Philo of Alexandria," *Temenos* 27 (1991): 122–23.

rable and implacable will make them feel that in all things great and small they are as nothing. *For the charioteer who has mounted the winged chariot of this world will put his bridle upon them and pull back with force the hitherto slackened reins till they are taut, tighten the muzzles, and with whip and spur recall to them the nature of that imperious authority,* which the kindness and gentleness of the ruler had caused them to forget, as bad servants do. For such misconstrue the mildness of the masters as failure to govern, and ape the state of those who have not master, *until the owner stems the full flood of the disease, by applying punishments in the place of remedies.* (*Somn.* 2.292–95; italics added)

Those who remain unrepentant and obstinate will not escape unscathed but the true master will afflict them with whip and spur in order to apply punishment as a remedy for prideful autonomy and independence. Philo seeks to increase his readers' fear of God's punishment as motivation to humility and moral improvement.

After recounting the various ways that several persons guilty of sacrilege met their untimely deaths Philo draws the conclusion that "it is reasonable to assert that they were the victims of divine justice" (*Prov.* 2.34). Untimely physical death could be explained as accidental coincidences but, for Philo, God was involved in history to bring punishments through natural causes. The interpretation of misfortune as divine judgment was widespread in Greco-Roman religion. Chaniotis notes, "[t]he fear of divine punishment for crimes, violations of sacred regulations, impiety, or anything else that might cause the anger of gods was omnipresent in Greek culture."[34]

It has been debated whether or not Philo thought there would be divine punishment and reward following death. Fred W. Burnett argues that, "In Philo there is no clear presentation of either an afterlife with rewards and punishments, as there is in Palestinian Judaism, or of a heaven and hell."[35] In contrast, Sandelin, commenting on *Praem.* 152, argues, "Idolaters who escape the death penalty will be punished in the after life."[36] In seeking to motivate fellow Jews not to engage in idolatry Philo praises the faithful proselyte and, in contrast, argues that "the nobly born who has falsified the sterling of his high lineage will be dragged right down and carried into Tartarus itself and profound darkness" (*Praem.* 152). Similarly, in *Questions*

---

[34] Chaniotis, "Constructing the Fear of Gods," 210. His discussion of epigraphic memorials of divine justice is particularly instructive (215–23).
[35] Fred W. Burnett, "Philo on Immortality: A Thematic Study of Philo's Concept of παλιγγενεσία," *CBQ* 46 (1984): 464. This does not mean that Philo did not hold to the immortality of the soul but that, "Philo gives no unequivocal, systematic discussion of his view of immortality" (464). Cf. Samuel Sandmel, *Philo of Alexandria: An Introduction* (Oxford: Oxford University Press, 1979), 116–17.
[36] Sandelin, "The Danger of Idolatry," 143, cf. 123. ,

and Answers on Exodus Philo argues that people with unrestricted passion would be "drawn downward ... to the depths of Tartarus" (*QE* 2.40). In *Cher.* 2 he seems to clearly discuss the reality of eternal punishment: "to him that is weighed down and enslaved by that fierce and incurable malady, the horrors of the future must needs be undying and eternal: he is thrust forth to the place of the impious, there to endure misery continuous and unrelieved." Elsewhere, however, Philo uses Tartarus as a metaphor for the present imprisonment of materialistic people. The earthly body and desires are the "true Tartarus" (*QG* 4.234).

Clint Burnett concludes that, "for Philo, then, Tartarus was a place of literal punishment for the wicked, but it was also true that a life devoted to materialism was already an existence in a state of Tartarus."[37] Recent work on reincarnation in Philo, however, calls this conclusion into question and it is possible that Philo saw the repeated cycle of living death through reincarnation as the fulfillment of souls being dragged into Tartarus.[38] Because, however, Philo never explicitly discusses reincarnation by way of acceptance or rejection it is also possible to read him as espousing a conditional immortality which is forfeited through the death of the soul.[39] Regardless, there is a growing consensus that there is no Hell in Philo as traditionally understood.[40] Yli-Karjanmaa concludes his study of reincarnation in Philo with questions for further research related to the severity of the danger: "Are some souls incurable like in Plato? If so, what is their fate—can Winston's suggestion of an endless series of reincarnations be upheld for them or do they face, e.g., annihilation?"[41]

We are now in a position to briefly comment on the four main elements of a successful fear appeal according to the Extended Parallel Process Model, a model used extensively to develop and evaluate fear appeals in

---

[37] Clint Burnett, "Going through Hell: ΤΑΡΤΑΡΟΣ in Greco-Roman Culture, Second Temple Judaism, and Philo of Alexandria," *Journal of Ancient Judaism* 4 (2013): 376.

[38] Yli-Karjanmaa, *Reincarnation in Philo of Alexandria*, 185, 242–43.

[39] On the lack of explicit endorsement of reincarnation in Philo see Yli-Karjanmaa, *Reincarnation in Philo of Alexandria*, 2–3. Yli-Karjanmaa explains this phenomenon as a result of Philo's unwillingness to explicitly follow Plato on a point that was so foreign to his Jewish heritage (244–45). On conditional immortality see Conroy, "Philo's 'Death of the Soul,'" 25–26; Zurawski, "Hell on Earth," 204–7; Jason von Ehrenkrook, "The Afterlife in Philo and Josephus," in *Heaven, Hell, and the Afterlife: Eternity in Judaism, Christianity, and Islam: Volume 1: End Time and Afterlife in Judaism*, ed. J. Harold Ellens (Santa Barbara, CA: Praeger, 2013), 104.

[40] Zurawski, "Hell on Earth," 203; Ehrenkrook, "The Afterlife in Philo and Josephus," 104–5.

[41] Yli-Karjanmaa, *Reincarnation in Philo of Alexandria*, 248.

the social scientific literature.[42] A successful fear appeal needs to convince a hearer that the danger is severe (threat severity), they or a loved one is susceptible to the danger (threat susceptibility), the proposed solution works (response efficacy), and the proposed solution is possible to implement (self-efficacy; the easier the better). In Philo's own use of fear appeals to motivate his readers toward moral perfection in virtue he regularly stresses the severity of the danger. Whether it led to eventual annihilation or de-evolution into a bestial form, the death of the soul was severe and everyone was susceptible to the danger. He insists that his proposed solution would work, the pursuit of virtue through philosophy would enable a person to overcome the passions and gain the immortal life of love and affection toward God unencumbered by a body (*Fug.* 58). He recognizes that the solution is not necessarily easy and would require vigilance (*Post.* 72), but he seeks to motivate his hearers with the assurance that success was possible.[43]

The Necessity of Fear is Audience Specific

At several points Philo distinguishes between different groups of people. Some people do not need to be motivated by fear but for others fear is the only motivation which will penetrate their dullness and stubbornness. The significance of individual differences has been widely investigated by social scientists evaluating the effectiveness of fear appeals.[44] "No messages produce uniform effects across a spectrum of audiences"; individual differences affect an individual's evaluation of severity, susceptibility, response efficacy, and self-efficacy.[45]

In *On Dreams* Philo explains that the Scripture used anthropomorphisms to describe God because some people are dull and unable to

---

[42] Cf. Maloney, Lapinski, and Witte, "Fear Appeals and Persuasion," 206–19; Witte, "Putting the Fear Back into Fear Appeals," 329–49; Witte, "Fear Control and Danger Control," 113–34.

[43] In general, Philo's soteriology could be described as synergistic: "the soul needs to make progress on its own but recognize its dependence on God's grace in order to be saved" (Yli-Karjanmaa, *Reincarnation in Philo of Alexandria*, 243).

[44] Cf. Hyunyi Cho and Kim Witte, "A Review of Fear-Appeal Effects," in *Perspectives on Persuasion, Social Influence, and Compliance Gaining*, ed. John S. Seiter and Robert H. Gass (Boston: Allyn and Bacon, 2004), 223; Robin L. Nabi, David Roskos-Ewoldsen, and Francesca Dillman Carpenter, "Subjective Knowledge and Fear Appeal Effectiveness: Implications for Message Design," *Health Communications* 23 (2008): 191.

[45] Cho and Witte, "A Review of Fear-Appeal Effects," 223.

understand or conceive of God in any other way. The use of fear for motivation is necessary for such people.

> [Some] are altogether dull in their natures, incapable of forming any conception whatever of God as without a body, people whom it is impossible to instruct otherwise than in this way, saying that as a man does so God arrives and departs, goes down and comes up, makes use of a voice, is displeased at wrongdoings, *is inexorable in His anger, and in addition to all this has provided Himself with shafts and swords and all other instruments of vengeance against the unrighteous. For it is something to be thankful for if they can be taught self-control* [σωφρονίζω] *by the terror held over them* [ἐπικρεμασθέντι φόβῳ] *by these means.* (*Somn.* 1.236–37; italics added)

Philo certainly thinks it is better to worship God for the right motives (for God's own sake) but even worship from fear, a lesser motive, is better than no worship at all. A fearful response from someone who only cares about avoiding God's punishment is not ideal but is sufficient to avert the punishment and may actually succeed in transforming the person to eventually worship God from better motives than fear.

> But God cannot suffer injury, and therefore He gladly invites all who set themselves to honour Him under any form whatsoever, and in His eyes none such deserves rejection. Indeed one might almost say that to those whose souls have ears God speaks plainly as follows: "My first prizes will be set apart for those who honour Me for Myself alone, the second to those who honour Me for their own sakes, either *hoping to win blessings or expecting to obtain remission of punishments*, since, though their worship is for reward and not disinterested, yet all the same its range lies within the divine precincts and does not stray outside. But the prizes set aside for those who honour Me for Myself will be gifts of friendship; to those whose motive is self-interest they do not show friendship but that I do not count them as aliens. For I accept both him who wishes to enjoy My beneficial power and thus partake of blessings and *him who propitiates the dominance and authority of the master to avoid chastisement. For I know well that they will not only not be worsened, but actually bettered, through the persistence of their worship and through practicing piety pure and undefiled. For,* however different are the characters which produce in them impulse to do My pleasure, no charge shall be brought against them, since they have one aim and object, to serve Me." (*Abr.* 127–30; italics added)

Speaking on God's behalf, Philo claims that fear of punishment is an important and sufficient (although not the perfect) motivation for moral development.

Even though fear is necessary for some, if not many, people, it is a lesser motivation. "Praise cannot be duly given to one who obeys the written laws, *since he acts under the admonition of restraint and the fear of punishment* [νουθετούμενος ἀνάγκῃ καὶ φόβῳ κολάσεως]. But he who faithfully observes the unwritten deserves commendation, since the virtue which he displays is freely willed" (*Spec.* 4.150; italics added). Philo elsewhere

praises those who do what is right "not through fear but of their own free will, for a right action if self-prompted is everywhere held in higher honour than if done under compulsion" (*Spec.* 4.193).
He develops this in more detail in *That God is Unchangeable.*

> But they whose natural wit is more dense and dull, or whose early training has been mishandled, since they have no power of clear vision, need physicians in the shape of admonishers, who will devise the treatment proper to their present condition. Thus ill-disciplined and foolish slaves receive profit from a master who frightens them [φοβερὸς δεσπότης ὠφέλιμος], *for they fear his threats and menaces* [τὰς γὰρ ἐπανατάσεις καὶ ἀπειλὰς αὐτοῦ δεδιότες] *and thus involuntarily are schooled by fear* [φόβῳ νουθετοῦνται]. All such may well learn the untruth, which will benefit them, if they cannot be brought to wisdom by truth. … So then the lawgiver, thereby being now approved as the best of physicians for the distempers and maladies of the soul, set before himself one task and purpose, to make a radical excision of the diseases of the mind and leave no root to sprout again into sickness which defies cure. In this way he hoped to be able to eradicate the evil, namely *by representing the supreme Cause as dealing in threats and oftentimes shewing indignation and implacable anger, or again as using weapons of war for His onslaughts on the unrighteous. For this is the only way in which the fool can be admonished.* And therefore it seems to me that with the two aforesaid maxims, "God is as a man," and "God is not as a man," he has linked two other principles closely connected and consequent on them, *namely fear and love. For I observe that all the exhortations to piety in the law refer either to our loving or our fearing the Existent* [τὰς γὰρ διὰ τῶν νόμων εἰς εὐσέβειαν ὁρῶ παρακελεύσεις ἁπάσας ἀναφερομένας ἢ πρὸς τὸ ἀγαπᾶν ἢ πρὸς τὸ φοβεῖσθαι τὸν ὄντα]. And thus to love Him is the most suitable for those into whose conception of the Existent no thought of human parts or passions enters, who pay Him the honour meet for God for His own sake only. *To fear is most suitable to the others.* (*Deus* 63–69; italics added)

Philo creatively describes divine fear producing punishment and threats as anthropomorphic language. For Philo, such language is a necessary deception because so many people are dull and sluggish and would not respond to any other motivation.[46] Philo again attributes such fear producing threats and punishments to God's beneficence.

Negative Perspectives on Fear

Katherine Hockey develops a comparison between Philo and the Stoics in regard to shared attitudes toward the passions, including a negative view

---

[46] Jean Daniélou comments, "Accordingly, ἀγάπη appears as belonging to the perfect in Philo also, to those from whose eyes the scales have fallen regarding all anthropomorphism in God, because they no longer need to be treated as children" (*Philo of Alexandria*, trans. James G. Colbert [Cambridge: James Clark, 2014], 168).

of fear.[47] She notes that Philo could warn of fear turning someone away from the straight road (ἀποστρέφοντος καὶ ἀποκλίνοντος τὴν ἐπ᾽ εὐθείας ὁρμὴν φόβου; *Mos.* 2.139) and how a virtuous person is truly free because "[h]e stands defiant and triumphant over love, fear [φόβῳ], cowardice, grief and all that sort" (*Prob.* 21). Freedom from the fear of death is the ultimate freedom (*Prob.* 22; cf. *Prob.* 111; *Ios.* 68–70) and wise people who prioritize and order their lives in accordance with virtue do not fear other people (*Prob.* 154). The soul must find freedom from fear.

> For if the soul is driven by desire, or enticed by pleasure, or diverted from its course by fear [φόβῳ], or shrunken by grief, or helpless in the grip of anger, it enslaves itself and makes him whose soul it is a slave to a host of masters. But if it vanquishes ignorance with good sense, incontinences with self-control, cowardice with courage [δειλίαν δὲ ἀνδρείᾳ], and covetousness with justice, it gains not only freedom from slavery but the gift of ruling as well. (*Prob.* 159)

Philo certainly holds that a certain kind of fear should be rejected by the wise in the pursuit of perfection. A broader exploration of Philo's attitudes toward fear, however, require a qualification of Hockey's claim that Philo is in continuity with the Stoics in seeing fear primarily as a negative passion.[48] Irrational fear should be rejected by the wise, but Philo has a much wider appreciation for the positive role of rational fear. Stoic philosophy does recognize the value of a certain kind of rational fear which they label εὐλά- βεια ("caution").[49] Philo recognizes the difference in value between rational and irrational fear, but, unlike the Stoics, he does not lexically differentiate positive and negative fear. Φοβός, for example, could be positive or negative for Philo depending upon the context and the object. Fear of God is always good but a proper fear of punishment by human authority figures can also play a positive and valuable role in the betterment of individuals and society as a whole. Philo likely views φοβός positively in contrast to Stoic philosophy because the LXX uses φοβός with God as an object in such a positive way throughout. In broader Greek usage (not influenced by the LXX) φόβος often indicates an irrational fear (especially when modified by κένος) while δέος and δείδω generally indicate a more reasonable fear.[50] Philo's apparently contradictory comments on fear, both positive and

[47] Hockey, *The Role of Emotion*, 183. Although not the main influence, there are many points of continuity between Philo and Stoic thinking. See Wasserman, *The Death of the Soul*, 45–47; Sharon Weisser, "Why Does Philo Criticize the Stoic Ideal of *Apatheia* in *On Abraham* 257? Philo and Consolatory Literature," *CQ* 62 (2012): 242–59.

[48] Hockey, *The Role of Emotion*, 183.

[49] Hockey, *The Role of Emotion*, 180–181; cf. Diogenes Laertius, *Vitae* 7.112–116.

[50] See, in particular, Patera, "Reflections on the Discourse of Fear," 110, 116, 122; cf. Chaniotis, "Constructing the Fear of Gods," 205–34.

negative, is not evidence of inconsistency but rather reflects different objects and purpose. When the fear is of God or a rightful authority and has the purpose of motivating people toward virtue and moral development it is valuable even if it is a lesser motivation than love.

Fearful Confidence

Even though it is better for people to approach and seek God through love and other pure motives Philo recognizes that this cannot ever really happen without some degree of fear because of the great gulf between who God is and who human beings are. He makes the following comments in reflection on the blending of fear and confidence in Abraham's question to God in Gen 15:2; the broader discussion indicates that Moses shared this blend of fear and confidence.

> Yet I, who proclaim my confidence, confess in turn my fear and consternation [ἀλλ᾽ ὁ λέγων ἐγὼ θαρρεῖν πάλιν ὁμολογῶ δεδιέναι καὶ καταπεπλῆχθαι], and still the fear and the confidence are not at war within me in separate camps [καὶ οὐκ ἔχει τὴν ἄμικτον ἐν ἐμοὶ μάχην φόβος τε καὶ θάρσος], as one might suppose, but are blended in a harmony [ἀλλὰ τὴν ἀνακεκραμένην συμφωνίαν]. I find then a feast which does not cloy in this blending [ἀπλήστως οὖν εὐωχοῦμαι τοῦ κράματος; or "I drink insatiably of this well-mixed cup"[51]], which has schooled my speech to be neither bold without caution, nor cautious without boldness [ὃ με ἀναπέπεικε μήτε ἄνευ εὐλαβείας παρρησιάζεσθαι μήτε ἀπαρρησιάστως εὐλαβεῖσθαι]. (*Heir* 28–29 [Colson and Whitaker, LCL])

Short of perfection, the most one could hope for in this life is a well-mixed cup of fear and confidence. Abraham and Moses are as close as it comes to perfection for Philo and are clear models for emulation.[52]

In *On Rewards and Punishment* Philo has an extended discussion of future hope based on scriptural promises. Increasing moral development toward virtue in humankind will lead to transformation in the world which will include the domestication of previously violent and dangerous animals (*Praem.* 85–92). This will lead to a time of peace and prosperity guaranteed by the coming of an irresistible messianic figure in fulfillment of the LXX of Num 24:7. This figure will lead securely because he will perfectly combine dignity, terror, and benevolence in his rule.

[51] C. D. Yonge, *The Works of Philo: Complete and Unabridged,* updated ed. (Peabody, MA: Hendrickson, 1995), 278.
[52] Annette Y. Reed, "The Construction and Subversion of Patriarchal Perfection: Abraham and Exemplarity in Philo, Josephus, and the *Testament of Abraham*," *JSJ* 40 (2009): 193; Satlow, "Philo on Human Perfection," 506–11.

For "there shall come forth a man," says the oracle, and leading his host to war he will subdue great and populous nations ... who will win not only a permanent and bloodless victory in the war but also a sovereignty which none can contest, *bringing to its subjects the benefit which will accrue from the affection or fear or respect which they feel.* For the conduct of their rulers shows three high qualities which contribute to make a government secure from subversion, namely *dignity, strictness* [δεινότητα; harshness, sternness, severity], *benevolence,* which produce the feelings mentioned above. For respect is created by dignity, *fear by strictness* [τὸ δὲ δεινὸν (κατασκευάζει) φόβον], affection by benevolence, and these when blended harmoniously in the soul *render subjects obedient to their rulers.* (*Praem.* 95–97; italics added)

Some would submit to this future ruler out of affection, fear, or respect; for Philo the motivation wouldn't matter since the end goal would be achieved: proper obedience to the rightful ruler. Philo acknowledges that perfect stability could not depend upon fear alone. It was necessary for the perfect ruler to have a perfect blend of dignity, terror, and beneficence in order to produce an ongoing and sustainable obedient response motivated by a mix of respect, fear, and good will. Even though Philo is reflecting on utopian hopes for a future state of existence based upon the biblical prophecies, he still foresees the necessity of fear in this period of restoration.

Conclusion

Philo was not afraid of fear. He saw it instead as a necessary part of humankind's moral development toward the virtues and perfection. Philo's view of God as the ultimate authority and master over humanity gives God the unquestioned right to punish and motivate people to perfection with fear-inducing threats. God is not a vicious and mean tyrant but the threats and punishment are necessary for God to fulfill his role as humanity's benefactor. God, as humanity's benefactor and master, uses punishment and threats to reform the sinner when possible and perfect the broader community through fear of punishment.

With these foundational beliefs in place, Philo utilized fear producing threats, often in "if, then" constructions, to motivate his own readers with the consequences of their choices. He often focused on the natural consequences which one could expect to reap in this life but he was not afraid to go beyond this to describe God's active punishment of sinners.

In Philo's rhetorical use of fear he clearly recognized that fearful argumentation was audience specific. Not everyone would need to be motivated by fear to the same degree but for some people that was the only kind of motivation which had a chance of breaking through their dullness.

However, even those with pure motives who were well on their way to perfection would never be able to completely live without fear of God in this life—even Moses and Abraham lived with a well-mixed blend of fear and confidence.

This survey of Philo's theoretical and practical reflection on the rhetorical use of divine threat demonstrates that he shared many ideas with the broader Greco-Roman religious and political landscape. He also articulated many ideas which are being discussed by argumentation theorists and social scientists interested in fear appeals today. Philo's religious context makes his insights in this area particularly relevant for New Testament studies. The New Testament is filled with warnings, divine threats, and fear appeals but has less explicit reflection on the logic of divine fear appeals. The New Testament authors are primarily practitioners while Philo provides explicit reflection on how and why divine fear appeals were seen as effective in a first century context.

Tyndale Theological Seminary
Badhoevedorp, The Netherlands

PHILO AND THE FATHERS ON MUSIC

EVERETT FERGUSON

Philo, the Alexandrian Jewish philosopher of the early first century, makes numerous references to music, but few studies have been devoted to this subject.[1] I will take representative passages from the corpus of Philo's writings and then offer a comparison and contrast of Philo with some of the church fathers. For this presentation I will do something I will not let my students do and appear to treat the Philonic corpus as a single body and early Christian literature as of one piece, but the purpose is tracing some of the common ideas in Philo and early Christianity. The point is not that the fathers were indebted to Philo, although in individual cases they may be influenced by him, but that both bodies of literature reflect a common cultural and philosophical background.

Philo on Music

Many of Philo's comments on music reflect current philosophical views on the subject. This may be seen in the way Philo relates musical harmony to the harmony of the cosmos, the ethical harmony of the soul, and harmony in the community. The Pythagoreans, followed by Plato and then by musical theorists, spoke of the "music of the spheres" and correlated the mathematical relations of the position of the heavenly bodies with the ratios of musical intervals.[2] Philo puts these ideas in a biblical, theological context and says that the creation is the "true music, the original and

---

[1] Louis H. Feldman, "Philo's View on Music," *Journal of Jewish Music and Liturgy* 9 (1986): 36–54; repr. in *Studies in Hellenistic Judaism* (Leiden: Brill, 1996), 504–28; Siegmund Levarie, "Philo on Music," *The Journal of Musicology* 9 (1991): 124–30; Everett Ferguson, "The Art of Praise: Philo and Philodemus on Music," in *Early Christianity and Classical Culture. Comparative Studies in Honor of Abraham J. Malherbe*, ed. John T. Fitzgerald, Thomas H. Olbricht, and L. Michael White (Leiden: Brill, 2003), 391–426, from which much of this material on Philo is drawn.

[2] Plato, *Resp.* 530d–531b; *Tim.* 34b–36d; Ps. Plutarch, *Mus.* 44 (=*Mor.* 1147a); Ptolemy, *Harmony* 3.4.95; Aristides Quitilianus, *Music* 2.8.66–68; 3.7.105; 9.107–27.133; 14.79–82.

model" from which human beings derived "this most necessary and beneficial art" (music).[3] The world is God's instrument with which he makes harmonious melody.[4] The harmony of the movement of the stars parallels the music made by birds and human beings.[5]

Music was important for Philo because of its effect in promoting the harmony of the soul and of the whole person.[6] Music "heals what is disproportionate, immoderate, and discordant in us."[7] Many philosophers espoused this ethos theory of music.[8] Philo, moreover, used the language of music to describe a person who thinks, speaks, and does good: observance of the ten commandments results in the soul being "an instrument that makes music harmoniously in all its parts for a melodious life and blameless concert."[9] Thus the human being, especially the soul, is likened to a musical instrument.[10] A corollary of the effects of music on a person was that it could have a harmful influence in arousing lust and promoting idolatry.[11]

The harmony of the self corresponded to the harmony of the community. The city is like a soul, and the best constitution is like a hymn to God;[12] and the unity of a people is like a symphony.[13] The correlation of musical imagery with establishing and sustaining community also had philosophical precedent.[14]

Music for Philo existed primarily for praising God. He often brought together the music of the cosmos with human praise.

Both heaven and the mind have the capacity to declaim praises, hymns, and blessings to the Father who is the One who brought them into being. For the human being was assigned the excellent reward above all other living things to worship the One who is, while the heaven is always melodious, producing all-musical harmony by the movements of its parts....

---

[3] Philo, *Opif.* 78. All translations from Philo are from PLCL.

[4] Philo, *Conf.* 56.

[5] Philo, *QG* 3.3.

[6] Philo, *Conf.* 16; cf. *Spec.* 1.343, for song charming away passion.

[7] Philo, *Cher.* 105.

[8] Warren D. Anderson, *Ethos and Education in Greek Music* (Cambridge: Harvard University Press, 1966).

[9] Philo, *Spec.* 4.134; cf. *Migr.* 104.

[10] Philo, *QE* 2.20—God wishes one to be a harmony of all sounds like a musical instrument.

[11] Unworthy pleasures—Philo, *Agr.* 35; *Spec.* 2.193; association with idolatry—*Spec.* 1.28–29.

[12] Philo, *Conf.* 108.

[13] Philo, *Conf.* 55, 58.

[14] Plato, *Resp.* 424c; *Leg.* 701a–b.

The heaven, then, the archetypical instrument of music, appears to have been tuned perfectly for no other purpose than that the hymns being sung to the honor of the Father of all might be accompanied musically.[15]

This is a striking thought: that the hymns sung by the mind and voice of human beings have the equivalent of instrumental accompaniment in the movements of the heavenly bodies. A similar passage adds the note of Moses's harmony in soul in describing his singing praise to God in the presence of angels while accompanied by God's instrument, the cosmos:

> He [Moses] began to praise God in song [Deut. 32:1–43], rendering thanks-giving. ... Gathering together a divine assembly, the elements of the universe and the most essential parts of the cosmos, the earth and heaven, one the home of mortals and other the house of the immortals, in their midst he sang his hymn of praise with all harmony and every kind of symphony so that both human beings and ministering angels might hear ... [Moses] was able like the sun, moon, and the all holy chorus of the other stars to harmonize his soul so as to make music in accompaniment with God's instrument, the heaven and all the cosmos. (*Virt.* 72–75)

Philo affirms that "the best and most perfect product of all right actions brought to birth is the hymn to the Father of the universe."[16]

Philo gives some indication of the vocal musical practices of Jews, indeed more than is usually acknowledged. It is true that he makes no allusion to the music in the Jerusalem temple nor explicitly to practices in houses of prayer or synagogues. Some have concluded that there is in fact no evidence of Psalmody in the synagogues for the New Testament period, so Christian singing must have derived from Jewish home or sectarian practices.[17] Such skepticism discounts too readily the possibility that the Qumran community and the Therapeutae described by Philo shared syna-gogue as well as temple influence. And, as regards the practice of the houses of prayer in Alexandria, there is a discounting or ignoring a passage in Philo that would suggest that singing was a normal part of Jewish community and liturgical life in Alexandria.

At the season of Tabernacles there occurred the trial leading to the deposition of the prefect of Egypt, Flaccus, who had allowed a pogrom against the Jews and the desecration of their houses of prayer. When news of the arrest of Flaccus arrived, the Jews "extending their hands to heaven,

---

[15] Philo, *Somn.* 1.35–37.

[16] Philo, *Plant.* 135. "What is more fitting for one to do than to return to the Benefactor words, songs, and hymns?"—*Sobr.* 58.

[17] J. A. Smith, "The Ancient Synagogue, the Early Church and Singing," *Music and Letters* 65 (1984): 1–16; J. W. McKinnon, "On the Question of Psalmody in the Ancient Synagogue," *Early Music History* 6 (1986): 159–91.

sang hymns and songs of victory to God." "All through the night they
continued in hymns and odes." At dawn they went to the beach, since their
synagogues had been taken from them, and offered prayer to God.[18]

There are incidental references in Philo's writings to what may be liturgical practices. He mentions "the leaders and precentors of the chorus that
sings the hymn of victory and thanksgiving."[19] Philo often makes reference
to Exod 15, "*the* song" sung by Israel on its escape from the Egyptians at the
Red Sea.[20] He elaborates with details not explicitly in the biblical text on the
division of the people into two choirs, one of men led by Moses and one of
women led by Miriam, singing antiphonally the same song but also with
the different voices of male and female blending harmoniously.[21]

This description of Exod 15 may be influenced by Philo's knowledge of
the Therapeutae, whose practice he says was copied from this example. The
all-night vigil of the community that concluded their festival on the fiftieth
day was spent in song. The men and women of the community formed
separate choruses, each led by a precentor or leader. They sometimes sang
together as one chorus, sometimes they sang with "responsive and
antiphonal strains, blending the bass sound of the men with the treble of
the women."[22]

> [Performing] a harmonious and truly musical symphony. Truly beautiful are
> the thoughts, truly beautiful the words, reverent are the chorus members. The
> goal of the thoughts, the words, and the choruses is godliness. (*Contempl.* 83–
> 88)

In addition to this report of the men and women combined to sing as one
chorus and also singing responsively and antiphonally (or was this a
double expression for responsorial singing?), Philo earlier mentioned that
the president of the gathering sang a solo and after him other individuals
sang while the rest listened and then sang the closing phrases in response.[23]

---

[18] Philo, *Flacc.* 121–122. In his commentary on the passage, Pieter W. van der Horst,
Philo's Flaccus: The First Pogrom, PACS 2 (Leiden: Brill, 2003), 203, concurs: "That the Jews
sing and pray here implies that this kind of worship was also what they would commonly
do in a synagogue service." Jutta Leonhardt, *Jewish Worship in Philo of Alexandria*
(Tübingen: Mohr Siebeck, 2001), chap. 2, covers Philo's references to psalm and hymn
singing.

[19] Philo, *Ebr.* 121.

[20] Philo, *Leg.* 2.102, 103; *Plant.* 48; *Sobr.* 13. He calls Deuteronomy 32, because of its
length, the "Great [or Greater] Song"—*Leg.* 3.105; *Post.* 121, 167; and frequently.

[21] Philo, *Agr.* 79–83; *Conf.* 35–36; *Mos.* 1.180 and 2.256–257.

[22] Similar wording in the account in *Mos.* 2.256–257. For the different voices of
different persons blended into a harmonious symphony cf. *QE* 2.120 and 2.38.

[23] Philo, *Contempl.* 80.

Hence, Philo's account of the Therapeutae provides examples of solo, responsorial, antiphonal, and unison singing.

The Babylonian Talmud, with similar reference to Exod 15, offers three different interpretations of how Israel might have rendered their song after crossing the Red Sea: (1) in the manner of an adult reading the *Hallel*, with the congregation responding to each line with a common refrain; (2) in the manner of a minor reading the *Hallel*, with the congregation responding by repeating the line spoken; and (3) in the manner of a schoolmaster reciting the *Shema* ("Hear, O Israel") in a synagogue, with the congregation joining in after the leader begins.[24] Philo adopts this last interpretation of Exod 15: Moses led off and then all Israel sang together.[25]

There is no reference to the presence of any instrument in the musical practice of the Therapeutae, and rabbinic souces later indicate vocal activities only in the synagogue assemblies.[26] Playing instruments was seen as a violation of the sabbath prohibition against work.[27] The rabbis regarded vocal music as superior to instrumental.[28] Instruments were absent from the services of the synogogue, but they were not banned from Jewish society,[29] although there was opposition by some rabbis to instruments even for entertainment.[30]

Louis Feldman notes one respect in which Philo apparently differed from the rabbis in regard to musical practice: the participation by women as well as men. He cites only the opinion of the third-century rabbi Samuel that "a woman's voice is a sexual incitement" to support the conclusion that a man was not permitted to hear her sing and so women did not sing in the synagogue.[31] Philo's references, on the other hand, to the women as well as the men singing in Exod 15 seem to indicate that this was significant for him, even claiming that the combination of male and female voices makes "the sweetest harmony."[32]

---

[24] b. Sotah (Suspected Adulteress) 30b.

[25] Philo, *Mos.* 2.257. Is this an indication of congregational song in Philo's synagogue?

[26] m. Ta'an. (Days of Fasting) 3.9–4.4 for reciting the Hallel Psalms; cf. b. Ta'an. 27b–28a.

[27] b. Sukkah (Feast of Tabernacles) 50b–51a; t. Shabb. (Sabbath) 13; m. Erubim (Sabbath Limits) 10.13 (tying the string of a musical instrument allowed in the temple on a Sabbath but not in the provinces).

[28] b. Arakh. (Vows of Valuation) 11a; later the *Midrash on the Psalms* 92.7; 149.5.

[29] J. W. McKinnon, "The Exclusion of Musical Instruments from the Ancient Synagogue," *Proceedings of the Royal Musical Association* 106 (1979–1980): 77–87.

[30] b. Gittin (Bills of Divorce) 7a and Sotah (Suspected Adulteress) 48a.

[31] Feldman, *Studies in Hellenistic Judaism*, 524–25 with reference to b. Ber. (Benedictions) 24a.

[32] Philo, *Mos.* 2.256.

Philo offered an evaluation of different types of music: he preferred string over wind instruments, vocal over instrumental music, and "silent singing" (the thoughts of the mind) over vocal music. Of the various instruments, Philo considered the lyre the best and the standard for other instruments: "The seven-stringed lyre, which corresponds to the choir of the [seven] planets, produces notable harmonies, and is (one might say) the chief of all the instruments for making music."[33]

Nevertheless, Philo contrasts the music made on "pipes [the principal wind instrument of the time], kitharas [the principal stringed instrument], and other instruments" with the music of "the instrument of nature," the voice.[34] He describes the "spoken word" as "the father of music and of all musical instruments," for "the faculty of speech is the first and most perfect instrument," possessing "harmonies and the various kinds of melodies in order that it might be a pattern made beforehand for those instruments later fashioned artificially."[35] He proceeds to praise the music of God's creatures, and especially of the human voice, over music on instruments:

> However much pipes, lyres, and other such instruments may make melodious sounds, they fall as much short of the music of nightingales and swans as a copy and imitation does of an original pattern ... for the music of human voices cannot be compared to that produced in any other way, since they have the exceptional gift, which is so honored, of clear articulation. (*Post.* 105–108)

He then contrasts the sounds pleasing only to the ear with articulate speech, whether spoken or sung, which is able to appeal also to the mind by its thoughts.[36]

For Philo higher even than speech are the thoughts of the mind.[37] Hence, Philo sometimes gives expression to the philosophical concept of "silent singing," that is praise to God with thoughts in the mind but not expressed with the voice. Philo's interpretation of the name of Judah makes him the "leader of those who sing the thanksgiving hymn not with the sound of the voice but with the mind."[38] Most people show their thanksgiving to God by building temples and offering gifts and sacrifices, but the proper expression is by "praises and hymns, not those the audible voice

---

[33] Philo, *Opif.* 126; cf. *Leg.* 1.14, "In music the seven-stringed lyre is generally regarded as the best of instruments."

[34] Philo, *Sobr.* 36.

[35] Philo, *Post.* 103–104. He specifies the windpipe as set up to be "a pattern for every kind of musical instrument."

[36] Cf. Philo, *Plant.* 131 on the voice used with or without melody.

[37] Philo, *Her.* 4–5; cf. *Leg.* 3.44.

[38] Philo, *Ebr.* 94; "thanksgiving hymn" also in §105.

sings, but those the unseen and most pure mind resounds [echoes] and lifts up."[39] In a remarkable passage that approximates Rom 12:1 Philo writes:

> Even if worshippers provide nothing else, by bringing themselves they offer the best and most perfect sacrifice, the fullness of what is noble and good, honoring God their Benefactor and Savior with hymns and thanksgivings, sometimes with the organs of speech, sometimes without tongue and mouth, in the soul only, making their thoughts narratives and loud cries that only one ear, the divine, can hear. (*Spec.* 1.272)

Indeed, even the human mind is inadequate to the praise of God:

> O Master, how can anyone hymn you? With what mouth, what tongue, what organ of speech, what principal part of the soul? If the stars become a single chorus, what song will they sing that is worthy?" (*Mos.* 2.239)

Greek philosophers provided the context for this evaluation of different types of music. Concerning the depreciation of the pipe (*aulos*), Pythagoras was reported to have banned this instrument from his communities,[40] and Plato excluded it from his ideal state.[41] Aristides Quintilian in the third century summed up earlier views on music in declaring that string instruments represent the higher regions of the soul and are superior, but wind instruments resemble the lower regions (through their use of breath) and so are inferior.[42] Although instruments played a prominent part in Greek religious practices,[43] philosophers regarded vocal music as superior. Plato had already lamented degenerate music, both instrumental and vocal.[44] Plutarch affirmed the superiority of the combination of song with instruments over instruments alone.[45] Pseudo-Plutarch, *On Music*, expresses a thought similar to Philo's: "It is an act of piety and a main purpose for human beings to hymn the gods, who granted only to them articulate speech."[46] Philosophers, furthermore, developed the idea of worship with the mind and regarded this as the highest form of sacrifice.[47] Apollonius of Tyana declared, "We should make use in relation to [God] solely of the higher speech, I mean of that which issues not by the lips; and from the

[39] Philo, *Plant.* 126.
[40] Iamblichus, *Life of Pythagoras* 111.
[41] Plato, *Resp.* 399d.
[42] Thomas J. Mathiesen, *Aristides Quintilianus On Music in Three Books* (New Haven: Yale, 1983), 37, with reference to book 2.1 (115). Cf. 2.19 (155–57).
[43] J. A. Haldane, "Musical Instruments in Greek Worship," *GR* 13 (1966): 98–107.
[44] Plato, *Leg.* 3.700e; similarly Plutarch, *Quaet. conv.* 7.5 (*Mor.* 704cff.).
[45] Plutarch, *Quaest. conv.* 7.8 (*Mor.* 713b–f).
[46] Pseudo-Plutarch, *Mus.* (*Mor.* 1131d).
[47] Everett Ferguson, "Spiritual Sacrifice in Early Christianity and Its Environment," *ANRW* 23.1: 1153–56.

noblest of beings we must ask for blessings by the noblest faculty we possess, and that faculty is the mind, which needs no organ."[48] Porphyry, the third-century Neoplatonic opponent of Christianity, systematized previous philosophical thought on sacrifice: (1) the demons receive the usual sacrifices; (2) the heavenly gods, planets and stars, receive offerings of honey and fruit but not animals; (3) the intellectual gods, the highest of God's offspring, are honored by hymns of speech; and (4) the highest God, is offered nothing by fire nor any of the things of sense, not even words, for silence and pure thoughts concerning him are his proper worship, that is the lifting up to him of the soul, which is the holy sacrifice and hymn to him.[49]

Philo referred to the book of Psalms as "hymns" or "songs."[50] He did so to avoid the Greek meaning of *psalmos*, the sound made by plucking on a stringed instrument, which differed from the Jewish and then Christian usage with reference to the songs (words) of the book of Psalms. He often used several words for vocal music with little distinction in meaning. Thus he speaks of "praise, hymns, and songs fitting for God."[51] With the substitution of psalms for "praise" this becomes a close parallel to Eph 5:19, "psalms, hymns, and spiritual songs."

With this observation I pass to some of the extensive patristic parallels to Philo on the subject of music.

Church Fathers on Music[52]

Christians join the heavenly bodies in praise of the Creator. As Origen says,

> We sing praise to God and his only Son, as do also the sun, moon, and stars, and all the heavenly host. For all these form a divine choir and with just human beings sing praise to the God over all and his only Son.[53]

---

[48] *Sacrifices*, quoted by Eusebius, *Praep. ev.* 4.13.

[49] Porphyry, *Abst.* 2.34–37.

[50] Philo, *Migr.* 157; *Contempl.* 25; and uniformly in his Psalm quotations. On Philo's use of the Psalter see David T. Runia, "Philo's Reading of the Psalms," *SPhiloA* 13 (2001): 102–20.

[51] Philo, *Leg.* 3.26.

[52] For the following sections on the harmony of the universe, the human person, the community, and musical praise I draw heavily on my article "Toward a Patristic Theology of Music," *StPatr* 24 (1993): 266–83; Peter Jeffery, "Philo's Impact on Christian Psalmody," in *Psalms in Community*, Harold W. Attridge and Margot E. Fassler (Atlanta: Society of Biblical Literature, 2003), 147-87.

The Pythagorean parallel between the harmony of the universe and musical harmony is in the background of many patristic statements referring to music.[54] Athenagoras gives a monotheistic thrust to the idea:

> Thus if the world is a harmonious instrument, rhythmically moved, I worship not the instrument but the one who tuned it and strikes the strings and sings to its accompaniment the melodious strain. (*Plea* 16.3)

Clement of Alexandria picks up the theme with the specifically Christian interpretation that the Logos makes music on the universe:

> [The Logos] composed the universe into melodious order, and tuned the discord of the elements to harmonious arrangement so that the whole world might become harmony.... And having tuned by the Holy Spirit the universe, and espcially humankind, who composed of body and soul is a universe in miniature, [the Logos] makes melody to God on this instrument of many tones. (*Protr.* 1.5) [55]

The harmony of the celestial bodies coincided with the ethical harmony of the human person. Clement of Alexandria, like Philo, included music among the educational disciplines to be appropriated by God's people, for "music is to be employed for the ordering and adornment of character."[56] Gregory of Nyssa, with the thought that a human being is a miniature cosmos, moved from the musical harmony of the cosmos to an analogous description of human nature in musical terms.[57] Theodoret summed up the thought of many when he explained that under the Law of Moses the people played various musical instruments, but these things apply to Christians spiritually: "We are able to express a pleasant sound and to be ourselves a harmonious instrument and to praise God through all our faculties of the senses and intellect."[58] Melody, according to Athanasius, both represents and achieves the harmony of the soul.

---

[53] Origen, *Cels.* 8.67. Cf. Ignatius, *Eph.* 19.2 for the sun, moon, and stars forming a chorus to the birth of Jesus. Robert A. Skeris, *Chroma Theou: On the Origins and Theological Interpretation of the Musical Imagery Used by the Ecclesiastical Writers of the First Three Centuries* (Altötting: A. Coppenrath, 1976), notes that the imagery of the stars as a chorus was used by the Stoics but was older (177–78, n. 122).

[54] Théodore Gerold, *Les pères de l'église et la musique* (Strasbourg: Impremerie alsacienne, 1931), 72–80.

[55] Cf. Athanasius, *C. Gent.* 42; Gregory of Nyssa, *Inscriptions of the Psalms* 1.3. Basil, *Hexaemeron* 3.3, and Ambrose, *Hexaemeron* 2.2–3, although describing the elements as forming a harmonious choir, were skeptical about the stars producing actual music.

[56] Clement of Alexandria, *Strom.* 6.11.89.

[57] Gregory of Nyssa, *Inscriptions of the Psalms* 1.3.19–21 on the cosmos and 1.3.22–24 on human nature.

[58] Theodoret, *Psalms* 33.2.

> The harmonious recitation [of the Psalms] is a symbol of the ordered and calm constitution of the mind.... So also singing well trains the soul and leads it out of disturbance to equanimity. (*Ep. Marcell.* 29) [59]

Niceta of Remisiana put the thought succinctly, when he said that the songs of the church "put out, rather than excite the passions."[60]

Harmony with God required not only harmony within the soul but also harmony between body and soul. This required, according to good Greek philosophical precedents, that the rational soul control the senses of the body. According to Gregory of Nyssa the body is an instrument used by the mind.[61] Augustine's expression is that the soul rules, the body obeys.[62] Athanasius compared the senses to the strings of the lyre, each with its own sound, and the mind to the skilful musician who brings these sounds into harmony.[63] There must be agreement between the words sung and the thoughts in the heart. John Chrysostom explained the phrase "in your hearts to the Lord" (Eph 5:19) as follows: "It means giving attention with the understanding, for those who do not pay attention merely sing, sounding the words while their hearts roam elsewhere."[64] Harmony of the self required, moreover, an agreement between words and life. Augustine said: "Let not your voice alone sound the praises of God, but let your works also be in harmony with your voice."[65]

The harmony of the celestial spheres corresponded not only to the harmony of the individual but also to the harmony of the church. Congregational participation in the singing exemplified the unity of the church and the harmony of human beings with God. Clement of Alexandria declares, "The union of many into one, bringing a divine harmony out of the many scattered sounds, becomes one symphony, following one Choir-

---

[59] Cf. 27 on the contrast of harmony and disharmony in the self. H.-J. Sieben, "Athanasius über den Psalter," *Theologie und Philosophie* 48 (1973): 157–73; Everett Ferguson, "Athanasius' 'Epistola ad Macellinum in interpretationem Psalmorum,'" *StPatr* 16 (1985): 295–308.

[60] Niceta, *On the Utility of Hymn Singing* 7.

[61] Gregory of Nyssa, *Making of Man* 9. Skeris, *Chroma Theou*, 131, 135, for the Neopythagorean fondness for the imagery of the body as the instrument of the soul.

[62] Augustine, *Psalms* 146.2.

[63] Athanasius, *C. Gent.* 31.

[64] John Chrysostom, *Hom. Eph.* 19 on Eph 5:19; cf. idem, *Psalms* 42.1; *Hom. Col.* 9 on Col 3.2; *Hom. 1 Cor.* 35 on 1 Cor 14:15; Athanasius, *Ep. Marcell.* 29; Niceta, *On the Utility of Hymn Singing* 13.

[65] Augustine, *Psalms* 147.2. Similarly John Chrysostom, *Psalms* 147.1, "It is not sufficient simply to make melody to please God with praise, but the life, prayer, and attention of the one singing must please God."

leader and Teacher."[66] The harmony came not from sameness but variety of sounds. Augustine expressed it this way:

> The saints of God will have their differences, accordant, not discordant, that is agreeing, not disagreeing, just as sweetest harmony arises from sounds differing indeed, but not opposed to one another. (*Psalms* 150.4)

Jerome had anticipated the point:

> "Chorus" is the term used when many sing together in unison and may be compared to the cithara which with many separate chords produces one sound … [The phrase] "in antiphonal response" indicates that, as the prophet sings, the entire multitude responds in the praise of God. It is the mystery of the church that is being prefigured, the church gathered together from many nations so that, from separate places and from diverse regions and customs, one choir may sound forth the praise of God. (*Homily* 65 on Ps. 87 [88])[67]

In a parallel passage, Jerome makes a negative point:

> Wherever there is a choir many voices blend into one song. In the same way that separate chords produce a single effect, so, too, do separate voices harmonize as one. In other words, when the faithful gather together, they form the Lord's choir. Let them praise his name in choir. Where there is dissension, where there is jealousy, there is no choir. (*Homily* 59 on Ps. 149.3)[68]

Accordingly, Basil of Caesarea makes this application:

> Who can still regard as an enemy one with whom he has sent forth one voice to God? … Psalmody harmonizes the people into a symphony of one chorus. (*Psalms* 1.2)

As is suggested in several of these quotations, the church fathers present Christian music as directed to the praise of God and, in significant addition to Philo, also to Christ. Niceta is typical: "The songs which the church of God sings … are pleasing to God, since everything about them is directed solely to the glory of the Creator."[69] Leo the Great says, "We have sung with one voice the Psalm of David to give praise to Christ the Lord."[70]

The human self is the true instrument to be used in praising God. Clement of Alexandria set the tone of many later comments: "A beautiful breathing instrument of music the Lord made a human being, after his own

[66] Clement of Alexandria, *Protr.* 9.88.
[67] Translation by Marie Liguori Ewald, *The Homilies of Saint Jerome*, Fathers of the Church 57 (Washington: Catholic University of America Press, 1964), 56.
[68] Ewald, *The Homilies of Saint Jerome*, 424.
[69] Niceta, *On the Utility of Hymn Singing* 7.
[70] Leo, *Sermon* 3.1.

image."[71] The musical instruments of the Psalms were commonly allegorized. Theodoret, for instance, gave this interpretation of the kithara, a stringed instrument.

> We [the churches] play the divine melody with the spiritual kithara. We make our bodies rational kitharas, and we use instead of chords the teeth, instead of brass the lips; higher pitched than any plectrum the tongue when moved performs the harmonious sound of the notes. The mind moves the tongue like a musician skilfully changing the sound. This kithara is more pleasing to God than a lifeless one. (*Psalms* 98.5)

A common interpretation referred the kithara to the body and the psalterion, another string instrument, to the spirit or soul.[72]

John Chrysostom interpreted the instruments of Psalm 150 to mean "As the Jews are commanded to praise God with all musical instruments, so we are commanded to praise him with all our members—the eye, the tongue, the ear, the hand."[73]

Praise offered in song was a spiritual sacrifice. Chrysostom continues, "Let us praise God continually ... for this is our sacrifice and offering."[74] Niceta explains that hymn singing is "a spiritual sacrifice that is greater than all sacrifices of victims," for instead of shedding the blood of irrational animals, "from the soul and a good conscience rational praise is offered up."[75] This praise of God in song unites the worshipers with the angels in their praise. "The voice of mortal humans is blended with the harmony of the angelic choirs in heaven."[76] "The chanters of the church imitate the angelic hosts and continually sing praises to God."[77]

The church fathers who spoke to the matter were generally negative toward instruments of music. John Chrysostom wanted to replace secular music in the home with Psalms.[78] He contrasted the aulos (a wind instrument), kithara, and pipes at a banquet with hymns and Psalm singing at a Christian one.[79] Gregory of Nazianzus sets Christian practices over against pagan practices: "Let us take up hymns instead of timbrels, Psalmody in-

---

[71] Clement of Alexandria, *Protr.* 1.5.

[72] Everett Ferguson, "The Active and Contemplative Lives: The Patristic Interpretation of Some Musical Terms," *StPatr*16 (1985): 15–23.

[73] John Chrysostom, *Psalms* 150.

[74] John Chrysostom, *Psalms* 150.

[75] Niceta, *On the Utility of Hymn Singing* 7.

[76] Eusebius, *Laud. Const.* 10.

[77] Cyril of Jerusalem, *Catechetical Lectures* 13.26.

[78] John Chrysostom, *Psalms* 41.2–3.

[79] John Chrysostom, *Hom. Col.* 1 on Col 1:5.

stead of lewd dances and songs, thankful acclamation instead of theatrical clapping."[80]

One exception to the generally condemnatory tone about instruments was Clement of Alexandria, who follows the philosophers and Philo in speaking more favorably of the string instruments than of the wind instruments. In discussing conduct at banquets (not church services, it should be noted), Clement offers an extended discussion of music.[81] He would banish the shepherd's pipes and the aulos from the "temperate banquet." He offers an allegorical interpretation of the instruments in Psalm 150 as parts of the human body, for human beings are "truly a peaceable instrument." "We employ the one peaceable instrument, the word alone, by which we honor God." After quoting Col 3:16–17 about singing Psalms, hymns, and spiritual songs, Clement offers this qualification, "Even if you want to sing or make melody to the kithara or lyre, there is no blame." The approval of the harp and lyre contrasts with the earlier rejection of the pipe and aulos, in keeping with philosophical opinion, but the very wording indicates that other Christians thought differently from Clement even in the context of home entertainment.

Eusebius gives a typical statement of the superiority of vocal music over instrumental:

> Of old at the time those of the circumcision were worshipping with symbols and types, it was not inappropriate to send up hymns to God with the psalterion and kithara and to do this on sabbath days.... We [now] render our hymn with a living psalterion and kithara [the human body in contrast to lifeless instruments], with spiritual songs. The unison voices of Christians would be more acceptable to God than any musical instrument. Accordingly in all the churches of God, united in soul and attitude, with one mind and in agreement of faith and piety, we send up a unison melody in the words of Psalms. (*Psalms* 91.2–3)

In contrasting music in the New Testament with that in the Old, Niceta says, "For the sound of these [trumpets, harps, cymbals, and timbrels] we now have a better substitute in the music from the mouths of people."[82]

Early Christian literature for the most part does not pick up the philosophical idea of "silent singing," but there are approximations to it. Chrysostom wanted the whole life to be directed toward God:

---

[80] Gregory of Nazianzus, *Or.* 5, *Against Julian* 2.

[81] *Instructor* 2.4.42–44. Charles H. Cosgrove, "Clement of Alexandria and Early Christian Music," *JECS* 14 (2006): 255–82.

[82] Niceta, *On the Utility of Hymn Singing* 9.

It is possible in every place and at every time to sing praise according to the understanding.... If you are a craftsman, you are able to sing praise while seated at your place of work and while working.... It is possible without the voice to sing praise with the inner mind. For we do not sing praise to men but to God who is able to hear the heart. (*Psalms* 41.2–3; cf. 145.2–3)

Paulinus of Nola favored the notion of silent singing.[83] Niceta of Remesiana, although agreeing that there is nothing wrong with singing in the heart, expressly opposed the idea that silent singing could replace vocal singing and so wrote his treatise *On the Utility of Hymn Singing*.[84] Generally, the emphasis in the fathers was on the mind and heart accompanying the vocal singing.[85]

As with Philo and the rabbis, the church fathers report only vocal music in a liturgical setting.[86] This is true of Clement of Alexandria himself. Inside the assembly one "hymns immortality."[87] He lists acts of worship as

Always giving thanks in all things to God through righteous hearing and divine reading, true inquiry, holy oblation, blessed prayer, praising, hymning, blessing, singing, such a soul is never separated from God at any time. (*Strom.* 6.14.113.3)

Hippolytus speaks of the "proper day ... in the house of God" when "all are praying there and singing to God."[88] Basil of Caesarea's account of a vigil involving antiphonal, responsorial, and unison singing shows some similarities to Philo's account of a vigil by the Therapeutae.[89]

There were contrasting views in the church on the subject of women singing in church. Jerome, in opposition to Pelagius, said women should sing at home, not in church.[90] Female catechumens in Jerusalem preparing for baptism were counseled "to sit together, either singing or reading quietly, so that their lips speak, but others' ears do not hear the sound," on the grounds of a conflate quotation of 1 Tim 2:12 and 1 Cor 14:34.[91] Ambrose had to take 1 Cor 14:34 into account in defending women singing,

---

[83] Paulinus of Nola, *Letter* 15.4.
[84] Niceta, *On the Utility of Hymn Singing* 1–2.
[85] Athanasius, *Ep. Marcell.* 29; Basil, *Psalms* 28; 29.3; John Chrysostom, *Hom. Eph.* 19 on Eph 5:19; John Chrysostom, *Hom. Col.* 9 on Col. 3:2.
[86] E.g., in addition to passages cited in other contexts, Ignatius, *Rom.* 12.2 (not describing a liturgical assembly but apparently drawing its imagery from such); cf. his *Eph.* 4; Tertullian, *Test.* 9.4; *Apostolic Constitutions* 2.57.6; 3.8.4.
[87] Clement of Alexandria, *Paed.* 3.11.80.4.
[88] Hippolytus, *Comm. Dan.*
[89] Basil of Caesaarea, *Ep.* 207. Discussed in my "Congregational Singing in the Early Church," *Acta Patristica et Byzantina* 15 (2004): 144–59.
[90] Jerome, *Pelag.* 1.25.
[91] Cyril of Jerusalem, *Procatechesis* 14.

but he emphasized that the whole congregation participated in reciting the Psalms:

> The singing of praise is the very bond of unity, when the whole people join in a single act of song. The strings of the harp are of varying lengths, but in the congregation that great Musician, the Spirit, cannot err. (*Psalms* 1, *Exposition* 9)

Ambrose follows Greek commentators in comparing the congregation's harmony to musical instruments, in stressing unity, and in emphasizing that all—young and old, men and women—participated.[92]

Conclusion

The church fathers, like Philo, shared with philosophers a correlation between human music and the music of the spheres, the harmony of the individual person, and the harmony of the community. Philo and the fathers had in common the interpretation of the human person as an instrument. The majority of the church fathers agreed with Philo that women as well as men participated in the singing in the assembly of the church. Similar to Philo, but with qualifications, the fathers also agreed with philosophers in the ranking of kinds of music: string music superior to wind and percussion music (Clement of Alexandria), vocal music superior to instrumental music, and the necessity of the thoughts of the mind to accompany vocal sounds. Philo and Christians emphasized the priority of praise toward God in music.

The church fathers make frequent and impressive statements of what vocal music, particularly psalmody, accomplishes. These are things that words, when set to melody or chanted, can do. Instruments cannot do them, and when accompanying the words may actually interfere with them.[93]

Abilene, Texas, U.S.A.

---

[92] John Chrysostom, *Psalms* 145.2; 150; cf. Basil, *Hex.* 4.7.

[93] In particular see John Chrysostom, *Psalms* 41; Theodoret, *Questions and Answers for the Orthodox* 10; Niceta, *On the Utility of Hymn Singing* 5–7; and Proclus, *Homily* 2, *On the Incarnation*. Others include, Basil, *Psalms* 1; Athanasius, *Ep. Marcell.* 32–33.

The Studia Philonica Annual 31 (2019): 201–226

SOLOMON JUDAH RAPOPORT'S MASKILIC REVIVAL OF PHILO OF ALEXANDRIA: RABBI YEDIDYA HA-ALEXANDRI AS A PIONEER OF JEWISH PHILOSOPHY*

ZE'EV STRAUSS

Introduction

Leopold Löw (1811–1875), chief rabbi of Szeged and editor of *Ben-Chananja: Monatsschrift für jüdische Theologie*, dedicated fifteen successive paragraphs of chapter 11[1] of the first volume of his *Ha-Mafteaḥ: Praktische Einleitung in die Heilige Schrift und Geschichte der Schriftauslegung, ein Lehrbuch für die reifere Jugend, ein Handbuch für Gebildete* (1855) to Philo of Alexandria, designated as "Philo der Jüngere" (§§247–261).[2] Despite Löw's critical assessment of Philo's method of allegorical exegesis as unscientific,[3] his overall positive portrayal of his "philosophical Midrashim" and their

---

* I would like to thank both Carlos Lévy and Yakir Paz for reading the drafts of this paper and giving me insightful comments on it. I am also grateful to Chaim Elly Moseson for patiently assisting me in some of the English translations from the Hebrew.
[1] The full title of the chapter's subheading covers a whole array of themes of the Jewish Hellenistic thought-world: "Das Eindringen der griechischen Sprache. Die Alexandriner. Ezekias. Philo der Aeltere. Aristobul. Philo der Jüngere. Der philosophische Midrasch" (Leopold Löw, *Ha-Mafteaḥ: Praktische Einleitung in die Heilige Schrift und Geschichte der Schriftauslegung, ein Lehrbuch für die reifere Jugend, ein Handbuch für Gebildete* [Nagykanizsa: J. Markbreiter, 1855], 129.
[2] Löw juxtaposes "Philo der Jüngere" to "Philo der Aeltere," which is in turn a designation for the Jewish Hellenistic Poet Philo.
[3] Löw, *Ha-Mafteaḥ*, 136: "Solcher Gestalt glaubte er manches in der Schrift zu finden, was ein schlichter, frommer Sinn nicht darin findet, und was eine wissenschaftlich gereifte Schriftauslegung für eitle Spielerei erklären muß." Cf. George Y. Kohler's remarks on Löw's drawing on Philo within the framework of his Kabbalah research: *Kabbalah Research in the Wissenschaft des Judentums (1820–1880): The Foundation of an Academic Discipline*, Europäisch-jüdische Studien 47 (Berlin: de Gruyter, 2019), 177–89.

prevalent traditional Jewish content is rather striking.[4] He concludes his presentation of Philo's thought with the following brief supplementary remark, in which he informs his readers of the latest developments in the scholarly research on Philo that had been undertaken by central nineteenth-century Jewish intellectuals:

> The works of Philo, forty-three in number, are often published and translated into Latin. Azaria dei Rossi was the first of the Jewish intellectuals to draw on him and discuss him. He calls Philo Jedidja (God's friend) the Alexandrian (ידידיה האלכסנדרי). While he praises and extols him in some respects, in some others, he accuses him of straying from the path of faith. Philo was defended from this accusation by Rapoport.—Krochmal also attempted to find some of Philo's doctrine and exegesis in Talmudic passages and Midrashim. Josef Flesch translated several Philonic writings into Hebrew.[5]

The three main Jewish intellectuals to whom Löw refers—namely, Solomon J. L. Rapoport (alias SHIR; 1790–1867), Naḥman Krochmal (alias RaNaK; 1785–1840), and Josef Flesch (1781–1839)—are all adduced as examples of thinkers who, during the first half of the nineteenth century, endeavored to rehabilitate Philo as a Jewish philosopher and exegete whose allegorical interpretations of the Bible were in broad agreement with the traditional Jewish thought-world. Rapoport—one of the key figures of the Haskala and the *Wissenschaft des Judentums*—is singled out as someone who took it upon himself to ward off Azaria dei Rossi's accusations that Philo diverged from the classic Jewish *Weltanschauung*.[6] It is obvious why Krochmal and

---

[4] Even though Löw designates Philo's allegorical interpretations as "philosophische Midraschim," he nonetheless enumerates their five essential deviations from the typical Midrashim of Jewish tradition: Löw, *Ha-Mafteaḥ*, 133 (§251).

[5] "Die Werke Philo's, dreiundvierzig an der Zahl, sind öfters aufgelegt und ins Lateinische übersetzt worden. Zwischen den jüdischen Gelehrten war Azaria dei Rossi … der erste, der dieselben benützte und besprach. Er nennt den Philo Jedidia (Gottesfreund) den Alexandrier (ידידיה האלכסנדרי); und während er ihn in mancher Rücksicht lobt und rühmt, beschuldigt er ihn, in manchen Stücken von der Bahn des Glaubens abgeirrt zu sein. Gegen diese Beschuldigung wurde Philo von Rapoport in Schutz genommen. — Krochmal hat versucht, manche Lehre und Auslegung Philo's auch in den Talmuden und Midraschim nachzuweisen. Joseph Flesch hat mehrere philonische Schriften ins Hebräische übertragen" (Löw, *Ha-Mafteaḥ*, 142; my translation). His mention of Philo's forty-three works appears to be predicated on Azaria dei Rossi's assertion in the beginning of *Words of Understanding*'s chapter 4 of Azaria dei Rossi, *The Light of the Eyes*, trans. Joanna Weinberg [New Haven: Yale University Press, 2001], 111). Cf. Weinberg's explanation of dei Rossi's specific enumeration of Philo's writings: "This figure is given in Gelenius's edition of Philo. It does not include the *Quaestiones et solutiones* on Genesis and Exodus but subdivides parts of the *De specialibus legibus* into separate books." (Weinberg, *Light of the Eyes*, 111, n. 2)

[6] For a detailed examination of Philo's reception within the intellectual movement of the *Wissenschaft des Judentums*, see Maren R. Niehoff, "Alexandrian Judaism in Nineteenth

Flesch are cited as examples of this apologetic trend. Krochmal devoted almost an entire chapter ("Ḥidot Mini Kedem") of his main historiographical work *More Nevokhei ha-Zeman* to Philo, where, under the section titled "Kovetz le-Ma'amarim be-Talmudim ve-Midraschot le-Tzorekh Bi'ur Shitat Yedidya ve-ha-Aleksandrim," he attempted to unearth the numerous ethical and metaphysical elements of Philo's system that coincide with central notions of rabbinic literature.[7] Even more obvious is Löw's reference to Josef Flesch, the "father of the Moravian [Jewish] Enlightenment."[8] Flesch was above all known for his life's work, which was almost exclusively dedicated to Hebrew translations of and detailed commentaries on Philo, consistently denoted as either *Rabbi Yedidya ha-Alexandri* or *ha-Rav ha-Meḥaber*.[9] In these translations, Flesch goes a step further than Krochmal: he not only assumed and demonstrated the conceptual agreement between Philo and the rabbis, but also that between Philo and the central thinkers of the Middle Ages and the Haskala.

On the other hand, and against this backdrop, it might seem quite perplexing that Löw deems Rapoport worthy of allusion in the same breath as the aforementioned maskilim in the context of the studies of Philo from the Jewish perspective. In the following article, I set out to substantiate this point of view. In so doing, I will also attempt to supplement Isaac Barzilay's monograph on Rapoport's thought *Shlomo Yehudah Rapoport (Shir) and His Contemporaries*[10] with a significant missing piece: Rapoport's utmost admiration for Philo and his thought, whose allegorical exegeses of Scripture anticipates the Greco-Islamic metaphysical and ethical teachings of medieval Jewish philosophy, specifically those of its greatest proponent

---

Century *Wissenschaft des Judentums*: Between Christianity and Modernization," in *Jüdische Geschichte in hellenistisch-römischer Zeit. Wege der Forschung: Vom alten zum neuen Schürer*, ed. Aharon Oppenheimer, Schriften des Historischen Kollegs 44 (Munich: Oldenbourg, 1999), 9–28; Niehoff, "Alexandria," in *Enzyklopädie jüdischer Geschichte und Kultur* 1 (2011), 31–32; Deborah R. Sills, "Re-Inventing the Past: Philo and the Historiography of Jewish Identity" (Ph.D. diss., University of California, Santa Barbara, 1984).

[7] Naḥman Krochmal, *More Nevokhei ha-Zeman*, ed. Yehoyada Amir (Jerusalem: Carmel Publishing House, 2010), 168–76.

[8] Michael Miller, *Rabbis and Revolution: The Jews of Moravia in the Age of Emancipation* (Stanford: Stanford University Press, 2011), 89.

[9] For a more detailed analysis of Flesch's Hebrew translations of Philo, see Ze'ev Strauss, *Rabbi Jedidja ha-Alexandri und die Maskilim: Die Wiederentdeckung der Religionsphilosophie des Philon von Alexandria in der osteuropäischen Haskala*, Jewish Thought, Philosophy and Religion 7 (Berlin: de Gruyter, forthcoming).

[10] Isaac E. Barzilay, *Shlomo Yehudah Rapoport (Shir), 1790–1867, and His Contemporaries: Some Aspects of Jewish Scholarship of the Nineteenth Century* (Tel Aviv: Massada Press, 1969). For Rapoport's biography, see also Andreas Brämer, "Rapoport, Solomon Juda Löb," in *RGG* 4 (2007), 38.

and authority, Maimonides. The objective at hand will be pursued in three successive steps. Initially, I will reveal Rapoport's close involvement in Flesch's sweeping project of translating Philo's writings into Hebrew.[11] I will then discuss the links between Rapoport and Krochmal as they pertain to the examination of Philo's philosophy. Like Krochmal, Rapoport, known as one of the "pioneers of the new historiography,"[12] wished to exploit Philo's ancient thought for the sake of developing his own unique historiographical account of Judaism. Finally, I will focus on Rapaport's own assertions relating to the Jewish Alexandrian, drawing mainly on his *Realenzyklopädie 'Erekh Milin* (1852). Through these different thematic junctures, I will put forward the argument that Rapoport played a pivotal role in the propagation of Philo's thought among Jewish intellectuals. I will aim to show that Rapoport advanced within maskilic circles a perception of the Alexandrian exegete as a genuine Jewish thinker whose philosophical innovation and historical significance could be compared with any of the achievements of other past Jewish intellectuals. Consequently, I wish to argue that Rapoport—one of "the great authorities of Jewish scholarship" in the Haskala[13]—served as the missing link between Krochmal and Flesch, mediating between them various ideas concerning Philo's intimate correlation with Jewish tradition.

1. *Rapoport's Role within Josef Flesch's Hebrew Translations of ha-Rav Yedidya ha-Alexandri*

The most comprehensive and profound treatment of Philo's thought within the Haskala is undoubtedly that of Josef Flesch. During the second part of the 1820s and throughout nearly all the 1830s, Flesch directed almost all of his intellectual endeavors towards one goal: translating the writings of Philo of Alexandria into Hebrew and methodically commenting on them through countless recourses to the entirety of the rich Jewish tradition.[14] At

---

[11] Shmuel Feiner also notes this fact in his *Haskalah and History: The Emergence of a Modern Jewish Historical Consciousness* (Oxford: Littman Library of Jewish Civilization, 2001), 72: "Solomon Judah Leib Rapoport (1790–1867) maintained contacts with maskilim in Moravia; for example, he gave much encouragement to Joseph Flesch (1781–1841) for his research and his translations of Philo's writings."

[12] Feiner, *Haskalah and History*, 3. Cf. also 125–38; Barzilay, *Shlomo Yehudah Rapoport*, 38, 51, 61, 111.

[13] Barzilay, *Shlomo Yehudah Rapoport*, 85.

[14] Flesch had most likely simply followed the Latin Turnebe-Hoeschel-Gelen edition of Philo's writings published by Pierre de la Rouière (1613). The strongest indication for this fact is in his direct quotation from Pierre de la Rouière's preface in the Turnebe-

the core of this immense undertaking lies Flesch's marked aim of tracing the "Jewish" features which constitute the quintessence of Philo's thought. In doing so, he attempts to paint an almost entirely unified image of the Alexandrian interpreter of Scripture as an unmitigated rabbinic figure from the Second Temple period, thus restoring Philo to his rightful place alongside the great thinkers of the Jewish tradition. These efforts yielded two major publications: (1) In 1830, his Hebrew translation of *Quis rerum divinarum heres sit*, composed by none other than *ha-rav Jedidja ha-Alexandri*, was published by Moshe Landau's Prague printing house under the title *Min ha-Yoresh Diverei Elohim Mevo'ar Bo ha-Ḥizyon Bein ha-Vetarim 'al Derekh Mashal Ḥiduti*. (2) In 1838, he published another translation of Philo under the title *Ḥayyei Moshe (be-Hitḥalkut Gimel Sefarav)*, which was significantly wider in scope: he had not only translated *De vita Moysis* into Hebrew and provided it with a commentary, but he also did the same for *De Decalogo*, *De vita contemplativa*, and *Quod omnis probus liber sit* (§§75–87).[15] In fact, one finds here two books in one. This becomes apparent if one looks at the later section of the work devoted to Philo's depiction of two Jewish sects, the Therapeutae and the Essenes, since he also designated this part as a separate book, namely as *Katot Mini Kedem*.

At this point, one may pose the question of how the abovementioned facts relate to Rapoport and our theme at hand. We may find a direct answer in Flesch's preface to *Ḥayyei Moshe* ("Petaḥ Davar"):

> And I was even more urged to undertake this task of translation by my close friend the dear rabbi, poet and erudite philosopher, our teacher the rabbi, Shlomo Yehuda Loeb Rapoport from the city of Lviv (and he has recently been appointed to the rabbinate of the glorious city, holy community of Ternopil, may God establish his position for eternity). For he has roused me in one of his pleasant letters to gird up the writer's case on my loins and to offer up many such [translations] to our peoples, and to rouse their hearts to piety. He himself intends to send me the sweet nectar of his words containing this great man's biography [sc. that of Philo] as an introductory essay to all of [Philo's] specific writings (and [Rapoport's] statements cited in this book will attest this fact, glittering like the heaven's radiance for all readers of the opening part of this book). I have therefore set out with strenuous effort, to fulfill this, for my spirit

---

Hoeschel-Gelen edition: Philo, *Min ha-Yoresh Diverei Elohim Mevo'ar bo ha-Ḥizyon Bein ha-Vetarim 'al Derekh Mashal Ḥiduti*, trans. Josef Flesch (Prague: Moshe ha-Levi Landau, 1830), 14. Flesch's Hebrew translations are from the Latin, but he also seems to have been proficient in Greek, as he occasionally refers to notions found in the original texts. He translates Philo into Hebrew quite loosely, for his main goal is to render Philo as Rabbi Yedidyah ha-Alexandri, a traditional Jewish sage.

[15] Philo, *Ḥayyei Moshe*, trans. Josef Flesch (Prague: Moshe ha-Levi Landau, 1838).

will not rest until I have implemented and carried out his heart's wishes, and realised all that he desires.[16]

From Flesch's own account, Rapoport, who at that time was regarded as one of the chief scholarly authorities on Jewish history, is depicted as the central driving force behind his Hebrew translations of Philo's works from 1838. The indifference with which the Jewish communities reacted to Flesch's translation left him deeply discouraged about his ambitious endeavor. His correspondence with Rapoport, which encouraged him to pursue his planned undertaking with even more rigor, seems to have been a decisive turning point for the better in this respect. This description reveals three important characteristics regarding Rapoport's attitude towards the Alexandrian philosopher: (1) Rapoport seems to have already read several of Flesch's Hebrew translations of Philo and to be well versed in his thought. Aside from his published translations, Flesch also claims to have translated some of Philo's other works into Hebrew, such as *De confusione linguarum* and *Legatio ad Gaium*.[17] (2) Rapoport was apparently of the opinion that Philo's philosophy does not simply agree with the central tenets of Jewish belief, but that it could also have quite a sweeping effect on Jewish communities and lead them to become more virtuous and pious (*le-ha'ir levavam yaḥad be-yir'at elokim*). When speaking of Philo, he refers to him as one of "our ancient sages" (*mi-zikenei ḥakhameinu*).[18] (3) Rapoport's role in this intellectual project does not seem to be merely to give words of encouragement. He probably shared his own stance relating to this "great man" (*ish gadol*) with Flesch and intended to write a biography of Philo for him which would have served as the introduction to all of Flesch's translations.[19]

As Flesch informs us in the aforementioned citation, he cites part of a letter Rapoport wrote to him in the introduction to his translation of *De vita Moysis* called "Devar Eḥad la-Dor." There, Flesch wrote:

> And I rely upon one of my endorsers who strengthened me in this respect, my close friend the dear rabbi, poet and erudite philosopher our mentor and rabbi, Shlomo Loeb Rapoport from the city of Lviv. He is indeed like the sphere of the sun traversing the heavens, for after I sent him one of the translations on the topic of the sects of the ancients for an analysis, he roused me in his exalted reply to gird up the writer's case on my loins and provide more of these

[16] Flesch, *Ḥayyei*, 1–2.
[17] Flesch, *Ha-Yoresh*, 9.
[18] Flesch, *Ḥayyei*, 18.
[19] Rapoport had already gained much-needed experience in writing such biographies, which won him much recognition in the Jewish scholarly world, including the German *Wissenschaft des Judentums*: Barzilay, *Shlomo Yehudah Rapoport*, 36, 50; Feiner, *Haskalah and History*, 112.

precious [translations] to our peoples, and this is what he wrote: 'I have read your exquisite translations from *De vita contemplativa*. I am, however, of the opinion that the size of this booklet is too limited, and is not large enough to be printed on its own. My present advice to your rabbinic honor is that you add another translation to this one. Concerning the content of the book, its poetic style along with its introduction is noticeably clearer and more fluent than your booklet *ha-Yoresh* [sc. *Quis rerum divinarum heres sit*].' Thus far [were his words]. After considering his advice and concluding that it was good — and indeed our sages already sensed this in relation to the books of the prophets, from whose words we live, and compiled the Twelve Minor Prophets into one single volume saying that each one of them on its own will be dispersed for they are too small [*bBB* 14b]. Besides this, after realising that the benefit of the above mentioned work is not very great for anyone except historians I therefore decided to give up and desist from the above translation. I therefore set out to take on the present translation, from which extensive elucidations of several biblical verses will branch out; new interpretations, of which none of the ancient exegetes thought; and despite the fact that this book [of Philo] was left for a long time among books of little worth.[20]

The following passage offers us an even more detailed glimpse into Rapoport's key position as *the* authoritative figure in Flesch's second book, which was comprised of annotated Hebrew translations of Philonic treatises. Through an allusion to a simile in b. Yoma 20b, Flesch expresses the dominant authoritative impact Rapoport had had on his intellectual undertaking. He does so by simply equating Rapoport with the sun dividing the heavens and thereby casting a pall over the entirety of the criticism uttered by his Jewish environment, which had questioned him and his unorthodox endeavors.[21] As Rapoport's response discloses, Flesch had sent him his translation of *De vita contemplativa* in order to receive his scholarly assessment of his new translation and his intention to publish a book consisting of Philo's historic writings on the Jewish sects. Rapoport's response is positive on the one hand, but quite critical on the other: he praised the work for being much better than his *Min ha-Yoresh Diverei Elohim* in terms of its quality, but at the same time, he passed a very harsh verdict on Flesch's plans for immediate publication. Rapoport maintained that the scope of this work was too limited. At the end of his introduction to *Kutot Mini Kedem*, Flesch cites an even larger portion of Rapoport's answer. There, the rabbi of Lviv claims that Flesch's small number of new translations do not add up to a coherent book. For this reason, he urges Flesch to include more translations of Philonic works—specifically suggesting adding *Legatio ad Gaium*—that will make his compilation worthy of being called a book: "... and if you publish this entire volume it might be

---

[20] Flesch, *Hayyei: Devar Ehad la-Dor*, II–IV.
[21] Flesch., *Devar Ehad la-Dor*, II.

large enough to be called a book, and the pages will not be scattered and lost."[22] Even though Flesch had not followed all of Rapoport's firm advice,[23] he emphasizes the fact that he had adopted almost all of his suggestions for improvements.[24] In the quoted letter, Rapoport makes four further recommendations in order that Philo's works will successfully gain a strong foothold in the "Jewish bookcase": (1) The entire *Corpus Philonicum* is to be translated into Hebrew. Rapoport agreed, for instance, that he would write a biography of Philo for Flesch's project only on condition of him translating all the Philonic writings ("… and how can you request of me to provide a biography of the writer and author for only these few translated pages. For I have made myself quite clear in advance that I would compose his biography only once you have completed, God willing, the translations of all the writings of this great sage").[25] (2) Those texts which included a considerable number of unfamiliar Greek concepts were to be greatly simplified so that they would prove comprehensible for the common Jewish reader. (3) Flesch should remove the supplementary translation whose Hebrew name was *Torat Adam ha-Ma'ala* (Περὶ εὐγενείας: *Virt.* 187–227).[26] Since this Philonic treatise might only have proven beneficial to a few Jewish intellectuals, Flesch acquiesced to this request.[27] (4) In his commentaries on Philonic treatises, Flesch should also refer to modern researchers.[28]

---

[22] Flesch, *Hayyei*, 18. The employment of the term *'alim* to mean "pages" is a strong indication that this was indeed genuinely written by Rapoport: cf. "Al Mot ha-Rav ha-Hakham ha-Gadol ha-Hoker ha-Filosof Morenu ve-Rabbenu ha-Rav Rabbi Nahman Krohmol Zikhrono li-Verakha," *Kerem Hemed* 6 (1841): 48 ("לא יחדל מכתוב בכל יום איזה עלים…"). For Rapoport's role in the Hebrew journal *Kerem Hemed*, see Barzilay, *Shlomo Yehudah Rapoport*, 33, esp. 42–43, 89; Moshe Pelli, *Kerem Hemed: 'Hochmat Israel' as the 'New Yavneh.' An Annotated Index to Kerem Hemed, the Hebrew Journal of the Haskalah in Galicia and Italy (1833–1856)* (Jerusalem: The Hebrew University Magnes Press, 2009), 24–25, 44.

[23] He does not, for example, see fit to incorporate *Legat.* in this book: Flesch, *Hayyei*, 18 n. 1.

[24] See, for example, Flesch, *Hayyei*, 18 n. 2.

[25] Flesch, *Hayyei*, 18.

[26] Flesch, *Hayyei*, 17–18. In Flesch's Latin Turnebe-Hoeschel-Gelen edition of Philo's writings (1613) Περὶ εὐγενείας is translated along with *Contempl.* ("de vita Contemplativa, sive supplicium virtutibus").

[27] Flesch, *Hayyei*, 18 n. 1.

[28] Flesch, *Hayyei*, 17–18.

2. "Dark Sayings of Old": Krochmal's Revival of Philo
and Its Impact on Rapoport

Another maskil who must have deeply shaped Rapoport's attitude towards Philo was Naḥman Krochmal, with whom he had an intense intellectual relationship. Heinrich Graetz had already regarded the intellectual affiliation between the two Eastern European maskilim to be exceptionally worthy of mention in the section of his *Geschichte der Juden vom Beginn der Mendelssohn'schen Zeit (1750) bis in die neueste Zeit (1848)* entitled *Die galizianische Schule*: "There were above all two men who made generous use of the proficiencies passed down to them from Germany: *Naḥman Krochmal* and *Salomon Judah Rapoport*, both called upon to fill up the gap which the members of the Jewish *Wissenschaft* in Germany and France could not have supplemented.... They were the founders of a new school, which one may call the *Galician* school."[29] According to Graetz, the two were in close contact around the time of Krochmal's arrival in Lviv in 1808, with Krochmal serving as a mentor and a source of intellectual inspiration for the younger Rapoport: "From his adolescence and reaching deep into his adulthood, almost three decades, Rapoport covered the distance from Lemberg to Zhovkva at least once a month in order to seek the researcher Krochmal, who was all at once bold, timid, and rich in ideas, and engage him in scholarly discussions. For Krochmal, the interaction with his gifted young friend had already become a necessity to such a great degree that he sought him in Lemberg whenever he was researching a topic, in order to attain clarity by means of exchanging ideas with him."[30] From these conversations, lasting nearly three decades, there emerged what Graetz considers to be nothing less than the "Geburtszeit der jüdischen Wissenschaft nach der

[29] Heinrich Graetz, *Geschichte der Juden: von den ältesten Zeiten bis auf die Gegenwart*, vol. 11: *Geschichte der Juden vom Beginn der Mendelssohn'schen Zeit (1750) bis in die neueste Zeit (1848)* (Leipzig: Oskar Leiner, 1870), 482: "Zwei Männer waren es besonders, die das Pfund, das sie von Deutschland empfangen hatten, reichlich wucherten: *Nachman Krochmal und Salomo Jehuda Rapoport*, beide gewissermaßen berufen, eine Lücke auszufüllen, welche die Pfleger der jüdischen Wissenschaft in Deutschland und Frankreich nicht hatten ergänzen können ... Sie waren die Stifter einer neuen Schule, welche man die *galizianische* nennen kann" (emphasis in original; my translation).

[30] "Von seinem Jünglingsalter an bis tief in sein Mannesalter hinein, fast drei Jahrzehnte, pflegte Rapoport den Weg von Lemberg nach Zolkiew mindestens alle Monate einmal zurückzulegen, um den zugleich kühnen und zaghaften, gedankenreichen Forscher Krochmal aufzusuchen und sich mit ihm in wissenschaftlichen Gesprächen zu ergehen. Der Umgang mit seinem begabten jungen Freunde war bereits für Krochmal so sehr Bedürfnis geworden, daß er, so oft ihn ein Forschungs-thema beschäftigte, ihn in Lemberg aufsuchte, um im Gedankenaustausch mit demselben zur Klarheit zu gelangen" (Graetz, *Geschichte der Juden*, 494; my translation).

geschichtlichen Seite."[31] Rapoport's own account thereof in his eulogy to Krochmal, 'Al Mot ha-Rav ha-Ḥakham ha-Gadol ha-Ḥoker ha-Filosof Morenu ve-Rabbenu ha-Rav Rabbi Naḥman Kroḥmol Zikhrono li-Verakha—upon which Graetz seems to base much of his depiction—affirms this portrayal to a large extent: "On the hand, he was an acknowledging father and kinsman to me from the time of my adolescence; on the other, he was a close friend to me and someone with whom I had a [deep] acquaintance."[32] As Harris and Barzilay already point out in reference to this testimony,[33] Krochmal's charismatic brilliance compelled deep admiration from the adolescent Rapoport:

> Thirty years have elapsed since I met him and saw his face for the first time. This transpired while he was in the big city in search of physicians, for he was unwell. His spirit proved strong, however. In my conversations with him, I was endowed with the spirit of wisdom and knowledge and was almost transformed into a completely different man, so capable was he at kindling his great passion for each science and language in the hearts of his interlocutors.[34]

It seems quite evident that Rapoport's deep interest in Philo stems in large part from this intellectual encounter with Krochmal. As Rapoport's account demonstrates, he had a very intimate knowledge of Krochmal's chief philosophical interests and the varying phases of his intellectual development in this respect.[35] Even more illuminating concerning the matter at hand is Rapoport's familiarity with Krochmal's attempt—after much encouragement from him and other pupils—to put his philosophical worldview into writing. From this effort resulted his masterful work More Nevokhei ha-Zeman,[36] a book he actively began writing in the early 1830s.[37] Rapoport's description of his efforts to embolden Krochmal to widen the very limited scope of his writing repertoire bears a remarkable resemblance to the manner in which he also encouraged Flesch to substantially broaden the scope of his project relating to Philo. Given these circumstances, one may take it for granted that Rapoport was well acquainted with Krochmal's

---

[31] Graetz, Geschichte der Juden, 494. Cf. Barzilay, Shlomo Yehudah Rapoport, 37.

[32] Rapoport, Mot, 41 (my translation).

[33] Jay M. Harris, Nachman Krochmal: Guiding the Perplexed of the Modern Age, Modern Jewish Masters Series 4 (New York: New York University Press, 1991), 9–10; Barzilay, Shlomo Yehudah Rapoport, 26.

[34] Rapoport, Mot, 45 (my translation).

[35] Rapoport, Mot, 46–47.

[36] Rapoport, Mot, 48.

[37] Yehoyada Amir, "Bein Meḥkar, Hagut ve-Sifrut Kodesh be-Mishnato shel Rabbi Naḥman Krochmal," in Jewish Thought and Jewish Belief, ed. Daniel L. Lasker (Beersheba: Ben Gurion University Press, 2012), 113; Barzilay, Shlomo Yehudah Rapoport, 12, 26, 29, 63 n. 7.

innovative approach to Philo's thought and the particular manner in which it is reflected in the twelfth gate (*Sha'ar Y[od]"B[eit]*) of his *More Nevokhei ha-Zeman*.[38] The notable resemblance between Krochmal and Flesch in conjunction with their employment of Ps 78:2 ("I will expound a theme, hold forth on the lessons of the past [אפתחה במשל פי אביעה חידות מני קדם]")[39] as the title for their treatment of Philo seems to be further evidence of this: Krochmal titled his chapter on Philo "Ḥidot Mini Kedem" and subsequently went on to quote Ps 78:3 ("things we have heard and known, that our fathers have told us [אשר שמענו ונדעם ואבותינו ספרו לנו]").[40] Flesch's approach was almost identical: he called his book regarding Philo's historical writings on the Jewish sects "Katot Mini Kedem" and proceeded to quote Ps 78:3–4a ("things we have heard and known, that our fathers have told us. We will not withhold them from their children, telling the coming generation [אשר שמענו ונדעם ואבותינו ספרו לנו לא נכחד מבניהם לדור אחרון]") on the next page. This is rather odd in light of the fact that neither Krochmal nor Flesch explicitly refers to the other's treatment of the Jewish Alexandrian. A very plausible explanation for this exceptional similarity can be that Rapoport mediated some of Krochmal's ideas relating to Philo's agreement with rabbinical sources to Flesch, or *vice versa*. Of course, this similarity does not necessitate this specific inference, but might simply point to the fact that both Flesch's and Krochmal's manuscripts and approaches were circulating among maskilic groups at that time. Still, Rapoport's intimate acquaintance with both Krochmal's and Flesch's interpretations of Philo and his active role therein, while at the same time exhibiting a deep fascination with his philosophy, seems to prompt the conclusion that he did function as a central mediator and propagator of newly formed maskilic approaches to understanding his body of work.

---

[38] For a more detailed analysis of the topic at hand, see Fischel Lachower, "Nigla ve-Nistar be-Mishnato shel RaNaK," in *'Al ha-Gevul ha-Yashan ve-ha-Ḥadash. Massot Sifrutiot*, ed. Fischel Lachower (Jerusalem: Bialik Institute, 1951), 211–63; Roland Goetschel, "Philon et le judaïsme hellénistique au miroir de Naḥman Krochmal," in *Hellenica et Judaica: Hommage à Valentin Nikiprowetzky*, ed. André Caquot, Mireille Hadas-Lebel, and Jean Riaud (Leuven: Peeters, 1986), 371–83.

[39] The English translations of Ps 78:2–4 are taken from the NJPS version.

[40] Krochmal, *Nevokhei*, 165.

3. Rapoport's 'Erekh Milin: Philo, Maimonides, and
the Jewish Origins of Negative Theology

Due to Flesch's premature death, he did not manage to complete his life's work: a translation of Philo's *œuvre*. This state of affairs had a further specific implication which is quite relevant to our theme at hand: Rapoport had not written his proposed piece on Philo's biography. Beyond that, we possess no systematic writing by Rapoport in which he exclusively conveys his perception of Philo. However, by focusing on several passages taken from his most important (unfinished) work *'Erekh Milin*, an encyclopedia of *termini* from both *Talmudim*, midrashic literature, and the *Toseftot*,[41] we can reconstruct in broad outline the central elements of his view of Philo. There, most notably in his entry on Alexandria ("Alexandria shel Mitzraim" / "Alexandria in Egypt"), he devotes some attention to the Alexandrian biblical exegete. Already in the previous entry dedicated to Tiberius Julius Alexander, Philo's well-known nephew, he refers to some historic facts relating to the Alexandrian philosopher: "And the brother of Alexander the Alabarch was the great sage Philo … denoted as *Yedidya* by the composer of *Me'or 'Einayim*."[42] Also, at the beginning of his next entry, while referring to Philo in connection with the question of how many Jews were living in Alexandria, Rapoport designates him as "the great sage" (*ha-ḥakham ha-gadol*).[43] This denotation in itself reflects his very favorable attitude towards Philo, which becomes all the more apparent if one recalls Azaria dei Rossi's reluctance to describe the Alexandrian as a sage in the concluding words of his treatment of Philo: "I shall not call him Rav or sage, heretic or sceptic. My only name for him shall be Yedidya the Alexandrian."[44] In his next

---

[41] For further analysis of the historical meaning of Rapoport's *'Erekh Milin*, see Barzilay, *Shlomo Yehudah Rapoport*, 25–26, 42, esp. 47–48.

[42] Salomon L. Rapoport, "Alexandria," in *Sefer 'Erekh Milin 'al Seder Alef"Beit kolel Bi'ur kol Shemot 'Azmayim shel Anashim me-'Amim, Aratzot vu-Mekomot, Yamim vu-Neharot, Kinuyei ha-Kavod be-Israel kefi Mishmarotam ve-Matzveihem, Katot ha-Shonot ascher Beineihem, ve-Sha'ar Milin ve-'Inyanim, shelo Nitba'aru 'od Milfanim Kekhol Tzorkham, Habaim be-Targumim Aramiyim, bi-Shenei ha-Talmudim, ba-Toseftot u-va-Midrashim* (Prague: Moshe ha-Levi Landau, 1852), 96 (my translation).

[43] Rapoport, "Alexandria," 98.

[44] Dei Rossi, *Light*, 165. For a more detailed examination of dei Rossi's treatment of Philo, see Giuseppe Veltri, "The Humanist Sense of History and the Jewish Idea of Tradition: Azaria de' Rossi's Critique of Philo Alexandrinus," *Jewish Studies Quarterly* 2 (1995): 372–93; Joanna Weinberg, "The Quest for Philo in Sixteenth-Century Jewish Historiography," in *Jewish History: Essays in Honour of Chimen Abramsky*, ed. Ada Rapoport-Albert and Steven J. Zipperstein (London: Halban, 1988), 163–87; Naomi G. Cohen, "Philo Judeaus and the Torah True Library," *Tradition: A Journal of Orthodox Jewish Thought* 41 (2008): 31–48, esp. 34–39; Ralph Marcus, "A Sixteenth Century Hebrew Critique of Philo

reference to Yedidya ha-Alexandri, Rapoport alludes to the vast number of translations of Philonic writings that are currently being produced,[45] probably also having Flesch's translations in mind. Through this statement regarding the attention Philo has received from numerous cultures, Rapoport could stress his importance.

Rapoport's core ideas relating to Philo's Jewish philosophy in this entry are first uncovered in conjunction with the fourth section on Jewish Neo-platonism in Alexandria. One of the characteristics of this Jewish school of thought, as Rapoport explains, is its intention to link the biblical narratives with philosophy. Rapoport goes on to tackle the problematic status of Philo's allegorical exegesis within Jewish tradition by reverting to the authoritative figure of Maimonides, whose philosophical interpretations of the Hebrew Bible find broad consensus among religious Jews and exhibit astonishing parallels to those of Philo:

> The wondrous fact is that our master ha-RaMBaM, may his memory be blessed—who had never read Philo's books, for he did not know Greek—followed him precisely in all the matters of the Torah. Like Philo, he thought that human perfection is predicated upon the attainment of more and more negations of all the attributes of the creator's essence. In this manner, both of them have an identical philosophical interpretation of the biblical *eheye asher eheye*; see hereof Dähne's *Jewish Philosophy of Religion in Alexandria*, page 138. There, you will find that Philo's statements are identical in every respect to those of Maimonides' *Guide* (1:63). The author of *The Light of the Eyes* has already drawn attention to this great similarity.[46]

There are four important points to be made regarding this quotation:

1. Rapoport's claim that Maimonides followed Philo's philosophical reading of Scripture throughout all of his biblical exegesis without even knowing him is nothing less than astounding. The particular point of commonality Rapoport chooses to highlight is their similar position regarding negative theology, which both of them, in his opinion, linked to their understanding of Exod 3:14. By virtue of this analogy, Rapoport attempts to show that in his most fundamental notions regarding the concept of God,

---

(Azariah dei Rossi's 'Meor Eynayim,' Pt. I, cc. 3–6)," *Hebrew Union College Annual* 21 (1948): 29–71; David M. Rosenberg-Wohl, "Reconstructing Jewish Identity on the Foundations of Hellenistic History: Azariah de' Rossi's *Me'or 'Enayim* in Late Sixteenth Century Northern Italy," (Ph.D. diss., University of California, Berkeley, 2014), esp. 109–38.

[45] Rapoport, "Alexandria," 99.

[46] Rapoport, "Alexandria," 99 (my translation): " והנפלא שאדוננו הרמב״ם ז״ל אשר לא ראה

ספרי פילון, כי לא ידע בלשון יוני, הלך ממש בדרכו בכל עניני התורה, כמהו הוא חושב לתכלית שלמות האדם

אם הוא משיג יותר ויותר שלילות כל התארים מעצמות הבורא, ועי״ז שניהם שוים בפירוש המושכל של המקרא

אהי׳ אשר אהי׳. ע׳ מזה דאהנע על הפילוסופיא הדתית של היהודים באלכסנדריא צד 138, תמצא דברי פילון

שוים ממש לדברי המורה (א׳ ס״ג), וכבר העיר על הדמיון הרב בעל מ״ע (רפ״ה)."

Philo advocated for ideas which would later become prevalent and accepted within the Jewish thought-world.[47]

2. As Rapoport's reference to Azaria dei Rossi's implies, his comparison between Philo and Maimonides in relation to their similar understanding of Exod 3:14 takes the fifth chapter of *Imrei Bina* ("There appear to be four defects with which Yedidyah may be charged that are not in accordance with our Torah") as its point of departure. In this chapter, dei Rossi alludes to Philo's anticipation of Maimonides's metaphysical reading of Exod 3:14, in which God is equated with the necessary existent: "Instead of the expression, *I will be that which I will be* (Ex. 3:14), he renders, *the existing being which is the existing being*. Such an interpretation anticipates the explanation of the expression given in the first part of the *Guide* when the author renders *I Am has sent me to you* (Ex. 3:15) as *The existing being sent me to you* [emphasis in the original]."[48]

3. If one keeps in mind Rapoport's sheer admiration for Maimonides, which, in Barzilay's words, "knew no bounds,"[49] then this juxtaposition stands out even more prominently. Through this comparative depiction, it becomes all the more apparent that Rapoport deeply revered not only Maimonides, but also his Alexandrian predecessor from the turn of eras. "The very synthesis of Judaism and worldliness, faith and rationalism"

---

[47] For the view of Philo as the founder of apophatic theology, see Harry A. Wolfson, *Philo: Foundations of Religious Philosophy in Judaism, Christianity and Islam*, 2 vols., rev. ed. (Cambridge: Harvard University Press, 1962), 94–126, esp. 119; Carlos Lévy, "Philo of Alexandria," in *The Stanford Encyclopedia of Philosophy* (Spring 2018 Edition), ed. Edward N. Zalta. Online: https://plato.stanford.edu/archives/spr2018/entries/philo/ (in the section "Negative Theology and Providence"); Maren R. Niehoff, *Philo of Alexandria: An Intellectual Biography* (New Haven: Yale University Press, 2018), 209–24 (chapter 11: "An Utterly Transcendent God and His Logos"). On the Middle Platonic sources of Philo's apophatic theology, see David T. Runia, "Early Alexandrian Theology and Plato's *Parmenides*," in *Plato's* Parmenides *and Its Heritage, Volume 2: Reception in Neoplatonic, Jewish, and Christian Texts*, ed. John D. Turner and Kevin Corrigan (Atlanta: Society of Biblical Literature, 2010), 175–88; Runia, "The Beginnings of the End: Philo of Alexandria and Hellenistic Theology," in *Traditions of Theology: Studies in Hellenistic Theology, Its Background and Aftermath*, ed. Dorothea Frede and André Laks, Philosophia Antiqua 89 (Leiden: Brill, 2002) 296–99; John M. Dillon, *The Middle Platonists. 80 B.C. to A.D. 220*, 2nd ed. (London: Cornell University Press, 1996), 155–58; John Whittaker, "Neopythagoreanism and Negative Theology," *Symbolae Osloenses* 44 (1969): 112; Mauro Bonazzi, "Towards Transcendence: Philo and the Renewal of Platonism in the Early Imperial Age," in *Philo of Alexandria and Post-Aristotelian Philosophy*, ed. Francesca Alesse, SPhA 5 (Leiden: Brill, 2008), 236–46; Jaap Mansfeld, "Compatible Alternatives: Middle Platonist, Theology and the Xenophanes Reception," in *Studies in the Historiography of Greek Philosophy*, (Assen/Maastricht: Van Gorcum, 1990), 178–99.

[48] Dei Rossi, *Light*, 131.

[49] Barzilay, *Shlomo Yehudah Rapoport*, 103.

which led to Rapoport's reverence of Maimonides[50] was also the underlying feature he discovered in Philo's writings. Yet Rapoport's remarkable admiration for Philo is not simply derived from his attitude towards Maimonides. Rather, he seems to view the ancient Alexandrian exegete as nothing short of the founder of Jewish philosophy and as a great metaphysical innovator, who, approximately twelve centuries before Maimonides, had developed some philosophical doctrines which would not become established teachings within Jewish tradition until much later.

4. The quoted passage makes it abundantly clear that Rapoport, like his teacher Krochmal, acquired much of his knowledge of Philo's philosophy from August F. Dähne's *Geschichtliche Darstellung der jüdisch-alexandrinischen Religionsphilosophie* (1834), which systematically expounds on the Philonic apophatic theology.[51] A closer look at the page to which Rapoport refers from the first volume of this scholarly work makes it evident that Rapoport premises a large extent of his above-mentioned depiction upon it:

> Very closely linked to the unfathomableness of God—yes, differing almost entirely in name only—is the second implication, which Philo inferred from the necessarily postulated absolute removal of all attributes from the Godly essence. This is the statement—which he later repeatedly maintains—that man can make no use of a name which would be ascribed to the highest being in the proper sense.... The passage from Moses to which Philo generally ties this standpoint is the abovementioned verse Exod 3:14: ἐγώ εἰμι ὁ ὤν, upon which he prefers to draw in this respect because it seems at the same time to provide a reason as to why the highest being cannot as such be attributed a human name.[52]

Through this juxtaposition of a specific formulation from this passage by Dähne with Rapoport's description of Philo's and Maimonides's stance on

---

[50] Barzilay, *Shlomo Yehudah Rapoport*, 103.

[51] For Dähne's description of Philo's apophatic theology, see also August F. Dähne, *Geschichtliche Darstellung der jüdisch-alexandrinischen Religionsphilosophie* (Halle: Buchhandlung des Waisenhauses, 1834), 119–26, 128–30, 133–42, 153.

[52] "Sehr nahe mit dieser Unerfaßlichkeit Gottes zusammenhangend, ja, fast nur dem Ausdrucke nach von ihr unterschieden, ist die zweite Folgerung, welche Philo aus der als nothwendig angenommenen absoluten Entfernung aller Eigenschaften von dem göttlichen Wesen zog. Es ist die bei ihm dann in der spätern Zeit oft wiederkehrende Behauptung, daß vom Menschen kein Name gebraucht werden könne, der dem höchsten Wesen im eigentlichen Sinne zukäme ... Die Stelle des Moses, an welche Philo diese Ansicht anknüpfen pflegte, ist die schon früher einmal berührte Exod. III. 14: εγώ εἰμι ὁ ὤν, die er hierbei um so lieber benutzte, da sie zugleich mit dem Belege auch den Grund dafür anzugeben schien, warum dem höchsten Wesen kein menschlicher Name im eigentlichen Sinne beigelegt werden könne" (Dähne, *Religionsphilosophie*, 138; my translation).

apophatic theology, this apparent dependence is even further substan-tiated:[53]

<table>
<tr>
<td>... if he grasps more and more the negations of all attributes from the essence of the Creator ... [אם הוא משיג יותר ויותר שלילות כל התארים מעצמות הבורא] (Rapoport, *Alexandria*, 99)</td>
<td>... which Philo inferred from the necessarily postulated absolute removal of all attributes from the Godly essence [die zweite Folgerung, welche Philo aus der als nothwendig angenommenen ab-soluten Entfernung aller Eigenschaften von dem göttlichen Wesen zog]. (Dähne, *Religionsphilosophie*, 138)</td>
</tr>
</table>

Like Rapoport's depiction, Dähne's account also mentions the conjunction of Philo's interpretation of Exod 3:14 with his doctrine of negative theology. The passage from Dähne also seems to point to the fact that Rapoport wishes to underpin the resemblance between Philo and Maimonides (*Guide*, 1:63) in relation to their correlation of God's inherent namelessness with a philosophical interpretation of Exod 3:14.

By drawing upon Dähne, Rapoport can broaden the scope of dei Rossi's initial comparison even further. In doing so, he can reveal the exact extent of the overlapping features of Philo's and Maimonides's philosophy. To this effect, he turns to emphasize the general mindset that Maimonides shares with Philo regarding the underlying allegorical meaning of Scrip-ture. Rapoport seems to want to particularly accentuate the moral doctrines that Philo derives from this allegorical sense entailed in the Bible.[54] The fact that Rapoport refers to Dähne in this respect hardly comes as a surprise. His monographic treatment of Philo's system devotes a whole section to the moral elements of his thought entitled "Die Ethik Philo's" (pp. 341–423). Rapoport goes on to pinpoint the ethical focus which Maimonides lays on his allegorical interpretation of Scripture, using a passage from a letter he wrote to one of his sons as an illustration ("In similar manner, it is well-known what Maimonides, may his memory be blessed, wrote in his letter to his son: And know that Pharaoh the king of Egypt is in truth the evil inclination").[55] In this letter, Maimonides views the biblical figure of Pharaoh as a symbol of *Yetzer ha-ra'* and Egypt as a symbol of the corporeal. Accordingly, for Maimonides, the Israelites epitomize human reason led by Moses, embodying the Godly reason, to overcome Pharaoh's Egypt; that is,

[53] For Rapoport's appreciation of and expertise in Maimonidean philosophy, see Barzilay, *Shlomo Yehudah Rapoport*, 38, 44, 57–59, 90, 103–5.

[54] Rapoport, "Alexandria," 100.

[55] Rapoport, "Alexandria, 100.

the rule of evil inclination and the corporeal.[56] It is hardly a mere coincidence that Rapoport singles out this example of Maimonidean exegesis: he must have encountered numerous instances in Dähne's book where descriptions of Philo's allegorical view of Egypt as a manifestation of the corporeal and the sensual that the Israelites, as the beholders of God guided by Moses as a symbol of the divine reason, overcome:

> The allegorizing Alexandrians were all agreed as to the additional mystical sense that was to be attributed to this exodus from Egypt. They regarded Egypt with its flesh-pots as the place of lusts, as a symbol of the sensual life which man must overcome and whence he may approach the spiritual and the Godly; however, the choir of Moses and Miriam on the higher bank symbolizes the rapture which man—or rather not man, but the pure spirit—experiences once he has reached the higher regions of the Godly.[57]

Rapoport concludes this specific comparison with the assurance that Maimonides, despite his ethical-allegorical understanding of Scripture, at the same time also firmly believed in the basic truths of the biblical narratives ("Although there is no doubt that Maimonides, may his memory be blessed, also believed in the literal sense of the [biblical] stories, as I have explained elsewhere")[58]. The rather remarkable fact is that Rapoport thought it necessary to make this comment about Maimonides and *not* about Philo, as if this aspect was already well established in the latter's case.

Rapoport's comparison between Philo and Maimonides consists of three interrelating points: (1) that Maimonides's metaphysical reading of Scripture in its core elements is aligned with Philo's speculative exegesis; (2) that Maimonides and Philo have quite a similar ethical-allegorical understanding of the Bible; (3) that both Jewish philosophers presuppose the double meaning inherent in Holy Scripture—the one truth literal, the other allegorical—without disqualifying one layer of truth over the other.

---

[56] Maimonides, *Iggerot ve-Sche'elot vu-Teshuvot* (Amsterdam: Shelomo Ben Yosef Kats Props Mokher Sefarim, 1712), 1.

[57] "Was nun aber ferner diesem Auszuge aus Aegypten für ein mystischer Sinn unterzulegen sei, darüber war man unter den allegorisirenden Alexandrinern einig. Aegypten mit seinen Fleischtöpfen galt ihnen als Sitz der Lüste, als ein Symbol des sinnlichen Lebens, aus welchem der Mensch heraustreten müsse dem Geistigen und Göttlichen entgegen; der Chor aber des Moses und der Mirjam auf den höhern Ufern versinnbildlichte das Entzücken, welches der Mensch, oder vielmehr nicht mehr der Mensch, sondern der reine Geist empfinden müsse, wenn er in den höhern Regionen des Göttlichen angelangt sei" (Dähne, *Religionsphilosophie*, 461–62; my translation). Cf. also 147, 394, and 422. For further analysis of the allegorical meaning of Egypt in Philo's biblical exegesis, see Sarah J. K. Pearce, *The Land of the Body: Studies in Philo's Representation of Egypt*, WUNT 208 (Tübingen: Mohr Siebeck, 2007).

[58] Rapoport, "Alexandria," 100.

There is a very discernable undertone of admiration voiced in Rapoport's perception of Philo's philosophical achievements. Philo's speculative reading of the Bible enables Rapoport to historically account for the tradition of Jewish philosophy not as a patchy, discontinuous phenomenon that merely originated under foreign influences in the Middle Ages, but as having roots reaching deep into the antique sources from the Second Temple period. In this sense, Philo represents to Rapoport the substantial anticipation of what constitutes the teachings at the heart of Jewish philosophy subsisting in all its varying stages and historical manifestations. Hegel's *Lectures on the History of Philosophy* are also worth mentioning in this context, inasmuch as they trace the Maimonidean philosophy back to Philo's allegorical exegesis of Jewish Scripture.[59]

4. *Rapoport, the 'Azaria dei Rossi of Our Century':*[60]
Overcoming Azaria dei Rossi's Critique of Philo

Reading further into Rapoport's remarks on Philo in his encyclopedic entry on Alexandria, one finds the reference point for Löw's aforementioned assessment, which contends that Rapoport attempted to fend off dei Rossi's criticism of the Jewish Alexandrian. We come across the following statement from him: "Despite all these sayings, all of the defects the rabbi and author of *Me'or 'Einayim* (ch. 5) stacked against Yedidya or Philo the

[59] Georg W. F. Hegel, *Werke in zwanzig Bänden mit Registerband. Theoriewerkausgabe (TWA)*, vol. 19: *Vorlesungen über die Geschichte der Philosophie II*, ed. Eva Moldenhauer and Karl M. Michel (Frankfurt am Main: Suhrkamp, 1986), 523–24: "Wie bei den Kirchenvätern und Philon ist das Geschichtliche dabei zugrunde gelegt; und dies ist metaphysisch behandelt … dagegen finden wir bei Moses Maimonides sehr strenge abstrakte Metaphysik, die sich nach Art Philons mit den mosaischen Büchern und deren Explikation verknüpfte." For a more detailed analysis of this link, see Ze'ev Strauss, *Die Aufhellung des Judentums im Platonismus. Zu den jüdisch-platonischen Quellen des Deutschen Idealismus, dargestellt anhand von Hegels Auseinandersetzung mit Philon von Alexandria*, Quellen und Studien zur Philosophie 137 (Berlin: de Gruyter, 2019), 174–76. On Philo and Hegel see also: Cyril O'Regan, "Hegel's Retrieval of Philo: Constitution of a Christian Heretic," *SPhiloA* 20 (2008): 101–27; Dirk Westerkamp, *Die philonische Unterscheidung. Aufklärung, Orientalismus und Konstruktion der Philosophie* (München: Fink Verlag, 2009), 91–144 (chapter 2: "Die philonische Unterscheidung. Hegel und die prinzipientheoretische Konstruktion der jüdischen Philosophie"), esp. 133–37; Jens Halfwassen, *Hegel und der spätantike Neuplatonismus. Untersuchungen zur Metaphysik des Einen und des Nous in Hegels spekulativer und geschichtlicher Deutung*, Hegel-Studien 40 (Bonn: Felix Meiner Verlag, 1999), 35–37, 41, 59–61, 69–71, 76, 98, 131, 134, 162–66, 223, 274, 293–96, 316–17.

[60] This description of Rapoport was coined by none other than Leopold Zunz, in *Die Monatstage des Kalenderjahres, ein Andenken an Hingeschiedene* (Berlin: M. Poppelauer, 1872), 57. Cf. also Barzilay, *Shlomo Yehudah Rapoport*, 36–37.

Alexandrian, since it appears that he did not follow the sages of Israel situated in the Holy Land, will be dispersed."[61] As is known, dei Rossi levels four central points of critique against Philo: (1) not using the Hebrew Bible as the authoritative point of departure for his own exegeses, but rather its Greek translation, the Septuagint; (2) postulating a *prima materia* and in doing so ruling out the "orthodox Jewish" position of *creatio ex nihilo*; (3) viewing some of the biblical stories as allegories, while excluding the possibility of their literal sense; (4) not referencing the tradition that was transmitted orally. In the closing paragraph of this chapter, dei Rossi connects these deviant tendencies of Philo to the Boethusians, a heretical Jewish sect that he identifies with the Essenes:[62] "It is true that we cannot claim that he was an adherent of the Saducean sect.... Thus, in my opinion, when somebody attacks him by issuing an evil report about him, he would be justified in identifying him as one of the other heretics, that is, the Boethusians."[63] It is precisely this concluding remark that Rapoport wishes to refute. This he tries to accomplish by pointing out the crucial difference between Philo's *Stillschweigen* and that of the Saducees regarding the exegetical rabbinic tradition in the Holy Land: "This resulted solely from error and lack of knowledge, and not because they did not listen to the [learned] teachers which was the grave sin of the Saducees in the land of Israel. Even if he had heard that the [learned] teachers in the land of Israel interpreted the biblical texts not in accordance with their literal meaning, but rather according to traditions they had, he did not know that they took such traditions to be a fundamental principle, but thought that their words were merely homilies."[64] The pivotal distinction between Philo and the heretical Saducean and Boethusian sects was that unlike them, the Alexandrian unknowingly overlooked the authoritative and binding status of the oral tradition that had originated in Israel at that time. By virtue of this viewpoint—Rapoport conclusively notes—Philo, who sacrificed himself for the good of his nation, can be won back for Judaism and return to its fold as one of its most prolific thinkers:

---

[61] Rapoport, "Alexandria," 101 (my translation). In his encyclopedic entry for "Etrog," Rapoport apparently considered it worthwhile to recapitulate the main points of his defense of Philo almost *verbatim* (Rapoport, *'Erekh Milin*, 257).

[62] "By means of identifiable evidence, I have come to the conclusion (as will be clarified later) that the Essenes were none other than the Boethusians who receive unfavorable mention by our rabbis" (dei Rossi, *Light of the Eyes*, 102; cf. 110).

[63] Dei Rossi, *Light of the Eyes*, 144–45. As Weinberg points out, Rapoport's understanding of the heretical nature of these sects is based on Maimonides' estimation that both the Sadducees and Boethusians "rejected the tradition," a heresy that according to Maimonides is to be traced back to the Karaites (dei Rossi, *Light of the Eyes*, 144 n. 153).

[64] Rapoport, "Alexandria," 101 (my translation).

In this manner, we have gained this great sage and righteous man in every way, for he has done much for the people of Israel. He went to Rome to repeal the decrees [issued against the Jews], as is known from his own accounts, since this man is one of our close relatives, one of our saviors [Ruth 2:20b], and he that will remain shall be for our God [Zech 9:7b]. And he bestows honor on our Jewish brothers, who pride themselves on him in the eyes of the other nations.[65]

A most revealing passage regarding Rapoport's quarrel with Azaria dei Rossi's critical assessment of Philo is also to be found in his article about the famous *paytan* Eleazar Kalir entitled "Zeman ve-Makom R' El'azar ha-Kalir, ve-'Inyanei Piyyutav ve-Piyyutei Zulato, u-Kezat 'Inyanei ha-Tefilot," which was published in *Bikurei ha-'Ittim* in 1830. In footnote 20 of this article—where he elucidates the Jewish custom of introducing *piyyutim* into prayer—he reiterates his defense of Philo more emphatically and from yet another angle, that of Philo's depictions of Jewish sects, expounding on it further:

> I have already proven in my book *'Erekh Milim*, with clear evidence against the author of *Me'or 'Einayim* (chap. 3), that the Essene sect, which is mentioned in the books of Philo the Jew and Josephus, are not the Boethusians mentioned in the *Shisha Sedarim*, since it is not remarked anywhere in Philo's or Josephus's writings that the Essenes deny the oral Torah in the explicit manner that this is said about the Sadducees. In his work *Quod omnis probus liber sit*, Philo wrote that all of their customs in each matter, which could exclusively be transmitted by means of Godly enthusiasm, were passed down to them from their forefathers. Similarly, in his work *De vita contemplativa*, Philo wrote that they [sc. the Essenes] have many ancient books entailing numerous sublime subject-matters, into which they delve and in which they immerse themselves. It is possible that those books were testaments of *Ma'ase Bereschit* and *Ma'ase Merkava*; see below. For this reason, I thought it obvious that this sect is part of the sect of the Pharisees, differentiating merely in people who are fiercer in their piety and their more ascetic life. They are [in accordance with] most of the wise *Ḥasidim* of antiquity found in the *Mishnayot*. The vast number of *Mishnayot* in chapter 6 of [*m.*] *'Abot* are based on them, and Philo therefore wrote in the abovementioned work about the [ascetic] grief-filled lives of these people, who eat nothing but a slice of bread with salt and drink a small quantity of water [*m. 'Abot* 6:4].... I also thought it to be right that the Essenes be denoted as "the vatikin [who] would conclude the recitation of *Shema* with sunrise" in *Shisha Sedarim* (*b. Ber.* 9b), and there they were also called the "holy community of Jerusalem." Many passages in Josephus and Philo reveal the Essenes' conformity to their prayer [rituals].[66]

There are four aspects of this passage that warrant our attention:

---

[65] Rapoport, "Alexandria," 101 (my translation).
[66] Rapoport, "Zeman ve-Makom R' El'azar ha-Kalir, ve-'Inyanei Piyyutav ve-Piyyutei Zulato, u-Kezat 'Inyanei ha-Tefilot," *Bikurei ha-'Ittim* 10 (1830): 118 (my translation).

1. Even though it appears that Rapoport exclusively "acquits" the Essenes and the Therapeutae of dei Rossi's charges of heresy—conflating both Jewish sects[67]—his "acquittal" of Philo also plays quite a central role. Rapoport's line of defense here is very similar to the one he employs for Philo in *'Erekh Milin*: the worldview of these sects rests on ancient traditions that were simply handed down to them,[68] which is why one cannot hold them liable for not explicitly acknowledging the oral rabbinic traditions developing in Judea in their time. Beyond this, it is not stated at any point in either Philo or Josephus that they openly dismissed the oral teachings of the rabbis. The reason for the striking similarity between both of Rapoport's defenses lies in his assumption—following dei Rossi in this case[69]—that Philo was closely associated with the Essene sect. Primarily basing himself on Philo's testimonies, Rapoport argues that the Essenes and the Therapeutae were branches of the Pharisees,[70] living in complete harmony with the principles of the ancient Ḥasidim whose ascetic *modus vivendi* is documented in the Mishnaic tractate *Avot*. Their mystical teachings also, as Rapoport wished to suggest, appear to be aligned with the secret tenets of both *Ma'ase Bereschit* and *Merkava*, mentioned in m. Hag. 2a.

It is noteworthy that this is precisely the perspective advanced by Krochmal in his treatment of Philo. In his "Ḥidot Mini Kedem," he links the ancient Ḥasidim, also in the particular manner they are described in m. 'Abot 6:4, to Philo's idealizing portrayal of the ascetic lifestyle of the Therapeutae, most likely having the account of their eating and drinking

---

[67] Dei Rossi also postulates that the Therapeutae were part of the Essenes: dei Rossi, *Light of the Eyes*, 107. Cf. Weinberg's remark on dei Rossi's selective interpretation of the Therapeutae as Essenes, which overlooks fundamental differences between both sects: Weinberg, *Light of the Eyes*, 107 n. 56. A similar debate is also present in modern scholarship. See, for example, Joan E. Taylor, *The Essenes, the Scrolls, and the Dead Sea* (Oxford: Oxford University Press, 2012), 22–48 (chapter 2: "Philo of Alexandria").

[68] Rapoport seems to derive this assessment from *Contempl.* 29: "They have also writings of men of old, the founders of their way of thinking, who left many memorials of the form used in allegorical interpretation and these they take as a kind of archetype and imitate the method in which this principle is carried out [ἔστι δὲ αὐτοῖς καὶ συγγράμματα παλαιῶν ἀνδρῶν, οἳ τῆς αἱρέσεως ἀρχηγέται γενόμενοι πολλὰ μνημεῖα τῆς ἐν τοῖς ἀλληγορουμένοις ἰδέας ἀπέλιπον, οἷς καθάπερ τισὶν ἀρχετύποις χρώμενοι μιμοῦνται τῆς προαιρέσεως τὸν τρόπον]." (PLCL 9:129).

[69] Dei Rossi, *Light of the Eyes*, 153–54: "I am therefore now in the position to prove that Yedidyah, whose case we are presently examining was affiliated with their sect." See also 158.

[70] Cf. dei Rossi, *Light of the Eyes*, 108: "But unlike the Pharisees, they [sc. the Essenes] did not hold the tenet that the [Oral] Tradition was also enjoined on us together with the Written Torah."

practices in *Contempl.* 36–37[71] in mind.[72] These prolific Galician maskilim are also in complete agreement regarding the parallel they draw between the Therapeutae (§27)[73] and the *Vatikin* (b. Ber. 9b) in relation to their common custom of reciting prayers at sunrise:

... I also thought it to be right that the Essenes be denoted as "the vatikin [who] would conclude the recitation of *Shema* with sunrise" in *Shisha Sedarim* [six orders] (*b. Ber.* 9b), and there they were also called the "holy community of Jerusalem." Many passages in Josephus and Philo reveal the Essenes' conformity to their prayer [rituals]. ... In the work *De vita contemplativa,* Philo wrote that the Essenes would pray twice a day, at evening and morning time. At sunrise they pray for this day that it will successfully and willingly fill their thoughts with divine light ... [

It is taught [in the *Baraita*] that "the vatikin ... would conclude it—the recitation of *Shema*—with sunrise ... in order to link salvation [*Yig'al Israel* blessing] to prayer and thus pray in the course of the day". "R[abbi]" Y[ose] ben Elyakim attested on behalf of the holy community in Jerusalem: The one who links the salvation blessing with prayer will not be harmed the entire day" (*b. Ber.* 9b)

[קריאת–אותה גומרין היו ... ותיקין תנא
גאולה שיסמוך כדי ... החמה הנץ עם–שמע
ריב"ן העיד ביום. מתפלל ונמצא לתפלה,
כל :דבירושלים קדישא קהלא משום אליקים
היום כל ניזוק אינו [...] לתפלה גאולה הסומך
ב').(ברכות)כולו].(Krochmal, *Nevokhei,*
174; emphasis in the original)

ושערתי [... בש"ס נקראים שהם לנכון
ב')(ברכות
החמה הנץ עם ק"ש גומרים שהיו ותיקין
ושם,
ונודע דבירושלים. קדישא קהלא ג"כ נקראו
מקומות בהרבה לתפלתם אי האיס"האיש הסכמת
כתב הפרישות חיי ובמאמר ... ופילא. ביוספיון
ביום פעמים שני מתפללים היו אי שהאיס"פילא
זה יום על יתפללו השמש בעלות ובערב. בבקר
אלהי באור מחשבותם למלא ונכון]ומוצלח
(Rapoport, *Zeman ve-Makom R' El'azar ha-Kalir,* 118–19 n. 20)

The juxtaposition at hand is quite illustrative. It clearly exposes the manner in which Krochmal's very fragmentary employment of rabbinic verses in

---

[71] PLCL 9:135: "Still they eat nothing costly, only common bread with salt for a relish flavoured further by the daintier with hyssop, and their drink is spring water."

[72] Krochmal, *Nevokhei,* 171. Cf. also Avrom B. Gotlober, *Toledot ha-Kabbala ve-ha-Ḥasidut* (Zhytomyr: A. S. Shodov, 1869), 41. For a more penetrating analysis of m. 'Abot and Philo's depiction of Jewish sects, see Maren R. Niehoff, '"Not Study Is the Main Objective, but Action' (Pirqe Avot 1:17): A Rabbinic Maxim in Greco-Roman Context," in *The Faces of Torah: Studies in the Texts and Contexts of Ancient Judaism in Honor of Steven Fraade,* ed. Michal B. Siegal, Tzvi Novick, and Christine Hayes, JAJSup 22 (Göttingen: Vandenhoeck & Ruprecht, 2017), 469–71.

[73] PLCL 9:127: "Twice every day they pray, at dawn and at eventide; at sunrise they pray for a fine bright day, fine and bright in the true sense of the heavenly daylight which they pray may fill their minds. At sunset they ask that the soul may be wholly relieved from the press of the senses and the objects of sense and sitting where she is consistory and council chamber to herself pursue the quest of truth."

his chapter on Philo could be complemented by Rapoport's finalized formulations on the topic, without explicitly mentioning Philo or his writings on the sects.

This approach taken by both Rapoport and Krochmal[74] was later directly adopted, *mutatis mutandis*, by the maskil Avrom Ber Gotlober (1811–1899). In his monograph *Toledot ha-Kabbala ve-ha-Ḥasidut* (1869), he devotes almost an entire chapter to showing that the Essenes were the first *Ḥasidim*.[75] In the following chapter, he proceeds to evaluate the Therapeutae in an analogous fashion: like the Essenes, they were also a faction of the Pharisees whose customs and mystical doctrines resembled those of the original *Ḥasidim*, illustrated in the Mishnah.[76] In this respect, Philo is elevated to an even higher pedigree, inasmuch as Gotlober regards his Jewish philosophy—following Krochmal's[77] and probably also Rapoport's indications[78]—as one of the main unblemished sources and testimonies for Kabbalistic thought in its original form, which Gotlober also understands as *Shitat ha-Ḥasidut*.[79]

2. Content-wise, Rapoport believes that the numerous parallels between the prayers of the Therapeutae, a branch of the Essenes, and *piyyutim* such as *Ahava Rabba* and *Ahavat 'Olam* prompt the hypothesis that the Essenes were actually the ones who authored these Jewish liturgical poems.[80]

3. With these comments, Rapoport exhibits his profound interest in Philo's historical writings. Through these testimonies, he aims to shed light on some pivotal components and intellectual developments of Second Temple Judaism. These remarks may uncover some of the ideas that would have been included in the biography of Philo that he intended to prepare for Flesch's Hebrew translations of the Alexandrian's works. It is also very plausible that Rapoport's observations showed Flesch, who at this very time was also a modest contributor to *Bikurei ha-'Ittim*,[81] the extraordinary relevance of such treatises and suggested the concept for his second book, *Katot Mini Kedem*. Given that this assumption was to a certain extent

---

[74] See, for example, Gotlober, *Toledot ha-Kabbala ve-ha-Ḥasidut*, 34 n. 2, 37 n. 1, 38, 39.

[75] Gotlober, *Toledot ha-Kabbala ve-ha-Ḥasidut*, 30–37.

[76] Gotlober, *Toledot ha-Kabbala ve-ha-Ḥasidut*, 38, 40, 42.

[77] Krochmal, *Nevokhei*, 173–74.

[78] See also Rapoport, "Zeman ve-Makom R' El'azar ha-Kalir," 119.

[79] Gotlober, *Toledot ha-Kabbala ve-ha-Ḥasidut*, 42. Cf. Kohler, *Kabbalah Research in the Wissenschaft des Judentums*, 31, 42, 184, 249–50.

[80] Rapoport, "Zeman ve-Makom R' El'azar ha-Kalir," 119.

[81] For example, he had published a brief entry on the etymology of the term *Lot* in the previous volume of *Bikurei ha-'Ittim*: Josef Flesch, "Davar el Meḥkarei Lashon 'Avar," *Bikurei ha-'Ittim* 9 (1829): 56.

correct, it would seem rather evident why Flesch sent Rapoport, of all people, parts of the manuscript of his translations of and commentaries on Philo's writings on the Jewish sects.

4. The fact that Rapoport deemed it fit to lay out his vindication of Philo on three separate occasions attests to just how eminently important this issue was for him. The prospect of Philo and his rich body of work being further excluded from the traditional group of sources which constituted the "classical" Jewish thought-world must have seemed to Rapoport to be absolutely dismal. It was precisely this inclusion of the Alexandrian philosopher as an inherent part of Jewish tradition that, in Rapoport's view, would not only lead to a broadening of the historical consciousness of its culture, but also, and *a fortiori*, a deepening of the foundation of its spiritual content. For Rapoport, "a staunch rationalist,"[82] these very contents, emerging from the methodical rationalization of Judaism through Greek philosophy, rendered the Jewish faith all the more special and valuable.

Conclusion

The main thrust of Rapoport's concise analysis of Philo is not only that it dares to go a step further than dei Rossi's mostly favorable treatment of the Jewish Alexandrian, but also that it does so quite explicitly on three different occasions by directly challenging the strong reservations against Philo's unorthodox Jewish thought voiced in chapter 5 of *Imrei Bina*. This explicitness is exactly what helps us to cast further light on the most renowned treatment of Philo in the philosophy of the Haskala: Krochmal's "Hidot Mini Kedem," a very fragmentary and at times incomprehensive chapter on Philo and Jewish Alexandrian philosophy. In this respect, one thing seems quite certain: Rapoport's perception of Philo is broadly aligned with that of Krochmal. It is not merely his drawing upon Dähne as his main secondary source regarding Philo's philosophy that prompts this assumption, but rather the *manner* in which he utilizes this source to underpin the Jewish ethics of the Philonic system. Considering this, one may assess Rapoport's attitude towards Philo, as outlined in *'Erekh Milin*, as an important complementary piece to the understanding of Krochmal's "Hidot Mini Kedem."

[82] Barzilay, *Shlomo Yehudah Rapoport*, 105.

Drawing on Krochmal,[83] Amos Funkenstein, in his *Perceptions of Jewish History*, argues that the entire intellectual movement of the Haskala was primarily predicated upon its rigorous re-analysis of central sources of medieval Jewish philosophy: "No elaborate proof is needed to convince us that the early Haskala manifested itself through a renewed dedication to medieval philosophical writings.... The Enlighteners saw in the medieval philosophers their own predecessors."[84] While this contention is, in itself, for the most part true, it fails to account for another very significant aspect of the historical consciousness of the maskilic philosophers: the renewed attention the philosophy of Hellenistic Judaism, represented almost exclusively by Philo, was gaining among the Jewish Enlighteners, who were thus venerating new philosophical heroes from antiquity such as Philo and attempting to reintroduce them into the core culture of Judaism. By reverting to Philo's ancient Ἰουδαϊκὴ φιλοσοφία,[85] the above-discussed maskilim were relentlessly pursuing the same basic objective as Mendelssohn: to unearth the "spirit of true Judaism" ("Geist ... des ächten Judentums")[86] in its "ancient, original" sense.[87]

This interpretation from Rapoport, one of the most prominent nineteenth-century maskilim and a substantial contributor to the *Wissenschaft des Judentums*, constitutes a pivotal moment within the rapid rediscovery of Philo's Jewish philosophy in the Haskala, taking Mendelssohn's *Netivot Shalom* as its crucial starting point.[88] Given that some of the chief premises

---

[83] Amos Funkenstein, *Perceptions of Jewish History* (Berkeley: University of California Press, 1993), 243–47.

[84] Funkenstein, *Perceptions of Jewish History*, 238–39.

[85] It is true that Philo uses this expression only once in the entire corpus of his writings—in his particularly favorable portrayal of Publius Petronius—but it still reveals an important aspect of his view of Judaism as a *philosophia perennis*. For a very learned discussion of Philo's Jewish thought as *philosophia perennis* within the context of Azaria dei Rossi's *Me'or 'Einayim*, see Giuseppe Veltri, *Renaissance Philosophy in Jewish Garb: Foundations and Challenges in Judaism on the Eve of Modernity*, Supplements to The Journal of Jewish Thought and Philosophy 8 (Leiden: Brill, 2009), 83–91. On Philo's view, see David Winston, *The Ancestral Philosophy: Hellenistic Philosophy in Second Temple Judaism*, ed. Gregory E. Sterling, BJS 331/SphilMS 4 (Providence: Brown Judaic Studies, 2001).

[86] Moses Mendelssohn, *Jerusalem, or On Religious Power and Judaism*, trans. Allan Arkush; introduction and commentary by Alexander Altmann (Hanover, N.H.: University Press of New England, 1983), 100. For the original German, see Moses Mendelssohn, *Gesammelte Schriften. Jubiläumsausgabe*, vol. 8: *Jerusalem oder über religiöse Macht und Judentum*, ed. Ismar Elbogen, Julius Guttmann, Eugen Mittwoch, Alexander Altmann, Eva J. Engel, and Daniel Krochmalnik (Bad Cannstatt: Frommann-Holzboog, 1983), 167.

[87] See Mendelssohn, *Jerusalem, or On Religious Power and Judaism*, 102.

[88] As Barzilay claims, Rapoport "was a great admirer of Mendelssohn and undoubtedly read the *Biur*" (Barzilay, *Shlomo Yehudah Rapoport*, 27; cf. 49). For Mendelssohn's drawing upon Philo in his *Bi'ur* and other works, see Ze'ev Strauss, "The Ground Floor of

of the Hegelian *Philosophiegeschichte* and *Religionsphilosophie* were widely accepted at that time, Philo's antique and tremendously influential philosophy was promptly gaining ground among Jewish thinkers. In terms of intellectual history as a whole—and also in Hegel's estimation thereof—Philo occupies a crucial position, since his speculative religious philosophy anticipates central thought patterns later found in both Christian and Neoplatonic doctrines.[89] Philo's ancient Jewish thought, in its newly formed Hebrew guise, provided Rapoport with a completely new scientific terminology through which he could better account, historiographically speaking, for the profound, comprehensive, and innovative phenomenon of Jewish philosophy; this being, at its core, entirely independent of the Christian and Islamic philosophical traditions. By invoking Philo's Jewish philosophy as an authoritative historical source, a maskil such as Rapoport could decisively establish a standpoint to which Krochmal had already alluded in his chapter on Philo: that at the basis of all critical moments of the history of ideas are Jewish roots, which in turn ultimately emanate from the all-encompassing regulative principle of the spirit of Israel (*nefesh israel ha-kelalit*).[90]

Center for Jewish Studies Heidelberg /
Heidelberg University, Heidelberg, Germany

Judaism: Scepticism and Certainty in Moses Mendelssohn's *Jerusalem*," in *Yearbook of the Maimonides Centre for Advanced Studies* 3 (2018): 186–94.

[89] For further analysis of this theme, see Strauss, *Die Aufhellung des Judentums im Platonismus*, 164–86 ("Philons Wirkungsgeschichte: Vom Neuplatonismus über Kabbala und Gnosis bis hin zur jüdischen und christlichen Philosophie").

[90] Krochmal, *Nevokhei*, 167.

BIBLIOGRAPHY SECTION

PHILO OF ALEXANDRIA
AN ANNOTATED BIBLIOGRAPHY 2016

D. T. Runia, M. Alesso, E. Birnbaum, A. C. Geljon, H. M. Keizer,
J. Leonhardt-Balzer, M. R. Niehoff, S. J. K. Pearce, S. Weisser,
S. Yli-Karjaanmaa

2016[1]

A. Afterman, *"And They shall be one Flesh": On the Language of Mystical Union in Judaism*, Supplements to the Journal of Jewish Thought and Philosophy 26 (Leiden 2016), esp. 25–48.

The subject of the monograph is the development of the notion of mystical union in Jewish thought. The author argues that the idea of union with God primarily originated in Philo and that he is the source of the *henōsis* mysticism in the later Neoplatonic tradition. Chapter 2 'From Philo to Plotinus: The Emergence of Mystical Union' is a slightly rewritten version of the 2013 article with the same title. See *SPhiloA* vol. 28, p. 393. (ACG)

[1] This bibliography has been prepared by the members of the International Philo Bibliography Project under the leadership of D. T. Runia (Melbourne). The principles on which the annotated bibliography is based have been outlined in *SPhiloA* 2 (1990) 141–142, and are largely based on those used to compile the 'mother works,' R-R, RRS and RRS2 (on the inclusion of works in languages outside the scholarly mainstream see esp. RRS2 xii). The division of the work this year is as follows: material in English (and Dutch) by D. T. Runia (DTR), E. Birnbaum (EB), A. C. Geljon (ACG) and S. J. K. Pearce (SJKP); in French by Sharon Weisser (SW); in Italian by H. M. Keizer (HMK); in German by J. Leonhardt-Balzer (JLB); in Spanish and Portuguese by M. Alesso (MA); in Scandinavian languages (and by Scandinavian scholars) by S. Yli-Karjanmaa (SYK); and in Hebrew and by Israeli scholars by M. R. Niehoff (MRN). We welcome as a new member of the team Dr Sami Yli-Karjanmaa, who has taken over the role of Torrey Seland. Acknowledgement must be made of the assistance given by the related bibliographical labours of L. Perrone (Bologna) and his team in the journal *Adamantius* (Studies on the Alexandrian tradition). Other scholars who have responded to requests this year are Giovanni Benedetto, Andrew Benjamin, Smaranda Marcelescu and Torrey Seland. This year I once again owe much to my former Leiden colleague Marten Hofstede, who laid a secure foundation for the bibliography through his extremely thorough electronic searches. However, the bibliography remains inevitably incomplete, because much work on Philo is tucked away in monographs and articles, the titles of which do not mention his name. Scholars are encouraged to get in

T. ALEKNIENÉ, *A l'approche du divin: dialogues de Platon et tradition platoni-cienne*, Vestigia 42 (Fribourg 2016).

The author, Professor of Ancient History at the Lithuanian University of Educational Sciences in Vilnius (in 2019 integrated into Vytautas Magnus University), has collected together eleven French-language articles written in the period 1999 to 2016, all of them related to the theme of the different stages of the path leading to the divine and the effects that such an approach has on those that experience it. The primary authors who are studied are Plato and his later follower Plotinus. But in the Preface the author also notes that a large part of her research has focused on the question of whether Plotinus gained knowledge of the writings of Philo during his studies in Alexandria, a positive answer to which she considers 'quite probable' (p. vii). Five of the contributions are directly relevant to Philonic studies, nos. 7–11. Three of these have been previously published: 'L'enigme de la 'patrie' dans le Traite 1 de Plotin: heritage de l'exégèse philonienne?' (2007; see sum-mary at *SPhiloA* vol. 22, pp. 209–210); 'L'«extase mystique» dans la tradition platonicienne: Philon d'Alexandrie et Plotin' (2010; summary at *SPhiloA* vol. 25, p. 170); La prière à l'Un dans le Traité 10 (V, 1) de Plotin et la tradition philosophique grecque' (summary at *SPhiloA* vol. 29, p. 225). The remaining two studies have not previously been published and are summarised elsewhere in this bibliography. (DTR)

T. ALEKNIENÉ, 'Quelle est cette fuite? Le *Théétète* de Platon, Philon d'Alexandrie et l'invention de l'exégèse platonisante,' in T. ALEKNIENE (ed.), *A l'approche du divin: dialogues de Platon et tradition platonicienne,* Vestigia 42 (Fribourg 2016) 271–320.

Until Plotinus the Platonist philosophers who address the famous passage of Plato's *Theaetetus* 176b do not show much interest in the motif of escape. Philo is the first to give this theme a prominent place in his exegesis and to understand it as the migration of the soul towards God. In light of the similarities between Philo and Plotinus (such as the stress on the motif of escape and its metaphoric and ecstatic character), it is plausible to consider Philonic influence on Plotinus. Philo's original strategy in allegorically interpreting the Homeric poems is also stressed. As opposed to other philosophical sources, Philo does not use the poems as a means to illustrate philosophical tenets, but offers an allegorical reading bearing on the spiritual journey of the soul. In this respect also, his influence on the Neoplatonic tradition should be considered. (SW)

T. ALEKNIENÉ, 'Le propos d'Héraclite: «Les cadavres sont plus vils que le fumier» (fr. 96 DK) chez les auteurs grecs anciens,' in T. ALEKNIENE (ed.), *A l'approche du divin: dialogues de Platon et tradition platonicienne,* Vestigia 42 (Fribourg 2016) 321–341, esp. 329–333.

---

touch with members of the team if they spot omissions or wish to have their own publications included (addresses below in 'Notes on Contributors'). In order to preserve continuity with previous years, the bibliography retains its own customary stylistic conventions and has not changed to those of the Society of Biblical Literature used in the remainder of the Annual.

A study of the reception and usage of Heraclitus' saying: 'Corpses are more fit to be thrown out than dung' (22A96 DK) by Greek authors. After a brief mention of the occurrences of the Heraclitean fragment in Strabo (the first author to mention it) and Plutarch, the author turns to Philo of Alexandria. Philo mentions or evokes the fragment (such as in *Fug.* 61, *QG* 1.81 and *Her.* 29–30) in order to illustrate the futility and nothingness of human mortal life as compared to divine life. Other Platonist authors, such as Plutarch, Celsus, or the emperor Julian, also use the fragment, but in order to convey the dualism between the soul, which is divine, and the body. Christian thinkers such as Origen and Julian, the 4th century Arian theologian, reject the contempt for the human body that emerges from the Heraclitean fragment. (SW)

M. ALESSO, 'Qué significa la divina providencia en la teología de Filón de Alejandría,' *Circe de clásicos y modernos* 20 (2016) 113–129.

The paper investigates the way in which Philo conceives the role of Divine Providence (πρόνοια τοῦ θεοῦ) as responsible for the design, existence and administration of the created universe. The contents discuss the following topics: (1) What is providence? (2) Providence in Greek philosophy; (3) What is Divine Providence according to Philo; (4) Provident God is not the cause of the evil; (5) Providence in the historical treatises; (6) Divine providence in patriarchal society. Philo interprets the biblical narratives about Moses and the patriarchs, and also the history of the Jewish people under the hypothesis that they reveal the Providence of God. However, although this idea appears in some passages of Septuagint, Philo does not base it on the biblical passages. His doctrine on Providence results from a synthesis between biblical conceptions and Platonic and Stoic philosophical arguments. He derives the idea of Providence from the biblical narratives that indicate the care and interest that God has for the world and his people, but he expounds these narratives in terms of the categories of Greek thought. (MA)

D. J. ARMITAGE, *Theories of Poverty in the World of the New Testament*, Wissenschaftliche Untersuchungen zum Neuen Testament 2.423 (Tübingen 2016), esp. 175–190.

The monograph is a lightly revised version of the author's 2015 University of Nottingham dissertation supervised by Prof. R. Deines. Its aim is to determine how approaches to poverty in New Testament texts are distinctive when seen against the background of interpretations of poverty in the Greco-Roman and Jewish contexts. These latter occupy the first 191 pages of the book, with Philo the last writer discussed. He is regarded as a useful control, particularly for gauging the subterranean influences of Greek philosophy in the New Testament. Philo was almost certainly very rich, but he does not adopt an attitude towards the poor of elite detachment. Not only does he indicate that he has witnessed poverty in Alexandria, especially during the crisis of 38–41 CE, but he also regularly commends the Law for expressing the virtue of φιλανθρωπία (love for humanity). The emphasis here is on the poor as fellow human beings. When, however, he evaluates poverty as an abstraction, he takes a different approach, which is influenced by Greek philosophy. God exercises providential oversight over all events, without this leading to any kind of Stoicizing fatalism. Bad things such as poverty can happen through intermediate agencies or through the exercise of human freedom. But at the same time Philo deprecates the importance of material things. If humanity recognises that it does not actually own anything, then material deprivation loses its power to shape well-being. The author concludes that the key priorities of Philo's formative traditions—Judaic and Hellenistic—are juxtaposed but not fully synthesized. 'He [Philo] emphasizes the importance of assisting the poor, but also argues that poverty ultimately does not matter (p. 190).' (DTR)

L. ARMOUR, 'Religious Experiences and their Frameworks of Intelligibility: Community and Universality in the Writings of Philo of Alexandria,'
in R. FEIST and R. SHUKLA (edd.), *Essays on Religious and Political Experience*
(Leuven 2016) 191–212.

Religious experiences are of different kinds but they require a context, which is usually
provided by religious tradition. With his different levels of interpretation—the literal,
scholarly, and allegorical—Philo exemplifies an approach that can encompass the specific
experience of a community and the more universal experience of the spirit. Several
features of Philo's thought and work enable him to bridge different cultures. The story of
Moses has an Egyptian background that may have been influenced by Akhenaten's
revolutionary belief in Aten as the only God. Philo reads this story in terms of Greek
philosophy but he also constructs a trinitarian view consisting of God, 'the ground of all
being'; the Logos, 'the ordering of the activity of God in the world'; and 'a Holy Spirit
which can infuse and guide other minds and spirits' (p. 201). This construction makes
possible a link between Jews and Christians, but Philo's understanding of the infinite as
'the cause of the world' (p. 204) also makes it possible for people of different religions to
relate to this cause. Philo thus offers a framework that renders 'religious experience
intelligible' and he tries to 'universalise the understanding of that experience so as to make
it mesh with Greek rationality' (p. 207). Contrary to the opinions of several scholars, this
attempt at universalization is also aimed at 'overcoming the male-dominated visions of
ancient Judaism' (ibid.), as can be seen, for example, from Philo's treatment of the concept
of *sophia* and especially of Sarah, who symbolizes wisdom, virtue, and unity, including
'the unity of man and woman' (p. 210). (EB)

R. VON BENDEMANN (ed.), *Philo von Alexandria – Über die Freiheit des
Rechtschaffenen*, Kleine Bibliothek der antiken jüdischen und christlichen
Literatur (Göttingen 2016).

The volume presents a German translation of *Quod omnis probus liber sit*. The author
begins with an introduction on Philo as a representative of Hellenistic diaspora Judaism,
on his writings, on the treatise's dating, genre and content, its structure and argument, on
Philo's method and on the translation. The treatise is a monograph, not a dialogue, and it
should not be seen as an early work. The translation is based on the Greek text of Leopold
Cohn. Von Bendemann divides the text into an introduction (1–15) and three main parts
(16–58; 59–97; 98–157), and a conclusion (158–160), allowing the reader to follow clearly
the train of Philo's thought. (JLB)

A. BENJAMIN, 'Barring Fear: Philo and the Hermeneutic Project,' *Epoché:
A Journal for the History of Philosophy* 20 (2016) 307–326.

The aim of the paper is to investigate the role of allegory in Philo and specifically in
Migr. It proceeds through the twofold move of arguing that, even though Philo remains a
Platonist and that his language is Platonic in orientation, what occurs is a transformation
of seeing, which is an immediate activity, into reading, which is always mediate. The
second element stems from this insistence on mediation. It results in freeing allegory from
the hold of the allegorical/literal opposition. Allegory is transformed as a result in the
name of an ineliminable allegoresis, conceived as that which opens up the interpretation
and allows it to move beyond the opposition of the literal and the allegorical. The author
sums up as follows (p. 323): 'The text opens beyond its own immediate concerns. The

hermeneutic therefore is not a form of continuity in which there is an unchecked proliferation of meaning. Rather, it is a continual opening in which what comes to the fore must be subject to processes of interpretation, transformation and deliberation and thus it is that within which the distinction between the literal and the allegorical is destabilized by the process of allegoresis.' (DTR; partly based on author's abstract)

P. BILDE, *Collected Studies on Philo and Josephus*, edited by E.-M. BECKER, M. H. JENSEN, and J. MORTENSEN, Studia Aarhusiana Neotestamentica 7 (Göttingen 2016).

A collected volume of previously published studies by the distinguished Danish scholar, who died in May 2014. It contains a Prologue and 11 studies which were selected by the author himself before his death. Four of the studies focus on Philo and give detailed analyses of Philonic texts: 1: 'The Roman Emperor Gaius (Caligula)'s Attempt to Erect his Statue in the Temple of Jerusalem' (1978; summary RR 7806); 6: 'The Essenes in Philo and Josephus' (1998; summary 9816); 10: 'Philo as a Polemist and a Political Apologist: An Investigation of his Two Historical Treatises Against Flaccus and The Embassy to Gaius' (2009; summary of 2007 German version at *SPhiloA* vol. 22 p. 214) ; 11: 'Der Konflikt zwischen Gaius Caligula und den Juden über die Aufstellung einer Kaiserstatue im Tempel von Jerusalem' (2012; summary at *SPhiloA* vol. 27, p. 214). A further study, no. 9: 'The Jews in Alexandria in 38–41 CE,' also touches on Philo as one of the Jewish sources of 'the circumstances and situation of the Jews in Alexandria at a very brief period of time, around the year 40 CE, more precisely the years 38–41' (published in 2006, not summarised in our bibliography). The volume also includes appreciations of Bilde's scholarly achievement by S. Mason and M. Müller. See further the review of this collection by G.E. Sterling in *SPhiloA* vol. 30, pp. 198–201. (DTR)

D. J. BINGHAM, '"We have the Prophets": Inspiration and the Prophets in Athenagoras of Athens,' *Zeitschrift für Antike und Christentum (Journal of Ancient Christianity)* 20 (2016) 211–242.

In discussing the views of the early Christian apologist Athenagoras on the inspiration of the prophets, the author agrees that Philo was an important influence (p. 241): 'Certainly there are significant parallels with Philo, both lexical and conceptual. His discussions concerning the divine inspiration of the prophets, the state of ecstasy, the role of the Spirit, the effect upon reason, and the musical metaphor find some degree of resonance in our apologist. It is almost unimaginable that Philo was not in his mind.' But beside Philo (together with Hellenic sources such as Plato and Plutarch), there are also other sources in the Septuagint, other Jewish texts, New Testament, and early Christian texts (especially Justin and Ignatius), that should be taken into account. (DTR)

E. BIRNBAUM, 'Some Particulars about Universalism,' in K. B. STRATTON and A. LIEBER (edd.), *Crossing Boundaries in Early Judaism and Christianity. Ambiguities, Complexities, and Half-Forgotten Adversaries: Essays in Honor of Alan F. Segal*, Journal for the Studies of Judaism Series 177 (Leiden 2016) 117–137.

The terms 'universalism' and 'particularism' cannot adequately describe expressions of either early Christianity or early Judaism, especially because 'at some point, a defining factor must distinguish between outsiders and insiders' (p. 118). Instead of using these terms, one should focus on the specific ways that religious systems are or are not open to others. The author demonstrates this approach in connection with three issues typically associated with universalism and particularism: chosenness, proselytism, and salvation. Having tried in an earlier study to characterize Philo as universalistic or particularistic (see RRS 9608), the author now believes that one should avoid these terms entirely and instead acknowledge his views in all their complexity. Thus, Philo can be seen as open to others in that he 'allows for the possibility that wise and virtuous non-Jews might be able to "see God"' and therefore might theoretically be part of 'Israel,' and he also welcomes as Jews proselytes, who worship God by observing His laws (p. 136). Philo also, however, denounces non-Jews who are polytheists, idolaters, and animal worshippers. If the terms 'universalistic' and 'particularistic' are 'inadequate just for Philo, … but one spokesperson for Judaism, how much greater is their inadequacy for the entire Jewish—or Christian—tradition!' (p. 137). (EB)

E. Birnbaum, 'What in the Name of God Led Philo to Interpret Abraham, Isaac, and Jacob as Learning, Nature, and Practice?,' in G. E. Sterling (ed.), *The Studia Philonica Annual Vol. 28 [= Studies in Philo in Honor of David Runia]* (Atlanta 2016) 273–296.

The translation of Exod 3:14–15 from Hebrew into Greek created problems not inherent in the Hebrew, in which the tetragrammaton YHWH in verse 15 is linked with God's statement in v. 14, *ehyeh asher ehyeh* ('I am who I am'). In Greek the tetragrammaton was translated as Κύριος, or 'Lord,' and the link between God's name and his statement in v. 14 became obscured. As Philo declares in *Abr.* 50–51, it also became possible to understand God's name as 'God of Abraham, God of Isaac, and God of Jacob.' In §51 Philo explains that the three patriarchs are symbols of excellence gained through teaching, nature, and practice, respectively, and that it is fitting that the divine name be linked with these abstract qualities because 'it is more suitable that the eternal should be called by what is imperishable rather than what is mortal …' (§55). Philo mentions that some people associate these excellences with the (mythological) three Graces. Based on principles explained by J.L. Kugel about biblical interpretation and the 'life' of exegetical motifs, the author hypothesizes that the interpretation of the Graces as teaching, nature, and practice was transferred into Jewish tradition and applied to the patriarchs so that God's name could be understood as associated with abstract qualities instead of the mortal patriarchs. In Philo's work the three patriarchs as symbols of teaching, nature, and practice, respectively, became a widespread motif that he took for granted and used for different purposes throughout many of his exegetical writings. (EB)

R. Bloch, 'Philo and Jeremiah: A Mysterious Passage in *De Cherubim*. A Response to Gregory E. Sterling,' in H. Najman and K. Schmid (edd.), *Jeremiah's Scriptures*, Supplements to the Journal for the Study of Judaism 173 (Leiden 2016) 431–442.

The author begins by acknowledging the meagreness of evidence concerning Philo's relationship with the prophet Jeremiah, but he agrees with G. Sterling (to whose paper his is a response) that asking the question about that relationship is worthwhile. He focuses on *Cher.* 49 as the most interesting of Philo's three citations from Jeremiah, and sets it in its exegetical context of Gen 4:1/Jer 3:4. In Philo's allegory, these verses speak of God engendering virtue in the human soul. The author discusses Philo's self-declared enrolment as a disciple of Jeremiah the 'hierophant' and notes the discrepancy between this statement and Philo's almost never actually using the book of Jeremiah. Further, he notes the negativity towards Egypt in the prophet and doubts that Philo's sympathy for him had anything to do with the latter's reported stay in that land. He also advocates caution with regard to the assumption of Jeremiah having been especially venerated by the Jews in Egypt. (SYK)

G. M. BONNEY, 'Philo of Alexandria: Some Traces of his Exegesis of Sin and Evil in Genesis in some Christian Authors,' *Vetus Testamentum et Hellas* 3 (2016) 96–116.

This article can be regarded as a companion piece to the article of M. Cimosa published in the same fascicle. It turns from the exegesis of Philo himself on the subject of sin and evil to the influence that he had on early Christian writers. It commences by noting that many publications about early Christian interpretation of the Bible and some on Jewish exegesis have ignored to their cost the role of Philo, for 'the *Philo ecclesiasticus* of Jerome was first exalted before being excluded from Christian theology' (p. 96). After an extensive discussion of the cultural and religious background of the Christians in Alexandria, the article examines in more detail some traces of Philo's exegesis of sin and evil in Genesis in the interpretation of Irenaeus and Didymus. The author then draws some conclusions about his influence on the Church Fathers. (DTR; partly based on the author's abstract).

P. BORGEN, 'Alternative Aims and Choices in Education: Analysis of Selected Texts,' in G. E. STERLING (ed.), *The Studia Philonica Annual Vol. 28 [= Studies in Philo in Honor of David Runia]* (Atlanta 2016) 257–271.

The article discusses the topic of education in selected Philonic texts: *Leg.* 3.162–168, which deals with the right and wrong motivation for pursuing education and philosophy, as well as two texts illustrating these motivations: the noble one is discussed in light of *Congr.* 71–80 that deals with the symbolism of Hagar as preliminary studies and Sarah as philosophy, and the ignoble one through *Legat.* 166–178, 203–206 where Philo writes of the Alexandrian slave Helicon and his career-oriented education. The author concludes that it is beneficial to read Philo's historical works together with the exegetical ones, as the same themes (e.g. the Jerusalem Temple) are approached from different angles in the various genres. (SYK)

J. M. BRODERICK, 'Custodian of Wisdom: The Marciana Reading Room and the Transcendent Knowledge of God,' *Studi Veneziani* 73 (2016) 15–94.

This extensive article studies the Renaissance painted ceiling of the Reading Room of the Marciana Library in Venice. The author's thesis is that the twenty-one roundels of the ceiling of the Reading room, painted by seven different artists, should be interpreted as a coherent program that gives expression to the academic interests, moral values, and political ideals of Venice at a particular time in its history. The ceiling in its entirety thus conveys a pedagogic message. The core of this message is formed by the second to fifth groups of three roundels, which portray humanity's quest for a transcendent under-standing of reality. It is proposed that the initial group of three roundels viewed on enter-ing the room, painted by Giovanni de Mio, 'form a theological prologue which privileges the 'Mosaic philosophy' of Philo of Alexandria as a means of reconciling Hellenistic thought with Christian doctrine and subsuming the philosophy that underpins the entire program into an acceptable religious framework' (p. 19). Specifically, two of the paintings deal with the origin of the sensible world and would seem to be influenced by Philonic thought, showing the generation of the intelligible cosmos and the existence of the models for the corporeal world within the Divine Intellect. Another contains tablets of the Mosaic Law as a revelation of God's knowledge. It is also noted that the Library contains twelve codices of Philo's works and that the first printed editions of these works appear in the decades preceding its construction. If this bold thesis is correct, then the author has uncovered a remarkable example of Philonism influencing the iconography of high Renaissance art. See also the Note in *SPhiloA* vol. 29, pp. 268–269. (DTR)

F. CALABI, "'It would not be Good that the Man should be Alone": Philo's Interpretation of Genesis 2:18 in *Legum Allegoriae*,' in G. E. STERLING (ed.), *The Studia Philonica Annual Vol. 28 [= Studies in Philo in Honor of David Runia]* (Atlanta 2016) 239–256.

The article proposes a reading of Philo's interpretation in *Leg* 2 of μόνος (from Gen 2:18, 'it is not good that the man should be alone') along Aristotelian lines. It commences with a discussion on Philo's concept of μόνος as applied to God (*Leg.* 2.1: being alone in its full sense applies only to God) and as applied to the human being. This leads to a careful analysis of Philo's views on the human being "after the image" and "moulded of the earth," and on the relationship between the intellect (Adam) and sense perception (Eve). Various scholarly interpretations are reviewed of Philo's different approaches (notably in *Leg.* 2, *Opif.*, *QG*) to these themes. Where Philo in *Leg.* 2.3 speaks about the monad in reference to God, this has been considered a Platonic discussion. Calabi argues, however, that a strong Peripatetic atmosphere pervades *Leg* 2, echoed in the use of terms as ἕξις, δύναμις and ἐνέργεια. She concludes that 'many passages in *Leg.* 2, 1–70 are quite, even if of course not totally, "Peripatetic," ... for Adam's being alone means being "in potency." It is not good that man—imperfect, composite, in need of help—should be alone, it is good that he should emerge from potentiality and actualize his *dunameis*, while God is one, alone, simple, without need of any helper, perfect (p. 256).' (HMK)

F. CALABI, 'Tra verità e apparenza: i sogni di Giuseppe in Filone di Alessandria,' in P. GALAND and E. MALASPINA (edd.), *Vérité et apparence: mélanges en l'honneur de Carlos Lévy, offerts par ses amis et ses disciples*, Latinitates 8 (Turnhout 2016) 321–331.

Inspired by Carlos Lévy, Calabi examines Joseph's dreams and Philo's study of the enigma related to the dreams. There are three types of dreams, those caused by God, but obscure to humans; prophetic dreams which predict the future and are open to the earthly intellect, inspired by God, such as the dream of Jacob; and the obscure predictions which require specialist allegorical interpretation, such as those of Joseph, which require a dream-critical approach. Joseph faces the deception of appearances, which hinders the approach to truth. Philo expounds how the allegorical interpretation transcends the literal one, revealing that Joseph is caught by ambition, in the realm of the senses, symbolised by Egypt, unlike the dreams of his father Jacob. Therefore, he is uncertain and says: 'it seems to me.' He is divided between vanity and dream on the one hand and truth and reason on the other. His dreams are evident on a first level of cognition, but they are obscure with regard to the truth. (JLB)

F. CALABI, 'Il Parmenide e Filone di Alessandria,' *Chôra: Revue des Études Anciennes et Médiévales* 14 (2016) 251–267.

The article investigates the possibility of discovering a relationship between Plato's *Parmenides* and Philo, although Philo never explicitly mentions or quotes the work. There is a debate among modern scholars as to what knowledge Philo may have had of the dialogue. Runia thinks that the *Parmenides* was not well known in the first century CE. Whittaker holds that Philo may have referred to the first hypothesis of the *Parmenides* with regard to divine transcendence through the mediation of the Platonizing Pythagoreanism of his time. Dillon sees a strong influence of the dialogue on the Alexandrian Platonism that preceded Philo. Calabi herself believes that there are lines of reasoning in Philo comparable to the first two hypotheses of the *Parmenides*. It may be impossible to determine if we have to do with a direct influence or an indirect one, and even whether or not the influence derives from Plato at first hand. What the author wants to investigate is whether Philo in his negative theology uses arguments (reformulated and adapted to his biblical exegesis) that recall Plato's dialogue. Placing side-by-side passages from the *Parmenides* (notably 137c–138b, 139b,e, 143a, 145a, 146a) and various passages from Philo, notably *Leg.* 2.1–4 on the (im)possibility of seeing or knowing God, she illustrates how Philo's interpretations echo various traditions among which the Platonic tradition from the *Parmenides* is prominent. (HMK, based on the author's abstract)

J. O. CARROLL, *Philo and Paul: Experiencing Divine Wisdom* (diss. University of Aberdeen 2016).

This study, consisting of two parts, explores Philo of Alexandria and the apostle Paul's understanding of the experience of divine wisdom. Following an examination of Philo's presentation of the gymnasium as an ideal institution (Chapter One), Part One examines Philo's portrayal of the biblical patriarch Abraham as the exemplar of an overarching process of *paideia*, a process that finds its *telos* in the experience of divine wisdom. In Chapters Two and Three (which discuss the treatises *Migr.* and *Her.*), key elements of Philo's process of *paideia* are gleaned from the Alexandrian's literal and allegorical interpretation of events surrounding the Abrahamic narrative. In these treatises, God provides the means for Abraham to engage in a system of *paideia* that will find its *telos* in an encounter with the λόγος of God, an encounter that results in the experience of divine wisdom. Chapter Four (which discusses the treatise *Congr*.), presents Philo's integration of his ideal educational process (the encyclia) by using Abraham solely as the allegorical personification of the mind, mostly disregarding the literal interpretation of the biblical text. Chapter Five explores Philo's thematic arrangement of specific vignettes in the life of Abraham (in *Abr.*) for the purpose of either presenting (1) an individual/soul in transition still engaged in his process of paideia, or (2) an individual who has reached the *telos* of this process, the experience of divine wisdom, and acts accordingly as an exemplar of God's virtue to the rest of humanity. The second major part of this study, explores a specific locus in Pauline thought, 1 Cor 1–4 for the purpose of presenting the apostle's understanding of the experience of divine wisdom. The author returns to Philo in the study's concluding Chapter Twelve, which presents a synoptic comparison of major themes present in both Philo's and Paul's understanding of this experience. (DTR; based on author's abstract)

M. Cimosa, 'Philo of Alexandria: His Exegesis of some Aspects of Sin and Evil in the Septuagint Version of the Book of Genesis,' *Vetus Testamentum et Hellas* 3 (2016).

The paper first introduces Philo's life and works against his Alexandrian background, posing the question whether he was a 'Philo judaeus' or a 'Philo graecus.' The author then traces aspects of Philo's exegesis of Gen 3–6 on the origin and history of evil, focusing mainly on the treatises of the Allegorical Commentary from *Leg.* to *Deus*, but also referring to *QG*. His guides in this discussion are the Commentary on the Septuagint Genesis by M. Harl (R-R 8620) and the Italian translation of Philo's Allegorical Commentary by R. Radice (R-R 2604). He concludes with a brief presentation of Philo's theological framework within which these themes should be placed, together with a rather confusing listing of Philo's so-called 'tetralogy' of treatises on the subject, i.e. *Cher.*, *Sacr.*, *Post.*, *Gig.* and *Deus* (five treatises!), but not including *Det.* (pp. 94–95, but contrast the list on p. 75 where *Post.* is left out). The article is complemented by the contribution of G.M. Bonney in the same fascicle. (DTR)

H. C. Clifford, '"And They Saw the Place where the God of Israel Stood": Exodus 24:10 LXX in the Writings of Philo of Alexandria,' in J. Flebbe (ed.), *Holy Places in Biblical and Extrabiblical Traditions. Proceedings of the Bonn-Leiden-Oxford Colloquium on Biblical Studies*, Bonner Biblische Beiträge 179 (Göttingen 2016) 125–143.

The author studies the relevance of Mount Sinai in Philo's writings. Philo quotes Exod 24:10 LXX four times, all four in the context of allegorical interpretation. In all four passages 'the place where God stood' is an expression of God's immutability. The place itself is a mediator, basically the Logos, and twice is interpreted in terms of the powers in the Logos. In all cases, God cannot really have been seen. This can be compared to other contemporary interpretations of the text, including when Philo sees the place where God stood as a reference to the Temple (*Somn.* 1.62). (JLB)

W. L. Craig, *God Over All: Divine Aseity and the Challenge of Platonism* (Oxford 2016), esp. 18–24.

The title of this philosophical and theological monograph centres on a little-known term. Aseity denotes the characteristic of being 'from oneself (*a se*) only,' i.e. having an existence dependent on nothing else. It applies to God the creator in the Judaeo-Christian tradition. The question addressed in the book is whether this doctrine is challenged by the existence of Platonic entities, mathematical objects such as ideal numbers and geometrical shapes. In setting out the biblical and theological underpinnings of the doctrine of divine aseity, the author commences with the prologue to the Gospel of John with its universally quantified statement that 'all things came into being through him and without him not one thing came into being' (John 1:3). The Gospel writer may not have thought about whether this statement included abstract objects, but there is little doubt that he thought that everything apart from God and his Logos came into being through the Logos. The question is, however, whether John was unaware of the existence of such objects, since he lived at the time of Middle Platonism, which exerted influence on Hellenistic Judaism. This leads into a section on Philo's thought. A brief account is given of his doctrine of the Logos and his use of prepositional metaphysics (which also occurs in the prologue). Philo explicitly describes the Logos as the place of the world of the ideas (*Opif.* 16–20, 24), which means that the intelligible world must be considered dependent for its existence on God. From this the following conclusion is drawn: 'Given the close similarity of the Logos doctrine of John's prologue to Philo's doctrine, it is not at all impossible that the author of the prologue was aware of the relation of the Logos to the realm of ideas (p. 23).' Certainly, for him 'there are no uncreated, independently existing eternal objects, for God exists uniquely *a se*' (p. 24). (DTR)

L. De Luca, 'Il serpente di bronzo secondo Filone Alesandrino in *Leg.* 2.79–81,' *Adamantius* 21 (2015) 173–184.

In *Leg.* 2.79–81 Philo gives an original interpretation of the bronze serpent (Num 21:4–9) made by Moses to counteract 'the snakes that kill' which were sent by God to punish the Israelites. According to Philo, the snake has a double meaning: on the one hand, as Eve's serpent, it represents vice, on the other, as Moses' serpent, it represents virtue. Philo considers Moses' bronze serpent on both the ethical and the noetic level: representing temperance, it is cure for the passions, but it also stands for the intelligible 'idea,' to be contemplated as a moral model, and to be imitated in order to eliminate every vice. Philo's exegesis, imbued with elements coming from the Greco-Roman world and the Jewish tradition, recurs in the interpretations of early Christian writers, such as Tertullian, Origen, Gregory of Nazianzus, Gregory of Nyssa, Ambrose of Milan, and, in an original rework-ing, in the *Physiologus*. They interpret the bronze serpent in relation to John 3:14–15 and are influenced especially by the ethical and pharmacological aspects of Philo's exegesis. (HMK; based on the author's abstract)

L. De Luca, 'Nuove prospettive su Filone Alessandrino,' *Rivista di Filo-sofia Neo-scolastica* 108 (2016) 997–1004.

Report of two sessions dedicated to Philo that were part of the 2015 Annual Meeting of the Society of Biblical Literature in Atlanta, U.S.A. Of the session entitled 'Philo, Plutarch, and the New Testament' (co-sponsored by Corpus Hellenisticum Novi Testamenti), a detailed account is given of the contributions of G.E. Sterling ('When East and West Meet: Eastern Religions and Western Philosophy in Philo of Alexandria and Plutarch,' cf. else-where in this bibliography); R. Cox ('Through Others: The Dirty Work of Heavenly Intermediaries in Philo, Plutarch, and Early Christianity'); and G. Reydams-Schils ('Philo and Plutarch on Philautia'). The report continues with the session dedicated to Philo's *De Plantatione*, giving an account of the presentations of A.C. Geljon ('Sample Translation and Commentary on Philo's *De plantatione*'); M.R. Niehoff ('Writing a Commentary on a Philonic Allegorical Commentary'); D.T. Runia ('The Place of the Treatise *De plantatione* in Philo's Allegorical Commentary'); J.R. Royse (The Text of Philo's *De Plantatione*); and S. Yli-Karjanmaa (*Plant.* 1–27: The Significance of Reading Philonic Parallels'). (HMK)

B. Decharneux, 'Les interdits alimentaires dans le *De specialibus legibus* IV de Philon d'Alexandrie,' in S. Peperstraete (ed.), *Animal et religion*, Problèmes d'histoire des religions 23 (Bruxelles 2016) 107–112.

In keeping with his usual practice, Philo provides a philosophical reading of the dietary laws in *Spec.* 4, connecting them with the practice of temperance and seeing them as extoll-ing the state of the Aristotelian mean. The dietary laws have, for Philo, a propaedeutic value, and aim at preparing the soul's elevation towards God. (SW)

P. B. Decock, 'Philo's *De decalogo*: Educating to Respect the Socially Disadvantaged,' *Acta Theologica (South Africa)* 23 (2016) 94–109.

This article aims to demonstrate (1) Philo's presentation of the laws of the Decalogue as 'part of a process of therapy and transformation of both the person and the community' (p. 95); (2) that those who live by these laws, according to Philo, will increasingly live in harmony with God and with nature and reason, and the attainment of a virtuous life; (3) that Philo understood the laws as intended to 'move people' away from vice and towards virtues. For Philo, the transformation of individuals, rather than the structures of society, will cultivate respect and care for the socially disadvantaged. (SJKP)

P. B. Decock, 'Philo of Alexandria: Holiness as Self-possession and Self-transcendence,' *HTS Teologiese Studies–Theological Studies (online journal, South Africa)* 72, no. 4 (2016), 7 pages.

Taking as his starting-point Pierre Hadot's interpretation of ancient philosophy at the time of Philo as a form of practical ἄσκησις aiming at the care of self in a twofold movement of interiorisation and exteriorisation, the author attempts to show how Philo draws on these aspects in order to develop his conception of human progress as a journey towards perfection or holiness. The first movement of interiorisation brings with it exercises that allow the person to transcend the passions and the influence of the body. This moral transformation is complemented by intellectual transformation, as seen in the example of Abraham's journey. This also involves transcending human language, the human words of the Torah serving 'as the gate to Logos, but only a gate' (p. 4). The second process of universalisation is interpreted in terms of the educative process towards perfection which is achieved through living according to nature as manifested in nature and in the Laws of Moses. Human perfection, to be equated with holiness, is the imitation of God's perfection, and is crowned with praise and thanksgiving. The author concludes that 'the two-fold aim of Graeco-Roman philosophy as articulated by Hadot proves to be a useful grid to explore Philo's philosophical reading of the scriptures and his understanding of human perfection' (p. 6). (DTR)

C. Delgado, 'Ecos del *Ión* platónico en los escritos de Filón de Alejandría,' *Emérita: Revista de Lingüística y Filología Clásica* 84 (2016) 73–97.

This work studies the presence of the *Ion* by Plato in the Philonic corpus by means of an intertextual analysis involving the study of key texts. It is observed that Philo has made a profound use of the Platonic motive of divine inspiration, as witnessed in the following steps: (1) divine inspiration is an experience that the inspired can relate, but not explain; (2) that such person experiences an initial lack of ability (ἀπορία), but then abundant resources come to him (εὐπορία) accompanied by a state of ignorance in relation to the contents that are inspired within him; (3) that the sudden and intermittent nature of the inspiration is proof that the message is not the result of a steady disposition of the inspired person and, therefore, it is necessary to believe that the authorship is not his or, at least, not exclusively or primarily his; (4) that inspiration requires a prior psychological state of ἔκστασις consisting of a dispossession of rational faculties, so that the inspired subject is only an instrument for communicating or interpreting a message. (MA)

C. Delgado, 'Una reminiscencia platónica en Filón de Alejandría (*R.* 2.377–9) en *Spec.* 1.28–30,' *Exemplaria Classica* 20 (2016) 117–131.

Through a textual and hermeneutic analysis, this paper attempts to show that Philo, as indicated in the text *Spec.* 1.28–30, had good knowledge of the critique of mythology put forward by Plato in *Rep.* 377–379. The author reaches this conclusion firstly by observing the existing textual parallels between both sections, and secondly by paying attention to the conceptual relations that are found between them. The connection between both treatments emerges from the reconstruction of the theoretical scheme by means of which the two thinkers undertook their criticism. It is concluded that the Philonic criticism of myth is substantially indebted to the corresponding Platonic critique. (MA)

J. Dillon, 'Philo and the *Telos*: Some Reflections,' in G. E. Sterling (ed.), *The Studia Philonica Annual Vol. 28 [= Studies in Philo in Honor of David Runia]* (Atlanta 2016) 111–119.

The goal of the article is to clarify Philo's place in the philosophical debate concerning the τέλος ἀγαθῶν, or 'the overarching purpose linking together and giving coherence to the particular 'goods' which a human being might pursue.' More specifically, the author's main question is how Philo reconciled (1) the Stoic ideal of living in accordance with Nature and the Stoa's inclusion of bodily and external goods in their *telos* with (2) the Platonist ideal of assimilation to the good and the exclusive emphasis on spiritual goods. The author concludes that Philo subscribed to both of the two ideals mentioned but reinterprets the former to mean the latter. Philo's *telos* also included the Pythagorean goal of following God. (SYK)

M. Donato, 'Philon lecteur de l'Éryxias ?,' *Revue de Philologie, de Littérature et d'Histoire Anciennes* 90 (2016) 69–79.

Contrary to the view that *Plant.* 171 is a precise reference to the ps.Platonic dialogue *Eryxias* (397e5–7), the author argues that this passage, in which the value of wealth is said to depend on the moral value of the one who possesses it, most likely has a doxographical origin and most probably echoes the Stoic doctrine of the 'indifferent things.' (SW)

J. A. Draper, 'Darkness as Non-being and the Origin of Evil in John's Gospel,' in C. Keith and L. T. Stuckenbruck (edd.), *Evil in Second Temple Judaism and Early Christianity*, Wissenschaftliche Untersuchungen zum Neuen Testament 2.417 (Tübingen 2016) 122–141, esp. 124–130.

The author derives Philo's understanding of good and evil from *Opif.* He focuses on Philo's Middle-Platonist theory of creation with its distinction between the creation of the immaterial and the material world and on the interpretation of the fall. Creation is order and measure, associated with light, while chaos is associated with darkness. For this reason God made a separation between light and darkness. Philo is aware of ideas of cosmic conflict associated with creation, but in his view there is no such conflict in the creation of the immaterial world on day one. Evil only enters the world through the human passions, which conquer the senses and lead to disharmony in the harmonious order of the human being and the world. Eve's true sin is to have chosen the tree of knowledge of good and evil instead of the tree of life, symbolising virtue. The snake in the fall narrative is the symbol of pleasure, which is conquered by raising the bronze serpent (*Leg.* 2.79), which symbolises temperance. The author's interest in Philo is for the purpose of placing the Gospel of John in the context of the ancient Jewish discourse on Gen 1 and the role of darkness in creation. (JLB)

P. Druille, 'Filón y las inscripciones griegas de los siglos II-I a.c.: la existencia de la 'gerousía' en Alejandría,' *Circe, de clásicos y modernos* 20 (2016) 131–145.

The Jewish γερουσία of Alexandria was an aristocratic council of elders, endowed with power in matters of government and jurisdiction over the Jewish community of the Egyptian city. But its existence at the beginning of the first century is doubtful. The aim of this work is to analyze the existence of the γερουσία in the Jewish community of Alexandria during the last period of the Ptolemaic era and the first decades of Roman empire on the basis of the relation between *Flacc.* 74 and the inscriptions *SGE* 34.1532 and *SB* 1.2100 from the second and first centuries BCE, now translated for the first time into Spanish. The paper also examines the technical concepts connected with this institution and its functioning. (MA)

A. N. Evans, 'Jesus 'the Word' as Creator in John 1:1–3: Help for Evolutionists from Philo the Hellenistic Jew,' *Scriptura* 115 (2016) 1–10.

The article sets out in a fairly popular style the claim that 'that Jesus walked the earth is undeniable, but without Greek philosophy his identification as God and Creator of the world as stated in John 1:1c–2 would have been impossible' (p. 8). How John was able to make that claim about the Logos can be better understood with reference to Hellenistic Judaism and particularly the thought of Philo. After giving some background in Greek philosophy (Heraclitus, Plato, the Stoics) and the Hebrew Bible (wisdom writings), the central part of the paper outlines the role of the concept of the *logos* in Philo's account of creation with special reference to *Opif.* Even though the term *logos* does not appear in Genesis, 'John conceives of the coming into being of the world in terms of Philo's Hellenistic concept of the presence of the Logos as mediator in humanity as part or spark of God' (p. 8), thereby conveying the mediation between the divine and the human in a novel way. (DTR)

E. Fiano, 'Adam and the Logos: Aphrahat's Christology in *Demonstration* 17 and the "Imponderables of Hellenization,"' *Journal of Ancient Christianity* 20 (2016) 437–468.

The fourth century Syriac theologian Aphraates is generally regarded as secluded from Hellenic influence. However, a close reading of a passage in his treatise *Demonstration* 17 on the subject 'that Christ is God and Son of God' shows that this is not the case. He reads into the double account of Adam's creation in Gen 1:26–27 and 2:7 a two-stage process, which he then further develops by applying to Adam the 'prolation of the Logos,' a process in which the Logos becomes immanent in a manner parallel to the psychological distinction between the λόγος ἐνδιάθετος and the λόγος προφορικός. These ideas go back to Philo's exegesis of the biblical texts, as is illlustrated by a number of passages and with reference to interpretations by H.A. Wolfson and J. Dillon. The author does not argue that Aphraates was directly influenced by Philo, but rather that 'the twofold stage of the Logos became part of common intellectual parlance in the Hellenic and Roman worlds' (p. 454–

455), resulting in a variety of theological outcomes. Aphraates applies the doctrine of the prolation of the Logos to the figure of Adam and, it is further argued, integrates it with an Adamitic Christology. (DTR)

E. FILLER, 'Philo's Threefold Divine Vision and the Christian Trinity,' *Hebrew Union College Annual* 87 (2016) 93–113.

The paper compares Philo of Alexandria's philosophical discussion of the status of God with Christian theology, esp. the Trinitarian controversy. It focuses on a study of the three angels 'standing near Abraham' at Mamre (Gen 18), as interpreted in the writings of Philo and several of the Church Fathers. The comparison shows a profound gap between Philo's theology and Christian theology, with the exception of Origen, who did continue the Alexandrian tradition. Characteristically, the latter was declared a heretic, a move which underscores the fundamental differences between Philo and Christian theology. (MRN)

E. FILLER, 'Platonic and Stoic Dialectic in Philo,' *Elenchos: Rivista di studi sul pensiero antico* 37 (2016) 181–208.

The paper addresses the question of Philo's rare allusions to Plato's later dialogues and asks whether ideological reasons for this lack are discernable. It is suggested that Philo avoided these dialogues because they contain a lot of logical dialectics and were thus superfluous to his overall project of using philosophical ideas in support of his exposition of the Torah. Philo is not prepared to accept the merely technical and formal aspects of philosophy, and especially those of dialectic used by the 'sophists' of his age, because they would likely lead some of its practitioners to pervert the truth, both philosophical and scriptural. (MRN)

H. FRANKEMÖLLE, *Vater im Glauben? Abraham/Ibrahim in Tora, Neuem Testament und Koran* (Freiburg 2016), esp. 272–277.

The author argues that Philo's Abraham reception is aimed at Greek, non-Jewish readers. Abraham is an example of a life worthy to be emulated. Although of Chaldean origin, he recognises the true God and leaves his home of idolatry and false perceptions. He mediates true knowledge of God by contemplating the world and is the model for all proselytes. Philo reads Abraham's circumcision allegorically, thus avoiding an exclusive interpretation as a Jewish identity marker. Philo's reception of Abraham has remained largely without impact in the rabbinic tradition. (JLB)

C. J. P. FRIESEN, 'Dying Like a Woman: Euripides' Polyxena as Exemplum between Philo and Clement of Alexandria,' *Greek, Roman, and Byzantine Studies* 56 (2016) 623–645.

In his *Hecuba* Euripides describes the fate of the Trojan princess Polyxena, who is sacrificed after the capture of Troy. Euripides presents Polyxena as accepting her fate with courage and gracefulness. His depiction problematizes the relationship between gender and heroic courage. On the one hand, Polyxena is depicted as a bride of Hades; on the other, her action shows an autonomy which is characteristic of heroic men. Centuries later Euripides' description was appropriated by Philo and Clement. Both authors deploy her as a gendered paradigm of virtue, but in strikingly different directions. Philo presents

Polyxena as an example of a martyr who dies in a masculine way (*Prob.* 116). This fits very well his view that spiritual advancement is progress away from the feminine toward the masculine. Clement presents Polyxena's death quite differently. She is a model for the Christian wife who values modesty over seductiveness (*Strom.* 2.137–147). (ACG)

C. J. P. Friesen, 'Getting Samuel Sober: The 'Plus' of LXX 1 Sam 1:11 and its Religious Afterlife in Philo and the Gospel of Luke,' *Journal of Theological Studies* 67 (2016) 453–478.

In the LXX version of 1 Sam 1:11 we find an additional clause that is absent in the MT: 'wine and strong drink [Samuel] shall not drink.' Having discussed the textual traditions of these words, the author discusses the function of Samuel's abstinence as a model for piety, paying particular attention to Philo of Alexandria and the Gospel of Luke. Philo sees Samuel as an example of spiritual virtue, interpreting his name as meaning 'appointed by God.' His abstinence from wine plays a role in the question of whether the sage will get drunk, which is treated in *Plant.* and *Ebr.* The discussion of the views of philosophers leads to the conclusion that a wise person may get drunk. Moses, however, forbids two classes of persons to drink wine: adherents of the great vow and ministering priests. This problematizes the conclusion drawn earlier. Consequently, Philo reads the regulation concerning priests (Lev 10:9) allegorically. In the same way he interprets the sobriety of Samuel (his only biblical example of an adherent to the great vow) allegorically as a spiritual drunkenness that characterizes the ascent of the soul (*Ebr.* 143–153). In the Gospel of Luke, in contrast, Samuel provides a model for the asceticism of John the Baptist. Both authors, however, subordinate abstinence from alcohol to the higher spiritual ideal, 'sober inebriation' in the case of Philo, the messianic banquet for that of Luke. (ACG)

F. Galet-Maignan, 'Identités et frontières dans la «Legatio ad Caium» de Philon d'Alexandrie,' in H. Berthelot, A. Boiché and P.-A. Caltot (edd.), *Vivre et penser les frontières dans le monde méditerranéen antique: actes du colloque tenu à l'Université Paris-Sorbonne, les 29 et 30 juin 2013*, Scripta Antiqua 89 (Bordeaux 2016) 213–223.

At first the *Legat.* presents the Roman Empire as a harmonious and unified entity in which the Jews and Romans converge within a vision of the world characterized by the 'passage of borders.' Philo furthermore praises Augustus' moral qualities as well as his 'Hellenization' of the barbarian world. However, when Philo turns to Caligula, this harmony appears to be shattered. Caligula's reprehensible tearing down of the borders between God and humankind, between reason and folly, destroys the foundations of the Roman identity. In this new outlook, the Jewish people and the Jewish identity are now clearly distinguished from that of the Roman and are expressed in opposition to Caligula. (SW)

A. C. Geljon, 'Mag een wijze dronken worden? Philo van Alexandrië over dronkenschap [Dutch: May a wise person become drunk: Philo of Alexandria on drunkenness],' *Hermeneus* 88 (2016) 111–115.

In this article the author offers a short overview of Philo's discussion on whether a wise person may get drunk, a question Philo deals with in the last part of *Plant.* Philo presents his discussion in the form of a *thesis*: first, he offers an introduction, second, he presents arguments *pro*, and finally arguments *contra* are formulated. Defending the view that a wise person may get drunk, Philo uses technical and non-technical arguments. Some technical arguments are based on the etymology of the word μεθύειν (being drunk). The presentation of counterarguments is very short and it is likely that the last part is missing. (ACG)

A. C. GELJON, 'Abraham in Egypt: Philo's Interpretation of Gen 12:10–12,' in G. E. STERLING (ed.), *The Studia Philonica Annual Vol. 28 [= Studies in Philo in Honor of David Runia]* (Atlanta 2016) 297–319.

The article deals with the episode of Abraham and Sarah in Egypt, where their marriage is threatened by Pharaoh (Gen 12:10–20). The story is retold by Philo both literally and allegorically in *Abr.* 89–106. Philo's retelling is compared to the LXX and Josephus' rewording (*Ant.* 1.161–168). The comparison shows that Philo retells the story in a free way, adding details that are not found in the Bible. Furthermore, he omits Abraham's lie about Sarah, because this detracts from Abraham's noble character. Philo presents Pharaoh as a wicked person with bad intentions and indulging in intemperance, whereas in Genesis Pharaoh is not pictured in this negative way. Josephus also retells the story in a free way. In the allegorical exegesis Abraham symbolizes mind and Sarah virtue. A discussion of the story does not occur in the Allegorical Commentary or the *Quaestiones*. A variation of the story can be found in the episode of Abraham and king Abimelech (Gen 20). Discussing this story in *QG* 4.60–70, Philo offers the same allegorical reading of Abraham as the virtue-loving mind and Sarah as virtue. Abimelech is presented in just the same way as Pharaoh in the passage discussed earlier. (ACG)

E. S. GRUEN, 'Jewish Literature in the Second Sophistic,' in E. S. GRUEN (ed.), *Constructs of Identity in Hellenistic Judaism. Essays on Early Jewish Literature and History*, Deuterocanonical and Cognate Literature Studies 29 (Berlin 2016) 488–503.

This article, commissioned for *The Oxford Handbook of the Second Sophistic* which appeared in 2017, was first published in the volume of collected essays on Hellenistic Judaism summarised elsewhere in this bibliography. The Jews in the early Imperial period regarded themselves as exceptional, and their Greek and Roman fellow citizens agreed with them. These perceptions or constructs, however, did not match conditions on the ground. Diaspora Jews far outnumbered those in Palestine and for them isolation was not an option. The subject matter of their literary production was distinct, but in order to produce it they used the genres of classical culture. It was not a cosy fit. Tensions and strains must have existed. After these introductory words, Philo is the first author discussed (pp. 489–492). His treatise *Prob.* seems to show that he was unselfconsciously comfortable in the culture of the Hellenes, but reading between the lines it is plain that the comfort was not complete. He is obliged to remind his readers that his commitment to Jewish teachings remains unshaken. Another example is his idiosyncratic description of Moses' education in *Mos.* 1.21–24, which shows both an attachment to Hellenic education and the need to go beyond it. In fact 'Philo's blend of Hellenism and Judaism was less of a smooth process than a tense negotiation' (p. 492). (DTR)

E. S. GRUEN, *Constructs of Identity in Hellenistic Judaism*, Deuterocanonical and Cognate Literature Studies 29 (Berlin 2016).

Collected volume of essays on Hellenistic Judaism written by the distinguished ancient historian over the period 1993 to 2015. Most of the essays in one way or another illustrate the thesis, succinctly and provocatively stated at the conclusion of his survey article on Hellenistic Judaism (p. 75): 'They [i.e. the Jews in Diaspora] successfully negotiated their own place within the world of Greco-Roman society: they were appropriationists rather than assimilationists. And they shunned the melting pot.' Philo is a constant point of reference, though only one article focuses on him primarily, namely 'Caligula, the Imperial Cult and Philo's *Legatio*' (2012, summarised in vol. 29, p. 190). On the hitherto unpublished article on 'Jewish Literature and the Second Sophistic,' which has a section devoted to Philo see the summary elsewhere in this bibliography. See further the Index of People, Places, and Subjects p. 547. (DTR)

L. GUSELLA, 'Le temple dans l'œuvre de Philon d'Alexandrie: le parcours de l'exégèse philonienne du modèle céleste jusqu'au sanctuaire de l'âme,' in M.-L. CHAIEB and J. ROUX (edd.), *Quand Dieu montre le modèle: interprétations et déclinaisons d'un motif biblique* (Paris 2016) 357–371.

Conciliation is what mainly characterizes Philo's enterprise: conciliation between different cultures, between the social and the theoretical lives, between the allegorical and literal reading of the Bible. This same conciliating and inclusive vein is found in Philo's reflection on the temple. Philo distinguishes between three kinds of temple: first, the temple of Jerusalem, built by men; second, the genuine temple of God, i.e. the cosmos; and third, the temple as an allegory of the soul. (1) *Mos.* 2.136–140, focuses on the 'portable sanctuary,' whose archetypal model was given to Moses to contemplate. In this context, Philo especially stresses the meaning of the numbers in the temple's construction. In *Spec.* 1.66–78, he rather focuses on the function of the temple as well as on the spiritual level of the person who comes to make an offering. Finally, *Legat.* 184–348 conveys the universal scope that the temple bears for Philo. (2) The true temple, however, is the cosmos (see esp. *Spec.* 1.66). In this context, Philo particularly emphasizes the analogy between the various elements of the constructed temple and the world. (3) Finally, the virtuous soul represents a kind of microcosm that functions as the spiritual temple of God. Philo stresses in this respect the importance of the spiritual cult, characterized by the offering of one's purified soul as a sacrifice to God. The author concludes by noting the inclusive mode of Philo's interpretation, his 'profoundly Jewish soul,' as well as early Christianity's abrogation of the ideal of a material cult of God. (SW)

C. HEZSER, '"For the Lord God is a Sun and a Shield" (Ps. 84:12): Sun Symbolism in Hellenistic Jewish literature and in Amoraic Midrashim,' in L. UZI and C. HEZSER (edd.), *Jewish Art in its Late Antique Context*, Texts and Studies in Ancient Judaism 163 (Tübingen 2016) 213–236, esp. 219–222.

Philo is studied as a representative of Hellenistic Jewish literature. Philo associates the sun with God. He mentions the chariot and the zodiac and thus provides background information for this imagery in ancient synagogues, especially in *Somn.* 1.72–95. The sun is the visible representation of God and the archetype of all light. It is unchanging and rules the universe. Elsewhere the sun is an imitation of eternity. Yet the sun remains a multivalent image, symbol of God, but not an independent god. It can also represent virtue and righteousness. Philo uses common visual language allegorically and symbolically to express his monotheistic theology. (JLB)

A. VAN DEN HOEK, and J. J. HERRMANN Jr., 'Chasing the Emperor: Philo in the *Horti* of Rome,' in G. E. STERLING (ed.), *The Studia Philonica Annual Vol. 28 [= Studies in Philo in Honor of David Runia]* (Atlanta 2016) 171–204.

The article probes the value of Philo's *Legat.* for its value in illuminating the historical context of Gaius' Rome and, specifically, the settings in which the encounters took place between Philo's embassy and the emperor, namely the gardens (*horti*) of Agrippina, of Maecenas and of Lamia. Detailed consideration of the architectural and material evidence for these gardens (with photographs of sculptures and other remains from the gardens of Maecenas and Lamia) allows us to better understand Philo's descriptions of his encounters with the emperor in these settings. By leading the Alexandrian delegations through his private gardens, which had thematic resonance with famous aspects of Alexandria, the emperor perhaps intended to offer privileged access to high-ranking guests as a mark of favour towards them, with a view to promoting his claim to divinity. If so, the visits to the emperor's gardens made no positive impression on Philo's delegation. Philo describes his exit from the gardens as an escape from 'such a theatre combined with a prison' (*Legat.* 370). This architectural metaphor has 'an uncanny echo of a construction in the *horti*' (p. 187), which suggests that the gardens did influence Philo's impressions of the emperor, but not as Gaius had intended. (SJKP)

T. C. HOKLOTUBBE, 'Great is the Mystery of Piety: Contested Claims to Piety in Plutarch, Philo, and 1 Timothy,' in N. DESROSIERS and L. C. VUONG (edd.), *Religious Competition in the Greco-Roman World*, Writings from the Greco-Roman World. Supplement series 10 (Atlanta 2016) 155–165.

In 1 Tim 3:16 the author characterizes Christian understanding of the divine as a 'mystery of piety.' Scholars have understood this phrase to refer to God's secret plan of salvation, which was revealed in the Christ-event. Consideration of the terms 'piety' and 'mystery' within a broader philosophical context, however, shows that these terms were used to highlight an author's own correct understanding of the divine against other views. Thus Philo adopted the Greek virtue of piety in part to counter anti-Jewish remarks by such people as Apion. In a passage like *Cher.* 42, Philo presented Jewish Scripture as containing divine mysteries that promote piety among initiates. Philo used the two terms 'piety' and 'mystery' to legitimate Jewish teachings in a Hellenistic society and to put forward his own understanding with authority. Plutarch similarly employed these terms to bolster his own philosophical interpretation of the Egyptian cult of Isis and Osiris above competing interpretations. Seen in this context, 1 Tim's use of 'piety' and 'mystery' can be understood as a strategy to persuade his audience of the rightness of his views against rival claims about piety and the divine. (EB)

C. R. HOLLADAY, 'Spirit in Philo of Alexandria,' in P. DRAGUTINOVIC, K.-W. NIEBUHR and J. B. WALLACE (edd.), *The Holy Spirit and the Church according to the New Testament. Sixth International East-West Symposium of New Testament Scholars, Belgrade, August 25 to 31, 2013*, Wissenschaftliche Untersuchungen zum Neuen Testament 354 (Tübingen 2016) 341–363.

The contribution studies Philo's use of the concept of πνεῦμα. The term has anthropological, cosmological and theological connotations, but Holladay focuses on the spirit of God, which is primarily discussed in Philo's Exposition of the Law. The spirit of God is the life breath, one of the created things. It belongs to the incorporeal part of the human being and is what renders it immortal. The divine spirit makes humans want to live virtuously. It also holds the universe together. It is the rational spirit which brings a sacrifice. In the Allegorical Commentary Philo studies the way in which God breathes the spirit into the mind. The spirit also implies strength and power, especially the mind's ability to reason. Humanity has two natures, blood and spirit. God's spirit can also be the pure knowledge or wisdom, especially in the context of the knowledge which Moses has. In most humans the divine spirit remains for a while, only in Moses it abided permanently. The human soul is imprinted by the divine spirit in order to become the image of God. In the *Quaestiones* Philo mentions the distinction of the blood and spirit and defines humans as consisting of earth and heaven, heaven being equivalent to the divine spirit. In addition to the divine spirit Philo also discusses the prophetic spirit, mainly in the Exposition and the Allegorical Commentary. It is a spirit which expels reason as well as sorcery and wickedness, and guides the mind to the truth. (JLB)

S. HONIGMAN, 'The Ptolemaic and Roman Definitions of Social Categories and the Evolution of Judean Communal Identity in Egypt,' in Y. FURSTENBERG (ed.), *Jewish and Christian Communal Identities in the Roman World*, Ancient Judaism and Early Christianity 92 (Leiden 2016) 25–74, esp. 64–70.

This study focuses on the role of state policy—and the official definition of person and group status—in shaping the development of Jewish/Judean communal identities in antiquity, with specific attention to the very different definitions of personal status that were created in Egypt under the Ptolemies and under Roman administration. As part of a wide-ranging discussion, the author explores how changes in defining social status in Roman Egypt influenced Philo's way of imagining the Judean diaspora. Philo's mapping in *Flacc.* of the social groups in conflict in Alexandria in 38 CE—split between Greeks and Egyptians—referred back to the situation in the Ptolemaic era, when Judeans were classed as a sub-group of the privileged class of the Greeks, and 'could act on an equal footing with other Greek communities' in Alexandria, while Egyptians were inferior to them (p. 66). His conception of the interconnected fate of all Judeans everywhere (*Flacc.* 46, 49) is influenced not only by by the model of Roman colonies, but also, and primarily, by the treatment by Roman authorities of Judeans in the empire. Under Roman rule, the legal demotion of Egypt's Judeans as a sub-group of Greeks led to the perception—and self-perception—of Judeans as a minority group which gradually came to define itself in religious terms. Decisive in this development were the aforementioned settlement of Claudius and Vespasian's creation of the fiscus Iudaicus following the fall of Jerusalem. (SJKP)

T. IACONO, *Filone di Alessandria De sobrietate: introduzione, traduzione e commento* (M.A. thesis University of Padua 2016).

This thesis of 156 pages begins with a thorough introduction to Philo's person and work in general, and to the treatise *Sobr.* in particular (place in Philo's oeuvre, date, structure, and text constitution). There follows an elegant and readable Italian translation of the treatise with the Greek text printed alongside it (Cohn-Wendland, with on 18 occasions a variant reading). Pages 57–149 present a running commentary, focusing on the lines of argument and explaining Philo's exegesis; textual issues are dealt with where necessary. The author highlights (p. 22) that *Sobr.* 34–43 amounts to a paraphrase of

Aristotle's *N.E.* 1103a-b (illustrated in detail in the commentary), and that this extended appropriation so far appears not to have been identified by scholars. (HMK)

A. Kamesar, 'ΔΗΛΩΣΙΣ and ΑΛΗΘΕΙΑ: The Septuagint, Philo, and Some Late Rhetorical Texts,' in P. F. Beatrice and B. Pouderon (edd.), *Pascha Nostrum Christus: Essays in Honour of Raniero Cantalamessa* (Paris 2016) 17–26.

Philo, in interpreting the terms δήλωσις and ἀλήθεια in the Septuagint as symbols of respectively the λόγος προφορικός and the λόγος ἐνδιάθετος, was putting to use associations that already existed between the two terms in the Greek Bible (where they translate *urim* and *thummim*, Exod 28:30 and elsewhere) and each of the two *logoi*. This is true even if such associations are attested only in later sources, or may hypothetically posited with the aid of later sources (introductions to and commentaries on the works of the second century rhetor Hermogenes, as well as Plutarch, Heraclitus the Allegorist, and Philo himself). It cannot be established with certainty that the associations between δήλωσις and ἀλήθεια and each of the two *logoi* are part of the explanation why the original translators of the Pentateuch chose to translate *urim* and *thummim* with those two terms. Nevertheless, this possibility must be strongly considered. For it would certainly be an interesting coincidence if, by relying on etymological translation alone, the seventy translators assigned to the λογεῖον of the high priest the same δήλωσις and ἀλήθεια later associated with the twofold *logos, prophorikos* and *endiathetos*. (HMK)

A. Kamesar, 'Philo and Ps.Longinus: a Case of Sublimity in Genesis 4,' in G. E. Sterling (ed.), *The Studia Philonica Annual Vol. 28 [= Studies in Philo in Honor of David Runia]* (Atlanta 2016) 229–238.

There are many points of contact between Ps.Longinus and Philo, prominent among which is the concept of literary ὕψος, or sublimity (greatness of thought involving the use of figures). Ps.Longinus offers Gen 1:3 as example and Philo notes the presence of sublimity in Gen 4:10 (the voice of Adam's blood cries out, cited at *Det.* 79). It appears that Philo is there referring to the metaphor of personification. This would imply that blood is an inanimate entity, which is in contrast with the exegesis Philo offers. Having examined the exegetical context of the passage, the author concludes that the reference to sublimity is best understood as separate from the discussion of the content. This conclusion can be confirmed from later church fathers. (ACG)

A. Kirsch, *The People and the Books: 18 Classics of Jewish Literature* (New York 2016), esp. 45–74.

In a chapter entitled 'Reading against the Grain,' Kirsch discusses Philo's writings among eighteen classics of Jewish literature from antiquity to the present. These classics also include, among others, Deuteronomy, the Book of Esther, Josephus's *Jewish War*, and Pirkei Avot. Philo's work shows 'how difficult it was, and still is, to reconcile secular thought with the wisdom of Jewish tradition' (pp. 45–46). By contrast with the Chanukah story about Jewish resistance to Greek culture, Philo represents a different, more positive response to this culture. Besides his valuable account of events in *Flacc.* and *Legat.*, these treatises convey Philo's position as a dedicated Jew 'living in a multicultural city in a multinational empire' (p. 55). Philo's treatise on creation brings together belief in God as creator and as equivalent to the laws of nature. According to Philo the Mosaic laws are 'the most perfect laws ever given to mankind [and offer] the best way to live for everyone' (p. 65). In 'The Allegory of the Laws,' Philo brings out the hidden philosophical meaning of Scripture, a meaning that often pertains to the struggle between body and soul. His symbolic approach to Scripture 'diminishes' but 'never quite dismisses ... the contingency and specificity of [Jewish] history' (p. 73). (EB)

S. KOTTEK and H. PAAVILAINEN, 'Embryology in the Works of Philo,' *Korot* 23 (2015–2016) 99–107.

The article initially provides a general introduction to Philo and his life, and then reviews Philo's different statements about seed, the growing of the embryo and the *spermatikos logos*. All of these topics are discussed with introductory comparisons to Greek medicine and rabbinic traditions. (MRN)

M. D. LARSEN, 'Listening with the Body, Seeing through the Ears: Contextualizing Philo's Lecture Event in *On the Contemplative Life*,' *Journal for the Study of Judaism* 47 (2016) 447–474.

Philo's description in *Contempl.* 75–79 of a lecture event—specifically, an exposition of Scripture among the Therapeutae—represents speaker and audience as conforming to established rules connected to giving and listening to a lecture in elite circles in the high Roman Empire. For the purposes of this study, those rules are based on details extracted from Plutarch, Pliny the Younger, Seneca and Tacitus. Based on Seneca's teaching on lecture style, Philo's speaker/lecturer (the 'President') 'gives an ideal Roman performance' (p. 457). Comparison with Roman sources also shows that, as Philo constructs them, the men and women of the Therapeutae who actively listened to the exposition by their 'President' were 'imbued with and exhibited proper *Romanitas* through listening and cultivation of masculine philosophical virtues.' Moreover, by describing the Therapeutae as performing the 'ideal Roman lecture praxis,' Philo aimed to situate this community among, perhaps even above other elite communities in the high Roman Empire. (SJKP)

D. W. LEON, 'The Face of the Emperor in Philo's *Embassy to Gaius*,' *The Classical World* 110 (2016) 43–60.

Following a brief discussion of events in 38 CE Alexandria connected to the eruption of violence inflicted by Greeks on Jews, this article explores Philo's *Legat.* as a response to those events, focusing on Philo's commentary on Roman government in this context. Much of the treatise is devoted to an extended critique of the emperor's character and rule. Philo is particularly interested in the subject of communication between the emperor and the provinces and in how unprecedented failures in communication under Gaius reveal fundamental problems in the government of the empire: 'In particular, he makes extensive use of the tension between the emperor as a symbol—of authority, stability, law, peace, and prosperity—and the emperor as a real person with moods and quirks and prejudices to underscore the fundamental instability of imperial rule imposed from afar' (p. 46). Philo's concern corresponds to a growing sense of anxiety among the Italian elite of this period and appeals to a 'shared experience of a breakdown in traditional governing practices together with a shared sense of hopelessness in the face of a new political world order' (p. 46). Philo's Gaius represents a key example of the dangers of Roman rule:

provincial government that depends on direct access to the emperor will fail when such access can no longer be relied upon. (SJKP)

J. LEONHARDT-BALZER, 'Philo and the Garden of Eden: An Exegete, his Text and his Tools,' in S. KREUZER, M. MEISER and M. SIGISMUND (edd.), *Die Septuaginta — Orte und Intentionen. 5. Internationale Fachtagung veranstaltet von Septuaginta Deutsch (LXX.D), Wuppertal 24.–27. Juli 2014*, Wissenschaftliche Untersuchungen zum Neuen Testament 361 (Tübingen 2016) 244–257.

This detailed study of Philo's references to the garden of Eden provides not only an account of his interpretation of that place, but also reflects more generally on Philo's approach to the biblical text in first century Alexandria. Philo refers to Eden twenty times, not leaving out any of the six biblical references. Frequently he associates the term with 'luxury,' τρυφή, which is associated with Eden in Gen 3:23–24. He rejects the idea that Eden could be a place of luxury or pleasure and interprets the term as referring to true joy (χαρά) instead, the joy of the virtuous who rejoice in the worship of God. A study of Philo's quotations of the biblical text shows that he is conservative in his use of the text, but occasionally uses a different text from the LXX. Some variants are due to lack of interest in precision, others due to a different text, again others due to Philo's theological interest. Some variants, however, are highly consistent, providing the same interpretation and deliberately using the same psalms to interpret a certain Pentateuchal text in order to make a very specific point. This indicates the use of textual tools, such as concordances or glossaries, comparable to a florilegium on the Genesis passages and any text related to them. (JLB)

C. LÉVY, 'De l'epochè sceptique à l'epochè transcendentale: Philon d'Alexandrie fondateur du fidéisme,' in A.-I. BOUTON-TOUBOULIC and C. LÉVY (edd.), *Scepticisme et religion: constantes et évolutions, de la philosophie hellénistique à la philosophie médiévale*, Monothéismes et philosophie (Turnhout 2016) 57–73.

The paper raises the question whether the term fideism rightly applies to Philo and if so, in which meaning of the term. The answer is positive, in that Philo in fact emerges as the originator of what the author calls 'biblical fideism.' Philo is the first monotheist thinker who has devoted attention to scepticism. On the one hand, he endorses a critical attitude towards scepticism, but he also uses it in order to establish faith. Philo sees the sceptic as a manifestation of the sophist who, in his eyes, represents a distortion of the legitimate desire of knowledge. However, Philo also appropriates the twofold outlook of the sceptic—not with a view to *isosthenia* (equipollence of beliefs) as in scepticism, but rather in order to affirm the limitation of human knowledge. This limitation is imposed by God's *logoi* and enables Philo to maintain the nothingness of the human being alongside the all-powerfulness of God. Philo thus develops a 'transcendental *epochè*': a voluntary attitude, which imitates the stability of God, while referring everything back to Him. (SW)

C. LÉVY, 'Continuity and Dissimilarity in Middle Platonism: Philo and Plutarch about the Epicurean *ataraxia*,' in G. E. STERLING (ed.), *The Studia Philonica Annual Vol. 28 [= Studies in Philo in Honor of David Runia]* (Atlanta 2016) 121–136.

The purpose of the article is to investigate the attitude to Epicureanism of the near contemporaries Philo and Plutarch, and in particular their views on the key term which summarises the *telos* of Epicurean philosophy, ἀταραξία (freedom from disturbance). This question allows the author to cast light on the transition from Hellenistic philosophy to the Imperial period when Platonism becomes dominant. The term itself is absent in Philo's works, for which—given its centrality—there must be a reason. Philo's attitude towards Epicureanism is complex. He agrees that all the sensations are true and that pleasure occupies an important place in human life, but at the same time he emphasises that they both must be repressed because they tend to exceed the limits that must be attached to them. Philo in fact avoids the term *ataraxia* because its use would be to give ethical autonomy to the Epicurean *telos*, whereas he wants to point out its contradictory nature. Philo in fact prefers the term ἠρεμία (quietude, inner peace), which he uses in relation to God in *Post.* 129, a view that in fact Lucretius would agree with. For Philo, however, the methods that the Epicurean uses to attain ἀταραξία only apply to the person making progress (the προκόπτων). To advance further requires divine grace. Unlike Philo, Plutarch does use the term ἀταραξία, but this does not mean that his position is essentially different from that of Philo. A number of texts are discussed in which he criticises the concept. The article concludes with three points. (1) Both thinkers elaborate the polemics against the Epicurean doctrine with Platonic themes. (2) There is a real contintuity between them and the earlier New Academics, notably Cicero. (3) Philo goes further than Plutarch in his absolute rejection of the term ἀταραξία. This certainly had the philosophical purpose of showing that 'the Greek language was rich enough not to need the contradictory concept coined by Epicurus. But it could be that Philo was also influenced by the Jewish idea that to refuse the name is the best way to refuse existence (p. 136).' (DTR)

C. LÉVY, 'Philon d'Alexandrie face à l'altérité. Le problème des sagesses barbares,' in S. H. AUFRÈRE (ed.), *Alexandrie la divine. Sagesses barbares: Échanges et réappropriation dans l'espace culturel gréco-romain* (Geneva 2016) 313–338.

Philo's attitude towards barbarian wisdom is complex. As is well exemplified by the writings of Cicero, by Philo's time, the classic Greek-barbarian dichotomy was undergoing a profound transformation, due to the emergence of a third component: the Romans, whose main feature is exceptionality according to Cicero. On the one hand, Philo thinks about the world and the nations through the classic distinction between the Greeks and the barbarians (with which he acknowledges that the Jews are associated); on the other hand, he conceives of the Jews as external to, and as transcending, this dichotomy. Although he both opposes the standard depreciation of the barbarian wisdom by showing that some barbarians were able to preserve the original harmony between man and nature (a harmony which was also originally held by the Greeks) and uses the prestige of the barbarian wisdom in order to affirm the superiority of the wisdom of Moses, he nevertheless fundamentally opposes the Jews to the rest of humanity. For Philo, the Greek-barbarian construct characterizes an immanent perspective on the world—a world marked by an internal strife that could be resolved thanks to the attractiveness and universal character of the Jewish law. However, Philo does not attain on this basis a universal approach to ethics. The wisdom of Moses is not entangled in the false illusion that human rationality by itself can reach the truth. The Jewish law in fact transcends nature and establishes a vertical relationship to God. (SW)

A. LIVNEH, 'Jewish Traditions and Familial Roman Values in Philo's *De Abrahamo* 245–254,' *Harvard Theological Review* 109 (2016) 536–549.

This article offers a close reading of Philo's encomium of Sarah in *Abr.* 245–54 and contextualizes it both within Jewish exegetical traditions and contemporary Roman discourses. While certain inner-biblical connections had already been adduced by previous Jewish interpreters, Philo's choice of the encomiastic genre as well as his emphasis on conjugal love, Sarah's accompaniment of Abraham even in times of battle, and her speech about Hagar are novel. The paper argues that the unique features of Philo's interpretation can be explained by recourse to contemporary Roman discourses, especially Augustan family ideals, the *Laudatio Turiae* and Musonius Rufus' philosophy of marriage. (MRN)

J. MACHIELSEN, 'Sacrificing Josephus to Save Philo: Cesare Baronio and the Jewish Origins of Christian Monasticism,' *International Journal of the Classical Tradition* 23 (2016) 239–245.

The Catholic church historian Cardinal Cesare Baronio (1538–1607) makes a sharp contrast between Josephus' Essenes and Philo's Therapeutae and argues that the latter, whom he calls Essenes, had converted to Christianity. In addition, Baronio offers an explanation why Christians might have been called 'Essenes.' (DTR)

S. MARCELESCU-BADILITA, 'Prophétie et mystique chez Philon d'Alexandrie,' in S. C. MIMOUNI and M. SCOPELLO (edd.), *La mystique théoretique et théurgique dans l'antiquité gréco-romaine. Judaïsmes et Christianismes,* Judaïsme ancien et origines du Christianisme 6 (Turnhout 2016) 355–372.

By focusing on the figure of Abraham especially as it emerges in *Her.*, the author shows the close relationship between prophecy and mysticism in Philo's exegesis. In contrast to the messianic activism which characterized the Judaism of his time, Philo conceives of prophecy as a privileged relationship between God and the wise person, in which the latter functions as God's instrument (*organon*). At the heart of the prophetic experience is the intellect that leaves room for divine possession. (SW)

C. MARKSCHIES, *Gottes Körper. Jüdische, christliche und pagane Gottesvorstellungen in der Antike* (Munich 2016), esp. 63–66.

Philo is listed as an example of the unselfconscious reception of the Platonic teaching that God is bodiless. Unlike Plato and Aristotle, however, Philo does not regard God as perceptible either. God is unlike humans and therefore biblical anthropomorphisms must be read allegorically. God does not inhabit space or time either. He is eternal. (JLB)

J. W. MARTENS, 'The Meaning and Function of the Law in Philo and Josephus,' in D. M. MILLER and S. J. WENDEL (edd.), *Torah Ethics and Early Christian Identity* (Grand Rapids, MI 2016) 27–40.

In the Hellenistic context in which Philo and Josephus wrote, the question came to the fore of the relationship between the particular laws of the Jews and universal higher laws, such as the law of nature (νόμος φύσεως), living law (νόμος ἔμψυχος), and unwritten law (ἄγραφος νόμος). Because Philo believed in a transcendent God who created both nature and law, he (Philo) equated the laws of Moses with the law of nature and thought that these laws should be followed by everyone. While the allegorical meaning of the law was more important to him, Philo held that literal observance was also necessary. Philo resolved the 'tension between the historic character of written law and the preexistence of the law of nature' by grouping together all forms of the 'higher law' and claiming that certain people, like the patriarchs, were able to follow this without having a written code, of which they were in fact the archetypes (p. 31). He also believed that some people in his own time could follow the law of nature without familiarity with Mosaic law (as in for example *Spec.* 2.42–48). Although Josephus also mentions the law of nature and 'hints at a universality underpinning' the Mosaic laws (p. 37), he does not develop a concept of the law of nature philosophically but instead uses it apologetically, especially to criticize acts of suicide and parricide and failure to give the dead a burial. (EB)

J. P. Martín (ed.), *Filón de Alejandría Obras Completas* Volumen IV (Madrid 2016).

This volume is a continuation of the series *Filón de Alejandría. Obras completas*, a translation into the Spanish language, with introductions and notes, of the complete works by Philo. It forms part of the Project *Philo Hispanicus*, directed by the renowned Philonist José Pablo Martín, who died on 10 January 2015. Volume IV begins with a general presentation (pp. 9–17) by the editor, followed by six treatises: *Sobre los sueños* I-II (*Somn.* 1–2), *Sobre José* (*Ios.*), *Sobre Abraham* (*Abr.*), all translated by Sofia Torallas Tovar; *Sobre las virtudes* (*Virt.*) translated by Pura Nieto; and *Premios y castigos* (*Praem.*) translated by José Pablo Martín. All the treatises are prefaced by introductions which explore questions regarding Philo's thought and its relations to late antiquity and medieval culture, as well as discussing topics relating to particular aspects of the treatises. (MA)

O. W. McFarland, *God and Grace in Philo and Paul*, Novum Testamentum Supplements 164 (Leiden 2016).

A slightly revised version of the Durham doctoral thesis completed in 2013. The revised title gives more emphasis on the central subject of divine grace. See the summary in *SPhiloA* vol. 28, p. 412. (DTR)

K. Metzler, *Prokop von Gaza Der Genesiskommentar. Aus den „Eclogarum in libros historicos Veteris Testamenti epitome" übersetzt und mit Anmerkungen versehen*, Die griechischen christlichen Schriftsteller der ersten Jahrhunderte N.F. 23 (Berlin 2016).

Magnificent edition—partly *editio princeps*—of the *Commentary on Genesis* by Procopius of Gaza (c. 465–529). This work is partly a *catena* (a 'chain' in the sense of being a massive interlinked collection of excerpts from Patristic and other writings), partly an epitome because it is an abridged version of those works, and partly a commentary because in its final form it does give a running commentary on the biblical text which is cited at the head of each section. Procopius' work is remarkable because it excises every single reference to the original authors and also does not contain, apart from the first fourteen lines, any text representing the author's own voice. It is thus an enormous task to identify the source of all the materials so expertly stitched together. In an extensive introduction the editor discusses the author and the nature of his work, followed by earlier editions and translations (only the Greek up to Gen 18:3 had been previously edited by Cardinal Mai (1831), the rest was only available in the Latin translation of Klauser (1555), so from Gen 18:4 onwards this edition is the first of the Greek text ever to be published). The Introduction then surveys the manuscripts resulting in a stemma on p. lxxxviii. The remainder of the Introduction analyses the sources of the excerpts. The Philonic excerpts are discussed on pp. cxix–cxx. They are all derived from the *Quaestiones in Genesim*, the full Greek text of which has been lost. So these fragments are most valuable for our knowledge of the original work and were extensively used in F. Petit's edition (1978 = R-R 1814). The Greek text of the Commentary on Gen 1–50 occupies 460 pages, with the sources of the excerpts printed on the inside margins (many remain unidentified). In a companion volume published in 2017 the editor presents a German translation of the text. This second volume contains the indices which will allow the reader to locate the Philonic passages, which are in fact 106 in number. For a review of both volumes, which gives more information on the Philonic contents of the *Commentary*, see D.T. Runia, *SPhiloA* vol. 29, pp. 260–264. (DTR)

J. Moreau, 'Une première théologie de la création : le *De opificio mundi* de Philon d'Alexandrie (1–37).' in B. Bakhouche (ed.), *Science et Exégèse: Les interprétations antiques et médiévales du récit biblique de la création des éléments (Genèse 1,1–8)* (Turnhout 2016) 65–78.

An analysis of *Opif.* 1–37 is proposed with the intention of showing that, for Philo, piety and philosophy are two sides of the same coin. Philo picks out the best philosophical options in order to rationally explicate the biblical text. By presenting a profound combination of philosophy and exegesis, Philo creates an initial form of theology. Scripture, however, forms both the departure point and the destination of his enterprise. (SW)

S. Morlet, *Les chrétiens et la culture. Conversion d'un concept (Ier–VIe siècle)* (Paris 2016).

This book seeks to show the way in which the classical notion of 'culture' was reworked by early Christian authors. In this context, the author recalls Philo's approach to *paideia* (chapter 1: Les défenseurs de la culture) and addresses his attitude towards mathematics, music and astronomy. Philo uses philosophical and scholarly mathematical speculations in order to interpret the biblical text (chapter 4: Arithmétique et géométrie). He moreover distinguishes between different types of music: bad music that turns to the senses, and good music that produces harmony in the soul. But Philo also echoes the Pythagorean theory of the 'music of the universe,' which serves as the archetype of terrestrial music (chapter 5: La musique). Philo conflates astronomy with astrology, which he considers as a worthless science embedded in the sensible realm, but he is ready to confer on it a more positive function in his interpretation of Abraham's spiritual journey (chapter 6: L'astronomie). Philo's attitude to these different branches of knowledge are all echoed in later Christian sources. (SW)

N. Naveros Cordova, *Philo's Εὐσέβεια and Paul's Πνεῦμα: The Appropriation and Alteration of Hellenistic Jewish and Greek Philosophical Traditions in Their Ethical Discourses* (diss. Loyola University, Chicago 2016).

The dissertation, prepared at Loyola University under the supervision of Prof. T. H. Tobin, S.J., examines Philo and Paul's ethical discourses using two key concepts, in Philo εὐσέβεια (piety) and in Paul πνεῦμα (spirit), within the larger Hellenistic Jewish and Greco-Roman contexts. Philo and Paul have much in common in the way they configure their own ethics. Both Hellenistic Jews privilege consistently and intentionally the place of piety and spirit in their respective ethical discourses, and also both move beyond the parameters of Hellenistic Jewish and Greek philosophical traditions. In the Greek philosophical ethical systems of Plato, Aristotle, and the Stoics, piety is often catalogued as a subordinate virtue under the generic virtue of justice. In Philo, however, piety is not only the 'queen of all the virtues'; piety becomes a foundational virtue of the intelligible world. This is demonstrated in five ways: piety for the service of God and human beings; piety as the source virtue; piety as the opposite of impiety; the practice of piety; and the special relationship between piety and love of humanity. In the case of Paul, the concept of spirit is examined in the seven genuine letters. In both the Hellenistic Jewish and Greek philosophical traditions, spirit is not an ethical concept; indeed, it is in Paul that the concept adopts an ethical understanding. While in Philo's ethics the virtue of piety is intrinsically linked with both the λόγος and the Mosaic Law, in Paul the concept of spirit is closely associated with Christ and the love commandment or Law of Christ. Significantly, the ethical role that each element plays is very similar in both ethical discourses. This study also illumines how the ethical role of piety and spirit is described in Platonic categories, by which Philo—more than Paul—is deeply affected, especially in terms of the development of Middle Platonism. Philo's 'divinization' of piety and its privileged place in his ethics are mainly expressed in Platonic categories, whereas Paul's 'Christification' of God's Spirit and his description of the qualities and powers given to his primary concept are expressed using both Platonic and Stoic language. However, the similarities with reference to these Greek philosophical traditions in Paul's ethics exist only at the terminological level, and not in content. (DTR; based on the author's abstract)

M. R. Niehoff, 'Justin's *Timaeus* in Light of Philo's,' in G. E. Sterling (ed.), *The Studia Philonica Annual Vol. 28 [= Studies in Philo in Honor of David Runia]* (Atlanta 2016) 375–392.

The article relies on Philo to throw light on Justin's overlooked use of Plato's *Timaeus* in the context of Roman discourses. It is argued that Philo and Justin faced remarkably similar intellectual challenges, as both arrived in Rome and addressed Roman audiences, defending their religion as a philosophy of life. Their use of the *Timaeus* plays a similar role in this context: both adduce this dialogue to build a creation theology, which is enriched by Stoic elements and speaks to the concerns of Roman audiences. (MRN)

C. Nougué and L. Monteiro Dutrá, *Fílon de Alexandria. Da Criação do Mundo e outros escritos* (São Paulo 2016).

The book offers for the first time in Portuguese the translation of the treatises *De Opificio Mundi, De Aeternitate Mundi, Quod Deus sit immutabilis* and *De Providentia*. The translation is fluent and well edited. However, there are few notes, with rare explanations of choices between manuscript readings and the editors' corrections, which might be explained by the fact that the original text that serves as the basis for the work was taken from the *Thesaurus Linguae Graeca* digital library. There are very few notes indicating parallels with other Philonic texts or explanation of difficult passages in relation to Philo's thought. The introductory text that precedes the translated treatises makes clear that it is written from a particular religious perspective, namely Catholic. After locating Philo in the history of thought, with an emphasis on his views on the knowledge of God and the world, Nougué discusses the life and works of the Alexandrian. It is evident that he depends heavily on the general introduction of R. Arnaldez in the French translation series (R-R 2202) and on the exposition of G. Reale in his *History of Ancient Philosophy* (R-R 7839, RRS 9056). (MA)

F. Oertelt, 'Befreiung der Seele – zur Deutung des Exodus bei Philo von Alexandria,' in J. Gärtner and B. Schmitz (edd.), *Exodus: Rezeptionen in deuterokanonischer und frühjüdischer Literatur*, Deuterocanonical and Cognate Literature Studies 32 (Berlin 2016) 269–288.

Although the interpretation of the Exodus of the people of Israel out of Egypt does not take much space in Philo's writings (cf. *Mos.* 1), the concept of the exodus as the soul's departure from the realm of the senses is an important concept throughout his work, especially in the Allegorical Commentary. The book Exodus is called Ἐξαγωγή, the departure from a country. Philo describes the exodus as departure from the barbaric xenophobia and slavery in Egypt, which the Jews suffered instead of the protection of strangers and the hospitality that could have been expected among civilized people (*Mos.* 1.35–39). The plagues are a warning and punishment for the Egyptians and a lesson of piety for the Jews (*Mos.* 1.96–146). The description of the exodus itself is drastically shortened in Philo's account. In the Allegorical Commentary the exodus is interpreted as the soul's migration from the senses and the passions towards the understanding of God, but this transition is mainly linked to the figure of Abraham (*Heres* 271–272; *Migr.* 14–15). This individualising interpretation turns the exclusive communal experience between God and his people into a timeless event, a universally accessible process of learning. (JLB)

S. Pearce, 'Notes on Philo's Use of the Terms ἔθνος and λαός,' in G. E. Sterling (ed.), *The Studia Philonica Annual Vol. 28 [= Studies in Philo in Honor of David Runia]* (Atlanta 2016) 205–226.

This article offers a detailed analysis of Philo's use of the terms ἔθνος and λαός as applied to the Jews and their ancestors. Philo uses both terms interchangeably to refer to the ancient Hebrews. λαός never appears in Philo's accounts of the Jewish people as a whole in the context of contemporary events. His use of ἔθνος as applied to Jews strongly emphasises the piety and conceptions about God which should define membership of this people. (SJKP)

J. Petitfils, *Mos Christianorum: the Roman Discourse of Exemplarity and the Jewish and Christian Language of Leadership*, Studien und Texte zu Antike und Christentum 99 (Tübingen 2016), esp. 87–140.

Against the background of the Roman discourse of exemplarity, whereby Roman writers promoted and inculcated Roman ideals through presentation and discussion of ancestral examples, Petitfils studies how the following sources from non-Roman native traditions adapted this discourse for their own ends: Philo, Josephus, 1 Clement, and the *Letter of the Churches of Vienne and Lyons*. Ch. 4 (pp. 87–140) is devoted to 'Moses as an *Exemplum* of Native Leadership in Philo's *De Vita Mosis* and Josephus' *Antiquities* 2–4.' Compared with the biblical portrayal, both writers significantly embellish Moses' character and position in such areas as noble lineage, education and eloquence, and especially piety, which they consider a supremely important virtue. The discussion of piety in Philo's account includes such topics as Philo's general view of God, his view of God in *Mos.* 1–2, and manifestations of piety in *Mos.* 1–2. Philo also emphasizes Moses' balance between reason and emotions. Both Philo and Josephus similarly play down or eliminate negative details, like Moses' being prohibited from entering the promised land. While both writers show parallels with Roman exemplary discourse such as is exhibited in Valerius Maximus' depiction of the Scipio family, Josephus displays more characteristics of this discourse than Philo. (EB)

M. Pucci Ben-Zeev, 'Philo on the Beginning of the Jewish Settlement at Rome,' in D. M. Schaps, U. Yiftach and D. Dueck (edd.), *When West Met East. The Encounter of Greece and Rome with the Jews, Egyptians, and Others: Studies Presented to Ranon Katzoff in Honor of his 75th Birthday* (Trieste 2016) 69–90.

The article offers a detailed analysis of Philo's statement in *Legat.* 155 about the origins of the Jewish community in Rome, which is said to have emerged from emancipated slaves who had arrived as prisoners of war. These statements are critically examined in the context of Roman practices, which suggest that war prisoners would not have come in large numbers to the capital and that emancipation of such slaves would have been more difficult than Philo suggests. His report is thus taken as an apologetic move, designed to highlight Augustus' beneficence towards the Jews of Rome. (MRN)

I. L. E. Ramelli, *Social Justice and the Legitimacy of Slavery: the Role of Philosophical Asceticism from Ancient Judaism to Late Antiquity*, Oxford Early Christian Studies (Oxford 2016), esp. 76–96.

The monograph aims to connect the themes of asceticism, the rejection of slavery as an institution, and the embrace of social justice in ancient philosophy, Jewish Hellenism and Christian antiquity. In a lengthy first chapter the author sets out the background of these topics in ancient philosophy and ancient judaism. Philo is first used as crucial evidence for the thought and practice of the Essenes and Therapeutae. It is clear that these groups rejected slavery on the grounds that it violates the law of equality. Philo's presentation of these groups later exerted influence on Gregory of Nyssa. As for Philo himself, however, it appears that he is closer to the Stoic view that juridical slavery is an indifferent matter and so he does not renounce the ownership of slaves. For Philo slavery is above all a moral thing, so juridical slaves can be people of the highest moral standing, whereas juridically free people can be enslaved to the passions. Also when interpreting the biblical record, Philo tends to make use of Stoic ideas, e.g. in his allegorical interpretations. (DTR)

I. L. E. RAMELLI, 'Hebrews and Philo on ΥΠΟΣΤΑΣΙΣ: Interlocking Trajectories?,' in P. F. BEATRICE and B. POUDERON (edd.), *Pascha Nostrum Christus: Essays in Honour of Raniero Cantalamessa* (Paris 2016) 27–49.

The article argues that a concept of ὑπόστασις found in Philo's *Aet.* contributed to Origen's specific notion of the individual substances or ὑποστάσεις (as opposed to their common divine nature or οὐσία) of the persons of the Trinity. Origen developed his notion in the context of his exegesis of Heb 1:3. The church father closely associated this text with Wisdom 7:25–26, and with Philo's reading of it. The article analyses *Aet.* 88 and 92 (passages speaking about the light, αὐγή, emitted by fire, which light is without a substance, ὑπόστασις, of its own). It discusses Philo's semi-hypostatic conceptualisation of the Logos/Wisdom of God in the context of his doctrine of the divine *dynameis*, which are important sources of influence on Origen (and on Clement of Alexandria). Philo uses various metaphors to illustrate the relationship of the Logos to God: shadow, mirror, emitted light, expression/seal. Heb 1:3 has the same two last-mentioned metaphors, describing the Son/Logos as the effulgence of God's glory and the express image of God's hypostasis. The author states that precisely the concept of hypostasis as individual substance forms a remarkable point of contact between Hebrews and Philo. Further parallels between Heb 1:3 and Philonic passages are discussed, as well as passages in Origen that contain the term ὑπόστασις or *substantia* and demonstrate the coeternity of the Son with the Father. The article concludes (p. 249): 'What seems certain is that Origen was inspired by both Hebr. 1,3 and Philo in the development of his enormously influential theological concept of hypostasis.' (HMK)

G. REYDAMS-SCHILS, '*Philautia*, Self-knowledge, and *Oikeiôsis* in Philo of Alexandria,' in P. GALAND and E. MALASPINA (edd.), *Vérité et apparence: mélanges en l'honneur de Carlos Lévy, offerts par ses amis et ses disciples*, Latinitates 8 (Turnhout 2016) 333–342.

The examination of Philo's condemnation of φιλαυτία (self-love) in light of both the Platonic-Socratic motif of self-examination and of the Stoic notion of appropriation (οἰκείωσις) shows that he transforms these strands into a theocentric doctrine. Plato in his *Laws* (731d6–732b4 and 715e–716d) draws a similar opposition to that found in Philo between self-love and the love of God. For Plato, the proper relation to oneself is that of care and knowledge (not of love), while for Philo, knowledge of self consists in realizing one's own nothingness and dependence on God. The Stoics (esp. Epictetus, *Diss.* 1.19.11–15) drew a distinction between two forms of self-interest: οἰκείωσις and φιλαυτία. Whereas the latter involves complete disregard for others, the former, in fact, centrally involves care for others. Though Philo's notion of οἰκείωσις differs from that of the Stoics, *QG* fr. 11 Marcus has shown that he combines Platonism and Stoicism in positing a transcendent God while emphasising his relational aspects. (SW)

J. D. ROSENBLUM, *The Jewish Dietary Laws in the Ancient World* (Cambridge 2016).

The author considers how Jews in antiquity defended kosher food laws and how outsiders, including Greeks, Romans, and early Christians, criticized these eating practices. Chapters are devoted to food laws in the Hebrew Bible, comments by outsiders in Greek and Roman sources, Jewish sources in the Hellenistic period, the New Testament, Jewish sources in the Tannaitic period, Amoraic sources, and Christian sources in the rabbinic/

patristic period. Justifications for kosher food laws are based on reason, revelation, allegory, or a combination of these categories. In Philo's time, the Hellenistic period, which witnessed the rise of 'the need to justify perceived traditional food practices,' 'authors presume revelation as a basis for these practices, but explicitly spell out reason as a foundational justification' (pp. 48–49). Explaining Jewish food laws, Philo himself emphasizes their link to temperance and their pedagogical value in imparting lessons about proper behavior. He discerns lessons about temperance, e.g., in the injunction to offer first fruits to God and to limit the kinds of animals that may be eaten, and he discerns lessons about proper behavior, e.g., in the injunction to avoid carnivorous animals and to refrain from cooking animal offspring in their mother's milk. Answering the emperor Gaius about why Jews abstain from pork, however, Philo simply replies that it is a matter of custom. (EB)

J. R. Royse, 'The Biblical Quotations in the Coptos Papyrus of Philo,' in G. E. Sterling (ed.), *The Studia Philonica Annual Vol. 28 [= Studies in Philo in Honor of David Runia]* (Atlanta 2016) 49–76.

The article commences with a brief description of the famous Coptos papyrus codex found in 1889, which not only contains the complete text of two Philonic treatises (*Sacr.* and *Her.*) and priceless early papyrus fragments of the New Testament used in its binding, but is also claimed to be earliest bound book still in existence. The codex's main contents represent the Philonic text at a very early stage of its transmission, probably in the third century CE. The *editio princeps* by V. Scheil is very inadequate and seriously hampered the use of the contents in the *editio maior* of Philo's works by Cohn and Wendland (who strangely never went to the trouble of studying the document themselves). The aim of the rest of the article is to examine the fate of Philo's biblical quotations in the two treatises in the light of the evidence that the papyrus furnishes. The first topic relates to the title of the book of Exodus, which is referred to twice at *Her.* 14 and 251. On both occasions Scheil's edition obscures the textual evidence. In fact the papyrus reads ἐξαγ(ωγῇ) and ἐξαγω(γῇ), confirming that Philo's preferred title for the book is Ἐξαγωγή rather than Ἔξοδος. In the remainder of the article the author examines the 33 biblical quotations in the two treatises: 18 from Genesis, 10 from Exodus, 2 from Leviticus, 2 from Numbers and 1 from Deuteronomy. He concludes (pp. 75–76) that these passages give 'an appropriate impression of the value of Pap's witness to Philo's biblical quotations. The readings that Pap preserves are from time to time erroneous, but very often they are testimony to Philo's actual words. Often indeed Pap transmits the true reading when other (sometimes all other) manuscripts have suffered corruption. And often Pap's readings themselves have not been adequately represented in Scheil's edition, and thus not by Cohn and Wendland in their edition.' (DTR)

D. T. Runia, 'Philo in Byzantium: An Exploration,' *Vigiliae Christianae* 70 (2016) 259–281.

The article gives the first comprehensive overview of the fate of Philo's writings and thought in the Byzantine period from 500 to 1500 CE. It sets out the evidence, based primarily on named references in a wide range of Byzantine sources, for the questions: (1) who read Philo and wrote about him; (2) what part of his legacy did they utilise; (3) why did they refer to him; (4) and what was their attitude to him as a Jewish author. Five conclusions are drawn: (1) During the Byzantine era Philo was regarded with respect as a thinker and writer, belonging to two canons, the Patristic canon for exegesis and theology, and the classical canon for style and language. (2) Philo is invariably recognised as a Jewish author, but this is almost never a source of criticism. (3) Philo's writings and thought are put to a variety of uses. His allegorical exegesis is little used, he is exploited for knowledge of Jewish practices at the time of the New Testament, and he is frequently mentioned in histories and chronicles of the time of Jesus. (4) Somewhat surprisingly the Byzantines were greatly interested in Philo from a literary viewpoint, viewing him as a model for style and language. (5) During the Byzantine period there are two extensive critiques of Philo by Photius and Theodore Metochites, but they are less penetrating than that of the Renaissance Jew Azariah de' Rossi. The article concludes with an Epilogue, which relates the remarkable Philonic heritage in Armenia from the 6th to the 13th century. (DTR)

D. T. RUNIA, 'Art. Philo Alexandrinus,' in R. DODARO, C. MAYER and C. MÜLLER (edd.), *Augustinus-Lexicon* (Basel 2016) 716–719.

Survey article on Augustine's knowledge of Philo and the presence of Philonic themes in Augustine's thought, with copious reference to bibliography on the subject. It is certain that the Church father had at least a limited acquaintance with Philo's writings, but there is no proof that he ever read any treatise in the original Greek. But there are many echoes of Philonic thought and exegesis in Augustine's *œuvre*, the majority transmitted via the Patristic tradition. Four main areas are briefly outlined: (1) protology; (2) further exegesis of Genesis; (3) the heavenly and earthly cities; (4) theology. (DTR)

D. T. RUNIA, 'La receptíon del *Fedón* de Platón en Filón de Alejandría (translated by M. ALESSO),' *Circe de clásicos y modernos* 20 (2016) 91–112.

A Spanish translation by M. Alesse of a paper presented by the author to the XIth Symposium Platonicum of the International Plato Society, held in Brasilia, Brazil in June 2016. The knowledge and use of the *Phaedo* by Philo is an important source of information about its interpretation at that time. Philo in fact never makes any direct references to the dialogue but he does quote a few snippets. It is apparent that Plato's use of language has influenced Philo, particularly in the rich use of compound adjectives. Philo draws a copious harvest of images from the dialogue: (1) the image of the body as a prison; (2) the image of the body as a garment for the soul; (3) the bondage that the soul must endure through its association with the body; and (4) the journey abroad (ἀποδημία) to another place (*Phd.* 67c), which is linked to the biblical theme of migration. Other general themes in the dialogue are also explored, such as the descent of the soul into the body in terms of metempsychosis or reincarnation. Finally, four passages are separately discussed: *Leg.* 1.105–108; *Gig.* 13–15; *Somn.* 1.138–139; and *Her.* 267–276. (DTR)

D. T. RUNIA, 'Ancient Doxography (Subject area: Classics),' in *Oxford Bibliographies Online*: Oxford University Press 2016).

Bibliography of studies on ancient doxography presented using the distinctive method of the Oxford Bibliographies Online database (http://www.oxfordbibliographies.com). This bibliography was commissioned as part of the section on Classical Studies. It consists of 18 sections, with a maximum of eight bibliographical items in each section. The first sections focus on the doxographical tradition itself, the latter part of the bibliography gives a historical overview of how that tradition developed. Scholarship on Philo is cited in the sections on the Hellenistic and the first century BCE. Every section and every item is briefly annotated. Most items are quite recent and in the English language, but some older works and studies in other languages are also included. The bibliography has been revised in 2019. (DTR)

D. T. Runia, M. Alesso, K. Berthelot, E. Birnbaum, A. C. Geljon, H. M. Keizer, J. Leonhardt Balzer, M. R. Niehoff, S. J. K. Pearce, and T. Seland, 'Philo of Alexandria: an Annotated Bibliography 2013,' *The Studia Philonica Annual* 28 (2016) 393–448.

The yearly annotated bibliography of Philonic studies prepared by the members of the International Philo Bibliography Project covers the year 2013 (108 items), with addenda for the years 2000–2012 (8 items), and provisional lists for the years 2014–2016. (DTR)

L. J. Sanders, 'The Causes of the Alexandrian Pogrom and the Visit of Agrippa I to Alexandria in 38 CE,' in I. Robinson, N. S. Cohn and L. DiTommaso (edd.), *History, Memory, and Jewish Identity,* North American Jewish Studies (Boston 2016) 2–30.

According to author the visit of Agrippa I to Alexandria in 38 CE is much more significant than is usually recognised in ancient sources and modern interpretations of events. Josephus, for example, is surprisingly silent about Agrippa's intervention in Alexandria at this time, while Philo portrays Agrippa's arrival in the city as a matter of mere chance. There are reasons to question Philo's emphasis on the marginal character of Agrippa's visit. Most importantly, Philo may have done so in order to remove from his narrative any evidence connected to Agrippa's role as an agent of Caligula sent to intervene in the Alexandrian conflict. It is argued that Agrippa's visit was no mere chance, but politically motivated: namely, 'to meet with the Jewish community of the city and to help it in its struggle against the Alexandrians, doing so, moreover, as official representative of the emperor' (p. 15). Hostility to Agrippa in Alexandria came not only from certain Alexandrian Greeks but also from Alexandrian Egyptians. The anger expressed by the mob attacking Agrippa may have expressed 'native Egyptian bitterness at the eclipse of ancient Egyptian monarchs as well as of wistful Greek memory of former Ptolemaic kings' (p. 24). Support for such a conclusion, it is argued, may also be deduced from some of Apion's arguments as given by Josephus. The evidence thus suggests that Agrippa's arrival refuelled ancient sources of conflict between Jews and non-Jewish residents of Egypt which went back to the Ptolemaic era. (SJKP)

M. A. Sassine, 'The Phenomenology of the Creative Imagination: Philo of Alexandria and Ibn 'Arabi,' in A.–T. Tymieniecka and P. Trutty-Coohill (edd.), *The Cosmos and the Creative Imagination,* Analecta Husserliana (The Yearbook of Phenomenological Research) 119 (Cham, Switserland 2016) 83–92.

How does a name arise out of infinite possibilities? The author posits that the human relation to the infinite is revealed through language and that the place where this occurs is in the creative imagination. For Philo the infinite and ultimate reality is τὸ ὄντως ὄν, but he also introduces an active Logos which finds expression in the world. This is illustrated through the theology presented in *Abr.*, where the Father is in the middle of two beings, the creative and the royal power. This trinitarian structure is bound together in a relation of intelligibility within the infinite by the Logos, i.e. speech. But this speech is not of the same order as human speech. It has to be responded to, as is illustrated by Philo's retelling of the story of Abraham and Sarah. The power of the new names they receive is that these names say something about them, which has to be grasped by the creative imagination and so inspires new possibilities. In Ibn 'Arabi the 'Creative feminine' takes the central place and it is tempting to see it as a development of Philo's creative Logos, whether they are drawing on similar sources or not. (DTR)

W. SCHMIDT-BIGGEMANN, 'Lingua Adamica and Speculative Philology: Philo to Reuchlin,' in A. BLAIR and A.-S. GOEING (edd.), *For the Sake of Learning: Essays in Honour of Anthony Grafton*, Scientific and Learned Cultures and Their Institutions 18 (Leiden 2016) 572–580.

The notion of Adamic language expresses an understanding that language has a divine origin. Philo was the first to interpret Gen 2:18–20 regarding Adam's naming of the animals. According to Philo, the two stories of the creation of humanity signify the creation of a spiritual, androgynous Adam and a separate, earthly Adam made of body and soul. Having the ability through divine grace of perceiving 'the inner essence of things,' this latter Adam 'named all things' (p. 574). In the early modern era Reuchlin incorporated Philo's concept of Adamic language into his theories of Christian kabbalah, which aimed to reconstruct Adamic language before the Fall. Belief in the divine origin of language, represented by these notions from Philo to Reuchlin, held sway until it was challenged in the eighteenth century. (EB)

G. SCHÖLLGEN ET AL. (edd.), *Reallexikon für Antike und Christentum Band 27 Pelagius–Porträt* (Stuttgart 2016).

A. Felber, Art. Pflanzung, 532–544 (esp. 536–537 (planting); D. T. Runia, Art. Philon von Alexandreia, 605–627 (summary in *SPhiloA* vol. 30, p. 149); J. Zachhuber, Art. Physis, 744–781, esp. 756–759 (nature); M. Erler, Art. Platonismus, 837–955, esp. 866–868 (Platonism). (DTR)

T. SELAND, 'The Expository Use of the Balaam Figure in Philo's *De vita Moysis*,' in G. E. STERLING (ed.), *The Studia Philonica Annual Vol. 28 [= Studies in Philo in Honor of David Runia]* (Atlanta 2016) 321–348.

The article investigates the ways in which, and the purposes for which, Philo discusses the figure of Balaam in *Mos.*, mainly in book 1. The author considers *Mos.* 1.263–299 as Philo's 'rewriting' the story of Num 22–24, although he does not want to classify the treatise as a whole as 'rewritten Bible.' He argues that Philo has specific purposes in his presentation, namely to resist magical divination in his own environment. Philo does this by portraying (particularly in the Allegorical Commentary) Balaam basically as a sorcerer, but one who experienced such God-possession that he could not but utter prophecies. The author argues that in Philo Balaam's temporary prophecy is on a par with the prophets of Israel and that his magical features do not serve to promote Moses' prophetic superiority. According to Seland, Philo's labeling Balaam as a sophist reflects contemporary concerns as well, although there is no scholarly consensus on whether the presence of a real Sophistic movement was felt at Alexandria. (SYK)

M. SPINELLI, 'O conceito grego da ἐγκύκλιος παιδεία e sua difusão no período helenístico [Portuguese: The Greek concept of ἐγκύκλιος παιδεία and its diffusion in the Hellenistic era],' *Hybris: Revista de Filosofía* 7 (2016) 31–58, esp. 44–46.

This paper focuses the concept of ἐγκύκλιος παιδεία used in ancient Greece to indicate the general education received by young people. Philo's views are given particular attention on pp. 44–46. Two concepts prominent in *Congr.* are analysed: the ἐγκύκλιος ἐπιστημῶν and ἐγκύκλιος μουσικῆς. Philo uses these concepts to show that it is necessary to follow a basic school cycle for the purpose of a propaedeutic fortifying of young people's minds. He thus justifies the applicability of the disciplines of Greek schooling (grammar, geometry, astronomy, rhetoric, music and logical theories) to Jewish schooling. (MA)

G. E. STERLING (ed.), *The Studia Philonica Annual [= Studies in Philo in Honor of David Runia],* Vol. 28 (Atlanta 2016).

This volume, which honors pre-eminent Philo scholar and co-editor of *The Studia Philonica Annual* David Runia, contains 16 articles in the following areas: the text of Philo's works (by J.R. Royse and A. Terian), Philo and Hellenistic philosophy (J. Dillon, C. Lévy, G.E. Sterling, J. Mansfeld), Philo and the world of Rome (A. van den Hoek, S. Pearce), Philo and interpretation of the Pentateuch (A. Kamesar, F. Calabi, P. Borgen, E. Birnbaum, A.C. Geljon, T. Seland), and Philo and early Christianity (T.H. Tobin, S.J.; M.R. Niehoff). In two introductory pieces, Sterling presents a biographical essay and a 30 page bibliography of Runia's publications from 1979 to 2016. The volume also contains an annotated bibliography of works on Philo that appeared in 2013 and some that appeared earlier. For summaries of the contributions mentioned here, see this bibliography under authors' names. At the beginning of the volume is a reproduction of a 2014 portrait of David Runia by Sydney artist Evert Ploeg. (EB)

G. E. STERLING, 'A Soaring Mind: The Career of David T. Runia,' in G. E. STERLING (ed.), *The Studia Philonica Annual Vol. 28 [= Studies in Philo in Honor of David Runia]* (Atlanta 2016) 3–13.

This essay introducing the *SPhiloA* volume in honor of David Runia (see the next entry) surveys his life and career, leadership role among scholars, and publications. In the first section, Sterling names members of Runia's family, including his wife, Gonni, who has typeset all issues of *SPhiloA* and joined him in hosting Philo scholars from around the world. Although born in the Netherlands, Runia grew up in Australia, where he lived from 1956 to 1977, and he 'received his primary, secondary, and tertiary education' (p. 4). As a doctoral student from 1977 to 1983 at the Free University in Amsterdam, he was strongly influenced by the French scholar Valentin Nikiprowetzky and produced his doctoral dissertation, 'an intellectual *tour de force*,' on Philo's use of Plato's *Timaeus* (p. 6). Runia continued his professional life mainly in the Netherlands, where he served as a researcher, professor, and administrator before returning to Australia in 2002 to become Master of Queen's College at the University of Melbourne, from which he retired in 2016. Both countries showered him with prestigious honors. Two activities that characterize Runia's scholarly leadership are his revival and editorship (now co-editorship) of *SPhiloA* and his continuation of bibliographic efforts on Philo through establishment and leadership of the International Philo Bibliography Project. Sterling concludes with high praise for Runia's many publications, collaborative endeavors, gifts of friendship, and 'soaring mind'—a title drawn from *Opif.* 69–71, in which Philo describes the mind's increasing yearning to reach a vision of God. (EB)

G. E. STERLING, 'David T. Runia: A Bibliography of his Publications, 1979–2016,' in G. E. STERLING (ed.), *The Studia Philonica Annual Vol. 28 [= Studies in Philo in Honor of David Runia]* (Atlanta 2016) 15–45.

The editor of the Festschrift in honor of David Runia has compiled a comprehensive list of his publications (not just in relation to Philo) covering the years 1979 to 2016. It lists them per year of publication in the following categories: books (51, including 33 volumes produced in collaboration with other scholars); articles and chapters (153); reference articles (51); and book reviews (88). (EB)

G. E. STERLING, 'When East and West Meet: Eastern Religions and Western Philosophy in Philo of Alexandria and Plutarch of Chaeronea,' in G. E. STERLING (ed.), *The Studia Philonica Annual Vol. 28 [= Studies in Philo in Honor of David Runia]* (Atlanta 2016) 137–150.

A study of Philo's and Plutarch's understanding of the First Cause or Principle, and of three factors that led them to reach similar although not identical conclusions about God. The first factor is philosophical monotheism, in the formulation of which Eudorus, working in Alexandria in the first century BCE, had a key role (the One, or God, as the highest principle, above the Monad and Dyad). For Eudorus and Philo, and for Plutarch's Egyptian teacher Ammonius and Plutarch himself, the Deity is One, transcendent, and First Cause. The second factor or common area is philosophical religion. Philo used his philosophical thinking to explain Jewish law; Plutarch, a priest of Apollo in Delphi, formulated a philosophical explanation of the cults and myths of Apollo and of Isis and Osiris. A third factor was the acceptance of a common, primitive wisdom that philosophy could uncover. For Philo (an Easterner), this wisdom or universal truth was hidden in the (eastern) writings of Moses (not in the writings of all peoples of the East) as well as in the (western) thought of Plato, for Plutarch (a Westerner), it was present among both Greeks and barbarians. For both, there was a unity of knowledge, and the instrument to uncover it was allegory. (HMK)

G. E. STERLING, 'Jeremiah as mystagogue : Jeremiah in Philo of Alexandria,' in H. NAJMAN and K. SCHMID (edd.), *Jeremiah's Scriptures*, Supplements to the Journal for the Study of Judaism 173 (Leiden 2016) 417–430.

The author undertakes to explain two exceptional features encountered in *Cher.* 49: only here does Philo introduce a citation of a prophetic text by naming the prophet (Jeremiah), and nowhere else does he connect a prophet so closely with Moses, calling them both mystagogues. The author considers three possible relationships that Philo may have thought to have existed between Moses, Jeremiah, and Egypt: (1) the similarities of the biographical details; (2) the possible special significance of Jeremiah for Egyptian Jews because of the prophet's being taken there (Jer 43:7 MT); and (3) similar roles assigned to, and other connections between, Moses and Jeremiah, as well as the latter's even being buried there according to legendary accounts. The author concludes that while Jeremiah was not on the same level as Moses, Philo seems to have known and utilized traditions that made Jeremiah 'the Jewish prophet of Egypt.' See also the responses to this paper by R. Bloch and F. Tóth summarized elsewhere in this bibliography. (SYK)

G. E. STERLING, '"A Law to Themselves": Limited Universalism in Philo and Paul,' *Zeitschrift für die Neutestamentliche Wissenschaft* 107 (2016) 30–47.

Universalizing tendencies in Philo and Paul suggest that there may have been Jewish traditions that recognized that pagans could hold valid understandings of the deity. Sterling examines several areas in Philo's thought that reflect universalizing tendencies: In discussing creation, Philo declares that the Mosaic law is in harmony with the cosmos and thus someone might live in accordance with this law by following the law of nature, as did the ancestors who lived before the written laws. Philo also speaks of 'Israel' as being able to see God, according to its etymology, and he seems to recognize that through Greek philosophy, some non-Jews could attain knowledge of God and live righteously. Criticizing pagans and Jews in Rom 1:18–3:20, Paul seems to incorporate arguments based on ideas that Gentiles might obey a kind of natural law and that circumcision might be of the heart rather than of the flesh. In these ways, he expands the understanding of Israel/Jew 'beyond ethnic Israel' (p. 42). Underlying both authors is the presence of Jewish traditions that view a relationship between Mosaic and natural law, that understand the concept of conscience as a guiding or rebuking force, and that recognize that law can be observed literally and/or symbolically. Although these authors hold different approaches to the right understanding of God, both have a limited universalistic vision in that they believe that such an understanding is potentially available to everyone, even though not all people actually have this understanding. (EB)

G. J. STEYN, 'Introductory Notes on Philo of Alexandria's "Proverbs" and Idiomatic Expressions,' in R. X. GAUTHIER, G. KOTZÉ and G. J. STEYN (edd.), *Septuagint, Sages and Scripture: Studies in Honour of Johann Cook*, Vetus Testamentum Supplements 172 (Leiden 2016) 294–322.

This article examines Philo's use of proverbial sayings by Philo. The author identifies three major groups: Group A consists of sayings that are attested in and are linked to the book of Proverbs; Group B consists of proverbial expressions with attestation from Greek classical authors; Group C consists of proverbs that are of unknown origin and without attestation in our extant corpus of Greek literature. In the analysis of the sayings attention is paid to the introductory formula, the possible origin and the situation within the Philonic context. The author concludes, among other things, that the majority of Philo's sayings are attested in extant classical Greek literature. Furthermore, it is striking that only a small number of wisdom sayings were quoted from LXX Proverbs and none, for instance, from Ben Sira or the Wisdom of Solomon. (ACG)

A. TERIAN, 'Philonis *De visione trium angelorum ad Abraham*: A New Translation of the Mistitled *De Deo*,' in G. E. STERLING (ed.), *The Studia Philonica Annual Vol. 28 [= Studies in Philo in Honor of David Runia]* (Atlanta 2016) 77–107.

The main part of the article presents a new Armenian text and English translation of the fragment conventionally known as *De Deo*, but which the author now gives the title already suggested by Aucher, *De visione trium angelorum ad Abraham* (On the appearance of the three angels to Abraham). The text is based on the Venetian ms. 1040, collated with the Matenadaran ms. 1500, the former representing the Western and the latter the Eastern Armenian tradition. Variants are given in an apparatus criticus and a few preliminary remarks are made on editorial practice. There is no commentary. The first part and longer part of the article provides a lengthy critique of the previous English translaton by F. Siegert, which was based on an attempted retroversion of the Armenian text back to Greek. The author argues that the 'interlinear' relation between the Armenian and the original Greek is not as close as often thought. The translators used a variety of techniques, some of which kept close to the Greek but others which moved away from it (e.g. using two or even more nouns to represent a single Greek term), as shown in the study of R. Sgarbi. So one is compelled 'to consider Siegert's Greek retroversion of *De Deo* simply [as] a translation' (p. 85). An illustration of the difficulty of determining Greek terms based on the Armenian is provided by studying in detail the three verbs associated with 'seeing' in the fragment and considering their equivalents in those Philonic treatises extant in both languages (with a priority given to *Abr.* because of the proximity of the subject matter). He concludes that 'determining a precise Greek equivalent for each of the Armenian words in the fragment is a complex exercise and well-nigh unworkable' (p. 85). Not only the method of retroversion but also further oddities in Siegert's translation have necessitated the new version in the present article. Finally the author takes issue with Siegert's dating of the fragment to Philo's later works. This dating is based on the mistranslation of an Armenian particle. It is more likely that the fragment belongs to the earlier Allegorical Commentary. (DTR)

H. TERVANOTKO, *Denying her Voice: the Figure of Miriam in Ancient Jewish Literature*, Journal of Ancient Judaism Supplements 23 (Göttingen 2016), esp. 229–248.

As part of a very thorough examination of Miriam as a literary character in ancient Jewish texts, five Philonic texts are studied. But first some introductory remarks are directed to Philo's views on women, particularly the relationship that he sees between gender and the characteristics of the human soul. A complicating factor is that he does not deal with all women in an even way. Not all women are treated as γυνή (woman). A few women enter the category of rationality or intellect (νοῦς), and for these he uses the term παρθένος (virgin). A key question, therefore, is how he understands Miriam in relation to the dichotomy. The first text *Contempl.* 87 is located in a historical text. Here the female Therapeutae are elevated to an unusual level of exemplarity and called παρθένοι. Though Miriam is not explicitly described as a virgin, it is hard to imagine that she has a lower status than her followers. She is portrayed as an ideal female figure. The four other texts, *Leg.* 1.76, 2.66–67, 3.103, and *Agr.* 80–81, are all in allegorical texts. In the first three Philo describes Miriam as a symbol of foolishness, shamelessness and sense perception. In the fourth she shows leadership, but is subordinated to Moses. Philo's depiction of Miriam is thus not uniform and not easy to analyse. Through the influence of the two portrayals in Exod 15 and Num 12, she is sometimes interpreted as a woman and sometimes placed in the category of virgins. Much depends on her relationship with the figure of Moses. In his portrayal Philo can be shown to be dependent on some earlier texts. He is selective in the traditions that he takes over, e.g. the fact that he neglects her family and presents her as an unmarried woman. He removes any references that could indicate an independent role and prefers to interpret her only on a symbolic level. (DTR)

T. H. Tobin S.J., 'Reconfiguring Eschatological Imagery: The Examples of Philo of Alexandria and Paul of Tarsus,' in G. E. Sterling (ed.), *The Studia Philonica Annual Vol. 28 [= Studies in Philo in Honor of David Runia]* (Atlanta 2016) 351–374.

The author seeks to compare the use of eschatological imagery and language by 'two rather different Hellenistic Jews,' Philo and Paul. For Philo, he focuses on *Praem.* which he takes to describe Philo's thoughts on eschatology in terms of the this-worldly fate of the Jewish people. The *Sibylline Oracles* are brought in as relevant background material for understanding Egyptian Judaism and the Jews' deteriorating relationship with their environment, as seen in the uprising of 115–117 CE in particular. The author also sees several parallels between the Oracles and *Praem.* and elaborates on what he considers Philo's eschatological interpretations of Lev 26, Num 24:7 and Deut 28 and 30. According to the author this biblical basis sets Philo apart from the *Sibylline Oracles* and represents his revision of their openly insurgent traditions. The author concludes that there are both differences and similarities between Philo and Paul. Both wrestled with the tension between a universal *eschaton* and the particularistic ultimate fate of Israel, but their eschatologies differ significantly and they came up with different solutions. (SYK)

F. Tóth, 'Jeremiah as Hierophant: Jeremiah in Philo of Alexandria—a Response to Gregory E. Sterling,' in H. Najman and K. Schmid (edd.), *Jeremiah's Scriptures*, Supplements to the Journal for the Study of Judaism 173 (Leiden 2016) 443–469.

The author begins by noting how little there is to go by when discussing Philo's use of the prophet Jeremiah: only three quotations. Yet he agrees with Sterling (to whose paper his is a response) that the peculiar passage *Cher.* 49 bearing on Jeremiah's relationships with both Philo and Moses is worth examining. The author aims to complement Sterling's analysis of the evidence by focusing on the mystery language occurring in *Cher.*, as well as the treatise's rhetorical structure and argumentation. He sets it in the context of its genre, the Allegorical Commentary, and the exegetical methods applied there. He notes that only Moses and Jeremiah are called 'hierophants' by Philo. He concludes, 'the special mention of Jeremiah's name is therefore determined by content, motivated by the line of argumentation and inspired by autobiography.' (SYK)

L. Troiani, 'Augusto e l'elogio di Filone Alessandrino,' in G. Negri and A. Valvo (edd.), *Studi su Augusto: in occasione del XX centenario della morte* (Torino 2016) 129–137.

In *Legat.* 143–47 Philo pronounces a eulogy of Augustus, attributing him superhuman qualities that may surprise us on the lips of an outspoken monotheist with little esteem for politicians. It is the Emperor's role of arbiter and peacemaker that for Philo, belonging to a minority, legitimates his authority. The contemporary Jewish historian Nicolaus of Damascus underlines Augustus' role in the creation of a new mentality. Augustus represents a military monarchy, with all its accompanying tough aspects (some of those perceptible also between Philo's lines). Historians of following generations begin to list the unsuccessful or ambiguous aspects of his life and person. All-important for Philo, however, was an Augustan politics of understanding Jewish needs. (HMK)

N. VALIM DE SENA, 'Violência, monumentalidade e poder: o conflito alexandrino de 38 d.c. [Portuguese: Violence, monumentality and power: the Alexandrine conflict of 38 AD],' *Romanitas, Revista de Estudos Greco-latinos* 7 (2016) 69–87.

The author analyses the relationship between violence, monumentality and power in *Flacc.* and *Legat.* Some buildings (gymnasium, theatre and synagogue) were destroyed, appropriated and repurposed during the pogrom of 38 CE. The paper seeks to demonstrate the importance of space in expressing the identity of Greeks, Egyptians and Jews in Alexandria. Despite the assimilation of cultural elements, living in this city meant that communities were both close to each other but also very different, which caused each group to generate strategies and practices to affirm, strengthen and defend their identity. This interaction led to acts of violence among different groups, with social status being sustained in the spatial domain. (MA)

A. VILLENEUVE, *Nuptial Symbolism in Second Temple Writings, the New Testament and Rabbinic Literature: Divine Marriage at Key Moments of Salvation History*, Ancient Judaism and Early Christianity 92 (Leiden 2016), esp. 93–108.

The monograph examines the ancient Jewish concept of the covenant between God and Israel portrayed as a marriage moving through salvation history. It is rather surprising that after the rich nuptial symbolism of the Hebrew Bible there is a relative scarcity of nuptial imagery in late Second Temple sources. The only author at the time to make a significant contribution to its development is Philo. The author is particularly interested in the role of the cherubim. Philonic texts discussed are *Cher.* 20, 27–29 and 49, together with *Ebr.* 30–31. The cherubim symbolise the union of the two powers of God, but also the *hieros gamos* between the male and female powers of the divinity. Other texts portray the cherubim as a paradigm for human marriages. Philo's interpretation of the cherubim in terms of a theosophical dualism is thus inspired by the sacred marriage of God and Wisdom in wisdom literature and it is the earliest indication that the two cherubim in the Temple consisted in a male and a female figure. The cherubim not only keep banished humanity out of Eden. As symbols of Wisdom's union with the soul, they also invite humanity back in through the divine impregnation of virtue in the Temple. (DTR)

J. C. DE VOS, *Rezeption und Wirkung des Dekalogs in jüdischen und christlichen Schriften bis 200 n. Chr*, Ancient Judaism and Early Christianity 95 (Leiden 2016), esp. 87–114.

The Decalogue plays a large role in Philo's writings. He is the first author who dedicates a whole treatise to the subject and uses the ten commandments as structuring principle for his discussion of the Special Laws. *Decal.* begins with comments about legislation and the revelation of the Decalogue. Then Philo discusses the number ten and the twofold structure of the commandments. After that they are interpreted individually and then linked to other commandments of the Pentateuch. Philo ends with general comments. It is not clear which of the two versions Philo used, as he only quotes numbers 6 to 8 (*Decal.* 36; *Spec.* 3.8; 4.78). Probably he used both. Philo treats the commandments as headings of the laws (*Congr.* 120). This division is not merely structural (against Amir). Philo is the first exegete who explicitly assigns laws to the biblical twofold division of the

Decalogue and who gives reasons for this: God himself has created the division, because through the number two it represents the logical and the illogical part of the soul, the first part being assigned to general laws and the second to those applying specifically to humans. The author also provides a brief summary of the interpretation of the individual commandments. The last commandment receives much attention from Philo because of the role of desire as negative passion in Stoic philosophy. (JLB)

B. WYSS, 'From Cosmogony to Psychology: Philo's Interpretation of Gen 2:7 in *De opificio mundi, Quaestiones et solutiones in Genesin* and *Legum allegoriae*,' in J. VAN RUITEN and G. H. VAN KOOTEN (edd.), *Dust of the Ground and Breath of Life (Gen 2:7). The Problem of a Dualistic Anthropology in Early Judaism and Christianity*, Themes in Biblical narrative 20 (Leiden 2016) 99–116.

The author takes as her aim to compare Philo's exegesis of Gen 2:7 in the three treatises, to note similarities and to explain differences. She paraphrases and contextualises the three main passages (*Opif.* 134–135; *Leg.* 1.31–42; and *QG* 1.4–5 more briefly), also utilising Philo's interpretations of Gen 1:26–27 where available. *Opif.* is seen as a Jewish representative of the literature on Plato's *Timaeus* that focuses on the literal interpretation of the creation. The main subject in *Leg.*, on the other hand, is the anthropological interpretation of Gen 2–3 that concentrates, in particular, on the constitution of the human soul. In her reading, Philo's exegesis of Gen 2:7 becomes a description of the mind in its pre-incarnate state. (SYK)

S. YLI-KARJANMAA, "Call Him Earth:' On Philo's Allegorization of Adam in the *Legum allegoriae*,' in A. LAATO and L. VALVE (edd.), *The Adam and Eve Story in the Hebrew Bible and in Ancient Jewish Writings Including the New Testament*, Studies in the Reception History of the Bible 7 (Turku 2016) 253–293.

The author develops further, and applies in the context of *Leg.*, certain notions introduced in his monograph *Reincarnation in Philo of Alexandria* (summary in *SPhiloA* vol. 30, p. 159, cf. also vol. 28, pp. 431–432), namely the model of the fall and rise of the soul in Philo's thought in general and the concept of the corporealization of the mind in particular. A major goal is to demonstrate that Philo's allegorization of the Paradise story mainly operates at the universal, as opposed to the protological, level. *Leg.* 3.52 (exegesis of Gen 3:9) is seen as an important nexus in the treatise, one that the author regards as alluding to Philo's interpretations of several other verses in Gen 2–3 dealing with virtue vs. wickedness, life vs. death and wisdom vs. ignorance. The author also argues the dichotomy in *Leg.* 1.31–32 between a heavenly and an earthly human is based on the distinction between Gen 2:7b and 2:7a that Philo makes in his allegory. He discusses parallelisms between *Leg.* and Plato's *Timaeus* as well as the Book of Wisdom to strengthen his point. (SYK)

C. ZIEGERT, 'In Pursuit of the Perfect Bible: Attitudes to Bible Translation in Hellenistic Judaism,' *Bible Translator* 67 (2016) 365–379.

Three ancient Jewish-Greek sources contain reflections on the nature of translating Scripture from Hebrew to Greek, and the attitudes that these sources evince toward this endeavor are pertinent for today. To protect a particular translation from being revised, the Letter of Aristeas adapts the prohibition of Deut 4:2 against adding to or subtracting from Scripture. Likewise some people today hold a preference for what they consider to be the 'only reliable' translation. In *Mos.* 2.25–44 Philo too adapts the Deuteronomic prohibition to describe what he considers the prophetic task of the translators. In his view, the Greek translation was aided by divine intervention and the original and translation were related 'like an archetype and its image' (p. 373). Similarly today some people regard a certain translation to be divinely inspired and as close to the original as possible. In translating his grandfather's work, the grandson of Ben Sira observes that Greek may not be able to render either the meaning or the rhetorical force of the Hebrew exactly. The grandson also observes that the Greek translation of the Bible differs 'not a little' from the Hebrew (p. 375). His recognition that 'a perfect translation is an illusion' (p. 377) offers a model to contemporary translators. (EB)

J. Zurawski, *Jewish Paideia in the Hellenistic Diaspora: Discussing Education, Shaping Identity* (diss. University of Michigan 2016).

While the integral role of *paideia* in Greek, Roman, and early Christian history has been widely recognized, the place of *paideia* in Jewish thought and the resultant influence on late antique Christianity, and thus on Western education as a whole, has been largely neglected. This study examines the theories of ideal Jewish education from three contemporaneous, but unique Diaspora Jews—Philo of Alexandria, the author of the Wisdom of Solomon, and Paul of Tarsus—particularly in light of the role of the Greek Septuagint translations. The purpose is not to locate a unified concept of Jewish Hellenistic *paideia*, but to allow the views of each author to stand on their own. The diverse educational theories all developed out of a complex amalgam of Jewish and Greco-Roman influences, brought together and reimagined thanks to the Septuagint and the consistent use of *paideia* as a translation for the Hebrew *musar*. The translators of the ancient Hebrew scriptures handed down to future generations a textbook and a teacher, a lens through which later Jewish thinkers could merge and morph ancestral traditions with contemporary Platonic and Stoic philosophy in the creation of new and innovative paideutic concepts. With their textbook in hand, these authors would deploy their ideal notions of *paideia* as a means of contemplating on and shaping the self and Jewish identity. *Paideia*, then, becomes the mechanism by which the most highly valued constituents of Jewish ethics and culture are formed and employed. The diverse developments in Jewish education explored reveal the varied dynamics both within the Jewish community and between the Jews and the wider cultural world. *Paideia* became the perfect surrogate, a common, universal good which could touch on every facet determinative in the construction of the self. (DTR; based on the author's abstract)

Extra items from before 2016

J. S. ALLEN, 'The Despoliation of Egypt: Origen and Augustine—From Stolen Treasures to Saved Texts,' in T. E. LEVY, T. SCHNEIDER and W. H. C. PROPP (edd.), *Israel's Exodus in Transdisciplinary Perspective* (New York 2015) 347–356.

The article deals with the interpretative history of the despoliation of Egypt by the Jews when they left Egypt (Gen 15:14; Exod 3:21–22; 11:2–3; and 12:35–36). Basing himself on Gen 15:14, Philo sees the baggage the Israelites take from the Egyptians as travel provisions; in allegorical terms the provisions represent Greek encyclical education, which nourishes the soul (*Her.* 272–274). He insists that Alexandrian Jews should utilize the encyclia in their strivings toward divine knowledge instead of exploiting it to further social and/or political ambition. Origen was familiar with Philo's exegesis and he offers a similar exegesis, in which the Egyptian treasures represent the classical education and philosophy (*Philoc.* 13). The lines of interpretation laid down by Origen are followed by Augustine (*Doctr. chr.* 2.40.60–61). (ACG)

K. CZAJKOWSKI, 'Jewish Attitudes towards the Imperial Cult,' *Scripta Classica Israelica: Yearbook of the Israel Society for the Promotion of Classical Studies* 34 (2015) 181–194.

Philo's evidence in *Legat.* 355–357 is the point of departure for this examination of Jewish attitudes to the Imperial cult. Using evidence from papyri and other sources, the author suggests that we should question the assumed norm (as witnessed by Philo) for Jews in the Greco-Roman period, which perhaps rests on an outdated understanding of what imperial cult involves, and argues for a much more diverse picture of Jewish attitudes. (DTR)

D. DE BRASI, 'Der *politikos aner* als *pantos oneirokritikos* bei Philon von Alexandria: Prolegomena zu einer Interpretation der Schrift De Iosepho,' *Elenchos: Rivista di studi sul pensiero antico* 36 (2015) 115–139.

Ios. is the only Philonic treatise explicitly devoted to politics. Philo's attitude to politics is ambivalent. He is partly positive and certainly aware of contemporary political theory, but his views on politics according to the author are fundamentally negative: politics is regarded as only an 'addition' to virtue and wisdom. All political activity occurs within the human realm. This realm is uncertain and confused, and therefore the activity of the statesman resembles 'daydreaming,' and the politician is a slave of the people, and even if he is good, he is merely an 'interpreter of dreams.' (JLB)

P. B. DECOCK, 'Philo of Alexandria: a Model for Early Christian 'Spiritual Readings' of the Scriptures,' *HTS Teologiese Studies / Theological Studies (online journal, South Africa)* 71, no. 1 (2015) 8 pages.

A synoptic account of Philo's interpretation of scripture as a spiritual exercise that aims to achieve the transformation and growth of the person towards the good life, with citation of key passages from his writings. Key themes of Philo's spiritual reading are outlined: the priority of God and of the health of the soul, the importance of human progress, the acceptance of human 'nothingness' in order to know God, the responsibility to choose, human effort initiated and completed by nature, the human journey as a journey towards deeper harmony with God and with nature and with the self. It is no wonder that Christian spiritual writers such as Origen found Philo's approach a very inspiring model. (DTR)

P. B. Decock, 'Education as Formation in Early Christianity: The Place of Philo of Alexandria,' *Grace and Truth: A Journal of Catholic Reflection for Southern Africa* 32 (2015).

There is a long and strong tradition that education has as its aim the formation of the person towards likeness to God. A starting point for this is already found within Greek philosophy. This view was integrated into the Hellenistic Jewish and Early Christian understanding of the creation of the human person in the image of God and towards the likeness of God. Philo of Alexandria, though Jewish, is one of the key figures in the development of the early Christian understanding of education. The paper explores Philo's allegorical commentary and reflection on Genesis 16:1–6, a passage about Abraham, when he was unable to beget children from Sarah and was advised by Sarah to turn to her slave girl, Hagar. The Christian tradition was strongly inspired by Philo's approach. (DTR; assisted by author's abstract)

P. Druille, 'La definición del concepto de justicia en *Leyes Particulares* 4, 135–238 de Filón de Alejandría: contexto, connotación y traducción,' *Stylos*, no. 24 (2015) 143–155.

The aim of the paper is to show that the reading of *Spec.* 4.135–238 allows us to observe how Philo defines the concept of δικαιοσύνη on the basis of the classical Greek formulation and includes it within the list of the four cardinal virtues established by Plato. Through this procedure Philo uses the terms of Greek philosophy that he believes most appropriate to explain Jewish law and for elaborating his own interpretation of justice. But he also relates δικαιοσύνη to other virtues that are not part of the four cardinal virtues of Greek thought. In addition, he applies the term in differing contexts, that is, psychic, judicial, political, theological, and especially legal, as befits the world-view of his own Jewish community of Alexandria. At the same time he uses δικαιοσύνη to signify divine justice and its particular areas of application. (MA)

C. Hayes, *What's Divine about Divine Law? Early Perspectives* (Princeton 2015).

Biblical and Greco-Roman conceptions of divine law represent two distinct discourses. The biblical notion, while complex, views divine law as arising from divine will and directed to a particular community. Greco-Roman notions distinguish between 'the unwritten natural or divine law,' which is grounded in reason and seen as universally true, and 'positive human law,' which can be arbitrary, is particular, must be enforced, and does not necessarily lead to virtue (p. 3). Hayes explores three responses to the dissonance between these two conceptions in Second Temple and Hellenistic Jewish literature, in letters of Paul, and in classical rabbinic literature. The apologetic response of Second Temple literature 'culminates in the writings of Philo, who identifies the Mosaic Law with the natural law and confers upon it the attributes of rationality, truth, universality, and

The Studia Philonica Annual 31 (2019)

fixity' (p. 5; see also pp. 111–124). Contrary to Philo, Paul describes Mosaic law similarly to human law 'as particular, temporary, nonrational, and not conducive to virtue' (ibid.). By contrast to these two positions, the rabbis reject ideas of natural law and instead embrace divine law as particular, arbitrary, and subject to moral critique. Philo's identification of divine and natural law raises the question of why a special revelation of laws to a specific community is necessary. Hayes finds Philo's answer in his interpretation of the two accounts of the creation of humanity. Unlike the first, noncorporeal Adam, the second, earthly Adam and his descendants require 'commands and prohibitions (to bring the wicked to virtue) and recommendations and instruction (to bring the ignorant to virtue)' (p. 136). Mosaic law thus becomes 'a second-best accommodation to the nature of human-kind as twice-fallen: fallen first from a purely spiritual into a bodily or corporeal existence and fallen again into a life dominated by sense perception and the passions' (p. 137). (EB)

G. Hertz, 'L'ouïe, «ce sens aveugle» : le statut de l'ouïe dans la vie pratique et religieuse chez Philon d'Alexandrie,' *Pallas: Revue d'Études Antiques*, no. 98 (2015) 155–181.

An examination of the physiology and psychology of hearing in Philo is presented, as well as of its relationship to *pistis*. After an examination of Philo's conception of the soul, the author addresses the relationship between Philo and Plato's depiction of hearing in the *Timaeus*. It appears that despite his use of a Platonic language and images, Philo departs from the *Timaeus* in his understanding of hearing. However, although one could have expected Philo to follow the Jewish tradition in conferring more importance to hearing than to seeing, the contrary is in fact true. Because of its relationship to the sensible realm, its passivity, its localization and slowness, hearing cannot be trusted (ἄπιστος). Philo associates hearing with what is feminine (as opposed to vision, which is masculine), and even to idolatry. (SW)

C. Hezser, *Jewish Slavery in Antiquity* (Oxford 2005).

Extensive use of Philonic evidence is made throughout this monograph, a detailed and comprehensive examination of the place of slavery in ancient Judaism. Contrary to some statements in scripture, Philo makes a clear distinction between slaves and animals, e.g. at *Spec.* 2.69 he says that no one is a slave by nature. It is reason that distinguishes slaves from animals and relates them to other human beings. His opposition to natural slavery is shared with the Stoics and with Paul. But it is uncertain whether he was 'influenced by the Stoics, or reached his views on the basis of biblical exegesis and his own moral thinking' (p. 59). Consistent with these views is the admonition to treat slaves mildly. But he does regard the possession of slaves, esp. those who are non-Jewish, as indispensable. Later in the study the author treats the symbolic use of slavery (Part IV), again referring frequently to Philonic texts. (DTR)

K. Jażdżewska, 'Dialogic format of Philo of Alexandria's *De animalibus*,' *Eos (Poland)* 102 (2015) 45–56.

Coming chronologically midway between the dialogues of Cicero and of Plutarch, Philo's *Anim.* is an important witness to the development of the philosophical dialogue in the early Imperial period. But it has been very little studied. In fact *Anim.* shares a number of features with the dialogues of these two figures. They include the following (p. 54): 'the presence of an author and his friends as interlocutors in the dialogue, a contemporary setting, a preference for *oratio continua*, an engagement in the polemics of post-classical philosophical schools, the modelling (to a greater or a lesser extent) of dialogic conversations and interlocutors on Platonic dialogues and characters, and imbuing reports of contemporary philosophical discussions with Platonic reminiscences.' A difference is that Philo does not name any of the schools or philosophers involved. The author makes much of Terian's observation, a debt which she acknowledges, that Philo deliberately imitates Plato's *Phaedrus*, and so gives himself the role of Socrates. Instead of having a humorous, ironic persona, however, Philo adopts an authoritative stance. (DTR)

O. KAISER, *Philo von Alexandrien: Denkender Glaube—Eine Einführung,* Forschungen zur Religion und Literatur des Alten und Neuen Testaments 259 (Göttingen 2015).

This is the first German introduction to Philo, written by a distinguished Old Testament scholar at the very end of his career. It has three parts: 1. Life and works; 2. Environment; 3. Teaching. Kaiser aims to show the importance of faith for Philo. In introducing Philo's world he not only wishes to locate him in the philosophical context of his time but also includes disparate everyday topics in his environment which are mentioned by Philo, such as the family, virgins, adultery, and inheritance laws as well as market-places and important buildings in Alexandria and their role in the pogrom under Flaccus. In spite of this amount of detail there is only a very brief reference to allegory in Philo and nothing on the key passage *Migr.* 89–93. Other topics discussed are teacher and student, education, philosophers, history of philosophy, geometry, astronomy and astrology, poets and their gods, the practical jobs, professional sports and music, war, arms and soldiers, the fringe groups of society (slaves, prostitutes, pederasts and criminals), plants and animals. There is only a short section, however, on the public evidence of Jewish life. Kaiser argues that Philo's contemplative faith aims at eternal life and aims at proving this in the final part which discusses Philo as exegete, his Middle Platonic cosmology, teaching about God, anthropology, ethics, politics, and his expectation of salvation. The book ends with a survey of those aspects of Philo's thought relevant for the New Testament. See further the review of the book by G.E. Sterling in *SPhiloA* 30 (2018) 191–195. (JLB)

O. KAISER, *Das höchste Gut : Philos Hochschätzung der Freundschaft im Horizont ihrer antiken Geltung* (Stuttgart 2015).

The author's aim is to give an overview of Philo's idea of friendship in the context of ancient authors on the topic. After a brief introduction to Philo's life and work, he gives a short account of Philo's idea of friendship, shown in free speech (παρρησία) as opposed to flattery. Philo knows the universal ancient definition that everything is held in common among friends. Therefore, Essenes and Therapeutae embody friendship in a particular way. The greater part of this short book is an overview of friendship in classical and Greco-Roman philosophy and of early Christian ideals of friendship, together with New Testament references to παρρησία. (JLB)

Y. LIEBES, 'Clothed Nudity: The Esoteric Cult of Philo [Hebrew],' *Jerusalem Studies in Jewish Thought* 24 (2015) 9–28.

Philo of Alexandria says that Nadab and Abihu were naked when they made their sacrifice, but on the other hand they were also clothed, since he insists that the garments in which they were borne out (Lev 10:4) were their own and did not belong to the carriers.

This contradiction may be solved by further delving into the significance of nudity for Philo. Nudity symbolizes direct and private communion with God outside institutionalized religion, and therefore it must be covered and hidden from the eyes of the multitude (in describing this matter Philo uses the vocabulary of Greek stadiums and theaters). The meaning of this clothed nudity is developed further in Philo's description of the high priest's entrance into the holy of holies; he enters naked although he is also clad (in four garments instead of the usual eight). In this case the meaning of clothed nudity could not be exactly the same as that mentioned above, since the priest is told precisely how to enter, in order to avoid the fate of Nadab and Abihu (Lev 16). However, it may be interpreted similarly: the tension between nakedness and clothing symbolizes the tension between established religion and individual mysticism. In discussing the nudity of Adam and Eve Philo again contradicts himself, now possibly to avoid revealing that his mystical ideal transcends both good and evil. Such concealment points to still another level at which Philo's clothed nudity should be interpreted, namely the esotericism ascribed by Philo to Scripture, and likewise the esoteric manner of Philo's own writing, which the author has expounded in previous articles. In this respect Philo is comparable to other Jewish classics, especially the Zohar. (DTR; based on the author's abstract)

T. H. LIM, *The Formation of the Jewish Canon*, Anchor Bible Reference Library (New Haven 2013), esp. 119–147.

Challenging the theory that the Jewish canon developed in stages, Lim instead studies authoritative writings within the context of different communities. After a review of the earliest canonical lists and notices, he devotes chapters to the Torah in the Persian and early Hellenistic periods, the Letter of Aristeas and its early interpreters, the Wisdom of Jesus ben Sira and 2 Maccabees, the Dead Sea Scrolls, the Essenes and Therapeutae, and the Gospels and Pauline letters. Philo is discussed primarily in comparison with the Letter of Aristeas and as a source about the Essenes and Therapeutae. Three major areas of difference between the Letter and Philo's account of the translation of the Hebrew Bible into Greek in *Mos.* 2.25–44 include the impetus for the translation—(according to Philo, the impetus was to introduce Jewish laws to the Greeks rather than 'to fill a gap in the library,' p. 80)—, the translation process (according to Philo individual translators worked in seclusion rather than consulting with other committee members), and Philo's report of an annual festival on the island of Pharos, which is missing from the Letter. Unlike the Letter, Philo also emphasizes the divine inspiration underlying the translation. Philo himself identifies the holy books primarily with the Pentateuch while his description of the holy books of the Therapeutae includes law, prophetic oracles, psalms, and other books. Lim regards this description as 'highly idealized' and believes that it 'could refer to two, three, or four internal divisions' (p. 155). (EB)

A. MICHALEWSKI, *La Puissance de l'intelligible: la théorie plotinienne des Formes au miroir de l'héritage médioplatonicien*, Ancient and Medieval Philosophy 51 (Leuven 2014), esp. 56–60.

This book sketches the history of interpretation concerning the nature of the intelligible Forms from Antiochus to Plotinus. In this comprehensive survey Philo is discussed with reference to his understanding of the Forms as the instruments of God used in the creation of the world. Philo is first and foremost an exegete of the Bible who considers God to be the cause of all things. The Forms are the thoughts of God, produced and created by Him as an intelligible model to be used to produce the sensible world. (SW)

N. J. Moore, *Repetition in Hebrews: Plurality and Singularity in the Letter to the Hebrews, Its Ancient Context, and the Early Church*, Wissenschaftlichen Untersuchungen zum Neuen Testament 2.388 (Tübingen 2015), esp. 46–54.

The book discusses the way repetition is portrayed in Hebrews and argues it is characterized as ineffective only in relation to Christ (whose mission was once and for all) The discussion on Philo locates the letter historically. Philo is discussed as one representative of Middle Platonism (the other being Plutarch) and also diaspora Judaism. The author begins with the connotations of plurality in Philo: sometimes it has positive aspects (e.g., manifold wisdom), but often it represents imperfection and even wickedness in comparison with divine singularity. He notes Philo's appreciative references to the great quantity of sacrifices offered by the Jews, but also his emphasis on the right intention of the act. Other aspects discussed include the connection of recollection and repentance to repetition as well as Philo's positive comments on the recurring cultic acts. (SYK)

J. Otto, '*Paideia* in Genesis: Interpreting Sarah and Hagar with Philo and Clement of Alexandria,' in W. J. Torrance Kirby, R. Acar and B. Bas (edd.), *Philosophy and the Abrahamic Religions: Scriptural Hermeneutics and Epistemology* (Newcastle upon Tyne 2013) 29–44.

The article discusses Philo's and Clement's interpretation of Sarah and Hagar. Philo interprets Sarah as wisdom (φρόνησις) and the highest virtue (ἀρετή). Abraham is an example of the person who learns by instruction and by taking Sarah as his wife, he becomes wise and acquires virtue. Philo sees Hagar as a symbol of the culture gained by the primary learning of the encyclical school course. Clement takes over Philo's allegorical interpretation but he reworks it. He sees Sarah as wisdom that rules philosophy. Hagar no longer represents the specifically introductory education as she did in Philo but *paideia* more broadly. Philosophy is subsumed into the category of the propaideutic. In Clement's reformulation, philosophy is not at one with wisdom, the higher lover represented by Sarah in Philo's allegory. Philosophical training is equated with Abraham's union with his foreign slave. Clement praises secular Greek philosophy for its preparatory usefulness, but it must be subordinated to Christian wisdom. (ACG)

D. Roure, 'Nm 21,4–9 en la interpretació al·legòrica de Filó d'Alexandria [Catalan],' in A. Puig i Tàrrech (ed.), *Relectures de l'Escriptura a la llum del Concili Vaticà II (2) "La serp d'Aram,"* Scripta Biblica 15 (Tarragona 2015) 155–172.

The article studies how Philo deals with the theme of the serpent that is described in Numbers 21:4–9. In *Opif.* and *Leg.* passion is compared to animal nature. Philo applies it to the man who lets himself be seduced by pleasure and become slave to a grievous passion which is hard to heal similar to the slavery in Egypt (*Leg.* 2.84). Therefore the passion-fighter must wage an endless and relentless war against intemperance and pleasure (*Opif.* 163–164) because temperance (σωφροσύνη) is not the possession of all the people but only of the man loved by God (θεόφιλος) (*Leg.* 2.79). In *Agr.* 96, however, the serpent of Moses, is the disposition quite contrary to pleasure, it is the strength of the spirit, which explains why it is represented as being made of very strong material like brass. (MA)

K.-G. Sandelin, 'The Letter of Eudaemon: An Exercise in Historical Fiction,' in S.-O. Back and M. Kankaanniemi (edd.), *Voces Clamantium in Deserto: Essays in Honor of Kari Syreeni*, Studier i exegetik och judaistik utgivna av Teologiska fakulteten vid Åbo Akademi 11 (Åbo 2012) 281–292.

The article is an amusing *jeu d'esprit* offered by the distinguished New Testament and Philonic scholar to a colleague as part of a Festschrift. As the sub-title indicates, it is presented as an 'exercise in historical fiction' (to be distinguished from 'fictional history,' p. 292). It consists of a letter written by Eudaemon, the fictional younger brother of Tiberius Julius Alexander, to the historian Josephus. It recounts the events of his life and particularly his interaction with the early Christians, including the apostle Paul whom he meets in Corinth. He begins the letter with the words 'Call me Isaac.' This unexpected move is explained two pages later: his father gave him the aspirational (Greek) name Eudaemon because his uncle Philo had seen this biblical figure as 'a representative of the happy category of human beings who are spiritually taught by God without human mediation' (p. 283). Wisely he adds that he himself doubts whether he has been given such happiness. The views of Philo are a *Leitmotif* of the piece, repeatedly invoked in order to shed light where appropriate on the Jewish world of life and thought described in the letter. (DTR)

J. M. Soskice, 'Creation and the Glory of Creatures,' *Modern Theology* 29 (2013) 172–185, esp. 177–181.

The article explores pre-histories of the doctrine of creation *ex nihilo*. According to the author, Philo is 'interesting to us because we see in play in his writings all the principles central to the doctrine of divine transcendence that is enshrined by *creatio ex nihilo*' (p. 78) The argument is illustrated briefly in examples from Philo's representation of God as Creator in *Opif.* and in Philonic expressions that 'border on creatio ex nihilo' in discussions of divine sovereignty. Philo's views on naming God are also relevant in this context. He exemplifies the treatment by Greek-speaking Jews of the doctrine of *creatio ex nihilo* as 'a biblically-inspired piece of biblical metaphysics,' and not simply a teaching of Hellenistic philosophy. (SJKP)

A. Standhartinger, 'Selbstsorge und politische Praxis in Philo von Alexandriens Schrift über die Therapeutinnen und Therapeuten,' in A. Bieler, C. Gerber, S. Petersen and A. Standhartinger (edd.), *Weniger ist mehr. Askese und Religion von der Antike bis zur Gegenwart* (Leipzig 2015) 115–130.

The chapter addresses Philo's account of the Therapeutae as an example of ancient Jewish forms of asceticism. Ascetic practices are known in the ancient world and the Jews are no exception. Fasting women play a role in Jewish Hellenistic literature; examples in Philo can be found among the Essenes and Therapeutae. Standhartinger first summarises *Contempl.* Then, following Taylor's book on the Therapeutae, she argues on the basis of the peculiarity of the account, especially on the female Therapeutae, that they are historical. Philo's account is located in ancient philosophical criticism of excess and represents an attempt at a religious socio-political vision, the union of religion and culture. (JLB)

G. J. Steyn, 'The text form of LXX Genesis 28:12 by Philo of Alexandria and in the Jesus-Logion of John 1:51,' *In die Skriflig* 49.2 (2015) 1–7.

This article is part of a larger project that investigates the text form of the Torah quotations common to the *corpus Philonicum* and that of the New Testament. It focuses on the only Torah quotation that the evangelist John and Philo have in common, that is Gen 28:12, part of Jacob's dream where a ladder is mentioned on which angels were ascending and descending. This verse is quoted by Jesus in his saying to Nathanael in John 1:51. Philo gives a full quotation of this verse in *Somn.* 1.3 with two shorter quotations following in *Somn.* 1.133 and 2.19. It emerges that Philo follows very closely the known LXX version, but there are a few major differences between John's version on the one hand and those of the LXX and Philo on the other. The differences should be ascribed to the editorial hand(s) of the Johannine school, rather than to an alternative LXX text form. (ACG)

A. Ziakas, 'Φίλων και δουλεία,' *Ηθική. Περιοδικό Φιλοσοφίας* 10 (2014) 30–42.

Short discussion of the notion of slavery in Philo, concentrating on the figure of Esau. Philo distinguishes between two forms of slavery: slavery of the soul and bodily slavery. He sees Esau as the prototype of the person who is a slave by nature. What is irrational is by nature a slave. There exists a class of people who are by nature slave and this class has been made by God. Other people are righteous from their birth. The slavery of Esau turns out to be a beneficial slavery. The bad nature of Esau can be corrected by obeying his master. Philo holds the Stoic view that slavery is not a condition of the body but of the soul. (ACG)

A. Ziakas, 'Η στωική θεώρηση της δουλείας από τον Φίλωνα τον Αλεξανδρέα,' *Φιλοσοφεΐν* 11 (2015) 89–98.

Philo's view on slavery has been influenced by Stoic thought. According to the Stoics no one is by nature a slave: the bad person is a slave because he does not have the power to act according to his will. Furthermore, they are of the opinion that all persons are akin to each other. Philo distinguishes two types of slavery: a bodily slavery, when a person has a master, and a slavery with respect to the soul, when a person is enslaved to the passions. Real freedom consists in acting in a rational way and doing nothing contrary to virtue. The wise are few and are characterized as friends of God. The most prominent example is Moses. (ACG)

SUPPLEMENT

A Provisional Bibliography 2017–2019

The user of this supplemental Bibliography of the most recent articles on Philo is reminded that it will doubtless contain inaccuracies and red herrings because it is not in all cases based on autopsy. It is merely meant as a service to the reader. Scholars who are disappointed by omissions or are keen to have their own work on Philo listed are strongly encouraged to contact the Bibliography's compilers (addresses in the section 'Notes on Contributors').

2017

S. A. ADAMS, 'Philo's *Questions* and the Adaptation of the Greek Philosophical Curriculum,' in J. M. ZURAWSKI and G. BOCCACCINI (edd.), *Second Temple Jewish "Paideia" in Context*, Beihefte zur Zeitschrift für die neutestamentliche Wissenschaft 228 (Berlin 2017) 167–184.

T. ALEKNIENÉ, 'Le parent comique du monastère: à propos du *De vita contemplativa* de Philon d'Alexandria,' in A. VAN DEN KERCHOVE and L. G. SOARES SANTOPRETE (edd.), *Gnose et manichéisme. Entre les oasis d'Égypte et la route de la soie: hommage à Jean-Daniel Dubois*, Bibliothèque de l'École des Hautes Études Sciences Religieuses 176 (Turnhout 2017) 647–668.

G. A. ANDERSON and M. BOCKMUEHL (edd.), *Creation ex nihilo: Origins Development, Contemporary Challenges* (Notre Dame, IN 2017).

J. ANNAS, *Virtue and Law in Plato and Beyond* (Oxford 2017).

H. W. ATTRIDGE, 'What's in a name?: Naming the Unnameable in Philo and John,' in J. BADEN, H. NAJMAN and E. TIGCHELAAR (edd.), *Sibyls, Scriptures, and Scrolls. John Collins at Seventy*, Supplements to the Journal for the Study of Judaism 175 (Leiden 2017) 1.85–95.

R. AUVINEN, *Philo and the Valentinians: Protology, Cosmogony, and Anthropology* (diss. University of Helsinki 2017).

M. A. BARBÀRA, 'L'esegesi patristica del 'Vino' del Cantico dei Cantici,' *Augustinianum* 57 (2017) 569–591.

M. BARETTA and F. CALABI, *Filone: Vita di Mosè* (Rimini 2017).

P. C. BEENTJES, 'With All Your Soul Fear the Lord' (Sir. 7:27)": Collected Essays on the Book of Ben Sira II*, Contributions to Biblical Exegesis & Theology 87 (Leuven 2017).

J. BEN-DOV, 'Time and Natural Law in Jewish-Hellenistic Writings,' in J. BEN-DOV and L. DOERING (edd.), *The Construction of Time in Antiquity: Ritual, Art, and Identity* (Cambridge 2017) 9–30.

K. Berthelot, 'Regards juifs alexandrins sur les religions,' *Revue de l'histoire des religions* 234 (2017) 635–660.

G. Boccaccini and J. Zurawski (edd.), *Second Temple Jewish "Paideia" in Context*, Beihefte zur Zeitschrift für die neutestamentliche Wissenschaft 228 (Berlin 2017).

C. Böhm, *Die Rezeption der Psalmen in den Qumranschriften, bei Philo von Alexandrien und im Corpus Paulinum*, Wissenschaftliche Untersuchungen zum Neuen Testament 2.437 (Tübingen 2017).

M. Böhm, 'Zum Glaubensverständnis des Philo von Alexandrien. Weisheitliche Theologie in der 1. Hälfte des 1. Jahrhunderts n. Chr.,' in J. Frey, B. Schliesser and N. Ueberschaer (edd.), *Glaube. Das Verständnis des Glaubens im frühen Christentum und in seiner jüdischen und hellenistisch-römischen Umwelt*, Wissenschaftliche Untersuchungen zum Neuen Testament 373 (Tübingen 2017) 159–181.

A. Botica, 'Windows of the Soul in the Worldview of Philo of Alexandria,' *Perichoresis* 3 (2017) 3–20.

G. Buch-Hansen, 'Beyond the New Perspective: Reclaiming Paul's Anthropology,' *Studia Theologica* 71 (2017) 4–28.

D. K. Burge, *First-Century Guides to Life and Death: Epictetus, Philo and Peter*, Paternoster Biblical Monographs (Milton Keynes 2017).

F. Calabi, 'L'agricoltura divina in Filone di Alessandria e in Numenio,' *Études Platoniciennes (electronic publication)* 13 (2017).

F. Calabi, 'Il bene migliore del bene in Filone di Alessandria,' *Chôra* 15 (2017) 111–126.

F. Calabi, 'L'arte come paradigma ideale in Filone d'Alessandria,' *Materiali di Estetica* 4 (2017) 76–95.

A. Canellis, *Jérôme Préfaces aux livres de la Bible*, Sources Chrétiennes 592 (Paris 2017).

L. Capponi, 'The Common Roots of Egyptians and Jews: Life and Meaning of an Ancient Stereotype,' in L. Arcari (ed.), *Beyond Conflicts. Cultural and Religious Cohabitations in Alexandria and Egypt between the 1st and the 6th Century CE*, Studien und Texte zu Antike und Christentum 103 (Tübingen 2017) 323–338.

P. Church, *Hebrews and the Temple. Attitudes to the Temple in Second Temple Judaism and in Hebrews.*, Novum Testamentum Supplements 171 (Leiden 2017).

J. G. Cook, 'Philo, *Quaestiones et solutiones in Genesin* 4.102 and 1 Cor 10:3,' *Novum Testamentum* 59 (2017) 384–389.

L. Cortest, *Philo's Heirs: Moses Maimonides and Thomas Aquinas* (Boston 2017).

L. DE LUCA, *Il Dio architetto e la Grande Città: il mondo come projetto divino nel De opificio mundi di Filone Alessandrino (Opif. 17–20)* (diss. Università degli studi Roma Tre 2017).

B. DECHARNEUX, 'L'architecture comme paradigme philosophique dans le *De Opificio* de Philon d'Alexandrie (*Opif. 17–22*),' *Diversitate si Identitate Culturala in Europa* 14.2 (2017) 11–26.

B. S. DECHARNEUX, 'Divine Powers in Philo of Alexandria's *De opificio mundi*,' in A. MARMODORO and I.-F. VILTANIOTI (edd.), *Divine Powers in Late Antiquity* (Oxford 2017) 127–139.

J. DECLERCK, 'Le Parisinus gr. 923: un manuscrit destiné à l'empereur Basile Ier (867–886),' *Byzantion: Revue Internationale des Études Byzantines* 87 (2017) 181–206.

P. B. DECOCK, 'Migration as a Basic Image for the Life of Faith: The Letter to the Hebrews, Philo and Origen,' *Neotestamentica* 51 (2017) 129–150.

P. B. DECOCK, 'Studying Physics: Reading Origen and Philo,' *Journal of Early Christian History* 7 (2017) 96–115.

M. DELCOGLIANO, 'Phinehas the Zealot and the Cappadocians: Philo, Origen, and a Family Legacy of Anti-Eunomian Rhetoric,' *Annali di Storia dell'Esegesi* 34 (2017) 107–123.

C. DELGADO, "El texto no se discute, se interpreta'. Hermenéutica en Platón y Filón de Alejandría,' *Anales del Seminario de Historia de la Filosofía (Madrid)* 34 (2017) 49–64.

C. DELGADO, 'El uso de los discursos falsos. Una justificación platónica en Filón de Alejandría (*República 376–414* y *Sobre la inmutabilidad de Dios 51–69*,' *Circe, de clásicos y modernos* 21 (2017) 1–15.

E. DEMEUSE, '*Nostre Philon*: Philo after Trent,' *The Studia Philonica Annual* 29 (2017) 87–109.

J. M. DILLON, *The Platonic Heritage: Further Studies in the History of Platonism and Early Christianity* (London; New York 2017).

L. DOERING, 'Philon im Kontext des palästinischen Judentums,' in M. R. NIEHOFF and R. FELDMEIER (edd.), *Abrahams Aufbruch. Philon von Alexandria, De migratione Abrahami*, SAPERE 30 (Tübingen 2017) 147–166.

P. DRUILLE, 'El enemigo público: causas y consecuencias del uso de la metáfora de la enemistad en los escritos de Demóstenes y de Filón de Alejandría,' in R. MIRANDA (ed.), *Metáfora y episteme: hacia una hermenéutica de las instituciones* (Neuquén 2017) 89–110.

P. DRUILLE, 'La estructura del sistema judicial en la época de Ptolomeo II Filadelfo,' in R. MIRANDA and H. LLEL (edd.), *Actas del I Congreso Internacional. Instituciones e interdisciplina. Alcances jurídicos, económicos y epistemológicos* (Santa Rosa, Argentina 2017) 285–293.

R. FELDMEIER, 'Gotteserkenntnis durch Selbsterkenntnis. Philons *Migratio* in ihrem religionsgeschichtlichen Kontext,' in M. R. NIEHOFF and R. FELDMEIER (edd.), *Abrahams Aufbruch. Philon von Alexandria, De migratione Abrahami,* SAPERE 30 (Tübingen 2017) 187–202.

E. FRIEDHEIM, 'Quelques notes sur la signification historique du silence Philonien à propos de la Bibliothèque d'Alexandrie,' in C. RICO and A. DAN (edd.), *The Library of Alexandria: A Cultural Crossroads of the Ancient World* (Jerusalem 2017) 245–255.

C. J. P. FRIESEN, 'Theatrical Ambivalences in Philo of Alexandria,' *Journal of Ancient Judaism* 8 (2017) 241–256.

C. J. P. FRIESEN, 'Virtue and Vice on Stage: Theatrical Ambivalences in Philo of Alexandria,' *Journal of Ancient Judaism* 8 (2017) 241–256.

M. GOFF and E. WASSERMAN (edd.), *Pedagogy in Ancient Judaism and Early Christianity. Early Judaism and Its Literature*, Early Judaism and Its Literature 41 (Atlanta 2017).

E. S. GRUEN, 'Jewish Literature,' in D. S. RICHTER and W. A. JOHNSON (edd.), *The Oxford Handbook of the Second Sophistic* (Oxford 2017), esp. 640–642.

M. HADAS-LEBEL, 'Juif ou grec?: Le cas Philon et le cas Paul,' *Revue des Études Juives* 176 (2017) 175–187.

J. HEIL, 'Die Konstruktion der hispanischen-jüdischen Geschichte der ersten Jahrhunderte. Ein Versuch,' *Temas Medias (Buenos Aires)* 25 (2017) 39–61.

R. HIRSCH-LUIPOLD, 'Unterwegs zu Weisheit und Heil. Philons Interpretation von Abrahams Auszug als Zeugnis der religiösen Philosophie,' in M. R. NIEHOFF and R. FELDMEIER (edd.), *Abrahams Aufbruch. Philon von Alexandria, De migratione Abrahami,* SAPERE 30 (Tübingen 2017) 167–186.

G. HOLTZ, *Die Nichtigkeit des Menschen und die Übermacht Gottes: Studien zur Gottes- und Selbsterkenntnis bei Paulus, Philo und in der Stoa*, Wissenschaftliche Untersuchungen zum Neuen Testament 377 (Tübingen 2017).

P. W. VAN DER HORST, *150 Book Reviews (Ancient Judaism, Early Christianity, and Hellenism)* (posted online at Academia.edu 2017).

J. JAY, 'Spectacle, Stage-Craft, and the Tragic in Philo's *In Flaccum*: A Literary-Historical Analysis,' *Journal of Ancient Judaism* 8 (2017) 222–240.

O. KAISER, 'Die kosmische Bedeutung des jüdischen Hohenpriesters im Denken Philos von Alexandrien,' in G. G. XERAVITS, J. ZSENGELLÉR and I. BALLA (edd.), *Various Aspects of Worship in Deuterocanonical and Cognate Literature*, Deuterocanonical and Cognate Literature Yearbook 2016/17 (Berlin 2017) 319–339.

O. KAISER, *Studien zu Philo von Alexandrien. Edited by Markus Witte*, Beihefte zur Zeitschrift für die alttestamentliche Wissenschaft 501 (Berlin 2017).

I. Katsos, 'Why Study Philo today?: A Hundred Years of Philonic Scholarship in Retrospect and Prospect,' *Reviews in Religion and Theology* 24 (2017) 6–15.

A. Klostergaard Petersen, 'Dissolving the Philosophy-Religion Dichotomy in the Context of Jewish Paideia: Wisdom of Solomon, 4 Maccabees, and Philo,' in J. M. Zurawski and G. Boccaccini (edd.), *Second Temple Jewish "Paideia" in Context,* Beihefte zur Zeitschrift für die neutestamentliche Wissenschaft 228 (Berlin 2017) 185–204.

J. Kucicki, 'Portraits of Pilate in Jewish Historical Works and Christian Canonical Writings. Part One: Pilate according to Josephus Flavius and Philo,' *Journal of the Nanzan Academic Society Humanities and Natural Sciences* 14 (2017) 91–109.

B. Lang, 'Jesus among the Philosophers: the Cynic Connection Explored and Affirmed, with a Note on Philo's Jewish-Cynic Philosophy,' in A. Klostergaard Petersen and G. H. van Kooten (edd.), *Religio-Philosophical Discourses in the Mediterranean World: From Plato, through Jesus to Late Antiquity,* Ancient Philosophy & Religion 1 (Leiden 2017) 187–218, esp. 212–218.

B. Lang, *Philo von Alexandria: Das Leben des Politikers oder Über Joseph. Eine philosophische Erzählung,* Kleine Bibliothek der antiken jüdischen und christlichen Literatur (Göttingen 2017).

V. Laurand, 'La justice chez Philon d'Alexandrie,' in A.-I. Bouton-Touboulic (ed.), *L'amour de justice, de la Septante à Thomas d'Aquin* (Bordeaux 2017) 37–47.

J. Leonhardt-Balzer, 'Die Funktion des Mahles für die Gemeinschaft bei Philo und Josephus,' in D. Hellholm and D. Sänger (edd.), *The Eucharist – Its Origins and Contexts. Sacred Meal, Communal Meal, Table Fellowship in Late Antiquity, Early Judaism, and Early Christianity,* Wissenschaftliche Untersuchungen zum Neuen Testament 376 (Tübingen 2017) 253–273.

J. Leonhardt-Balzer, 'Mose als Mittler bei Philo von Alexandrien,' in M. Sommer, E. Eynikel, V. Niederhofer and E. Hernitschek (edd.), *Mosebilder: Gedanken zur Rezeption einer literarischen Figur im Frühjudentum, frühen Christentum und der römisch-hellenistischen Literatur,* Wissenschaftliche Untersuchungen zum Neuen Testament 390 (Tübingen 2017) 123–142.

J. Leonhardt-Balzer, 'Diaspora Jewish Attitudes to Metropoleis. Philo and Paul on Balanced Personalities, Split Loyalities, Jerusalem, and Rome,' in S. Walton, P. R. Trebilco and D. W. J. Gill (edd.), *The Urban World and the First Christians* (Grand Rapids 2017) 86–98.

C. Lévy, 'From Cicero to Philo of Alexandria: Ascending and Descending Axes in the Interpretation of Stoicism and Platonism,' in T. Engberg-Pedersen (ed.), *From Stoicism to Platonism: the Development of Philosophy, 100 BCE to 100 CE* (Cambridge 2017) 179–197.

G. Lozza, 'Il sogno secondo Filone di Alessandria,' in E. Baricci (ed.), *Sogno e Surreale nella Letteratura e nelle Arti Ebraiche* (Milan 2017) 117–127.

S. Marculescu, 'Philon, exégète de la Bible,' in L. Mellerin (ed.), *Lectures de la Bible (Ier–XVe siècle)* (Paris 2017) 187–193.

K. Martin Hogan, 'Would Philo have Recognized Qumran Musar as Paideia?,' in M. Goff and E. Wasserman (edd.), *Pedagogy in Ancient Judaism and Early Christianity*. Early Judaism and Its Literature 41 (Atlanta 2017) 81–100.

E. Matusova, '"Seeing" God in Alexandrian Exegesis of the Bible: From Aristobulus to Philo', in E. Dafni (ed.), *Gottsschau—Gotteserkenntnis*, Wissenschaftliche Untersuchungen zum Neuen Testament 387 (Tübingen 2017) 63–86.

A. M. Mazzanti, 'Gli avvenimenti storici come rivelazione: l'incipit della *Legatio ad Caium* di Filone di Alessandria,' *Acta Antiqua Academiae Scientiarum Hungaricae* 56 (2017) 177–190.

A. M. Mazzanti, 'Filone di Alessandria e Giustino: la costituzione umana e il Logos,' *PATH (Rivista semestrale della Pontificia Accademia Teologica, Vatican City)* 16 (2017) 9–33.

O. McFarland, 'Divine Causation and Prepositional Metaphysics in Philo of Alexandria and the Apostle Paul,' in J. R. Dodson and A. W. Pitts (edd.), *Paul and the Greco-Roman Philosophical Tradition*, Library of New Testament Studies 527 (London 2017) 117–133.

F. Mirguet, *An Early History of Compassion in Hellenistic Judaism* (Cambridge 2017), esp. chap. 1.

J. Moreau, 'A Noocentric Exegesis: The Function of Allegory in Philo of Alexandria and Its Hermeneutical Implications,' *The Studia Philonica Annual* 29 (2017) 61–80.

P. Nagel, 'Towards a Better First-Century CE Understanding of the Term "Kyrios": Contributions from Philo and Paul,' *Journal of Early Christian History* 7 (2017) 89–107.

H. Najman, 'Jewish Wisdom in the Hellenistic period: Towards the Study of a Semantic Constellation,' in A. Feldman, M. Cioatà and C. Hempel (edd.), *Is There a Text in this Cave? Studies in the Textuality of the Dead Sea Scrolls in Honour of George J. Brooke*, Studies on the Texts of the Desert of Judah 119 (Leiden 2017) 459–472.

H. Najman, 'Philo's Greek Scriptures and Cultural Symbiosis,' in M. Popović, M. Schoonover and M. Vandenberghe (edd.), *Jewish Cultural*

Encounters in the Ancient Mediterranean and Near Eastern World, Supplements to the Journal for the Study of Judaism 178 (Leiden 2017) 190–200.

H. Najman and B. G. Wright, 'Perfecting Translation: The Greek Scriptures in Philo of Alexandria,' in J. Baden, H. Najman and E. Tigchelaar (edd.), *Sibyls, Scriptures, and Scrolls: John Collins at Seventy,* Supplements to the Journal for the Study of Judaism 175 (Leiden 2017) 897–915.

H.-G. Nesselrath, 'ΠΕΡΙ ΑΠΟΙΚΙΑΣ Text und Übersetzung,' in M. R. Niehoff and R. Feldmeier (edd.), *Abrahams Aufbruch. Philon von Alexandria, De migratione Abrahami,* SAPERE 30 (Tübingen 2017) 28–113.

M. R. Niehoff, 'Ist Philon ein typischer Vertreter des Diasporajudentums?,' in M. R. Niehoff and R. Feldmeier (edd.), *Abrahams Aufbruch. Philon von Alexandria, De migratione Abrahami,* SAPERE 30 (Tübingen 2017) 133–145.

M. R. Niehoff, 'Between Social Context and Individual Ideology: Philo's Changing Views of Women,' in E. M. Schuller and M.-T. Wacker (edd.), *The Bible and Women: An Encyclopedia of Exegesis and Cultural History: Volume 3.1 Early Jewish Writings* (Atlanta 2017) 187–203.

M. R. Niehoff, 'Philon d'Alexandrie à Rome: les conséquences intellectuelles d'un voyage,' *Semitica et Classica: International Journal of Oriental and Mediterranean Studies* 10 (2017) 81–93.

M. R. Niehoff, 'Zwischen gesellschaftlichem Kontext und individueller Ideologie: die Entwicklung des Frauenbildes bei Philo von Alexandria,' in E. Schuller and M.-T. Wacker (edd.), *Frühjüdische Schriften,* Die Bibel und die Frauen 3.1 (Stuttgart 2017) 174–190.

M. R. Niehoff and R. Feldmeier (edd.), *Abrahams Aufbruch. Philon von Alexandria, De migratione Abrahami,* SAPERE 30 (Tübingen 2017)

P. van Nuffelen, '*De migratione Abrahami* und die antike Exilliteratur,' in M. R. Niehoff and R. Feldmeier (edd.), *Abrahams Aufbruch. Philon von Alexandria, De migratione Abrahami,* SAPERE 30 (Tübingen 2017) 203–218.

J. Otto, 'Origen's Criticism of Philo of Alexandria,' *Studia Patristica* 92 (2017) 121–130.

Y. Paz, 'Examining Blemishes: The Μωμοσκόποι and the Jerusalem Temple,' *The Studia Philonica Annual* 29 (2017) 81–86.

S. Pearce, 'The Cleopatras and the Jews,' *Transactions of the Royal Historical Society* 27 (2017) 29–64.

S. Pearce, 'Philo of Alexandria and the LXX,' in A. Salvesen and T. M. Law (edd.), *The Oxford Handbook of the Septuagint* (Oxford 2017) 1–24.

J. D. Penniman, *Raised on Christian Milk: Food and the Formation of the Soul in Early Christianity,* Synkrisis: Comparative Approaches to Early Christianity in Greco-Roman Culture (New Haven 2017), esp. 62–70.

L. Pérez, *La regulación de la sexualidad en Las Leyes Particulares 3 de Filón de Alejandría* (Santa Rosa, Argentina 2017).

L. Pérez, 'El mundo es la gran ciudad: cosmología y política de los estoicos a Filón,' in R. Miranda (ed.), *Metáfora y episteme: hacia una hermenéutica de las instituciones* (Neuquén 2017) 111–135.

L. Pérez, 'El léxico de la sexualidad en Filón de Alejandría: observaciones sobre la traducción,' *Stylos* (2017) 186–197.

L. Pérez, 'Metáforas de la virtud y el vicio en el alma en los textos de Filón,' in R. Miranda and H. Llel (edd.), *Actas del I Congreso Internacional. Instituciones e interdisciplina. Alcances jurídicos, económicos y epistemológicos* (Santa Rosa, Argentina 2017) 272–284.

T. A. Pino, 'An Essence–Energy Distinction in Philo as the Basis for the Language of Deification,' *Journal of Theological Studies* 68 (2017) 551–571.

C. Pisano, 'Moses »Prophet« of God in the Works of Philo, or How to use Otherness to Construct Selfness,' in L. Arcari (ed.), *Beyonds Confllicts. Cultural and Religious Cohabitations in Alexandria and Egypt between the 1st and the 6th Century CE*, Studien und Texte zu Antike und Christentum 103 (Tübingen 2017) 361–375.

H. M. van Praag, *Slecht zicht: een hommage aan de twijfel [Dutch: Poor sight: paying homage to doubt]* (Eindhoven 2017).

T. L. Putthoff, *Ontological Aspects of Early Jewish Anthropology: the Malleable Self and the Presence of God*, The Brill Reference Library of Judaism 53 (Leiden 2017).

I. Ramelli, 'The Mysteries of Scripture: Allegorical Exegesis and the Heritage of Stoicism, Philo, and Pantaenus,' in V. Černušková, J. L. Kovacs and J. Plátová (edd.), *Clement's Biblical Exegesis: Proceedings of the Second Colloquium on Clement of Alexandria (Olomouc, May 29–31, 2014)*, Vigiliae Christianae Supplements 139 (Leiden 2017) 80–110.

J. Riaud, 'Le messianisme de Philon d'Alexandrie,' in D. Hamidovic, X. Leveils and C. Mézange (edd.), *Encyclopédie des messianisme juifs dans l'antiquité*, Biblical Tools and Studies 33 (Leuven 2017) 287–302.

P. van 't Riet, *Philo van Alexandrië: de belangrijkste joodse wijsgeer uit de tijd van Jezus—wegbereider voor het christendom* (Zwolle 2017).

M. Rizzi, 'The Bible in Alexandria: Clement between Philo and Origen,' in V. Černušková, J. L. Kovacs and J. Plátová (edd.), *Clement's Biblical Exegesis: Proceedings of the Second Colloquium on Clement of Alexandria (Olomouc, May 29–31, 2014)*, Supplements to Vigiliae Christianae 139 (Leiden 2017) 111–126.

J. M. Rogers, *Didymus the Blind and the Alexandrian Christian Reception of Philo*, The Studia Philonica Monograph Series 8 (Atlanta 2017).

J. M. ROGERS, 'Origen in the Likeness of Philo: Eusebius of Caesarea's Portrait of the Model Scholar,' *Studies in Christian-Jewish Relations* 12 (2017) 1–13.

G. ROSENBERG, 'Philo of Stockholm. The Unrequited Love of Rabbi Marcus Ehrenpreis,' *European Judaism* 50 (2017) 1–8.

G. ROSKAM, 'Nutritious Milk from Hagar's School: Philo's Reception of Homer,' *The Studia Philonica Annual* 29 (2017) 1–32.

D. ROURE, 'Filón de Alejandría, espíritu y método,' in A. del Agua Pérez (ed.), *Revelación, tradición y escritura: a los cincuenta años de la «Dei Verbum»* (México 2017) 520–538.

J. R. ROYSE, 'The Text of Philo's *De plantatione*,' *The Studia Philonica Annual* 29 (2017) 139–158.

D. T. RUNIA, 'From Stoicism to Platonism: The Difficult Case of Philo's *De Providentia* I,' in T. Engberg-Pedersen (ed.), *From Stoicism to Platonism: the Development of Philosophy, 100 BCE to 100 CE* (Cambridge 2017) 159–178.

D. T. RUNIA, 'Synesius of Cyrene's Homily 1 and the Alexandrian Exegetical Tradition,' in E. MINCHIN and H. JACKSON (edd.), *Text and the Material World: Essays in Honour of Graeme Clarke*, Studies in Mediterranean Archaeology 185 (Uppsala 2017) 329–338.

D. T. RUNIA, 'The Structure of Philo's *De plantatione* and its Place in the Allegorical Commentary,' *The Studia Philonica Annual* 29 (2017) 115–138.

D. T. RUNIA, 'Special Section. Philo's *De plantatione*: Introduction,' *The Studia Philonica Annual* 29 (2017) 111–114.

D. T. RUNIA, M. ALESSO, E. BIRNBAUM, A. C. GELJON, H. M. KEIZER, J. LEONHARDT BALZER, M. R. NIEHOFF, S. J. K. PEARCE, T. SELAND and S. WEISSER, 'Philo of Alexandria: an Annotated Bibliography 2014,' *The Studia Philonica Annual* 29 (2017) 185–243.

D. T. RUNIA and G. E. STERLING (edd.), *The Studia Philonica Annual*, Vol. 29 (Atlanta 2017).

J. R. RUSSELL, 'The Bible and Revolution: Some Observations on Exodus, Psalm 37, Esther, and Philo,' *Judaica Petropolitana* 7 (2017) 109–134.

I. RUTHERFORD, 'Concord and Communitas: Greek Elements in Philo's Account of Jewish Pilgrimage,' in M. R. NIEHOFF (ed.), *Journeys in the Roman East: Imagined and Real*, Culture, Religion, and Politics in the Greco-Roman World 1 (Tübingen 2017) 257–272.

Z. SAGBO, *La providence chez Eusèbe de Césarée: étude analytique et évaluation théologique* (Cesena 2017).

J. SHAW, *Philo of Alexandria and the Cain and Abel narrative: Structure and Typology in Philo's exegesis of Genesis 4.1–8* (MA thesis University of Wales 2017).

K. Silver, *Alexandria and Qumran. Back to the Beginning* (Oxford 2017).

F. Simeoni, *Trascendenza e cambiamento in Filone di Alessandria. La chiave del paradosso* (diss. Padua 2017).

F. Simeoni, 'Au-delà du Changement: l'immuabilité Divine. Le concept de changement et le Dieu immuable dans la pensée de Philon d'Alexandrie,' *Camenulae (Sorbonne)* 18 (2017).

M. Z. Simkovich, *The Making of Jewish Universalism: From Exile to Alexandria* (Lanham, MD 2017).

A. Standhartinger, 'The School of Moses at Table: Sympotic Teaching in Philo's *De vita contemplativa*,' *Lexington Theological Quarterly (Online)* 47 (2017) 67–84.

G. E. Sterling, 'Philo's School: The Social Setting of Ancient Commentaries,' in B. Wyss, R. Hirsch-Luipold and S.-J. Hirschi (edd.), *Sophisten in Hellenismus und Kaiserzeit: Orte, Methoden und Personen der Bildungsvermittlung*, Studien und Texte zu Antike und Christentum 101 (Tübingen 2017) 123–142.

G. E. Sterling, '"The Most Perfect Work": The Role of Matter in Philo of Alexandria,' in G. Roskam and J. Verheyden (edd.), *Light on Creation. Ancient Commentators in Dialogue and Debate on the Origin of the World*, Studies and Texts in Antiquity and Christianity 104 (Tübingen 2017) 243–257.

G. E. Sterling, '"The Most Perfect Work": The Role of Matter in Philo of Alexandria,' in G. A. Anderson and M. Bockmuehl (edd.), *Creation ex nihilo: Origins Development, Contemporary Challenges* (Notre Dame, IN 2017) 99–118.

G. E. Sterling, 'The School of Moses in Alexandria: An Attempt to Reconstruct the School of Philo,' in G. Boccaccini and J. Zurawski (edd.), *Education in the Ancient World*, Beihefte zur Zeitschrift für die neutestamentliche Wissenschaft 228 (Berlin 2017) 141–166.

G. J. Steyn, 'Quotations from Scripture and the Compilation of Hebrews in an Oral World,' *Journal of Early Christian History* 4 (2017) 68–87.

M. E. Stone, *Secret Groups in Judaism* (Oxford 2017), esp. ch. 5.

E. Taub, 'La inacción política como comunidad de saber: una lectura de *La vida contemplativa* de Filón,' *Las Torres de Lucca: Revista Internacional de Filosofía Política* 10 (2017) 215–239.

J. E. Taylor, 'Real Women and Literary Airbrushing: The Women "Therapeutae",' in E. M. Schuller and M.-T. Wacker (edd.), *The Bible and Women: An Encyclopedia of Exegesis and Cultural History: Volume 3.1 Early Jewish Writings* (Atlanta 2017) 205–223.

J. E. TAYLOR, 'Frauen in der Realität und in literarischer Retusche: die Frauen unter den Therapeuten in Philos "De vita contemplativa" und die Identität dieser Gruppe,' in *Frühjüdische Schriften, Die Bibel und die Frauen* 3.1 (Stuttgart 2017) 191–210.

S. WEISSER, 'Knowing God by Analogy: Philo of Alexandria against the Stoic God,' *The Studia Philonica Annual* 29 (2017) 32–60.

F. WILK, '*De migratione Abrahami* als Kontext des Neuen Testaments,' in M. R. NIEHOFF and R. FELDMEIER (edd.), *Abrahams Aufbruch. Philon von Alexandria, De migratione Abrahami*, SAPERE 30 (Tübingen 2017) 219–244.

J. WORTHINGTON, 'Gendered Exegesis of Creation in Philo (*De Opificio Mundi*) and Paul (1 Corinthians),' in J. R. DODSON and A. W. PITTS (edd.), *Paul and the Greco-Roman Philosophical Tradition*, Library of New Testament studies 527 (London 2017) 199–219.

A. WYPADLO, ' Die Basileia Gottes im Opus Philonicum,' *Theologische Revue* 3 (2017) 179–192.

S. YLI-KARJANMAA, 'Philo of Alexandria,' in H. TARRANT, F. RENAUD, D. BALTZLY and D. A. LAYNE (edd.), *Brill's Companion to the Reception of Plato in Antiquity* (Leiden 2017) 116–129.

S. YLI-KARJANMAA, 'The Significance of Reading Philonic Parallels: Examples from the *De plantatione*,' *The Studia Philonica Annual* 29 (2017) 159–184.

J. M. ZURAWSKI, 'Mosaic Torah as Encyclical Paideia: Reading Paul's Allegory of Hagar and Sarah in Light of Philo of Alexandria's,' in M. GOFF and E. WASSERMAN (edd.), *Pedagogy in Ancient Judaism and Early Christianity*, Early Judaism and Its Literature 41 (Atlanta 2017) 283–308.

J. M. ZURAWSKI, 'Mosaic Paideia: The Law of Moses within Philo of Alexandria's Model of Jewish Education,' *Journal for the Study of Judaism* 48 (2017) 480–505.

2018

S. A. ADAMS, 'Movement and Travel in Philo's *Migration of Abraham*: The Adaptation of Genesis and the Introduction of Metaphor,' *The Studia Philonica Annual* 30 (2018) 47–70.

T. ALEKNIENÉ, 'Le *Phédon* de Platon et la notion de mort de l'âme dans l'œuvre de Philon d'Alexandrie ,' *Freiburger Zeitschrift für Philosophie und Theologie* 7 (2018) 25–43.

M. ALESSO, 'Qué es Israel en los textos de Filón,' *Circe de clásicos y modernos* 14 (2018) 15–30.

B. ALEXANDERSON, *Critique de texte et interprétations d'œuvres de Philon d'Alexandrie: De sacrificiis Abelis et Caini (Sacr.), Quod deterius potiori insidiari soleat (Deter.), De posteritate Caini (Poster.)* (Gothenburg 2018).

A. APPELBAUM, 'A Fresh Look at Philo's Family,' *The Studia Philonica Annual* 30 (2018) 93–113.

N. BANNER, *Philosophic Silence and the 'One' in Plotinus* (Cambridge 2018) esp. 119–120, 173–175.

V. BARANOV, 'Classical Philosophy in the Homily on the Transfiguration of the Lord by Andrew of Crete,' *Schole-Filosofskoe Antikovedenie I Klassiches-kaya Traditsiya [Schole-Ancient Philosophy and the Classical Tradition]* 12.2 (2018) 433–443.

B. BEECKMAN, 'Apologetics against the Devaluation of the Mosaic Law in Early Judaism? An Indication of an Anti-Hellenistic Stance in LXX–Proverbs and the Works of Philo of Alexandria,' *Scriptura: Journal for Contextual Hermeneutics in Southern Africa* 117 (2018) 1–10.

D. BOESENBERG, 'Retelling Moses's Killing of the Egyptian: Acts 7 in its Jewish Context,' *Biblical Theology Bulletin* 48.3 (2018) 148–156.

A. BOICHÉ, *L'écriture de l'exégèse dans le* De somniis *de Philon d'Alexandrie* (diss. Sorbonne, Paris 2018).

H. K. BOND, 'Philo of Alexandria and Mark 15:1–15a: Pontius Pilate, a Spineless Governor?,' in B. C. BLACKWELL, J. GOODRICH and J. MASTON (edd.), *Reading Mark in Context: Jesus and Second Temple Judaism* (Grand Rapids, MI 2018).

G. BOYS-STONES, *Platonist Philosophy 80 BC to AD 250: An Introduction and Collection of Sources in Translation,* Cambridge Source Books in Post-Hellenistic Philosophy (Cambridge 2018).

C. BUFFA, 'Le défi de la fraternité dans le "De Josepho" de Philon d'Alexandrie,' in M.-J. THIEL and M. FEIX (edd.), *Le défi de la fraternité. The Challenge of Fraternity. Die Herausforderung der Geschwisterlichkeit,* Theologie Ost-West: Europäische Perspektiven (Zürich 2018) 207–217.

M. C. BUROW, *Colossians, Cosmology and Christ: A Study into Colossians 1:15–17 with Insights from Plato's* Timaeus, *Philo of Alexandria and Middle Plato-nism* (diss. Australian Catholic University 2018).

F. CALABI, 'L'harmonie originaire entre hommes et animaux, sa coupure et sa restauration à la fin des temps chez Philon d'Alexandrie,' in M. CUTINO, I. IRIBARREN and F. VINEL (edd.), *La restauration de la création: Quelle place pour les animaux?,* Vigiliae Christianae Supplements 145 (Leiden 2018) 81 101.

A. CANELLIS, 'La Lettre 64 de Saint Jérôme et le symbolisme des couleurs: les vêtements sacerdotaux d'Exode, 28, 1–43,' *Vigiliae Christianae* 72 (2018) 235–254, esp. 248–254.

R. Carlson, 'Hannah at Pentecost: On Recognizing Spirit Phenomena in Early Jewish Literature,' *Journal of Pentecostal Theology* 27 (2018) 245–258.

D. Christopher, *The Appropriation of Passover in Luke-Acts*, Wissenschaftliche Untersuchungen zum Neuen Testament 2.476 (Tübingen 2018).

M. B. Cover, 'A New Fragment of Philo's *Quaestiones in Exodum* in Origen's Newly Discovered *Homilies on the Psalms*? A Preliminary Note,' *The Studia Philonica Annual* 30 (2018) 15–30.

M. Cutino, 'Les animaux dans le récit du déluge (Gen 6–9) et ses interprétations patristiques,' in M. Cutino, I. Iribarren and F. Vinel (edd.), *La restauration de la création: Quelle place pour les animaux?*, Vigiliae Christianae, Supplements 145 (Leiden 2018) 63–80, esp. 65–71.

P. B. Decock, 'Journeys towards Fullness of Life: A Comparison between Philo and the Apocalypse of John: Different Approaches to the Study of Mystical Texts,' in J. J. Collins, P. G. R. De Villiers and A. Yarbro Collins (edd.), *Apocalypticism and Mysticism in Ancient Judaism and Early Christianity*, Ekstasis. Religious Experience from Antiquity to the Middle Ages 7 (Berlin 2018) 167–186.

P. M. C. Elliott, *Ambrose of Milan and his Use of Philo of Alexandria in His Letters on the Hexaemeron* (diss. Hebrew Union College—Jewish Institute of Religion (Ohio) 2018).

B. Embry, R. Herms, and A. T. Wright, *Early Jewish Literature: an Anthology* 2 vols. (Grand Rapids 2018).

D. Forger, 'Divine embodiment in Philo of Alexandria,' *Journal for the Study of Judaism* 49 (2018) 223–262.

Z. Foroozfar and G. Elmi, 'The Position of the Human in the System of Creation in the Point of View of Philo of Alexandria and Mulla Sadra,' *Comparative Theology* 8.18 (2018) 19–21, 85–96.

S. D. Fraade, 'Early Rabbinic Midrash between Philo and Qumran,' in M. L. Satlow (ed.), *Strength to Strength: Essays in Appreciation of Shaye J. D. Cohen* (Providence R.I. 2018) 281–294.

M. Gargiulo, *The Philonian Exegesis from the Encounter of Culture to the Encounter of Religous Traditions: the Case of the Quaestiones*, Lectures on Philo. Convegno di Studi Rimini-Rome: October 16–18, 2017 (Rimini 2018).

M. Goodman, *A History of Judaism* (Princeton 2018), esp. 171–181.

S. K. Gribetz, 'The Festival of Every Day: Philo and Seneca on Quotidian Time,' *Harvard Theological Review* 111 (2018) 357–381.

E. S. Gruen, 'Philo and Jewish Ethnicity,' in M. L. Satlow (ed.), *Strength to Strength: Essays in Appreciation of Shaye J. D. Cohen* (Providence RI 2018) 179–196.

P. B. Hartog, 'Space and Travel in Philo's *Legatio ad Gaium*,' *The Studia Philonica Annual* 30 (2018) 71–92.

M. HILLAR, 'Philo of Alexandria,' in T. ANGIER, C. MEISTER and C. TALIA-
FERRO (edd.), *The History of Evil in Antiquity 2000 BCE to 450 CE* (London,
New York 2018).

V. JEŽEK, 'Michael Psellos and Philo of Alexandria,' in K BOUDOURIS (ed.),
Proceedings of the XXIII World Congress of Philosophy (Charlottesville VA
2018) 6.11–15.

A. JOOSSE, 'Philo's *De migratione Abrahami*: The Soul's Journey of Self-
Knowledge as Criticism of Stoic *oikeiôsis*,' in C. FERELLA and C. BREYTEN-
BACH (edd.), *Paths of Knowledge. Interconnection(s) between Knowledge and
Journey in the Greco-Roman World*, Berlin Studies of the Ancient World 60
(Berlin 2018) 111–136.

R. L. KORSTANGE, *The Pre-existence of the Human Soul in Philo of Alexandria*
(diss. Hebrew Union College Cincinnati 2018).

E. KOSKENNIEMI, *Greek Writers and Philosophers in Philo and Josephus: A Study
of Their Secular Education and Educational Ideals*, Studies in Philo of Alexandria 9 (Leiden 2019).

N. LACOSTE, *Waters of the Exodus: Jewish Experiences with Water in Ptolemaic
and Roman Egypt*, Supplements to the Journal for the Study of Judaism
190 (Leiden 2018).

R. LAHAM COHEN, 'La literatura rabínica a la luz de Filón de Alejandría,'
Circe, de clásicos y modernos 22 (2018).

P. LAMPE, 'Caesar, Moses and Jesus as 'God', 'godlike' or 'God's Son':
Constructions of Divinity in Paganism, Philo and Christianity in the
Greco-Roman World,' in D. F. TOLMIE and R. VENTER (edd.), *Making
Sense of Jesus*, University of the Free State Theological Explorations
(Bloemfontein 2018) 19–27.

D. LANZINGER, "A Sabbath Rest for the People of God' (Heb 4.9): Hebrews
and Philo on the Seventh Day of Creation,' *New Testament Studies* 64
(2018) 94–107.

J. R. LEVISON, 'Ascent and Inspiration in the Writings of Philo Judaeus,' in
J. J. COLLINS, P. G. R. DE VILLIERS and A. YARBRO Collins (edd.),
Apocalypticism and Mysticism in Ancient Judaism and Early Christianity,
Ekstasis. Religious Experience from Antiquity to the Middle Ages 7
(Berlin 2018) 129–154.

C. LÉVY, 'Philo of Alexandria,' in E. N. ZALTA (ed.), *The Stanford Encyclopedia of Philosophy (Spring 2018 Edition)* (online 2018).

W. LOADER, '"Not as the Gentiles": Sexual Issues at the Interface between
Judaism and Its Greco-Roman World,' *Religions* 9 (2018) 22 p. (online).

L. LUGARESI, *Realtà e metafora dello spettacolo nella riflessione di Filone. Tra
eredità biblica e cultura ellenistica*, Lectures on Philo (Rimini 2018).

E. Matusova, 'The Origins of Translation Theory: The LXX among Jewish Greek Writers,' in M. Meiser, M. Geiger, S. Kreuzer and S. Sigismund (edd.), *Die Septuaginta – Geschichte, Wirkung, Relevanz. The Proceedings of the 6th international conference in Wuppertal (21–24 July 2016)*, Wissenschaftliche Untersuchungen zum Neuen Testament 405 (Tubingen 2018) 557–572.

L. J. Mix, *Life Concepts from Aristotle to Darwin: on Vegetable Souls* (Cham, Switzerland 2018), esp. 79–90.

D. Mrugalski, 'Bóg niezdolny do gniewu. Obrona apathei Boga w teologii aleksandryjskiej: Filon, Klemens i Orygenes [Polish: A god incapable of anger. Defending the apatheia of God in Alexandrian theology: Philo, Clement and Origen],' *Verbum Vitae* 33 (2018) 279–314.

T. Naumann, *Ismael. Israels Selbstwahrnehmung im Kreis der Völker aus der Nachkommenschaft Abrahams*, Wissenschaftliche Monographien zum Alten und Neuen Testament 151 (Göttingen 2018) XIII, 554 S.

N. Naveros Córdova, *Philo of Alexandria's Ethical Discourse: Living in the Power of Piety* (Lanham MD 2018).

M. R. Niehoff, *Philo of Alexandria: an Intellectual Biography*, The Anchor Bible Reference Library (New Haven 2018).

M. R. Niehoff, 'Colonizing and Decolonizing the Creation: A Dispute between Rabbi Hoshaya and Origen,' in M. Blidstein, S. Ruzer and D. S. Ben Ezra (edd.), *Scripture, Sacred Tradition and Strategies of Religious Subversion. Studies in Discourse with the Work of Guy G. Stroumsa* (Tübingen 2018) 113–129.

M. R. Niehoff, 'Philo and Josephus Fashion Themselves as Religious Authors in Rome,' in E.-M. Becker and J. Rüpke (edd.), *Autoren in religiösen literarischen Texten der späthellenistischen und frühkaiserzeitlichen Welt: Zwolf Fallstudien*, Culture, Religion and Politics in the Greco-Roman World 3 (Tübingen 2018) 83–103.

J. Otto, *Philo of Alexandria and the Construction of Jewishness in Early Christian Writings*, Oxford Early Christian Studies (Oxford 2018).

L. Pérez, 'La escatología personal en Filón de Alejandría: inmortalidad y destino del alma,' *Nova Tellus* 36 (2018) 9–38.

J. M. Petitfils, 'A Tale of Two Moseses: Philo's *On the Life of Moses* and Josephus's *Jewish Antiquities* 2–4 in Light of the Roman Discourse of Exemplarity,' in S. R. Johnson, R. R. Dupertuis and C. Shea (edd.), *Reading and Teaching Ancient Fiction: Jewish, Christian, and Greco-Roman Narratives* (Atlanta 2018) 163–164.

P. Richardson, *Temple of the Living God. The Influence of Hellenistic Philosophy on Paul's Figurative Temple Language Applied to Corinthians* (Eugene OR 2018).

T. RODRÍGUEZ HEVIA, *Filón de Alejandría. De Ebrietate: el uso de los tópicos filosóficos griegos* (diss. Universidad San Dámaso, Madrid 2018).

J. R. ROYSE, 'Fragments of Philo of Alexandria Preserved in Pseudo-Eustathius,' *The Studia Philonica Annual* 30 (2018) 1–14.

T. RUDAVSKY, *Jewish Philosophy in the Middle Ages: Science, Rationalism, and Religion*, The Oxford History of Philosophy (Oxford 2018).

D. T. RUNIA, M. ALESSO, E. BIRNBAUM, A. C. GELJON, H. M. KEIZER, J. LEONHARDT BALZER, M. R. NIEHOFF, S. J. K. PEARCE, T. SELAND, and S. WEISSER, 'Philo of Alexandria: an Annotated Bibliography 2015,' *The Studia Philonica Annual* 30 (2018) 115–181.

D. T. RUNIA and G. E. STERLING (edd.), *The Studia Philonica Annual*, Vol. 30 (Atlanta 2018).

H. SCHMID, *Christen und Sethianer: Ein Beitrag zur Discussion um den religionsgeschichtlichen und den kirchengeschichtlichen Begreiff der Gnosis*, Vigiliae Christianae Supplements 143 (Leiden 2018), esp. 151–154.

G. SCHÖLLGEN ET AL. (edd.), *Reallexikon für Antike und Christentum Band 28 Poseidon–Reue* (Stuttgart 2018).

J. G. Mueller, Art. Priester, 112–155, esp. 128–129 (priest); I. Tanaseanu-Döbler, Art. Profanus, 207–231, esp. 225–228 (profane); M. Frenschkowski, Art. Prophet, 274–339, esp. 284–285 (prophet); J. C. Thom, Art. Pythagoras, 496–522, esp. 508 (Pythagoras); C. Ritter, Art. Rachel und Lea, 625–637, esp. 627–628 (Rachel and Lea); M. Wacht, Art. Reichtum, 830–855, esp. 841–842 (wealth).

C. STEAD, 'Logic and the Application of Names to God,' in M. BRUGAROLAS (ed.), *Gregory of Nyssa Contra Eunomium I: An English Translation with Supporting Studies*, Vigiliae Christianae Supplements 148 (Leiden 2018) 341–356, esp. 349–353.

G. E. STERLING, 'The Structure of Philo's Allegorical Commentary,' *Theologische Literaturzeitung* 143 (2018) 1225–1238.

G. E. STERLING, 'Dancing with the Stars: the Ascent of the Mind,' in J. J. COLLINS, P. G. R. DE VILLIERS and A. YARBRO COLLINS (edd.), *Apocalypticism and Mysticism in Ancient Judaism and Early Christianity*, Ekstasis. Religious Experience from Antiquity to the Middle Ages 7 (Berlin 2018) 155–166.

G. E. STERLING, 'Philo of Alexandria's *Life of Moses*: An Introduction to the Exposition of the Law,' *The Studia Philonica Annual* 30 (2018) 31–46.

G. E. STERLING, 'Thunderous Silence: The Omission of the Sinai Pericope in Philo of Alexandria,' *Journal for the Study of Judaism* 49 (2018) 449–474.

G. J. STEYN, 'Psalm quotations by Philo of Alexandria. Some observations,' in *Die Septuaginta – Geschichte, Wirkung, Relevanz. 6. Internationale Fachtagung veranstaltet von Septuaginta Deutsch (LXX.D), Wuppertal 21.–24. Juli 2016*, Wissenschaftliche Untersuchungen zum Neuen Testament 405 (Tübingen 2018) 464–480.

R. Svetlov, and E. Alymova, 'Концепция естественного права: от Платона к Филону [The Concept of Natural Law: from Plato to Philo],' *Schole-Filo-sofskoe Antikovedenie I Klassicheskaya Traditsiya [Schole-Ancient Philosophy and the Classical Tradition]* 12 (2018) 643–658.

J. E. Taylor, 'Scrolls and Hellenistic-Jewish Literature: Philo,' in G. J. Brooke and C. Hempel (edd.), *T&T Clark Companion to the Dead Sea Scrolls* (London 2018) 139–155.

H. Tervanotko and E. Uusimäki, 'Sarah the Princess: Tracing the Hellenistic Afterlife of a Pentateuchal Female Figure,' *Scandinavian Journal of the Old Testament* 32 (2018) 271–290.

T. H. Tobin, 'Philo of Alexandria's Interpretations of the Episode of the Golden Calf,' in E. F. Mason and E. F. Lupieri (edd.), *Golden Calf Traditions in Early Judaism, Christianity, and Islam,* Themes in Biblical Narrative 23 (Leiden 2018) 73–86.

N. Treu, *Das Sprachverständnis des Paulus im Rahmen des antiken Sprachdiskurses,* Neutestamentliche Entwürfe zur Theologie 26 (Tübingen 2018).

E. Uusimäki, 'A Mind in Training: Philo of Alexandria on Jacob's Spiritual Exercises,' *Journal for the Study of the Pseudepigrapha* 27 (2018) 265–288.

K. Vibe, *The Spirit of Faith: A Comparative Study of Philo's and Paul's Reading of the Abraham Story* (diss. Oslo 2018).

J. C. de Vos, 'Murder as Sacrilege: Philo of Alexandria on the Prohibition of Killing [pp.],' in H. Löhr and J. C. de Vos (edd.), *"You shall not kill": the Prohibition of Killing in Ancient Religions and Cultures,* Journal of Ancient Judaism. Supplements 27 (Göttingen 2018) 142–158.

S. Weisser, 'Do We Have to Study the Torah? Philo of Alexandria and the Proofs for the Existence of God,' in M. Blidstein, S. Ruzer and D. S. Ben Ezra (edd.), *Scripture, Sacred Tradition and Strategies of Religious Subversion. Studies in Discourse with the Work of Guy G. Stroumsa* (Tübingen 2018) 65–87.

A. Wypadlo, 'Die philosophisch-allegorische Deutung der Migration Abrahams durch Philo von Alexandrien in De Virtutibus 211–219 und in De Abrahamo 68–88. Migration als monotheistischer Erkenntnisprozess,' in R. von Bendemann and M. Tiwald (edd.), *Migrationsprozesse im ältesten Christentum,* Beiträge zur Wissenschaft vom Alten und Neuen Testament 218 (Stuttgart 2018) 99–121.

N. H. Young, '"The King of the Jews": Jesus before Pilate (John 18:28–19:22),' *Australian Biblical Review* 66 (2018) 31–42.

A. Ziakas, *Η δουλεία στον Φίλωνα τον Αλεξανδρέα [Modern Greek: Slavery in Philo of Alexandria]* (diss. National University of Athens 2018).

2019

F. ALESSE and L. DE LUCA (edd.), *Philo of Alexandria and Greek Myth: Narratives, Allegories, and Arguments*, Studies in Philo of Alexandria 10 (Leiden 2019).

A. C. GELJON and D. T. RUNIA, *Philo On Planting: Introduction, Translation and Commentary*, Philo of Alexandria Commentary Series 5 (Leiden 2019).

J. GLUCKER, 'Hebraica sunt, non leguntur: Some Emendations to Philo by the Late Yehoshua Amir,' *Archiv für die Geschichte der Philosophie* 101 (2019) 135–144.

P. S. HORKY, 'Cosmic Spiritualism among the Stoics, Pythagoreans, Jews and Early Christians,' in P. S. HORKY (ed.) *Cosmos in the Ancient World* (Cambridge 2019) 270–294, esp. 281–286.

M. R. JOHNSON, 'Aristotle on Kosmos and Kosmoi,' in P. HORKY (ed.), *Cosmos in the Ancient World* (Cambridge 2019) 74–107, esp. 83–87.

M. KISTER, 'Son(s) of God: Israel and Christ: A Study of Transformation, Adaptation, and Rivalry,' in G. V. ALLEN, K. AKAGI, P. SLOAN and M. NEVADER (edd.), *Son of God. Divine Sonship in Jewish and Christian Antiquity* (University Park, PA 2019) 188–224.

E. KOSKENNIEMI, *Greek Writers and Philosophers in Philo and Josephus: A Study of Their Secular Education and Educational Ideals*, Studies in Philo of Alexandria 9 (Leiden 2019).

D. LANZINGER (ed.), *Philon von Alexandrien. Das Leben des Weisen/De Abrahamo. Eingeleitet, übersetzt und mit begleitenden Essays versehen*, SAPERE (Tübingen 2019).

G. SCHÖLLGEN ET AL. (edd.), *Reallexikon für Antike und Christentum Lieferungen 226–229* (Stuttgart 2019).

L. Doering, Art. Sabbat, 257–280, esp. 266–267 (Sabbath); A. Felber, Art. Samen, Saat, 475–512, esp. 480–481 (Semen, Seed).

BOOK REVIEW SECTION

GEORGE BOYS-STONES, *Platonist Philosophy 80 BC to AD 250: An Intro-duction and Collection of Sources in Translation.* Cambridge Source Books in Post-Hellenistic Philosophy. Cambridge: Cambridge University Press, 2017. xiv and 648 pages. ISBN 97804521838580 (hardcover); 97805215547390 (paperback). Listed price £142 (hc), £30 (pb).

The young English scholar George Boys-Stones burst onto the academic scene in 2001 with his book *Post-Hellenistic Philosophy*, in which he put forward the hypothesis that the guiding thought of the philosophy of this period was the concept of philosophy as the recovery of ancient wisdom (see the review by John Dillon in this Annual, vol. 14 [2002]: 236–38). Now, nearly two decades later, he takes up this period again and slightly narrows his focus to Platonist philosophy, treating the thought of what is generally known today as "Middle Platonism," a term with which he does not in principle disagree, though not using it in his title. The book has a distinguished Cantabrigian lineage. Its only predecessor in the series Cambridge Source Books in Post-Hellenistic Philosophy was the volume *Peripatetic Philosophy 200 BC to AD 200* with the same subtitle by the late Robert Sharples, published in 2010. That book in turn took its cue from the well-known sourcebook of Anthony Long and David Sedley, *The Hellenistic Philosophers* (1987), which has become the standard work for the study of that period of ancient philosophy.

The present work under review stands in that lineage, but also diverges from its predecessors in a number of respects. Most importantly, whereas the first two for the subjects treated in individual chapters first presented a selection of texts, followed by a commentary, Boys-Stones divides each chapter into *three* parts. First there is a general discussion, untitled as such, which is further divided in sub-topics. This is followed by a section entitled Notes and Further Reading, printed in smaller type and also sub-divided further, in which he presents further comments on ancient authors and texts relevant to the topic, as well as extensive references to and comments on the relevant scholarship. Finally, starting on a new page he presents a section of Texts, in larger type again, up to a maximum of nearly fifty and varying from a few lines to a page or more. This sequence is very delibe-rate. Boys-Stones's primary purpose is to understand Platonism in terms of its philosophical beliefs and their justification, rather than considering it chiefly in terms of its sources in earlier philosophy and in the writings of Plato himself. This means that the background of Platonic exegesis is downplayed. The method of placing his own commentary separate and first is a key technique for achieving his main aim. The starting point is what he calls "the dialectical context," asking "how Platonists in the post-Hellenistic period argued their corner" (p. 5). The texts have been selected in dialogue with the commentary (and often referred to in it) so that each informs the other, but the reader is warned to be on guard, since different texts might have been chosen. Stated somewhat crudely one might say that, in comparison with his predecessors, Boys-Stones's method in handling the textual evidence is more deductive, whereas their approach was more inductive. The notes are very full, providing a remarkable (and refreshingly non-Anglocentric) overview of past and current scholarship. The views of others are stated dispassionately, but the author definitely does not hold back with his own judgments. As a result the book has become rather compendious, more than double the length of that of Sharples. Like its predecessor, it does not publish the Greek and Latin texts on which the translation is based, thus not following the example of Long and Sedley, who published a separate volume with the texts. But Boys-Stones has very usefully made available an online file which contains the original texts using the same pagination as in the published work, which may be found on the book's CUP website (see Resources).

The first chapter treats Plato and the history of philosophy. It well illustrates Boys-Stones's approach. The upshot of Hellenistic philosophy was a stalemate: the argument from disagreement dictated that there was no way to the truth. Platonists came to believe there was a way out, the commitment to a belief in transcendent causes. The ascription to Plato of absolute doctrinal authority should not be regarded as a credo but rather as a working hypothesis. Moreover, Plato was not unique in his systematic exposition of the truth. Earlier generations had also had some success in this quest. *Pace* Sedley, Plato did not just have the authority of the founder of a school. There was something distinctive in the absolute commitment to his texts as infallible reference-points for philosophical questions. His authority was even expressed in religious language, though this did not place it beyond discussion or justification. A series of twelve texts accompany this interpretation, the most important being from a philosopher who was not strictly speaking a Platonist, Numenius.

After a further introductory chapter on "Making sense of the dialogues," there follow seventeen chapters discussing the core doctrines of Platonism during this period. The organisation of these chapters reflects an interpretation of what was most important in the Platonists' thought. Boys-Stones does not follow the conventional division into logic, physic, and ethics. Instead part one is devoted to Cosmology, beginning with the crucial doctrine of the primacy of non-material causes, followed by chapters on matter and the paradigm forms. The key role of the Creator God, endorsed by all Platonists, is next, linked to theories of creation. Important chapters on the World Soul and Individual Souls follow, then a thorough treatment of the scala of Living Beings. Cosmology ends with chapters on Providence and Fate. Part two, entitled Dialectic, examines epistemology, logic (of relatively little interest to Platonists), the categories, and the hierarchy of sciences. Part three on Ethics has chapters on The Goal, including the ideal life, ethical virtue and the management of the passions, and a brief chapter on Politics. A final, slightly anomalous chapter devoted to the System of the Chaldean Oracles rounds off the main body of the book.

No single author or work dominates the selection of texts. At the end of the book there is a valuable catalogue of Platonists, with type in capitals indicating whether one self-identified as a "Platonist philosopher" or not. Alcinous's *Handbook*, Plutarch, and Numenius (though not, as we saw, a Platonist) are prominent. Later Platonists such as Porphyry and Proclus are not included, but the evidence they provide on their predecessors is listed in the Index of Sources and References.

Readers of this Annual will of course be interested to see the place that Philo of Alexandria occupies in the volume. His entry in the catalogue rightly notes a high regard for Plato, but no self-description as a Platonist. It was later Christian writers who described him as "a zealous student of Plato and Pythagoras" (Eusebius). A list of references to him in the Notes and further reading shows that his evidence is briefly discussed in the majority of chapters, which also generally contain one or more brief extracts from his writings. The discussions do not go deep, but when read in their context are consistently well-informed and show sound judgment. Philo's evidence is perhaps most important for chapter ten on Living Beings, and here it is a pity that the recent discussions on reincarnation in Philo were not (or could not be) taken on board.

All in all, this volume represents an impressive contribution. Its distinctive methodology establishes it beside and as a more compact alternative for the massive (and still uncompleted) project of *Der Platonismus in der Antike* of Dörrie–Baltes with its greater attention to the role of Platonic exegesis. I personally found the emphasis on philosophical engagement enlightening and stimulating. Only occasionally does it go too far and introduce an anachronistic note. This occurs particularly in the treatment of soul, when the World Soul is interpreted as a "distributory mechanism"

(p. 213) and the individual soul as "a quality of some body" (p. 254) which necessarily must possess a soul vehicle. The volume is well organised and readers will soon find what they are looking for. All students of ancient Platonism, including Philonists, will be keen to have this volume on their shelves.

David T. Runia
Australian Catholic University
The University of Melbourne, Australia

José Pablo Martín, Pura Nieto Hernández, and Sofía Torallas Tovar, eds., *Filón de Alejandría: Obras Completas*. Volume IV. Madrid: Trotta, 2016. 461 pages. ISBN 9789498796100. Softcover. Listed price 30,00 €.

The collection *Obras Completas de Filón de Alejandría* (*OCFA*) is the result of *Philo Hispanicus*, a research project directed by the late Prof. José Pablo Martín, a renowned member of the National Scientific and Technical Research Council and Professor Emeritus of the National University of General Sarmiento (Argentina). The research project team is composed by members of national and international universities with a prominent academic career, who have been called to translate into Spanish the fifty-one treatises that make up Philo's work. From the eight volumes that make up this collection, volumes 1 and 5 were published in the year 2009, and volumes 2 and 3 were published in the years 2010 and 2012 respectively. In each of these books, the research team offers a direct and literal Spanish translation from the Greek text of Philo's treatises edited by Cohn, Wendland, and Reiter (1896–1915), with introductions that constitute real systematic studies that deal with issues not much explored about Philo's thinking and his relationship with the ancient, late ancient, and medieval culture.

Volume 4 is not an exception. It starts with a general "Presentación" (pp. 6–17) written by José Pablo Martín, who addresses different issues that arise from the complexity of the treatises translated in the book. Two of those issues are: a) the type of material selected for this edition, and b) the differences found between the form and the content of the volume's treatises in comparison with the other collections' texts. Regarding the first issue, *OCFA IV* is made up by six works: *On Dreams* 1–2, *On the Life of Abraham*, *On the Life of Joseph*, *On the Virtues*, and *On Rewards and Punishments*. Based on the editor's criteria, *On Dreams* 1–2 constitute an independent and subordinate series to the Allegorical Commentary as they show a different reading method. They leave aside the *lectio continua* of the previous treatises and follow a thematic arrangement focusing on Genesis's verses that are about Issac's, Jacob's, and Joseph' dreams and the interpretations derived from each of them. The treatises *On the Life of Abraham, On the Life of Joseph, On the Virtues* and *On Rewards and Punishments* belong to the Exposition of the Law, which is a series comprised of ten treatises distributed in four parts: (1) cosmogonical, (2) historical-genealogical, (3) legislative, and (4) ethical-eschatological. *On the Life of Abraham* and *On the Life of Joseph* belong to the historical-genealogical section, while *On the Virtues* and *On Rewards and Punishments* belong to the ethical-eschatological section. The editor justifies the inclusion of the texts from the second and fourth part in volume 4 because of their similarity with the rest of the OCFA's volumes. He upholds that, even though *On the Life of Abraham, On the Life of Joseph, On the Virtues,* and *On Rewards and Punishments* are unequal treatises as regards the treatment of the biblical text, their narrative nature and their thematic content allow for an ethical interpretation that shows commonality between the four treatises.

In relation to the second issue addressed by Martín, the editor does not find any lexical, syntactic or rhetorical differences among the six treatises of this volume and the other printed works. However, based on the works' order and the contextual data recorded, the editor finds differences in the internal development of the narrative works. Philo's change in focus becomes evident in the last treatise of the narrative series. Indeed, *On Rewards and Punishments* contains references to Messianism and eschatology that bring the Alexandrian's thinking closer to that found in the political Judaism of other locales. In the treatises that belong to the cosmogonical and historical-genealogical divisions of the Exposition, as well as the first three treatises of the legislative part, internal data point to a peaceful Alexandria, characterized by its inhabitants' civic and social stability. This is not the case in the last part of the Exposition, written by Philo after the first persecution against the Jews in the year 38 CE. The results of this event decided the future of the Jewish community in the Egyptian city, and made the author deal with new challenges mainly related to the enforcement of the law, whose answer was the grounds of the arguments deployed in the six treatises of volume 4. The first four writings included in this edition, *On Dreams* 1–2 (pp. 21–127) and *On the Life of Abraham* and *On the Life of Joseph* (pp. 131–241), were in the charge of Sofía Torallas Tovar. In her "Introducción" to *On Dreams* 1–2 (pp. 21–29), the editor claims that the series was originally made up by three books, of which the first one has been lost. This treatise would have concentrated on Isaac's dreams (Gen

26:24), while the present *On Dreams* 1 focuses on Jacob's dreams (Gen 28:10–17; 31:11–13) and *On Dreams* 2 on Joseph's (Gen 37:40 and 41).

On Dreams 1–2 make up an independent series close to the Allegorical Commentary. In her introductory studies to *On the Life Abraham* and *On the Life of Joseph* (pp. 131–137; 187–192), Torallas Tovar interprets these works with attention to the distinctive elements in each of them. *On the Life of Abraham* presents the patriarch as seen in Gen 12–19 and 21–24. It combines a literal explanation with an allegorical one and employs an apologetic rhetorical tone. Philo values Abraham as the incarnation of God's law and, in this sense, as the living law or the perfect soul paradigm. To the contrary, *On the Life of Joseph* deals with its protagonist as seen in Gen 37:39–47 and 50, interspersing political-philosophical comments of Greek influence. Respected as a model of judiciousness in the political scene, Philo's Joseph in this treatise is an archetype of a good politician that identifies with the "ideal del monarca helenístico" (p. 190).

The remaining treatises of volume 4, *On the Virtues* and *On Rewards and Punishments* (pp. 245–334; 337–386), were in the charge of Pura Nieto Hernández and José Pablo Martín. In her "Introducción" to *On the Virtues* (pp. 245–262), Nieto Hernández reflects on the bravery, humanity, repentance or conversion, and nobility that Philo adds to a universal apologetic speech. Moreover, the author argues that this treatise's objective is to demonstrate that the Mosaic Law does not only deliver benefits for the Jewish community, but also for all humanity. Based on this line of thought, in the "Introducción" to *On Rewards and Punishments*, José Pablo Martín enquires about the originality of the Exposition's last treatise. Martín notes that the text is distributed in two sections—"premios y castigos" (p. 337), and "bendiciones y maldiciones" (p. 337)—associated with the idea of Israel as the chosen people and with the "mesianismo" issue (pp. 342–344) that characterizes the works of Philo's maturity.

Each of the introductory studies is followed by a translation of its corresponding treatise from the Greek. In all cases, these have been divided in short sections or chapters. The translations as much as the introductions have numerous notes with bibliography and useful explanations for the reader interested in certain topics. The book finishes with a thorough bibliographic section that details "Ediciones, comentarios y traducciones," the "Fuentes clásicas," the "Bibliografía crítica," and a general index preceded by several particular indexes of biblical quotations, Philonic passages, ancient and modern authors, Greek terms, and topics that open up several ways to deal with the reading of this edition.

OCFA IV, like volumes 1, 3 and 5, is of indispensable importance for specialists in Jewish Studies and for those interested not only in ancient and late, but also in medieval culture. The content of the six treatises, as well as the substantive introductions written by team members in this edition, demonstrates the influence of Hellenistic ideas and their adaptation to Jewish framework. Philo redefines the Platonic, Aristotelian, and Stoic legacy and assigns a Jewish value that will be received by the Fathers of the Church as the founding vector of Christian theology. It enlightens the particular circumstances of the Jewish community in Alexandria. This context and the Hellenistic ideas that Philo applies to his biblical reading make his texts fundamental in the evolution of Western thinking.

Paola Druille
Universidad Nacional de La Pampa
Argentina

JANG RYU, *Knowledge of God in Philo of Alexandria*. WUNT 2.405. Tübingen: Mohr Siebeck, 2015. xiv and 311 pages. ISBN 9783161530067. Softcover. Listed price 89,00 €.

A revised version of a 2013 Oxford dissertation supervised by Markus Bockmuehl, this monograph offers a broad survey of Philo's theological epistemology. Most notably, it attempts to identify epistemologies specific to the Allegorical Commentary and the Exposition of the Law. The epistemological roles of divine inspiration and the mysteries are also considered in detail.

Following an introductory review of scholarship, Ryu examines a variety of epistemological themes in the Allegorical Commentary, beginning with the nature and limitations of the human mind, and the overcoming of those epistemic limitations through noetic ascent. His discussion of the divine gifts of sense perception and knowledge contains many helpful insights (pp. 35–41). Notable as well are his identification of four primary limitations of the mind: ontology (i.e., only that which is divine can know the divine); the deceptiveness of the senses, which often calls for their complete excision; and the mind's ignorance, both of itself and of divine causality (pp. 55–57).

Unfortunately this chapter on the Allegorical Commentary also suffers from a number of missteps, mistakes, and misrepresentations: (1) While discussing the Logos Ryu fails to mention the crucial texts, *Leg.* 3.96 and *Her.* 230–231, which establish the Logos as the image of God, and humans as created in the image of the image (pp. 45–46). (2) An excursus on the Therapeutae quickly veers off topic and ignores such important epistemic texts as *Contempl.* 10–14, 27, 66–68, 78, and 89 (pp. 51–55). Of utmost significance in these sections is Philo's depiction of an ascetic mastery of the senses, though one which ironically affirms the senses' teleological role in surmounting the sense-perceptible realm, thereby "seeing the invisible through the visible" (*Contempl*. 78). (3) Ryu's summary of Stoic, Academic, and Platonic epistemologies misrepresents the optimism of the Stoics ("the Stoics defined knowledge in a way that rendered all things as *acataleptic*. Nothing can be apprehended" [p. 58]), fails to situate Platonic episte-mology in metaphysics and ascetic praxis, ignores Middle Platonism, and almost entirely focuses on Academic scepticism (pp. 58–62). (4) A clear appraisal of Philo's philosophical allegiances is never provided. Though on occasion Philo espouses Academic scepticism, as Ryu claims, the epistemo-logies of Plato and the Stoics are more fully integrated into his exegetical program. For example, one of Philo's most interesting epistemological innovations, which Ryu neglects to mention, is his importation of the Stoic "cognitive impression" (καταληπτικὴ φαντασία) into a Platonic epistemo-logical milieus, thereby lending epistemic certainty to noetic perception.

The next chapter treats the epistemology of the Exposition. It is divided into three sections, corresponding to Philo's accounts of creation, the patriarchs, and Moses. In the "creation" section, a discussion of Platonic metaphysics and epistemology is offered at last (pp. 80–83), followed by an idiosyncratic consideration of "Stoic Perspectives on Platonic Views of the Mind" (pp. 84–85), and finally a discussion on Philo's "engagement" with philosophic views, in which Ryu puzzlingly fails to discuss epistemology, and instead focuses on creation *ex nihilo* (pp. 85–86). Stoic and Platonic elements in the accounts of the creation of the "heavenly" and "earthly" humans are noted (pp. 87–97), and depiction of the noetic ascent of *Opif.* 69–71 is subjected to some scrutiny (pp. 97–100). One gets the impression that Ryu's assertion of the primacy of divine agency in this text is based on a selective presentation of the evidence (p. 99). In his consideration of the "patriarchs," Ryu discusses Abraham's *visio Dei* in *Abr*. 107–122, and notes the symbolic triad of "instruction" (Abraham), "nature" (Isaac), and "prac-tice" (Jacob). Unfortunately he overlooks *Praem*. 36–46, a *visio Dei* text in the Exposition that attributes to the "person of practice" (i.e., Jacob) an episte-mic experience that surpasses the one described in *Opif.* 69–71. This account begins with vigorous human striving, but then "suddenly" (ἐξαίφνης) turns, when a divine beam of light illuminates the "noetic realm [κόσμος νοητός] ruled by its charioteer" (*Praem*. 37). The practicer's initial attempt to see the deity is frustrated by overwhelming divine luminosity, just as in *Opif.* 69–71. A refutation of divine impassibility then follows, with the "sincerity" of Jacob's "yearning" eliciting "mercy" (ἐλεέω) from the "Father and Savior," who allows Jacob a "vision of himself, in so far as it is possible" (*Praem*. 39).

The remainder of the text then backpedals from this synergistic epistemology, repeatedly insisting that the *visio Dei* will not admit any human
"cooperation" (συνεργέω, *Praem.* 45). This text, when taken in its entirety
(including the concluding retraction!), perfectly captures the complexities
and ambiguities of Philo's theological epistemology, and it should have
been considered in detail.

The "Moses" section of this chapter begins with a lengthy consideration
of the Law of Nature and the Law of Moses. No reference is made to the
work of Hindy Najman or John W. Martens (pp. 120–29). While discussing
the "true vision" (φαντασίας δ' ἄληθοῦς) of *Spec.* 1.38, Ryu casually observes
that "the faculty of sight must play a pivotal role in one's aspiration to
know God, a point which probably traded on proximate theories of vision
in non-Jewish philosophy" (p. 134). This short remark represents the book's
sole mention of the existence of philosophic/scientific theories of sight. The
integral role of sight and vision to Philo's epistemology and contemplative
praxis is so obvious and well known it can go almost without saying. But
not in a book about epistemology. Equally egregious is Ryu's failure to discuss the "spiritual senses." In particular, the spiritual sense of sight, which
functions as the operative faculty in noetic contemplation, is pervasive in
Philo.

The second half of the book discusses divine inspiration and the
language and imagery of the mysteries. Attending both topics are two
somewhat contradictory depictions of divine inspiration, which Philo holds
in tension: the "divinely-inspired enhancement of human reason," and "the
divinely-inspired eviction of human reason" (p. 151). Ryu's preliminary
treatment of the philosophic appropriation of mystery language might
have offered a slightly more detailed consideration of the topic in Plato.
Three sentences is hardly enough, given its prominence in the dialogues,
and the extent of Plato's influence on Philo. Though Philo is occasionally
critical of the mysteries (cf. *Spec.* 1.319–323), more commonly he uses their
language and imagery to represent the highest epistemological attainments,
even the *visio Dei* (cf. *Sacr.* 60–62; *Contempl.* 11–12). Instead of providing a
useful survey of this important and interesting Philonic theme, Ryu
devotes the bulk of this chapter to a discussion of Protagoras's relativistic
epistemology ("humans are the measure of all things"). He then uncon-
vincingly attempts to read a refutation of that epistemology into two texts
that contain mystery language: *Cher.* 42–52 and *Gig.* 50–55. The final text
considered in this chapter, *Fug.* 80–86, resolutely denies God's involvement
in evil, and then exhorts the "initiates and hierophants of holy mysteries"
to "drive out" those who entertain thoughts "that heaven forbids us to
hear," and speak things "that should never be uttered" (85). Philo thus

short-circuits theodicy, perhaps seeing it as a Protagorean attempt at solving the "mystery" of undeserved suffering.

Chapter five focuses on divine inspiration. This is possibly the best part of the book. It begins with a treatment of the theme in Plato (pp. 180–81), and includes excellent discussions of Philo's autobiographical account of ecstatic states of inspiration in *Migr*. 34–35, as well as the inspiration of the authors of scripture and the translators of the LXX (cf. *Prob*. 80; *Mos*. 2.37). Ryu's claim, that "more often than not," Philo "insists" that "the divinely designated agent of inspiration" is the "divine spirit," is unsubstantiated (p. 186). He appeals to texts that describe God's "breathing upon" (κατά-πνέω, *Plant*. 23), "inspiration" (ἐπιθειάζω, *Sacr*. 10; *Deus* 139), and "indwelling" (ἔνθεος, *Deus* 138), yet only *Gig*. 55 makes a conclusive identification of the divine πνεῦμα as the source of inspiration. The remainder of the chapter is spent demonstrating the innovative thesis that Philo's depictions of inspiration that are based on priestly figures and Exodus feature an enhanced rationality (*Sacr*. 59–62; *Migr*. 84; *Fug*. 90–91), while the patriarchs of Genesis elicit portrayals that emphasize the displacement of human reason, ecstatic inspiration, and even supra-rationality (*Her*. 249–265; *Fug*. 167–168; pp. 193–213). Somewhat puzzling is Ryu's repeated characterization of divine inspiration as a "metaphor" (pp. 6, 21, 177, 184, 213, 216, 222–223, 236). Though surely the language and imagery of the mysteries is metaphorical, the phenomenological detail found in autobiographical texts like *Cher*. 27, *Migr*. 34–35, and *Spec*. 3.1–6, would seem to indicate that Philo considered his own experiences of divine inspiration to be quite real.

Contributions notwithstanding, the effort invested in this dissertation might have borne more fruit if each of the four main chapters had provided an in-depth analysis of a dozen or so significant texts. From those texts some overarching tendencies might have emerged. Instead, Ryu seems to have begun his investigation with an already formed thesis, which then constrained the scope of his inquiry.

Scott D. Mackie
Venice, California

CHRISTIANE BÖHM, *Die Rezeption der Psalmen in den Qumranschriften, bei Philo von Alexandrien und im Corpus Paulinum*. WUNT 2.437. Tübingen: Mohr Siebeck, 2017. xii + 284 pages. ISBN: 9783161546648. Softcover. Listed price 84,00 €.

The present volume—a study of the reception and interpretation of the Psalms in three Jewish corpora from the late Hellenistic and early Roman periods—is a revision of the author's 2015 doctoral dissertation under Prof. Dieter Sänger at the Christian-Albrechts-Universität zu Kiel. As the title indicates, the scope of the project is divided between 11QPsᵃ, Philo's Allegorical Commentary, and the undisputed Pauline epistles. These respective corpora are treated, in titular order, in chapters one, two, and three. The study ends with a short comparative fourth chapter, which reformulates the conclusions of the former three and seeks common ground between these divergent works in an "inner-Jewish discourse" about the Psalms.

Of the three main chapters, the longest (78 pages) is the study of 11QPsᵃ—a noteworthy Qumran psalter manuscript that differs remarkably in order and content from the proto-Masoretic text type. The second longest chapter is the study of the Pauline corpus (72 pages). The chapter on Philo is the shortest of the three, roughly half the length of the former two (41 pages). The conclusion, consisting largely of summaries of the individual sections and some comparative analysis, seems a formality at 16 pages. The study includes an appendix listing textual differences between Pauline quotations from the Psalms and the LXX Göttingen psalter, a bibliography, and three indexes. Each of the three main chapters offers a self-standing study, which can be serviceably consulted independently from the others. In each chapter, Böhm uses the same structure and analytical method. First, a list of all Psalms (in 11QPsᵃ) or Psalms' citations (in Philo and Paul) is presented. Each of these constituent parts or citations then receives a contextualization, from which Böhm extracts evidence of the redactor's or author's "interpretive horizon" (*Deutehorizont*, p. 217) and exegetical concerns. As the author admits, this process is in a certain way awkward, given the generic differences between the Psalms manuscript, on the one hand, and the Philonic commentaries and Pauline letters, on the other.

Despite such difficulties, a clear picture of each author or interpretive community and its concerns emerges from Böhm's study. 11QPsᵃ, in her view, represents a sectarian reworking of the proto-Masoretic psalter to mirror the religious concerns of the Qumran community. First among these changes, according to Böhm, is (1) the "Davidification" (*Davidisierung*) of the psalter (p. 21)—a point that can be seen both in the "Davidic" character of the Psalms clusters that begin and end the manuscript, as well as in the inclusion of the 2 Sam 23:(1–)7 and the "Compositions of David" in column XXVII. This "Davidification" comports with the messianic and eschatological hopes of the Qumran community. Second, Böhm argues that 11QPs[a] evinces (2) a sectarian transformation of the "Pilgrimage Psalter" (*Wallfahrtspsalter*: Ps 121–132, 119), which removes the cultic telos of the proto-Masoretic sequence (Ps 133) and replaces it with the Torah-centric Ps 119. The redactor thus rearranges the psalter to reflect Essene critiques of the Jerusalem temple cult and the community's ersatz pilgrimage *away from* the temple and into the wilderness, in order to study the Law aright.

Philo's Psalms' citations, which Böhm finds almost exclusively in the Allegorical Commentary, are interpreted with a different horizon in view. Philo uses these Psalms to reveal truths about God, his wisdom, and his Logos, on the one hand; and about the human soul, on the other. Such an interpretive horizon is in keeping with Philo's project in this commentary series: the allegory of the soul. In Philo's view, the Psalms derive their authority not primarily from their authorship by David, but by the hymnodist's identity as a follower and companion of Moses. Philo's citations are in general atomistic (3–10 words) and often ignore or subvert the larger context of the Psalms in which they occur.

Paul, by contrast, seems to cite the Psalms in more wholistic ways which recall their original context, worldview, and spirituality. His citations are evoked to support, prove, or illustrate several themes: the Christ proclamation, Paul's theocentric anthropology, the Israel question, and God's action in creation and history. Disappointingly, if honestly, Böhm concludes that each of these three interpretive horizons is so far divergent from the other two as to reveal little commonality. Just how they represent a single, "inner-Jewish discourse" on the Psalms remains unclear (the final paragraph on p. 217 notwithstanding).

Much could be said about each of these three chapters. Keeping the readership of the present Annual in mind, I will focus my specific remarks on the first two, casting an eye on Paul in my assessment of the Philonic chapter. In her first and longest chapter, Böhm does an admirable job in laying out the contents and substructures in 11QPs[a]. Particularly the inclusion of the "Compositions of David" render Böhm's suggestion that this psalter represents an act of Psalms "interpretation" at least plausible. That said, Böhm's starting point—the thesis of Ulrich Dahmen that 11QPs[a] represents an intentional reworking and interpretation of the proto-Masoretic text-type—is an assumed first principle rather than a studied conclusion. Böhm barely mentions Peter Flint's work under Eugene Ulrich, which would suggest a different picture: that 11QPs[a] represents a contemporaneous and independent text-type to the proto-Masoretic version.

Were this the case, Böhm's conclusions about the psalter's sectarian reworking would need to be rethought. Similarly, in her assessment of the Davidic framing of 11QPs^a, Böhm does not conclusively overcome objections (raised by Armin Lange in his review of Dahmen in *ZAW* 117 [2005]: 441) that the fragmentary beginning of 11QPs^a renders such structural assessments hazardous. Many of Böhm's corroborating arguments about the Qumran "community" being reflected in (e.g.) changes from the singular to the plural subject in individual Psalms' verses are too minor to be probative.

Readers of this Annual will be most interested in the second chapter of this study. Its scope and aim naturally recall David T. Runia's 2001 study of the subject, published in these pages (*SPhiloA* 13 [2001]: 102–121), as well as Naomi Cohen's 2007 monograph. A comparison of Böhm's study with Runia's (which Böhm knows) will help to frame the contribution of the work under review. Böhm begins, like Runia, with a comprehensive list and thumbnail analysis of all Philo's citations from the Psalms. Surprisingly, Böhm only lists 18 citations (cf. Runia's 20), omitting, with little to no discussion, Runia's citations A12 (*Her.* 290, LXX Ps 83[84]:11) and A20 (*QG* 4.232 [Latin], LXX Ps 64[65]:2). These omissions have the unfortunate effect of making her study immediately less comprehensive than Runia's. Additionally, Böhm omits all paraphrases of the Psalms, of which Runia finds 10 and suggests that there may be more. This second omission results in a skewing of the Philonic evidence toward the Allegorical Commentary. Böhm's rationale for such an omission—that the allusions lack an explicit citation formula—overlooks the generic difference between the Allegorical Commentary, in which Philo often cites his proofs, and the Exposition of the Law, in which (although still a commentary work) Philo prefers to use paraphrase. In omitting the Exposition and the search for further allusions to the Psalms, Böhm misses an opportunity and ignores an important part of the Philonic evidence. Additionally, Böhm's analysis of Philo's citations of the Psalms could have been pursued with greater attention to commentary patterns. While Böhm often offers an excellent *thematic* contextualization of the citation within the treatise, she does not always offer an *exegetical* contextualization in light of the primary and secondary lemmas. In her treatments of *Migr.* 157, for example, there is no explicit reference to Num 11:4, the secondary biblical lemma, which the two tertiary Psalms serve to amplify (Philo seemingly adduces Psalms as tertiary biblical lemmas in *Fug.* 59 and *Somn.* 2.242–246 as well).

Criticisms aside, Böhm's comparison of these three corpora opens several new avenues for research. Most intriguing, though underexplored, is the contrast between the "Davidification" of the psalter in 11QPs^a and what one might call the "Mosesification" of the psalter in Philo. Second, Böhm's mapping of Philo's use of the Psalms in a Pentateuchal commentary may shed new light on texts like Rom 4, in which Paul concatenates Gen 15:6 with LXX Ps 31. Third, Böhm's study offers some preliminary analysis of Psalms' verses that Philo cites in two different treatises, sometimes with different allegorical significance (LXX Ps 22[23]:1 in *Agr.* 50, 52 and *Mut.* 115; and LXX Ps 36[37]:4 in *Plant.* 39 and *Somn.* 2.242). That these duplicated verses occur first in the Noahic cycle and then are reused in the later treatises of the Abrahamic cycle could offer some clues about Philo's compositional process. For raising these and other important observations, Böhm deserves our thanks.

> Michael B. Cover
> Marquette University
> Milwaukee, Wisconsin

Sean A. Adams and Seth M. Ehorn, Eds., *Composite Citations in Antiquity. Volume One: Jewish, Graeco-Roman, and Early Christian Uses.* LNTS 525. Edinburgh: T&T Clark, 2016. xiv + 242 pages. ISBN 9780567657985. Listed price $117 (hc); $36 (pb).

The work under review is the first of two volumes focusing on the nature of composite citations in ancient world. The second volume, published in 2018, focuses exclusively on the New Testament. The volume under review may thus be considered foundational to the more recent and specific one. Since these are the first works devoted primarily to composite citations in antiquity, the editors provide a helpful working definition: "a text may be considered a composite citation when literary borrowing occurs in a manner that includes two or more passages (from the same or different authors) fused together and conveyed as though they are only one" (p. 4). This definition is sufficiently broad to encapsulate both combined and conflated citations, but sufficiently narrow to distinguish composite citations from a simple chain of quotations.

The editors have structured the volume well. After an introductory chapter that provides helpful definitions and outlines the scope of the work, the first section treats composite citations in the "pagan" (my term) world (chapters 2–4). Chapters 5–8 cover Jewish sources. Finally, chapters 9–10 deal with Christian sources, with a concluding chapter of reflection by Christopher Stanley, whose work inspired the present investigation.

In chapter 2, Sean Adams raises the intriguing possibility that composite citation was an art taught in school, surveying citations of Homer from the Classical period to Late Antiquity. Adams also shows that composite citation could function essentially the same as any quotation (1) to summarize a larger body of text; (2) to enhance the author's argument; and (3) to elevate the style of the author's work. Chapter 3 focuses exclusively on Plutarch, an author known to have read and quoted from a vast body of literature. Ehorn discusses Plutarch's confessed interest in making notebooks from which he could draw excerpted quotations, but in fact finds few composite citations. Chapter four focuses on Cicero, Seneca, and Pliny, and provides a useful survey of their quotation methodologies. However, only one composite citation is located in Cicero, and none in Seneca or Pliny. One wonders why these ancient authors warrant a separate chapter when they yield such little evidence.

The second section treats Jewish authors, beginning with Philo (chapter 5). James Royse notes the editorial challenges inherent in the identification of composite quotations, especially the absence of quotation marks. Next, he highlights the common Philonic practice of ellipsis. Although ellipses technically fall within the scope of the volume's definition of a composite citation, I agree with Royse that they should be treated separately. The intent of ellipsis is not to combine two different texts, but merely to skip unessential information within the same context (this point is not sufficiently appreciated by all the authors in the volume). When thus delimited, Royse notes that "the only sure examples of composite quotations are when the different portions of the quotation (typically the beginning and end) are from fairly distant portions of the biblical text" (81). Royse therefore imposes a stricter definition for a composite quotation than the editors stipulate. Consequently, Royse is able to locate only four composite citations in Philo (in order of treatment, *Sacr.* 87; *Leg.* 3.8, 108; *Mut.* 187). Royse's chapter is a careful, helpful explication of Philo's quotation methodology.

Turning to the Damascus Document, Jonathan Norton discusses the so-called "Admonition" section (cols. I–VIII, XIX–XX). Although he assures the reader there are more, Norton treats only two examples of composite citation (p. 110). He then generally surveys CD's use of Scripture, and promises to do more with composite citations in a later publication (p. 110). This is a confusing promise in light of the volume's stated purpose. The editors co-author chapter 7 on the Septuagint Apocrypha. Although they can locate only four composite citations in this body of literature, Adams and Ehorn offer a useful and thorough discussion of each passage. Chapter 8 is a survey of composite citations in the Pseudepigrapha, but only three examples are discussed. These three are not determined to be rhetorically significant in the contexts of the works in which they occur.

Chapter 9 treats Justin Martyr's composite citations. Here we finally locate an author who makes copious use of composite citations. Philippe Bobichon in fact remarks, "Among the various citations constitutive of these two texts [scil. *1 Apol.* and *Dial.*], many—if not most of them—are composite" (p. 159). This is even more significant when we consider "more than half of the *Dialogue* and approximately one third of the *Apology*" consists of scriptural quotations (p. 161). Justin is the first author in history for whom composite citation is typical of his quotation methodology. Finally, Martin Albl discusses composite citations in light of the early Christian testimonia hypothesis, but in fact identifies only two composite citations. The final chapter is a response by Christopher Stanley, "a retrospect and prospect."

The volume overall is well-edited, but a few errors remain. For example, Ehorn consistently misaccents the term ὑπομνήματα as "ὑπομνημάτα," indicating that the mistake is more than a misstroke. He also refers to "Plato's *Legatio*" (p. 56), instead of "Plato's *Leges.*" There is the occasional grammatical error (e.g., "… presented as if were a continuous piece of text," p. 68), and run-on sentence ("Legal material in the HB is not organized or systematized, however, in the Second Temple period, scribes assumed …," p. 152). On the same page there is also a spelling error of "others" for "other." These, however, are minor defects in what is otherwise a clean, coherent, and well-edited work.

Another point relates to consistency. It appears the editors intend to use the terms "citation" and "quotation" more or less as equivalents, with the understanding that the quotations in question are composite. "Citation" is defined by the editors as including one or more of the four following criteria: "(1) an explicit attribution to an author or speaker; (2) the use of an introductory formula; (3) a noticeable break in syntax between the citation and its new literary context; or, (4) if the citation is well-known in antiquity or cited elsewhere by the same author it can reasonably be considered a citation" (p. 3). However, two chapters (those of Royse and Norton) routinely use the term "composite quotation" in place of "citation." Especially since Royse, for example, seems to employ a more restrictive definition, one wonders whether the terms should be distinguished.

As for the big picture, the volume certainly fills a void in scholarship, and will be responsible for creating another dimension of quotation analysis. However, one wonders why two volumes were deemed necessary for the investigation of composite citations. Five of the nine central chapters in the volume lament the paucity of composite citations in the sources they surveyed (pp. 55, 59, 141, 186). With the exceptions of Adams, who surveys a period of some 700 years, and Bobichon, who covers Justin Martyr, no other contributor considers more than four examples of composite citations, whether in a single author or in an entire literary corpus. Indeed the evidence seems to point to the conclusion that, while composite citation is not unknown in "pagan" and Jewish literature, it does not play a substantial role in anyone's quotation methodology. Given this reality, the work ends up being a survey of ancient quotation methodology, with comparatively brief sections directly treating composite citations.

In addition, one wonders if ancient writers and readers found the *composite* nature of a citation all that significant. Garrick Allen remarks with regard to Jewish pseudepigraphic works, "Overall, at least in these cases, the composite-ness of a quotation does not contribute substantially to its rhetorical effect" (p. 154). This comment, it seems to me, could apply to virtually all the contributions in the volume (with the possible exception of Justin Martyr). There appears to be little interpretative significance in the composite-ness of a citation for most of the ancient authors who receive coverage. Perhaps the New Testament and early Christian literature, however, represent a significant shift in the number and importance of composite citations.

For readers of Philo specifically, Adams and Ehorn teach us an important lesson: the manner of the quotation has potential significance. It is not enough for the interpreter to consider whether a citation is verbatim or an allusion, or whether the quotation represents the LXX, a variant to the LXX, or Philo's own manipulation. We now must consider whether Philo has combined citations, either to harmonize similar verses of Scripture, or to enhance the credibility of his case. We must examine the composite-ness of the citation as a potentially important, if rare, tool in the interpreter's bag. For this reason we should be grateful for the authors calling our attention to the complexity of ancient citation methodology in general, and the composite features of ancient citations in particular.

Justin M. Rogers
Freed-Hardeman University
Henderson, Tennessee

PIETER B. HARTOG, *Pesher and Hypomnema: A Comparison of Two Commentary Traditions from the Hellenistic-Roman Period*. Leiden: Brill, 2017. xv ɪ 356 pages. ISBN 9789004353541. Hardcover. Listed price $152.00.

The present volume, a revised version of the author's KU Leuven doctoral thesis, compares seventeen commentaries (*hypomnemata*) on the *Iliad* written in Greek that reflect Alexandrian philological scholarship with sixteen commentaries (*pesharim*) written in Hebrew dealing with passages from the Hebrew Bible that focus on eschatology. The *hypomnemata* on the *Iliad* were preserved on papyrus in Egypt and date from the early Hellenistic period through the third or fourth century CE. The *pesharim* were found among the Dead Sea Scrolls in the Judean wilderness during the Roman period. They offer serial exegesis of biblical texts (e.g., Habakkuk, Isaiah, Zephaniah, and Psalms) and thus are known as "continuous" *pesharim*. *Pesher and Hypomnema* places these different but roughly contemporaneous commentary traditions into conversation, exploring the origins of biblical commentary writing and the interaction between broader Greek and local Jewish cultures.

The book consists of a substantial Introduction and three main sections that discuss the *pesharim* and *hypomnemata* from different angles. The Introduction orients the reader to the ancient commentaries and describes the conceptual framework underlying the analysis. The *hypomnemata* are first situated briefly within the context of Alexandrian scholarship. Then follows a lengthier discussion of potential contexts for understanding the *pesharim*, including rabbinic and apocalyptic texts, Ancient Near Eastern dream/ omen and textual interpretation, and lastly Alexandrian Greek scholarship, the significance of which is emphasized without denying the possibility of other influences. In describing the relationship between the *pesharim* and Alexandrian scholarship, the concept of "glocalization" is invoked, defined as the "intricate interplay between global and local cultures and traditions" (p. 18), with the global culture in this case being the widespread ethos dominated by Hellenism and the local culture being the Judean Jewish community that produced the *pesharim*. In this framework, Alexandrian Jews are seen as a key channel of thought between Hellenistic culture in Egypt and Jews in Palestine.

The first main section begins with a chapter on the intellectual cultures reflected in the *hypomnemata* and *pesharim*, particularly what these texts might tell us about the activities of scribes, scholars, and teachers in their respective contexts. This is followed by a chapter detailing the physicality of the *hypomnemata* and another on the physicality of the *pesharim*, looking at factors such as the dimensions of the texts, orthography, corrections, use of abbreviations, employment of signs, and sense dividers. Not surprisingly, scribal corrections appear in both sets of commentaries. Special attention is drawn to the use of critical signs in both *hypomnemata* and *pesharim* as evidence of intellectual exchange between the groups behind these texts. It is suggested that by employing signs, the authors of the *pesharim* attempted to evoke the image of Alexandrian scholarship (p. 100). This seems plausible based on the evidence presented; at the same time, it is unclear whether there is any functional similarity between the signs in the *pesharim* and the critical signs in Alexandrian scholarship.

The second main section deals with the basic structure of commentary writing (i.e., base text plus interpretation) as a phenomenon in antiquity and in the two corpora under discussion. After an introduction to the section, two chapters follow on "Structure and Scholarship in the *Hypomnemata*" and "Structure and Interpretation in the *Pesharim*." Issues raised in each chapter include the selection of passages, the explanation of difficult words, paraphrase, references to and quotations from other sources, and the presentation of differing interpretations. Historical contact between the *pesharim* and *hypomnemata* is seen in the very fact of the lemma-comment structure, as well as in shared elements such as the treatment of individual words, paraphrase, formulaic terminology, and the presence of multiple interpretations. Significant differences are also noted, for example: the *hypomnemata* formally introduce not only quotations from Homer and other literary texts but also readings from other manuscripts and opinions of various scholars, which are often presented without final resolution as to the correct interpretation. In the *pesharim*, on the other hand, references to other biblical texts are not typically introduced in a formal way but are woven into the primary explanation, glossography is not primarily a matter of explaining the meanings of words (as in the *hypomnemata*) but of identifying elements in the base text with contemporary events or persons, the only clear technical term is the word פשר, and the only alternative "interpretations" cited are the views of figures such as the "Spouter of the Lie" (e.g., 1QpHab), which are unequivocally rejected. By the end of this section, my sense as a reader was that the differences are greater than the similarities.

I received the same overall impression from the third section, which deals with hermeneutics. The introductory chapter for this section presents a system for categorizing interpretive "resources" that is based on A. Samely's *Rabbinic Interpretation of Scripture in the Mishnah* (Oxford: Oxford University Press, 2002). Categories include "perspectivization" (interpreting the base text in view of the commentator's interests), "analogy" (transferring features between texts based on some commonality), and the broad category "structure" that includes (among other aspects) appeal to or disregard for the co-text, resolving inconsistencies, and attention to word order. After this introduction, the *hypomnemata* and the *pesharim* are each given a chapter-length "hermeneutical profile." These chapters contain a great deal of useful information and many insightful observations. Similarities are noted in a few areas such as analogical reasoning and resources related to individual words. Again, differences seem prominent:

the commentators of the *hypomnemata* see Homer as a self-conscious author, and so they cite parallels from elsewhere in Homer and pay attention to the Homeric co-text. These Greek commentators seek to resolve contradictions in Homer's text, discuss manuscript variations, and exhibit wide ranging interest in Greek culture. As for the *pesharim*, the herme-neutical resources employed and the interpretations produced are quite different, with their eschatological focus, ideological commitments (including to the Teacher of Righteousness), and prophetic-fulfillment application to the present.

Pesher and Hypomnema contributes significantly to our understanding of these individual texts and offers a useful paradigm for thinking about networks of scholarship in antiquity. Although the author strives for balance between presenting similarities and differences, the picture that emerges is one of substantial dissimilarity between the interpretive approaches of the *hypomnemata* and *pesharim*. Given the limited evidence we have for commentary writing in antiquity, the theory is not unreasonable that Alexandrian scholarship served as a model of sorts for the authors of the *pesharim*. But overall, it is essential to recognize how much the authors of the *pesharim* adapted the model of scholarly commentary to fit their specific aims.

Philo's works are invoked as an example of Jewish biblical commentaries written after the *pesharim* that confirm the continuing appeal of commentary writing among Jews (pp. 5, 11). Philo is also mentioned in connection with Hellenized Jews in Egypt who were in a position to bring Classical scholarship to Palestine (pp. 14, 25). In particular, it is observed that Philo appropriated the commentary form and certain scholarly techniques from Alexandrian scholarship while at the same time criticizing those who followed this scholarship too rigidly (pp. 23–24). In an early footnote, Philo is taken to illustrate that we should not draw too sharp a distinction between allegorical and philological interpretation in the Hellenistic context (p. 4). Given the important role ascribed to Hellenistic Judaism in mediating Greek scholarship to Palestine, it is somewhat surprising that Philo's commentaries do not receive more attention in the main body of this book.

On the one hand, the relative lack of attention to Philo is understandable, since *Pesher and Hypomnema* is a focused work that originated as a doctoral thesis. On the other hand, a clearer picture of how classical commentary writing entered the Jewish world could be achieved by widening the scope of inquiry to include Philo, other Hellenistic Jewish sources, and other examples of ancient Greek exegesis, such as Galen's commentaries and the *Mythographus Homericus* (as noted on p. 32). As for the specific scope and aims of the present work, *Pesher and Hypomnema* is a well-executed study that will generously reward any reader with interest in ancient exegesis.

Michael Graves
Wheaton College,
Wheaton, Illinois

MARTIN GOODMAN, *A History of Judaism*. Princeton, NJ: Princeton University Press, 2018. xxix + 623 pages. ISBN 9780691181271. Hardcover. Listed price $40.00.

Martin Goodman, Professor of Jewish Studies at the University of Oxford, has distilled the results of a lifetime's study, teaching, and experience of Judaism into this magnificent volume, which presents the reader with a diachronic account of the religion and practices of Judaism as it developed up to the present day. As he emphasizes in the introduction, a history of Judaism is not a history of the Jews, and so should have religious ideas and practices as its main focus, rather than trace the political and cultural history of their adherents. But the two are necessarily entwined.

Where should one start such a history? With Moses, or with Abraham, or even with Adam? Goodman has a clever solution. He starts with Josephus and presents the earlier history of Judaism through the lens of the Jewish historian's account. Josephus thus dominates the first two parts of the book, which take the story up to the fall of Jerusalem and the beginnings of rabbinic Judaism. Philo of Alexandria, Josephus's senior by about fifty years, is given a more modest role, but one that is not without some importance. In chapter six, entitled "Jewish Doctrine Takes Three Forms," the account that Josephus gives of the three main Jewish αἱρέσεις takes centre stage (with Philo brought in when the Essenes and the Therapeutae are discussed). The following chapter seven is called "The Limits of Variety" and it will come as no surprise that Goodman starts that chapter with Philo's description of the extreme allegorists in *Migr.* 89–92. Further along in this chapter a dozen pages are devoted to Philo.

It is intriguing to observe how one of the leading historians of Second Temple Judaism presents the figure of Philo. The portrait that Goodman gives is generally sympathetic, but with a clear slant. Three times he is emphatically introduced as the "philosopher Philo" (pp. 33, 46, 170), and on one occasion we even read the "Platonizing philosopher Philo" (p. 128). The longer passage devoted to him under the sub-heading "Allegorizers" (pp. 170–181) begins by locating him in his Alexandrian context. It is claimed that "the abstruse philosophy of Plato ... was not popular in the first century CE, and Philo's predilection for his writings was idiosyncratic" (p. 172). This is to minimize the importance and extent of Alexandrian Platonism, but since Philo is a chief witness for the revival of interest in Plato in that city, Goodman could justifiably claim that the argument for such a development is circular. The role of exegesis in Philo's writings is emphasized, but what is distinctive in Philo's case in the context of contemporary Judaism is the role of philosophy, particularly as it comes to the fore in allegorical interpretation. This leads, when combined with the demands of Jewish religion, to contradictions and inconsistencies, for example in the theological doctrine of "extreme transcendentalism" (p. 174) and in the role of the divine Logos. Philo is not "the first or the last Jew to base an idiosyncratic interpretation of the Torah on explicit allegorizing," we read (p. 177), but what is distinctive about him, and very visible in his treatment of the laws, is the emphasis on their rationality and the excellence of their moral implications.

The importance of Philo for Goodman thus lies in the way that he illustrates an extreme variety of ancient Judaism under the strong influence of Hellenism. Given the lack of continuity between Aristobulus in the second century BCE and Philo, he does not think that there is a reason to view them as belonging to a distinctive school, but the popularity of the allegorical mode of exegesis can be deduced from Philo's frequent references to other exegetes. It would appear that Philo's allegorizing writings were largely ignored by his fellow Jews, but this should not be taken to mean that he was a marginal figure, as shown by his immersion in the religious life of the community and, we might add, his foray into politics. Earlier, in his account of the Therapeutae, a note of criticism comes to the fore. "There has ... been," we read (p. 137), "much suspicion that these ascetic philosophers were an invention of Philo," but of the all details in his account there is one that especially inspires confidence, namely the inclusion of women as full members. "Since Philo was elsewhere strikingly antagonistic to women as 'selfish, excessively jealous, skilful in ensuring the morals of a spouse and in seducing him by endless charms,' his particularizing the full role of women among the Therapeutae is unlikely to have come from his imagination, let alone his description of the practicalities in allowing men and women to worship together in chaste fashion" (*Contempl.* 32–33 is then quoted). My aim here is not to defend Philo's views on women, which are often quite indefensible, but to point out that the above argument, though broadly convincing, is not entirely fair. The quoted words are in fact from his account of the Essenes in the *Hypothetica* (11.14). Colson adds a note to his translation in the Loeb Classical Library edition

(9.442): "This diatribe must not, I think, be taken as Philo's definite opinion, but rather as what might be plausibly argued by the Essenes." One could easily argue that something of Philo's biases comes through, but the above attribution leaves out an essential detail.

Philosophically minded Jews return from time to time in the book. References to Philo occur in connection with the Karaite Benjamin b. Moses al-Nahawandi, Maimonides, and Herman Cohen. It is all part of the fascinating sweep of Goodman's narrative. This volume cannot be recommended highly enough as a comprehensive, responsible, and captivating account of a religious tradition that continues to this very day, and no doubt still has a fascinating future ahead of it.

David T. Runia
Australian Catholic University
The University of Melbourne,
Australia

ANDREI A. ORLOV, *Yahoel and Metatron: Aural Apocalypticism and the Origins of Early Jewish Mysticism.* TSAJ 169. Mohr Siebeck: Tübingen, 2017. xii and 238 pages. ISBN 9783161554476. Hardcover. Listed price 114.00€.

Andrei Orlov's volume, *Yahoel and Metatron*, seeks to demonstrate the impact that aural components of apocalyptic experiences had on the development of early Jewish mysticism. The volume is neatly divided into three chapters. First, Orlov reviews the Antecedents and Influences, then one chapter each is dedicated to the study of Yahoel and Metatron respectively. In a succinct introduction, Orlov explains why the study focusses on these two celestial beings. Their enigmatic natures led to much ancient speculation about them, which in turn has led to considerable scholarly attention focusing on the general similarities between them. His goal is to discern

> the differences between the "aural" features of Metatron's profile associated with Yahoel lore and other non-aural aspects of the Metatron lore that might have their roots in the "visual" Enochic mold of Jewish apocalypticism. Proper attention to these different theophanic characteristics, sometimes barely discernable in Metatron's profile, might reveal some distant memories of Yahoel and Enoch as iconic representatives of two distinctive ideologies, one connected with the ideology of the Name and the other with the ideology of the Form. (p. 4)

Orlov begins the first chapter with an examination of aural ideology in the Hebrew Bible beginning with the anthropomorphic character of biblical theophanies, especially in the Priestly source, that were later challenged by the Deuteronomic source that instead "promulgated the anti-corporeal 'aural' ideology" (p. 12). The early polemic between the focus on the form and the Name can be seen as early as texts like Exod 33:17–20. Many post-biblical texts contain references to mediators of the Name, but as Orlov points out, "the earlier existence of such mediatorial developments, in which certain heroes were associated with the divine Name, cannot be ruled out." This leads to a review of those mediators in the subsequent sections with the goal of understanding "the elusive connections between Yahoel's and Metatron's onomatological profiles" (p. 16).

The first mediator figure examined is the Angel of the Lord, who has his roots in Exodus (23:20–22). Orlov points out two key aspects of the portrayal of the Angel of the Lord. First, the Angel of the Lord is perhaps the first and best-known figure to be identified with the Divine Name. The Angel of the Lord is "often considered to be the most prominent individual angel in the Hebrew Bible" who provides "the foundational blueprint for future Jewish and Christian portrayals of the divine Name mediators, including Yahoel and Metatron" (p. 17). Second, the aural aspects of Exod 23 are noted, especially that Moses is to listen to the Angel's "voice." These two aspects are seen in many of the other figures that are examined subsequently.

The two figures examined next, Moses and the high priest, are noteworthy in that they are both human beings who are portrayed as mediators of the divine Name. Moses in particular is central to the Exodus events and the Angel of the Lord traditions. The archangel Michael and a perhaps more unlikely mediator of the Name, Shemihazah, are examined briefly, followed by the enigmatic figure, the Son of Man and another human figure, the patriarch, Jacob. Next, the lesser known figure called Little Yao (as seen in the heterodox Christian text, the *Pistis Sophia*) is examined.

Readers of this Annual will be especially interested in the section that is most directly connected with Philo, "The Logos as the Mediator of the Name." Here, Orlov examines texts like *Agr.* 51 and *Migr.* 174. In these texts, the Logos is identified with the Angel of the Lord, and the imagery suggests the Logos acts as a mediator of the divine Name. Orlov notes that, "these Philonic developments, in which the Logos is closely associated with the divine Name, continue to exercise a formative influence on early Christology" (p. 52) in texts such as John 1. Thus, the impact of Philonic thought on the development of these traditions is significant, and comes at a crucial moment in the development not only of the Jewish traditions, but also in nascent Christian thinking, both the developing orthodoxy and likely heterodox traditions alike.

The final section of the first chapter examines Jesus as the Mediator of the Name. Orlov notes that the scope of the present study "does not allow a full presentation of all available early evidence" about Jesus. Instead, this section is "limited solely to several brief illustrations of each discernable mode of the Name's mediation through the figure of Jesus" with a focus on those that "are particularly relevant for our treatment of Yahoel and Metatron" (pp. 53–54). The modes discussed about Jesus are his personification as the Divine Name, Jesus as the Name that sustains Creation, Jesus as the Angel of the Lord, and Jesus as clothed with the Divine Name.

In a brief summary of the first chapter, Orlov notes the that the imagery of the Angel of the Lord traditions was foundational for many later representations of individuals who mediated the divine Name. In addition, he notes that the imagery related to many of these mediators was of their being "clothed" with or embodying the divine Name. These key observations then set the stage for the close examination of Yahoel and Metatron that follows in the subsequent two chapters.

The examination of Yahoel in chapter two focuses on the *Apocalypse of Abraham*, while the examination of Metatron in chapter three focuses on the presentation of him in the Hekhalot materials (especially *Sefer Hekhalot*). Each chapter contains the same sub-sections: after their respective Roles and Titles are discussed, Philo then considers each respectively as mediators of the Name, as embodiments of the deity, as choirmasters, as revealers of secrets, as Sar Torah, as heavenly high priests, as sustainers of creation, as guide and guardian of the visionary, as liminal figures, as remover of human sins, as finally as "Second Powers." The number of parallels is striking. Orlov notes that his approach, which looks at similarities and differences between the roles and titles of the two figures, is intentional as a means of structuring the comparison (p. 71). Orlov used such a structure in his study of the Enoch-Metatron traditions, and not only did it prove useful, but it also helped to discern "the rabbinic and Hekhalot afterlife of early apocalyptic motifs." While there are few titles in common between the two figures, there are numerous common roles. At the end of chapter two, Orlov concludes that Yahoel "remains a controversial figure, at once affirming the divine presence through mediation of the Tetragrammaton and challenging its overt veneration" (139–40). Contrastingly, in chapter three, Orlov concludes about Metatron that: "The account of Metatron's exaltation and demotion recorded in *Sefer Hekhalot* can be viewed as a monumental landmark in a long-lasting polemical dialogue between the Kavod and the Shem paradigms—a contestation that started many centuries before the Aher story originated in Jewish lore" (p. 203).

The book's conclusion, while seemingly brief, is both succinct in its review of what has been added to the field by this valuable monograph, but is also rich with suggestions of possibilities for further study, and as Orlov concludes, "further explorations of this aural apocalyptic imagery will provide additional insights into the origins of early Jewish mysticism" (p. 210).

In *Yahoel and Metatron*—as with his numerous other scholarly works— Orlov demonstrates his knowledge of ancient Jewish and Christian litera- ture and makes important contributions to the study of both Jewish apocalypticism and Jewish mysticism. In particular, Orlov has argued persuasively that the aural component of Jewish apocalypticism exercised a decisive and formative influence on the development of early Jewish mysticism. In doing so, he has also set the stage for subsequent works that examine the aural component of apocalypticism in other bodies of litera- ture, such as the early Christian and gnostic texts.

Kevin Sullivan
Illinois Wesleyan University
Bloomington, Illinois

GUDRUN HOLTZ, *Die Nichtigkeit des Menschen und die Übermacht Gottes: Studien zur Gottes- und Selbsterkenntnis bei Paulus, Philo und in der Stoa.* WUNT 1.377. Mohr Siebeck: Tübingen, 2017. xiv + 471 pages. ISBN 9783161550089. Hardcover. Listed price 169,00 €.

"Not of human beings, but of God" (Rom. 2:29): this is a principle of Pauline theology, but Philo would have agreed to it as well. Gudrun Holtz, Associate Professor for New Testament at the University of Tübingen, takes this observation as a starting point for a broad examination of this motif. The basic idea of her book is that Paul's criticism of "boasting" (καύχησις) and Philo's conceptualization of "self-love" (φιλαυτία) have a "common core" as both authors emphasize the "nothingness" of human beings com- pared to the supremacy of God. Holtz further suggests that this "common core" should be explained as an indirect influence of Alexandrian tradi- tions on Paul. The author advances her argument in ten chapters, which are subsumed under two parts (except for chapter 1, which presents the outline of the book). Part 1 (chapters 2–5) develops the basic idea of the book by analysing and comparing the relevant passages in Paul's and Philo's writings. Part 2 (chapters 6–10) is devoted to the Stoic philosophy of the self and its possible influence on Paul and Philo.

Holtz starts with an analysis of two key passages, in which Paul discusses the problem of human self-exaltation (chapter 2). The first passage is 1 Cor 1–4, where Paul deals with factions in the Corinthian community. As Holtz demonstrates, the core of Paul's argumentation is that knowledge of God is only possible because God himself reveals this knowledge. Boasting (καυχάομαι), on the other hand, is considered an illegitimate attitude because it amounts to a self-exaltation of the human being against God's wisdom. This idea is further developed in the second passage, 2 Cor 10–13, where Paul distinguishes illegitimate self-aggrandisement from a legitimate form of boasting that highlights one's own weakness and thus one's dependency on the strength (δύναμις) of Christ.

In chapter 3, Holtz turns to Philo. She discusses a wide range of instances in which Philo elaborates on his understanding of φιλαυτία. As she notes, this notion means more than just "self-love" and is thus difficult to translate. Philo's use of the term has some parallels in Plato and Plutarch but is nevertheless unique because he combines the philosophical tradition with biblical anthropology. His understanding of φιλαυτία is closely connected to the way he conceptualizes the knowledge of God. Although Philo acknowledges that there is something like a "natural" theology, he highlights that the ascent of the soul to God is only possible because God provides this possibility as a gift. Human beings are not subjects of knowledge about God, but rather the objects of his revelation. This, in turn, means that thinking oneself to be the subject and trusting too much in one's own reason and senses is, in Philo's eyes, hubris. The biblical archetype of this self-deceiving attitude is Cain (cf. *Det.* 32–34). He is a "self-lover" (φίλαυτος), whereas Abraham is the archetypal God-lover (φιλόθεος) who admits his own nothingness (οὐδένεια; cf. *Her.* 26–30).

In chapter 4, which is partly identical with a previously published article by the author (see Gudrun Holtz, "Von Alexandrien nach Jerusalem: Überlegungen zur Vermittlung philonisch-alexandrinischer Tradition an Paulus," *ZNW* 105 [2014]: 228–263), Holtz raises the question of how the similarity between Paul's understanding of καύχησις and Philo's concept of φιλαυτία can be explained. Both Paul and Philo develop the idea of human nothingness in a similar way, use similar formal structures and terms, and partly draw upon the same traditions. In seeking an explanation for this, Holtz evaluates three models that have been brought forward in previous scholarship: direct dependency, oral tradition, and shared background. Her own reconstruction is a variant of the second model: She considers the Greek-speaking synagogues in Jerusalem the most probable place where Paul came into contact with Philonic thought.

These results may also have consequences for the reconstruction of the origin and context of Paul's doctrine of justification, as Holtz outlines in chapter 5. She argues that the essence of this doctrine is basically identical with the above-mentioned "Pauline-Philonic core": the subject of justification is God whereas human beings are only receivers of his grace. This leads Holtz to conclude that the doctrine of justification, as it is found in Galatians and Romans, is Paul's reinterpretation of a basic conviction that is evidenced already in his first letter (cf. 1 Thess 1:1.6; 2:13).

Chapter 6 lays the groundwork for the second part of book which aims at inscribing the results into the broader horizon of Stoic philosophy. Drawing mostly upon Seneca's and Epictetus's works, Holtz points out that the "care of the self" (cura sui, ἐπιμέλεια αὐτοῦ) plays an important role for both of these thinkers. How this concept is adapted by Philo is the focus of chapter 7, in which Holtz provides an exegesis of *Leg.* 3.1–48. She demonstrates that Philo, on the one hand, makes ample use of the Stoic psychology of the soul, whereas, on the other hand, he strictly refutes its underlying anthropology: It is not the human being that cares for him- or herself, but it is God who cares for the human being. Philo's anthropology, which Holtz paraphrases as "dei cura hominis" (p. 337), is thus meant to be a Scripture-based alternative to the Stoic "cura sui." This difference corresponds to differences in theology, as is set out in chapter 8. Philo's God is much more strictly separated from the sphere of human beings than the God of Seneca and Epictetus. In chapter 9, Holtz once again turns to Paul; she argues that Paul in general participates in the same intellectual discourse of the early Imperial era as Philo, but, in contrast to the latter, he does so without direct reference to Stoic concepts. Chapter 10 summarizes finally the results and concludes with an approval of Gregory Sterling's famous reiteration of Coleridge's statement: "Philo has not been used half enough."

Overall, Holtz carefully guides her readers through a remarkable number of ancient texts and sheds light on their interrelation. Particularly interesting is her suggestion that Jerusalem should be regarded as the point of contact between Philonic and Pauline tradition. Given the fact that there is clear evidence for Greek-speaking synagogues in Jerusalem, among them an "Alexandrian" one (cf. Acts 6:9), it would indeed be surprising if Paul had *not* encountered at least some Alexandrian traditions during his time in Jerusalem. This could serve as a starting point for further research on possible relations between the works of both authors. My main point of criticism concerns Holtz's methodological approach to Philo: she does not follow the current trend in Philonic scholarship that Philo's three commentary series should be considered each in their own right and thus be analysed separately. Although she indicates briefly that she is aware of the fact that the three series might have different contexts and addressees (p. 217), this does not have much impact on her interpretation. Holtz cannot, of course, be blamed for not knowing Maren Niehoff's recent biography on Philo because it appeared after Holtz's book. However, Niehoff had already published her key insights regarding the chronology of Philo's writings and their respective contexts in 2011 (see her monograph *Jewish Exegesis and Homeric Scholarship in Alexandria* (Cambridge: Cambridge University Press, 2011) 133–185, and her article in the present Annual, vol. 23 [2011]: 1–12). Making use of these considerations would have allowed Holtz to enhance her insights through a diachronic perspective and to inquire whether there is a development *within* Philo's thinking (as she does for Paul). One may also ask: If Niehoff is right that Philo's Exposition cannot predate his arrival in Rome in 38 CE, can these later writings still be kept on the list of possible influences on Paul if it is assumed that his encounter with Philonic thought goes back to his pre-Christian phase (i.e. before 33 CE)? This might have been worthy of a methodological discussion. These critical remarks notwithstanding, the book under review is a highly significant contribution to scholarship and will surely inspire further studies on both Paul and Philo.

Daniel Lanzinger
Rheinische Friedrich-Wilhelms-Universität
Bonn, Germany

JENNIFER OTTO, *Philo of Alexandria and the Construction of Jewishness in Early Christian Writings*. Oxford Early Christian Studies. Oxford: Oxford University Press, 2018. xii and 231 pages. ISBN 9780198820727. Hardcover. Listed price: $84.50.

This revised dissertation interestingly examines how Philo was represented by Clement, Origen, and Eusebius. The introduction stresses Philo's representation of Christianity as philosophy from mid-second century.[1] Otto expresses doubts that some of Philo's Jewish successors became followers of Jesus and shared his writings with Christians; as an alternative to the presence of Philo's works in the "Catechetical school," she suggests the transmission of Philo's oeuvre in the philosophical schools which dissemi-

---

[1] See "Ethos and Logos," *VC* 69.2 (2015): 123–56.

nated the Pythagorean-Platonic corpus to early Christians (p. 26).[2] Both ways of transmission, I find, may have coexisted together. That Philo was transmitted within philosophical circles is consistent with Otto's observations on Ammonius, Origen's and Plotinus's master, who taught philosophically advanced Christians and Hellenes.

Turning to chapter one: I agree with Otto's suggestion that Ammonius disproves that "Platonic philosophers and Christian theologians would not interact with each others' circles" (p. 45).[3] A systematic comparison between Origen and Plotinus and a project on the interactions between "pagan" philosophical and patristic notions of apokatastasis will further this investigation. Otto points to philosophers interested in "barbarian philosophy" (pp. 46–47): I would include "paga"' (Pythagoraean-) Platonists Numenius and Amelius, the latter commenting on John's Prologue, arguably with Origen's _Commentary_ in mind.[4] Philo, indeed, influenced Patristic philosophers-exegetes more than patristic authors generally.[5]

In chapter two, on Clement's writings, Otto examines "Israel" (Christians pursuing the knowledge of God), _Hebraioi_ (historical), and _Ioudaioi_ (recent and contemporary Jews, including Philo). She discusses the studies of van den Hoek and Runia about Clement on Philo and my article in this Annual, "Rome-Alexandria Connection" (_SPhiloA_ 23 [2011]: 69–95). Philo's biblical exegesis is, for Otto, "Pythagorean" (p. 63). This concurs with what I discovered about Clement, Origen, and Nyssen (_SPhiloA_ 20 [2008]: 55–99): Philo's theological themes passed on to patristic authors through his exegesis. Otto emphasises the notion of the Logos in Clement, which I have extensively analyzed.[6] Clement called Philo, like Numenius, "the Pythago-

---

[2] My words "the link between Philo and the early Christian community of Alexandria, although historically unfounded, reflects however the probable Jewish roots of Alexandrian Christianity, before the transformation that occurred at the beginning of the second century" (_SPhiloA_ 23 [2011]: 78–79) are misinterpreted: I was speaking of Eusebius's reading of Philo's _Contempl._ as a (pretended) document of Alexandrian Christianity, not suggesting that Philo's writings were exclusively transmitted by Jewish-Christians.

[3] See also Ramelli, "Origen, Patristic Philosophy, and Christian Platonism," _VC_ 63 (2009): 217–63; "Origen and the Platonic Tradition," _Religions_ 8.2 (2017): 1–20; "Origen, Greek Philosophy, and the Trinitarian Meaning of Hypostasis," _HTR_ 105 (2012): 302–50; _The Christian Doctrine of Apokatastasis_ (Leiden: Brill, 2013); "Proclus and Apokatastasis," in _Proclus and His Legacy_ (Berlin: de Gruyter, 2017), 95–122.

[4] Ramelli "'Revelation' for Christians and 'Pagans' and their Philosophical Allegoresis," lecture at the conference _Ancient Revelation_, Durham University, 25–27 June 2019, forthcoming.

[5] Ramelli, "Philo as One of the Main Inspirers of Early Christian Hermeneutics and Apophatic Theology," _Adamantius_ 24 (2018): 276–92.

[6] Ramelli, "The Logos/Nous One-Many between 'Pagan' and Christian Platonism," StPatr (forthcoming).

rean" because Pythagoreanism was a venerable Greek tradition dependent on Jewish wisdom, and upheld the same secrecy Philo found in Scripture (p. 87). I find the same parallel in Origen: both Plato and Scripture used myths and enigmata and require allegoresis to reveal the truth to the worthy alone.[7]

Otto deems *Congr.* 78–80 the source of *Strom.* 1.5.30. Origen's Letter to Gregory/Theodore (*Philoc.* 13), I think, was also inspired by *Congr.* 78–80 and should be read in that light. Otto rightly notes that, while Philo rejected Egyptian animal worship, Clement allegorized it (p. 77). Indeed, as I have argued elsewhere, Clement relied on Chaeremon's allegorization of Egyptian mythology (and hieroglyphics), known to Origen. Otto receives Tzvetkova-Glaser's thesis that Christian exegesis sometimes influenced Rabbinic exegesis (p. 100); I concur, and have added further examples (*BMCR* 2011).

Clement's declaration that "there is no *gnōsis* without *pistis*: *pistis* is the ground of truth" (*Strom.* 2.6.31.3 [78]) makes the same point as Bardaisan, possibly a teacher of Clement: faith grounds knowledge (Ramelli, *BLC* 3). Otto rightly deems the Therapeutae in *Contempl.* assimilated to Pythagoreans (p. 88). I furthered this view in *Social Justice and the Legitimacy of Slavery* (Oxford: Oxord University Press, 2016, Introduction; Ch. 1): the Therapeutae were concerned with justice owing to purity laws, but Philo attaches philosophical ideas to their notion of justice. This proved influential on the link between social justice and philosophical asceticism, for which I argue there.

In chapter three, Otto argues that Origen took from Philo the meaning of "Israel" as "seeing God" (p. 113). His conviction, in the *Commentary on Romans*, in my estimation is that the totality of the nations/"pagans" and Israel will eventually be saved. The main target of Origen was Christians observing Jewish practices. Otto is correct that Celsus was a Middle Platonist (p. 104): Origen called him "Epicurean," I suspect, being easier for him to refute an Epicurean than a Platonist (as I argued in *JTS* 68.1 [2017]: 348–50).

Origen often refers to Philo as a predecessor, τις τῶν πρὸ ἡμῶν; Otto agrees citing my "Philo as Origen's Model" (pp. 115–27). Nyssen uses this expression in a passage against preexistence and metensomatosis, generally taken to refer to Origen, but likely targeting others (probably "pagan"

---

[7] See Ramelli, "The Philosophical Stance of Allegory in Stoicism and its Reception in Platonism," *IJCT* 18 (2011): 335–71.

Neoplatonists and/or Manichaeans).[8] Otto is correct that "predecessor" is not necessarily an endorsement of Philo (p. 128); indeed, I observe that Nyssen used this expression to *criticize* those who supported metensomatosis, which he rejected. But Origen was adopting Philo's allegoresis: he disliked that Philo was no Christian, but adopted the hermeneutics of an authoritative antecedent in biblical philosophical (Platonizing) allegoresis.

Origen overtly claimed Philo and Aristobulus as predecessors.[9] Philo's influence on Origen's exegesis is structural but also extends to exegetical details.[10] Origen's explicit appeals to Philo always occur in connection with fundamental exegetical strategies, conveying theological truths.[11] Otto deems such appeals an effort to define the continuities and distinctiveness of Christianity vs. Judaism. This is a component of Origen's references to Philo, but does not obliterate the value of Origen's appeals to Philo as an authoritative antecedent—explicitly in *Contra Celsum*, and significantly, appearing in connection with fundamental exegetical strategies, which Origen appropriated and come from Philo. This is confirmed by the attempt, by "pagan" Platonists (Celsus, Porphyry), to sever Origen's allegoresis of Scripture from its Jewish antecedents and connect it exclusively to Stoic allegoresis. Origen's appeal to Philo as antecedent should be inscribed within his anti-Marcionite polemic. Marcionites rejected the Jewish heritage; Origen appealed to it, but in its philosophico-allegorical strand, as a basis for his allegoresis and theology.

Allegoresis allowed Philo to interpret Scripture in light of Platonism, Stoicism (although Philo discarded Stoic immanentism), and Pythagoreanism. These are the same philosophical strands (in addition to Aristotelian concepts) in light of which Origen read Scripture. Philo found in Scripture the Platonic doctrine of the Ideas (Exod 33:18 [*Spec.* 1.41.45–48]; Exod 25:40 [*QE* 2.82; Mos. 2.74–76]). Both Philo and Origen—mostly interested in Philo's Platonizing Allegorical Commentary—interpreted Scripture allegorico-philosophically, but rejected a sheer allegorization of Scripture (dismissing the literal level), practiced by pre-Philonic Jewish, "gnostic," Stoic, and "pagan" Middle/Neoplatonic allegorizers.

---

[8] Ramelli, "Gregory of Nyssa," in *A History of Mind and Body in Late Antiquity* (Cambridge: Cambridge University Press, 2018), 283–305.

[9] Ramelli, "Philo as Origen's Declared Model," *SCJR* 7 (2012): 1–17. For a catalogue of Origen's *loci* depending on Philo, see Annewies van den Hoek, "Philo and Origen," *SPhiloA* 12 (2000): 44–121.

[10] Case studies in "Philosophical Allegoresis"; "Inspirers"; "Philo and Paul on Soteriology and Eschatology," forthcoming.

[11] Ramelli, "Allegoresis of Scripture in Philo," not cited by Otto.

Unlike Clement, Origen prefers Paul's interpretation of Gal 5 on Sarah and Hagar to Philo's (p. 119),[12] and was selective in the use of Philo's exegesis (p. 134). Likewise, Nyssen often preferred Origen's interpretation to Philo's, but through Philo's exegesis, important theological aspects are conveyed. Therefore, it should be noted that Origen did not deem Philo's allegoresis innovative or especially authoritative (p. 198).

In the fourth chapter, Otto rightly argues that Eusebius's familiarity with Porphyry's oeuvre indicates that the exchange of ideas between the successors of Origen and Plotinus continued for a long time (p. 143). After an examination of Eusebius's use of *Hebraioi, Ioudaioi,* and *Christianoi,* Otto analyses Eusebius's Christian representation of Philo—an "honorary" Christian (Runia). Indeed, he was called "bishop" in a Byzantine *catena* and his writings were held in Roman libraries in the early Imperial age (*HE* 2.18.8). Eusebius's description of Philo as a witness to the sufferings of the Jews after the Crucifixion (p. 181) echoes Origen and, I would add, the Slavonic *Bellum Iudaicum.* According to Eusebius, Philo, speaking of the Therapeutae in *Contempl.,* meant early Christians (pp. 187–88): this has interesting social and gender implications and significance for the Rome-Alexandria connection.[13] Otto rightly concludes that Eusebius selectively approved Philo, to present the Christians as heirs of the Hebrew scriptures, by which Plato was inspired (p. 195). Clement, Origen, and Eusebius will feature, with others, in the *Oxford Handbook to the Reception of Philo,* which will surely offer new elements of reflection.

Ilaria L. E. Ramelli
Catholic University of the Sacred Heart
Milan, Italy

[12] See my "The Role of Allegory, Allegoresis, and Metaphor in Paul and Origen," *JGRChJ* 14 (2018) 130–57.
[13] See Ramelli, *Justice* and Ramelli, "Rome-Alexandria Connection."

The Studia Philonica Annual 31 (2019): 330–335

NEWS AND NOTES

Conference in Lyon, France on the Reception of Philo in Early Modern Europe

A ground-breaking conference on "Philo of Alexandria in Early Modern Europe, from the Renaissance to the Enlightenment (16th–18th Centuries): Reception and Appropriation of a Judeo-Hellenistic Corpus," was held in Lyon, France on 7–9 November 2018. It was organised by Professors Fréderic Gabriel and Smaranda Marcelscu of the Institute of the History of Representation and Ideas in the Modern Era (IHRIM) of the École Normale Supérieure (ENS), located in Lyon. At the conference two lines of research were pursued: the first approach involved philology and the history of the book; the second sought to explore the various uses of the Philonic corpus in exegetical and theological treatises, as well as in historical scholarship and controversies. The conference allowed two groups of scholars, Philonists and experts on early modern history of ideas, to engage with each other in a most fruitful dialogue, touching on areas that have hitherto remained almost totally unexplored. The conference also included excursions to the Municipal Library of Lyon and the Institut des Sources Chrétiennes, both of which possess many copies of works by and on Philo published in the 16th to 18th century. Scholars who gave papers were, apart from the convenors: Gregory Sterling (Yale University, USA), Michael Cover (Marquette University, USA), Marie-Luce Demonet (Tours), Luigi-Alberto Sanchi (Paris), Lucia Maddalena Tissi (Paris), Claudio Moreschini (Pisa), François Roudaut (Montpellier), Thomas Leinkauf (Münster), Nicholas Hardy (Birmingham), Scott Mandelbrote (Cambridge, UK), Brigitte Tambrun (Paris), Gianni Paganini (Vercelli, Italy), Matthieu Somon (Louvain), Joanna Weinberg (Oxford), Myriam Silvera (Rome), Pierre-François Moreau (Lyon), Giovanni Benedetto (Milan), David Runia (Melbourne), Martine Pécherman (Paris), Marco Rizzi (Milan), Jérémy Delmulle (Paris).

The convenors plan to publish the papers of the conference in the series Études Augustiniennes (Brepols).

The editors

The Philo of Alexandria Group of the Society for Biblical Literature

At the Society of Biblical Literature 2018 Annual Meeting in Denver, Colorado (November 17–20), the Philo of Alexandria Seminar held three sessions. The first, presided over by Ronald Cox (Pepperdine University), was an open session that included the following speakers and presentations: Courtney Friesen (University of Arizona), "Philo of Alexandria and the Masks of Heracles"; Tyler A. Stewart (Lincoln Christian University), "The Origin of Evil and Subordinate Creators: Philo's Exegesis of Gen 1:26 in Context"; Richard A. Zaleski (University of Chicago), "Philo's Double Paraphrase of the Parting of the Red Sea in *Mos.* 1.175–179 and 2.250–255"; and John Sehorn (Augustine Institute), "Philo and Origen on Moses as Prophet." Luiz Felipe Ribeiro (University of Toronto), who was scheduled to speak on "Pederast Playthings and Androgynous Souls: Philo Judaeus' Polemic against Socratic Pedagogic Pederasty in the *Symposium* (*Vit. Cont.* 57–64)," was unfortunately unable to attend.

The second session, composed of invited speakers who have completed commentaries for the Philo of Alexandria Commentary Series (PACS), was devoted to the theme, "Reflections on Writing a Commentary." Presided over by Gregory Sterling (Yale Divinity School), General Editor of the series, the session included the following speakers and topics: Ellen Birnbaum (Cambridge, MA), "Some Things I Learned from Co-writing a Commentary on Philo's *De Abrahamo*"; David Runia (University of Melbourne), "Writing Commentaries on Philo's Allegorical Treatises"; and Joan Taylor (King's College-London), "Writing a Commentary on *De Vita Contemplativa*." John Dillon (Trinity College Dublin) was unfortunately unable to attend, but he submitted a paper entitled "Philo as Rhetorician: Diatribe Moments in the *De Abrahamo*," which was read by Ronald Cox (Pepperdine University).

The third session was devoted to Philo's *On the Sacrifices of Cain and Abel*, a treatise being prepared for PACS by Justin Rogers (Freed-Hardeman University), who presented a sample of his commentary. Other speakers and their topics included James R. Royse (Claremont, CA), "New and Neglected Readings from *De sacrificiis* and Other Works of Philo"; and Scott Mackie (Chapman University), "'God Has Had Mercy on Me': Theology and Soteriology in *De sacrificiis Abelis et Caini*." Torrey Seland from Norway was scheduled to preside over this session but was regrettably not able to attend, and Ronald Cox (Pepperdine University) presided in his stead. The session concluded with a business meeting.

Each session provided ample time for discussion. On Monday evening, November 19, members and friends of the Philo Seminar extended their collegial fellowship over dinner at a nearby restaurant.

Anyone wishing to read the papers from the first and third sessions can find them online at http://torreys.org/philo_seminar_papers/, a website graciously hosted by Torrey Seland.

Ellen Birnbaum
Cambridge, MA

Conference in Münster, Germany on Philo of Alexandria
and Philosophical Discourse

"Philo of Alexandria and Philosophical Discourse," an international conference on Philo's debt to and appropriation of Hellenistic and Roman schools of philosophy, took place on 12–13 May 2019 at the Westfälische Wilhelms-Universität in Münster. The conference, organized jointly by A/Prof. Dr. Michael Cover (Humboldt Fellow, WWU Münster/ Marquette University) and Prof. Dr. Lutz Doering (WWU Münster), included international experts on Philo and ancient philosophy from three continents and eight different countries. The conference, planned in connection with Prof. Cover's Humboldt Fellowship and supported primarily by funds from the Alexander von Humboldt Stiftung in Bonn, had the dual aim of advancing Cover's Humboldt project and providing the groundwork for a larger *Sammelband*, including an even wider range of scholarly contributions.

The first day of the conference, held at the Evangelisch-Theologische Fakultät at the WWU Münster, consisted of two sessions. Papers in session one aimed to locate Philo within his larger scholarly and religious landscape: Gregory Sterling (Yale University), "Philo's Library and the Libraries of Philosophical Schools; Rainer Hirsch-Luipold (Universität Bern), "The Difficulty of Being Theologically and Philosophically Orthodox: Reincarnation and Afterlife as a Test Case." Session two moved from more general considerations to the focus on a single Philonic treatise, *Quod omnis probus liber sit*: Maren Niehoff (The Hebrew University), "Exemplary Ethics in Philo's *Every Good Man Is Free*"; Troels-Engberg Pedersen (University of Copenhagen; "Stoicism, Platonism and Judaism in the *Omnis Probus*: Philo's Authorial Stance").

The second day of the conference began with a third session, which likewise broke new ground in the field of Philo and ancient philosophical scepticism: Carlos Lévy (Paris-Sorbonne), a recent fellow of the Maimonides Centre for Advanced Studies at the Universität Hamburg, "Is Philo's Moses a Pyrrhonian Hero?"; Mauro Bonazzi (University of Utrecht), "Scepticism and Contemplation in Philo of Alexandria." The final session was devoted to a single paper, Michael Cover (Marquette University) presenting on Philo's philosophy of language, "What's in a Name Change? Neo-Pythagorean Arithmology and Middle-Platonic Namewrights in Philo's Orchard of Philosophy."

In addition to lively moderated questions and answers after each paper, David Runia (Australian Catholic University), in his capacity as invited respondent, offered feedback and fielded questions from speakers in all four sessions. The conference organizers are currently soliciting further contributions to round out the volume. The proceedings will be submitted for review with a respected publishing house.

Michael Cover
Marquette University

Report on the Seminar on Philo and Early Christianity,
Studiorum Novi Testamenti Societas (SNTS)

As reported in last year's Annual, a seminar on Philo and Early Christianity, directed by Gregory E. Sterling and Per Jarle Bekken, was accepted at the Studiorum Novi Testamenti Societas (SNTS) meeting in Pretoria, South Africa, 2017, to function from 2018 until 2022.

The second seminar with Gregory E. Sterling, Yale Divinity School, USA, and Per Jarle Bekken, Nord University, Norway, as convenors, took place at the SNTS meeting hosted by the Philipps Universität Marburg, Germany, 31 July to 2 August 2019. The papers were spread out over the three days of the conference. On Wednesday, 31 July Karl-Wilhelm Niebuhr (Germany) presented a paper on "Der Philosoph Hans Leisegang als Philon-Forscher," to which Gregory E. Sterling (USA) responded. On Thursday 1 August the presenter was Athanasios Despotis (Germany), "Aspects of Cultural Hybridity in Philo's Apophatic Anthropology and a Short Excursus on John," for which Paul Anderson (USA) was the respondent. On Friday 2 August it was the turn of Florian Wilk (Germany), who gave a paper entitled "Einflüsse von oder Parallelen zu philonischem Denken im ersten Korintherbrief des Paulus?" The respondent this time was Gottfried Schimanowski (Germany).

The papers were distributed beforehand to the participants that were registered for the seminar. In addition to a summarizing of the paper by the presenters and a prepared response, all sessions included ample time for discussion. The seminar at the society's next meeting in Rome, July, 28–31 2020, will be devoted to the topic Philo, Rome, and Early Christianity.

Per Jarle Bekken
Nord University, Levanger,
Norway

Maren Niehoff Wins the Polonsky Prize

The Polonsky Prizes were initiated in 2005 by Dr Leanrad Plonsky, a prominent member of the British Friends of the Hebrew University, who generously established the award to provide support for research in the Humanities. Each year up to four prizes—two for researchers who have published books, one for a post-doctoral researcher who has recently completed a dissertation, and one for PhD or Masters students who have published an article or had their MA thesis accepted.

This year the Polonsky Prize for Creativity and Originality in the Humanistic Disciplines was awarded to Maren R. Niehoff's monograph, *Philo of Alexandria. An Intellectual Biography* (New Haven: Yale University Press, 2018). The book was selected for the prize, because it is the first attempt to offer a comprehensive historical analysis of Philo's *œuvre* and provide answers to questions that have vexed scholarship since the inception of modern research. Philo poses a serious challenge to scholars, because he has left behind not only one of the most voluminous *œuvres* of antiquity, but also one of the most diverse. No other author of the turn of the Era accomplished as diverse tasks as systematic commentary, historiography, biography, philosophy and a general exposition of religion, including religious law. An additional challenge is the fact that Philo tells us very little about his own person and virtually nothing about the circumstances of his writing activity. Given this situation, scholars have specialized in one of the literary genres of Philo's work and drawn very partial, often misleading conclusions about its overall character.

The Intellectual Biography undertakes to face the challenge of Philo's *œuvre* by presenting a comprehensive analysis of each of his series of works in its cultural context, arguing that political, philosophical, theological and exegetical aspects must be understood in view of each other. Philo the historian cannot be isolated from Philo the biblical interpreter or philosopher.

The book reconstructs the chronology of Philo's works and shows that his visit to Rome, as the head of the Jewish embassy to Gaius Caligula, had a perceptible intellectual impact on him. The encounter with Roman audiences prompted him to exchange systematic Bible commentary for more general literary genres and a strictly transcendental Platonism for a more Stoic orientation. His notion of Judaism, too, changed and became more immanent, with emphasis on the Jews as good citizens and God as a helper involved in history.

The German and Hebrew translation of the Intellectual Biography will be published respectively in 2019 by Mohr Siebeck in Tübingen and in 2020 by Ha-kibbutz ha-Meuhadin in Tel Aviv.

The editors

Philo of Alexandria Commentary Series

After a period of quiescence the next volume in the Philo of Alexandria Commentary Series (PACS) is about to be published. Written by Albert Geljon (Utrecht) and David Runia (Melbourne), it is a sequel to their translation and commentary on the treatise *On Cultivation* published in 2013 (PACS 4). This volume translates and examines in detail the second treatise in the Noah cycle, *On Planting (De plantatione)*. It will be published by Brill in time for the annual meeting of the Society of Biblical Literature in San Diego in November 2019. It is expected that the next volume in the series, on the *Life of Abraham (De Abrahamo)*, prepared by John Dillon and Ellen Birnbaum (PACS 6), will be published in the course of next year. There are a number of volumes nearing completion, so it is expected that they will be appearing at shorter intervals in the future.

The editors

NOTES ON CONTRIBUTORS

MARTA ALESSO is Titular Professor of Greek language and literature in the Faculty of Human Sciences at the National University of La Pampa, Argentina. Her postal address is Pestalozzi 625, 6300 Santa Rosa, La Pampa, ARGENTINA; her electronic address is alessomarta@gmail.com.

ELLEN BIRNBAUM has taught and/or conducted postdoctoral research at several Boston-area institutions, including Boston University, Brandeis, and Harvard. Her postal address is 36 Highland Avenue, Cambridge, MA 02139, U.S.A.; her electronic address is ebirnbaum78@gmail.com.

GÁBOR BUZÁSI is Assistant Professor of Biblical Studies at Eötvös Loránd University (ELTE), Budapest. His postal address is: Ókortudományi Intézet (Institute of Ancient Studies), ELTE, Múzeum krt. 4/F, Budapest, HUNGARY; his electronic address is: buzasi.gabor@btk.elte.hu.

MICHAEL B. COVER is Assistant Professor of Judaism and Christianity in Antiquity at Marquette University. His postal address is: Marquette University, Department of Theology, P.O. Box 1881, Milwaukee, WI 53201-1881, U.S.A. His electronic address is michael.cover@marquette.edu.

MIKOLAJ DOMARADZKI is an Associate Professor in the Institute of Philosophy at Adam Mickiewicz University in Poznan. His postal address is ul. Szamarzewskiego 89c, Poznan, POLAND; his electronic address is mikdom@amu.edu.pl.

PAOLA DRUILLE is an investigator with the National Scientific and Technical Research Council (Argentina), tenured adjunct at the National University of La Pampa, and coeditor of the scholarly journal *Circe, de clásicos y modernos*. Her postal address is Mosconi 825, Santa Rosa (CP. 6300), La Pampa, ARGENTINA. Her electronic address is paodruille@gmail.com.

EVERETT FERGUSON is Professor Emeritus of Bible and Church History at Abilene Christian University, Abilene, Texas, U.S.A. His postal address is Wisteria Place, 3202 South Willis #428, Abilene, TX 79605, and his electronic address is fergusone@acu.edu.

ALBERT C. GELJON teaches classical languages at the Christelijke Gymnasium in Utrecht. His postal address is Gazellestraat 138, 3523 SZ Utrecht, THE NETHERLANDS; his electronic address is ageljon@xs4all.nl.

MICHAEL GRAVES is Armerding Professor of Biblical Studies at the Wheaton Center for Early Christian Studies at Wheaton College. His postal address is: Biblical and Theological Studies, Wheaton College, 501 College Ave, Wheaton, IL 60187, U.S.A. His electronic address is michael.graves@wheaton.edu.

HELEEN M. KEIZER is Dean of Academic Affairs at the Istituto Superiore di Osteopatia in Milan, ITALY. Her postal address is Via Guerrazzi 3, 20900 Monza (MB), ITALY; her electronic address is h.m.keizer@virgilio.it.

DANIEL LANZINGER is Wissenschaftlicher Mitarbeiter in the Seminar for New Testament Exegesis in the Catholic Theological Faculty at the Rheinische Friedrich-Wilhelms-Universität Bonn. His postal address is Neutestamentliches Seminar, Katholisch-Theologische Fakultät, Universität Bonn, Regina-Pacis-Weg 1a, 53113 Bonn, GERMANY. His electronic address is daniel.lanzinger@uni-bonn.de.

JUTTA LEONHARDT-BALZER is Honorary Senior Lecturer at the University of Aberdeen, UK. Her postal address is Heinrich-Heine-Str. 15, 65201 Wiesbaden, GERMANY; her electronic address is jutta.leonhardt-balzer@abdn.ac.uk

SCOTT D. MACKIE is a lecturer in the Department of Religious Studies at Chapman University. His postal address is 51 Rose Ave. #2, Venice CA 90291, U.S.A.; his electronic address is scottdmackie@gmail.com.

EKATERINA MATUSOVA is a Heisenberg research fellow at the Institut für antikes Judentum und hellenistische Religionsgeschichte at the university of Tübingen. Her postal address is: Institut für antikes Judentum und hellenistische Religionsgeschichte, Liebermeisterstraße 12, 72076 Tübingen, GERMANY. Her electronic addresses are: ekaterina.matusova@uni-tuebingen.de and ek.matusova@mail.ru.

Maren R. Niehoff is Professor in the Department of Jewish Thought at the Hebrew University, Jerusalem. Her postal address is Department of Jewish Thought, Hebrew University, Mt. Scopus, Jerusalem 91905, Israel; her electronic address is msmaren@mscc.huji.ac.il.

Sarah J. K. Pearce is Ian Karten Professor of Jewish Studies at the University of Southampton. Her postal address is Department of History, Faculty of Humanities, Avenue Campus, Highfield, Southampton SO17 1BF, United Kingdom; her electronic address is sjp2@soton.ac.uk.

Ilaria L. E. Ramelli has been Honorary Professor of Theology, Durham University; Senior Fellow, Oxford, Erfurt MWK, Sacred Heart University, Princeton; and Professor of Theology and endowed Chair, Angelicum, Rome. Her postal address is Sacred Heart University, Largo A. Gemelli 1, 20123 Milan, Italy; her electronic address i.l.e.ramelli@durham.ac.uk.

Justin M. Rogers is Associate Professor of Biblical Studies at Freed-Hardeman University, and Director of the FHU Graduate School of Theology. His postal address is: FHU Box 2, 158 E Main Street, Henderson, TN 38340, U.S.A. His electronic address is jrogers@fhu.edu.

David T. Runia is Honorary Professor at the Institute for Religion and Critical Inquiry, Australian Catholic University, Melbourne. He is also a Professorial Fellow in the School of Historical and Philosophical Studies at the University of Melbourne. His postal address is 4 Woodlands Drive, Ocean Grove VIC 3226, Australia; his electronic address is dtrunia@gmail.com.

Gregory E. Sterling is the Lillian Claus Professor of New Testament and the Reverend Henry L. Slack Dean of the Yale Divinity School. His postal address is 409 Prospect Street, New Haven, CT 06511, U.S.A.; his electronic address is gregory.sterling@yale.edu.

Alexander E. Stewart is Academic Dean and Associate Professor of New Testament Language and Literature at Tyndale Theological Seminary in the Netherlands. He is also a Research Associate of Prof. Dr. Jacobus (Kobus) Kok in the department of New Testament and Related Literature at the University of Pretoria, South Africa. His postal address is 's Gravesandestraat 18, 1171XP, Badhoevedorp, The Netherlands; his electronic address is astewart@tyndale-europe.edu.

ZE'EV STRAUSS is the holder of the The Lilli and Michael Sommerfreund Guest Professorship in Jewish Cultures at the Hochschule für Jüdische Studien Heidelberg and a Visiting Lecturer at the Philosophical Seminar of the Heidelberg University. His postal address is Landfriedstraße 12, 69117 Heidelberg, GERMANY; his electronic address is zeevstrauss@gmail.com.

KEVIN SULLIVAN is Associate Dean of Curricular and Faculty Development and Professor of Religion at Illinois Wesleyan University. His postal address is Mellon Center (CLA 363), Illinois Wesleyan University, P.O. Box 2900, Bloomington, IL 61702-2900, U.S.A. His electronic address is ksulliva@iwu.edu.

ABRAHAM TERIAN retired in 2008 as Professor Emeritus of Early Christianity and Armenian Patristics at St. Nersess Armenian Seminary. His postal address is 5478 N. Ferger Ave., Fresno, CA 93704, U.S.A.; his electronic address is terian@stnersess.edu.

SHARON WEISSER is Lecturer at the Department of Philosophy, Tel Aviv University. Her postal address is The Department of Philosophy, Tel Aviv University, P.O.B. 39040, Ramat Aviv, Tel-Aviv 69978, ISRAEL; her electronic address is weisser@post.tau.ac.il.

BEATRICE WYSS is a Postdoctoral Researcher at the faculty of Theology, University of Bern. Her postal address is Universität Bern, Theologische Fakultät, Länggass-Strasse 51, CH-3012 Bern, SWITZERLAND. Her electronic address is beatrice.wyss@theol.unibe.ch

SAMI YLI-KARJANMAA is an Academy of Finland Postdoctoral Researcher in the Faculty of Theology at the University of Helsinki. His postal address is Asemalammentie 103, FI-41370 Kuusa, FINLAND; his electronic address is sami.yli-karjanmaa@helsinki.fi.

The Studia Philonica Annual 30 (2019): 340–347

INSTRUCTIONS TO CONTRIBUTORS

Articles and book reviews can only be considered for publication in *The Studia Philonica Annual* if they rigorously conform to the guidelines established by the editorial board. For further information see also the website of the Annual:

http://divinity.yale.edu/philo-alexandria

1. *The Studia Philonica Annual* accepts articles for publication in the area of Hellenistic Judaism, with special emphasis on Philo and his *Umwelt*. Articles on Josephus will be given consideration if they focus on his relation to Judaism and classical culture (and not on primarily historical subjects). The languages in which the articles may be published are English, French and German. Translations from Italian or Dutch into English can be arranged at a modest cost to the author.

2. Articles and reviews are to be sent to the editors in electronic form as email attachments. The preferred word processor is Microsoft Word. Users of other word processors are requested to submit a copy exported in a format compatible with Word, e.g. in RTF format. Manuscripts should be double-spaced, including the notes. Words should be italicized when required, not underlined. Quotes five lines or longer should be indented and may be single-spaced. Texts in Greek *must* be submitted in SBL Greek and texts in Hebrew *must* be submitted in SBL Hebrew (both available at no cost from the SBL website). In all cases a PDF version of the document must be sent together with the word processing file. No handwritten Greek or Hebrew can be accepted. Authors are requested not to vocalize their Hebrew (except when necessary) and to keep their use of this language to a reasonable minimum. It should always be borne in mind that not all readers of the Annual can be expected to read Greek or Hebrew. Transliteration is permitted for incidental terms. If other language fonts need to be used, the font must be sent with the manuscript or contact should be sought with SBL Press.

3. Authors are encouraged to use inclusive language wherever possible, avoiding terms such as "man" and "mankind" when referring to humanity in general.

4. For the preparation of articles and book reviews the Annual follows the guidelines of the *SBL Handbook of Style*, Second Edition, Atlanta: SBL

Press, 2014. Here are examples of how a monograph, a monograph in a series, an edited volume, an article in an edited volume, and a journal article are to be cited in notes (different conventions apply for bibliographies):

> Joan E. Taylor, *Jewish Women Philosophers of First-Century Alexandria—Philo's 'Therapeutae' Reconsidered* (Oxford: Oxford University Press, 2003), 123.
>
> Ellen Birnbaum, *The Place of Judaism in Philo's Thought: Israel, Jews, and Proselytes*, BJS 290, SPhiloM 2 (Atlanta: Scholars Press, 1996), 134.
>
> Gerard P. Luttikhuizen, ed., *Eve's Children: The Biblical Stories Retold and Interpreted in Jewish and Christian Traditions*, Themes in Biblical Narrative 5 (Leiden: Brill, 2003), 145.
>
> G. Bolognesi, "Marginal Notes on the Armenian Translation of the *Quaestiones et Solutiones in Genesim* by Philo," in *Studies on the Ancient Armenian Version of Philo's* Works, ed. Sara Mancini Lombardi and Paola Pontani, SPhA 6 (Leiden: Brill, 2011), 45–50.
>
> James R. Royse, "Jeremiah Markland's Contribution to the Textual Criticism of Philo," *SPhiloA* 16 (2004): 50–60.

Note that abbreviations are used in the notes and also in bibliographies. Numbers should be given in full for ancient texts, for example, *Aet.* 107–110; for references to modern publications the conventions of the *SBL Handbook of Style* should be followed (see p. 18). When joining up numbers in all textual and bibliographical references, the en dash should be used and not the hyphen, that is, 50–60, not 50-60. For publishing houses only the first location is given. Submissions which do not conform to these guidelines will be returned to the authors for re-submission.

5. The following abbreviations are to be used in both articles and book reviews.

(a) Philonic treatises are to be abbreviated according to the following list. Numbering follows the edition of Cohn and Wendland, using Arabic numbers only and full stops rather than colons (e.g., *Spec.* 4.123). Note that *De Providentia* should be cited according to Aucher's edition, and not the LCL translation of the fragments by F. H. Colson.

Abr.	*De Abrahamo*
Aet.	*De aeternitate mundi*
Agr.	*De agricultura*
Anim.	*De animalibus*
Cher.	*De Cherubim*
Contempl.	*De vita contemplativa*
Conf.	*De confusione linguarum*
Congr.	*De congressu eruditionis gratia*
Decal.	*De Decalogo*
Deo	*De Deo*
Det.	*Quod deterius potiori insidiari soleat*
Deus	*Quod Deus sit immutabilis*

Ebr.	*De ebrietate*
Flacc.	*In Flaccum*
Fug.	*De fuga et inventione*
Gig.	*De gigantibus*
Her.	*Quis rerum divinarum heres sit*
Hypoth.	*Hypothetica*
Ios.	*De Iosepho*
Leg. 1–3	*Legum allegoriae I, II, III*
Legat.	*Legatio ad Gaium*
Migr.	*De migratione Abrahami*
Mos. 1–2	*De vita Moysis I, II*
Mut.	*De mutatione nominum*
Opif.	*De opificio mundi*
Plant.	*De plantatione*
Post.	*De posteritate Caini*
Praem.	*De praemiis et poenis, De exsecrationibus*
Prob.	*Quod omnis probus liber sit*
Prov. 1–2	*De Providentia I, II*
QE 1–2	*Quaestiones et solutiones in Exodum I, II*
QG 1–4	*Quaestiones et solutiones in Genesim I, II, III, IV*
Sacr.	*De sacrificiis Abelis et Caini*
Sobr.	*De sobrietate*
Somn. 1–2	*De somniis I, II*
Spec. 1–4	*De specialibus legibus I, II, III, IV*
Virt.	*De virtutibus*

(b) Standard works of Philonic scholarship are abbreviated as follows:

G-G   Howard L. Goodhart and Erwin R. Goodenough, "A General Bibliography of Philo Judaeus." In Erwin R. Goodenough, *The Politics of Philo Judaeus: Practice and Theory* (New Haven: Yale University Press, 1938; repr. Georg Olms: Hildesheim, 1967), 125–321.

PCH   *Philo von Alexandria: die Werke in deutscher Übersetzung.* Edited by Leopold Cohn, Isaac Heinemann *et al.* 7 vols. (Breslau: M & H Marcus Verlag; Berlin: de Gruyter, 1909–1964).

PCW   *Philonis Alexandrini opera quae supersunt.* Edited by Leopoldus Cohn, Paulus Wendland et Sigismundus Reiter. 6 vols. (Berlin: Georg Reimer, 1896–1915).

PLCL   *Philo in Ten Volumes (and Two Supplementary Volumes).* English translation by F. H. Colson, G. H. Whitaker (and R. Marcus), 12 vols., Loeb Classical Library. (London: William Heinemann; Cambridge, MA: Harvard University Press, 1929–1962).

PACS   Philo of Alexandria Commentary Series

PAPM   *Les œuvres de Philon d'Alexandrie.* French translation under the general editorship of Roger Arnaldez, Jean Pouilloux, and Claude Mondésert (Paris: Cerf, 1961–1992).

R-R	Roberto Radice and David T. Runia, *Philo of Alexandria: An Annotated Bibliography 1937–1986,* VCSup 8 (Leiden: Brill 1988).
RRS	David T. Runia, *Philo of Alexandria: An Annotated Bibliography 1987–1996,* VCSup 57 (Leiden: Brill 2000).
RRS2	David T. Runia, *Philo of Alexandria: An Annotated Bibliography 1997–2006,* VCSup 109 (Leiden: Brill 2012).
SPhA	Studies in Philo of Alexandria
SPhAMA	Studies in Philo of Alexandria and Mediterranean Antiquity
SPhilo	*Studia Philonica*
SPhiloA	*The Studia Philonica Annual*
SPhiloMS	Studia Philonica Monographs

(c) References to biblical authors and texts and to ancient authors and writings are to be abbreviated as recommended in the *SBL Handbook of Style* §8.2–3. Note that biblical books are not italicized and that between chapter and verse a colon is placed (but for non-biblical references colons should not be used). Abbreviations should be used for biblical books when they are followed by chapter or chapter and verse unless the book is the first word in a sentence. Authors writing in German or French should follow their own conventions for biblical citations.

(d) For giving dates the abbreviations BCE and CE are preferred and should be printed in regular large caps.

(e) Journals, monograph series, source collections, and standard reference works are to be be abbreviated in accordance with the recommendations listed in *The SBL Handbook of Style* §8.4. The following list contains a selection of the more important abbreviations, along with a few abbreviations of classical and philosophical journals and standard reference books not furnished in the list.

ABD	*The Anchor Bible Dictionary*, 6 vols. New York, 1992
AC	*L'antiquité classique*
ACW	Ancient Christian Writers
AGJU	Arbeiten zur Geschichte des antiken Judentums und des Urchristentums
AJP	*American Journal of Philology*
AJSL	*American Journal of Semitic Languages*
ALGHJ	Arbeiten zur Literatur und Geschichte des hellenistischen Judentums
ANRW	*Aufstieg und Niedergang der römischen Welt*
AnPhil	*L'année philologique*
BDAG	Bauer, W., F. W. Danker, W. F. Arndt, and F. W. Gingrich. *A Greek-English Lexicon of the New Testament and Other Early Christian Literature*. 3rd ed. Chicago: University of Chicago Press, 1999
BETL	Bibliotheca Ephemeridum Theologicarum Lovaniensium
BO	Bibliotheca Orientalis
BJRL	*Bulletin of the John Rylands Library*

BJS	Brown Judaic Studies
BMCR	*Bryn Mawr Classical Review* (electronic)
BZAW	Beihefte zur Zeitschrift für die alttestamentliche Wissenschaft
BZNW	Beihefte zur Zeitschrift für die neutestamentliche Wissenschaft
BZRGG	Beihefte zur Zeitschrift für Religions- und Geistesgeschichte
CBQ	*The Catholic Biblical Quarterly*
CBQMS	The Catholic Biblical Quarterly. Monograph Series
CCSG	Corpus Christianorum Series Graeca, Turnhout
CCSL	Corpus Christianorum Series Latina, Turnhout
CIG	*Corpus Inscriptionum Graecarum*. Edited by A. Boeckh. 4 vols. in 8. Berlin, 1828–1877
CIJ	*Corpus Inscriptionum Judaicarum*. Edited by J. B. Frey. 2 vols. Rome, 1936–1952
CIL	*Corpus Inscriptionum Latinarum*. Berlin, 1862–
CIS	*Corpus Inscriptionum Semiticarum*. Paris, 1881–1962
C P	*Classical Philology*
CPJ	*Corpus Papyrorum Judaicarum*. Edited by V. Tcherikover and A. Fuks. 3 vols. Cambridge MA, 1957–64
ClQ	*The Classical Quarterly*
CR	*The Classical Review*
CRINT	Compendia Rerum Iudaicarum ad Novum Testamentum
CPG	*Clavis Patrum Graecorum*. Edited by M. Geerard, 5 vols. and suppl. vol. Turnhout, 1974–1998
CPL	*Clavis Patrum Latinorum*. Edited by E. Dekkers. 3rd ed. Turnhout, 1995
CSCO	Corpus Scriptorum Christianorum Orientalium
CWS	Classics of Western Spirituality
DissAb	Dissertation Abstracts
DBSup	*Dictionnaire de la Bible*, Supplément. Paris, 1928–
DPhA	R. Goulet, ed., *Dictionnaire des philosophes antiques*, Paris, 1989–
DSpir	*Dictionnaire de spiritualité*, 17 vols. Paris, 1932–1995
EBR	*Encyclopedia of the Bible and Its Reception*. Edited by Hans-Josef Klauck *et al*. Berlin: de Gruyter, 2009-
EncJud	*Encyclopaedia Judaica*, 16 vols. Jerusalem, 1972
EPRO	Études préliminaires aux religions orientales dans l'Empire romain
FAT	Forschungen zum Alten Testament
FGH	*Fragmente der Griechische Historiker*. Edited by F. Jacoby *et al*. Leiden, 1954–
FRLANT	Forschungen zur Religion und Literatur des Alten und Neuen Testaments
GCS	Die griechischen christlichen Schriftsteller, Leipzig
GLAJJ	M. Stern, *Greek and Latin Authors on Jews and Judaism*. 3 vols. Jerusalem, 1974–1984
GRBS	*Greek, Roman and Byzantine Studies*
HKNT	Handkommentar zum Neuen Testament, Tübingen
HNT	Handbuch zum Neuen Testament, Tübingen
HR	*History of Religions*
HTR	*Harvard Theological Review*
HUCA	*Hebrew Union College Annual*
JAAR	*Journal of the American Academy of Religion*
JAOS	*Journal of the American Oriental Society*
JAC	*Jahrbuch für Antike und Christentum*

JBL	*Journal of Biblical Literature*
JHI	*Journal of the History of Ideas*
JHS	*The Journal of Hellenic Studies*
JIGRE	*Journal of Inscriptions in Greco-Roman Egypt*
JJS	*The Journal of Jewish Studies*
JQR	*The Jewish Quarterly Review*
JR	*The Journal of Religion*
JRS	*The Journal of Roman Studies*
JSHRZ	Jüdische Schriften aus hellenistisch-römischer Zeit
JSJ	*Journal for the Study of Judaism in the Persian, Hellenistic and Roman Periods*
JSJSup	Supplements to the Journal for the Study of Judaism
JSNT	*Journal for the Study of the New Testament*
JSNTSup	Journal for the Study of the New Testament. Supplement Series
JSOT	*Journal for the Study of the Old Testament*
JSOTSup	Journal for the Study of the Old Testament. Supplement Series
JSP	*Journal for the Study of the Pseudepigrapha and Related Literature*
JSS	*Journal of Semitic Studies*
JTS	*The Journal of Theological Studies*
KBL	L. Koehler and W. Baumgartner, *Lexicon in Veteris Testamenti libros.* 3 vols. 3rd ed. Leiden, 1967–1983
KS	*Kirjath Sepher*
LCL	Loeb Classical Library
LSJ	*A Greek-English Lexicon.* Edited by H. G. Liddell, R. Scott, H. S. Jones. 9th ed. with revised suppl. Oxford, 1996
MGWJ	*Monatsschrift für Geschichte und Wissenschaft des Judentums*
NCE	*New Catholic Encyclopedia*, 15 vols. New York, 1967
NETS	New English Translation of the Septuagint. Edited by Albert Pietersma and Ben Wright. New York: Oxford University Press, 2007
NHS	Nag Hammadi Studies
NT	*Novum Testamentum*
NovTSup	Supplements to Novum Testamentum
NTA	*New Testament Abstracts*
NTOA	Novum Testamentum et Orbis Antiquus
NTS	*New Testament Studies*
ODJ	*The Oxford Dictionary of Judaism.* Edited by R.J.Z. Werblowsky and G. Wigoder. New York 1997
OGIS	*Orientis Graeci inscriptiones selectae*
OLD	*The Oxford Latin Dictionary.* Edited by P. G. W. Glare. Oxford, 1982
OTP	*The Old Testament Pseudepigrapha.* Edited by J. H. Charlesworth. 2 vols. New York–London, 1983–1985
PAAJR	*Proceedings of the American Academy for Jewish Research*
PAL	*Philon d'Alexandrie: Lyon 11–15 Septembre 1966.* Éditions du CNRS, Paris, 1967
PG	Patrologiae cursus completus: series Graeca. Edited by J. P. Migne. 162 vols. Paris, 1857–1912
PGL	*A Patristic Greek Lexicon.* Edited by G. W. H. Lampe. Oxford, 1961
PhA	Philosophia Antiqua
PL	Patrologiae cursus completus: series Latina. Edited by J. P. Migne. 221 vols. Paris, 1844–1864
PTS	Patristische Texte und Studien

PW	Pauly-Wissowa-Kroll, *Real-Encyclopaedie der classischen Altertumswissenschaft.* 49 vols. Munich, 1980
PWSup	Supplement to PW
RAC	*Reallexikon für Antike und Christentum*
RB	*Revue biblique*
RBL	*Review of Biblical Literature*
REA	*Revue des études anciennes*
REArm	*Revue des études arméniennes*
REAug	*Revue des études augustiniennes*
REG	*Revue des études grecques*
REJ	*Revue des études juives*
REL	*Revue des études latines*
RevQ	*Revue de Qumran*
RGG	*Die Religion in Geschichte und Gegenwart,* 7 vols. 3rd edition Tübingen, 1957–1965
RhM	*Rheinisches Museum für Philologie*
RHR	*Revue de l'histoire des religions*
RSR	*Revue des sciences religieuses*
RTP	*Revue de théologie et de philosophie*
RVV	Religionsgeschichtliche Versuche und Vorarbeiten
SAPERE	Scripta Antiquitatis Posterioris ad Ethicam REligionemque pertinentia
SBLDS	Society of Biblical Literature Dissertation Series
SBLMS	Society of Biblical Literature Monograph Series
SBLSP	Society of Biblical Literature Seminar Papers
SBLTT	Society of Biblical Literature Texts and Translations
SC	Sources Chrétiennes
SCS	Septuagint and Cognate Studies
Sem	*Semitica*
SHJP	E. Schürer, *The History of the Jewish People in the Age of Jesus Christ.* Revised edition. 3 vols. in 4. Edinburgh, 1973–1987
SJLA	Studies in Judaism in Late Antiquity
SNTSMS	Society for New Testament Studies. Monograph Series
SR	*Studies in Religion*
ST	*Studia Theologica*
STAC	Studies and Texts in Antiquity and Christianity
Str-B	H. L. Strack and P. Billerbeck, *Kommentar zum Neuen Testament aus Talmud und Midrasch.* 6 vols. Munich, 1922–1961
SUNT	Studien zur Umwelt des Neuen Testaments
SVF	*Stoicorum veterum fragmenta.* Edited by J. von Arnim. 4 vols. Leipzig, 1903–1924
TDNT	*Theological Dictionary of the New Testament.* 10 vols. Grand Rapids, 1964–1976
THKNT	Theologischer Handkommentar zum Neuen Testament, Berlin
TRE	*Theologische Realenzyklopädie,* Berlin
TSAJ	Texte und Studien zum Antike Judentum
TU	Texte und Untersuchungen zur Geschichte der altchristlichen Literatur, Berlin
TWNT	*Theologisches Wörterbuch zum Neuen Testament.* 10 vols. Stuttgart 1933–1979.
TZ	*Theologische Zeitschrift*
VC	*Vigiliae Christianae*

VCSup	Supplements to Vigiliae Christianae
VT	*Vetus Testamentum*
WMANT	Wissenschaftliche Monographien zum Alten und Neuen Testament
WUNT	Wissenschaftliche Untersuchungen zum Neuen Testament
YJS	*Yale Jewish Studies*
ZAW	*Zeitschrift für die alttestamentliche Wissenschaft*
ZKG	*Zeitschrift für Kirchengeschichte*
ZKT	*Zeitschrift für Katholische Theologie*
ZNW	*Zeitschrift für die neutestamentliche Wissenschaft*
ZPE	*Zeitschrift für Papyrologie und Epigraphik*
ZRGG	*Zeitschrift für Religions- und Geistesgeschichte*